Writing Women in Jacobean England

Writing Women in Jacobean England

Barbara Kiefer Lewalski

Harvard University Press
Cambridge, Massachusetts
London, England   1993

Publication of this book has been aided by a grant from the Hyder Edward Rollins Fund.

This book is printed on acid-free paper, and its binding materials have been chosen for strength and durability.

Library of Congress Cataloging-in-Publication Data

Lewalski, Barbara Kiefer, 1931-
  Writing women in Jacobean England / Barbara Kiefer Lewalski.
    p. cm.
  Includes bibliographical references and index.
  ISBN 0–674–96242–7 (alk. paper)
  1. English literature—Early modern, 1500–1700—History and
criticism. 2. English literature—Women authors—History and
criticism. 3. Women and literature—England—History—17th century.
  I. Title.
PR113.L53 1993
820.9'9287'09032—dc20
92–9506
    CIP

For Kenneth F. Lewalski
Feminist *avant la lettre*

Contents

Acknowledgments   xi

Introduction: Women, Writing, and Resistance in Jacobean
England   1

I THE ROYAL OPPOSITION

1 Enacting Opposition: Queen Anne and the Subversions
of Masquing   15

2 Scripting a Heroine's Role: Princess Elizabeth and the Politics
of Romance   45

3 Writing Resistance in Letters: Arbella Stuart and the Rhetoric
of Disguise and Defiance   67

II RE-WRITING PATRIARCHY

4 Exercising Power: The Countess of Bedford as Courtier, Patron,
and Coterie Poet   95

5 Claiming Patrimony and Constructing a Self: Anne Clifford
and Her *Diary*   125

6 Defending Women's Essential Equality: Rachel Speght's
Polemics and Poems   153

III LITERARY RE-VISIONS

7 Resisting Tyrants: Elizabeth Cary's Tragedy and History   179

8 Imagining Female Community: Aemilia Lanyer's Poems   213

9   Revising Genres and Claiming the Woman's Part: Mary
     Wroth's Oeuvre   243

     Afterword: The Politics of Jacobean Women's Writing   309

     Appendix A: Elizabeth, Lady Falkland, and the Authorship
     of *Edward II*   317

     Appendix B: Presentation Copies of Lanyer's *Salve Deus
     Rex Judaeorum*   321

     Notes   323

     Index   413

Illustrations

Queen Anne of Denmark, by Paul Van Somer. In the collection of the Duke of Buccleuch and Queensberry, K. T., and reproduced by his permission. 14

Elizabeth and Frederick of Bohemia as Champions of Protestantism; engraver unknown. National Portrait Gallery, London. 44

Arbella Stuart; posthumous engraving issued in 1619 by John Whittaker, Senior. National Portrait Gallery, London. 66

Lucy, Countess of Bedford, as a masquer, attributed to John De Critz. Reproduced from the Collections at Woburn Abbey, by permission of the Marquess of Tavistock and the Trustees of the Bedford Estates. 94

The Clifford "Great Picture," probably executed by Jan van Belcamp. At Appleby Castle, Cumbria; reproduced courtesy of Abbot Hall Art Gallery, Kendal, Cumbria, U.K. 124

Title Page, Rachel Speght, *A Mouzell for Melastomus* (1617). By permission of the Houghton Library, Harvard University. 152

Elizabeth, Lady Falkland. A wash drawing by Athow from a painting by Paul Van Somer. In the Sutherland Collection, Ashmolean Museum, Oxford, and reproduced by permission of the Ashmolean. 178

Title page, Aemilia Lanyer, *Salve Deus Rex Judaeorum* (1611). Reproduced by permission of The Huntington Library, San Marino, California. 212

Lady Mary Wroth with archlute; artist unknown. At Penshurst. Reproduced by permission of the late Viscount De L'Isle, V.C., K.G. 242

Acknowledgments

This book owes more than I can possibly acknowledge to the devoted cadre of scholars far and near who are now working on early modern women's writing—especially members of the Harvard Seminar on Women in the Renaissance and Reformation; the Brown University Women Writers Project and its editors Susanne Woods and Elizabeth Hageman; and several graduate students past and present (especially Naomi Miller and Jennifer Carrell). Some sections of the book have greatly benefited from the responses of Conference audiences: MLA panels, the Reading (England) Conference on Politics, Patronage and Literature, the English Institute, the Renaissance Society of America, and the University of Chicago Centennial Colloquium on the Renaissance.

Many librarians and archivists—at the Huntington Library, the Newberry Library, the Houghton and Widener Libraries, the British Library, the Bodleian, the Public Record Office, the Guildhall Library (London), the Cumbria Record Office (Kendal), the Center for Kentish Studies (Maidstone, Kent), the National Portrait Gallery, the Witt Library of the Courtauld Institute, the Ashmolean Museum, the Scottish National Portrait Gallery, the Abbot Hall Art Gallery (Kendal)—helped me locate and gain access to obscure materials, and facilitated this research at every stage. I especially want to thank owners of several private collections for allowing me access to materials in those collections and granting permission to quote from papers or reproduce portraits: the Marquess of Tavistock and the Trustees of the Bedford Estates for papers relating to Lucy, Countess of Bedford (and for her portrait), from the collection at Woburn Abbey; the Marquess of Salisbury for the Cecil Papers at Hatfield House; Lord Hothfield of Drybeck Hall for letters and papers relating to Lady Anne

Clifford; the Duke of Buccleuch and Queensberry, K. T., for the portrait of Queen Anne; and the late Viscount de L'Isle, V.C., K.G., for the De L'Isle MSS from the Penshurst collections and the portrait of Lady Mary Wroth.

Materials in some parts of this book appear in the following essays, in an earlier form: "Of God and Good Women: The Poems of Aemelia Lanyer," in *Silent but for the Word: Tudor Women as Writers, Translators, and Patrons,* edited by Margaret Hannay (Kent State University Press, 1985); "Lucy, Countess of Bedford: Images of a Jacobean Courtier and Patroness," in *Politics of Discourse: The Literature and History of Seventeenth Century England,* edited by Kevin Sharpe and Steven Zwicker (University of California Press, 1987); "Re-Writing Patriarchy and Patronage: Margaret Clifford, Anne Clifford, and Aemilia Lanyer," *Yearbook of English Studies* 21 (1991); and "Writing Women and Reading the Renaissance," *Renaissance Quarterly* 44 (1991). I want to thank the editors and publishers for use of these materials.

This book has received skillful attention at the Harvard University Press, from editor Margaretta Fulton, copyeditor Amanda Heller, and production editor Donna Bouvier. My research assistant Susan Thornberg read proof with remarkable care and dispatch.

The dedication records, as always, my greatest debt.

Writing Women in Jacobean England

Introduction: Women, Writing, and Resistance in Jacobean England

This book examines nine women whose active involvement with Jacobean culture can be read through some texts of their own making. Thanks to a decade or so of feminist and cultural studies focused on gender and the social construction of identity, we now know a good deal about how early modern society constructed women within several discourses—law, medicine, theology, courtiership, domestic advice.[1] We also know a good deal about how major English poets and dramatists of the period—Shakespeare, Jonson, Donne, Spenser, Milton—dealt with issues of gender and the representation of women in complex literary texts.[2] But because we have only begun the recovery and analysis of elusive women's texts, many of them unpublished, uncertain of attribution, and in obscure archives,[3] we still know very little about how early modern Englishwomen read and wrote themselves and their world. And the few texts we do have were virtually unknown before the present decade.

For the study of women's writing, the unfortunate balkanization of our intellectual landscape creates large problems. Several scholars are now attending to Renaissance women's texts, publishing essays and collections of essays about particular authors and issues as well as anthologies and surveys of women's writing.[4] They are also producing much-needed scholarly editions and critical biographies.[5] But this work has not received much attention from traditional scholars of Renaissance literature, or from newer scholars of early modern ideology and culture in their analyses of class, race, gender, and power relations.[6] As a consequence, the newly important women's texts are often too narrowly contextualized—studied chiefly in relation to other women's texts, or to modern feminist theory, or to some aspects of the period's patriarchal ideology. Yet these texts urgently need to be read with the full scholarly apparatus of textual analysis, historical synthesis, and literary interpretation in play, since they come before us bare and unaccommodated, without the accretion of scholarship and critical opinion through the ages that so largely determines how we understand and value literary works. Another consequence is that early modern women's voices, perspectives, and texts are seldom brought to bear upon questions that have become central for literary scholars of the period: the power of social and cultural institutions, the ideology of absolutism and patriarchy, the formation of subjectivity, the forms of authorial "self-fashioning," the possibility and manifestations of resistance and subversion. It remains the case, as Carol Neely has observed, that the new Foucaultian Renaissance world picture we now invoke tends to be as monolithic as the old one: hierarchical, patriarchal, absolutist, unsubvertible.[7]

The nine women of my study—Queen Anne, Princess Elizabeth, Arbella Stuart, the Countess of Bedford, Anne Clifford, Rachel Speght, Elizabeth Cary, Aemilia Lanyer, and Mary Wroth—were actively involved in cultural production in Jacobean England. I seek to situate them within the complex web of Jacobean society and its institutions, and in relation to the literary traditions (genres, topics, styles) which they employ and alter. Their texts afford us some purchase on their conceptions of self, role, womankind, the Jacobean ethos, and their own writing. Their lives and their texts illuminate and contextualize one another, inviting the perception of common patterns. One such pattern, I was somewhat surprised to discover, is the strong resistance mounted in all these women's texts to the patriarchal construct of women as chaste, silent, and obedient,[8] and their overt rewriting of women's status and roles.

Why the Jacobean era? Received wisdom has it that this era was a regressive period for women, as a culture dominated by a powerful Queen gave way to a court ethos shaped by the patriarchal ideology and homosexuality of James I.[9] In theory—King James's theory articulated in *The Trew Lawe of Free Monarchie* and *Basilikon Doron*—the absolute power of God the Supreme Patriarch is imaged in the absolute monarch of the state, and in the husband and father of a family. A woman's subjection, first to her father and then to her husband, supposedly imaged the subjection of all English people to their monarch, and of all Christians to God.[10] Education for women is said to have declined in this period, by comparison with the humanist classical education some Tudor women enjoyed.[11] And beyond question the Jacobean era saw an outpouring of antifeminist or overtly misogynist sermons, tracts, and plays detailing women's physical and mental defects, spiritual evils, rebelliousness, shrewishness, and natural inferiority to men in the hierarchy of being.[12] These circumstances suggest how dominant elements of Jacobean society sought to construct women. We need to ask, however, whether women generally accepted and internalized that construction. These women's texts indicate that, in some cases at least, they did not.

Remarkably enough, it is in the repressive Jacobean milieu that we first hear Englishwomen's own voices in some numbers. In France, Italy, and Spain the sixteenth century saw the emergence of such notable women writers as Marguerite of Navarre, Louise Labé, Veronica Franco, Gaspara Stampa, and Vittoria Colonna; but their English contemporaries turned much more readily to translation than to original composition.[13] However, several Jacobean women—Lanyer, Speght, Cary, Wroth—produced and also published original poems, drama, and prose of some scope and merit, while others wrote themselves and their experiences through letters, memoirs, and other forms of expression. This breakthrough to female authorship, and especially the oppositional nature of that writing, prompts the question, how is it that these women all managed to develop a strong sense of self, to claim an identity as authors, and to produce texts which consistently though variously resist, oppose, and rewrite patriarchal norms?

Jacobean women did not of course float free of the ideology and institutions that structured Jacobean society. Their development of a sense of self, while embedded within social institutions, bears a certain analogy to the patterns Natalie Davis has studied in some sixteenth-century Frenchwomen.[14] One useful theoretical grid for viewing Jacobean women's resistance is Gramsci's analysis of how a dominant ideology may be contested by subaltern or marginal groups; another is the Marxist concept of negotiation for meaning and power by marginal groups who challenge a hegemonic system.[15] But the most illuminating perspective on their oppositional stances and texts is provided by the recent political upheavals all over Eastern Europe, testifying to the fact that inner resistance and a critical consciousness can develop even while ideological conformity is being rigorously enforced. I want to urge the importance of the textual gestures through which these Jacobean women claimed an authorial identity and manifested their resistance within their repressive culture.

Jacobean women did not see themselves as a cohesive group defined by gender, and those I mean to discuss are hardly representative of women in other or even the same ranks of society. For a more comprehensive sociological account of early modern women's lives, we must look to the social historians' accumulation and analyses of facts and statistics about social patterns and private life.[16] Yet several of these women (Lanyer, Speght, Wroth, Clifford) register some consciousness of common gender interests, while Lanyer and Speght explicitly claim to voice the wrongs and complaints of many women. They rewrite discourses which repress or diminish women—patriarchy, gender hierarchy, Petrarchism, Pauline marriage theory, and more—by redefining or extending their terms or infusing them with new meaning: this is the way any orthodoxy is first opened to revisionism.

Why these particular Jacobean women? All but two are royal or noble, and those two are gentlewomen with some court connections. Most of them were interrelated within the kinship bonds of aristocratic families or associated within patronage networks. They are, obviously, a social and cultural elite. But the only texts we have through which to explore how Jacobean women read and began to write themselves and their culture are by women of position, education, and privilege. In addition to these nine women I might have included a few others. The mothers' manuals of Elizabeth Jocelin, Dorothy Leigh, and the Countess of Lincoln provide examples of women extending the sphere of domestic power allotted them in the patriarchal family.[17] The diaries of Margaret Hoby and Grace Sherrington, Lady Mildmay, detail the large responsibilities for household management, the education of their own and others' children, medical treatment of the sick, and the many other activities that constituted an aristocratic woman's domestic province.[18] The Scots dream-vision poem of Elizabeth Melville, Lady Culross, displays a woman's spiritual equality in the form of a rigorously Calvinist, female *Pilgrim's Progress*.[19] I have, however, opted to focus on a smaller group of highly articulate women whose resistance takes various but striking forms: defining an oppositional role vis-à-vis patriarchal institutions; claiming rights, status, and power not usually accorded women; projecting in literary texts a fantasy of overt resistance and rebellion, of dominant or separate female communities, or of feminist politics and values; claiming genres and rewriting literary discourses for women's voices and stories. Several of these women found impressive literary means to contest the places assigned them in Jacobean patriarchal culture.

I look first to the cultural work carried on by the three royal ladies, all of whom placed themselves directly and publicly in opposition to King James, providing at the highest level examples of female resistance to the greatest patriarch. As head of state, Queen Elizabeth had been a female prince with all the powers, actual and symbolic, of both a male monarch and a courtly lady. In sharp contrast, Anne of Denmark was a queen consort, valued principally as the mother of royal progeny; and she was thoroughly marginalized in both the public and the personal sphere by James's ideology of patriarchal rule and his emotional ties to a series of homosexual favorites. In response she developed an oppositional role, manifested in her separate court, entourage, and patronage, her Roman Catholic proclivities, her pro-Spanish politics, and especially in the masques she commissioned, produced, helped create, and performed in. Personating black-faced Africans and militant queens, Anne of Denmark and her ladies subverted the expected representation of the King as the radiating source of all goods by displaying themselves as agents of energy, power, virtue, and transformation. The King's daughter Elizabeth, as Electress Palatine and later as the ill-fated Queen of Bohemia, enacted in her letters and her life a romance role as Protestant heroine. Assuming the mantle of her dead brother Prince Henry, she became a galvanizing symbol for international Protestantism in the Thirty Years' War, and the catalyst for opposition in England to James's pacific politics. The King's cousin Arbella Stuart defied James by a secret and forbidden marriage to William Seymour which strengthened her claim to the English throne; then, in male disguise, she made a boldly romantic though unsuccessful flight to France with him. Her numerous letters claim some personal autonomy in the very different but similarly constraining roles of courtier and prisoner: many subject Jacobean court society to trenchant and ironic inspection, while others are fascinating exercises in the rhetoric of disguise and concealment.

Next I turn to three women who demanded inclusion within the spheres of power: they rewrite patriarchy by using contemporary institutions and interpreting contemporary discourses so as to claim within them rights and status normally denied women. Lucy (Harrington) Russell, Countess of Bedford, constructed for herself a very powerful role as Queen Anne's favorite courtier and as the major patroness of the period. She was a force to be reckoned with in the disposition of offices and favors at both courts; she associated herself closely with the Queen's subversive masques and Princess Elizabeth's oppositional politics; she patronized and participated in coterie literary exchanges with the major poets of the period, exercising some influence over their poems; and in her familiar letters she offers a wryly ironic perspective on Jacobean court life. Beyond that, she claimed for herself the status of coterie poet, evidently seeking and obtaining in her own circle a reputation for the wit and *sprezzatura* long expected of male courtiers.

Anne Clifford, Countess of Dorset, Pembroke, and Montgomery, undertook over several decades to sue in the law courts for her rights of inheritance to Clifford lands and titles. She thereby challenged the terms of her father's will on the basis of an ancient entail, resisting the importunities of husband, male relatives, judicial and ecclesiastical authorities, and the King himself. Her legal and domestic struggles and the development of her sense of self are recorded in several works of biography, autobiography, and family history, and especially in her Jacobean *Diary*—virtually the earliest English secular diary to deal with the analysis of emotions, motives, experiences, and judgments of people and events.[20] Her diary opens up the relation between writing and resistance, between authoring a text and authoring a self.

The London minister's daughter Rachel Speght is the first English woman polemicist who can be securely identified, based on her forthright claims of authorship.[21] Her defense of women participates in the rancorous Jacobean pamphlet controversy over women's nature and worth. Reinterpreting the often-cited biblical texts, her tract forces the prevailing Protestant discourse to yield a more liberalizing view of women that affirms their natural and spiritual equality to men. Her later dream-vision poem allegorizes her education—her fierce desire for learning, the obstacles she encountered, her delight in her studies; the poem includes a vigorous and uncompromising defense of women's education in any and all subjects. Speght's explicit claim of authorship in both works indicates that this London daughter did not internalize class or gender constraints about writing or publishing; like Isabella Whitney in the 1560s and 1570s,[22] she may have sought to earn money from her books, thereby assuming something like professional status.

Next I turn to three women who claimed the major genres and wrote their resistance, their fantasies, and their imaginative visions in complex literary terms, producing works of considerable aesthetic interest. Elizabeth Cary, Lady Falkland, was the first Englishwoman to write a tragedy, *Mariam* (in the Senecan mode), and also the first to write a full-scale history, *Edward II* (in the Tacitean mode). Both texts explore issues important in the Jacobean state and in Cary's difficult personal life, as a secret and then a professed Roman Catholic: the claims of conscience, the analogy of domestic and state tyranny, the justifications for resistance to tyrants, the power of passive resistance. They do so, moreover, in genres considered dangerous because they traditionally probe such issues.[23] In both works a queen-wife is subjected to domestic and political tyranny. Cary's tragedy profoundly challenges patriarchal control within marriage, as the heroine claims a wife's right to self-definition and the integrity of her own emotional life. The history, long attributed erroneously to Cary's husband, Henry, Lord Falkland, contains a remarkably sympathetic and complex portrait of Edward II's Queen, Isabel, as an able rhetorician, military commander, and reforming ruler who is almost justified in leading an armed rebellion against her King and husband.

The gentlewoman Aemilia Lanyer, daughter and wife of court musicians and the cast-off mistress of Queen Elizabeth's Lord Chancellor, was the first Englishwoman to publish a substantial volume of original poems, *Salve Deus Rex Judaeorum*. She represents herself as defender and celebrant of an imagined community of good women, sharply distinguished from male society and its evils, which reaches from Eve to the contemporary Jacobean patronesses she addresses. In her multiple poetic dedications she makes an overt bid for patronage much as a male poet-client might; but she rewrites the patronage system to invite female patronage for a female client. Her title poem treats Christ's Passion as a locus exibiting the contrast between the good women associated with that event and the weak and evil men; it incorporates a notable defense of Eve as relatively guiltless by comparison with Adam and Pilate, culminating in a forthright declaration of gender equality. Her country-house poem—perhaps predating "Penshurst"—is Lanyer's fantasy of a classless society inhabited solely by women.

Lady Mary Wroth, niece of Sir Philip Sidney and the Countess of Pembroke and daughter of the courtier-poet Sir Robert Sidney, was the most prolific and self-conscious woman writer of the period. She claimed her status as author by family inheritance and used it transgressively to replace heroes with heroines at the center of several major genres and to transform their values accordingly. Her three works are all firsts for an Englishwoman, making their respective kinds into vehicles for women's experience. Her Petrarchan lyric sequence *Pamphilia to Amphilanthus* takes over the genre long dedicated to the analysis of the male lover's passions, pains, fantasies, and frustrations, and uses it to give voice and subjectivity to the woman lover, celebrating her self-construction through a self-chosen ideal of constancy. Her very long romance *Urania* overturns monolithic female stereotypes by presenting a range of women's responses to life and love, as well as many spheres for women's exercise of agency and power: as rulers, counselors, lovers, scholars, storytellers, poets, seers. The work also emphasizes enduring bonds between women and between the generations while representing male lovers as by nature fickle and unconstant. As a roman à clef (in some parts) it unleashed a storm of controversy: a few episodes allude to notorious scandals in court circles, while others encode Wroth's adulterous relationship with her first cousin William Herbert, to whom she bore two illegitimate children. Wroth's pastoral tragicomedy *Love's Victory* appropriates another genre traditionally used as a vehicle for male desire, nostalgia, and political commentary, making it register an implicit feminist politics: the work depicts a nonhierarchical pastoral world whose ideality and security depend on female friendships, female agency, and female control.

Several factors, I suggest, helped to destabilize the repressive cultural forces and empower these women. For one thing, a larger space for cultural activity was opened to aristocratic women when Queen Elizabeth's death removed her from the scene as an overwhelming cultural presence while leaving in place a powerful female example. For another, there is evidence of some counterweight to patriarchy provided by female communities—mothers and daughters, extended kinship networks, close female friends, the female entourage of Queen Anne. For yet another, most of these women received a reasonably good education (modern languages, history, literature, religion, music, occasionally Latin). Several read widely, deriving especially from romances and histories more expansive terms for imagining women's lives; and as writers they sometimes claimed the vernacular as women's special province. Also, the status and reputation of the important Elizabethan patroness-poet the Countess of Pembroke provided a model and sanction for the literary activities of a new generation of women, as Lanyer and Wroth explicitly recognized.[24]

At another level, while Jacobean patriarchy and absolutism were enormously powerful as ideology, that power was often undermined in practice by conflicting demands and loyalties. The women of my study all experienced conflicts among the various authorities that claimed a woman's duty—her own family, her husband, her King, her religion—or conflicts between her own desire and obedience to any of these. Such conflicts register, as Karl Weintraub phrases it, a destabilizing competition between compelling cultural forms:[25] they force choices and thereby foster the growth of self-consciousness. A woman's pride in her own family connections might dictate resistance to a husband's wishes and commands (as was sometimes the case with Queen Anne and Anne Clifford); and it might validate both sexual license and authorship (as was the case with Mary Wroth). Family pride and ambition coupled with personal desire might lead to open flouting of a king-patriarch's commands (as was the case with Arbella Stuart). Service to God, the Protestant cause, and a beloved husband might dictate ideological opposition to a king and father (as was the case with Princess Elizabeth). The claims of a Catholic conscience might justify opposing a whole phalanx of Protestant patriarchs (as was the case with Elizabeth Cary). When the patriarchs do not line up neatly in support of one another, women must choose, and their struggles to do so may serve as a catalyst for self-definition, resistance, and writing.

Moreover, Christian and especially Protestant orthodoxy held within it a large potential for destabilization in its insistence on every Christian's immediate relationship with God and primary responsibility to follow conscience in every action. There is of course plenty of support in the Pauline epistles and elsewhere in the Bible for patriarchy and a wife's subjection to her husband. One locus classicus is Ephesians 5:22–24: "Wives, submit yourselves unto your own husbands, as unto the Lord. For the husband is the head of the wife, even as Christ is the head of the church . . . Therefore as the church is subject unto Christ, so let the wives be to their own husbands in every thing." But some texts inscribe a very differ-

Women, Writing, and Resistance in Jacobean England   9

ent politics, for example, Galatians 3:28: "There is nether Jew nor Greek, there is neither bond nor free, there is neither male nor female: for ye are all one in Christ Jesus." Not until the Familists, Diggers, and Quakers at midcentury would the radical implications of such texts find application in social theory, but they anchor the arguments for women's spiritual equality by which Speght and Lanyer undermine the presumption of women's natural inferiority and necessary subjection to men. Several of the women I examine here confidently claimed the support of God the Supreme Patriarch (much as Foxe's female martyrs had done) against the various earthly patriarchs who claimed to rule them in his stead.

Another enabling factor may be the amazing variety of female images offered in contemporary literature and especially on the stage: clever and resourceful widows such as Middleton's Valeria; ambitious plotters who dominate their husbands such as Lady Macbeth; "roaring girls" such as Middleton and Dekker's Moll Cutpurse; numerous cross-dressed heroines such as Rosalind and Jessica; learned princesses skilled in legal and rhetorical argument such as Shakespeare's Portia or Sidney's Pamela; lady knights whose swords are mighty in the pursuit of adventure and love such as Spenser's Britomart or Tasso's Bradamante and Clorinda; powerful queens who lead their forces on the battlefield such as Fletcher's Bonduca (Boadicea) and Heywood's Amazon Penthesilea; shrews, often enough justified, such as Shakespeare's Emilia and Paulina; lively city wives and shopkeepers, whores honest and dishonest, vigorous tavernkeepers such as Mistress Quickly; courtesan-heroines such as Webster's Vittoria Corombona; widows who govern states and marry to please themselves such as the Duchess of Malfi. If such texts are read against marriage sermons and domestic conduct literature, and with Foucaultian assumptions about the irresistible power of ideology, it is easy enough to produce the familiar argument that all the subversive images of female power, wit, and rebellion are finally contained by the catastrophes in the tragedies or the marriage finales in the comedies, and that patriarchal power is reinforced by allowing and then controlling such gestures.[26] But if we admit the power of literary and dramatic images to affect the imagination, we might expect the very presence of such a galaxy of vigorous and rebellious female characters to undermine any monolithic social construct of woman's nature and role.[27] There is some evidence that women took the oppositional support they needed or wanted from books and plays. Women of all social classes went to the theater, and the Queen herself was passionate about it, attending plays of all sorts with her female entourage; the French ambassador claimed that she especially favored satirical plays "in order to enjoy the laugh against her husband."[28]

There is also the gap or slippage between ideology and common experience and observation. As Margaret Ezell's studies have shown, English-women throughout the seventeenth century exercised a good deal of actual power: as managers of estates in their husbands' absences at court or on military and diplomatic missions; as widows managing their own estates and those of their minor children or wards; and as wives and mothers who sometimes dominated their men by sheer force of personality or outright defiance.[29] Edward Coke's wife, Lady Elizabeth Hatton, was a notorious case of such defiance: she refused to take Coke's name, sent an armed band to try to rescue their daughter from the disastrous marriage he had arranged for her, and at length separated from him.[30] Also, as has often been noted, the anxiety about women's unruliness so frequently voiced by King and clergy in this period is patently a response to something. One major target for such denunciation was the fad of female cross-dressing: if the tracts are to be believed, not only lower-class or underworld figures such as the notorious Long Meg of Westminster and Moll Cutpurse, but even noblewomen and citizens' wives were affecting doublets, swords, broad-brimmed hats, and short hair.[31] This was read as a challenge to gender hierarchy—and the gesture could indeed insinuate that clothes and custom (not intrinsic nature) make the man or woman. The effect was to enact gender ambiguity in the streets, suggesting that women might assume masculine roles and privileges as easily as doublet and sword. Also, it is probably no accident that several of the women writers defied gender norms in their personal lives: both Lanyer and Wroth bore illegitimate children; the Countess of Bedford lived apart from her husband; Clifford defied the male authorities in prosecuting her lawsuits. Their personal experience of resisting gender norms surely reinforced, and was reinforced by, their literary challenges to those norms.

My method in this study is deliberately eclectic, in accordance with my belief that these texts need to be situated within many contexts—biographical, historical, literary, theoretical. Several of the issues I engage (representation, cultural repression, identity, agency, authorship, resistance) have been focused by feminist, Marxist, and new historicist theory, but with all these writers I begin empirically, with an attempt to find and marshal whatever scanty information exists about them and their texts. Also, I have tried to read the works as responsibly as possible, using techniques of formalist analysis to begin a consideration of them in aesthetic as well as political terms. We need to know much more about these texts before we can address questions of aesthetics very securely, but it is already evident that Cary, Lanyer, and especially Wroth are writers of considerable merit.

What broader understandings might we gain about Jacobean England and about literature and culture from attending to these writing women?

I hope it will be evident that the womens' texts examined here richly repay scrutiny both in literary and in cultural terms, and that we need to search out more such texts and study them better; also, that such womens' voices need to be listened to carefully as we develop and revise our theories about women and gender in early modern England. These texts allow us to complicate our understanding of terms such as patriarchy, female patronage, subversion and containment, absolutism and resistance with a range of period-specific female examples. If the exercise proves illuminating, it will argue for an examination of early modern women's roles and writing not only century by century and country by country but even generation by generation, so as to write a more careful and comprehensive cultural history. The tantalizing question "Did Women Have a Renaissance?" is probably best addressed through the old journalistic questions: When? Where? How? What kind? How much?

Also, by attending to the several kinds of resistance inscribed in these women's texts, we may be led to recognize important aspects of early modern literature and culture that the overused new historicist formula, subversion and containment, may obscure. My emphasis here will be clear enough: I have more interest in resistance than subjugation, more interest in attending carefully to what these women manage to express than in reading through them (again) the all-too-true story of what the culture managed to repress. Although these women writers were subsequently ignored or suppressed, I take it that their literary gestures of resistance matter, and that those gestures (often subtly coded)[32] have resulted in fascinating texts. Obviously these Jacobean women did not and could not change their world, but they were able to imagine and represent a better one.

Attention to these women writers will also help us recognize that authorship may be the process as well as the product of asserting subjectivity and agency. I believe that for most of them writing itself was a major means of self-definition. In this study I have tried to let several women's voices be heard as they begin a dialogue with the literary tradition, with one another, and with the men shaping politics and culture in Jacobean England.

I

THE ROYAL OPPOSITION

Queen Anne of Denmark, by Paul Van Somer.

1 ～♂♂

Enacting Opposition: Queen Anne
and the Subversions of Masquing

The Jacobean establishment had not one but three centers of power, with the courts of Queen Anne (1575–1619) and (later) Prince Henry standing in some oppositional tension vis-à-vis the King's court. For the first time since Henry VIII there was a separate Queen's household with new places for female as well as male courtiers, and separate channels for patronage and cultural production. That institutional separation was intensified by King James's attitudes, interests, and sexual proclivities, which led the Queen to develop over time various strategies to maintain her own worth and dignity. One major strategy was her use of the court masque as a vehicle for self-affirmation and for subversive intervention in Jacobean politics.

The marriage of King James of Scotland and Princess Anne of Denmark began as a romantic tale with James's dashing sea voyage to rescue his fourteen-year-old bride, who was delayed by storms en route to Scotland. After the wedding in 1589 he accorded her due public honor as Queen of Scotland and later of Great Britain; he maintained generally amicable relations with her (as the newsy letters exchanged between them testify),[1] and he fathered seven children by her (of whom three survived infancy). But the homosexual and patriarchal ethos of his court excluded her from any significant place in his personal or political life. A succession of male favorites—Esmé Stuart, James Hay, Philip Herbert (Montgomery), Robert Carr (Somerset), George Villiers (Buckingham)—supplied James's romantic interests and served as primary channels of influence and patronage, while he devoted much of his time and thought to hunting and theological disputation. In 1606 the poet John Harington observed that James's court was increasingly a locus of scandal, riot, and debauchery:

I neer did see such lack of good order, discretion, and sobriety, as I have now done . . . the gunpowder fright is got out of all heads, and we are going on hereabouts, as if the devil were contriving every man should blow up himself by wild riot, excess, and devastation of time and temperance.[2]

James spelled out his rigidly patriarchal notions of marriage and kingship in the *Basilikon Doron,* advising his presumptive heir, Prince Henry, about a queen's proper marital subordination and entire exclusion from political activities or influence:

> And for your behaviour to your Wife, the Scripture can best give you counsell therein: Treat her as your owne flesh, command her as her Lord, cherish her as your helper, rule her as your pupill, and please her in all things reasonable; but teach her not to be curious in things that belong her not: Ye are the head, shee in your body; It is your office to command, and hers to obey; but yet with such a sweet harmonie as shee should be as ready to obey, as ye to command; . . . suffer her never to meddle with the Politicke government of the Commonweale, but holde her at the Oeconomicke rule of the house; and yet all to be subject to your direction.[3]

Although James did not manage to impose these terms on his Queen, the Protestant clergy sought from the outset to construct her role along similar lines. In a coronation year sermon Thomas Playfere, Lady Margaret Professor of Divinity at Cambridge, attributed the "present felicitie and glory of this realme" to James alone, praising Anne for excellence "in due proportion conformable to himself."[4] Andrew Willet's sermon of that year offered the Queen somewhat greater scope as moral helpmeet after the biblical model, urging her to be to James "as Deborah to Baruch, as Hyuldah to Josias, as Esther to Ahuseuroth," and to exhibit the piety of Rebecca, the zeal of Miriam, the wisdom of the matron of Abel, the charity of the Shunammite.[5] Some years later William Cowper firmly insisted on the Queen's wifely subjection: she should reverence her husband "as the rocke from whence shee was taken, but much more love and honour him as the Head, under whom she lives," and thereby guarantee the welfare of the royal children and the common benefit of the subjects.[6]

Almost from the outset, however, Queen Anne resisted these restrictive terms through various gestures of opposition and also by fostering cultural myths and practices which enhanced her own dignity and power. She was no Queen Elizabeth, but neither was she the frivolous lightweight of the usual historians' portrait. As Leeds Barroll has emphasized, she came from a sophisticated court. Her father, Frederic II of Denmark, was the patron of Tycho Brahe and built the observatory at Hveen for him. Her mother,

Sophie, studied the sciences, patronized scholars and artists, and fought hard to retain some power at court during her son's minority. Her brother, Christian IV of Denmark, despite his notorious drunken carousing with James on his 1606 state visit to England, was a monarch of substantial accomplishment.[7] Queen Anne's sense of herself, her consciousness of wrongs, her oppositional political gestures, her attitudes and quirks of character are pointed up in an eighteenth-century memoir, falsely attributed to one of Princess Elizabeth's ladies-in-waiting but evidently based on stories and materials handed down in the Erskine family, longtime intimates of James's:

> None of his [the King's] Caresses comforted her, for the little Share he was willing to give her in Affairs of Government, though she often extorted his Consent to the Points she insisted upon, by Importunity, Clamour, and Perseverence . . . She took all her Information on trust, from those who courted her Favour, and, as they generally happened to be of a contrary Party to those whom the King thought his faithfullest Friends, she gave him frequent Uneasiness . . . She was sincere in her Professions, and scorned to dissemble with any body; nothing could make her break her Word, though she was apt to give it hastily: She was humane to those in Distress, and very affable to all who approached her with the Respect she thought due her, as one of the greatest Princesses in *Europe,* but extremely sensitive on any Failure in that point . . . She was always fond of Shows and Diversions, and after she had been some time in *England* gave herself almost wholly up to them; finding it vain for her to attempt managing the State-affairs, which the *English* Council, still more than the King, prevented her doing, yet for several Years, she interfered more than they liked . . . She knew the King's Character better than almost any body did, and had a great Influence over him, when he was not under that of any particular Favorite, and those he always pretended to choose, upon her Recommendation; yet she was grieved at the little Esteem she thought he had for her, though, one would think, she could not but be sensible it was not personal to her, but to the whole Sex, (whom he was taxed with looking on, as necessary Evils) . . . She grew to despise him for his Want of Spirit, and took . . . little Care to conceal her mean Opinion of him.[8]

Much of this is confirmed in contemporary accounts. The Queen's oppositional attitudes and gestures of resistance arose chiefly from her desire to assert her own value and importance as something more than James's Queen. The circumstances of her life offered limited opportunities to construct such a role, but the masques and entertainments she sponsored afforded better ones. Such gestures also had broader ramifications. Even as Prince Henry's oppositional court became a locus for reformist Protestant ideology and hopes, so the Queen's presence and court provided a locus, unstable but yet influential, of female resistance to Jacobean patriarchy.

Modes of Resistance

The Queen's resistance took various forms. For one thing, in her progresses and public appearances she developed a distinct persona which was reinforced by the responses of the populace. On her 1603 progress from Scotland to London to ascend the English throne, she found she greatly enjoyed the splendid entertainments offered her at the cities and country houses along the way, enacting to perfection the role of warm, gracious, lovely and beloved Queen and presenting a sharp contrast to James's much-criticized aloofness and reserve.[9] A year later, reports of the deferred coronation progress from the Tower to Whitehall again underscore the contrast: "Our gratious Queene Ann, milde and curteous, plaste in a chariot of exceeding beauty, did all the way so humbly and with mildenes salue her subjects, never leaving to bend her body to them, this way and that, that women and men, in my sight, wept with joy."[10]

Early tributes and works dedicated to Anne display some awkwardness in constructing her person and role as they labor to please both King and Queen. In the coronation year and shortly after, several texts inappropriately transfer to her the classical divine epithets, Petrarchan praises, and pastoral topoi developed for Queen Elizabeth. Hugh Holland dedicated his *Pancharis* (1603), originally intended for Queen Elizabeth, to the new monarchs, applying to Anne the Elizabethan Petrarchan terms "silver Cynthia" and "Queene of Love and Beauty."[11] She was "sweete Cynthia" also for the Scots poet Alexander Craigie, who claimed her as patron.[12] Ben Jonson's elegant "entertainment" for Queen Anne and Prince Henry at Althorpe found for her the appropriate new title "Oriana" (*Oriens Anna*), predicting with wild hyperbole that she would "excede, whom she succeeds, our late Diana." His Satyr speaker laments the absence of the King but is content to find his image in Henry and to honor Anne as the womb that gave birth to that image.[13] Jonson's entertainment for the King and Queen at Sir William Cornwallis's Highgate (May 1, 1604) has the pastoral gods Aurora, Flora, Maia, and Mercury praise James as "master of the ocean" and the Queen as Oriana, emphasizing her "state and comeliness" and her noble blood; it ends with familiar comic banter as Pan presses drink on them both and jests about the Queen's fondness for it.[14]

Some other entertainments and dedications addressed the Queen in the terms she liked best, emphasizing her independent worth and dignity through her own family (as the daughter and sister of Kings) and praising her entourage, her noble virtues, and her maternity. In Jonson's portion of the entertainment offered to King, Queen, and Prince by the City of London in the 1604 coronation procession, Genius accords Anne "no less a part / In this day's greatness" than the King. Apostrophizing her as "Glory of Queens . . . You Daughter, Sister, Wife of several Kings / Besides alliance, and the style of mother, / In which one title you drown all your other," he proposes that she take on the role of the City's advocate with James.[15] On the same occasion Grant Dugdale employed similar formulas, and also honored the Queen and her entourage, "lovely Ladies, the onely wed-starres of the world for beautye and good graces."[16] In 1608 George Chapman praised Anne as the source of all Prince Henry's merit: "Sole Empress of Beautie, and Vertue / . . . With whatsoever Honor wee adorne / Your Royall Issue; we must gratulate yow / Imperiall Soveraigne. Who of you is borne, / Is you. One Tree, make both the Bole and Bow."[17] In 1613 John Florio, Privy Councilor and "Reader of the Italian tongue" to Queen Anne, deftly complimented her linguistic gifts with a hyperbolic Italian sonnet praising her magnanimity and virtue as "above divine," and her maternity as the glorious source of the nation's joy, security, and good.[18] Making a bid for the Queen's patronage that same year, George Wither first invoked the familiar formula "Daughter, Wife, Sister, Mother to a King; / And Empresse of the North." But he honored her especially for the wisdom, bounty, and courtesy she manifested in valuing his honest satirical writings.[19]

In the first dedication to her 1611 volume of poetry, the Queen's only female celebrant, Aemilia Lanyer, constructed her in much more expansive terms. Taking Anne as the embodiment and conduit of all the (female) virtues and powers associated with the classical goddesses, Lanyer also expanded her maternal role, inviting the Queen to see herself as nurturer of artists, defender of women, judge of biblical exegesis, and special patron of Lanyer herself as a female poet concerned to defend women:

> Renowned Empresse, and great Britanes Queene,
> Most gratious Mother of succeeding Kings;
> Vouchsafe to view that which is seldome seene,
> A Womans writing of divinest things:
> . . . . .
> From *Juno* you have State and Dignities,
> From warlike *Pallas*, Wisdome, Fortitude;
> And from faire *Venus* all her Excellencies,
> With their best parts your Highnesse is indu'd:
> . . . . .
> The Muses doe attend upon your Throne,
> With all the Artists at your becke and call.
> . . . . .

Behold, great Queene, faire *Eves* Apologie,
Which I have writ in honour of your sexe,
And doe referre unto your Majestie,
To judge if it agree not with the Text:
And if it doe, why are poore Women blam'd,
Or by more faultie Men so much defam'd?[20]

There is no record of the Queen's response, if any, to Lanyer's book, but Lanyer evidently expected her to approve these terms of address—a not unwarranted hope, given Anne's oppositional activities in several public and private arenas.

Queen Anne's more direct forms of resistance centered on her children and household, the Roman Catholic religion, court appointments, theater patronage, and political maneuvering. As Queen of Scots, Anne was rumored to have loved and plotted with the rebel lords James proscribed as traitors—the dashing Bothwell and the Ruthven brothers. The scandalous rumors are unsubstantiated, but the Queen showed considerable sympathy for the rebel lords and fiercely protected ladies of her chamber associated with them.[21] Her frequent opposition to and quarrels with the King's most trusted advisers and favorites were usually motivated by concern for her just due or slighted dignity, or by loyalty to friends and clients, though sometimes also by larger issues; they are recorded in a series of pithy, spirited, and sometimes humorous notes penned in the Queen's own hand. On one occasion shortly before her coronation in England, she sharply protested James's leniency in pardoning two noblemen who had had the temerity to quarrel in her presence: "Sir . . . I could not but think it strange that any about your Majestie durst presume to bring neer where your majestie is, on[e] that had offered me such a publicke scorne, for honore gois befor lyfe."[22]

Her most important early struggle involved Prince Henry, born in February 1594 and a few months later given over by the King to be raised (as he himself had been) by John Erskine, Earl of Mar, and his wife. Anne raged at the King, pleaded to be given the care of her child, contrived various plots to obtain him, and was so distressed that she had a miscarriage in July 1595. The King, always fearful of plots and treason, adamantly refused, arguing that "if some faction got strong enough, she could not hinder his boy being used against him, as he himself had been against his unfortunate mother."[23] In 1603, after James departed for England, the Queen led armed troops to Stirling Castle to reclaim Henry; when repulsed she had another miscarriage and flatly refused to come to England until Henry was formally returned to her, and by someone other than the hated Mar. To avoid acute embarrassment at his coronation, James had to capitulate to all her terms. His letter to Anne on this occasion alludes to the persistent rumors that she was a closet papist, and (typically) disallows her claims to independent status and dignity through her own family:

> My Hairte . . . I can say no more but proteste upon the peril of my salvation and damnation, that nather the Erle of Marr nor any flesh living ever informed me that ye was upon any Papish or Spanish course . . . I thank God, I carrie that love and respecte unto you quhich by the law of God and nature I ought to do to my wyfe and mother of my children, but not for that ye are a King's dauchter, for quhither ye waire a King's or a cook's dauchter ye must be all alike to me, being once my wyfe . . . I beseache you excuse my rude plainness in this; for casting up of your birthe is a needless impertinent argument to me.[24]

Though she was raised a Lutheran, Queen Anne's attraction to Roman Catholicism involved her both early and late in oppositional politics. Her failure to take the Sacrament at her English coronation in the Abbey (July 25, 1603) fueled rumors about her conversion. Her closest friend in Scotland, Henrietta Stuart, the Catholic Countess of Huntley, was reportedly instrumental in her conversion; one Father Abercrombie claimed to have received her into the Church around 1600; several ambassadors reported that she told them in confidence of her conversion; letters and gifts were exchanged between Anne and Pope Clement VIII in 1601 and 1604, and again in 1609 in relation to marriage plans for Prince Henry; and priests were creditably reported to be in attendance at her court.[25] In Scotland James exploited the Queen's religious inclinations to win the support of the Catholic peers as a counterpoise to the Kirk and the Protestant extremists. In England, however, her overt pro-Spanish advocacy disrupted the careful balance that the pacific and politic James sought to maintain between Spain and France, and between the warring Catholic and Protestant states of Europe. The Queen strongly supported a marriage between Prince Henry and the Infanta Anna of Spain, and later between Henry and a Medici Princess of Florence. For Princess Elizabeth she supported the suit of the recently widowed Philip III of Spain, and at first opposed that of the Protestant Elector Palatine. For more than a decade she forwarded her Spanish policy through her sponsorship of court masques, continually and flagrantly favoring the Spanish ambassador with invitations and precedence over the French ambassador, who complained bitterly that the King of England was not master in his own house.[26]

Whatever the depth or duration of her commitment to Roman Catholicism, it made her a focus of intrigue and offered her an independent sphere of action. Roman Catholic writers often intimated or asserted that she was one of their own, who might further Catholic interests. Citing reports of the Queen's "vertuous inclination" and her habit of importing Catholic books of piety and devotion from abroad, one "R.W." offered her his *Dialogues of S. Gregorie,* to redress a (supposed) neglect: "None at all for ought that I can learne, much lesse that professeth the religion of S. Gregorie, hath hitherto presented any booke to your Princely person."[27] More expansively, Michael Walpole urged Queen Anne to model herself on Queen Esther, in order to save her co-religionists and return England to the Roman fold:

> By her mediation with King *Assuerus,* the nation of the *Jewes* was delivered from an universall overthrow: and why should not Queene *Anne* prevaile as farre with King *James* for Ancient and Christian Catholikes? Can any doubt, but that he would extend the Golden Rod of Clemency, toward his dearest spouse? Yea rather divide his Kingdome, then deny her request? . . . The very attempting of this Noble & Godly enterprise deserveth immortall prayse: *Henricus rosas; Jacobus regna,* oh, that we might adde, *Anna Ecclesias!*[28]

In the sphere of patronage and appointments, the Queen fought hard to choose her own court and household officers. She tried unsuccessfully to preempt the King's and Cecil's choice for her Lord Chamberlain in 1603, but won the battle to retain two favorite Scots ladies-in-waiting and her Danish maid Anna. En route to London in 1603 Anne was met in Berwick by an official welcoming party of English noblemen and noblewomen;[29] but of the English ladies she warmed only to those who had rushed on their own to Scotland to meet her—especially the Countess of Bedford and her mother, Lady Harington, Lady Dorothy Hastings, and Lady Elizabeth Hatton. Sir Thomas Edmonds's letter of June 15 reports the King's angry response to the Queen's independent line:

> Some courses which she hath taken . . . doe verie muche discontent the Kinge; namelie, for conferringe the place of her Chamberleyn (to the which Sir George Carew was recomended) on one Mr. Kennedy, a Scottishe gentellman, of whom the King hath very ill conceipt, and, as it is said, used these wourdes against him; that if he should find that she doe bring him hither to attend her in that place, that he woulde breake the staffe of his Chamberleynshipp on his hedd, and so dismisse him . . . It is sayd that the Kynge taketh the like offence at the coming of dyvers others that be in her companie . . . It is said that she hath hitherto refused to admitt my Ladye of Kildare and the Ladye Walsingham, to be of her privye chambr, and hath onlye as yett sworne my Ladye of Bedfourd to that place.[30]

In the event she had to forgo Kennedy and accommodate the great English ladies. On February 2, 1604, Edward Somerset, Earl of Worcester, reported the official appointments in what he terms "the feminine common welthe," as well as the continued vying for favor and notice within it:

> Youe must knowe we have ladyes of divers degrees of favor; some for the privat chamber, some for the drawing chamber, some for the bed chamber, and some for neyther certeyn, and of this nomber is onely my La. Arbella and my wife. My Lady of Bedford howldethe fast to the bed chamber . . . My Lady of Derbee the yonger, the Lady Suffolke, Ritche [Rich], Nottingham, Susan [de Vere], Walsingham, and, of late, the Lady Sothwell for the drawing chamber; all the rest for the private [privy] chamber, when they are not shut owt, for mayny tymes the dores ar lokt; but the plotting and mallice amongst them is sutche, that I thinke envy hathe teyd an invisibl snake abowt most of ther neks to sting on another to deathe. For the presence [chamber] there are nowe 5 mayds [of honor]; Cary, Myddellmore, Woodhouse, Gargrave, Roper; the sixt is determyned, but not come.[31]

But within the official household the Queen continued to distinguish her own favorites—the Ladies Bedford, Rich, and Hatton—who attracted her especially, Anne Clifford intimates, by their youth, liveliness, and enterprise.[32]

Over the years, Queen Anne's choice of favorites and close friends, female and male, was often grounded in oppositional politics as well as personal attraction. She found her interests and influence threatened by the Catholic Howards as well as by Robert Carr (Somerset), who were in the ascendant at James's court; accordingly, despite her Catholic inclinations, she chose her closest associates from the Essex-Sidney faction of internationalist Protestants, whose hopes centered on her son Prince Henry. They were major patrons of literature and the arts in the period, and most of them were kin to her favorite and most influential courtier, the Countess of Bedford. Robert Sidney, Viscount Lisle of Penshurst and later Earl of Leicester as well as brother to Sir Philip Sidney, became Anne's Lord Chamberlain, responsible for the entertainments, plays, and other festivities at her court (the King's initial choice, George Carew, was relegated to Vice-Chamberlain).[33] Another male friend was William Herbert, Earl of Pembroke (son of the Dowager Countess of Pembroke, Mary Sidney Herbert), who was the King's Lord Chamberlain after 1615; still another was Sir Walter Ralegh, whom the Queen greatly admired, visited in the Tower, received medicines from, and tried hard to save. The husband of her chief female favorite, Lucy Harington Russell, the Countess of Bedford, was seriously implicated in the Essex conspiracy; another favorite, Penelope Rich, was Sidney's "Stella" and sister to Essex.[34] The Countess of Bedford's parents, Lord and Lady Harington, were chosen as tutor-guardians for Princess Elizabeth.[35]

The Queen's oppositional stance was signaled publicly in her patronage and support of the Children of the Queen's Revels; between 1603 and 1608 they presented at Blackfriars a series of politically daring and satiric plays that often brought down official wrath and punishment on the playwrights involved. Among the worst offenders were Ben Jonson's *Eastward Ho;* John Day's *Isle of Gulls;* Samuel Daniel's *Philotas;* George Chapman's *Widow's Teares, Charles Duke of Byron,* and *Monsieur D'Olive;* John Marston's *Dutch Courtesan,* and a lost play attributed to Marston, *The Silver Mines.*[36] The special status and freedom of the Children's company was due directly to the Queen's patronage: they were licensed not by the Master of the Revels but by the Queen's own client and appointee, Daniel, a collaborator manifestly sympathetic to her own oppositional posture. Far from serving as censor, Daniel himself contributed to the theater's controversial repertoire with his daring Senecan play *Philotas,* understood to allude in sympathetic terms to Essex's rebellion.[37] That the Queen gave active as well as passive support to the oppositional theater and encouraged anti-Jamesian satire is evident from the French ambassador Beaumont's dispatch of June 14, 1604: "Consider for pity's sake what must be the state and condition of a prince, whom the preachers publicly from the pulpit assail, whom the comedians of the metropolis bring upon the stage, whose wife attends these representations in order to enjoy the laugh against her husband."[38]

Queen Anne also involved herself at times in direct political maneuvers and plots. Her dislike for Robert Carr (Somerset) kept pace with his meteoric rise to power as the King's favorite; and she found occasion to protest bitterly what she took to be mockery and insults from him.[39] Her hostility intensified upon Somerset's notorious marriage to Frances Howard (in the wake of her scandalous divorce from Essex's son), a liason which strengthened Carr's power and the Howard hegemony. So Anne was persuaded in 1615 to join forces with Pembroke, Archbishop of Canterbury George Abbot, and several Protestant lords to promote a new favorite, George Villiers. Abbot recounted her role in this conspiracy (made possible because James sought to involve her in his choice and thereby avoid a reprise of her feud with Somerset), and credited the Queen with clearer perceptions about the outcome than the others had:

> King James, for many insolencies, grew weary of Somerset . . . We could have no way so good to effectuate that which was the common desire as to bring in another in his room . . . It was now observed, that the King began to cast his eye upon George Villiers, who was then Cup-bearer, and seemed a modest and courteous youth. But King James had a fashion, that he would never admit any to nearness

about himself but such an one as the Queen should commend unto him, and make some suit on his behalf; that if the Queen afterwards, being ill-treated, should complain of this dear one, he might make his answer, "It is long of yourself, for you were the party that commended him unto me." Our old Master took delight in things of this nature.

That noble Queen (who now resteth in Heaven) knew her Husband well; and having been bitten with Favorites both in England and Scotland, was very shie to adventure upon this request . . . I laboured much, but could not prevail; the Queen oft saying to me, "My Lord, you and the rest of your friends know not what you do. I know your Master better than you all; for if this young man be once brought in, the first persons that he will plague must be you that labour for him; yea, I shall have my part also. The King will teach him to despise and hardly intreat us all, that he may seem to be beholden to none but himself." Noble Queen! how like a prophetess or oracle did you speak!

Notwithstanding this, we were still instant, telling her Majesty, that the change would be for the better. For George was of a good nature, which the other was not; and if he should degenerate, yet it would be a long time before he were able to attain to that height of evil, which the other had. In the end, upon importunity, Queen Anne condescended, and so pressed it with the King, that he assented, which was so stricken while the iron was hot, that in the Queen's Bed-chamber, the King knighted him with the rapier which the Prince did wear.[40]

Queen Anne immediately had him sworn a Gentleman of the Bed-Chamber, circumventing a last-ditch effort by Somerset to give him the lesser office of Groom.

Over the years Anne's relations with Villiers (soon to be Buckingham) remained cordial; she adopted James's pet name for him ("my kind dog") and occasionally sought small favors by his influence.[41] But he ignored her appeal in 1618 to save Ralegh from execution—her last serious political cause:

My kind dogge,
If I have any power or credit with you, I pray you let me have a trial of it at this time, in dealing sincerely and earnestly with the king that Sir Walter Ralegh's life may not be called in question, if you do it so, that the success answer my expectation, assure your self that I will take it extraordinarily kindly at your hands.[42]

She made other fruitless efforts in Ralegh's behalf, appealing to the King directly on personal grounds that "as he tendered her health to spare him for that she had receved great goode by his receits."[43] Nor did she fare better in her highest political ambition—to be appointed Regent when the King visited Scotland in the spring of 1617. True to his notions about women's place, James entrusted the government to Lord Keeper Bacon.[44]

The Queen's resistance manifested itself also in separatism—defining a distinct and relatively independent sphere of activities and interests with her own entourage. While separate residences and households for queen consorts are customary, James's homosexuality as well as other familial circumstances led to Queen Anne's progressive withdrawal to her own court and affairs. The King and Queen ceased to cohabit in 1607, after their sixth child, Mary (born in April 1605), died of a violent fever; the year before a seventh child, Sophia, had died a few hours after birth, and the Queen suffered a long, life-threatening illness. Thereafter Anne came to Whitehall only for state occasions and for the traditional festivities of Christmastide, spending the rest of the year at her several residences—Somerset House (renamed Denmark House),[45] Hampton Court, Oatlands, Greenwich—or on progress. As early as January 1605 Dudley Carleton commented on the Queen's court as a separate and competing locus of interest and power, to which the King's officers gravitated during the King's frequent hunting expeditions: "The Lords of the Council are tyed to attendance at the Queen's Court, and they have a letter from the King to be more diligent in his affairs."[46] In 1608 James wrote a curious letter, partly in cipher, to his new Lord Treasurer, Robert Cecil, jestingly reproving the nobles' involvement with the Queen's court and affairs:

> Ye and youre fellowis thaire are so proude nou that ye have gottin the gyding againe of a Feminine Courte in the olde fashon, as I know not hou to deale uith you; ye sitte at youre ease and directis all; the newis from all the pairtis of the uorlde comes to you in youre chamber, the King's owin resolutions dependis upon youre posting dispatches.[47]

The Queen was devastated by Prince Henry's sudden death in 1612, at age eighteen; a few months later she saw her newly married daughter Elizabeth leave England forever. According to the indefatigable commentator on court affairs John Chamberlain, a "pacification" between King and Queen followed upon these losses: James magnanimously forgave Anne for shooting his favorite hound by mistake during a hunting trip in July 1613, and gave her a diamond and also Greenwich into her jointure.[48] The Queen enjoyed hunting, but arthritis and gout increasingly kept her from sharing James's favorite activity. In 1616 poor health and (Chamberlain thought) grief over Prince Henry caused her to miss the ceremonies creating Charles Prince of Wales.[49]

The Queen's separate interests ran to progresses, entertainments, attending the theater, dancing and games with her ladies, architectural planning, and masques—activities which allowed her some scope for self-affirmation, for affecting Jacobean culture, and for resistance. Her most significant cultural activities were the entertainments and court masques she planned with Daniel, Jonson, and Inigo Jones, the primary recipients of her patronage over several years. After the progress from Scotland in 1603, her most extended independent progress was in the spring and summer of 1613, to Bath, Bristol, and Wells. She went in great state, obviously enjoying the lavish entertainments and the pleasure of being sole center of attention.[50] At Caversham House near Bath, home of Lord and Lady Knollys (Lord Chamberlain Suffolk's daughter), she was so delighted by Thomas Campion's elegant entertainment that she "vouchsafed to make herselfe the head of their revels, and graciously to adorne the place with her personall dancing."[51] After taking the waters at Bath she proceeded to Bristol, where the lavish entertainments, pageants, and sea fights caused her to exclaim that "she never knew she was a Queen till she came to Bristoll." Chamberlain records her delight in all this, and her determination to "make many more such progresses."[52] She also planned architectural projects with Inigo Jones, beginning work in 1613 on the Queen's House or "House of Delight" in the Park at Greenwich, where she spent more and more time as her health worsened.[53]

Queen Anne died of dropsy on March 2, 1619, at age forty-five, after several months of illness. During her last years she became more earnest in her Catholic practice, keeping priests within call at Hampton Court and fitting up a beautiful chapel at Oatlands.[54] Yet death took her by surprise, so that she could not arrange her affairs as she might have desired. She left a very considerable fortune but (despite much urging) no written will: there were reports that she intended a casket of jewels for Princess Elizabeth and wanted her brother the King of Denmark for executor, but in the event she could only answer yes to Prince Charles's questions as to whether he was to have everything. Deathbed accounts (probably fictionalized) claimed for her a good Protestant death, with the Archbishop of Canterbury and the Bishop of London prompting her to renounce all confidence in the saints and in her own merits.[55] Some of her servants (including her trusted Danish Anna) helped themselves to valuable jewels. The Howard ladies squabbled over the place of chief mourner (it went finally to Alatheia Howard, Countess of Arundel). The funeral was postponed for several weeks until the exchequer could afford the high costs of mourning apparel and other trappings, during which time relays of mourners kept watch over the corpse at Denmark House.[56] It took place at last on May 13, beginning with a solemn and splendid procession on foot to Westminster Abbey, which according to Chamberlain soon became a "tedious sight" as the ladies "came laggering along even tired with the length of the way and the waight of theyre clothes"—sixteen yards of black broadcloth for the Countesses.[57] The King, who hated gloomy occasions, declined to attend, remaining with Buckingham at Theobalds. He wore no mourning, refused to recognize his wife's deathbed legacies to Charles, and gave a good portion of her estate to Buckingham.[58] Nor was any monument ever erected over Queen Anne's grave in Westminster Abbey.

The Queen's Subversive Entertainments

Queen Anne made her chief contribution to Jacobean culture through her early patronage of Ben Jonson and Inigo Jones, and her participation in the creation and development of the court masque. In the first Jacobean decade masques and entertainments were a primary means by which the Queen affirmed herself and intervened in Jacobean politics. While entertainments of various sorts had been a staple of Queen Elizabeth's progresses, the court masque became a major genre in the early years of James's reign, and Queen Anne was midwife to it. She commissioned, produced, and performed with her ladies in the first masques. Contemporary references crediting the Queen with a designing hand in several of the masques are generally dismissed as conventional puffery, and of course she was not in any usual sense a third partner with Jonson and Inigo Jones. But Jonson's own comments indicate that she often proposed the governing concept for a masque—the idea of black-faced Africans in the *Masque of Blackness,* or the idea for an antimasque in *Queenes.* The Queen and her masquing ladies may also have offered other suggestions as the masques took shape.

The Jacobean masque is usually treated as a mythic idealization of James, a Neoplatonic representation of his concept of sovereignty. Seated in his chair of state, where he enjoys the only perfect perspective and his gaze encompasses and controls the entire spectacle, he displays what the masque texts and the symbolic action show: that the monarch is the radiating source of all power, virtue, and benefits.[59] Stephen Orgel observes that "the monarch, always the ethical centre of court productions, became in a physical and emblematic way the centre as well"; or, in Jonathan Goldberg's terms, the masque serves as a mirror, its personages reflecting and elucidating the King's majesty.[60] In the masques written for Prince Henry—*Oberon* and *Barriers*—we have come to recognize the strains and contradictions that complicate this scenario, as Jonson seeks in them to accommodate the very different interests and political agendas of Prince and King.[61] But we have not much considered the subversive elements in the earliest Jacobean masques, arising from the Queen's dominant presence as planner, promoter, performer, and first audience.[62] For the first decade or so, it seems that the Stuart masque Orgel describes has not yet taken normative form, that the masque is instead a site for contestation about gender, power, and status.

We need not suppose contestation and subversion to be fully conscious on the Queen's or the authors' parts, or to be in the service of a consistent political agenda—save that of enhancing the Queen's status. They are produced by the need to please multiple audiences—King, Queen, male courtiers, court ladies—and from the complexities of shared authorial responsibility with the Queen-patron. The effect was to subvert the representation of James as exclusive locus of power and virtue by means of texts and symbolic actions which exalt the power and virtue of the Queen and her ladies—and, by extension, of women generally. That the Queen herself is in some way responsible for these subversive features is indicated by their presence in both Daniel's and Jonson's masques and entertainments for her. Moreover, Queen Anne regularly used her role as presenter of court masques to intervene in diplomatic politics. Since quarrels over precedence made it virtually impossible to invite the Spanish and French ambassadors together, the Queen could flaunt her support for Spanish Catholic interests through her masque invitations to the Spaniard—thereby enraging the French ambassador and often profoundly embarrassing James.

The first masque the Queen organized was Daniel's *Vision of Twelve Goddesses,* presented on January 8, 1604, at Hampton Court, as part of the Christmastide ceremonies.[63] Daniel became the special poet of the Queen and her court; he was appointed Special Licenser of the Queen's Revels in 1604 and by 1610 had been made Groom of her Privy Chamber. In the dedication to the printed text of *The Vision,* Daniel credits the Countess of Bedford with persuading the Queen to give him that commission, and proposes to validate her judgment by explaining to "captious Censurers" the symbolic meanings of the action, personages, costumes, and spectacle; he also defends his notion of masque as a static symbolic pageant filled with "pompe and splendor."[64] This masque began the ambassadorial jockeying for position and the Queen's partisanship, as Carleton explains to Chamberlain on January 15, 1604:

> The French and the Spanish ambassadors . . . hard hold for the greatest honor, which the Spaniard thinks he hath carried away by being first feasted . . . and invited to the greatest mask; and the French seems to be greatly discontented that he was flatly refused to be admitted to the last, about which he used unmannerly expostulations with the king and for a few days troubled all the court; but the queen was fain to take the matter upon her, who as a masker had invited the

Spaniard . . . and to have them both there could not well be without bloodshed.[65]

According to the masque conceit, twelve goddesses present various gifts and blessings of heaven to King James and his reign, which is symbolized by a Temple of Peace in tribute to his self-characterization "Pacificus." Daniel's notes indicate that the Queen chose to personate Pallas (whose gifts are Wisdom and Defense); her favorites the Countess of Bedford, Lady Rich, and Elizabeth, Lady Hatton, were, respectively, Vesta (Religion), Venus (Love and Amity), and Macaria (Felicity). The other personages were Juno (Power and Empire), Diana (Chastity), Proserpina (Riches), Concordia (Union of Hearts), Astraea (Justice), Flora (the Beauties of the Earth), Ceres (Plenty), and Tethis (Power by Sea).[66]

But although these allegorical gifts compliment James, the Queen and her ladies introduce a subversive element.[67] For one thing, their very presence as performers makes the female body the locus of action and meaning—in striking contrast to the public theater, where boy actors took the women's parts. Here the ladies are the spectacular center of attention in their satins, cloth of gold and silver, and splendid jewels, for which (Carleton writes) "they were beholden to Queen Elizabeth's wardrobe."[68] Moreover, they are the active forces, the earthly embodiments of the deities who bring to James qualities and gifts which (by implication) his reign does not yet have. Given the iconographic representation, it might seem that these qualities, like the outward finery, are a heritage from Queen Elizabeth.

Queen Anne's choice of Pallas as her persona is also significant: Juno or Venus might have seemed more obvious (and acceptable) choices. Pallas, the virgin warrior and goddess of wisdom, would evoke Queen Elizabeth to a contemporary audience, carrying associations of female power and militant internationalism that were anathema to James. The Pallas figure would also invite classical associations, linking Queen Anne with the awesome and invincible warrior-goddess whose breastplate bore the terrible head of Medusa. The presenter, Iris, accords Pallas-Anna controlling power—"all-directing *Pallas* (the glorious Patronesse of this mighty Monarchie)"—and intimates that she brings into the new realm the glorious Elizabethan qualities. The Queen's short skirts, appropriate to the female warrior, elicited Carleton's disapproving jest: "Only Pallas had a trick by herself; for her clothes were not so much below the knee but that we might see a woman had both feet and legs, which I never knew before." The masque was not well liked: Daniel complained that it was subjected to "sinister interpretation."[69] One reason may be that the spectators had some ill-defined but uneasy sense of currents of power radiating from the Queen rather than the King.

Ben Jonson's first masques were also for the Queen and her ladies. His *Masque of Blacknesse* (especially in conjunction with its sequel, the *Masque of Beautie*) seems to center firmly on the King: the conceit presents beauteous daughters of Niger come to gain the perfection of their beauty—white skins—from Albion-James, the Sun-King of "Britania." *Blacknesse* was the Queen's Twelfth Night masque for 1605; it concluded a season of festivities celebrating the wedding of the King's current favorite, Sir Philip Herbert, to Lady Susan de Vere, and the creation of Prince Charles as Duke of York. Presented at Whitehall by the Queen and eleven of her ladies—the Countesses of Bedford, Derby, and Suffolk, and the Ladies Rich, Bevill, Howard of Effingham, Elizabeth Howard, Walsingham, Wroth, Anne Herbert, and Susan De Vere Herbert—it marked the first collaboration between Jonson and Inigo Jones.[70] Everybody commented on the cost, one ambassador observing, "It cost ye K. betweene 4. and 5000[li] to execute ye Q. fancye."[71] This time the ambassadorial quarrels over precedence were to be resolved by inviting all ambassadors privately, but the French ambassador refused to come on these terms. The Spanish and Venetian ambassadors were then invited to sit by the King in state, at which gesture, wrote Carleton, "Monsieur *Beaumont* quarrells so extreamly, that he saith *the whole Court is Spanish.*"[72]

In his published text Jonson explicitly credits the Queen with the governing idea: "Because it was her majesty's will to have them blackamores at first, the invention was derived by me."[73] Moreover, she bore the brunt of the adverse criticism the idea received. Dudley Carleton termed the blackface "a very lothsome sight," detailing his objections to Sir Ralph Winwood:

> At Night we had the Queen's Maske in the Banquetting-House, or rather her Pagent. There was a great Engine at the lower end of the Room, which had Motion, and in it were the Images of Sea-Horses with other terrible Fishes, which were ridden by Moors: The Indecorum was, that there was all Fish and no water. At the further end was a great Shell in form of a Skallop, wherein were four seats; on the lowest sat the Queen with my Lady *Bedford;* on the rest were placed the [other] ladies . . . Their Apparell was rich, but too light and Curtizan-like for such great ones. Instead of Vizzards, their Faces, and Arms up to the Elbows, were painted black, which was Disguise sufficient, for they were hard to be known; *but it became them nothing so well as their red and white, and you cannot imagine a more ugly Sight, then a Troop of lean-cheek'd Moors.*[74]

The vehemence of this response may be rooted in the (perhaps subconscious) subversiveness of the Queen's governing concept. Representing

herself and her ladies as black African beauties, the Queen associates them
with alien cultural practices and primitive energies, with the feared and
desired "others" imagined by contemporary explorers, and perhaps with
the Amazons—always portrayed as dark-skinned and often assumed to be
located in Africa or America. Inigo Jones's costume sketches reinforce the
conjunction of exotic female beauty and wildness.[75] Their otherness is validated (at least temporarily) by their Father Niger, who blames Petrarchan
poets for arousing their foolish desire to conform themselves to European
courtly ideals of beauty (ll. 135–181).

At first glance their danger seems to be contained, and the transformative power seems to be vested where it should be, in James as Albion, son
of Neptune and Sun-King of "Britania"—the place the nymphs must discover and visit in order to gain their desired white skins. With James's
union of the two kingdoms, the proper name of this isle is "Britania"
(l. 242):

> Britania (whose new name makes all tongues sing)
> Might be a Diamont worthy to inchase it,
> Rul'd by a Sunne that to this height doth grace it:
> Whose beames shine day and night, and are of force
> To blanch an AETHIOPE, and revive a Cor's.
> His light scientiall is, and (past mere nature)
> Can salve the rude defects of every creature.
>
> (ll. 251–257)

But in the myth of this masque the Sun-King's powers (whatever their
force) are not displayed: the Ethiops are not blanched but remain at the
end of this masque black as they began. Also, the long process they are to
undergo in order to effect the change problematizes the source of the
transformative power, connecting it with female forces and the nymphs'
own ancestor rather than with Britain's Albion. Aethiopia (the Moon) is
the female director of the entire scheme: she instructs the nymphs to remain for a year the guests of Ocean—the father of the nymphs' own Father, Niger, and the source from which Venus was begotten—and to perform the rites she precribes at each full moon:

> Thirteene times thrise, on thirteene nights,
> (So often as I fill my *sphaere*
> With glorious light, throughout the yeere)
> You shall (when all things else doe sleepe
> Save your chast thoughts) with reverence, steepe
> Your bodies in that purer brine,
> And wholesome dew, called Ros-marine:
> Then with that soft, and gentler fome,

Of which, the *Ocean* yet yeelds some,
Whereof bright Venus, beauty's Queene,
Is said to have begotten beene,
You shall your gentler limnes o'er lave,
And for your pains, perfection have.
                                         (ll. 334–346)

As Moon goddess, Aethiopia recalls Queen Elizabeth as Cynthia, further reinforcing the association of these ladies with female danger and power. In Jonson's first masque, as in Daniel's, the Queen's authorial and directorial presence proves subversive.

The sequel was postponed for two years, its place taken by wedding masques in which the marital unions are linked with the union of kingdoms that James had effected.[76] *The Masque of Beautie* was presented at last on January 10, 1608—postponed from Twelfth Night ostensibly because the new Banqueting House at Whitehall was not yet ready, but in fact because the Queen's Spanish politics were again causing trouble. The French ambassador was outraged that the Queen had again passed him over while personally inviting the Spanish and Venetian ambassadors.[77] There was some talk of canceling the masque, but it went forward, though the King was reportedly so angry that he left for his hunting trip without speaking to Anne. The Venetian ambassador wrote that the Queen produced this masque "at her own charges," thereby claiming unequivocally the role of producer and hostess.[78]

In his published text Jonson again credits the Queen with the controlling idea: she commanded "that I should thinke on some fit presentment, which should answer the former, still keeping them the same persons, the daughters of NIGER, but their beauties varied, according to promise, and their time of absence excus'd, with foure more added to their number."[79] The new masque accordingly calls for sixteen masquers, but besides the Queen only four of the original twelve from *Blacknesse* took part: the Countesses of Bedford, Derby, and Montgomery (formerly Susan de Vere), and Lady Walsingham. The new cast included Arbella Stuart, the Queen's old favorite Elizabeth Hatton, and some newly prominent younger ladies, among them Anne Clifford. It also included several known or reputed Catholics: Alatheia Howard, Countess of Arundel, and the four daughters of the Earl of Worcester.[80] The Venetian ambassador, invited, then disinvited to smooth over the brouhaha, then invited again, praised the Queen not only as a spectacular performer but also as "authoress" of the masque:

I must just touch on the splendour of the spectacle, which was worthy of her Majesty's greatness. The apparatus and the cunning of the stage machinery was a miracle, the abundance and beauty of the lights immense, the music and the dance most sumptuous. But what beggared all else and possibly exceeded the public expectation was the wealth of pearls and jewels that adorned the Queen and her ladies . . . So well composed and ordered was it all that it is evident the mind of her Majesty, the authoress of the whole, is gifted no less highly than her person. She reaped universal applause and the King constantly showed his approval.[81]

That general approbation suggests that this masque seemed unproblematic—though in fact the strains arising from the Queen's "authorial" presence are quite evident. *Beautie* begins properly enough with elaborate compliments to Albion-James, crediting him with the "great wonder" worked upon the ladies of Niger. A dialogic exchange between Boreas and Januarius at first convicts the ladies of ingratitude for failing to return on the day required, but then explains their delay by their efforts to rescue four of their sisters held in prison by Night. At length all return, and James is invited to regard them in their new splendor and "Love the miracle, which thy selfe hast done" (l. 160). The subtext would seem to insinuate the women's willing conformation of what is alien and threatening in female beauty and sexuality to the norms of Jacobean culture.

Yet despite all that, the active, transformative powers are displaced from James, and female power is emphasized. The nymphs leave their blackness in, and receive true beauty from, Ocean (their own ancestor Oceanus); the role of the Sun-King is left ambiguous. The rescue of the captured nymphs from Night is effected by their Queen, the silver moon Aethiopia: this adventure takes place offstage and is described as a contest between two potent female rulers for control of the women, leaving the Sun-King patriarch completely out of the equation. Finally, the "Beauty" the Ladies figure forth—the several qualities of serenity, joy, loveliness, dignity, delicacy, and so on, which are all conjoined in Harmonia, personated by Queen Anne—is invested with sweeping Platonic power for creation and conquest (of men): "It was for *Beauty*, that the World was made" (l. 288); "Beautie, at large, brake forth, and conquer'd men" (l. 395). Reversing the harshest slur of Jacobean misogyny, one of the concluding songs makes even more sweeping claims for the control of men by female power:

> Had those, that dwell in error foule,
> And hold that women have no soule,
> But seene these move: they would have, then,
> Said, *Women were the soules of men*.
> So they doe move each heart, and eye
> With the *world's soule*, true *harmony*.
> (ll. 368–373)

Finally, as the ladies are urged to make their permanent throne in Britannia, they are explicitly recognized as agents of national transformation. It is their Platonic beauty and harmony that will turn James's Britannia into Elysium: "So all that see your beauties sphaere / May know the '*Elysian* fields are here" (ll. 406–407).

In the interval between the performances of *Blacknesse* and *Beautie*, Samuel Daniel prepared a pastoral tragicomedy, *The Queen's Arcadia*, as one of the several entertainments laid on for the visit of the King and Queen to Oxford in August 1605. Chamberlain comments on the "well-performed" disputations in theology, law, medicine, and moral philosophy in which King James took part, on the dullness of most of the plays presented by the colleges, and on the special merit of Daniel's play for Queen Anne: "The day of departure an English pastorall of Samuell Daniells (presented before the Quene) made amends for all, being indeed very excellent, and some parts exactly acted."[82] For this work the Queen was neither collaborator nor participant, but she exerted influence nonetheless as primary audience: in commissioning Daniel the university certainly expected that the Special Licenser of the Queen's Revels would know how to please her. The work emphasizes the Queen's (and women's) worth, and the choric criticisms by Ergastus and Meliboeus invite application to the scandals and misogynist ethos of James's reign. The action treats the dishonoring and defamation of Arcadia's nymphs by the rake Colax, and their introduction to faddish arts and fashions by the sophisticated Techne. Arcadia is no longer the "gentle region of plaine honestie"; faith is destroyed as spotless nymphs are made the objects of male treachery and scandal; and the sexes fear and distrust each other. Meliboeus summarizes: "I have never knowne, / So universall a distemperature, / In all parts of the body of our state, / As now there is."[83] When the villain's plots are unmasked and the several pairs of lovers unite, Palamon voices the men's apology for misjudging women, directing it especially to the Queen as Pallas, recalling her chosen persona in Daniel's first masque:

> And pardon me you glorious company,
> You starres of women, if m'inraged heat
> Have ought profan'de your reverent dignitie;
> And thou bright *Pallas*, sov'raigne of al Nimphes,
> The royall Mistresse of our Pastorall Muse
> And thou *Diana* honour of the woodes,
> To whome I vow my songes, and vow my selfe,
> Forgive me mine offence.
>
> (Act V, scene iv; sig. K 3v)

The dedication to Queen Anne in the printed text (1606) denies any intent to deal with the "artes of Thrones," which poor shepherds are bound to misunderstand and misjudge (sig. A 2); the politic disclaimer identifies Anne with the royal power and state, but also removes her (as one excluded from direct political power) from the corruptions here displayed, associating her with the better values of Arcadian poets and scholars.

On February 2, 1609, the Queen's longest and most elaborate masque was performed, the Jonson–Inigo Jones *Masque of Queenes*. The central conceit involves the celebration and enthronement in the House of Fame of the twelve greatest Queens of history, whose virtue, martial prowess, and wise governance are now epitomized in Bel-Anna. This action is preceded by a long antimasque of twelve hags and witches (appealing to James's long-standing interest in witchcraft) whose spells and charms are readily dispelled by the appearance of the Queens.[84]

Queen Anne is again given responsibility for the plans and arrangements. Donne wrote to Sir Henry Goodyere in early November 1608 that before leaving on his hunting trip the King "left with the Queen a commandment to meditate upon a Masque for Christmas"; and on December 1 the King ordered the exchequer to pay out the sums needed for the project: "The Queene our deerest wife hath resolved for our greater honor and contentement to make us a Maske this Christmas attended by most of the greatest ladies of the kingdome."[85] Queen Anne's close involvement with the production extended to "daily rehearsals and trials of the machinery," according to the Venetian ambassador. She was evidently fascinated by the House of Fame, the most complicated masque structure yet devised, with "diverse running scaffoldes" and "great gates and turning doores belowe and a globe and sondry seates above for the Quene and Ladies to sitt on and be turned round about," all moved by a *machina versatilis,* or turning machine.[86]

The Queen had to forgo playing diplomatic politics this time. The masque was postponed until Candlemas in the hope that the Spanish Ambassador Extraordinary, Don Fernandez di Girone, would be gone; he had been sent to thank James for help with the truce in the Netherlands and was entitled to take precedence over Ambassadors in Ordinary. But the King did not want to annoy the by now greatly incensed French ambassador La Boderie—or his monarch, Henry IV—by further slights: Chamberlain comments that "the French ambassador hath ben so longe and so much neglected, that yt is doubted more wold not be well indured."[87] Di Girone left on February 1, and the masque took place the following day; La Boderie reported that the King was prepared to put off the masque till Shrove Tuesday if necessary.[88] He was the only diplomat invited, much to the consternation of the Venetian ambassador, Marc'Antonio Correr, whose report suggests the Queen's displeasure at being preempted in these matters: "The Queen let me know that she regretted that I had not been invited and pleaded that as the King paid the bill he desired to be the host. She says she is resolved to trouble herself no more with Masques."[89]

The masque of the famous Queens bears yet more strongly the imprint of Queen Anne's "authorship" in its subversion of the trajectory of power, and of James's own ideology of gender and male sovereignty. Jonson's text makes the usual gesture of shared authorship to Anne, this time crediting her with the idea for the chief literary innovation of the work, the anti-masque:

> It encreasing, now, to the third time of my being us'd in these services to her Majesties personall presentatio's, with the Ladyes whome she pleaseth to honour: it was my first, and speciall reguard, to see that the Nobilyty of the Invention should be answerable to the dignity of theyr persons . . . her Majestie (best knowing, that a principall part of life in these Spectacles lay in their variety) had commaunded mee to think on some *Daunce,* or shew, that might praecede hers, and have the place of a foyle, or false-Masque.[90]

At one level the intended effect seems to be to obviate the subversive as-sociations of the black Africans in *Blackness* by dividing the female image: on the one hand, the monstrous witches (personated by male actors) and on the other, the noble Queens. But there are intimations that the Queens appropriate rather than destroy the power of the witches. They themselves are figures of fierce violence, overturning gender norms. In myth Perseus, who introduces the Queens, served the warrior goddess Athena and brought Medusa's head to be emblazoned on Athena's breastplate. In like manner the Queens tie the witches' bodies before their chariots.[91]

These Queens are stereotypical counters in many medieval and Renais-sance defenses of women, but they are not allegories; their subversive im-pact here and elsewhere depends on the assumption that they were histor-ical women who fought battles and ruled kingdoms in their own right. Viewing them was hardly a happy prospect for James, haunted as he was by Queen Elizabeth and his mother, Mary Stuart, as well as by the royal claims advanced for his cousin Arbella Stuart. The merits of the Queens are validated by their presenters: first Perseus, the father of Fame and a figure for the *"heroicall,* and *masculine Vertue"* (l. 365) the Queens are said to embody, describes the Queens in their niches in Fame's Temple; then Fame herself presents them in their chariots in a triumphal procession. And while the masque spectators were not given the biographical accounts that Jonson provided in his elaborately annotated text for Prince Henry— accounts which emphasize their militancy, gender inversion, and con-quests of men—the descriptive epithets in the text would evoke for many the familiar stories of these Queens and their claims to fame. So would the magnificent and diverse costumes, which in some cases (Penthesilea, Thomyris, Candace) have distinctively martial elements.[92]

The order begins with the most ancient, Homer's "brave Amazon" (l. 399) Penthesilea, who fought with Achilles (portrayed by the Countess of Bedford). As leader she associates all the militant Queens who follow with the Amazonian myth of female power directed against men. The other Queens include Virgil's "swift-foot" Camilla, Queen of the Volcians, who fought for Turnus (Lady Catherine Windsor); Thomyris, Queen of the Scythians, who conquered and killed Cyrus (the Countess of Montgomery); Artemisia, Queen of Caria, honored by Xerxes for her fighting spirit, chastity, and governance (Lady Elizabeth Guildford); Berenice, Queen of Egypt, honored for magnanimity and bravery (Lady Anne Clifford); Candace, Queen of Ethiopia, celebrated for her martial spirit and singular affection to her subjects (Lady Anne Winter); Zenobia, Queen of Palmyrenes, noted for her divine courage, incredible beauty, and chastity (Countess of Derby). The rest—Voadicea (Boadicea), who fought for the Britons' liberty against the Romans; Hypsicratia, Queen of Pontus, who fought alongside her husband; "the wise and warlike Goth Amalasunta" (l. 408); and Valasca, Queen of Bohemia, who led women to slaughter their barbarous husbands and lords—were presented by one or another of the other designated masquers, the Countesses of Arundel, Huntingdon, and Essex, and Viscountess Cranbourne. The penultimate Queen, Valasca, is described in Jonson's notes as a comparatively recent European embodiment of the Amazon:

> The eleventh was that brave *Bohemian Queene, Valasca,* Who, for her courage, had the surname of *Bold.* That, to redeeme her selfe, and her *sexe,* from the *tyranny* of Men, which they liv'd in, under *Primislaus,* on a night, and at an hower appoynted, led on the Women to the slaughter of theyr barbarous *Husbands,* and *Lords;* And possessing them selves of theyr Horses, Armes, Treasure, and places of strength, not only ruld the rest, but liv'd, many yeares after, with the liberty, and fortitude of *Amazons.*   (ll. 643–654)

Queen Anne ends the procession, figured as Bel-Anna, Queen of the Ocean, and she is said (disconcertingly enough) to possess all the qualities and virtues "for which, One by One / They were so fam'd" (ll. 417–418). In an effort at containment, King James is then identified as the epitome of all this merit—as the light from whence Queen Anne "Confesseth all the luster of her Merit" (l. 431), and as the site in which all these examples are "contracted" (l. 437). But the attempted containment cannot succeed: these militant Queens whose force is directed against Kings and husbands need, and find, a female referent in Queen Anne, not in King James. The trajectory of power and compliment returns quite explicitly to the Queens in the final songs. It is their fame, and especially that of Queen Anne (who is the present repository of their virtues) that confers benefit on James's reign: "How happier is that Age, can give / A Queene, in whome all they do live" (ll. 747–748). And the Queens' virtue and good fame (including, presumably, Queen Anne's) will outlast empires (including, presumably, James's).[93]

On June 5, 1610, the Queen sponsored and performed in *Tethys Festival* by Samuel Daniel and Inigo Jones, an elegant, stately, and subtle masque-pageant showcasing all the royal family and celebrating Prince Henry's creation as Prince of Wales.[94] The Queen personated Tethys, Goddess-Queen of the Ocean and wife of Neptune, who comes, with thirteen nymphs representing rivers in England and Wales, to pay tribute to Prince Henry (Meliades) and James (the Ocean King). The antimasque presented twelve "little ladies," daughters of Earls and Barons, who performed, said John Fynett, "to the Amazement of all the Beholders, considering the Tenderness of their Years and the many intricate Changes of the Dance."[95] Then Zephirus (played by Prince Charles) delivered Tethys' gifts—a trident to the King and the rich sword of Astraea to Henry. In the masque proper Tethys and her thirteen nymphs appear in a magnificent gold- and jewel-encrusted maritime scene with caverns, giant seashells, silver whales, seahorses, fountains, spouting water, swans, thrones, and arches. Daniel notes that the dancers were assigned to specific rivers according to "their dignitie, Signiories, or places of birth": Princess Elizabeth (masking for the first time) was the Nymph of Thames, Arbella Stuart the Nymph of Trent.[96]

Along with her gifts Tethys offers advice to Prince Henry, reported by Triton: to exercise his "Emperie" within Alcides' pillars, and to enjoy miraculous riches (based on fishing) within those waters. She hereby promotes James's pacific policies in opposition to the internationalist Protestant wars and expansionist ventures favored by Henry and his supporters:

> For there will be within the large extent
> Of these my waves and watry Governmente,
> More treasure, and more certaine riches got
> Then all the *Indies* to *Iberus* brought;
> For *Nereus* will by industry unfold
> A Chemicke secret, and turne fish to gold.
>   (ll. 172–177)

In this case Anne's own pro-Spanish and Catholic interests would dictate the same policies. But even here the King's control is put in question. As giver of Astraea's sword, the Queen stands in for Astraea (and her recent embodiment in Queen Elizabeth), linking the promised return of the Golden Age to Henry—an association with less than complimentary implications for James's present rule. Also, while the Queen eschews in this context the martial associations of the Elizabethan ethos, she claims as her own the alternative sphere of power and worth: as the goddess Tethys (who gave the trident to James) she embodies the quintessentially female waters of the oceans and rivers, with all their wealth and peaceful industry. Her designation of these as "my waters" qualifies in some measure the lavish compliments to King and Prince, and the King's dominance. Tethys "joyes to bring / Delight unto his Ilands and his Seas" (ll. 105–106); she comes to "adorne" Henry's celebratory day "with her al-gracing presence" (ll. 129–130); her nymphs deck the "tree of victory" to bring "glory, to the Ocean King" (ll. 314–318). Tethys' gifts and graces signify the King's rights to the Ocean, but yet the masque presents that right as founded upon her gifts and graces.

The next two Queen's masques constrain Anne firmly to the King's ideology and interests. The masque she undertook for Christmastide 1610, *Love Freed from Ignorance and Folly* by Jonson and Jones, was postponed to make place for Prince Henry's productions: his *Barriers* took place on Twelfth Night 1610 and his *Oberon* on January 1, 1611. The Queen's masque was again postponed from Twelfth Night 1611 to February 3, either, the Venetian ambassador speculated, "because the stage machinery is not in order or because their Majesties thought it well to let the Marshall [Laverdin of France] depart first."[97] He did not, and attended along with the Venetian ambassador. The Queen's influence seems little in evidence in the conception of this work, and her eleven lady masquers are not identified. The central conceit is of an evil Sphinx holding Love captive; the Queen of the Orient (Anne) together with eleven Daughters of the Morn try to aid him but are themselves captured and imprisoned in darkness. At length the male Priests of the Muses solve the Sphinx's riddle (the answer is Albion, an allusion to the King's wisdom, majesty, and love); and by the power of that name all are freed. There is an antimasque of (female) Follies associated with the Sphinx, followed by the masque of the freed ladies. In this masque the banished Follies are gendered female and the masquing ladies have no power to affect the action; the King is unambiguously the source of the power to free love and beauty, and he is the right object of the ladies' quest. The subversions of a decade have been quelled in this elaborate Neoplatonic masque—from which all signs of the Queen's "authorship" have been excised.

The Queen was given, but probably did not much care for, the central, transforming role in Thomas Campion's *Maske* for the Somerset-Howard wedding on December 26, 1613. The work was produced at the King's behest and expense, flaunting his own unsavory sponsorship of that scandalous affair.[98] The conceit portrays knights en route to the wedding captured by vile enchanters—Deformed Error, Rumor, Curiosity, and Credulity. They are released only when the Queen breaks off and delivers to their squires a bough from the Tree of Grace and Bounty. A song by Eternity makes clear that Queen Anne performs the transformative act, a gesture of social acceptance intended to dispel the scandal:

> Bring away this Sacred Tree,
> The Tree of Grace, and Bountie,
>   Set it in Bel-Annas eye,
> For she, she, only she
>   Can all Knotted spels unty.
>
>   (sig. Bv)

The squires beg the "divine-touch't bough" from her "Sacred Hand," whose powerful effect will make manifest her glory (sig Bv). While this masque empowers the Queen, it constrains the use of her power to an unwelcome arena, given her strong dislike of Somerset and the Howards. The King's effective control of the entire enterprise is obvious throughout, and underscored at the end, as the gifts and blessings promised the King and the nuptial couple come from Jove and the Fates, sources in no way associated with the Queen.

After this the Queen produced no more Christmastide court masques, in part because Prince Henry—and later Buckingham—were eager to take charge, abetted by James, who much preferred to watch male dancers. In court masques after 1613 the Queen's ladies were relegated to the minor roles of dancing partners in the revels.[99] The Queen could no longer find a way to register her own worth and claims in such performances, and looked to other venues.

On February 3, 1614, at Denmark House the Queen presented Samuel Daniel's *Hymens Triumph* for the King and court, to celebrate the wedding of her maid of honor Lady Jane Drummond to Lord Roxborough.[100] She first projected a masque, but could not, it seems, mount it in time.[101] The pastoral tragicomedy she commissioned from Daniel was presented by actors, not the Queen and her ladies, but her influence is strongly felt in the drama's emphasis on female worth. It focuses on the courage, fidelity, and wit of Silvia, who escapes an unwanted arranged marriage, survives two years' captivity by pirates with honor intact, and returns home in male disguise to play a Viola-like role, wooing her own lover (who supposes her dead) on behalf of her mistress. Here several pairs of mismatched lovers, each of whom loves one who loves elsewhere, are contrasted with the utterly faithful Thyrsis and Silvia. And, as in Daniel's earlier tragicomedy, choral figures again lament the new corruption in Arcadia, as greed and pretense undermine true love and virtue. The work also contains Thyrsis' exalted praise of woman as the keystone of creation:

> And for a woman, which you prize so low,
> Like men that doe forget whence they are men;
> Know her to be th'especiall creature, made
> By the Creator of the complement
> Of this great Architect the world, to hold
> The same together, which would otherwise
> Fall all asunder: and is natures chiefe
> Vicegerent upon earth, supplies her state.
>   And doe you hold it weakenesse then to love?
> And love so excellent a miracle
> As is a worthy woman!
>
> (Act III, scene iv; sig. C 8v)

Dedicating the printed version of the work to the Queen, Daniel reviews her personal claims to greatness—her graciousness, her great lineage, her children—making no reference whatever to King James:

>   never yet was Queene
> That more a peoples love have merited
> By all good graces, and by having been
>   The meanes our State stands fast established
> And blest by your blest wombe, who are this day
>   The highest-borne Queene of *Europe,* and alone
> Have brought this land more blessings every way,
>   Than all the daughters of strange Kings have done.
> For, we by you no claimes, no quarrels have,
>   No factions, no betraying of affaires:
> You doe not spend our blood, nor states, but save:
>   You strength us by alliance, and your haires.
>
> (sig. A 2v)

Informal productions evidently continued at Denmark House. Chamberlain wrote to Carleton on February 16, 1616, that "the Queen's Musicians (whereof she hath more than a good many) made her a kind of Masque or Antick at Somerset House on Monday night last."[102] Entertainments were also laid on at Greenwich, among them the masque called *Cupid's Banishment,* attributed to Robert White and presented on May 4, 1617, "by younge Gentlewomen of the Ladies' Hall in Deptford." This was evidently a school attended by the daughters of some court personages, including (the text specifies) two of the Queen's goddaughters.[103] Dedication of the printed text to the Countess of Bedford recognizes her major role in planning such activities. The work is pedestrian, but again the theme of female worth is sounded: the presenter, Occasion, finds "confidence and Royall resolution / Of female worth" in the Queen's "bright Spheare of Greatnes"; the masque dances spell out *Anna Regina* first, then *Jacobus Rex* and *Carolus P.* Occasion ends the work by addressing the Queen as Pallas (the persona she claimed in her first masque), begging pardon from her and her entire "glorious Company, you starrs of women" for anything uttered "in prejudice of your most noble sex."[104]

Queen Anne's patronage and sponsorship were largely responsible for the emergence and development of that new form, the Jacobean masque, especially in its first decade; and her "authorial" presence exercised a powerful and often subversive influence on masques and entertainments until her death. The Queen's oppositional activities and subversions could not substantially alter her actual position in James's patriarchal regime, nor had she the intellectual power or political consciousness to mount a consistent oppositional policy. But she was able to make these limited, and perhaps partly subconscious, gestures of resistance because conflicting claims and structures allowed her some space for self-definition and self-assertion. Pride in the status she derived from her own family provided a counterweight to the ideology of Jacobean patriarchy. Attraction to Catholicism offered a competing source of authority and political interest. And her domestic circumstances led her increasingly to define (with her female entourage) a range of interests and activities quite separate from those of the King. The masques and entertainments the Queen produced or sponsored affirmed the worth of women, and her court was perceived as a separate female community, marginalized but yet powerful. Her masques and her court provided a site for contesting the gender ideology dominant in the King's court and on the public stage—serving, perhaps, as a kind of *école des femmes,* affecting the consciousness of at least some of the ladies involved. In any event, the Queen's oppositional stance offered a patently subversive royal example to Jacobean patriarchal culture.

Elizabeth and Frederick of Bohemia as Champions of Protestantism.

2 ～〇〇〆

Scripting a Heroine's Role: Princess Elizabeth and the Politics of Romance

King James's daughter, Elizabeth Stuart (1596–1662), was also an author of sorts, constructing her life and times in terms of a romance narrative. Her texts include the cultural roles she developed, as well as hundreds of letters, private and public. Yet if she was cast, and cast herself, as a romance heroine, she found Jacobean England and Counter-Reformation Europe to be inhabited by real dragons. She could not be a victorious Britomart or Pamela, but played out a narrative of struggle and final defeat. Nevertheless, by taking over and rescripting available romance roles, she located in them some space for self-definition and oppositional political action, becoming a potent symbol of resistance to Jacobean patriarchy. As a cultural icon she inspired numerous poems, masques, tributes, and polemics. And her own letters, while not high literature, are impressive rhetorical texts: they provide a critical perspective on, and a political engagement with, King James's policies and values as they plead her own case and cause.

In the late sixteenth and early seventeenth centuries women were targeted by writers and moralists alike as the prime readership for romances in verse and prose.[1] But in fact, young aristocrats of both sexes delighted in works such as the *Amadis de Gaule,* Sidney's *Arcadia,* Spenser's *Faerie Queene,* Jorge de Montemayor's *Diana,* Honoré D'Urfé's *L'Astrée.* King James himself was known to admire John Barclay's Latin *Argenis.*[2] Elizabeth's husband, Frederick, the Elector Palatine, writing to her (in French) from the wars, cast the two of them as romance characters: "My thoughts are always with my dear Astre whom I will love completely until death"; "Continue for ever to love your poor Celadon, and rest assured that his thoughts turn continually to his star."[3] These letters locate them both in-

side *L'Astrée*—Frederick as the lovelorn hero, Elizabeth as the "star" heroine whose name also associates her with the goddess who will bring back
the Golden Age, and with the first Queen Elizabeth, often celebrated as
Astraea.

Elizabeth's letters to Frederick apparently have not survived, though he
refers to them often in the hundreds of letters he wrote to her over many
years. But her letters to others reveal her own disposition to construct
herself and her world in romance terms; indeed, virtually her only literary
references are to romances and classical "lives." She refers to herself as a
"ladie errant" in a letter to her longtime admirer Sir Thomas Roe; in another she places him "in King Cambyse's Reign" (out of the *Cyropaedia*)
for his eloquence; and in yet another she refers to her eccentric friend the
Countess of Lowenstein as "my Dulcinea."[4] Concerned about a madcap
scheme by her son Rupert to colonize Madagascar and become its governor, she writes to Roe that this "Romance of Madagascar . . . sounds like
one of Don Quixots conquests where he promist his trustie squire to make
him king of an Island."[5] She reports the adventures of Queen Christina of
Sweden escaping in man's clothing as "this Romance." Still more revealing, she discusses the marital problems of her son Charles Lewis by assigning legendary or romance names to the principals: her daughter Sophie is Candace (the legendary martial Queen of Ethiopia), her son is
Tiribaze (out of Plutarch), his wife is Eurydice (and also a "patient Gricill"
for the wrongs done her though not her bearing of them); others are
Artaxerxes, Arsace, and Berenice.[6]

While romance is a conservative form in its valorization of hierarchy
and female virginity, Frederick's letters point to its potential uses in apocalyptic politics—a potential also present in book one of the *Faerie Queene,*
which brought together romance, contemporary politics, and apocalyptic
prophecy.[7] As Northrop Frye notes, romance could be liberating for its
noble readers by allowing them an imaginative escape from the rigid structures of society: in romance "kings and princesses are individuals given
the maximum of leisure, privacy, and freedom of action. In real life, of
course, royal figures have even less of such things than other people."[8]
Romance was likely to be especially liberating for royal and noble women:
in romance, though not often in life, they rule kingdoms, have exciting
adventures, match with their true lovers, display boldness and wit. And
while they may suffer violence and dire catastrophe, they do so nobly,
courageously, admirably.

In Jacobean England, Princess Elizabeth was accorded various epithets:
Elizabeth Rediviva, Queen of Hearts, Winter Queen. They name romance
roles pressed upon her from her happy childhood, through her fairytale
wedding to her preferred suitor, to her short reign as Electress Palatine
and Queen of Bohemia, to her long life in exile as figure of pathos, object

of chivalric devotion, and symbol of Protestant resistance. Until her marriage she seems to have been an actor in scenes scripted by others, but showing signs of an emerging self-awareness. After it she took on deliberately the role of warrior queen in support of the Elector's claims and the cause of international Protestantism, and became for much longer the galvanizing spirit for Protestant opposition in England to James's pacific politics.

Born in Scotland on August 19, 1596, she (like Prince Henry) was given into foster care immediately, to Lord and Lady Livingstone at Linlithgow.[9] In England the Countess of Bedford's parents, the Haringtons of Exton, had charge of her care and education. At their estate, Coombe Abbey in Warwickshire, she spent an apparently happy childhood doing her lessons, riding, reading the Bible, attending religious services, visiting Prince Henry (whom she evidently idolized), and penning formal, carefully inscribed notes to her father and brother that seem intended in part to display her skill in English, Italian, and especially French composition.[10] Harington took his educational duties seriously, undertaking to offer Elizabeth "such service as is due to her princely endowments and natural abilities." She had a music master, Dr. John Bull, and tutors for French and Italian, writing and dancing; records indicate that she played the virginals, and that she was given "the Book of Martyrs, a great Bible, and divers other volumes of histories" to read.[11] Since James himself often urged his children to practice their music and dancing, she was probably accomplished in both.[12] The French ambassador testified to her excellent French when he undertook to negotiate her marriage with the Dauphin: "She is handsome, graceful, well nourished, and speaks French very well, much better than her brother."[13] She had at first to converse with her husband in French, and his letters to her were usually in that language. She may or may not have studied Latin as a girl: the eighteenth-century Frances Erskine memoir, citing James's well-documented disapproval of learned women, claims that he forbade her to study Latin and Greek, but a later correspondent credits her with the ability to write and speak Latin.[14] Possibly James approved of Latin for a daughter who might well ascend to the throne.

She also learned to make verses: an exercise for Harington of uncertain date—thirty-three quatrains on the *vanitas* theme—is hardly poetry, but it does show her capacity to keep meter and find rhymes in a somewhat taxing verse form. The verses express conventional religious sentiments:

> I. This is joye, this is true pleasure,
>   If we best things make our treasure,
>   And enjoy them at full leasure,
>   Evermore in richest measure.
>   . . . . .

> V. Earthly things do fade, decay,
>   Constant to us not one day;
>   Suddenly they pass away,
>   And we can not make them stay.
>   . . . . .
> XVIII. O how frozen is my heart!
>   O my soule, how dead thou art!
>   Thou, O God, we maye impart,
>   Vayne is humane strength and art.
>   . . . . .
> XXV. What care I for lofty place,
>   If the Lord grant me his grace,
>   Shewing me his pleasant face,
>   And with joy I end my race.[15]

Fate offered the Princess a romance adventure at the age of nine. The Gunpowder plotters intended, after blowing up the King and Prince with the Parliament, to seize Princess Elizabeth, force her to change religion, and marry her to a suitable Catholic husband. She was spirited away just two hours before the kidnappers arrived.[16] Harington reports with pride how nobly his pupil played the part of right-minded heroine: "Her Highness doth often say, 'What a Queen should I have been by this means? I had rather have been with my royal father in the Parliament-house, than wear his crown on such condition.'"[17]

Over the next several years Princess Elizabeth was invested with a broad range of political and symbolic values. A Latin panegyric on James and his family in 1608 constructed her, in blatantly hyperbolic terms, as Elizabeth Rediviva:

> Her wit is acute, her memory tenacious, her judgment discerning, beyond her tender years. In piety she equals Flavia, the daughter of Clementius, the Roman consul; in her knowledge of a variety of languages she is to be compared, or rather preferred, to Zenobia the Palmyrian queen, to Aretia, and Cornelia. She also diligently cultivates music, and is a great proficient in the art . . . In fine, whatever was excellent or lofty in Queen Elizabeth, is all compressed in the tender age of this virgin princess, and if God spare her to us, will be found there accumulated.[18]

In 1611 the female poet Aemilia Lanyer praised her "goodly wisedome, though your yeares be greene," identifying her as a "modell" of Queen Anne's beauty and virtue, and honoring her especially as the vehicle for keeping alive Queen Elizabeth's virtues in the new age:

Most gratious Ladie, faire ELIZABETH,
Whose Name and Virtues puts us still in mind,
Of her, of whom we are depriv'd by death;
The *Phoenix* of her age, whose worth did bind
All worthy minds so long as they have breath,
In linkes of admiration, love and zeale,
To that deare Mother of our Common-weale.[19]

She was also associated, no doubt very willingly, with Prince Henry's internationalist Protestant values and politics, presiding with him at the tournament and magnificent feast he hosted for the King and court at Twelfth Night 1610. The entertainment, Jonson's *Barriers*, set Henry in the warrior line of Arthur, Edward III, Henry V, and Queen Elizabeth, and associated his sister with those same martial values:

That most princely *Mayd*, whose forme might call
The world to warre, and make it hazard all
His valure for her beautie, she shall bee
Mother of *nations*, and her Princes see
Rivals almost to these.[20]

Elizabeth danced the Nymph of Thames in her first masque, *Tethys Festival* (June 5, 1610), celebrating Henry's creation as Prince of Wales; she retained that persona in later tributes describing the Elizabeth-Frederick marriage as the marriage of Thames and Rhine.

The years 1610–1612 were much taken up with marriage negotiations. Although Elizabeth could not of course choose for herself, she had the good fortune of a romance heroine in obtaining the mate she wanted—owing in part to her brother. Early negotiations explored double marriages for Henry and Elizabeth in the French royal family, but those efforts collapsed with the assassination of Henry IV in 1610.[21] Elizabeth had suitors from Sweden, the German states, and England itself, but all were deemed unsatisfactory.[22] Queen Anne strongly supported overtures from the recently widowed Spanish King, Philip the Pious, but reports that Elizabeth would be expected to change her religion aroused English opposition, galvanized by Henry.[23] Another Catholic double match involved the ruling house of Savoy, but this proposal met strong opposition from Cecil as well as Henry.[24] At length James settled on the most eligible of the Protestant suitors, Frederick V, Elector Palatine, Senior Elector of the Holy Roman Empire, and head of the League of Protestant Princes. For balance, he planned to marry Prince Henry to a Catholic princess, thereby positioning himself to play his coveted role of mediator in the European religious controversies. Henry and his coterie strongly supported Frederick's suit, and a flurry of letters and emissaries passed between the Prince's court and Heidelberg. Henry was prepared to take a Catholic bride if he had to, but at one point he was reportedly plotting a countermove with his sister: to conduct her to Germany after her wedding and to choose there a Protestant bride for himself. The sister of Prince Otto of Hesse was mentioned.[25]

Frederick arrived in England on October 16, 1612, to woo and win his promised bride. Descriptions of his first meeting with the English royal family is the stuff of romance: Frederick the enamored lover, Elizabeth the modest but welcoming lady, Queen Anne the disapproving mother.[26] The court gossips were determined to have it a love match, and the young couple (both sixteen years old) seems to have obliged almost immediately. Chamberlain reports that Frederick's gracious and gentle behavior won favor with everybody except the disgruntled papists, and that he was constantly with Elizabeth at private suppers and theatricals, seeming "to take delight in nothing but her Company and Conversation."[27] The Queen's frosty reception continued, based partly on religion, partly on Frederick's inferior status: Palsgrave (Count) rather than King. One story had it that she taunted her daughter with the epithet "Goodwife Palsgrave," to which Elizabeth replied that she "would rather be the *Palsgrave's* Wife, than the greatest Papist Queen in *Christendom*."[28] The anecdote is again the stuff of romance, but the sentiments suit both parties: if they did not say these things, they should have.

Romance was soon displaced by tragedy, with Prince Henry's sudden, entirely unexpected death on November 6, 1612—apparently of typhoid fever.[29] Chamberlain reports the special closeness of Henry and Elizabeth, and the latter's romancelike attempts to visit her quarantined brother in disguise:

> The Lady Elizabeth is much afflicted with this losse, and not without goode cause; for he did extraordinarilie affect her, and during his sicknes still inquired after her, and the last wordes he spake in good sense, (they say) were, Where is my dear Sister? She was as desirous to visit him, and went once or twise in the evening disguised for that purpose, but could not be admitted.[30]

Court and country plunged into deepest mourning: a solemn funeral was mounted on December 7; a flood of epitaphs, elegies, lamentations, and mourning tracts poured from the presses,[31] far exceeding these for Queen Elizabeth's death, and recalling the literary response to the death of that other young Protestant hero, Sir Philip Sidney. Some feared the wedding of Elizabeth and Frederick might never take place.

But the hopes vested in Prince Henry were soon displaced onto his sister and her intended. They were formally betrothed December 27, 1612.

An unsubstantiated tradition holds that Shakespeare's *Tempest* was performed that evening, its wedding masque devised for the occasion.[32] Queen Anne stayed away, prompted by disapproval as well as gout, but contemporary letters note her change of heart—or decision to make the best of things—about the time Frederick was formally installed as Knight of the Garter on February 7, 1613: "The Queen doth discover her liking of this match over all others and . . . caresseth the Palsgrave whensover he cometh to her as if he were her own son."[33] As King James and Queen Anne were appropriating Frederick as surrogate son, the Protestant reform party was laying upon him the mantle of leadership just fallen from Henry IV of France and Prince Henry. And as Princess Elizabeth was being displayed as an emblem of familial glory—the beautiful, virginal, accomplished, splendidly ornamental daughter-bride—the reformist Protestants were portraying her as the incarnation of Prince Henry's spirit and that of her great namesake. In this prophetic conception, the wedding portended a militant, pan-Protestant alliance to curb Hapsburg power and secure the Reformation. The wedding ceremonies, entertainments, and tributes constructed that event in romance terms, inscribing Elizabeth on the one hand as an emblem of Jacobean order, but on the other as a prophetic symbol of Protestant apocalyptic hopes.

The wedding on Saint Valentine's Day 1613 in the chapel at Whitehall was under the sign of the emblematic. The wedding party was bedecked in sumptuous fabrics and dazzling, prodigiously expensive jewels; the bride was costumed as a fairy-tale princess, starring in what one account termed "these Tryumphes":

> The Lady Elizabeth, in her virgin-robes, clothed in a gowne of white sattin, richly embroidered . . . upon her head a crown of refined golde, made Imperiall by the pearles and diamonds thereupon placed, which were so thicke beset that they stood like shining pinnacles upon her amber-coloured haire, dependantly hanging playted downe over her shoulders to her waste [dishevelled and unbound, in sign of virginity]; between every plaight a roll or liste of gold-spangles, pearles, rich stones, and diamonds; and, withall, many diamonds of inestimable value, embrothered upon her sleeves, which even dazzled and amazed the eies of the beholders . . . Virgin bridemaids attended upon the Princess, like a skye of caelestial starres upon faire Phoebe.[34]

These emblems asserted the authority of King, father, and English Church: James, monarch and paterfamilias, gave the bride; and the Archbishop of Canterbury conducted the wedding service, "in all points according to the Book of Common Prayer." James's voyeuristic visit to the couple in bed the next morning replayed these gestures of authority in low-comedy domestic terms: according to Chamberlain, the King "did strictly examine him whether he were a true son-in-law, and was sufficiently assured." [35] At one point, however, Elizabeth was seen to break free of the emblematic, revealing by an irrepressible giggle her own subjectivity and desire: "While the Archbishop of Canterbury was solemnizing the Marriage, some Coruscations and Lightnings of Joy appear'd in her Countenance that express'd more than an ordinary smile, being almost elated to a Laughter." [36] It was an augury that, in defiance of genre norms, Elizabeth's role as romance heroine would begin, not end, with her wedding.

Donne's "Epithalamion" for the wedding seems designed to reinforce James's emblematic construction. The focus is on the ceremonial of the wedding day (and night): the bride is decked out in "Rubies, Pearles, and Diamonds" (l. 35); the Archbishop of Canterbury is conflated with Bishop Valentine; the couple is imaged as two phoenixes become one. The poem entirely eschews the prophetic, save for a cryptic address to Elizabeth as a "new starre that to us portends / Ends of much wonder"(ll. 39–40). Quite surprising in any epithalamion and especially in one for royalty is the fact that Donne makes almost no reference to progeny—eliding the reformist Protestant hopes so heavily invested in that progeny. [37] The courtiers' entertainment for the wedding evening (*The Lord's Masque* by Thomas Campion and Inigo Jones, a double masque for men and women) is couched chiefly in emblematic terms. After an antimasque of Frantics, or madmen, Orpheus and Poetic Furor call up Prometheus, who turns fiery stars into men masquers "fit for warres" and golden statues into women "fit for love." [38] The only prophetic element in this masque is the Sybil's Latin proclamation, addressed chiefly to Elizabeth as "future mother . . . of kings, of emperors"; it predicts that

> one mind, one faith, will join two peoples, and one religion, and simple love. Both will have the same enemy, the same ally, the same prayer for those in danger, and the same strength. Peace will favor them, and the fortune of war will favor them; always God the best help will be at their side. [39]

It is unclear whether the Latin is intended to add solemnity or to obscure the exact terms of the prophecy.

In their martial motifs and themes of Christian conquest, some entertainments for the wedding still bore the impress of Prince Henry's planning, though in muted form. He reportedly had planned tilts, barriers, and jousts, but the only martial exercise to survive was a running at the ring. [40] Elizabeth would also have had a more creative role: she was said to be planning and preparing to act in "a sumptuous ballet of sixteen maidens" that was to cost 12,000 crowns. [41] After Henry's death it did not go forward—whether because of her grief, or some presumption of unseemliness, or her need for Henry's support in the enterprise. On the Thursday prior to the wedding spectacular fireworks were staged, developing the Spenserian romance theme of Saint George rescuing an Amazon Queen from an evil magician, and clearing the world of evil enchantments (Saint George is the Garter emblem, pointing the allegory to the new Garter knight, Frederick, and his Princess). On Saturday a magnificent sea fight portrayed the English navy defeating a Turkish fleet and capturing a fort, with allusion to the hoped-for reconquest of the Holy Lands.[42] Both events were accident-ridden, and James was reportedly bored with them.[43]

Prince Henry had also commanded masques from the Inns of Court, and on February 15 the Middle Temple and Lincoln's Inn presented a masque by one of Henry's poets, George Chapman. Its themes—the blindness of Plutus [Riches] cured by the love of Honor, and homage offered to James by the priests of Virginia for bringing true religion to their land—urge the anti-Spanish, colonial expansionist program of the reformist Protestants.[44] James postponed until February 20 the other Inns of Court masque, written by Francis Beaumont and sponsored by Francis Bacon. Celebrating the marriage of Thames and Rhine, with Olympian knights and Jupiter's priests as masquers, it hints obliquely at Christian chivalry and was possibly intended (in Henry's design) to culminate in a barriers.[45] Henry's death probably accounts for the substitution of Campion's masque for the very remarkable apocalyptic masque published in a contemporary French pamphlet as the offering of Grey's Inn and the Middle Temple. In the latter, Atlas gives over the globe to Truth (Alithie, modeled on the woman clothed with the sun in the Apocalypse); masquers representing the continents of Europe, Asia, and Africa then pay homage to her, and heavenly cherubim present her with a sword and celebrate her victory. The argument spells out the allegory: "The world (quitting its errors) will come to give recognition to Truth which resides solely in England and the Palatinate."[46]

In many of the literary tributes and tracts celebrating the wedding, the Princess is portrayed as Elizabeth Rediviva, the new agent of Providence for Protestant reform. Thomas Heywood's *Marriage Triumph* compares her with Alcestis, Portia, Penelope, and especially Queen Elizabeth: "You equall her, in vertues fame / From whom you receiv'd your name."[47] Henry Peacham saw in her "ELIZAS Zeale, and Pietie . . . Heire of her Name, and Virtues," and prayed that her marriage might produce "a *Caesar* born as great as *Charlesmagne*.[48] In Joannis de Franchis's Latin epic— translated into English "that the Ladies may be partakers"—a council of the gods determines to save Religion, Cupid is sent to stir up love in Frederick and Elizabeth, and dreams move King James and Queen Anne to consent. Jove, declaring that the Princess derives her knowledge from Religion and her "name and manners" from Queen Elizabeth, prophesies that her marriage to Frederick will restore the "long-wisht-for golden age."⁴⁹ George Webb's tract *The Bride Royall* likens Elizabeth to the biblical mothers and heroines of Israel—Sarah, Rebecca, Rachel, Leah, Judith, Deborah—and to Queen Elizabeth, who restored true religion:

> Our present *Elizabeth,* this dayes Royall Bride, is of no lesse happy hopes: her Love unto her Name-sakes memorie, her imitation of her Vertues, her hatred of Popery and Superstition, her zeale to Gods glory, and sincere profession of the Gospell, her religious education from her infancie . . . It was the desire and often wish of this Gracious Princesse (if report of some of her neerest observants may be credited) that in her Marriage match, shee might be linked to a Prince professing the same Religion . . . No sonne of Antichrist; No vassal to the Pope . . . Doubtless the finger of God hath been here, This match is of his especiall chusing.⁵⁰

The reformist Protestant patriot and satirist George Wither was even more emphatic: one epithalamic poem proclaims that "beside thy proper merit / Our late *Eliza,* grants her Noble spirit. / To be redoubled on thee," and another prays that "from out your blessed loynes, shall come; / Another terror, to the *Whore of Rome.*"⁵¹

In large part Elizabeth's early married life continued in the romance vein, its events reported in detail to an England all too conscious that only the sickly Charles stood between Elizabeth and the English throne. Her progress through the Dutch provinces and German states and up the Rhine was attended by fireworks, entertainments, and celebrations, and her entry into Heidelberg, the chief Palatinate city, was staged as a triumph.⁵² But there are signs that she was trying to shape her assigned romance role to her own needs. She reveled in hunting parties and gained quite a reputation with her crossbow as a new Diana; she amused herself with a menagerie of monkeys and lapdogs; and she and Frederick commissioned Salomon Caus to lay out elaborate geometrical gardens with mechanical fountains, speaking statues, and musical grottoes.⁵³ Pregnant almost immediately, she refused to admit her condition to the world or even to herself, causing much consternation when she insisted on riding and hunting as hard as ever. She explained this behavior later as stemming from uncertainty and inexperience, but it suggests real ambivalence about giving over the role of romance princess for that of mother, as was expected of her.⁵⁴ The birth of the swarthy Frederick Henry on January 2, 1614 ("mon petit black babie"), touched off joyful celebrations and tributes in both the Palatinate and England. In the event, Elizabeth managed to combine both roles: Sir Henry Wotton reported to James in April 1616 that "your gracious daughter, retaineth still her former virginal verdure in her complexion and features, though she be now the mother of one of the sweetest children that I think the world can yield."[55]

Elizabeth's letters of these years reveal a growing maturity and self-awareness as she learned to cope with mundane troubles and to resist the constructions others would place on her. There were immediate financial constraints: Chamberlain thought the entourage sent to accompany her from England was "meanly attended by Ladies"; and she had to pawn some jewels so as to keep up with the requirements of gift giving en route.[56] She was wholly inept at managing her household and finances, being unable to resist "importunities, complaints, and tears" from all and sundry, according to Henry's loyal servant Hans Meinhard von Schomberg, who became her steward. She soon learned to trust him and tried to follow his sensible rules, often testifying that "I find none so truely carefull of me as that man."[57] His letter to Winwood (May 24, 1615) is a *cri de coeur* defending his procedures against English complaints and offering a revealing insight into the young couple's difficulties, as well as his own:

> I have brought up the Prince, reformed the court, installed madame, maintained the balance proper for the preservation of their highnesses, offended everybody to serve his majesty and madame, and so acted that his majesty can never, with truth, hear any reproach or reflection upon these personages, though married so young, assisted so little, left, flattered by everybody; and it is I alone who have had their burden upon my shoulders.[58]

Elizabeth had also to cope with Frederick's fits of melancholy (he was apparently a manic-depressive), and with the Dowager Electress's efforts to make her conform to German customs, which, she protests with some spirit, "I neither have binne bred to or is necessarie in everie thing I shoulde follow, neither will I doe it."[59] James's efforts to control the couple from afar made further trouble, especially his insistence that Frederick honor the promise James extracted from him to give Elizabeth precedence over himself, his mother, and the other German Princes.[60] Revealing letters from King James to Frederick and Elizabeth set her duties to the two patriarchs in her life in sharp conflict: James declares that she should be "humbly obedient to her husband" but that "in what concerns the quality and honor of her birth, she would not be worthy to live if she were to quit her place without my knowledge and advice."[61] Also, James continually called Elizabeth to account for her gift giving, her jewelry, and her servants' honesty.[62] Elizabeth's letters to her father repeat the formulas of filial duty, but she resists his more egregious interference—especially his objections to a projected marriage between Schomberg and her maid of honor, Anne Dudley. (This situation reads like another romance episode, the servants' love match reprising the royal one.)[63] With Dudley's death in child-birth Elizabeth lost a valued friend and companion of her own age. She asked James for a replacement of similar age and rank, but seemed genuinely pleased to gain instead a mother figure, her old guardian, the now-widowed Lady Harington, who arrived after the birth of her second and favorite child, Charles Louis, on December 22, 1617.[64]

The Bohemian crisis of 1618–1620, which touched off the Thirty Years' War, allowed Elizabeth to assume by choice and develop through her actions and her letters the apocalyptic romance role so often accorded to Frederick and herself—champions of Protestant Europe. When the Hapsburg Prince Ferdinand became King of Bohemia (and soon after Holy Roman Emperor), he refused to honor traditional guarantees to Protestants of liberty of conscience, provoking the famous Defenestration at Prague. This brought armies of the Protestant League and their head, Frederick, into the field against the Catholic Hapsburg armies, and the affair culminated in Frederick's election to the throne of Bohemia, an elective monarchy but one owing fealty to the Emperor. Frederick received contradictory advice from all sides as to whether he should accept and thereby challenge the Holy Roman Emperor directly; James, characteristically, delayed his response and was then furious when Frederick acted before hearing from him.[65] At last Frederick concluded that he ought not refuse "the legitimate and ordinary vocation from God," conveyed by the votes of the Bohemian estates.[66] Later accounts and Hapsburg caricatures blamed that decision and its disastrous outcome on Elizabeth's ambition, often portraying her as a fierce lioness importuning her mate to forage for her many cubs. More sympathetic contemporary comment suggests that she eschewed direct pressure but made her hearty support and approval evident.[67] To Frederick's letter telling her of the election, she reportedly replied that since God directs all, he doubtless sent this thing, that she would leave the decision to him, but should he accept the crown, she would be ready to follow the divine call, to suffer what God should ordain, and to pledge her jewels and all her worldly goods.[68]

Disastrous as Frederick's action proved, it was predicated on the wide-spread belief that in a crisis James would support his children and the Protestant cause, and that a decisive military intervention by England had some chance of checking Hapsburg power and resolving the Bohemian situation quickly. But Elizabeth and Frederick, like George Abbot the Archbishop of Canterbury, Edward Herbert, and other judicious English observers,[69] badly misjudged the strength of James's pacifism and the complex motivations behind his refusal to take decisive action in the matter. He detested Protestant radicalism and the challenge to political absolutism which it often fostered; he had no wish to support the Bohemians' revolt against their hereditary lord the Emperor; he wanted to strengthen ties with Hapsburg monarchical Spain through a Spanish marriage for Prince Charles and to distance England from the Republican Dutch (who supported the Elector); and he feared a protracted war that would necessitate seeking money from a Parliament concerned to limit his powers. Weighed against these interests, his Palatine children did not count for much: he refused to accord them the Bohemian royal title, refused to enter the war in their cause even after Spanish armies invaded the Palatinate, strictly limited support and authorization for volunteer forces, imposed strict censorship on English discussion of Bohemian affairs, and persistently delayed and undermined their decisions and actions by his constant but fruitless diplomatic negotiations with Spain. The English were shocked, as Chamberlain observed ironically to Carleton in January 1620, at the prohibition of public rejoicing over Elizabeth's new son, "which makes a speach fathered on the Prince of Orenge (and so told the King) to be much talked of, that he is a straunge father that will neither fight for his children or pray for them."[70]

During and after the Bohemian adventure Elizabeth was able, at last, to participate in constructing her own role as apocalyptic romance heroine— an Elizabeth Rediviva both martial and maternal. That symbolic role is epitomized in a contemporary engraving which represents Frederick and Elizabeth in their coronation robes; at their feet four lions (crowned); to the left Calvin, Luther, and Huss united in study of the Bible; to the right the Catholic clergy fleeing into the darkness. Entitled *The Triumph of Protestantism,* it carries the motto (from Psalm 118:23) "This is the Lord's doing, and it is marvellous." (See illustration, page 44.) After Frederick's elevation Elizabeth took on the role of Protestant heroine with courage and determination.[71] Although her fourth pregnancy was far advanced and Frederick urged her to stay in Heidelberg or return to England for a time, she insisted on sharing the Prague venture with him.[72] John Harrison's narrative of her departure for Prague draws out all its emotional and symbolic import to marshal English support:

No heart but would have been ravished to have seene the sweete demeanour of that great ladie at her departure: with teares trickling downe her cheekes; so mild courteous, and affable (yet with a princelie reservation of state well beseeming so great a majestie) lyke an other *Queene Elizabeth* revived also agayne in her, the only *Phoenix* of the world . . . shewing her selfe like that *virago* at *Tilburie* in *eightie eight:* an other *Queene Elizabeth,* for so now she is: and what more she may be in time, or her royall yssue, is in gods hands to dispose to his glorie, and the good of his church . . . It is the maner of the *Moores*

in their most deadlie battayles, to make choice of one of their chief-
fest, and fayrest virgins, to goe before them into the field: her to be
surprized and taken from them they hold it an everlasting shame, and
thearfore will fight it out to the last man. And shall we suffer our
sweete Princesse, our royall *infanta,* the only daughter of our soveraigne lord and king, to goe before us into the field and not follow
after her?[73]

At her splendid coronation in Prague on November 7, 1619, with the
crown of another Elizabeth, Saint Elizabeth of Hungary, she was proclaimed a nursing mother of the Church.[74] Six weeks after her coronation
she gave birth to Prince Rupert (later Rupert of the Rhine, of Civil War
fame). The next autumn her secretary, Sir Francis Nethersole, reported
with admiration that she steadfastly refused to leave beleaguered Prague
lest "her removing for her owne safety might be the occasion of much
danger, by discouraging the hearts of this people," and that she made
thereby "a conquest of all the heartes of this people." He also reported her
courage under fire: "There are dayly skirmishes, and we can in this town
heare the Canon play day and night, which were enough to fright another
queene. Her majesty is nothing troubled therewith."[75]

As loving and courageous wife, prolific mother, and gracious courtly
lady, Elizabeth also invested with substance the romance role Queen of
Hearts that was accorded her first during her fairy-tale progress as a bride.
The evaluation of contemporaries suggests that if Elizabeth was not the
prime mover in Frederick's Bohemian venture, she was the dominant force
in the marriage, in both the private and the public sphere. To many observers Frederick seemed weak by comparison: at his first appearance in
England, Chamberlain accounted him "much too young and small-
timbred to undertake such a taske" as his marriage and state responsibilities would involve.[76] Under the pressure of disappointment and defeat, he
frequently gave way to spells of melancholy and impulsive actions. Also,
his very real courage was often rendered ineffectual by faulty judgment
and generalship, most disastrously at the Battle of White Mountain on
November 8, 1620, at which Frederick lost Prague and all of Bohemia.
Not expecting attack, he made a surprise visit to Prague to see his wife
and the visiting English ambassadors, returning to find his army in utter
disarray and the city lost. Frederick's uncle Maurice, the martial Prince of
Orange who was their host during their exile in the Hague, did not mince
words on their comparative stature: "The Queen of Bohemia is accounted
the most charming princess of Europe, and called by some the Queen of
Hearts. But she is far more than that—she is a true and faithful wife and
that too, of a husband who is in every respect her inferior."[77] Yet Frederick's letters to Elizabeth and hers about him testify to a relationship of
mutual love, support, and respect. An example is Frederick's letter from

the battlefield on November 1, 1621, suggesting that it might be better for Elizabeth to depart from Prague in orderly fashion rather than in flight, but leaving it to her own judgment: "Croyez que je ne desire de vous forcer de partir; mais je vous en dis mon opinion."[78]

Elizabeth also won sympathy, support, and sometimes intense devotion from James's emissaries and other visitors: Lord Doncaster, Francis Nethersole, Sir Henry Wotton, Sir Thomas Roe, Sir Edward Conway, Richard Weston. By her courage she managed to rewrite the role proposed for her by the Jesuit satirists, who scoffed that the Winter King and Queen would vanish with the snows. After the debacle of the White Mountain, Elizabeth had indeed to flee in the snows, to bear her fifth child (Maurice, named for the Prince of Orange) as the unwelcome guest of the Elector of Brandenburg (who feared to offend the victorious Emperor), and at length to take sanctuary in the Hague. But her dignity and spirit in these hardships became a legend: James's ambassadors Conway and Weston praised her "unchangeable temper, as at once did raise up in all capable men this one thought—that her mind could not be brought under fortune"; and her secretary, Nethersole, confessed himself "rapt with the greatness of her Majestys spirit, and the goodnes of her disposition, and I am not alone in it."[79] In many minds the Winter Queen became an image of the woman of the Apocalypse fleeing into the wilderness, a figure of the distressed Church in this world.

Throughout this struggle Elizabeth took upon herself the task of lobbying vigorously for James's and England's support in a barrage of forthright, urgent, incisive letters to persons best placed or best disposed to help: James, Buckingham, Prince Charles, Roe, the Countess of Bedford. In them she inscribes her militancy and her several self-chosen roles, but adapts her rhetoric to the audience addressed. To James and others she emphasizes the claims of family, but her letters offer an increasingly critical reading of James's paternal promises and dispositions. Immediately following the offer of the Bohemian crown she wrote to Buckingham (September 1, 1619), asking him to hold before James the need to fulfill his professions of paternal love by offering present aid:

> The Bohemians being desirous to chuse him [Frederick] for their King, which he will not resolve of till he knowe his Majesties opinion in it. The King hath now a good occasion to manifest to the world the love he hath ever professed to the Prince heere. I earnestlie entreat you to use your best meanes in perswading his Majestie to shew himself now, in his helping of the Prince heere, a true loving father to us both.[80]

On January 27, 1620, she wrote James herself, emphasizing the support accruing to Frederick and the goodness of their cause:

> The King [Frederick] has departed today for Moravia and Silesia, and the other provinces, to receive their oath and hommage. I very humbly beg Your Majesty to have care of your son-in-law and me here and to assist us in this war; I hope that Baron Dona has already satisfied Your Majesty about the good cause of this country here.[81]

On September 25, 1620, as the battle raged in the Palatinate, Elizabeth wrote again to Buckingham, prompting him to urge upon James the dictates of proper family feeling as well as James's own loss of face by his fruitless diplomacy, in an effort to spur him to join the battle:

> I doubt not but you have alreadie heard how Spinola hath taken three townes of the King's in the Lower Palatinat; two of them are my jointur: he will, if he can, take all that countree. This makes me write to you at this time (because I am most confident of your affection) that you will move his Majestie now to shew himself a loving father to us, and not suffer his children's inheritance to be taken away. You see how little they regard his Ambassadours and what they say . . . I pray tell the King that the enemie will more regard his blowes than his wordes.[82]

On the same day she wrote to Prince Charles, voicing near-desperation and a clear-sighted awareness of the damage done their cause by the King's "slackness," which she urges Charles to reprove:

> I am sure you have heard before this, that Spinola hath taken some towns in the lower Palatinate, which makes me to trouble you with these lines, to beseech you earnestly to move his majesty that now he would assist us; for he may easily see how little his embassages are regarded. Dear brother, be most earnest with him; for, to speak freely to you, his slackness to assist us doth make the Princes of the Union [the German Princes] slack too, who do nothing with their army; the king hath ever said that he would not suffer the Palatinate to be taken; it was never in hazard but now.[83]

On November 27, 1620, shortly after the disastrous battle of White Mountain, Elizabeth wrote a long letter (probably to Carleton) in the role of a defeated leader boosting her supporters' morale by playing down the damage and affirming confidence in a final, providential victory:

> I am sure by this tyme you had the unwelcome newes of our armies defete which forced the king and me to leave Prague not without danger to have bene taken by the ennemie if they had followed us which they did not . . . I am not yet so out of hart though I confesse wee are in an evill estate, but that (as I hope) God will give us againe the victorie, for the warres are not ended with one battaile, & I hope

wee shall have better luck in the next. The good newes you write of the king my fathers declaring himself for the Palatinat. I pray God they may be seconded with the same for Bohemia. I am sure you wishe it as well as I.[84]

A few weeks later Elizabeth made a further desperate plea to James, insisting that he recognize how high the stakes are:

Your majesty will understand by the king's [Frederick's] letters how the Palatinate is in danger of being utterly lost, if your majesty give us not some aid. I am sorry we are obliged to trouble your majesty so much with our affairs, but their urgency is so great that we cannot do otherwise.[85]

After this her letters to James (usually in French) are dutiful but brief. During what proved to be their permanent exile in the Hague, Frederick and Elizabeth were dependent on James for some financial support, and he continued his ineffectual diplomacy. Accordingly, Elizabeth wrote occasionally in 1621–1623 urging him not to abandon them, repeating formulas of filial duty, thanking him for sending his portrait.[86] But she had become openly and bitterly disillusioned with her father. To Sir Thomas Roe she wrote on December 5, 1622, "My father hitherto hath done us more hurt than good." And her acerbic letter to Conway on September 6, 1623, about the latest humiliating treaty forced on Frederick by James, concludes: "You say the king must beleeve, he hath long beleeved, but hath gotten little, yet I hope his Majestie will one day see the falshood of our ennemies."[87]

Wielding the potent symbolic force of the distressed woman of the Apocalypse and Queen of Hearts, Elizabeth became a locus for Protestant resistance and oppositional politics in England for the rest of James's reign. The English were shocked that James vehemently refused to offer the family refuge in England when they were driven from the Palatinate, and even refused to allow Elizabeth to come for a visit.[88] But James evidently feared that her presence, as an emblem of dashed Protestant hopes, would exacerbate domestic discord and offer a rallying point for resistance. A volunteer expeditionary force under Sir Horace Vere (accompanied by the Earls of Essex and Oxford) had been allowed to go to Frederick's aid in 1620, but was forbidden to engage the Spanish general Spinola and was recalled early in 1623.[89] The 1621 Parliament voted sums for a war to regain the Palatinate, calling loudly for the King to declare war on Spain; and the nobility and clergy raised subscriptions.

Elizabeth was the galvanizing force for these efforts, appealing to her friends at court, to Protestant radicals, and to English gallants alike, encouraging their devotion, their polemic, and their military aid. She kept

up warm relations with her good friend the Countess of Bedford, thanking her for continuing support—including the gesture of congratulating
her as Queen of Bohemia despite James's prohibition:

> I see by your lines that you are still the same to me in your affection
> . . . I wish that others were of your mind. Then I hope there woulde
> be taken a better resolution for us heere than yett there is . . . I think
> I can easilie guesse who it is that doth chieflie hinder the King in
> resolving, but I am sure that though they have English bodies they
> have Spanish hartes.[90]

A letter from the Venetian ambassador, partly summarized and partly
quoted, makes clear that Elizabeth relied on the Countess as a confidant
who would faithfully serve her interests at court:

> I have seen a genuine letter of the Queen of Bohemia written to one
> of the leading countesses here, an intimate of hers, saying how she
> has reached the Hague after a long and toilsome journey where she
> enjoys more popularity among the people, with her husband, than
> she ever experienced anywhere else, and where she will stay a while,
> seeing she cannot come where she ought and asking the countess if
> she heard any talk of her coming to this kingdom to contradict it, as
> she certainly will not do for reasons which cannot easily be put upon
> paper, but which the lady can easily imagine. She adds: "Everyone is
> awaiting some good resolution from his Majesty; for my part I expect
> very little, but it will only redound to the triumph of our enemies
> who mock and jest at him."[91]

In the summer of 1620 Sir Thomas Roe, who became her dear friend,
courtly love servant, and constant correspondent over many years, pledged
in high chivalric style his undying devotion and service with pen or sword:
"I am ready to serve your majestie to death, to poverty, and if you shall
ever please to command, I wil be converted to dust and ashes at your
Majesties feete."[92] Her many letters to her "Honest Thom Roe" are
couched in terms of warm affection and gratitude, encouraging his continued diligence in "furthering of anie thing that is for the good of our Bohemian affairs."[93] She was Queen of Hearts also to Sir Henry Wotton,
who produced an elegant poetic tribute to her:

> *On his Mistris, the Queen of Bohemia*
> You meaner *Beauties* of the *Night*,
>   That poorly satisfie our *Eies*
> More by your *number,* then your light,
>   You *Common-people* of the *Skies;*
> What are you when the *Sun* shall rise?

You Curious Chanters of the Wood,
    That warble forth *Dame Nature's* layes,
Thinking your *Voyces* understood
    By your weake *accents;* whats your praise
When *Philomell* her voyce shal raise?

You *Violets* that first appeare,
    By your pure *purpel mantels* knowne,
Like the proud *Virgins* of the yeare,
    As if the *Spring* were all your own;
What are you when the *Rose* is *blowne?*

So, when my *Mistris* shal be *seene*
    In *form* and *Beauty* of her *mind,*
By *Vertue* first, then *Choyce* a *Queen,*
    Tell me, if she were not design'd
Th'Eclypse and *Glory* of her kind.[94]

In similar vein the gallants of the Inns of Court pledged their devotion in an elaborate Christmastide ceremony in 1621:

> The Lieutenant of Middle Temple played a game this Christmas time, whereat his Majestie was highly displeased. He made choise of some thirty of the civillest and best-fashioned gentlemen of the House to sup with him; and, being at supper, took a cup of wine in one hand and held his sword drawn in the other, and so began a health 'to the distressed Lady Elizabeth,' and having drunk, kissed his sword, and laying his hand upon it, took an oath to live and die in her service; then delivered the cup and sword to the next, and so the health and ceremonie went round.[95]

The polemicists, wits, and satirists also came out in force, defying James's censorship. Caricaturists represented James with empty pockets and an empty scabbard. Imported news sheets (which James tried in vain to stop) gave reports from the battlefronts. Thomas Scott's *Vox Populi* tracts portray Spain's glee over its Machiavellian deception of James in regard to the Palatinate and the Spanish marriage; other tracts cite James's words against himself in promising support to the Palatinate and to Protestantism; still others lament the wrongs done to "the most renowned and second Queene Elizabeth (for her constancie and spirit)."[96] George Wither was arrested for the anti-Spanish tirades in his *Wither's Motto,* as was John Reynolds for his *Vox Coeli,* in which the first Queen Elizabeth is made to denounce the Spanish marriage in train for Charles, and the Palatine policy.[97] The most devastating of these tracts, *Tom Tell-Troath* (1622), reports with feigned horror the widespread disaffection for the King but in fact justifies it, terming James "Head of the Church Dormant":

> They that take the affaires of your children abroade most to hearte . . . will hardlie be perswaded, that you are their father; because, they see, the lamentable estate, whereto you suffer thinges to run, comes nearer to destruction than the nature of fatherly correction . . . since they have not been able, all this while, to get their petition answered . . . In your Majesties owne tavernes, for one healthe that is begun to your selfe, there are ten drunke to the Princes, your forrayne children . . . I cannot forget, how I have seene soame, when they have lost all their money, fall a cursing and swearing at the loss of Prague and the Palatinate; as though all the rancour of their hartes lay there . . . Since your Majestie came to be our Soveraigne . . . we have lived to see that brave stock of soveraigne reputation, which our greate Queen, your predecessor, left us, quite banisht, and brought to nothing . . . Who would have thought, that wee should have lost, but rather infinitely gained, by changing the weaker sexe, for your more noble . . . But the event showes, wee are in nothing more miserable, then in that wee had so much reason to thinke our selves happy.[98]

This striking contrast of the two Queen Elizabeths to the vacillating male King represents women as the true, militant defenders of English Protestant values in the decadent Jacobean world. Conscious of such support, Elizabeth sent out some feelers early in 1623 about returning to England or sending over her eldest son, provoking rumors that she was plotting to be in place should Charles meet with disaster (as was often predicted) while he was in Spain wooing the Infanta. She had to give over this activist move, which put James in a panic and prompted an urgent plea from the Countess of Bedford to the British ambassador to the Hague, Dudley Carleton:

> For Gods sake preache more warines to the Queene whom she uses freedom to, else shee will undo her selfe, and make others afrayd how they interest them selves in her servis, though for my part I will never omitte makeing good my professions to her as becoms a faithfull and carefull servant.[99]

The Winter Queen kept her court-in-exile in the Hague for forty years. She bore more children (thirteen in all), exchanged devoted letters with her husband fighting under the command of Prince Maurice, and agitated through forceful letters for support in the Palatine wars. After Frederick's death in 1632 she turned her efforts to regaining the Palatinate for her son,

Charles Lewis.[100] In a letter dated March 20 (1634?) she pressed her kinsman the Marquis of Hamilton to influence King Charles to grant levies

> for the defence of the Palatinat and regaining what is yett to be recovered . . . [else] I shall never againe looke for anie good from your quarter, for the King my Brother will hardlie recover againe such an opportunitie, you see I write frelie to you and therefore I pray burne my letter and lett no bodie else see it.[101]

In a revealing exchange in 1636 with Archbishop Laud, Elizabeth justified her "unfeminine" preference for military action by referring to her sixteen years' experience with ineffectual diplomacy: "All I fear is that you will think I have too warring a mind for my sex; but the necessity of my fortune has made it."[102] She entertained a steady stream of visitors, among them the British ambassador Dudley Carleton, the Countess of Bedford, her courtly servant Christian of Bruswick, Buckingham, Roe, Edward Herbert, John Evelyn. She patronized the educational and utopian writing of the proto-Enlightenment thinkers Samuel Hartlib, John Dury, and Comenius.[103] And she wrote hundreds of letters—vivacious, witty, shrewd, informed, incisive—to King Charles, to John Donne (thanking him for the gift of his *Devotions*), to Thomas Roe (regularly), and to Buckingham, Montrose, Laud, and Charles Lewis, among many others. Reportedly she now could write and converse in German, Dutch, and Latin as well as French and Italian.[104] Soon after his accession Charles I began a war with Spain intending to reclaim the Palatinate, but soon gave over for want of resources. Charles Lewis was restored to a part of the Palatinate in 1648 in the Peace of Munster.[105] Elizabeth returned to England for the first time in 1661, invited by her nephew Charles II just a few months before her death on February 13, 1662.

While Elizabeth's symbolic force declined during her long exile, she was for many in Jacobean England a romance heroine come to life and transformed into a potent figure of resistance to James's politics and patriarchy. She came to represent true English, Elizabethan, and Protestant virtue and valor, embodied in a woman and poised against a vacillating, impotent, decadent male monarch in thrall to Spain. She collaborated actively in constructing that portrait through her life and letters, affording to Jacobean women (and men) a striking example of oppositional politics in which Jacobean patriarchy was challenged directly by the King's own daughter.

Arbella Stuart, by John Whittaker, Senior.

3 ☙

Writing Resistance in Letters: Arbella Stuart and the Rhetoric of Disguise and Defiance

No one, except Arbella Stuart herself on occasion, planned that she should star in a romance. Generally acclaimed as the most intelligent and learned lady in Jacobean England, she, like Princess Elizabeth, constructed herself through her cultural roles and her letters, but in her case both texts were written under much more rigid constraints. As a plausible claimant to the English throne and an object of suspicion for two monarchs, Arbella (1575–1615) must often have felt herself a pawn in scenarios devised by others. Nevertheless, she undertook several bold, though unsuccessful, acts of defiance in an effort to escape those scripts and devise her own narrative.[1] Her royal blood gave her acts, and her numerous lettters and petitions, some resonance in Jacobean culture, affording an example of resistance to patriarchal and monarchical power in a bid for some personal autonomy.

Sara Jayne Steen usefully classifies Arbella Stuart's letters into three categories: loosely structured, associational, and often angry complaints and recriminations; informal, affectionate, often bantering letters to her favorite uncle, Gilbert Talbot, and her aunt Mary; and formal, carefully structured, conventionally humble and submissive court letters.[2] Her letters are noteworthy for their witty and ironic comments on Elizabethan and Jacobean court society; for their unconscious self-representation combined with highly conscious self-fashioning; and for their rhetorical strategies of self-defense, ranging from obfuscation to self-abasement to insistent self-justification. They register her efforts to claim her life and wrest control of it from all those others, but they can do so only by indirection in the Elizabethan and Jacobean court. In them, Arbella Stuart works out a rhetoric of concealment as a strategy for retaining some limited power of self-determination in a repressive milieu.

Arbella's claim to the throne was based on her descent from Henry VII's daughter Margaret through her second marriage to the Earl of Angus; James I's line descended from Margaret's first marriage, to James IV of Scotland. Also, Arbella was born in England, whereas James's "alien birth" in Scotland might be invoked as a bar to succession. The other plausible claimants, the Seymours, were descended from Mary, the younger daughter of Henry VII, and also from Edward III. Arbella's formidable grandmother and guardian, Bess of Hardwick, educated her for a throne (English or foreign), and virtually imprisoned her for several years at Queen Elizabeth's behest. Queen Elizabeth played politics with Arbella's marriage prospects and her claims, but refused (except briefly) to have her at court. At his accession James I brought his cousin to court but kept her dependent on him, refusing to return her estates or arrange her marriage lest she become a threat to him. In two reigns Roman Catholic conspirators and agitators made her a focal point for their plots to displace the Protestant line, though Arbella remained a Protestant all her life and was not a party to these schemes. To succeed in such circumstances she needed qualities Bess of Hardwick had in abundance but which she unfortunately did not inherit: shrewd judgment, strong nerves, steely will, and sheer good luck.

Arbella Stuart was born in the autumn of 1575, the daughter of Charles Stuart, Earl of Lennox, and Elizabeth Cavendish, Bess of Hardwick's daughter by her second husband. At her father's death in 1576, James VI made the earldom extinct, bypassed Arbella, and bestowed the title and properties elsewhere—eventually on his favorite, Esmé Stuart. Efforts to press Arbella's claims to the Lennox properties were unsuccessful, leaving her and her mother dependent upon family resources and a small royal pension. The death in 1578 of her paternal grandmother, Margaret Lennox (mother also to Darnley), effectively removed Arbella from the influence of that Roman Catholic family; the death of her mother in 1582 brought her into the care of her redoubtable maternal grandmother, Bess of Hardwick.

Bess was then married to her fourth husband, Gilbert Talbot, seventh Earl of Shrewsbury, Earl Marshall of England, and custodian for Mary Queen of Scots, who lived a prisoner in the various Shrewsbury mansions (Sheffield Castle, Chatsworth, Worksop, Wingfield) from 1569 to 1586. Proximity and access to Mary Stuart (executed when Arbella was eleven) offered her a harsh lesson in the perils of being a rival claimant to an inhabited throne, but extended her experience of powerful women. She knew the Queen of Scots as the center of plots and power plays; the always formidable Queen Elizabeth; and her grandmother Bess, who outlasted four husbands, amassed a great fortune (starting with only £40), constructed and acquired magnificent houses and castles (notably Hardwick Hall and Chatsworth), and was a force to be reckoned with in both the domestic and the public sphere.[3] When Bess and Shrewsbury were embroiled in marital disputes, Arbella spent some time at Shrewsbury House, Chelsea, with her aunt Mary and uncle Gilbert Talbot (Bess's daughter married to Shrewsbury's son), for whom she always retained great affection.

As a prospective ruler Arbella received under Bess's supervision a rigorous classical education on the male model; she used Latin easily and competently in several letters. Her other studies were more common for highborn ladies: French and Italian, Chancery script, history and globes, the Bible and religious texts, the lute and virginals, dancing. She also embroidered and stitched, read literature, hunted and hawked, and (at Bess's insistence) learned to keep accounts.[4] When she was almost seven Bess wrote to Walsingham that Arbella "is of very great towardness to learn anything" and that Bess was taking special care for her education because of "the consanguinity she is of to her Majesty,"[5] but the letter did not elicit the hoped-for increase in Arbella's pension. At Arbella's first visit to court at the age of twelve, Burghley commented on her accomplishments: "She had the French, the Italian, played of instruments, danced, wrought and wrote very fair."[6] Sometime later John Harington (the translator of Ariosto) added his personal testimony to her fine education, and especially her linguistic and critical skills:

> Her virtuous disposition . . . her choice education, her rare skill in languages, her good judgment and sight in music, and a mind to all these free from pride, vanity, and affectation, and the greatest sobriety in her fashion of apparel and behaviour as may be, of all of which I have been myself an eyewitness, having seen her several times at Hardwick, at Chelsea, where she made me read the tale of Drusilla in Orlando unto her, and censured it with a gravity beyond her years. And first of all at Wingfield, when, being thirteen years old, she did read French out of Italian, and English out of both, much better than I could, or than I expected.[7]

During her ten-year seclusion at Hardwick (1592–1602) she learned Greek, Hebrew, and perhaps Spanish, and read Homer in the original as well as parts of the Hebrew Bible.[8] Over the years her letters are filled with allusions to the classics, Homer, Plutarch, Pliny, and Greek mythology.

From early childhood Arbella received marriage proposals, but nothing came of them. In 1581 a match with her cousin Esmé Stuart was considered (this union would have settled the Lennox property claim), but he was banished from Scotland in 1582. In 1583 Bess and Leicester agreed to a match between the eight-year-old Arbella and Leicester's four-year-old son Robert Dudley, but the child died a few months later. At this juncture the Queen forbade such private negotiations, holding Arbella, like herself, as a counter in the game of statecraft and encouraging speculation that she might indeed inherit the throne. The most serious negotiations, carried on by various factions over several years, involved Rainutio Farnese, son of the Duke of Palma, who had a distant claim to the English throne through John of Gaunt. Cecil and Walsingham saw that union as a means of neutralizing Palma's military support for Spain, and Catholic factions saw the possibility of regaining England for the Church. But when Palma died in 1592, his son was no longer a useful connection.[9]

Arbella had no say in any of these negotiations, or in several others that also came to nothing.[10] She probably did enjoy her seasons at court in 1587 and 1588, and especially in 1591 and 1592, when the Palma negotiations were in train and she was a focus of attention as a possible successor to Elizabeth. Later she recalled with pride that "it pleased hir Majesty to give me leave to gaze on hir, and by trial pronounce me an Eaglett of her owne kinde, as worthy . . . to carry hir Thunderbolt."[11] In 1588 she committed some fault that caused her to be, as she put it, "disgraced in the Presence at Greenwich, and discouraged in the Lobby at Whithall," and then banished from the court for three years.[12] Some sort of "haughtiness" may have been involved, as an unreliable report by the Venetian secretary Scaramelli claimed, but a more important cause, as she hinted obliquely in 1603, may have been the attention paid her by the Queen's favorite, Essex:

> And weare not I unthanckfully forgetfull, if I should not remember my noble frend [Essex] who graced me by her Majesties commaundment disgraced orphant, unfound ward, unproved prisoner, undeserved exile in his greatest and happy fortunes to the adventure of eclipsing part of her Majesties favours from him which weare so deare, so wellcome to him?[13]

That three-year banishment, whatever its cause, was soon followed by a de facto ten-year banishment (1592–1602) and near-imprisonment with Bess at Chatsworth and Hardwick. This was dictated in part by the Queen's unwillingness to confront the issue of her own mortality and the succession, but chiefly by the perceived need to keep Arbella secure in the plot-ridden atmosphere of the 1590s. In 1592 a dangerous plot was uncovered, involving English recusants and Spanish agents, to kidnap Arbella, spirit her out of the country, and marry her to a suitable Catholic. Rumors of similar plots abounded, fueled by Jesuit polemic about the succession.[14] In these circumstances Bess took her guardianship responsibilities very seriously, as is evident from her report to the Privy Council:

I wyll not have any unknowen or suspected person to come to my howse . . . I have litle resort to me, my howse is furnished with sufficient company, Arbell walks not late, at such tyme as she shall take ye ayre, yt shalbe neer the howse, and well attended on; she goeth not to any bodyes howse at all, I se hyr almost every howre in the day, she lyeth in my bed chamber, yf I can be more presise then I have bene I wilbe.[15]

Bess generously settled lands and money on Arbella so as to give her some financial independence, but gave her no personal freedom. She was cut off from companions of her own age of either sex, and her life centered on her tutors and chaplain, the occasional visits of relatives, the occasional performances of musicians or players, her own music making and reading, and the study of Greek and Hebrew.[16]

In 1602 Arbella, now twenty-seven years old, reached a breaking point: no marriage had been arranged for her, no invitations to court arrived, and Bess's wardship seemed daily more demeaning and insupportable. So she made a daring, though highly imprudent, decision to act for herself, galvanized perhaps by news of the Queen's failing health. Shortly before Christmas she sent a gentleman servant, John Dodderidge, to the Earl of Hertford with a proposition of marriage between herself and his grandson, the sixteen-year-old Edward Seymour. Her choice makes sense only as a bid for the succession. Whether or not Hertford had advanced the idea first, as Arbella later insisted, she evidently counted on his interest in linking together and thus reinforcing the claims of the only two real contenders (besides James) for the throne. Her expectation was probably based on Hertford's own surreptitious marriage in 1560 to Catherine Grey, in very similar circumstances.[17] But eight years in the Tower in consequence of that affair had left Hertford with no desire to make another attempt to put his family in the way of a crown through a dangerous marriage without royal consent, and he immediately apprised Cecil of Arbella's overture. Her elaborate plan was thereby aborted, the persons associated with it questioned, and a special emissary, Sir Henry Brounker, was sent to determine what plots were afoot at Hardwick.[18]

In grave danger, Arbella wrote a series of letters and confessions over the next several months that are often opaque, confused, and disjointed in subject and syntax—very different indeed from her usual brisk and lucid style. This may have been due, as many of her contemporaries and modern biographers have supposed, to a temporary mental breakdown[19]—though if so only, I think, in the final weeks. Rather, she seems to have been practicing the rhetoric of disguise—with some success, in that she kept herself out of the Tower and gained one primary objective: release from Hardwick. Her reported mental instability during the final months of

Elizabeth's reign effectively eliminated her as a viable candidate for the throne, but by this time James's succession was assured in any case.

Brounker was at Hardwick January 7–9, 1603. Arbella admitted verbally to what could be proved against her, but Brounker demanded her written account of the affair, which he found so "confused, obscure and in truth ridiculous" that he refused to accept it. He concluded that "her wits were somewhat distracted, either with feare of her Grandmother or conceit of her owne folly."[20] Still, as a means to avoid damaging admissions her seeming confusion worked well enough. Her letter to the Queen, sent back with Brounker, is sensible, if curt: it acknowledges in the most general terms that "most" of the things Brounker has charged her with are true, and begs pardon of the Queen's "Princely clemency."[21] Reassured by Brounker that the whole affair was simply Arbella's foolishness, Cecil and Stanhope (the Vice-Chancellor) exonerated Bess, ascribed Arbella's fault to "base Companions," and recommended greater freedom and more society for her. But they refused to settle her elsewhere, as both she and the now-exasperated Bess desired.[22] Seeing no escape, Arbella wrote again to the Queen, probably in late January or early February, thanking her effusively for her "most gracious interpretation of this accident" (the term displaces responsibility from herself) and explaining her actions as a strategy to call the Queen's attention to her sad plight:

> My exile out of your Majestyies presence . . . hath binne the onely motive both of this and many other occurrents . . . I call the Judge of all hearts to witnesse . . . if she [Bess] had not binne stricter than any childe how good discreet, and dutyfull soever, would willingly obey . . . so I have all the other wayes I could devise not by way of complaint but mone [moan] disclosed my most distressed state to your Majesty, of whom onely I have expected and with silent and stolne teares implored and expected reliefe.[23]

Arbella's next strategy was to pretend to have another secret lover and to be plotting another marriage, rightly thinking this the best means to keep the court interested in her plight. A letter to her grandmother at about the same time is filled with teasing intimations of a long-standing affair, along with what seem to be deliberate obfuscations. Protesting that she intended the Hertford proposal to be discovered, she defies Bess directly, promising to be "accountable to her Majesty, but not to your Ladyship, for all that ever I did in my life or ever will do," and offering to reveal to the Queen alone (through Brounker) "some secrettes of love concerning my selfe."[24] She alludes to her "dearest and best-trusted, whatsoever he be"; claims that he persuaded her to take up a "ridiculous and contemptuous stile . . . before he could persuade me to play the fool in good earnest"; describes him as "great with hir Majesty" and very secret; and claims she has "already unreservedly accepted" the love of "this worthy gentleman . . . and will never deny . . . nor will repent whatsoever befall."[25] She attributes to this mysterious "he" all the assumptions and expectations upon which her strategies were based—which suggests that she may be devising an allegory of her own intellect as an alter ego (gendered masculine). Her several references to deliberate riddling support this view, and it makes considerable sense of the apparent ravings:

> He taught me by the example of Samuell that one might plead one errand and deliver an other with a safe conscience. By the example of Sampson that one might and (if they be not too foolish to live in the world) must speake riddles to theyr frends and try the truth of offred love . . . He assured me hir Majesties offense would be converted into laughter, when hir Majesty should see the honest cunning of the contriver . . . He told me he would have me enter into some great action to winne my selfe reputation, try her Majesties love to me though neither of us doubted of it, try what my frends would do for me . . . I thinck it long till I may lett hir Majesty know his name . . . and none living shall understand my drift but hir Majesty, the noble Gentleman whose name I conceale, and whom it pleaseth them two to acquaint.[26]

That this is the rhetoric of concealment and not the ravings of a madwoman seems indicated by Arbella's letter a few days later (February 6) to Cecil and Stanhope, in which she refers to her "scribbled follies" as evidence of "how merry secure innocence can be even in the presence of a reverenced, and yet unappeased parent." Then, claiming the "Christian liberty" due any subject of a gracious sovereign, she asks with trenchant if truculent logic for clarification, implementation, and extension of the more liberal conditions of life which the Queen's letter had seemed to promise her:

> Whither it be hir Majesties pleasure I shall have free choice of my owne servants to take keepe and putt away whom I thinck good either telling or not telling the reason: And whither I may send for whom I thinck good or talke with any that shall voluntarily or upon businesse com to me, in private if they or I shall so desire . . . And whither it be not hir Majesties pleasure I should as well have the company of some yong Lady or gentlewoman for my recreation, and Schollers, Musick, hunting, hauking, variety of any lawfull disport . . . Whither if the running on of yeares be not discerned in me onely, yet if it be not hir Highnesses pleasure to allow me that liberty being the 6 of this February 27 yeares olde, which many Infants have to chuse theyr

own Guardian, as I desire to do my place of abode . . . And then if it please hir Majesty to impose an extraordinary yoke of bondage upon me . . . to lett me know the true causes whearfore . . . And to sett downe the time how long, and without ambiguity to prescribe me the rules whearby it pleaseth hir Majesty to try my obedience.[27]

Bess reported to Cecil on February 21 that Arbella was ill and had gone on a hunger strike: "She hath made a vowe not to eat or drink in this house at Hardwick, or where I am till she maye heare from hir Majestie." This tactic forced Bess to send Arbella to her uncle William Cavendish's house, Oldcotes, and to add her own plea that Brounker be sent back.[28]

Brounker returned on March 2 to confront Arbella with thirty-three questions seeking clarification of statements in her "merry" letter to Bess. But since he came as the agent of the Privy Council and not as the direct emissary of the Queen she had requested, she turned again to obfuscation. To every demand that she identify whom she meant when she referred to her "dearest," she answered "the King of Scots."[29] Though she wrested her texts ingeniously to make them fit, the identification was patently ridiculous. And that was evidently the point: James was perhaps the one man in the kingdom who could not be harmed by her naming, since no one would credit this long-married known homosexual as Arbella's secret lover. She sent back with Brounker a letter for the Queen or Cecil, again intimating that the love affair was only pretense:

> I presumed to draw Sir Henry Brounker hither to an Allegory which I have moralized to him, and howsoever it please her Majesty to interpret it, I protest I thought the matters I have declared worthy hir Majesty's knowledge, and durst not reveile them in plainer sort to any but hir Majesty . . . Experience had taught me theire was no other way to draw down a messenger of such worth from hir Majesty but by incurring some suspition and having no ground whearupon to work but this, and this being love.[30]

She categorically declares that she is and will remain "free from promise, contract, marriage, or intention to marry," unless forced to another course by "the continuance of these disgraces and miseries,"[31] and promises to trouble the Queen no more about her lands or marriage if given her due liberty and the Queen's favor. Bess, who clearly believed in the secret lover, also sent a letter apologizing for Brounker's failed mission and Arbella's state of mind, along with a heartfelt plea to be relieved of her charge.[32]

In the few days after Brounker left, Arbella sent several long letters after him which seem increasingly distraught, though their burden is clear enough: complaint that her intolerable situation has not improved. She cannot indulge in tirades against the Queen, or even Cecil and Stanhope (save for ironic asides charging these statesmen with nepotism),[33] but she lambastes Brounker in letter after letter for unkept promises and for toadying with "court-dazled eyes" to those in power. She no doubt knew that these letters would be passed on and that their mystifying allusions to her beloved and intimations of her possible suicide would keep the pressure on. In her letter of March 7 she complains of being kept by Bess from her "quondam study chamber" and the "comfort and good counsell, of my dead counsellers and comforters."[34] These letters employ learned references to describe her embattled and abandoned situation: she would endure a ten-year *Iliad*-like siege rather than reveal her beloved; under verbal onslaught from her grandmother she is a Virgilian Camilla, her waiting women are viragoes, and she escapes the fate of Eurydice by refusing to look back; she must "live like an Owle in the wildernesse since my Pallas will not protect me with hir shield."[35] Some other allusions are to "disgraced" Plutarch, and to Hebe, Ganymede, Ulysses, Esther, and the Song of Songs. She also playfully invokes the biblical ideal of *caritas* to explain her identification of James as her beloved:

> Because you know not the power of Divine and Christian love at Court . . . [you] cannot beleeve one can come so neere Gods precept who commandeth us to love our neighbour like our selfe, as to love an unkinde but other-wise worthy kinsman, so well as nobody else (it seemes to your knowledge) doth any but their paramours . . . But he [James] hath studied too much divinity to thinck either the word misapplied or the matter impossible to be most true and lawfully allowable, of any married man, which made you so captious and inquisitive, because you are more conversant in Court and in the Arcadian phrase which need no comment to you, then in the Church or our Churches translation of the Testament which commaundeth holy love and holy kisses.[36]

At this juncture she is clearly in great emotional distress: her letters make reference to her "travelling minde," and to her "scribling melancholy (which is a kinde of madnesse, and theare are severall kindes of it)."[37] But she is still, I think, quite sane. As with Hamlet or Poor Tom, apparent madness offers a cover for otherwise unspeakable defiance of authority. So Arbella's letter of March 9 ("this fatal Ash Wednesday," the liturgical anniversary of Essex's execution) flaunts her friendship with, sympathy for, and similarity in condition to Essex:

> The more you think to make the more you marre when all is donne I must take it [in] hand, and shape my owne cote according to my cloth . . . fitt for me, and every way becoming of that vertu in me whither it be a native property of that bloud I come of, or an infective vertu

of the E. of Essex . . . Shall not I, I say now I have lost all I can loose or allmost care to loose . . . who may well say I never had nor shall have the like frend [as Essex was], nor the like time to this to need a frend in Court . . . Had the Earle of Essex the favour to dy unbound because he was a Prince, and shall my hands be bound from helping myself in this distress?[38]

Reverting constantly to the arrest and questioning of her servants and the suicide of her first agent, Starkey, she reads her own situation, wrongs, and danger in the light of Essex's experience. Nor does she shrink from open defiance:

When it shall please hir Majesty to afford me those ordinary rights which other subjectes cannot be debarred of justly, I shall endeavour to receive them as thanckfully now as if they had binne in due time offred . . . [I will answer no more] for all the commandments and threatenings and wrongs and torments all the Councill, Rackmasters and all the ministers of hir Majesties indignation can powre upon me . . . till I be used like my selfe . . . who am not ignorant either of my birth or desert, nor sencelesse of wrong, nor hopelesse of redresse, which as it is my duty first to begg as I have done, and after a while to expect from her Majesty, so it is my duty to God to procure by all the lawfull meanes with speed because my weake body and travelling mind must be disburdned soone or I shall offend my God and I weare better offend my Prince . . . My words have binne already too offensively taken and too unjustly wrested by them that had least cause so to do. I am deafe to commaundments and dumbe to Authority.[39]

The following day (March 10) Arbella made an abortive attempt to escape from Hardwick with the aid of her uncle Henry Cavendish and a known Catholic, Henry Stapleton, who hoped in the final days of Elizabeth to place Arbella on the throne. But the principals got their signals crossed, and Bess's vigilance (reported by her to Cecil in great detail) prevented a second attempt. This affair prompted Brounker's return to Hardwick with more inquiries; he reported Arbella much less cooperative than before, probably because the Queen's death was imminent (it occurred on March 24) and so also the expiration of his warrant.[40] When Arbella's uncle Gilbert and aunt Mary Talbot entertained James at the Shrewsbury estate in Worksop in early April, they evidently pressed him about Arbella's sad situation, and he ordered her removal to Wrest Park, to the care of her kinsman Henry Grey, Earl of Kent.[41] On April 12 the Venetians reported that Arbella was "no longer mad"—further evidence that her "madness" was more politic than psychological.[42] As the Queen's kinswoman, Arbella was asked and expected to be a mourner at Elizabeth's funeral, but she declared with spirit that she would not be part of the public spectacle at the death of a Queen who had refused her access during her life.[43]

James invited his cousin to reside at court; probably she came for the coronation on July 25. Her life there was an improvement over the near-incarceration at Hardwick, but it was hardly ideal: without large financial resources of her own (she had about £1,400), without a powerful family network now that Bess's great days were over, without a power base at court because of her long seclusion in the country, and without a husband to provide some security and protection, she was wholly dependent upon the King and Queen, Cecil, Somerset, and others in favor. Her first concern had to be money, to enable her to survive in James's extravagant court. Several formal letters and petitions, often elegantly inscribed and very polite, recount her needs and beg prompt settlement of her royal pension. On June 23 she suggests the sum of £2,000 to Cecil as consonant with her necessities, and asks his help as "my honourable good friend both in procuring it as soon, and making the sum as great as may be."[44] Several letters to her aunt Mary Talbot report severe financial strain: the requisite New Year's gifts for 1604 (some "daffe Toy" for the Queen, a purse for James, nothing for others) will, she writes, "manifest my poverty more then all the rest of the yeare, but why should I be ashamed of it, when it is others faults and not mine?"[45] James first granted a pension of £800, increasing it over time to about £2,000 together with a provision of food for her houschold—hardly munificent considering the style a royal Lady had to maintain. Over the years Arbella also acquired splendid jewels as gifts, as well as some patents and monopolies.[46]

Almost immediately there were new plots and rumors of plots involving Arbella, but she had the wit to stay clear. The notorious "Main" Plot discovered in July 1603 intended the assassination of James and Cecil and the coronation of Arbella, using Spanish and Austrian money; when the chief conspirator, Lord Cobham, broached the matter to Arbella through his brother Lord Brooke, she at once turned the letter over to Cecil.[47] At the conspirators' trial in November, Arbella (seated in the gallery) was briefly threatened by the prosecutor, Edward Coke. Eager to railroad Ralegh he declared: "Your intent was to set up the Lady Arabella as a titular Queen and to depose our present rightful King." Ralegh derisively but decisively replied that he had no acquaintance with her and that he liked her least of any woman he ever saw. Cecil defended her rather more graciously:

> Here hath been a touch of the Lady Arbella Stuart, the King's near kinswoman, let us not scandal the innocent by confusion of speech.

> She is as innocent of all these things as I, or any man here: only she received a letter from my Lord Cobham to prepare her, which she laughed at and immediately sent to the King.[48]

Writing to Mary Talbot at Christmastide, Arbella angrily denounced "the vanity of wicked mens vain designes [that] have made my name passe through a grosse and suttle Lawyer's lippes of late";[49] she does not comment on the trials themselves. About this time there were new speculations about a marriage for Arbella: Count Maurice of the Netherlands was mentioned; also the King of Poland and the Prince of Anhalt, though the Queen's secretary, William Fowler, commented that Arbella "nothinge lyketh his [Anhalt's] letters nor his Latine."[50] But she had no impressive dowry, she was no longer in the bloom of youth, and James had no real interest in making a match for her.

Accordingly, for the next several years she was one of the Queen's entourage, not numbered among her closest companions but appointed Carver and Train-Bearer in recognition of her rank. She followed the court in its peregrinations, reporting wittily to her aunt and uncle Shrewsbury on its follies and her own involvement in them. Her playful banter, acerbic wit, ironic observation, and self-reflexive irony are irrepressible—a mask and escape valve for a highly intelligent woman who sees the absurdities around her with penetrating clarity but cannot alter or escape from them. Her wryly amused tone in these letters, especially the early ones to her uncle, evidences a conscious separation between her astute, learned, highly critical inner self and the public role she was called upon to play.

Despite her own past quarrels with Queen Elizabeth, she had only scorn for the female courtiers' malicious gossip about her: "Our great and gratious Ladies leave no gesture nor fault of the late Queene unremembered, as they say who are partakers of theyr talke, as I thank God, I am not."[51] She reports herself appalled by the new court manners ("But if ever theare weare such a vertu as curtesy at the Court, I marvell what is becom of it, for I protest I see little or none of it"); she exempts only Queen Anne, likening her gracious behavior to "that attractive vertu of our late Queene El."[52] She regales her uncle with accounts of sumptuous dinners, ladies' jewels, ambassadors' visits, and, as the nadir of inanity, the pastimes of the Queen's court:

> Will you know how we spend our time on the Queene's side? Whilst I was at Winchester, there weare certein Childe playes remembred by the fayre Ladies. Viz. "I pray, my Lord give me a course in your Parke"; "Rise, Pig, and go"; "One peny follow me," etc. and when I cam to court they were as highly in request as ever cracking of Nuts was. so I was by the Mistress of the Revelles not only compelled to

play at I knew not what, (for till that day I never heard of a play called *Fier*) but even perswaded by the Princely example I saw, to play the childe againe. This excercise is most used from 10 of the clock at Night till 2 or 3 in the morning; but that Day I made one, it beganne at twilight, and ended at suppertime. There was *an interlude,* but not so ridiculous (ridiculous as it was) as my letter.[53]

In the same letter she rises to a playfully ironic defense of women, identifying Shrewsbury with traditional views of women's natural moral infirmity and countering with a jest about the greater spiritual peril of the rich and noble—men like himself. She concludes, as so often, by turning the irony on herself:

I cannot deny so apparant a truth as that wickednesse prevaileth with some of our sex, because I dayly see some even of the fairest amongst us, misled and willingly and wittingly ensnared, by the Prince of Darknesse. But yet ours shall still be the purer and more innocent minde. Theare went 10,000 Virgins to heaven in one day; looke but in the Almanack, and you shall finde that glorious Day; and if you thinck there are some, but not many, that may prove Saints, I hope you are deceived. But not many rich, not many noble, shall enter into the Kingdom of Heaven. So that Richesse and Nobilitye are hindrance from Heaven as well as our natures infirmitye. You would thinck me very full of divinity or desirous to shew that little I have (in both which you should prove wrong) if you knew what businesse I have at Court, and yet preach to you.[54]

Writing to the Earl a few days later, she called on her classical reading for a riddling characterization of life at court:

I dare not write unto you how I do, for if I should say well, I weare greatly to blame; If ill, I trust you would not beleeve me, I am so merry. It is enough to change Heraclitus into Democritus, to live in this most ridiculous World, and enough to change Democritus into Heraclitus to live in this most wicked World. If you will not allow reading of riddles for a Christmas sport, I know not whether you will take this Philosophical folly of mine in good part, this good time.[55]

She clearly felt some resentment about "this everlasting hunting" and the other duties of "never-intermitted attendance on the Queene," pointing to the conflict with her scholarly interests: "I am as diligently expected, and as soone missed, as they that performe the most acceptable service. And because I must . . . return at an appointed time to go to my booke I must make the more hast hither."[56] William Fowler commented that her time was spent at "lecture, reiding, hearing of service, and preaching."[57] These serious interests evidently caused her to be labeled a Puritan, and she sometimes jestingly attributes Puritan proclivities to herself: in a bantering letter to her uncle she asks for "Puritanlike" directions to guide her behavior at court, alluding, it seems, to advice from him to curb her too caustic wit.[58]

Although her acerbic comments indicate that she kept her internal distance from the court, she played her part well enough to gain privileges befitting her rank. In 1605 she stood godmother to the newborn Princess Mary. In the same year she was granted a peerage for her uncle William Talbot, and this familial benefit made her peace with Bess.[59] After the visit in 1606 of the Queen's brother, King Christian of Denmark, Arbella wrote several Latin letters to him and to the Danish Chancellor, Christian Tris. A principal topic was King Christian's desire to take into his service her lutenist, one Thomas Cutting; her gracious reply emphasizes rather wistfully her great pleasure in Cutting's abilities, her oversight of his training, and her sorrow at losing him. To Queen Anne, who petitioned Arbella for this favor to her brother, she voiced the requisite delight to be of service, but managed to intimate that the Queen had incurred a considerable debt by asking such a large and really unnecessary sacrifice:

> Although I know well how far more easy it is for so great a prince to command the best musicians in the world than for me to recover one not inferior to this, yet do I most willingly embrace this occasion whereby I may in effect give some demonstration of my unfeigned disposition to apply myself ever unto all your royal pleasures.[60]

There is no evidence that Arbella recognized the subversive element in the Queen's masques, though she danced in two of them. She took no part in Daniel's *Vision of Twelve Goddesses* (1604) or Jonson's *Blacknesse* (1605), probably because she was not yet able to sustain the expense. On January 10, 1608, she danced in the *Masque of Beautie* as one of the nymphs who attain white skins; she was then resplendent in jewels which Carleton valued at more than £100,000.[61] Smallpox kept her from dancing in *Queenes*—perhaps fortunately, since James would hardly have relished seeing her in the role of a powerful Queen; she was back at court in time to see the production at Candlemas. Though already under some suspicion, she danced as the Nymph of Trent (a river in her native Derbyshire) in *Tethys Festival* (June 5, 1610), celebrating Prince Henry's installation as Prince of Wales.

Arbella was the recipient of several dedicatory poems and praises during these years, most of them complimenting her learning. She made her debut as patroness in 1598 while still at Hardwick, as dedicatee of a collection of songs and madrigals from her cousin Michael Cavendish, who lauded her "rare perfections in so many knowledges," and acknowledged her welcome "favours."[62] A bad sonnet by her great admirer William Fowler (1603) praises her "graces rare" and her heavenly devotion, which contrast sharply with the trash and toys around her.[63] Several works address her in Latin, in compliment to her classical education: Hugh Holland's sonnet (1603) praises her as a most illustrious virgin and lover of the Muses; David Hume's prose epistle (1605) celebrates her as the nursling of the Muses, who is furnished with virtue, piety, humanity, erudition, authority, and intelligence; John Owen's two epigrams acclaim her noble talents, virtue, and constancy.[64] In 1609 John Wilbye, a musician who was evidently in her service, dedicated his songs to her, acknowledging her "deep understanding" in all the arts and "particular excellency in this of music," and declaring himself "borne up by the daily experience of your most noble and singular disposition."[65] George Chapman addressed Arbella in one of the fourteen presentation verses for the first half of his *Iliad*. Alluding gracefully to her knowledge of Greek—her "former conference with his [Homer's] original Spirit"—he invites her, as "our English Athenia, Chaste Arbitresse of vertue and learning," to pass judgment on his work.[66] She was probably the only one of his dedicatees who could.

Aemilia Lanyer included Arbella among her nine female dedicatees in *Salve Deus Rex Judaeorum* (1611), pointing to learning as her distinguishing characteristic and inviting her to attend to Lanyer's book:

> Great learned Ladie, whom I long have knowne,
> And yet not knowne so much as I desired:
> Rare *Phoenix,* whose faire feathers are your owne,
> With which you flie, and are so much admired:
> True honour whom true Fame hath so attired,
>   In glittering raiment shining much more bright,
>   Than silver Starres in the most frostie night.
>
> Come like the morning Sunne new out of bed,
> And cast your eyes upon this little Booke,
> Although you be so well accompan'ed
> With *Pallas,* and the Muses, spare one looke
> Upon this humbled King, who all forsooke,
>   That in his dying armes he might imbrace
>   Your beauteous Soule, and fill it with his grace.[67]

As the years passed, Arbella grew increasingly resentful of James's failure to honor earlier promises to restore the Lennox lands to her and to arrange a marriage for her. In his report of 1607 the Venetian ambassador Nicoló Molin describes her situation very perceptively:

> The nearest relative the King has is Madame Arbella . . . She is twenty-eight [actually thirty-two]; not very beautiful, but highly accomplished, for besides being of most refined manners she speaks fluently Latin, Italian, French, Spanish, reads Greek and Hebrew, and is always studying. She is not very rich, for the late Queen was jealous of everyone, and especially of those who had a claim on the throne, and so she took from her the larger part of her income, and the poor lady cannot live as magnificently nor reward her attendants as liberally as she would. The King professes to love her and to hold her in high esteem. She is allowed to come to Court, and the King promised, when he ascended the throne, that he would restore her property, but he has not done so yet, saying she shall have it all and more on her marriage, but so far the husband has not been found, and she remains without a mate and without estate.[68]

Her tart, witty letters give covert testimony to her mounting discontent. At times her wit is simply a gesture of self-affirmation, the only one available to the impotent; at other times it registers a determination to find some remedy. When Bess of Hardwick died on February 13, 1608, Arbella came into an inheritance of £1,000; her report to Shrewsbury about buying a small house in Blackfriars as an escape from court alludes ironically to her still unmarried state: "For want of a nunnery, I have for awhile retired myself to the Friars."[69] A few months later in a letter to Shrewsbury she contrives a witty but bitter parable about the King's failure to restore her property, with jests about her aunt Mary's recent conversion to Catholicism and about herself as Pope Joan—an office that would allow her to offer authoritative interpretations and make appointments:

> I make it my end only to make you merry, and show my desire to please you even in playing the foole; for no folly is greater, I trow, then to laugh when one smarteth; but that my aunt's divinity can tell you St. Laurence, deriding his tormentors even upon the gridiron, bad them turne him on the other side, for that he lay on was sufficiently broiled, I should not know how to excuse myselfe from either insensiblenesse or contempt of injuries. I finde if one rob a house, and build a church with the money, the wronged party may go pipe in an ivy leafe for any redresse . . . Unto you it is given to understand parables, or to command the coment; but if you be of this opinion of the Scribes and Pharasees, I condemne your Lordship by your leave, for an heretike, by the authority of Pope Jone; for theare is a text saith, you must not do evill that good maye comme thearof . . . I

humbly pray your Lordship to bestow two of the next good personages [clergy benefices] of yours shall fall on me; not that I mean to
convert them to my owne benefit, for, though I go rather for a good
clerke then a worldlywise woman, I aspire to no degree of Pope Jone,
but some good ends.[70]

In the fall of 1609 she undertook a semiroyal progress through the Mid-
lands, in part to recuperate, in part to visit relatives and old friends from
her younger days, in part to begin inquiries about a countryhouse, and
perhaps also to renew association with the Seymours.[71]

Late in 1609 rumors about Arbella started circulating again: that she
had become a Catholic (given color by her attachment to the Countess of
Shrewsbury and to the Catholic Lady Skinner, her attendant during the
smallpox confinement); that she was planning to cross the seas with and
perhaps marry a Scot named Douglas; that she had sent money to and was
planning to marry the unscrupulous pretender to the throne of Moldavia,
Stephano Janiculo, who had conned a royal pension from James in 1607
and claimed when in Venice to be engaged to Arbella.[72] Ben Jonson's misogynist comedy *Epicoene* (November or December 1609) alludes to that
last rumor in a line about Jack Daw drawing portraits "of the Prince of
Moldavia, and of his mistris, mistris Epicoene."[73] Though the referent of
"his" is ambiguous, Arbella's reputation for "masculine" wit, learning,
Latinity, and interests no doubt reinforced her identification with the
cross-dressed spark Epicoene, and also with the female collegians. Arbella
felt the insult keenly enough to demand the play's suppression.[74] She was
called before King and Council to answer the rumors, and the Venetian
ambassadors heard that her replies were very prudent and wise: "She
would neither affirm nor deny that she had thought of leaving the kingdom; she meerly said that, ill-treated as she was by all, it was only natural
that she should think of going."[75] She came out of this well enough, with
a New Year's gift of plate worth £200 and money to pay her debts, but
James disregarded her request to commute her household allowance to
cash—thus effectively preventing her from living elsewhere.[76] She later
claimed she had received permission at this time to choose as husband any
subject in the realm, but it was of course understood that James would
have to approve the choice.[77]

Behind all this was Arbella's effort to work out a marriage with William
Seymour, the younger brother of that Edward she had tried for in 1603.
Except for the age difference (William was twenty-two, she thirty-five)
they were not mismatched: he was studious, a B.A. from Magdalen College, and later a physician and Chancellor of Oxford. Arbella clearly
wanted to marry to attain greater independence and to force the issue of
her lands; and she may well have hoped also to find love and emotional

fulfillment at last. She had evidently had some contact with William Seymour and may have formed an attachment to him.[78] But her fixation on
the Seymours (the one family that already had been, and would surely
continue to be, forbidden to her) has to be explained as an effort to give
her progeny—and possibly herself—some chance at the throne. She seems
to have believed the King's anger would eventually pass, that she would
be forgiven and restored to favor, and that she could then live as she
wished and act as circumstances dictated. But this rosy scenario reckoned
without James's increasing paranoia about plots and treason and his un-
yielding determination to uphold his absolute authority as patriarch and
King.

By mid-February rumors of the affair had reached the Council; both
parties were questioned and gave careful, probably prearranged, answers.
William claimed to have initiated the proposal as a younger son seeking
to make an advantageous match: he insisted that they both thought Arbella had been given permission to marry where she would but that neither meant to proceed without James's approval.[79] Arbella, according to a
Venetian ambassador's report, maintained her own reading of her situation and rights as long as she could, but was at last forced by James to
make an abject confession and ordered to give up all thought of marriage
with Seymour:

> Lady Arbella spoke at length, denying her guilt and insisting on her
> unhappy plight. She complained again that her patrimony had been
> conceded by the King to others . . . She was required to beg the
> King's pardon, but replied that seeing herself deserted she had imag-
> ined that she could not be accused if she sought a husband of her
> own rank. All the same, if error she had made she humbly begged
> pardon. This did not satisfy the King; he demanded an absolute con-
> fession of wrong and an unconditional request for forgiveness. That
> she complied with, and received fresh promises of money and leave
> to marry provided the King approved.[80]

She then returned to court activities, and on June 5 danced in *Tethys Festival*. But on June 22, despite all the warnings, she and William Seymour
contracted a clandestine marriage, assisted and witnessed by friends and
faithful servants. They enjoyed a seventeen-day respite before the marriage
was discovered, but on July 8 William was taken to the Tower and the next
day Arbella was consigned to the care of Sir Thomas Perry at Lambeth.
Contemporary gossips made snide comments about the lady's "hot blood,
that could not live without a husband."[81]

Arbella wrote numerous letters over the next several months, some of
them in several drafts, testifying to the care she thought necessary for her

self-presentation.[82] Several to Shrewsbury manifest concern for her servants, especially the imprisoned Hugh Crompton, Ann Bradshaw, and Edward Reeves, and pose anxious queries as to how the King would deal
with her.[83] Others are petitions to possible intercessors and to the King
himself: constructing her stance very carefully, she seeks in them to deny
or mitigate her guilt (often by representing her action as at worst an error), to emphasize her contrition and present sufferings as sufficient punishment, and to project the conviction that the King must sooner or later
pardon and restore the erring couple. Grounding all this is Arbella's insistence that the marriage is a fait accompli which cannot now be undone:
she persistently refuses to take the only tack that might have saved her—
the renunciation of her marriage on some contrived basis. An early and
much-corrected petition to the Lords of the Privy Council sounds all these
notes:

> I humbly beseech your Lordships . . . to testify unto his Majesty my
> hearty sorrow for his Majestys displeasure. Restraint from liberty,
> comfort and counsell of frends, and all the effects of imprisonment
> are in them selfes very grievous, and inflicted as due punishment for
> greater offences then mine . . . If our punishment weare to do his
> Majesty service or honour I should endure Imprisonment and my
> affliction with patience and alacrity. But being inflicted as a sygne of
> his Majestys displeasure, it is very grievous for us, whose error we
> hope his Majesty in his owne gracious disposition, will rather pardon,
> then any further expiate with affliction.[84]

Her ostensibly humble but in fact almost defiant petition to the King at
about the same time combines self-justification with resentment for
wrongs, and even implies that in keeping the couple apart, James is acting
like David with Uriah:

> I doe most hartelie lament my hard fortune that I should offend your
> Majestie the least . . . And though your Majesties neglect of me, my
> good likeing of this gent. that is my Husband, and my fortune drewe
> me to A Contract before I acquainted your Majestie, I humblie be-
> seech your Majestie to consider how impossible itt was for me to
> ymagine itt could be offensive unto your Majestie, having fewe Dayes
> before given me your Royall consent to bestowe my selfe on anie
> Subject of your Majesties. Besides never havinge been either prohib-
> ited any or spoken to for anie in this Land by your Majesty these 7
> yeares that I have lived in your Majesties house I could not conceive
> that your Majesty regarded my Mariage att all . . . I presume . . . your
> Majestie would not doe evill that good might come thereof . . .
> though our Princes maie have lefte some [precedents] as little imita-

ble for so good and gratious A Kinge as your Majestie as Davids dealinge with Uriah. But I assure my selfe if itt please your Majestie in your owne wisdome to consider thoroughlie of my cause there will no solide reason appeare to Debarre me of Justice and your princelie favour, which I will endeavour to Deserve whilst I breathe.[85]

Arbella's denials here and elsewhere of the seriousness of her offense no doubt infuriated James and indicate some willful self-delusion. But this is also a rhetorical posture, a self-representation that she hopes to persuade mediators and the King himself to accept. She registers thereby her stubborn resistance to the construction others would place on her motives and actions, insisting, beneath the rhetoric of deference, on telling her own story of her own life.

She expected a good deal from, and had some early testimony of, the Queen's support: Arbella's letter of July 22 laments that she is "debarred the happinesse of attending your Majesty," proffers thanks for "your Majesties gratious favour and mediation to his Majesty for me," and acknowledges that favor as "my greatest comfort and hope in this affliction."[86] In October, through her kinswoman Jane Drummond, the First Lady of the Queen's Bedchamber, she approached the Queen again. The letter to Drummond enclosed a petition to the King and a formal letter to the Queen that expresses great confidence in Anne's powers as mediator: "If it please hir Majesty to intercede for me, I cannot but hope to be restored to hir Majesties service and his Majestyies favour."[87] The carefully penned letter to the Queen terms her the "mirrour of our sexe," and reiterates Arbella's confidence in her "helpe and mediation . . . in a cause of this nature, so full of pity and commiseration."[88] Her several petitions to James employ the familiar courtier's formula—his presence is her greatest comfort on earth and deprivation of it is her greatest affliction—but her theme is usually self-justification, as in this (undated) address:

> I most humblie beseech your Majestie . . . to consider in what a miserable state I had binne if I had taken any other course, then I did, for my owne conscience wittnessinge before God, that I was then the wife of him, that nowe I am, I could never have matched with any other man but to have lived all the Dayes of my lief, as an harlott, which your Majestie would have abhorred.[89]

She concludes by emphasizing her expectation of eventual release: "In all humilitie attendinge your Majestyies good pleasure for that libertie."

A few days later (apparently) Arbella wrote again to Lady Drummond, impatient to know why her petitions did not meet with success: "I cannot rest satisfied till I may know what disaster of mine hindreth his Majesties goodnesse towards me, having such a mediatrix to pleade so just and honest a cause as mine. Therefore I pray you with all earnestnesse let me know freely what hath binne done concerning me."[90] How active Queen Anne was in Arbella's cause is unclear, but she apparently made some effort—which proved unsuccessful: Drummond reported from the Queen that "his majestie . . . gave no other ansuer then that yee had etne of the forbiddne tre." Queen Anne softened the blow somewhat by sending a token of her continuing favor. In response to Arbella's direct inquiry, Drummond offered her own pessimistic view of the situation, alluding to the case of Catherine Grey: "The exsample, how sum of your qualitie, in the lyk caus hes bein uset, maeks me fer that yee shall not find so essie end to your truble, as yee expect, or I wish."[91] Arbella sent the Queen a pair of hand-wrought gloves, but refused Drummond's clear-sighted, realistic appraisal, insisting that her case was unique and insinuating (by the reiterated "till") that her punishment would be temporary:

> The token of the continuance of hir Majesties favour towards me . . . hath so cheered me as I hope I shall be the better able to passe over my sorrow *till* it please God to move his Majestyies heart to compassion of me . . . I humbly beseech her Majesty to accept [the gloves, and] . . . hope those Royall handes will vouchsafe to weare them which *till* I have the honour to kisse, I shall live in a great deal of sorrow . . . I say that I never heard nor read of any bodies case that might be truly and justly compared to this of mine . . . and so I am assured that both theyre Majesties (when it shall please them duely to examine it in theyre Princely wisdomes) will easily discerne.[92]

Some time later, perhaps shortly before Christmas, Arbella wrote again to the Queen, referring to "my longe experience of your Majesties gratious favour to me," and urging the forgiveness appropriate to the season, "when his Majesty forgiveth greater offence."[93] The enclosed petition to the King implores pardon, calling up the analogue of sincere penitent and forgiving God. But even as Arbella agrees not to contest the King's view of her fault, she insists on her innocence of motive:

> Whereinsoever your Majestie will say I have offended I will not conteste, but in all humilitie prostrate my selfe at your Majesties feete, only I doe most humbly on my knees beseech your Majestie to beleeve that that thought never yett entered into my heart, to doe any thinge that might justlie deserve any parte of your indignaton, but if the necessitie of my state and fortune, together with my weakenes, have caused me to do somewhat not pleasinge to your Majestie. Most gracious Sovereign lett all be covered with the Shadow of your gratious benignitie, and pardoned in that heroical mynd of yours which is never closed to those who carrie a most loyall hart to your Sovereigntie.[94]

But the rhetoric of submission cloaked continued resistance. With the aid of loyal friends Arbella managed some communication with William and even some conjugal visits to him in the Tower.[95] In September Arbella thought herself pregnant and her doctor, Thomas Moundford, President of the College of Physicians, was called in, but it proved a false pregnancy. James at length determined to ensure the separation of the couple and so eliminate the danger of progeny. On January 21, 1611, the Venetian ambassador Correr reported the King's decision to send Arbella to Durham so as "to secure himself against dissatisfaction settling around her."[96] The warrant assigning her to the charge of the Bishop of Durham was issued March 13: it described her as one who has "highly offended us" and whose seclusion is required for the "honour and order of the state."[97] Arbella resolved at all costs to avoid going to Durham, where she had no friends or partisans, where she could not press her case, where the court would soon forget her, and where she could not see Seymour. Her first move was a bold legal appeal to the Lord Chief Justice (Fleming) and the Lord Chief Justice of Common Pleas (Edward Coke) for a writ of habeas corpus, based on the cogent argument that she had done nothing "deserving so long restraint or separation from my lawfull husband" and should not be denied the common right of all English subjects to be brought to trial in an appropriate court for alleged wrongdoing:

> My Lords,—Whereas I have binne long restrained from my liberty
> which is as much to be regarded as my life and am appointed as I
> understand, to be removed farre from these Courts of Justice wheare
> I ought to be examined tried, and then condemned or cleared to re-
> mote parts whose Courts I hold unfitte for the triall of my offence,
> this is to beseech your Lordships to inquire by an Habeas Corpus or
> other usuall form of Law what is my fault . . . And if your Lordships
> may not or will not of your selves graunt me the ordinary reliefe of a
> distressed subject then I beseech you become humble intercessors to
> his Majesty that I may receive such benefitt of justice as both his
> Majesty by his oath those of his blood not excepted hath promised
> and the Lawes of this Realme afford to all others.[98]

Law failing, Arbella turned to medicine. She escalated her distress into what she represented as a life-threatening illness that prevented travel beyond the first stage of the journey. Abetted by her faithful physician Moundford, she succeeded in convincing her attendants, the Bishop of Durham and Sir James Croft, that she was indeed seriously ill, though the King suspected her of mere "obstinacie."[99] Her stream of petitions to King and Council at this juncture won several postponements of the journey, allowing her to remain at Highgate and Barnet.[100] In one of them she thanks James humbly for "these Halcyon daies it hath pleased your Majesty to graunt me," begs the return of his favor, and signs herself "Your Majesties most humble and faithfull almost ruined subject and servant."[101]

In late April, as one deadline for departure approached, she sent Croft and Moundford to the King with a much-corrected and very carefully drafted petition; Moundford reported to the Bishop of Durham that it was penned "by her in the best terms, as she can do right well," and that it was "even commended by [James] himself with the applause of prince and Councill."[102] What evidently pleased the King was the appearance of abject submission: Arbella promised her "moste humble and dutifull obedience"; she cast James as her saviour ("certenlie I had sodaynlie perished if your Majestie had not speedelie had compassion of me in grauntinge me this time of stay for my recoverie"); and most important, she put a terminus on her delay in going to Durham ("if itt may please your Majestie of your gratious goodnes to add 3 weekes more, Mr. Doctor Moundford hopes I maie recover so much strength, as may enhable me to travell."[103] But the signs of covert defiance are still there: she admits no guilt, she denies obstinacy, she offers no apology for disobeying James's direct order, and she does not renounce her marriage. Below the surface her defiance is overt: on one copy of this letter angry marginal notations contest the obsequious statements she has forced herself to make. Beside her promise of obedience is a note declaring that her promise "without the Jorney is inoughe if the K: desire but his honor salved." Beside the statement that she will be ready to go north after three weeks is the angry disclaimer "as thoughe I had made resistans [to] goe, and so the Jorney more perilous & painefull by my selfe whereuppon I must confess I bely my selfe extreemely in this." Alongside her reference to "the dutie I owe you as my Soveryne" is the counterclaim "I take it to bee more then I owe by my allegiance to bee separated from my husband duringe his pleasure." Beside her reference to the King's "grace & goo[d]nes" is a tart "What man of grace this is I cannot guess." And beside the claim that James has "my obedyant hart" she comments ironically on his effort to control the heart "as thoughe none but this would serve."[104]

Arbella used her month's extension (to June 5) to plan a daring escape with Seymour to the Continent, abetted and financed by the Countess of Shrewsbury in conjunction with Catholic factions abroad. On June 3 Arbella got permission to visit William one last time, and instead escaped in male disguise, with doublet, peruke, black hat, cloak, and rapier. With her faithful servants Crompton, Markham, and Ann Bradshaw, she traveled by horseback and riverboat to the fishing village of Leigh, waited for a time for William (who had escaped from the Tower as planned but was unaccountably delayed), and then took ship for France.[105] The escape failed because there were no contingency plans in the event the parties failed to meet up. Arbella insisted on delaying the landing at Calais to wait for William (who had been forced by bad weather to make for Ostend), and her party was overtaken and captured by one of the English vessels sent in pursuit.[106] Her delays, despite the seamen's advice and her own danger, suggest that her relationship with William, whatever its initial motivation, now meant much more to her than simply an escape from dependency or a dynastic opportunity. After Arbella's capture William was no longer considered dangerous, and he lived undisturbed on the Continent for several years.[107]

Arbella went to the Tower, as did her aunt Mary, and all the servants who accompanied or abetted the escape were imprisoned. Winwood had reports in June that Arbella "answered the Lords at her examination with good judgment and discretion,"[108] but her case was made hopeless by her association with the Countess of Shrewsbury and her Catholic schemes. Though Arbella was not brought to trial, the case against her as a present and future threat to the state and the King's felicity was summarized by Francis Bacon at the Countess of Shrewsbury's Star Chamber trial on June 30, 1612. In the first place, Arbella had married without the King's consent,

> which had been a neglect even to a mean parent. But being to our Sovereign, and she standing so near to his Majesty as she doth, and then choosing such a condition as it pleased her to choose . . . it was not unlike the case of Mr. Seymour's grandmother [Catherine Grey] . . . That this flight or escape into foreign parts might have been seed of trouble to this state, is a matter whereof the conceit of a vulgar person is not incapable.
>
> For although my lady should have put on a mind to continue her loyalty, as nature and duty did bind her; yet when she was in another sphere, she must have moved in the motion of that orb, and not of the planet itself. And God forbid the King's felicity should be so little, as he should not have envy and enviers enough in foreign parts.[109]

Arbella remained in the Tower until her death four years later. Often ill, she was at first hard-pressed to pay the keepers for food and necessaries since her jewelry and money had been confiscated. A few (probably early) petitions to Cecil and others intimate that her hard conditions have brought her close to death, and ask relief. And in a much-corrected letter to her kinsman Viscount Fenton, she obliquely threatens to let herself die if conditions do not improve:

> I have binne sicke even to the death from which it hath pleased God miraculously to deliver me for this present danger . . . Be assured that neither physitian nor other but whom I think good shall comme

about me whilst I live till I have his Majesties favour, without which I desire not to live, and if you remember of olde I dare dy so I be not guilty of my owne death, and oppresse others with my ruine too if theare be no other way. as God forbid . . . I can neither get clothes nor posset ale for example nor any thing but ordinary diett, and complement fitt for a sicke body in my case when I call for it, not so much as a glister, saving your reverence.[110]

After a few months she received part of her royal pension as well as rent from her lands, and was attended by the faithful Bradshaw and other servants. At some nadir of despair she began to draft a cloying and wholly abject petition to the King, renouncing her actions and even her own subjectivity—terming herself an "it" rather than an "I." But then the pronoun changes, and the letter is torn away after a few lines. It was probably never completed and sent; even in these straits Arbella is unwilling, it seems, to construct herself in such terms:

In all humility—the most wretched and unfortunate creature that ever lived prostrates it selfe at the feet of the most mercifull King that ever was desiring nothing but mercy and favour, not being more afflicted for any thing than for the losse of that which hath binne this long time the onely comfort it had in the world, and which if it weare to do againe, I would not adventure the losse of for any other worldly comfort. mercy it is I desire, and that for Gods sake. Let either Freake [her embroiderer] or—[111]

For as long as she possibly could, she continued to hope for release. On the occasion of Princess Elizabeth's wedding, she bought four new gowns—one of them said to have cost £1,500—on the chance that this occasion might move the King to mercy; there is no record that the Princess interceded for Arbella, but if she did she was unsuccessful.[112] In November 1613 and in midsummer of 1614 there are oblique references to plots for her escape, evidently engineered by her faithful servants Crompton and Reeves, who were briefly imprisoned again. At about this time rumors circulated that Arbella was "crackt in her brain" and "far out of frame," inviting some observers then and later to conclude that she was insane in her last months.[113] She was no doubt emotionally distraught (as before at Hardwick), but it seems unlikely that her friends and servants would have risked themselves to rescue a madwoman. When the rescue plots failed and she was placed under increased restraints, she took the course she had earlier hinted to Fenton: she refused all medical examinations and treatments and virtually starved herself. On September 25, 1615, Arbella Stuart died at the age of forty. The recently revealed murder of Overbury in the Tower made a postmortem necessary. The six physicians headed by Moundford attributed her death to a "chronic and long sickness" and a "confirmed unhealthfulness of liver," exacerbated by her "extreme leanness" and "refusal of remedies."[114]

At the end, Arbella Stuart defied James and the conditions of her life by managing the only escape still within her power. Her resistance did not bring the crown within her grasp, or even permit her to realize her simpler dreams of marriage, liberty, and choice of life. Like most other Jacobean women and men, she found that the external circumstances of her life were firmly controlled by arbitrary royal and patriarchal power. But her self-presentation in her many letters registers inner resistance to and open defiance of that power. Her empowerment came from a sense of self-worth derived from lineage, education for rule, and classical learning; it manifested itself in an irrepressible wit, a keen sense of irony, and the skillful exercise of the rhetoric of disguise. Arbella Stuart's notorious rebellion offered the example of yet another royal lady challenging James's patriarchal and absolutist claims.

II

RE-WRITING PATRIARCHY

Lucy, Countess of Bedford, as a masquer, attributed to John De Critz.

4 ❧

Exercising Power: The Countess
of Bedford as Courtier,
Patron, and Coterie Poet

Lucy Harington Russell (1581–1627), wife of Edward, third Earl of Bedford, was the most important and most powerful patroness of the Jacobean court, except for Queen Anne herself.[1] Other ladies wielding some power at court, such as the (Howard) Countesses of Suffolk and Northampton, the Countess of Somerset, and the Duchess and Countess of Buckingham, did so chiefly by reason of a husband's or male kinsman's place. But the Countess of Bedford was a special case: as favorite lady-in-waiting to the Queen from her accession in 1603 to her death in 1619, she influenced the Queen's patronage directly and had the ear of the King's ministers and favorites. She seems to have constructed her role with some self-consciousness, as the counterpart of the changing role evolving for the Jacobean male courtier; absent the sexual relationship, she offers some parallel on the Queen's side to the King's favorites, Somerset and Buckingham. In so doing, she claimed a place in the courtiers' power games, and became a force to be reckoned with in the disposition of offices, the arrangement of marriages, and the shaping of Jacobean culture.[2] She also claimed the role of coterie poet, seeking and gaining a reputation for wit and talent much as a male courtier might—though for court ladies that was hardly a route to career advancement. But she evidently found the activity empowering and pleasant; and it seems to have enhanced her prestige as a powerful cultural presence.

As the dominant figure in Queen Anne's circle of female courtiers, she would appear to be a primary referent for her cousin Sir John Harington's snide description of the court ladies as "statly Heroyns [of] noble mynde":

> These entertayne great princes; these have lerned
> The tongues, toyes, tricks, of Room, of Spain, of Fraunce;

> These can Currentos and Lavoltas dance,
> And though they foot yt false tis nere discerned,
> The vertues of these dames are so transcendent,
>   Themselvs ar learnd, and their Heroyk sperit
>   Can make disgrace an honor, sinn a merit.
> All penns, all praysers ar on them dependent.[3]

The numerous accomplishments, the confident self-display in all company, and the potency of the patron's role fit Lucy Bedford exactly. But the allusions to sexual impropriety do not; they pertain rather to the likes of Frances Howard, Cecilia Bulstrode, Penelope Rich, and the Countess of Suffolk.

The Countess of Bedford was a consummate insider, but one whose situation and role offered some challenge to the norms of patriarchy and male patronage networks. For one thing, she gained eminence despite rather than because of her husband. The Earl was given to extravagant entertainment and display in youth, but in 1601 he was disgraced, heavily fined, and exiled from court for his part in Essex's rebellion. Even after the exile was lifted, his apparent preference for country life, his heavy debts, and his partial paralysis and stammer, occasioned by a fall from a horse in 1612, kept him from court.[4] Accordingly, Lucy Bedford's prominent role as Jacobean courtier and patron was due almost entirely to her own (Harington) family connections, and to her very considerable talents, brilliance, and style. In some arenas her challenge to Jacobean patriarchy was more overt: she associated herself closely with Queen Anne's subversive masques and Princess Elizabeth's oppositional politics. Also, she recast the role of literary patron, extending assistance more through court influence and coterie association than financial largess, and participating with her clients in coterie literary exchange.

Her largely self-designed role as courtier and patron was in part created, sustained, and revealed through literary images. They emerge in contemporary comments about her life at court, portraits painted of her, masques in which she danced, and numerous literary tributes to or about her. These sources afford some measure of her effect on the cultural scene—as subject and audience for literary works, as patron, as masquer, as coterie poet. Her letters and single extant poem provide more direct access to her own self-fashioning as female courtier and author, and offer as well a unique perspective on Jacobean society from that unusual perspective.[5]

Constructing Cultural Roles

The known facts of the Countess's life can be briefly summarized. Born at Coombe Abbey in 1581 to John Harington of Exton and Anne Kelway, she grew up in a religious and educated family, with a younger brother, John, and sister, Frances. She was kinswoman to Sir Philip Sidney and the Countess of Pembroke (through her grandmother, Lucy Sidney) and to John Harington of Kelston, poet and translator of Ariosto. In 1594, at age thirteen, she was married to Edward Russell, third Earl of Bedford (then twenty-one), bringing him a handsome marriage portion of £3,000 and the estate of Minster Lovell. A lavish life-style at court, extravagant entertainments, the expenses of the Garter ceremonies for the Earl, and an encumbered estate kept Lord and Lady Bedford continually in debt, even before the Earl's disastrous association with Essex's rebellion brought him a fine of £20,000 (later reduced by half).[6]

After the Essex debacle the Countess undertook to make her own way at court. In a brilliant and lucky coup, immediately upon the death of Queen Elizabeth Lucy and her mother hastened to Edinburgh to pay their respects to Queen Anne. Lucy was evidently an instant success, as her immediate appointment to the Queen's Bedchamber testifies; Lord and Lady Harington were given charge of Princess Elizabeth's education. Thereafter, the Countess of Bedford was the recognized favorite among the Queen's ladies; she also maintained a close friendship with Princess Elizabeth both before and after her marriage to the Elector Palatine in 1613. Lord and Lady Harington accompanied the Electress to Germany, and Lady Harington returned as her chief attendant in 1617; John Harington, Lucy's brother, became a close friend of the heir apparent, Prince Henry.[7] The death of Lady Bedford's father in 1613 and of her brother the following year made her heir to two thirds of the Harington estate. But this new status compounded her financial problems since the estate was encumbered by almost £40,000 debt.[8]

From 1608 to 1617 the Countess resided chiefly at Twickenham when she was not at court, making that estate a salon of sorts for female and male friends, most of whom were also courtiers. Her circle of female friends included her kinswomen Bridget, Lady Markham, and Cecilia Bulstrode, Ladies of the Queen's Bedchamber, and Jane Meutys (later Lady Cornwallis), who was the Countess's closest female friend and correspondent in later life. Male members of her entourage included Sir Henry Goodyere, Gentleman of the Privy Chamber to James and the Earl of Bedford's servant who acted for Lucy in acquiring Twickenham; and also Sir Thomas Roe, diplomatic emissary to the Turks, Cecilia Bulstrode's lover, and later the passionate supporter and friend of Elizabeth, the Winter Queen. She counted as her good friends and primary channels of influence at James's court the Earl of Pembroke, who was the King's Lord Chamberlain after 1615, and James, Marquis of Hamilton, who was Steward of the King's Household. Among the sometime residents at Twickenham were one "Mistress Goodyer" (a daughter or niece of Sir Henry) as a young waiting woman; Carew Gorges, son of the author and translator Sir Arthur Gorges; and Dr. John Burges, the Calvinist minister-physician who attended her during a serious illness in 1612–13.[9] Twickenham was host as well to writers and artists, though not on the scale of the Countess of Pembroke's Wilton, and as occasional guests rather than resident dependents. Donne visited her there on several occasions while he lived at Mitchem, and so probably did other writers and musicians among her clients—Jonson, Samuel Daniel, John Dowland, John Davies of Hereford, George Chapman.[10]

In 1612 a stroke left Lady Bedford speechless for a time and she was thought close to death. According to Chamberlain, this resulted in a conversion of sorts, prompted by Burges, and a changed way of life—at least temporarily: "Mary, she is somwhat reformed in her attire and forbeares painting. which, they say, makes her looke somewhat straungely among so many visards, which together with theyre fisled, powdred haire, makes them looke all alike.[11] After 1617 she resided chiefly at Moor Park (granted by the King to the Earl and Countess of Bedford in that year); there she designed and laid out the magnificent landscape gardens later praised by Sir William Temple as "the most beautiful and perfect, and altogether the sweetest place, which he had ever seen in England or in foreign countries."[12] In 1619 her patron Queen Anne died, and so did her mother. In that year also smallpox ravaged what remained of her beauty: Edward Howard reported that "the small pocks hath seased on the Lady of Bedford, and so seasoned her all over, that they say she is more full and fowle then could be expected in so thin and barre a body."[13] But she remained an active courtier and patron until the accession of Charles in 1625. The Earl of Bedford died at Moor Park on May 3, 1627, and was buried at Chenies; the Countess died later the same month, on May 27, and was buried with her own family at Exton. She had no living children: a son born in 1602 died a month later; a daughter born in 1610 lived only two hours; and there was no issue from other rumored pregnancies.[14]

The Countess won respect in her public role as courtier for her strength of mind, loyalty to family and friends, and occasional audacity. The young Lady Anne Clifford records in her diary for 1603 that "my lady of Bedford . . . was then so great a woman with the queen, as that everybody much respected her"; nearly a decade later Chamberlain testified that she retained that status: "She is now the Quenes only favorite."[15] In 1605 Robert Cecil paid grudging tribute to the Countess's tenacity of purpose and family loyalty (if not diplomatic delicacy) in a letter to Lord Harington calling a halt to her efforts to arrange a marriage between his daughter and her brother:

> I must be thus far bowld with my Lady the Countesse, as to say that
> if she hathe not more resembled her sex in loving her owne will than

she dothe in those other noble and discrett parts of her mynd (wherein she hath so great a portion beyond most of those that I have knowne) she myght have moved you to suspend the sending upp of any particularities at this tyme . . . I have not hidd it from herselfe, that I have found her so absolutely fixed uppon a resolution to allow of no reason which she finds not justly concurrent with your satisfaction.[16]

She did not succeed with that marriage, but on two later occasions she arranged weddings against strong parental opposition: that of Lord Hay and Lady Lucy Percy, youngest daughter of the Earl of Northumberland, in 1617; and that of Sir John Smith and Lady Isabella Rich in 1619, supplying her own bed for the consummation of the latter clandestine union.[17] She was constantly solicited about appointments at court, high and low: in 1618 one of Sir Dudley Carleton's well-wishers advised him to press his request for a secretaryship through "mylady of Bedford (who is above measure powerfull with both the Marquesses and mylord Chamberlaine)."[18]

An important aspect of the Countess's courtiership and patronage was her part in the Queen's oppositional masques, and in the development of court masque as a genre. Not only did she dance the major role (after the Queen's) in several masques and entertainments, but she also arranged and perhaps helped produce some of them. Samuel Daniel acknowledged that she obtained for him the commission from the Queen for the Christmas masque of 1604, in which the Countess also served as *rector chori,* or leader of the masquers.[19] A letter from Donne to Goodyere in November 1608 associates her with the Queen in planning the Christmas masque of that year (*The Masque of Beautie*).[20] John Chamberlain identified her to Carleton as "Lady and Mistress of the Feast" given by Lord Hay in honor of the French ambassador Baron de La Tour on February 22, 1617; therefore she probably arranged the entertainment of that evening, the Jonson masque *Lovers Made Men,* for which she served as *rector chori.*[21] She continued arranging entertainments for Queen Anne, including one that spring by the schoolgirls at Deptford.[22] In that office she may have had some responsibility for the subversive elements introduced into these masques by the Queen's "authorial" presence. The makers of masques of course had the royal family principally in view as the embodiment of their idealized images, and we do not know whether any masque roles were specifically imagined or created for the Countess. But her closeness to the Queen makes it likely that she often chose the roles she would portray; and she certainly projected through them an image of splendor, beauty, fantasy, and often of special privilege and power.

In Daniel's *Vision of Twelve Goddesses* (January 8, 1604) the Countess of Bedford portrayed Vesta—not at first glance the most honorific role, and one which placed her in the second rather than the first triad of goddesses in the procession. But in Daniel's account of the allegory Vesta represented Religion, garbed "in a white Mantle imbrodred with gold-flame," with "a burning Lampe in one hand, and a Booke in the other." Lady Bedford's role as Vesta-Religion associated her closely with the Queen (who portrayed Pallas), and her gift was specified as the primary support of the realm:

> Whose maine support, holy Religion frame:
> And *1 Wisdome, 2 Courage, 3 Temperance,* and *4 Right,*
> Make seeme the Pillars that sustaine the same.[23]

She took the preeminent role among the Queen's ladies in the Jonson–Inigo Jones *Masque of Blacknesse* (1605) and in its sequel, *The Masque of Beautie* (1608). In his highly critical report on *Blackness,* Carleton notes the Countess's place of honor: "At the further end was a great Shell in the form of a Skallop, wherein were four Seats; on the lowest sat the Queen with my Lady *Bedford;* on the rest were placed the [other] Ladies."[24] Jonson's notes indicate that the Queen represented Euphoris (Abundance), while Bedford was Aglaia (Splendor)—two of the three Graces. Together they carried a golden tree laden with fruit as a symbol of their conjoined qualities. In *Beautie* the Queen was Harmonia and the Countess of Bedford again, almost certainly, Splendor, the only personage to bear the same name as before and again presented first—"In a robe of *flame* colour, naked brested; her bright hayre loose flowing."[25]

The Jonson–Inigo Jones wedding masque, *Hymenaei,* celebrating the ill-starred nuptials of the Earl of Essex and Frances Howard shows Reason moderating the four affections and four humors, after which eight ladies representing the powers of Juno Pronuba come down to confirm the union. The Queen did not take part, but Lucy Bedford and the Countess of Rutland portrayed the two most important powers.[26] Lucy chose to be painted in the gorgeous costume designed for these lady masquers (see the illustration at the beginning of this chapter), described by Jonson in great detail:

> The Ladies *attyre* was wholly new, for the invention, and full of glorie; as having in it the most true impression of a *celestiall* figure: the upper part of *white* cloth of silver, wrought with JUNOES *birds* and *fruits;* a loose undergarment, full gather'd, of *carnation,* strip't with *silver,* and parted with a golden *Zone:* beneath that, another flowing garment, of *watchet* cloth of silver, lac'd with gold; through all which, though they were round, and swelling, there yet appeared some touch of their delicate *lineaments* . . . their haire . . . bound under the circle of a rare and rich *Coronet,* adorn'd with all varietie and choise of

jewels; from the top of which, flow'd a transparent *veile,* downe to the ground . . . Their shooes were *Azure,* and gold, set with Rubies and Diamonds; so were all their garments.[27]

In the spectacular Jonson–Inigo Jones *Masque of Queenes* (February 2, 1609) Lady Bedford's role as Penthesilea, Queen of the Amazons, is not likely to be accidental, despite Jonson's claim that the parts were disposed "rather by *chance,* then *Election.*" As the most ancient (and most subversive) Queen, the martial Penthesilea led the procession, figuring forth power linked to virtue, martial valor, and beauty, as Jonson indicates:

The most upward in time was Penthesilea. She was Queen of the Amazons . . . She lived and was present at the war of Troy, on their part against the Greeks, where, as Justin gives her testimony, "among the bravest men great proofs of her valour were conspicuous." She is nowhere mentioned but with the preface of honour and virtue, and is always advanced in the head of the worthiest women. Diodorus Siculus makes her the daughter of Mars. She was honoured in her death to have it the act of Achilles. Of which Propertius sings this triumph to her beauty: "to her whose bright beauty conquered the conquering hero, when the golden helmet left her brow bare."[28]

Inigo Jones's costume designs depict her with elaborately plumed classical helmet, sword, a virtually transparent corselet, and skirts of "deep pink color, deep morray [mulberry], skie color."[29]

During the next decade the Countess is mentioned only occasionally in relation to masques and entertainments.[30] Jonson identified her as a (speaking?) character—"Mogibell overbery"—in an undated, unpublished, and now lost pastoral drama, *The May Lord,* which may or may not have been produced.[31] It is possible that she eschewed the masquer's image for a time as a result of her illness of 1612, but in any case the Queen and her ladies were much less prominent as masquers after 1610, when Prince Henry and later Buckingham took over that function.[32]

The many addresses to Lady Bedford from would-be clients cannot be taken as a record of her actual patronage. But their number and diversity provide some indication of her perceived power as patron, and the works they offer assume her interest in a wide range of subjects. The dedicatory epistles and tributes give some indication of the terms thought appropriate for her praise, and of the qualities she herself liked to have emphasized. Many praised her as learned lady and poet, though she has less claim to the first distinction than Arbella Stuart, and less to the second than Mary Sidney, Elizabeth Cary, Aemilia Lanyer, or Lady Mary Wroth. Still, while all noble ladies of the period are praised for virtue, beauty, and generosity, the Countess is one of the three or four regularly celebrated as fit audience and worthy critic for works of literature and serious learning, and as a talented poet.

Some tributes commend her knowledge of languages and literature. Holyband, possibly her tutor for a time, dedicated a language book to the two-year-old Lucy, urging her to learn languages in obedience to her parents' wishes.[33] John Florio, sometime member of the Harington household, dedicated his *World of Words* (1598) to the Countess, praising her great proficiency in reading, writing, and speaking Italian, French, and Spanish, but especially her interest in the texts written in those languages.[34] Dedicating his translation of Montaigne's *Essays* (1603) to the Countess and her mother, among others, Florio (with evident exaggeration) claims that the young Lucy read, encouraged, and offered helpful suggestions for that work in progress.[35] She probably did not know Latin, and certainly not Greek, but was assumed to have interests in classical poetry and history in translation. George Chapman addressed her as "faire Patronesse, and Muse to Learning" in one of the dedicatory sonnets to his *Homer;* and Arthur Gorges's son presented his father's translation of Lucan's *Pharsalia* to her as "an honourable lover and Patronesse of learning and the Muses."[36] Speaking to her musical interests, Lucy's sometime client John Dowland commends her as "the worthiest Patronesse, of Musick," one who has exceptional musical knowledge and talents, and who embodies harmony itself by her conjunction of many virtues.[37] In 1614 Arthur Saul alluded to another of her courtly accomplishments in dedicating to her his treatise on chess.[38]

Several writers offered religious verse to her, praising the concurrence in her of learning and virtue, and often associating her talents and interests with those of her kinswoman the Countess of Pembroke. Around 1600 John Harington of Kelston sent some of his verse meditations to her along with three of the Countess of Pembroke's Psalms, declaring that "none coms more neere hir, then your self in those, now rare, and admirable guifts of the mynde, that clothe Nobilitie with vertue."[39] In the dedication to his *Divine Meditations,* John Davies of Hereford linked Lucy Bedford with the Countess of Pembroke and Elizabeth, Lady Cary, as the three Graces—"at once Darlings as Patronesses, of the Muses" and "Glories of Women"—commending Lucy particularly for "Wit and Sp'rit, in Beauties Livery."[40] The female poet Lanyer claims no personal acquaintance with the Countess but supposes that her virtue, knowledge, religious devotion, and "cleare Judgement" will commend Lanyer's divine poem to her:

> Me thinkes I see faire Virtue readie stand,
> T'unlocke the closet of your lovely breast,
> Holding the key of Knowledge in her hand,
> Key of that Cabbine where your selfe doth rest,

To let him in, by whom her youth was blest:
> The true-love of your soule, your hearts delight,
> Fairer than all the world in your cleare sight.[41]

Several other dedications construct the Countess as a religious woman of Calvinist leanings, associated through her family and her own proclivities with reformist elements in England and with the cause of international Protestantism abroad. These dedications do not offer personal praise, but implicitly commend her virtue and judgment by assuming that she will value these treatises and patronize their authors. In 1595 William Perkins offered her a meditation on death, reminding her of Solomon's adjuration to "remember thy Creator in the days of thy youth." In 1608 Thomas Draxe dedicated his treatise on predestination and the final conversion of the Jews to her.[42] After her illness and reported conversion in 1612 such offerings increased. Clement Cotton offered her his treatise on martyrs (1615) and his translation of Calvin's lectures on Jeremiah (1620).[43] In 1617 her chaplain, Nicholas Byfield, dedicated a set of sermons to her, many of which she had already heard "with great attention."[44] In 1621 John Reading proposed to her a meditation on the uses of sickness and health—appropriate in light of her recent bout with smallpox.[45] A striking portrait of the Countess at age thirty-eight (1620) attributed to Cornelius Jansen captures this sober religious persona: in a black dress adorned with black jewelry, against a somber black background, she holds an attitude of pensive meditation with her head reclining on her hand. But some hint of the earlier showy display remains in the gold coronet, the warm ash-blonde hair, the large and elegant lace ruff, cuffs, and handkerchief.[46]

As a major patroness at the center of Jacobean society, the Countess of Bedford had an important, if indirect, influence on literature and culture. How important that influence was, and how deliberate, are questions that can be answered only speculatively. She had some shaping influence upon the early development of the court masque through her own activities and her patronage of Daniel and Jonson. But she did not directly promote other literary kinds and experiments, as the Countess of Pembroke promoted quantitative verse, classicizing verse drama, prose romance, and religious lyric. The poetry which she inspired and invited was almost exclusively poetry of compliment, centered upon herself, her family, and her household. But her chief literary clients—Jonson, Donne, Daniel, Drayton—are the major poets of the age, so their poems for her are often complex and subtle. Those poems frequently embody the strains of the patron-client relationship—strains especially in evidence when the patron is a highborn and powerful woman. But there is no reason to suppose that Lucy Bedford was ignorant of this subtext in her clients' verse, or to agree with John Carey that her "stomach for flattery" makes it difficult "to take a very generous view of her intelligence."[47] To the contrary, the evolution of her patronage from Drayton to Donne affords some indication of her taste in poetry and in praise, as does her participation in poetic exchanges with Wotton and Donne. She seems to have provided a fit audience for such very different poets as Daniel, Jonson, and Donne, encouraging new poetic styles in satire as well as eulogy.

She did not long retain her first important poet client, Michael Drayton, who defined in simple, feudal terms his role as her courtly love servant and the recipient of her largess: without apparent basis he announced himself "bequeathed" to her at the death of his first patron, Sir Henry Goodyere of Polesworth. In 1594 he dedicated his legend of *Matilda* to the thirteen-year-old Lucy Harington, identifying her with his heroine, "adorned with the like excellent gifts, both of bodie and minde." He dedicated his epyllion *Endimion and Phoebe* (1595) to the newly married Countess of Bedford, alluding to the "sweet golden showers" she has rained upon him and imploring her to grace his Muse, "whose faith, whose zeale, whose life, whose all is thine."[48] He continued this obsequious posture as her feudal servant and creature in 1596 with the inscription of his collected legends to her: "If any thought of worth live in mee, that onely hath been nourished by your mild favours and former graces to my unworthy selfe, and the admiration of your more then excellent parts shyning to the world."[49] In his historical epic *Mortimeriados* (1596) he apostrophizes her as "rarest of Ladies, all, of all I have, / Anchor of my poore Tempest-beaten state / . . . My hopes true Goddesse, guider of my fate," and interrupts his epic twice to invoke her as his Muse.[50]

But the Countess seems to have tired of, and failed to reward, such heavy-handed and passé rhetoric. In 1597 Drayton dedicated the first pair of his *England's Heroicall Epistles* to her, but thereafter wrote no new dedications or praises to her and removed all references to her when he revised *Mortimeriados* as *The Barons Warres* (1603).[51] In 1606 he included in his revised version of *Idea the Shepheard's Garland* a bitter curse on the Countess as the faithless Selena, who abandoned the "faithfull Rowland" she once rewarded, to favor the "deceitefull *Cerberon*" (probably Ben Jonson):

> Let age sit soone and ugly on her brow,
> no sheepheards praises living let her have
> to her last end noe creature pay one vow
> no flower be strew'd on her forgotten grave.
>   And to the last of all devouring tyme
>   nere be her name remembred more in rime.[52]

The Countess's withdrawal of patronage from Drayton probably had something to do with her financial difficulties, and much to do with Drayton's own penchant for raising hackles in high places.[53] But the fact that she apparently made no effort to further his career in the Jacobean court also suggests that his Spenserian poetry and his conventional stance as her feudal servant had ceased to interest her.

By contrast, she played a significant role in advancing Samuel Daniel's career with the new court, although he was more closely associated with other patrons.[54] She would have been involved in planning the visit King James made to her family's house in Rutlandshire in April 1603 en route to his coronation: the entertainment was a reading of Daniel's *Panegyrike Congratulatory,* a grave and thoughtful praise of James for the virtues he ought to acquire, consonant with Daniel's established character as a moralist-historian in his *Civile Warres.*[55] Some months later she recommended him to the Queen for the Christmas masque of 1604, *The Vision of the 12. Goddesses.* In dedicating the printed text to the Countess, Daniel defended it against its many critics, so as to "cleere the reckoning of any imputation that might be layd upon your judgement, for preferring such a one, to her *Maiesty* in this imployment."[56] These opportunities opened the door to court appointments—in 1604 as Licenser to the Children of the Queen's Revels, in 1607 as Groom of the Queen's Bedchamber—and also to commissions to write other masques and dramas for the queen.

The Countess's interest in Daniel may have been prompted by the Florio connection (Florio was Daniel's brother-in-law). But she may also have been attracted to Daniel's high moral seriousness, his barely veiled critique of James, and the novelty of his weighty plain style as a vehicle for praise, displayed in the very fine verse letter to her published with the *Panegyrike.* In a serious tone intimating true regard, he takes Lucy as an exemplum through whom important moral lessons may be illustrated. Especially pleasing, I suspect, was Daniel's recognition of her difficult situation as female courtier, and his judicious praise of her for qualities she apparently liked to be praised for—intelligence and learning. Through these qualities, he indicates, she has largely escaped the restrictions of the female role:

> And this faire course of knowledge whereunto
> 　Your studies, learned Lady, are addrest,
> 　Is th'onely certaine way that you can goe
> Unto true glory, to true happines:
> · · · · ·
> 　And no key had you else that was so fit
> T'unlocke that prison of your Sex, as this,
> 　To let you out of weaknesse, and admit
> 　Your powers into the freedome of that blisse
> That sets you there where you may oversee
> 　This rowling world, and view it as it is,
> · · · · ·

How oft are we forc't on a cloudie hart,
   To set a shining face, and make it cleere.
   Seeming content to put our selves apart,
To beare a part of others weaknesses:
   As if we onely were compos'd by Arte,
   Not Nature, and did all our deedes addresse
T'opinion, not t'a conscience what is right:
. . . . .
And though Bookes, Madame, cannot make this minde
   Which we must bring apt to be set aright,
   Yet they do rectifie it in that kinde,
And touch it so, as that it turnes that way
   Where judgement lies:
. . . . .
   And therefore in a course that best became
   The cleerenesse of your heart, and best commends
Your worthy powres, you runne the rightest way
   That is on Earth, that can true glory give,
   By which when all consumes, your fame shal live.[57]

Ben Jonson also addressed several poems to the Countess, as a major patron herself and as part of the Sidney-Pembroke familial and political alliance whose patronage he courted assiduously over many years.[58] As early as 1599 Jonson included a passage in his "Epistle" for Sir Philip Sidney's daughter the Countess of Rutland, acknowledging Lucy Bedford's "timely favors" and his competition for them with another poet (probably Drayton). This odd insertion almost seems to invite competition between the two ladies as to which will prove the better patron to him. Jonson here transforms the poet-servant convention, substituting for Drayton's feudal obsequiousness his own characteristic stance of respectful compliment grounded upon proper self-regard:

You, and that other starre, that purest light,
   Of all LUCINA's traine; LUCY the bright,
Then which, a nobler heaven it selfe knowes not.
   Who, though shee have a better verser got,
   (Or *Poet,* in the court account) then I,
   And who doth me (though I not him) envy,
Yet, for the timely favours shee hath done,
   To my lesse sanguine *Muse,* wherein she'hath wonne
My gratefull soule, the subject of her powers,
   I have already us'd some happy houres,
To her remembrance; which when time shall bring

> To curious light, the notes, I then shall sing,
> Will prove old ORPHEUS act no tale to be:
> For I shall move stocks, stones, no lesse then he.[59]

The Countess evidently approved; her "favors" at Elizabeth's court continued into the next reign as she helped produce Jonson's masques and probably helped to promote him as principal maker of masques at James's
court. In 1605 he felt able to call upon her good offices when he was jailed
with George Chapman in 1605 for satirizing the King's Scots followers in
Eastward Ho.[60] And several exchanges during the Twickenham years
(1608–1617) suggest a more familiar relationship.[61]

Jonson's poetic addresses to Lucy Bedford often begin with interpretations of her name as a symbol of her wit and intelligence, and often give
special praise to her literary judgment. An ode addressed to her in manuscript apostrophizes her beauty and "illustrate brightness" but especially
celebrates "Her wit as quicke, and sprightfull / As fire; and more delightfull," and her "Judgement (adornd with Learning)."[62] He assumes her
delight in witty epigram: the deft "Epigram 84" gratefully acknowledges
her offer of a deer while reminding her, in a wry turn, that an offer is not
yet a gift:

> MADAME, I told you late how I repented,
>   I ask'd a lord a buck, and he denyed me;
> And, ere I could aske you, I was prevented:
>   For your most noble offer had supply'd me.
> Straight went I home; and there most like a *Poet,*
>   I fancied to my selfe, what wine, what wit
> I would have spent: how every *Muse* should know it,
>   And PHOEBUS-selfe should be at eating it.
> O *Madame,* if your grant did thus transferre mee,
>   Make it your gift. See whither that will beare mee.[63]

"Epigram 94," sent with a copy of Donne's satires, pays high tribute to
her literary taste and moral judgment in requesting and liking these
poems: his theme is "Rare poems aske rare friends."[64] The poem begins
and concludes with an apostrophe to her—"Lucy, you brightnesse of our
spheare, who are / Life of the *Muses* day, their morning-starre"—and takes
as proof of her place among the "best" the fact that she can read and enjoy
satire (which all sinners necessarily hate since they are its subject). But
more than that, as George Rowe points out,[65] her "daring" interest in
satire is a dangerous activity, since it exposes the corruptions of the court
she is part of—a court distinctly nervous about satire (witness *Eastward
Ho*):

> They, then, that living where the matter is bred
> > Dare for these poemes, yet, both aske, and read,
> And like them too; must needfully, though few,
> > Be of the best: and mongst those, best are you.
> > > (ll. 11–14)

It is hard to know how far to credit such tributes to the Countess's "advanced" literary taste and judgment, but she seems to have valued that reputation. And Jonson could certainly have praised her in other terms, had he supposed she desired that.

In one of his finest epigrams, Jonson assays Lady Bedford's mind and character in a tone of utmost judiciousness, thereby creating a literary image at once wonderful and credible. "Epigram 76" describes Jonson's ideal poetic mistress made flesh in Lucy Bedford, emphasizing her learning, her strong mind, and her most unusual freedom to control her own destiny. The terms are at once laudatory and remarkably appropriate to the special circumstances of her life:

> This morning, timely rapt with holy fire,
> > I thought to forme unto my zealous *Muse,*
> What kinde of creature I could most desire,
> > To honor, serve, and love; as *Poets* use.
> I meant to make her faire, and free, and wise,
> > Of greatest bloud, and yet more good then great;
> I meant the day-starre should not brighter rise,
> > Nor lend like influence from his lucent seat.
> I meant shee should be curteous, facile, sweet,
> > Hating that solemne vice of greatnesse, pride,
> I meant each softest vertue there should meet,
> > Fit in that softer bosome to reside.
> Onely a learned, and a manly soule
> > I purpos'd her; that should, with even powers,
> The rock, the spindle, and the sheeres controule
> > Of destinie, and spin her owne free houres.
> Such when I meant to faine, and wish'd to see,
> > My *Muse* bad, *Bedford* write, and that was shee.[66]

Something happened in 1609–10 that launched Jonson on a vein of antifeminist writing which put at some risk his relationship to the Countess. He was perhaps picking up on some heightened resentment of the female courtiers by the King and his followers, or perhaps responding to the special strains of courtiership and subservience (even on his redefined terms) to powerful court women. Or he may have reacted to an actual slight by exhibiting what David Riggs describes as his periodic need to defy social constraints and authority.[67] Sometime in 1609 he wrote a vitriolic epigram on Lucy Bedford's kinswoman and friend and the Queen's lady-in-waiting Cecilia Bulstrode ("The Court Pucell"). Apparently responding to some censure from her, Jonson harshly satirizes both her sexual adventures and her participation with male wits of the Twickenham circle in literary games of "News" and bawdy poetry:

> Do's the Court-Pucell then so censure me,
>   And thinkes I dare not her? let the world see.
> What though her Chamber be the very pit
>   Where fight the prime cocks of the Game, for wit?
> . . . . .
> What though with Tribade lust she force a Muse,
>   And in an Epicoene fury can write newes
> Equall with that, which for the best newes goes,
>   As aërie light, and as like wit as those?
> What though she talke, and cannot once with them
>   Make State, Religion, Bawdrie, all a theame?
> And as lip-thirstie, in each words expense,
>   Doth labour with the Phrase more then the sense?[68]

In his *Conversations with Drummond* Jonson claimed that the epigram was "stollen out of his pocket by a Gentleman who drank him drousie & given Mistress Boulstraid, which brought him great displeasur"[69]—chiefly, it would seem, from the Countess of Bedford. After Bulstrode died suddenly and painfully (August 4, 1609), Jonson tried to make amends with an epitaph commending her as a virgin who (most remarkably) had preserved her virginity at court, and who, moreover, "taught Pallas language; Cynthia modesty."[70] The performance was evidently intended to pacify the Countess by turning the "pucelle" into a virgin, thereby repairing her reputation after death.

Jonson's gesture suggests a scenario in which the Countess reacted so strongly to this malicious male put-down of her friend that he felt obliged to recant lest she do him harm at court. But the cynicism of this *volte-face* is obvious, and the less-than-complimentary reference to Pallas (Queen Anne) as needing a language lesson is hardly circumspect. Some months later Jonson's comedy *Epicoene* was produced. Arbella Stuart was the only court lady directly satirized, but many contemporaries must have associated Jonson's collegiate ladies with Lucy Bedford's circle at Twickenham, and their "President," Lady Haughty (who lives apart from her husband), with the Countess herself:

> *Truewit:* Then, if you love your wife, or rather, dote on her, sir: ô how shee'll torture you! . . . [She will] goe live with her she-friend,

or cosen at the colledge, that can instruct her in all the mysteries, of writing letters, corrupting servants, taming spies . . . [She will] be a states-woman, know all the newes, what was done at *Salisbury,* what at the *Bath,* what at court, what in progresse; or so shee may censure *poets,* and authors, and stiles, and compare DANIEL with SPENSER, JONSON with tother youth, and so foorth; or, be thought cunning in controversies, or the very knots of divinitie; and have, often in her mouth, the state of the question: and then skip to the *Mathematiques,* and demonstration and answere, in religion to one; in state, to another, in baud'ry to a third.[71]

What Lucy Bedford made of these works is not known, but there was no public rupture in the relationship. Perhaps, as she was not a named target in *Epicoene,* she did not take it personally. Perhaps she was willing to accept Jonson's gesture of tribute to her dead friend (sincere or not) as sufficient apology. Perhaps she was willing to extend considerable license to satire: Jonson had after all praised her highly for daring to like it even when its object was the court that was her orbit. Jonson's elegant praises of Lucy probably predate these satires, though we cannot be sure; in any case, except for the "Pucell" epigram, he included them all in the 1616 Folio.

The Countess had a closer relationship with Donne than with her other literary clients; indeed, for a time he was virtually her laureate. Sometime in 1607 or 1608 he was probably introduced into the Countess's circle by his good friend Sir Henry Goodyere. His letters of 1608–1612 report that he dined at Twickenham on several occasions; that the Countess stood godmother to his second daughter (who was named for her); that she was prompt and active in supporting him for an office he sought; that he sent literary works to her (some of his poetry, a translation she requested, some fashionable French poems from abroad); that she was often generous in relieving his needs; that he paid deathbed visits to Cecilia Bulstrode at Twickenham; and that he exchanged poems with the Countess on at least two occasions.[72] During these years he wrote to her several times; addressed six verse letters and two other occasional poems to her; titled his lyric "Twicknam Garden" after her estate; and wrote funeral elegies for her friends Lady Markham and Cecilia Bulstrode, as well as (in 1614) for Lucy's brother, John Harington.[73]

At one level theirs was a patron-client relationship, in which Donne received some financial assistance and some support in his constant (and unavailing) quest for secular office.[74] His letters voice many anxieties of clientage: his concern about pressing too many letters or verses upon the Countess; his uneasiness about addressing praises to other noble ladies; his worry that publishing some of his poems would demean him in her eyes; his tortuous explanations for his extravagant praise of Elizabeth Drury in the *Anniversaries*.[75] His expressions of admiration for the Countess also display his painful sense of dependency and social inferiority. He declared to Goodyere in 1609, "I have made her opinion of me the balance by which I weigh myself," and a little later, "I would write apace to her, whilst it is possible to express that which I yet know of her, for by this growth I see how soon she will be ineffable."[76]

The fact that Donne gained closer association with the Countess's coterie than did Daniel or Jonson made her relationship with him markedly different, blurring somewhat, though by no means obliterating, the great social divide between them. They exchanged poems and critiqued those poems as coterie friends. In a letter probably written in 1609, Donne requested some of Lucy's poems, complimenting them as excellent exercises on an "ill" subject:

> I . . . make a petition for verse, it is for those your Ladyship did me the honour to see in Twicknam garden, except you repent your making; and having mended your judgment by thinking worse, that is, better, because juster, of their subject. They must needs be an excellent exercise of your wit, which speak so well of so ill: I humbly beg them of your Ladyship, with two such promises, as to any other of your compositions were threatenings; that I will not show them, and that I will not believe them; and nothing should be so used that comes from your brain or breast.[77]

Her poems in this vein (courtly love poems? bawdy verse? contributions to the "News" game?) are unfortunately not extant. But it seems likely that Donne's "Twicknam Garden"—an exaggerated Petrarchan lament in which a weeping, sighing speaker bemoans his mistress's cruelty in the "paradise" of the Countess's garden—belongs to some such game of poetic exchanges on conventional love themes. Arthur Marotti suggests that "Aire and Angels," "The Feaver," and "The Funerall" may also have had such an origin. The title and themes of "A Nocturnall upon S. Lucies Day" suggest that this poem was also written for (though not about) the Countess.[78]

Donne's verse letters project an image of the Countess as able logician, metaphysician, and literary critic, in whom wit and religion are (as they should be) perfectly fused: "nor must wit / Be colleague to religion, but be it."[79] In Donne's hands the poem of praise underwent a sea change, transformed from conventional hyperbolic compliment or quasi-Petrarchan adulation into an audaciously witty but also serious metaphysical inquiry into the bases of human worth,[80] played off against the mundane transactions of courtiership. Although he also praised Elizabeth

Drury, the Countess of Huntingdon, Prince Henry, Lord Harington, and some others in similar terms, it might be argued that Donne developed his poetics of praise in the poems to the Countess of Bedford, since he addressed her first, and most often, in this vein. Specifically, he proposes to study, or meditate upon, or contemplate the Countess (as image of God, as powerful courtier and patron, as the single locus of virtue in a corrupt court); in doing so he offers to explore through her some general proposition about virtue, or religion, or death, or sorrow. At the same time, as recent criticism shows, the strains of clientage permeate these outrageously hyperbolic and logically contorted poems. David Aers and Gunther Kress see them encoding the alienation of the excluded intellectual through subtexts in which Donne asserts his own worth and undermines, even as he seeks to profit by, Lucy herself and the entire system of courtiership and patronage.[81] Marotti argues similarly that Donne's temperamental aggressiveness and discomfort with suitorship subvert the polite ritual of these poems, and the Countess herself, in both conscious and unconscious ways.[82]

The likelihood is that Lucy Bedford was aware of these witty subversions, and that Donne earned his association with her circle by his wit. As Marotti notes, Donne assumes in his poems that she "could appreciate his mischievously witty playing with the conventions of praise," and he turns this into a compliment to Lucy's intelligence and sophistication.[83] One ground for crediting her ability to appreciate Donne's strategies is suggested by Margaret Maurer's argument that Donne's poems consistently invite an analogy between Lucy's own uneasy situation as Jacobean courtier and his as her courtier-poet—the link between them being the daring *sprezzatura* of both their performances.[84] Moreover, her own letters, as we shall see, reveal her complex sense of her relationship to the court—sometimes keenly involved, sometimes detached, sometimes ironic, occasionally oppositional.

The verse letter "Reason is our Soules left hand, Faith her right / By these wee reach divinity, that's you" is probably Donne's first address to the Countess. It daringly (though temporarily) conflates her with God himself, applying to her the divinizing rhetoric King James so liked to arrogate to himself. Donne seeks to reach her first by reason, then by faith; to study her in her "Saints, / Those friends, whom your election glorifies," and then in her deeds; and finally to understand her goodness—which consists chiefly in "learning and religion / And vertue." The apparently outrageous hyperbole finds resolution in his recognition of her as "Gods masterpeece, and so / His Factor for our loves," that is, God's image and agent to attract mankind to love him (even as she was so often the "factor" or go-between in patronage transactions at court). The final lines urge her attention to the next life, while alluding wittily to his hopes from her in this one: "For so God helpe me, I would not misse you there / For all the good which you can do me here" (ll. 34–38). It is hard to believe, given the oppositional ethos so prominent on the Queen's side, that Lucy Bedford did not relish the jest whereby she supplanted James as primary analogue and image of God.

Often, Donne's verse epistles make the Countess the embodiment or incarnation of virtue, posing the question, how can (her) complete virtue exist in, act in, or manifest itself to an essentially wicked court? The poem "You have refin'd mee, and to worthyest things" takes the occasion of a visit to Twickenham to praise her and her country estate: "The Mine, the Magazine, the Commonweale, / The story 'of beauty,' in Twicknam is, and you" (ll. 69–70). The speaker explores the problematics of knowing those "worthyest things / (Vertue, Art, Beauty, Fortune)": he now understands through her alchemical "refining" that at court those qualities are wholly relative, known only by use and circumstance, not in their Platonic essence. There, in the exchanges of patronage, her transcendent virtue is a dark text requiring an exegete (Donne).[85] But at her country estate she is a true Sun making the court her Antipodes (ll. 19–25), and a true Deity making "new creatures" (l. 22). In this witty poem, Lucy Bedford and Twickenham are seen to supplant James's court as locus of value: the clear evidence of the senses testifies to the presence of beauty in that place and thereby (on Platonic grounds) to virtue also.

Other poems analyze the moral ambiguities of life at court. "T'have written then, when you writ" positions this poem in relation to a poem or letter of hers, then proceeds to identify her as the locus of virtue in an otherwise immoral court:

> I have beene told, that vertue' in Courtiers hearts
> Suffers an Ostracisme, and departs.
> Profit, ease, fitnesse, plenty, bid it goe,
> But whither, only knowing you, I know;
> Your (or you) virtue two vast uses serves,
> It ransomes one sex, and one Court preserves.[86]

Inviting her to "meditate" with him on the evils of the world, he daringly alludes to her possible (slight) participation in those vices, claiming that in the most virtuous, and so even in her, "Vertue hath some, but wise degrees of vice" (l. 76). With some illogic, however, he ends by warning her against such leaven: "Take then no vitious purge, but be content / With cordiall vertue, your knowne nourishment" (ll. 89–90). A verse letter to her "At New-yeares Tide" (1610), the season for exchanges of gifts at court, queries how the lowly Donne can worthily praise her (being perfect virtue). He presumes to expatiate on the doubts and trials God provides to try her so that she will be comprehensible to weaker mortals; he also dares to ventriloquize God, proffering her an extended moral lesson about court behavior, discretion, wariness, and virtue. The poem "Honour is so sublime perfection" begins by making explicit the basis of the patron-client relation: all honor (even to God himself) flows from low to high.[87] Again posing the question of how her perfect virtue can be manifested to or praised by the unworthy, Donne concludes by finding in her (and urging the continuance of) a perfect fusion of discretion and virtue, wit and religion, so that her external behavior truly mirrors her inner state: "*Beeing* and *seeming* is your equall care / And *vertues* whole *summe* is but *know* and *dare*" (ll. 32–33). He urges her to remain as she is, both "great and innocent."

Donne's poems occasioned by the deaths in 1609 of Lucy Bedford's close female friends and coterie associates develop a similar strategy. The verse epistle "You that are she and you, that's double shee," sent with an elegy on Lady Markham, applies to these female friends the Platonic commonplace on male friendship—"they doe / Which build them friendships, become one of two" (ll. 3–4); it concludes with the claim that all Lady Markham's virtues are now contracted in the Countess. The elegy analyzes the extent and limitations of death's power, concluding that it has no true power over the souls of the regenerate. Donne wrote two elegies for Cecilia Bulstrode: the first magnifies the power of death over all things; the second (evoked apparently by Lucy's poetic response to his first) analyzes the problem of sorrow in relation to such deaths.[88] The long "Obsequies to the Lord Harrington" (1614) is a meditation upon the uses of good men and the world's loss by their death. A covering letter refers to Lucy's changed situation—"your noble brother's fortune being yours"—suggesting that, even as he denies it, Donne hoped to reap some benefit from that fortune.[89]

The relationship between Donne and the Countess cooled somewhat after 1613: Donne looked increasingly to other patrons (the Drurys, other court ladies, Somerset), while the Countess's new religious seriousness after her illness made her more critical of Donne.[90] She raised scruples (for which he blamed Dr. Burges) about Donne's worthiness to take orders in the Church; and she was less generous than he apparently had been led to expect in helping him to settle his debts before he did so. Donne's letter to Goodyere elaborates on his suspicions and his disappointment, though he recognizes the Countess's financial problems:

> Of my Lady Bedford . . . I would say nothing of her upon record, that should not testify my thankfulness for all her graces. But . . . she had more suspicion of my calling, a better memory of my past life,

than I had thought her nobility could have admitted . . . yet I am afraid they proceed in her rather from some ill impression taken from Dr. Burges, than that they grow in herself . . . I am almost sorry, that an elegy [that for Lord Harington] should have been able to move her to so much compassion heretofore, as to offer to pay my debts; and my greater wants now, and for so good a purpose, as to become disengaged into that profession, being plainly laid open to her, should work no farther but that she sent me £30, which in good faith she excused with that, which is both parts true, that her present debts were burdensome, and that I could not doubt of her inclination, upon all future emergent occasions, to assist me . . . this diminution in her makes me see, that I must use more friends than I thought I should have needed.[91]

There was, however, no rift: Donne continued to refer to her as "the noblest Countess," and on January 7, 1621, he preached an eloquent sermon before her at Harington House. The text, "Loe, Though he slay me, yet will I trust in him" (Job 13:15), was certainly chosen for its applicability to her own trials in the recent death of her mother and her patron, the Queen.[92]

Letters and Poetry

Lady Bedford's own writings afford some insight into what it was to be a female courtier at the courts of King James and Queen Anne. Her representation of herself and her reading of her world can be glimpsed in her letters, public and private, especially the thirty-three written between 1613 and 1625 to her good friend Lady Jane Bacon—always addressed to "Dear Cornwallis," giving the lady the name and title of her noble first husband, who settled a fortune on her.[93] The self she constructs in and through her letters shows self-reliance, confidence in her own abilities, judgment and taste, strong religious faith, and great satisfaction with her remarkably independent life, so largely free from a husband's control and the constraints of the domestic sphere. The Earl of Bedford is almost never mentioned, but she makes a few rather wistful allusions to her childless state. Her closest family bond is with her aged mother, whom she admires and worries about during her attendance in Heidelberg upon the Electress Palatine.[94]

The Countess considers herself first of all a courtier, a public person at the center of affairs who wields influence for herself, her friends, and her political allies, and thinks that function important. Her court letters are filled with negotiations for appointments and marriages: a preferment to the Elector Palatine for one Will Gombleton; a secretaryship at home for the ambassador to the Hague Dudley Carleton; a chaplain for the Queen of Bohemia; a marriage for her niece; an appointment as Gentleman Usher for a son of Lady Bacon.[95] At times she voices some of the anxieties and compulsions Stephen Greenblatt traces in the "self-fashioning" gestures of contemporary male courtiers—especially the conflict between public duties and personal needs and desires. She often complains to Cornwallis about the strenuous demands of court attendance, but it is clear nevertheless that she relishes those demands:

> I deferred my wrighting to you till I cam into the contry, wheare within 8 days the K[ing] overtooke me; against whos coming, and during his stay att my house, all my tyme and litlle witt was so taken up about the busnes of house keepinge as itt made me lay all else aside. Within 3 days after . . . I mett with a peremtory commandement from the Queene to wayte upon her at Woodstocke, which I did, though with so ill health as I had much adoe to get heather to use the helpe of some phisicke.[96]

Writing to Carleton about the office he hopes for, she comments on the difficulty of knowing just whom to approach as political alliances shift: "I assure your Lordship even those that are nearer the well head, know not with what bucket to draw for themselves and thir freinds."[97] From time to time she comments about the course of public affairs—indicating, for example, that God has worked a great improvement in Prince Charles after the Spanish marriage fiasco: "I will give you my testimony that the Prince is the most improved man that ever I saw, and that my Lo. of Buckingham recovers much of what he had lost."[98]

The oppositional impulse which manifested itself in Lucy Bedford's connection with the Queen's subversive masques and in her notorious circle at Twickenham carried over as well into her patronage activities. She took up the cause of her Puritan chaplain-cum-physician John Burges, who, Chamberlain reported, had been responsible for her supposed conversion and was banished from the court for his pains:

> Burges (who is turned phisician) was much about her in her sickness, and did her more good with his spirituall counsaile, then with naturall phisike . . . the king . . . was so moved that he should dogmatise (as he called yt) in his court, that he commaunded the archbishop to look to yt who . . . injoined him not to practise within ten miles of London.[99]

She labored for and at length obtained Burges's reinstatement in 1616, and sought his advice on several occasions.[100]

At times she sees herself caught in a moral dilemma of courtiership, a conflict of loyalties. In a case where she thinks the Queen has been unjust in dismissing her friend Lady Roxborough from her service, she writes Cornwallis that she has had to register her protest by absenting herself from court: "Of the Queen's court I can say litle good, for her resolution to part with Roxbrough still continues . . . no measuer of favor could often invite me theather, whear ther is no hope of any good to be donne."[101]

Her politics were also oppositional. She aligned herself consistently with the Sidney-Pembroke faction against the Howards and Buckingham. Over the years she promoted the cause of the Elector Palatine and Elizabeth, whose plight became a *cause célèbre* in the struggles of international Protestantism against Rome and Spain and a focus for opposition to James at home.[102] In 1621 she made a hazardous sea voyage to visit Elizabeth in exile in the Hague,[103] and frequently wrote news and advice to her—always addressing her, against James's express command, as Queen of Bohemia. In 1622 she reminds Carleton of the dangers of writing openly, "since letters must passe more hands then yours," but assures him that her own advice to Elizabeth would never "perswade any thing to her disadvantage, whose good is as deare to mee as my owne lyfe."[104] In 1623 she writes urgently, warning (through Carleton) of dangerous rumors to the effect that Elizabeth planned an unauthorized visit to England while Prince Charles was in Spain, giving rise to fears that she wished to be on hand should circumstances call her to the throne:

> For Gods sake preache more warines to the Queene whom she uses freedom to, else shee will undo her selfe, and make others afrayd how they interest them selves in her servis, though for my part I will never omitte makeing good my professions to her as becoms a faithfull and carefull servant.[105]

Elizabeth depended upon the Countess for news and reports from the court, and gratefully acknowledged her continued efforts in the exiles' behalf.[106]

Apart from her role as courtier, the Countess also projects herself as a competent woman of affairs, with sufficient practical intelligence and business acumen to cope with the exigencies of her encumbered estate, her debts, and her legal problems. After a brief report to Cornwallis in 1614 on her husband's illness, she moves quickly to such matters:

> Now I thanke God I can say, that out of a very great and almost hopeles danger My Lord of Bedford hath recovered so much health and strength as we are out of all fear of him, and doe conseave that the violent fever he hath had hath done him some good for his palsy, his speach being better then itt was before he fell sick, though his

lamenes be nothing amended. His present state setts me at liberty to follow my terme busnesses, which daylie are multiplied upon me, and make me heavile feel the burden of a broken estate; yett doe I not doubt but by the assistance of Almighty God I shall ear long overcum all those difficulties which at the present contest with me.[107]

To meet some of her debts and expenses, she accepted long-standing personal loans from Lady Cornwallis, for which her letters often apologize.[108] From the King she sought and received £2,000 a year in 1619, and patents at various times on copper farthings, sea coal, and gold and silver thread; she also took a share in the Bermudas Company.[109] In 1621 she writes Cornwallis that she is at last getting her affairs in order by arranging to sell Coombe Abbey: "I intend to turn Combe wholly into money, bothe to make myself a free woman from debt, and with the rest of itt to rayse as good an estate for lyfe as I can, having now nonne but myselfe to provide for."[110]

On the personal side, she represents herself as a loyal and devoted friend to a few individuals (men as well as women): Jane Cornwallis and her husband, Nathaniel Bacon; William Herbert, Earl of Pembroke; James, Marquis of Hamilton. The relationship with her closest friend, Cornwallis, was cemented by frequent exchanges of letters, visits, and gifts.[111] She wrote several letters of comfort to Cornwallis, who was given to melancholy and apprehension during her pregnancies:

> It is one of my misfortunes, and such a one as I assure you I am very sensible of, to be thus farre from you . . . You must not consent to sincke under that melancoly . . . which I grieve hartely to heare hath already rought so ill effects upon your health, and so strong aprehencions in your minde, though I trust our good God will with a safe deliverance of a happy bearth restore you.[112]

In the exigencies of sickness and death her ready recourse was to seek for herself and offer her friends the consolations of religious faith.

She wrote often about death, analyzing her own grief and that of others with some precision, and assessing how religiously it is endured. Writing to Cornwallis after her mother's death in 1619, she compares that heavy but expected loss with her friend Pembroke's unexpected loss of his son:

> What a mother I have lost I need not tell you, that know what she was in herselfe, and to me. Yet God, that sees no affliction to worke sufficiently upon me, hath this last night added another heavie one to my former woe, having taken My Lord Chamberlain's sonne . . . Now itt is com to the trial I am confident he will show well tempered

effects of that religious resolution, and bear with pacience what the Almighty hath donne.[113]

Her report to Cornwallis on the death of the Marquis of Hamilton reveals the inextricable mix of personal regard and political usefulness in most of her relationships. She writes of him as both a dear friend and a powerful patron, lamenting his sad loss to the political alliance headed by Pembroke, and condemning by implication the favorite Buckingham and his cohort:

I acknowledge that I feele so to the quicke this last affliction God hath pleased to lay upon me as no worldly comfort will ever be able to prevaile against itt, for I have lost the best and worthiest freind that ever breathed, whom I could not love enoffe for what he was to me, nor sufficiently admire for what he was in himselfe and to all the world . . . for myselfe I must trewly say I am a maimed body and worse, and so is my Lo. Chamberlain [Pembroke], the last person left of power that I can relie on for the worth of his affection and friendship to me; and, to speake freely to you, the only honest harted man imployed that I know now left to God and his countrie.[114]

In quite another vein, her account of Lady Richmond's response to her husband's death, written to "entertaine" Cornwallis in one of her spells of melancholy, reveals Lucy Bedford's considerable flair for narrative, her sense of irony, and her capacity for acute psychological insight:

My La. of Richmond's losse, though it weare such a blow from Heaven as I must confesse I never knew given, will not kille her, of so strandge resisting stue are our hartes made. She was the happiest woman I thinke that lived . . . she had of glorie and greatnes as much as a subject was capable of, wealth of all kinds in abundance, health and extraordinary beautie even at this adge, and, above all, a noble husband, that was the love of her harte, and doted on her with the same pasion to the last ower of his lyfe that he did the first month of his being in love with her. Out of those loveing armes she rose not two owers before he died, and left him, as she thought, well, only troubled with a litle paine in his head, which made him desirous to sleep a litle longer . . . I much feared the first violence might have distracted her, but her pasion had so liberal vent as I thinke itt wrought the less inwardly. Her haire, in discharge of a vowe she had formerly made, she cutte off close by the rootes that afternoone, and told us of som other vowes of retirednes she had made if she should be so miserable as to outlive him, which I hope she will as punctually performe. For my part, I confesse I incouradge her to itt, which, som say, hereafter she will love me nothing the better for; but itt is the counsel I should take to myselfe in her case, and therfore I cannot spare to give itt.[115]

Lucy Bedford's letters also construct her as a person of artistic interests and taste. She is passionate about the garden she is laying out at Moor Park, soliciting Nathaniel and Lady Bacon for "som of the little white single rose rootes I saw att Brome," and any other "extraordinary" flowers they may have. At one point she declares herself "so much in love with" her gardens at Moor Park "as, if I wear so fond of any man, I wear in hard case."[116] Her passion for art collection, and especially for Holbeins, is indicated by her rather ruthless offer to bid for them (through her friend Lady Bacon) even as the owner is drawing his last breath, and to pay any price:

> I was told the last night that your father in law was like to die and that he had som peeses of painting of Holben's . . . I beseech you entreate Mr. Bacon, if they will be parted with to any, to lay hold of them afore hand for me . . . for I am a very diligent gatherer of all I can gett of Holben's or any other excellent master's hand; I do not care at what rate I have them for price, but shall thinke itt an extraordinary favor if Mr. Bacon can procure me those, or any others, if he know any such thereabouts, upon any conditions; whos judgement is so extraordinary good as I know nonne can better tell what is worth the haveing. Som of those I have, I found in obscure places, and gentleman's houses, that, because they wear old, made no reckoning of them; and that makes me thinke itt likely that ther may yett be in divers places many excellent unknown peeses, for which I lay wayghte with all my freinds; and when Mr. Bacon coms to London, he shall see that though I be but a late beginner, I have pretty store of choise peeses. Dear Madam . . . be not curious to thinke I may pay too much [for the Holbeins], for I had rather have them then juels.[117]

Lucy Bedford's single extant poem shows her claiming the status of coterie poet—an amateur talented enough to produce verses on appropriate occasions and exchange them with her circle. Like most members of her class she evidently regarded writing poetry as a social grace rather than a serious endeavor; she made no effort to save or collect her poems, nor do her letters make reference to her activities as literary patron or poet. Yet she clearly took pleasure in the activity, and evidently won respect for it, at least in her own coterie. The poem we have is from a poetic exchange with Donne in 1609, occasioned by the death of Cecilia Bulstrode; it is good enough to have been ascribed to Donne himself in the 1635 edition and often thereafter.[118] The exchange provides an insight into the poetic transactions of the Countess's circle: her elegy supplies a deft response and correction to Donne's first elegy for Bulstrode, and he then responds with another poem. Donne's first elegy begins by alluding to his holy sonnet "Death be not Proud" and to his elegy for Markham, recanting their argument, "Death I recant, and say, unsaid by mee / What ere hath slip'd, that might diminish thee."[119] At great length and with great vividness it describes the whole world as a universe of death, all life devoured by Death and served up to his table. But the horrors described elide Bulstrode herself and overbalance the rather pat consolation proclaiming that her death and new life in heaven are a defeat for Death.

In the episode of the Jonson epigram, the Countess apparently intervened to rescue her friend from the constructions placed upon her by a male wit. Here she intervenes with an elegy, one which offers to do better justice to Bulstrode as a person and as a regenerate soul than did Donne's powerful but rather impersonal poem. The Countess's poem, like Donne's in heroic couplets, begins by quoting (against its author) the first line of Donne's "Death be not Proud." Its argument is that the death of the just (as Bulstrode was) is a summons from God, not from Death. In the spirit of Donne's sonnet, the Countess affirms that Death cannot harm the just, that it has power only over the reprobate—defined in Calvinist terms as "people curst before they were." Then, referring obliquely to the scandals about Bulstrode, the Countess counters them with the visible evidences of her deathbed sanctity. The elegy ends strongly, with a couplet proposing the Pauline affirmation of victory over death as an appropriate celebratory hymn for Bulstrode:

> Death be not proud, thy hand gave not this blow,
> Sinne was her captive, whence thy power doth flow;
> The executioner of wrath thou art,
> But to destroy the just is not thy part.
> Thy comming, terrour, anguish, griefe denounce;
> Her happy state, courage, ease, joy pronounce.
> From out the Christall palace of her breast,
> The clearer soule was call'd to endlesse rest,
> (Not by the thundering voyce, wherewith God threats,
> But, as with crowned Saints in heaven he treats,)
> And, waited on by Angels, home was brought,
> To joy that it through many dangers sought;
> The key of mercy gentle did unlocke
> The doores 'twixt heaven and it, when life did knock.
>   Nor boast, the fairest frame was made thy prey,
> Because to mortall eyes it did decay;

A better witnesse than thou art, assures,
That though disolv'd, it yet a space endures;
No dramme thereof shall want or losse sustaine,
When her best soule inhabits it again.
Goe then to people curst before they were,
Their spoyles in Triumph of thy conquest were.
Glory not thou thy selfe in these hot teares
Which our face, not for hers, but our harme weres,
The mourning livery given by Grace, not thee,
Which wils our soules in these streams washt should be,
And on our hearts, her memories best tombe,
In this her Epitaph doth write thy doome.
Blinde were those eyes, saw not how bright did shine
Through fleshes misty vaile the beames divine.
Deafe were the eares, not charm'd with that sweet sound
Which did i'th spirit-instructed voice abound.
Or flint the conscience, did not yeeld and melt,
At what in her last Act it saw, heard, felt.
   Weep not, nor grudge then, to have lost her sight,
Taught thus, our after stay's but a short night:
But by all soules not by corruption choaked
Let in high rais'd notes that power be invoked.
Calme the rough seas, by which she sayles to rest,
From sorrowes here, to a kingdome ever blest;
And teach this hymne of her with joy, and sing,
   The grave no conquest gets, Death hath no sting.

The Countess here claims the right of a woman not only to offer a funeral elegy for her friend, but to critique through it the premier male poet of the age in this kind. Donne's second elegy on Bulstrode appears to "correct" the first in light of the Countess's poem.[120]

Given the period's restrictions on women, Lucy Bedford had scant opportunity to engage her considerable talents and strength of character toward large accomplishments. But she found some scope for them within the important social institutions of courtiership and patronage, whose cultural codes allowed noblewomen some access to power and influence. She could wield more power than most, in large part because of her unusual freedom from patriarchal familial constraints, through circumstances that gave her the privileged status of a wealthy, titled widow without in fact being one. She was able to a remarkable degree to "spin her owne free houres," and she used them to claim and exercise a unique role as female courtier at the Queen's and the King's court. She was part of the power structure, but her gender and her politics placed her in an oppositional relationship to James's patriarchal establishment.

As courtier, patron, masquer, and poet she created and elicited various idealized images of herself in literature and art, transforming herself into something of a cultural myth. The older literary code of Petrarchan adulation is not part of that myth; it is replaced by newer modes of praise (which she seems to have fostered), and in the case of Donne, by a relationship of coterie interchange. Lucy Bedford constructs herself in her masquing images, her clients' praises, and her own writings as a figure of power and influence, of splendor and grace, of literary and artistic discrimination, of intelligence and wit. She claims as well to be a hardworking courtier, a staunch Protestant, a good friend, a shrewd judge of people and affairs, a good businesswoman, and a poet capable of *sprezzatura* display. Her writings give little hint of the anxieties or strains she may have felt in projecting and sustaining her remarkable public persona. In any event, the Countess of Bedford is one Jacobean lady who laid claim to considerable political power and cultural status, and got away with it.

The Clifford "Great Picture," probably executed by Jan van Belcamp.

5 ❧

Claiming Patrimony and Constructing a Self: Anne Clifford and Her Diary

Anne Clifford (1589–1676) provides an instance of sustained public opposition to patriarchal authority and property settlements. Her struggle is recorded in several autobiographical works, among them a fascinating though fragmentary *Diary* covering the years when she felt herself most embattled (1616–1619).[1] While lawsuits over women's claims to property and inheritance were very common in the era, as the cases described in that curious tract *The Lawes Resolutions of Womens Rights* makes clear,[2] Anne Clifford's *Diary* offers a rare reading of one such situation by the women involved (Anne Clifford and her mother, Margaret Clifford, Countess of Cumberland). It thereby provides an intriguing insight into their construction of self and world as they contested Jacobean patriarchal ideology, supported on the one hand by a sense of female community, and on the other by the firm conviction that God the Divine Patriarch was on their side against the many earthly patriarchs who oppressed them. Anne Clifford's *Diary* shows her struggling for some limited self-realization within a field of highly complex familial and social forces and constraints which she only partially understands. It offers a most unusual representation (for the period) of a developing sense of self, evidently promoted in part by the struggle itself and in part by the challenge of interpreting it that diary writing posed. In writing down her *res gestae*, Anne Clifford asserted the significance of her female life.

By her first marriage in 1609 to Richard Sackville, Lady Anne Clifford became Countess of Dorset; by her second in 1630 to Philip Herbert, she became Countess of Pembroke and Montgomery. But she did not define herself or her place in society through these marriages and these illustrious titles. Rather, she claimed her true identity from her own family, as the "sole Daughter and Heir to my Illustrious Father," George Clifford, Earl of Cumberland, and Margaret (Russell), her adored mother and model. That identity was forged through decades of legal and personal battles in which Lady Anne and her mother set themselves against the Jacobean male establishment—their husbands, their Clifford relatives, powerful courtiers, the Archbishop of Canterbury, and the King himself—to maintain Lady Anne's legal claim by ancient entail to a large inheritance which her father's will left to his brother. Anne Clifford did not intend to challenge the patriarchal order as such, but rather to take full advantage of the exceptional legal circumstances that in this instance gave her a claim to offices and properties which would normally descend to a son or other male relative. Yet her struggle implied such a challenge by her emphasis upon a matrilineal heritage, and her assumption that a daughter is worthy and competent to hold such offices and properties in her own right. That struggle served as stimulus and focal point for Lady Anne's several projects in research and writing. The legal titles she sought and at long last obtained name the roles through which she defined herself: "Baroness Clifford, Westmoreland and Vesey, High Sheriffess of Westmoreland, and Lady of the Honor of Skipton in Craven."[3]

The social conditions constructing Anne Clifford's life, and her response to them, can be read from several kinds of contemporary records: letters, memoirs, court gossip, personal letters, a few dedications, Lady Anne's funeral sermon, her own collections and writings.[4] Anne and her mother compiled massive tomes of records and family papers (called "The Chronicles" in implicit analogy to chronicle histories of the life and times of princes), in part from pride in the family's illustrious history, but chiefly to reinforce Anne's own legal claims as sole heir.[5] About 1653 Anne Clifford wrote memoirs of her father and mother in the vein of Plutarch's moralized *Lives* but incorporating as well vignettes in the tradition of the literary "character"; at about the same time she wrote a lively and occasionally reflective secular autobiography.[6] These resources allow us to contextualize Anne's Jacobean *Diary,* the narrative it encodes, and the issues it raises.

Anne Clifford records on her mother's authority the date and place of her conception—May 1, 1589, "in the Lord Wharton's house in Channell Row in Westminster"—the curious detail serving to reinforce her claim as her father's only surviving legitimate child (*Life of Me,* 33). She was born in Skipton Castle in Craven, Yorkshire, January 30, 1590, when her father was at sea. George Clifford, third Earl of Cumberland (1558–1605), was Queen Elizabeth's official Champion in the tilt yard and a dashing adventurer and privateer who engaged in twelve sea voyages (including the Armada and Cádiz); he captured and despoiled Spanish and Portuguese merchant ships, helped launch the East India Company, and ran up enormous debts. In 1577 he married Margaret Russell, youngest daughter of his guardian, Francis, Second Earl of Bedford; in later years he had notorious affairs with other women and "parted houses" with his wife, though they reconciled when he begged her forgiveness on his deathbed.[7] Two sons died in childhood, leaving Anne the sole survivor. Anne's various memoirs record early and happy associations with the court, but this promising situation changed with the accession of James I, the open rift between her parents, and her father's death.

At George Clifford's death the title and properties pertaining to the Cumberland earldom legally reverted to his brother Francis, the nearest male relative. But Anne claimed other castles, estates, titles, and county offices—in Yorkshire the Barony of Clifford and the castle and estates of Skipton in Craven; in Westmoreland the castles and estates of Appleby, Brougham, Brough, and Pendragon, as well as the office of Sheriff. By writ of 4th Edward II (1310–1311) these lands were entailed to the "heirs of the body, lawfully begotten," of Robert de Clifford—that is, to the heirs general (daughters as well as sons). Some of the Westmoreland properties also constituted Margaret Clifford's jointure. Without breaking the entail (as he might have done), George Clifford willed those properties and offices to his brother, making a monetary provision of £15,000 for his daughter out of those estates, and giving her the reversion of the properties should his brother's male line fail. Anne's claim was sound according to two precepts enunciated in *The Lawes Resolutions:*

> A female may be preferred in succession before a male by the time wherein she commeth: as a daughter or daughters daughter in the right line is preferred before a brother in the transversall line, and that aswell in the common generall taile, as in fee simple . . . also a woman shall bee preferred *propter jus sanguinis* . . . land discended must alwaies goe to heires of the blood of the first purchaser, and the case may bee such that a female shall cary away inheritance from a male.[8]

Anne accounts for her father's actions and motives in terms of patriarchal values: "the love he bore his brother, and the advancement of the heirs male of his house" (*Life of Me*, 36).[9]

Margaret Clifford had herself appointed Anne's guardian, to protect her from the lucrative court traffic in wards and their fortunes, and specifically from her Cumberland uncle. She then sued out a writ of livery for the lands in the Court of Wards, and both traveled north to visit (and claim) the Westmoreland properties of Margaret Clifford's jointure.[10] Anne's marriage to Richard Sackville, under discussion for some time, was concluded in some haste on February 25, 1609, when his father's imminent death made it expedient to protect Sackville from the dangers of wardship;

two days later the newlyweds (both aged nineteen) became Earl and Countess of Dorset.[11] In 1609–10 Anne took her place in the Queen's entourage and danced in three court masques: as one of the Queen's attendants in Jonson's *Masque of Beautie* (January 14, 1609); as Berenice of Egypt (noted for her "magnanimity" and her beautiful hair) in the *Masque of Queenes* (February 2, 1610); and as the river Ayr (near her birthplace, Skipton) in Samuel Daniel's *Tethys Festival,* celebrating the creation of Henry as Prince of Wales (June 5, 1610).[12]

Subsequently, though she attended court occasionally, Anne spent much of her time at the Dorset country house in Knole, Sevenoaks, Kent, occupied with reading, writing, needlework, and domestic oversight. Dorset gave himself increasingly to lavish expenditures, costly dress, cockfighting, gambling, and a profligate life, including liasons with Lady Venetia Stanley and Lady Penniston, as well as a close (perhaps a homosexual) relationship with his gentleman-servant Matthew Caldicott.[13] As Anne's lawsuits dragged on for twelve years, Dorset, having many debts and his way to make at court, tried to force her to relinquish her claims in return for a cash settlement along the lines of her father's will, which was upheld in an initial legal ruling. He tried banishment to the country, rage, threats of separation, taking her daughter away from her—all to no avail. Early in 1617 King James handed down a settlement to which Dorset, George Clifford's brother Francis (now Earl of Cumberland), and his son and heir, Henry, all agreed. It gave the estates to the Cliffords, with reversion to Anne if the male line failed, and £20,000 in installments to Anne—that is, to Dorset, for as a married woman she was a "Feme Covert" with no power or control over her money or goods.[14] Payment of the final £3,000 depended, however, on her signing this agreement as a just settlement of all her claims, and she persistently refused to do so, though Dorset continued the personal and financial pressure. He kept her short of cash and even canceled her jointure in June 1617, restoring it only in 1623, the year before he died at age thirty-five—according to Chamberlain of a "surfeit of [sweet] potatoes," a supposed aphrodisiac which seems to have brought on dysentery.[15] Anne bore Dorset five children: three sons who died in infancy and two daughters, Margaret (1614) and Isabella (1622), who survived to adulthood. Clients' descriptions of her in the last years of her marriage to Dorset emphasize the expected female qualities—virtue and resolute patience in affliction.[16]

With its usual numerical precision, Anne's *Life of Me* reports that she lived a widow "six yeares, two monthes, and fower or five daies over," a period she finds replete with trials, enemies, new legal claims, and providential deliverances (46–48). Both Anne and her daughter Margaret nearly died of smallpox, which, she notes wryly, "did so martyr my face, that it confirmed more and more my mind never to marry againe, though the Providence of God caused me after to alter that resolution." In April 1629 she gave her daughter Margaret in marriage at age fourteen to John, Lord Tufton (soon to become Earl of Thanet). In June 1630, at age forty, and despite her martyred face, Anne remarried: her new husband was Philip Herbert, second son of Henry, second Earl of Pembroke, and Mary (Sidney). Philip was fourth Earl of Pembroke and Montgomery, Lord Chamberlain of the household to James I and Charles I, and a great favorite of both.[17] He was physically attractive, extravagant, and a passionate hunter, but also coarse, foul-mouthed, quarrelsome, a notorious libertine, and barely literate, though a sound judge of pictures and architecture.[18] In his *Memoirs* George Sedgwick, who served Pembroke and (later) Anne as clerk and secretary, raises the obvious question as to why this strong-minded woman chose to marry again and so unsuitably after she had achieved a widow's independence and full control of her own affairs. She credits Providence, while he invokes ironical fortune;[19] a more adequate explanation might be Anne's sense of vulnerability (without husband, son, or brother) and desire for an influential protector in dealing with the male power structure. Her uncle Cumberland's heir, Henry Clifford, having no son, was trying to break the revisionary clause in the settlement so as to bequeath the estates to his daughter; and her brother-in-law, the new Lord Dorset ("my extreme enemy"), had designs on the lands of her jointure.[20]

Anne bore Herbert two sons who died in infancy; after about two years they lived apart, Anne chiefly at Wilton, where the large-scale renovations in progress probably proved instructive for her own later architectural projects.[21] They cooperated in some matters of business. Herbert made her a generous jointure, joined her in making formal legal claims for her properties in 1632 and 1637, and relinquished his rights in the Westmoreland property and Skipton in favor of her daughter Isabella (whose hand he sought for his son against Anne's resolute and successful opposition). She aided him by remaining in Baynard's Castle during the Civil War years, in part to protect his property.[22] A staunch Royalist, she was wholly out of sympathy with Herbert's adherence to Parliament, but because of it she did not have to compound for her estates when she gained them at last, in 1643, after the death of her uncle Cumberland followed by that of his son Henry without a male heir. In 1647 she married her daughter Isabella to the Earl of Northampton, and despite the Interregnum turmoil went north in 1649 to take over her properties. In 1650 Pembroke died, leaving her again a widow but now fearing and beholding to none, and ready to enjoy the independence, status, and authority pertaining to that condition, as *The Lawes Resolutions* describes it: "Consider how long you have beene in subjection under the predominance of parents, of your husbands, now you be free in libertie, a free proprietris of your own Law . . . [your] estate [is now] . . . free from controlment."[23]

For more than thirty years Anne Clifford ruled her little domain as a (usually) benevolent autocrat, combining public and private roles—Lord of the Manor and Lady Bountiful, Sheriff of the County and grandmother, patriarch and matriarch. She began rebuilding her castles and ordering her estates immediately, defying the authority of Cromwell's occupying forces.[24] She held Common Prayer services in her chapels and defended her loyalty to King and established Church before General Thomas Harrison himself and committees of Puritan ministers, displaying what her funeral eulogist Bishop Edward Rainbowe termed "Heroick" courage "not so often to be found . . . in that Sex."[25] After the Restoration she rebuilt seven churches, six castles, and two almshouses for impoverished widows. She ran her estates herself, buying supplies locally to foster the economy of the region and often suing her tenants to recover contested rights. She dispensed patronage and largess to worthy divines, old servants, tenants, friends, even Dorset's bastard daughters.[26] She often entertained and kept prideful account of her numerous grandchildren and great-grandchildren (Margaret had ten living children and Isabella, who died in 1661, had one daughter). In the public realm she exercised the duties of the High Sheriffwick: overseeing and returning writs of election for Parliament, handpicking the MPs for Appleby and Westmoreland, convening and summoning the jury for the annual assizes courts.[27] Rainbowe found his interpretive key to Anne Clifford in the extraordinary completeness and autonomy of her life—qualities he found especially remarkable in a woman: "She was absolute Mistris of her Self, her Resolutions, Actions, and Time."[28] She died in 1676 at the age of eighty-six.

Empowering Influences

Anne Clifford's memoirs of 1653 represent her as a strong-minded, self-assured woman with a firm sense of personal worth, sitting in confident authorial judgment on all the men who held familial authority over her—father, uncle, husbands—and penning perceptive, fair-minded, and judicious evaluations of them. That representation invites the question, how was such an identity constituted within the institution and ideology of patriarchy? Her later writings emphasize several factors.

For one thing, she characteristically ranged the various patriarchal authorities against one another, thus opening space for subversion. She both accepted and challenged the patriarchal family structure as she sought to rewrite her place within it. Her constant emphasis on the web of Clifford family connections is dictated by family pride, but much more by the desire to substantiate her claims as her father's rightful heir. Even her physical appearance is made an argument for true descent from her father, but she also insists, significantly, on an equal inheritance from her mother:

> I was very happy in my first constitution both in mind and body, both for internal and external endowments, for never was there child more equally resembling both father and mother than myself. The color of mine eyes were black like my father, and the form and aspect of them was quick and lively like my mother's; the hair of my head was brown and very thick, and so long that it reached to the calf of my legs when I stood upright, with a peak of hair on my forehead, and a dimple in my chin, like my father, full cheeks and round face like my mother, and an exquisite shape of body resembling my father. But now time and age hath long since ended all those beauties, which are to be compared to the grass of the field.　　　　　(*Life of Me*, 34–35)

These attitudes inform her collection, annotation, and writing of family history. The title pages of her three massive volumes of records and biographical sketches, tracing the Veteriponts and the Cliffords back to the early thirteenth century, proclaim their primary purpose, to prove Anne's "right title . . . to the inheritance of her father and his ancestors."[29] Her memoir of her father has the same subtext, identifying him as the "last heir male of the Cliffords that was rightfully possessor of those ancient lands and honors"—thereby setting aside with a word those unrightful possessors, her uncle and cousin—and identifying herself as "his only daughter and sole heir that lived, the Lady Anne Clifford, now Countess Dowager of Pembroke, Dorset, and Montgomery."[30] In 1646, just after she came into her inheritance but before she could take possession of it, she commissioned a family picture (see the illustration at the beginning of this chapter) as a visual compendium of that history, complete with lengthy commentaries. Probably executed by Jan van Belcamp, who copied and adapted several extant portraits, the triptych's center panel presents Anne's mother and father with their two young sons (the presumptive heirs, now deceased), together with inset portraits of Clifford and Russell relatives; labels and coats of arms along either side trace the history, respectively, of the Clifford family and of Margaret Clifford's jointure lands in Westmoreland. The wings of the triptych show Anne—on the left as the young Clifford daughter at about age fifteen, on the right at age fifty-three, when the inheritance at long last fell to her.[31]

Anne was able to maintain great pride in, and a primary identification with, her father by persuading herself on the basis of the deathbed reconciliation that he expected and indeed intended the property to revert ultimately to her: "A little before his death he expressed with much affection to my mother and me a great belief that he had, that his brother's son would dye without issue male, and thereby all his lands would come to be mine; which accordingly befell."[32] Her memoir of Clifford exudes pride in his sea adventures, his intellectual qualities, and his general knowledge of all the arts, especially mathematics and navigation, "wherein he became the most knowing and eminent man, of a Lord, in his time."[33] While at Knole she also had the contemporary records and eyewitness accounts of all Clifford's sea voyages collected in a beautiful manuscript which is still a major source for them.[34] But she also subjects his character to judgment—balancing virtues and faults, noble and less-than-noble reasons for his financial straits—in the authoritative manner of a Plutarch:

> This Earl George was endowed with many perfections of nature befitting so noble a personage, as an excellent quickness of witt and apprehension, an active and strong body, and an affable disposition and behaviour. But, as good natures through humane frailty are often times misled, so he fell to love a lady of quality, which did by degrees draw and alienate his love and affection from his so virtuous and well deserving wife; so that at the length, for two or three years together before his death, they parted houses, to her extream grief and sorrow and also to his extream sorrow at the time of his death, for he dyed a very penitant man . . . He consumed more of his estate than ever any of his ancestors did by much. To which his continual building of ships, and his many sea voyages, gave great occasion to those vast expenses of his. And that which did contribute the more to the consuming of his estate was his extream love to horse-races, tiltings, bowling matches, shooting, and all such expensive sports.[35]

She erected a superb tomb for him at Skipton, with her own claims carved prominently on the stone.[36]

This identification strengthened her to resist the authority and claims of uncles, husbands, courtiers, and kings. It also enabled her, as she asserts with some pride and a deft quotation from Sidney's *Arcadia,* to detach herself from her two husbands' families and concerns:

> The marble pillars of Knowle in Kent and Wilton in Wiltshire were to me often times but the gay arbour of anguish. Insomuch that a wise man that knew the insides of my fortune [perhaps her cousin and friend Francis Russell, Earl of Bedford] would often say that I lived in both these my lords' great familys as the river of Roan or Rodamus runs through the lake of Geneva, without minging any part of its streams with that lake; for I gave myself wholly to retiredness, as much as I could, in both those great families, and made good

books and virtuous thoughts my companions, which can never discern affliction, nor be daunted when it unjustly happens.[37]

Though she took some pride in the greatness of her two husbands, these striking metaphors proclaim her stoic detachment and her internal and external resistance to the patriarchal authority her society vested in husbands.[38]

Another factor empowering her resistance to the patriarchs ranged against her was her firm conviction that Providence was directing all the courses of her life, and doing so in accordance with her father's true wishes. By her reading, the Divine Patriarch himself frustrated the machinations of the various earthly patriarchs, at every juncture thwarting "the sinister practices of my Enemies" in defense of her rights. She notes that her "long contention" with Dorset about her lands "brought many troubles upon me, the most part of the time after that I lived his wife," but concludes, typically, that "God protected and inabled me to pass through them all."[39] Her second marriage, to Philip Herbert, "was wonderfullie brought to pass by the providence of God for the Crossing and disappoynting the envie Malice and sinister practices of my Enemyes," despite the "anger and falling out" over his desire to marry Isabella to his son.[40] All the male issue of her uncle Francis Clifford and his son Henry died "by the providence of God," thus clearing the way for her to inherit.[41] This firm conviction that God himself supported her claims because she was in the right enabled her to oppose the patriarchal power structure at every point while at the same time demanding that it make a place for her as a species of female paterfamilias.

Another factor of primary importance to Anne Clifford's self-definition and sense of empowerment was her close identification with her mother, and her emphasis on a matrilineal heritage and kinship network. If she derived her social role and property rights from the patriarchy, through identification with her father, she claimed her moral and spiritual heritage from her beloved mother, whom she consciously took as model: "By the bringing up of my said dear mother, I did, as it were, even suck the milk of goodness, which made my mind strong against the storms of fortune."[42] Anne's memoir of her "saint-like" mother mingles hagiographic reverence with some precise description of her person and character—her "high spirit" bridled only by grace and civility, her good intellect and education, her interest in alchemy, the love she inspired from the worthy:

She was naturally of an high spirit, though she tempered it well by grace, having a very well favoured face with sweet and quick grey eyes, and of a comely personage. She was of a gracefull behaviour, which she increased the more by her being civil and courteous to all sorts of people. She had a discerning spirit, both into the disposition of humane creatures and natural causes, and into the affairs of the world. She had a great sharp natural wit, so as there was few worthy knowledge but she had some insight into them. For though she had no language but her own, yet was there few books of worth translated into English but she read them, whereby that excellent mind of hers was much enriched, which even by nature was endowed with the seeds of the four moral virtues, Prudence, Justice, Fortitude, and Temperance. She was a lover of the study and practice of alchimy, by which she found out excellent medicines, that did much good to many . . . She was dearly beloved by those of her freinds and acquaintance that had excellent witts and were worthy and good folks . . . [She] was truly religious, devout and conscientious, even from her very childhood, and did spend much time in reading the Scriptures and other good books, and in heavenly meditations and in prayers, fastings, and deeds of charity.[43]

Anne was profoundly grateful to her mother for beginning and carrying forward the lawsuits in her behalf, and admired her enormously for her "quiet mind in the midst of all her griefs and troubles" and her exemplary courage and firmness in opposing the patriarchal power structure in her daughter's cause:

In which suit she met with great oppositions, even from King James himself, who then reigned, and professed himself to be against her, and from some of the greatest men of power of that time in the kingdom; in which business she shewed she had a spirit too great to yeild to fortune or opposition, further than necessity compelled her to it; and so much constancy, wisdom, and resolution did she shew in that business that the like can hardly be paralleled by any woman.[44]

An exchange of letters between them in 1614–1616, when Margaret Clifford was in Westmoreland living on her jointure estates, reveals Margaret's role as primary strategist, comrade in arms, and emotional support for her daughter. Margaret's long letter of September 22, 1615, is typical:

You writ wisely and I fear too truly for the king and queen, whom you might have had in a more favorable sort, but it was one of your Lord and his friends strategems . . . I have written another [letter] to be delivered to them [the judges] . . . it were best by yourself, if my Lord's [Dorset's] tyranny let it not. Well it seems he hath not tasted of true spiritual comforts that so much forgets that saying of the apostle, he is worse than an infidel that provides not for his wife and family. Then he that hath not a heart to defend their rights, wants the true spirit of God . . . Lay all on me and neither cross him in words but keep your resolutions with silence and what gentle persuasion you can, but alter not from your own wise course . . . You have written to Masters Crackenthorpe which letter was opened by chance, that whether my Lord would let you or not, if I would have you come [to visit her in the North] you would come against his will. Dear heart be very wary what you say but most wary what you write for they desire to have advantage and to sever my Lord and you, as they let me from my Lord, for you are too near me in resemblance, not of faces but of fortune, which God make better, and me thankful that hath and does overcome in God, which he in mercy grant that you may do in the end.[45]

Anne's letters to her mother mingle filial reverence with conspiratorial address, often registering as well Anne's anxiety and emotional travail. In early 1615 she pleads her emotional state to excuse her failure to send a New Year's gift of handiwork to her mother: "I had nether lesuer to worke, or doe aney thing ellse, but weepe and greeve." In November of that year she reports that Dorset is pressing her hard, "but by the power of God I will continue resolout and constant"; later that month she complains of sore eyes from her constant griefs and terrors. Caught between loyalties, she urges her mother to a better opinion of Dorset, assuring her that he is a "very kind loving and deare father, and in every thing will I commende him, saving in this busnis of my Land, wher in I thinke some evil speret workes for in this he is as vialent as is possable." In late January 1616 she is clearly desperate: "I beecich [beseech] you sende me an annser with as much speede as you can, for I shall bee earnestly prest to doe it [accept the terms of the will] or else absolutley to denie it, which will make cich [such] a breche betwin my Lorde and mee, as will not esely be mended. I will doe nothing without your Ladyship's knollege."[46] A letter of April 26, 1616, to her mother agonizes over the conflict of loyalties:

What so ever you think of my Lorde, yet I have founde him, doe finde him, and thinke shall find him, the best and most worthest man that ever brethed, therfore, if it bee possible I beecich you have a beter opinion of him, if you knew all I doe, I am shuer you would beeleve this that I writ; but I durst not impart my mind when I was with you, bicause I found you so biter against him; or ellse I coud have told you so many arguments of his goodnis and worthe, that you shold have seene it planley your selfe.[47]

But she seems now to have attained some emotional equilibrium by recognizing the limits of possible resistance: "Bee assured that I will stande as constantley to my berthe right, as is possable for mee; but I can doe no more than I can, ther fore I can promes you no sortinty [certainty] of thes maters."[48]

Reinforcing Anne Clifford's sense of a matrilineal heritage was her perception of uncanny parallels between her mother's life and her own: their childhood residence in Northamptonshire, "which caused that mother and daughter ever after to love a country life";[49] their childlessness in early marriage; their joint projects—the family chronicles, the lawsuits, the almshouses. She also saw her elder daughter, Margaret, as a near-replica of Margaret Clifford "[She] grose [grows] everey day more like your Ladyship"; "My chillde your Litell selfe, is well I thanke God."[50] She had great confidence in Margaret's maternal protection, manifested in her prayers and prophetic powers. An example was Margaret's "divining dream" predicting that her as-yet-unborn daughter Anne would outlive her two brothers to inherit the ancestral lands—evidence, Anne thought, that her mother "had more converse with heaven . . . than with terrene and earthly matters," though the matter of the dream was the very earthly business of Anne's inheritance.[51]

Anne's efforts in autobiography and diary keeping may also have been fostered by Margaret Clifford, who herself wrote a brief introspective autobiography in a letter to her chaplain, Dr. Layfield.[52] Organized into seven decades, this poignant and melancholy "Seven Ages of Woman" represents Margaret Clifford's life under two metaphors—a dance (with backward and forward movements) and a pilgrimage of grief, inexplicably breaking off after the fifth decade, in 1589. The clerical addressee may partially explain Margaret's passive stance, as one buffeted by and patiently enduring the chances and changes of fortune; there is little sign here of the high spirits Anne attributes to her. Anne celebrated her matrilineal heritage by erecting several splendid monuments to Margaret Clifford: a statue in Appleby town, an octagonal obelisk by the side of the highway near Brougham Castle marking the place Anne said her last farewell to her mother in 1616; and a magnificent alabaster tomb in Appleby Church with a beautifully executed, life-size effigy.[53]

Anne also found some maternal protection and example in a larger female community. She spent some part of her childhood in the country (Lillford, Northamptonshire) with her great-aunt, Mrs. Alice Elmes, but had her "chief breeding" under her maternal aunt Anne (Russell) Dudley, Countess of Warwick, who was, she notes, "more beloved and in greater favour with the said Queen [Elizabeth] than any other lady or woman of the kingdom." This Countess, her other Russell aunt, Elizabeth, Countess of Bath, and her mother were, she observes with obvious pride, "the most remarkable ladys for their greatness and goodness of any three sisters in the kingdom."[54] In this female protective network Anne includes Queen Elizabeth, by whom she was "much beloved" as a child owing to her aunt's patronage. She also includes Queen Anne, who, she claims, "was ever in-clyneing to our part, and very gratious and favourable to us" in the controversies over the lands, thanks to early associations: "In my youth I was much in the Courte with her, and in Maskes attended her, though I never served her."[55]

Books and learning were also of primary importance to Anne Clifford's self-definition and her resistance. Anne's childhood governess was Mrs. Anne Taylor, and her tutor was the poet Samuel Daniel, who evidently joined the household sometime between 1595 and 1599. Account books indicate that she had a dancing master, that she was taught French and music, and that she participated in the craze for raising silkworms.[56] Her good education in "true religion and moral virtue and all other qualities befitting her birth" she attributes to her mother and to her mother's "chief agent" Daniel—"that religious and honest poet who composed the *Civil Wars of England*." Summarizing, she comments that she "was not admitted to learn any language, because her father would not permit it; but for all other knowledge fit for her sex none was bred up to greater perfection than she."[57] This evidently meant no Latin, since records show that she studied French, at least for a time. Her comment contains no open protest, yet in ascribing that prohibition so pointedly to her father, she invites the inference that she herself, her mother (whose education was similarly restricted), and perhaps Daniel did not share the prevalent notion that Latin was inappropriate for women.

It is not clear what other limitations she (apparently) accepted as "fit for her sex," but the Clifford "Great Picture" offers some indication of both the scope and the emphases of her reading—the best such record we have from a noblewoman of the period.[58] The left-hand panel depicts her at age fifteen with her lute and a considerable library of neatly arranged books, evidently texts she studied and valued as a young girl. Religion, philosophy, and science are represented by the Bible, Augustine's *City of God*, John Downame's *Christian Warfare*, the *Works* of Joseph Hall, the *Manual* of Epictetus, Boethius' *Consolation of Philosophy*, Gerard's *Herball*, Cornelius Agrippa's *Vanity of Sciences*, and Loys de Roy's *Variety of Things*. Several works of history and geography may reflect Daniel's influence: Eusebius' *History of the Church*, Camden's *Britannia*, Daniel's prose *Chronicle of England*, and Abraham Ortelius' *Maps of the World*. The rest is literature, especially romance and fiction: Ovid's *Metamorphoses*, Castiglione's *Courtier*, Montaigne's *Essays*, Cervantes's *Don Quixote*, the three parts of the *French Academy*, all of Chaucer's and Spenser's works, and Sidney's *Arcadia*. The right-hand panel depicts Anne at fifty-three with the books evidently im-

portant to her then, depicted in considerable disarray as if in constant use.
Religion and moral philosophy predominate: the Bible, Henry More's
Map of Mortalitie, Henry Cuff's *Age of Man's Life,* Bishop Henry King's
Sermons, William Astin's meditations and devotions, Donne's *Sermons,*
George Stroude's *Book of Death,* George Hakewell's *Apologie of the Providence and Power of God.* The moral philosophy is Stoic: Antonius' *Meditations,* Plutarch's *Morals,* and a translation of Pierre Charron's *Book of Wisdom.* Her interest in history is now represented by Guicciardini (in French
translation) and an English translation of Philippe de Comines's *History;*
her new interest in biography by Plutarch's *Lives;* and her great concern
with building by Henry Wotton's *Book of Architecture.* The literary works
reflect both current tastes and good judgment: Donne's Poems, Jonson's
Workes, Herbert's *Temple,* Fulke Greville's *Works,* John Barclay's *Argenis,*
George Sandys's poetic version of the Psalms and other biblical poems.

Neither circumstance nor (apparently) inclination led Anne to become
a major literary patron, though in her youth her mother's clients designate
her Margaret Clifford's heir as paragon of virtue and patron of serious
literary and theological works. Margaret's chief literary clients included
Spenser, Daniel, Thomas Lodge, Robert Greene, Henry Lok, and the female poet Aemilia Lanyer, who attributed her religious conversion and
poetic vocation to some period spent with Margaret and Anne at the
country estate of Cookham in Berkshire.[59] Among her theologian clients
were William Perkins, Richard Greenham, Thomas Saville, Samuel Hieron, and Peter Muffett.[60] Samuel Daniel's verse epistle (1603) to his erstwhile pupil Anne emphasizes the complexity of the role she has inherited
and challenges her to learn how to balance the virtuous actions belonging
to greatness with the limitations imposed by female nature and the fallen
state:

> Nor may you build on your sufficiency,
> For in our strongest partes we are but weake,
> Nor yet may over-much distrust the same,
> Lest that you come to checke it so thereby,
> As silence may become worse then to speake;
> Though silence women never ill became.[61]

Daniel's dedicatory sonnet of 1607 invites Anne to take up the role of
literary patroness, "I know you love the Muses, and you will / Be a most
faithfull Guardian and a just." So does Lanyer's long dedicatory poem in
Salve Deus, which emphasizes Anne's maternal legacy of virtue, beauty,
delight in the Word of God, and especially bounty (of which Lanyer not
very subtly proposes herself as recipient).[62] In the same year the young

theologian Anthony Stafford prefixed his *contemptus mundi* treatise *Staffords Niobe* with a wildly effusive dedication to Anne, professing such "astonishment" at her seeming perfection and sinlessness (surpassing Eve) that he almost commits the blasphemy of giving "as much honour and praise, to the Architecture as to the Architect."[63] The hyperbole in this bid for patronage from Dorset or from Anne does not surpass what we find in some of Donne's or Drayton's praises, but someone (perhaps Dorset) evidently thought it smacked of scandal or bad taste and had the dedication excised from all but one of the extant copies. If Anne did not imitate her mother as literary patron, she did pay special tribute to writers closely associated with the family. She honored her old tutor Daniel by introducing a portrait of him into the Great Picture, terming him "a man of Upright and excellent Spirit, as appeared by his Works." She also erected a tomb for him in Beckington Church (Somersetshire) with an inscription to "that Excellent Poett and Historian." In 1620 she erected a monument in Westminster Abbey for her mother's literary client Spenser, proclaiming him "THE PRINCE OF POETS IN HIS TYME / WHOSE DIVINE SPIRRIT / NEEDS NOE OTHIR WITNESSE / THEN THE WORKS WHICH HE LEFT BEHINDE HIM."[64]

Several associates testify to Anne Clifford's lively wit and broad intellectual interests. Donne, a client of Dorset's, who met her at Knole when visiting his benefice at nearby Sevenoaks, reportedly observed "that she knew well how to discourse of all things, from Predestination to Sleasilk"—evidently meaning that her learning and conversation ranged freely from female domestic matters to complex theological doctrine.[65] Sedgwick and Rainbowe emphasize her "great sharpness of Wit, a faithful Memory, and deep Judgment"; her "ability to discourse in all Commendable Arts and Sciences . . . with Virtuoso's, Travellers, Scholars, Merchants, Divines, States-men, and with Good Housewives in any kind"; her "library stored with very choise books"; and her "indefatigable" reading, especially in vernacular history and Scripture.[66] Rainbowe describes her rather amusing transformation of her bedchamber into a species of commonplace book, to serve as subjects of discourse for herself and her servants:

> She would frequently bring out of the rich Store-house of her Memory, things new and old, Sentences, or Sayings of remark, which she had read or learned out of Authors and with these her Walls, her Bed, her Hangings, and Furniture must be adorned; causing her Servants to write them in Papers, and her Maids to pin them up, that she, or they, in the time of their dressing, or as occasion served, might re-

member, and make their discants on them. So that, though she had not many Books in her Chamber, yet it was dressed up with the flowers of a Library.[67]

Unfortunately, she does not comment on the books she read. But we can infer something of what they meant to her from a remarkable letter of 1649 to the Dowager Countess of Kent, in which she associates herself with Selden in a common love of Chaucer and perhaps acknowledges the loan of his works, which she had read earlier at Knole:

> My love and service to worthy Mr. Selden, and tell him if I hade nott exelent Chacor's booke heere to comfortt mee I wer in a pitifull case, having so manny trubles as I have, butt when I rede in that I scorne and make litte of tham alle, and a little partt of his devine sperett infusses itt selfe in mee.[68]

It would be fascinating to know what she found so inspiriting in Chaucer: the *Legend of Good Women?* patient Griselda? the Wife of Bath? Whatever it was, she here appropriates her literary patrimony as boldly as she did her ancestral lands, echoing Spenser as she claims empowerment through the infusion of Chaucer's spirit.[69]

The Diary

Anne Clifford's *Diary* evidently served as a primary means of self-definition for her. She seems to have kept some kind of journal throughout her life, though most of the originals have been lost or destroyed except for a few entries for the last months of her life. The Jacobean *Diary* exists in two later copies, with entries for the years 1603, 1616–1617, and 1619 (the year 1618 is omitted). When its implications are teased out, this work offers an illuminating female perspective on Jacobean society, as well as on the development of one Jacobean woman's sense of self as she confronted and reflected on her own experience.

Recent theoretical and historical investigation has underscored the blurred generic boundaries between such forms as diary, memoir, letters, and formal autobiography in early modern England, and the emergence of self-conscious introspection in the spiritual diaries and autobiographies which flourished chiefly after the Restoration.[70] In the sixteenth and early seventeenth centuries diary keeping was common enough, but most extant diaries record the external duties and activities pertaining to men's public roles—travel diaries, military diaries, sea logs, astrologers' diaries, political records. The few domestic diaries, notably by Lady Margaret Hoby and Lady Grace (Sherrington) Mildmay, record women's household and family activities.[71] Such diaries focus on personal experience, but almost never contain intimate self-revelation. While Anne Clifford's *Diary* in some respects conforms to this norm, it also offers analytic comments and descriptions of her emotions, motives, and judgments of people and events. Except for Simon Forman's diary,[72] hers is the only English secular diary I know that does so at this early date.

By definition the diary is a private genre, yet it seems likely from the format that Anne intended hers ultimately for the Clifford chronicles; she may have decided to preserve the segment we have as a record for posterity of her most momentous years in the struggle over her lands. Although we do not have her original, the distinctive layout in the two manuscript copies is not likely to be the copyists' invention.[73] The text of the *Diary* is a running account focused chiefly on her own doings and family affairs, with very sporadic reference to public matters. In the wide margins surrounding that text on both sides is another running commentary (in the same voice though clearly added later) which partly expands upon the personal story, but also interweaves many more events from the larger social and public worlds—births, deaths, marriages, separations, court appointments, major scandals, public affairs—often introduced by the formula "About this time."[74]

The margins record, but do not expand upon, such events as these: Buckingham sworn of the Bedchamber; the Countess of Somerset sent prisoner to the Tower; the appointment of Sir John Digby as Vice-Chamberlain and Sir John Oliver as Lord Deputy of Ireland; the birth of Lady Montgomery's first son, Prince Charles created Prince of Wales; the death of Lord Chancellor Egerton; Marquis Damse slain in France, "which bred great alterations there"; expectations (in 1617) of a match for Prince Charles with Spain; Queen Anne at Greenwich and Oatlands during King James's trip to Scotland; "a great stir about my Lady *Hatton's* daughter—my Brother Sackville undertaking to carry her away with men and horses"; Sir John Digby on a long-expected journey to Spain; Lady Rich brought to bed of her first son and afterwards afflicted with small-pox; the death of Lord Cobham, "the last of the three that was condemned for the first conspiracy against the King at his first coming into England"; the Countess of Suffolk stricken with smallpox "which spoiled that good face of hers, which had brought to others much misery and to herself greatness which ended with much unhappiness"; the King's "fit of the stone" while the court ladies watched by the Queen's corpse; Barnwelt beheaded at the Hague, "which is like to breed alteration for the best for this man hath long been a secret friend to the Spaniards and an enemy to the English"; Lord Doncaster's mission to Germany to mediate the Bohemian crisis; Star Chamber proceedings against Lord and Lady Suffolk.

By adding the marginalia at some later stage, Anne Clifford seems to have sought to locate and position her own story more firmly within the larger drama of events. At the same time, the format asserts the significance of the personal narrative: it holds the center while the public and social world are (quite literally) marginalized. Anne Clifford's *Diary* provides an intriguing perspective on the engagement of personal experience with patriarchal ideology, and on the relation between authoring a text and authoring a self. While her later writings represent Anne as an assured, stable woman with a firm sense of personal worth, her Jacobean *Diary* presents that identity in process, constrained by powerful and complex social forces but struggling toward some limited redefinition of her female self, rights, and place in the world.

The year 1603 is presented in retrospect. The entries capture the wide-eyed thirteen-year-old girl's impressions of the flurry of court activity surrounding Queen Elizabeth's funeral and James I's coronation, at the same time supplying a more mature perspective on the changes these events brought about for her and her family. They highlight Anne's excitement and her personal disappointments, great and small. By Queen Elizabeth's death she missed her chance of preferment to the Privy Chamber through her aunt Warwick's good offices, "for at that time there was as much hope and expectation of me as of any other young lady whatsoever" (*Diary*, 3). She was held "too young" to join her mother and aunt and "a great company of lords and ladies" in the nocturnal watches by the Queen's corpse; and she was not allowed to be a mourner, "because I was not high enough, which did much trouble me then" (4–5). She was admitted to the church at Westminster for the splendid funeral, but forbidden to attend James I's coronation "because the plague was hot in London."[75] Her graphic description of the universal jockeying for position in those weeks highlights the Russell sisters' fears of their declining influence at court: "My Mother being all full of hopes, every man expecting mountains and finding mole-hills, excepting Sir R. *Cecil* and the house of the *Howards*, who hated my Mother and did not much love my Aunt Warwick" (5). She herself joined her mother, her aunt, and the other court ladies in rushing to Berwick-upon-Tweed to meet Queen Anne en route from Scotland, killing "three horses that one day with extremity of heat" (7). She observes, however, that the Countess of Bedford got there first, and that her star was in the ascendant: "[She] was so great a woman with the Queen as everybody much respected her, she having attended the Queen out of *Scotland*" (8).

Anne's account registers her delight in assuming a role among the court women—recording court gossip, visiting various palaces and country houses in attendance upon the Queen and the Princess Elizabeth.[76] But these great affairs play off against the strained domestic situation: Cumberland "had at this time as it were wholly left my Mother." She reports Margaret's presence at the magnificent entertainment he laid on at Grafton for the King and court, though she was "not held as mistress of the house, by reason of the difference between my Lord and her, which was grown to a great height" (10). She notes that when her parents met by chance in their roles as courtiers, "their countenance did show the dislike they had one of the other," and comments rather plaintively on her own uncomfortable situation: "Yet he would speak to me in a slight fashion and give me his blessing" (14). One remarkable entry proudly describes George Clifford exercising at York his hereditary right to carry the sword before the King, culminating with Anne's quite astonishing claim to the same privilege: "Because it was an office by inheritance . . . it lineally descended to me" (6). Whenever these events were written up, they are viewed through the prism of Anne's property claims.

The *Diary* resumes again in January 1616 with the intervening years and the year 1618 lost, or never written, or excised. These entries are contemporaneous with the events recorded; they set forth periodically though not daily Anne's activities and her relations with her husband and child, her mother, her Russell and Clifford relatives, her society, and the court. The controlling motif throughout is her protracted struggle, sustained only by her own determination, a few allies, and the help of God, against the demands from all sides (and especially from Dorset) that she relinquish her claims to the lands. She sees herself holding out against the entire power structure—though without the certitude of providential care and ultimate victory so prominent in her later memoirs.

Entries for early 1616 report several scenes of high drama as well as private encounters with well-intentioned advisers whose kindness made them especially difficult to withstand. On February 16 her Russell kinsman Francis, afterwards fourth Earl of Bedford, who was "exceedingly careful and kind to me" throughout the troubles, "came to me . . . and chid me and told me of all my faults and errors in this business; he made me weep bitterly."[77] On February 17 she reports a formal scene staged to intimidate, a visit from a phalanx of male kinsmen on both sides reinforced by the Archbishop of Canterbury:

> Upon the 17th my Lord Archbishop of *Canterbury,* my Lord *William Howard,* my Lord *Rous,* my Coz. *Russell,* my Brother *Sackville* and a great company of men . . . were all in the Gallery of *Dorset House* where the Archbishop took me aside and talked with me privately one hour and half and persuaded me both by Divine and human means to set my hand to their arguments. But my answer to his Lordship was that I would do nothing till my Lady and I had conferred

together. Much persuasion was used by him and all the company,
sometimes terrifying me and sometimes flattering me, but at length
it was concluded that I should have leave to go to my Mother and
send an answer by the 22nd of March next, whether I will agree to
this business or not.

Next day was a marvellous day to me through the mercy of God,
for it was generally thought that I must either have sealed to the
argument or else have parted with my Lord.   (19–20)

That entry registers her belief that she had managed to escape total surrender or the break-up of her marriage only by pleading the necessity to con-
fer with her mother, then resident in Westmoreland.

Entries during that visit in March and April point up Margaret's vital
role as adviser, and the strategies the two ladies developed to cope with
exigencies. On March 20 they sent back a direct refusal of the judges'
award, to which Dorset responded by commanding that his servants return to London without Anne. The ladies then drafted a letter to the effect
that Anne was obeying Dorset rather than her own wishes in staying, lest
she be charged with deserting her husband;[78] but after "much talk" for
two nights, they determined that she should return anyway, to avoid if
possible an open separation. As a further delaying tactic, Anne left with
her mother the papers she was supposed to sign. She records her "grevious
and heavy parting" with Margaret Clifford, and when she returned had
but a "cold welcome" from Dorset (23).

Diary entries for the following months recount Dorset's escalating persecution of his wife to force her to accept the proposed monetary settlement. At the beginning of May he threatened to leave her forever and
banish her from his residences. Then he ordered that their child be sent to
him in London; Anne thought of refusing, "but when I considered that it
would both make my Lord more angry with me and be worse for the
Child, I resolved to let her go . . . and wept bitterly" (25–26). But there
was worse to come: on May 9 Dorset wrote that "the Child should go live
at *Horseley* [with her Dorset aunts], and not come hither any more so as
this was a very grievous and sorrowful day to me." She wrote begging that
she might go to Horsely also, and not "to the Little House that was appointed for me," but this was refused (26–31). The *Diary* also records her
mounting anxiety during May over conflicting reports regarding her
mother's health, and finally, on May 29, reports "the heavy news of my
Mother's death which I held as the greatest and most lamentable cross that
could have befallen me" (29–32). The emotional pressure of April and May
must have been nearly unbearable, but these entries do not suggest des-
peration or nervous collapse.

Margaret Clifford's death made for a temporary rapproachment of interests between husband and wife, as Dorset sought to enhance their bar-
gaining position vis-à-vis the Cliffords by taking possession of the Westmoreland properties in Anne's name. He urged Anne to designate him as
her heir, assuring her "how kind and good a husband he would be to me";
she agreed but stipulated the clause "if I had no heirs of my own body"—
thus ensuring her daughter's rights (33–35). She traveled north to take
possession; Dorset followed soon after; and the child was restored to her,
"so that my Lord and I were never greater friends than at this time." Dorset also promised that he would make her "a jointure of the full thirds of
his living," and showed her a new will leaving virtually everything to the
child—"a matter I little expected" (37–39).

Anne reports graphically the crisis of Christmastide 1616–17, as the King
determined to settle the matter between Anne and the Clifford heirs. Dorset saw his interest in accepting the proposed financial settlement, and
Anne reports pressure from all sides to give over: "All this time of my
being at *London* I was much sent to, and visited by many, being unexpected that ever matters should have gone so well with me and my Lord,
everybody persuading me to hear and make an end."[79] She thankfully
takes note, however, of a few female partisans, some limited female soli-
darity.[80] Among them she counts the Queen, carefully recording her sur-
prisingly frank counsel: "[The Queen] promised me she would do all the
good in it she could . . . [and] gave me warning not to trust my matters
absolutely to the King lest he should deceive me" (48–49).

Whether or not the Queen exercised herself any further in this matter,
Anne Clifford acted on her shrewd advice in her meetings with James. The
entry of January 18 reports a dramatic private meeting with him:

> My Lord *Buckingham* . . . brought us into the King, being in the
> Drawing Chamber. He put out all that were there and my Lord and
> I kneeled by his chair sides when he persuaded us both to peace and
> to put the whole matter wholly into his hands, which my Lord con-
> sented to, but I beseech't His Majesty to pardon me for that I would
> never part from *Westmoreland* while I lived upon any condition what-
> soever. Sometimes he used fair means and persuasions and sometimes
> foul means but I was resolved before so as nothing would move me
> . . . All this time I was much bound to my Lord for he was far kinder
> to me in all these businesses than I expected, and was very unwilling
> that the King should do me any public disgrace.   (48–49)

On the twentieth, the formal session with the King went forward. Anne's
lively description of the scene registers her sense of being confronted with

an awesome assemblage of powerful men: the King, the Chief Justice, several peers holding court office, lawyers, the Cliffords, and Dorset. It also intimates some female support (or at least comfort) from the Countess of Bedford and Lady Ruthven:

> I went to my aunt *Bedford* in her lodging where I stay'd in Lady *Ruthven's* chamber till towards 8 o'clock about which time I was sent for up to the King into his Drawing Chamber when the door was lock'd and nobody suffered to stay here but my Lord and I, my Uncle *Cumberland,* my Coz. *Clifford,* my Lords *Arundel, Pembroke Montgomery,* Sir *John Digby.* For lawyers there were my Lord Chief Justice *Montague* and *Hobart Yelverton* the King's Solicitor, Sir *Randal Crewe* that was to speak for my Lord and I. The King asked us all if we would submit to his judgment in this case. My Uncle *Cumberland,* my Coz. *Clifford,* and my Lord answered that they would, but I would never agree to it without *Westmoreland* at which the King grew in a great chaff. My lord of *Pembroke* and the King's Solicitor speaking much against me, at last when they saw there was no remedy, my Lord fearing the King would do me some public disgrace, desired Sir *John Digby* would open the door, who went out with me and persuaded me much to yield to the King . . . Presently after my Lord came from the King when it was resolved that if I would not come to an agreement there should be an agreement made without me.
>
> (50–51)

Anne read this outcome as a victory—"Neither I nor anybody else thought I should have passed over this day so well as I have done"—for which she gives credit to those other patriarchs, God and her husband. She had managed to maintain her cause "led miraculously by God's Providence"; and she was saved from public disgrace at the King's hands when Dorset orchestrated her timely departure.

During the next several months as the matter hung fire, Anne records great emotional distress: she often found her soul "much troubled and afflicted" upon hearing "how much I was condemned in the world and what strange censures most folks made of my courses"; but she sought comfort from God "that always helped me," and from history—reading the family chronicles and comparing "things past with things present" (52–56). Dorset intensified his pressure to get her signature to the agreement (upon which his receipt of the full financial settlement depended). Anne often reports "a falling out about the land,"[81] but on April 17 she records with relief, "My Lord told me he was resolved never to move me more in these businesses, because he saw how fully I was bent" (64). That resolution broke down by Easter, when there was again a "great falling out," leading to strained marital relations: "This night my Lord should have lain with me, but he and I fell out about matters" (65). In May she felt especially beleaguered, hearing that Dorset had canceled her jointure and that "all *Westmoreland* was surrender'd to my Uncle *Cumberland*," with her Russell relatives agreeing to the settlement. In June she reports herself "extremely melancholy and sad" when Dorset proposed to leave all his land to his brother, "away from the Child" (68–72). July 3 she spent "weeping the most part of the day seeing my enemies had the upper hand of me"; and on July 9 she received the King's award, which was "as ill for me as possible" (72). Though the settlement was taken to be final, Anne preserved her legal claim (especially to the rights of reversion) by steadfastly refusing her signature. The following November she notes with some relief the King's "gracious" reception, removing the threat his continued enmity would pose to her social standing.[82]

In her *Diary* Anne sees herself as a loving wife who is forced to endure great suffering at the hands of her husband and much of society, but takes considerable pride in resisting the compliance demanded. She justifies her resistance in terms of the paradigm provided by Foxe's female martyrs, enacting a secular and self-interested version of their patient endurance and firm adherence to the right. The entry of April 5, 1617, shows her self-conscious adoption of this stance: "Sometimes I had fair words from him and sometimes foul, but I took all patiently, and did strive to give him as much content and assurance of my love as I could possibly, yet I told him I would never part with *Westmoreland* upon any condition whatever" (62).

Several cryptic diary entries suggest that her distress was exacerbated by the continued enmity of Matthew Caldicott, Dorset's favorite retainer: her note that they once lived privately at Buckhurst for several days probably implies a homosexual relationship (82). On Whitsunday, June 8, 1617, the matter reached a crisis: "My eyes were so blubbered with weeping I could scarce look up, and in the afternoon we fell out about *Mathew*"; the next day she took the extraordinary step of writing "to the Bishop of *London* against Matthew" (70–72). She seems to have won that round: some weeks later Matthew was suing for her forgiveness through Dr. Rann, the chaplain, and after complaining that she had received "so many injuries from him that I could hardly forget them," she sent word that "as I was a Christian I would forgive him" (73–76).

Another crisis occurred at Easter 1619, when she evidently felt herself so far out of charity with her husband and "so troubled as I held not myself fit to receive the Communion." She saw it as a special kindness that Dorset postponed the communion for the entire household, and responded to her concern about her financial insecurity after the cancellation of her jointure by "protesting to me that he would be a very good husband to me and that I should receive no prejudice by releasing my thirds."[83] Her anxiety was probably exacerbated by Dorset's increasingly public relationship with Lady Penniston, which was "much talked of abroad and my Lord was condemned for it."[84] In these weeks she often reports being "sad and melancholy," complaining to Dorset "how good he was to everybody else and how unkind to me."[85] After falling ill in late October 1619, she makes a point of the fact that she never left her own bedchamber until the following March—a gesture that seems to have been motivated by a wish to define in this small way the terms of her own life and to force Dorset to come to her. On December 18, after another "great falling out," he "came and supped with me in my chamber . . . for I determined to keep my chamber and did not so much as go over the threshold of the door" (108–109).

She obviously accepts as a fact of life that Dorset's interests, needs, and concerns are quite different from her own, that he will have affairs, that his wife and daughter are a relatively small part of his life—no doubt finding here some reprise of her own parents' domestic situation. While she laments his behavior to her, she does not question that it is authorized by his place as her husband and lord. She also seems to care for him—rejoicing in the occasions when he "came to lie in my chamber," keeping her tenth anniversary "as a day of jubilee"—and this attachment heightens the emotional cost of resisting his wishes (58, 65, 88). Remarkably, these attitudes subsist with a clear perception that she cannot trust Dorset to look out for her interests and those of her child—and a dogged determination to do this herself as best she can. The effort to confront and express these complex feelings in the *Diary* was surely a major factor in developing her sense of identity and self-worth.

The *Diary* also shows how Anne's relationship with her daughter contributed to her emerging sense of herself as positioned in a female line reaching from her mother to herself to the young Margaret. She certainly recognized that her status would be enhanced as the mother of a son and heir to Dorset, but she never expresses such a desire, though she reports possible pregnancies.[86] Instead, she seems to take on her own mother's role, concerned to raise an only daughter and secure her inheritance.[87] She refers to her daughter as "the Child" until her fifth birthday (July 2, 1619), and after that always by name and title, "my lady Margaret," apparently recognizing that day as marking the end of infancy.[88] Diary entries record Anne's grief when Dorset takes the child from her, and her joy at the girl's return (25–27, 36). They also register anxieties over the child's illnesses. During her bitter fits of "the ague" in 1617 Anne "could hardly sleep all night"; and in 1619 she worried about "some distemper in her head" which produced alarming effects: "My Lady *Margaret's* speech was very ill so as strangers cannot understand her, besides she was so apt to take cold and so out of temper that it grieved me to think of it" (51–54, 82, 110). Anne also records carefully the small milestones in her daughter's life: her visits to London in December 1616, "where my Lord Treasurer and all the company commended her"; the days (January 23 and April 28, 1617) when she first "put on her red baize coats" and "a pair of whalebone bodice"; the falls she had when her leading strings were cut (May 1); the day (June 22) that she had her hair trimmed by Adam the barber (51, 66, 72). Unfortunately, Anne does not indicate what arrangements she made for the child's education.

The *Diary* also offers some insight into the activities and interests important to Anne in these years—her sense of her place in the larger culture. When in London (at Dorset House) she reports her enjoyment of social functions, music, masques, plays, and art, though she seldom mentions particular works (17–20, 43–51, 78–85). She notes the burning of the Banqueting House at Whitehall and gives several entries to the death of Queen Anne, at whose funeral occasions she was a chief mourner (84, 93–102). But there is little of the lively reportage of 1603: her interpretive powers are engaged almost entirely by her own concerns, revealing, perhaps, the psychic cost of her constant struggle. Though she took part in a few mixed gatherings, her social activities chiefly revolved around a female court circle—the ladies Ralegh, Carr, Rich, Grey, Arundel, Derby, and Carey—with whom she exchanged visits, went to masques and dinners, played Glecko and other card games, and attended upon the Queen (43–51, 78–85). Following her mother's direction, she tried to play the politics of the female court: cultivating ladies in places of influence and sending the expected New Year's gifts and other lavish presents to the Queen, on one occasion "the skirts of a white satin gown all pearled and embroidered with colours which cost me four score pounds without the satin."[89]

While in exile at Knole, she recorded her quotidian domestic activities: small exercises of local patronage; occasional visits from and to the Sackville and Russell relations and various friends, including the Sidneys from nearby Penshurst;[90] the card games, especially Glecko, which she played with the household staff when aristocratic company was unavailable; the occasional new gown worn "because I was found fault with for wearing such ill clothes"; the constant needlework, always executed while one of her staff read aloud. She does not indicate whether she thought as well of Donne as he of her, but she made special note of the week (July 20–27, 1617) he preached at Sevenoaks and dined with her.[91] Occasionally the disparity between Dorset's situation and her own elicits poignant complaint:

All this time my Lord was in *London* where he had all and infinite great resort coming to him. He went much abroad to Cocking, to Bowling Alleys, to Plays and Horse Races, and commended by all the world. I stayed in the country having many times a sorrowful and heavy heart, and being condemned by most folks because I would not consent to the agreements, so as I may truly say, I am like an owl in the desert.   (28)

Her careful record of the books she read or had read to her during these hard years indicates how important they were to her self-realization and resistance, though she does not comment on them. No reading is reported during the stressful early months of 1616, but from September of that year she read steadily: "a great part of the History of the Netherlands," Montaigne's *Essays,* the *Faerie Queene,* Sidney's *Arcadia,* as well as Sandys's *Government of the Turks,* and Chaucer. In March 1617 she began reading the Bible with the chaplain, Mr. Rann, but Dorset interrupted this project when he claimed Rann's services, telling her "it would hinder his study so as I must leave off reading the Old Testament till I can get somebody to read it with me" (60–61). It is not clear whether Anne, Rann, or Dorset thought these Old Testament books too difficult for a woman to read without help, or whether Anne simply wanted the benefit of Rann's learned commentary. On Good Friday she chose a book of preparation for the Sacrament, and in 1619 (the year of the Easter spiritual crisis) she was deep in religious literature: Saint Augustine's *City of God,* Parsons' *Resolutions,* "my Lady's Book of Praise of a solitary life" (a treatise by John Harington dedicated to Margaret Clifford),[92] and Saragol's *Supplication of the Saints* "which my Lord gave me" (91). But by late June she was ready for Ovid's *Metamorphoses,* and in December for Josephus (90–91, 104, 111). *Diary* entries of these years also reveal her continuous attention to the family history projects: her father's sea voyages, and "the Chronicles." These intellectual pursuits probably offered Anne some escape from her troubles, and perhaps also some vicarious imaginative experience of female resistance and power.

Anne Clifford's life and writings deliver a remarkable challenge to contemporary patriarchal ideology as she presses vigorously for her legal rights. The *Diary* presents a self in process, constrained by powerful social forces but struggling toward definition. In it Anne claims the importance of her own life and highlights the factors that (increasingly) empower her: an abiding belief in the rights and privileges of family and class; a strong maternal model and some sense of female community; a firm conviction that Divine Providence is engaged on her behalf; a stimulus to self-awareness and imagination through reading; and the act of writing itself, constructing self and world in language. The catalyst seems to have been struggle: she seems to see herself engaged in an almost mythic battle, against mighty odds and against every social pressure—a kind of female David taking on the Goliath of the patriarchal power structure to claim the rights of a daughter to certain patriarchal titles, privileges, and property, and to preserve the interests of a female line. Her later exercise of these rights was due largely to her good luck in outlasting all the men who stood in her way. But the *Diary* records the emergence of a female self able to resist existing social norms and to struggle for those rights. We find here not overt rebellion against patriarchy but a subversive re-writing in which Anne Clifford laid stubborn claim to a place of power within it.

A

MOVZELL FOR

MELASTOMVS,

The Cynicall Bayter of, and foule
mouthed *Barker against*
EVAHS SEX.

Or an Apologeticall Anſwere to
that Irreligious and Illiterate
Pamphlet made by *Io. Sw.* and by him
Intituled, *The Arraignement*
of Women.

By *Rachel Speght.*

PROVERBS 26. 5.
*Anſwer a foole according to his fooliſhneſſe, leſt he bee wiſe in
his owne conceit.*

LONDON,
Printed by *Nicholas Okes* for *Thomas Archer*, and
are to be ſold at his ſhop in Popes-
head-Pallace. 1617.

Title Page, Rachel Speght, A Mouzell for Melastomus (*1617*).

6 ❦

Defending Women's Essential Equality: Rachel Speght's Polemics and Poems

Rachel Speght's importance has been seriously underrated. A well-educated young woman of the London middle class, she was the first Englishwoman to identify herself, unmistakably and by name, as a polemicist and critic of contemporary gender ideology. She took manifest pride in her published foray into the Jacobean gender wars as well as in her poems: a long *memento mori* meditation, and an allegorical dream-vision that recounts her own rapturous encounter with learning and also defends women's education. Her family connections were with the clerical and medical professions in London: her father was rector of two London churches; her husband was also a minister; and her godmother was the wife of the renowned City and court physician who attended and aided Arbella Stuart. We know almost nothing about the life circumstances that empowered Speght to take on the roles of polemicist and poet, though her writings and their context afford some basis for speculation.

Speght (1597?–?) is usually discussed as the first of three female contributors to a rancorous Jacobean skirmish in the centuries-old *querelle des femmes,* or debate over the nature and worth of womankind.[1] As Joan Kelly and others have argued, some defenses of, and especially by, women, beginning with Christine de Pisan and Cornelius Agrippa, staked out important feminist ground in consciousness if not in action. They challenged misogynist stereotypes; offered positive images of female warriors, rulers, and scholars; and exposed male bias and interest in subjugating women.[2] But as Linda Woodbridge shows, throughout the English Renaissance the formal polemic controversy over women owed more to rhetorical convention than to ideological conviction or emotional involvement: in substance, these tracts (pro and con) recycled hoary arguments from the past;

in form they relied heavily on the judicial oration and the outrageous paradox.[3] Many if not most of the writers were participants in an ongoing game of wit played by men for their own and (they seem to have supposed) women's amusement.

The major Jacobean controversy was touched off by an anonymous attack, the rambling, boisterous, tonally confused but lively *Araignment of Lewde, idle, froward, and unconstant women* (1615). It is a jumble of proverb lore, rowdy jokes, invective, authorities, anecdotes, and exempla about women's lechery, vanity, shrewishness, and worthlessness, cobbled together from the entire tradition of misogynist writing. In the first printing the title page carried no name, and the epistolary preface was signed "Thomas Tel-troth"; Speght's tract claims the exploit of unmasking the author as one Joseph Swetnam, a fencing master.[4] Swetnam's prefatory epistles seem deliberately calculated to provoke responses from women or their defenders, in the spirit of the rhetorical game. He says he expects to be "bitten" by women, who will go about to "reprove" his book, but warns them not to answer lest they reveal their galled backs to the world; and he threatens women with a yet fiercer "second booke, which is almost ready." Such remarks, together with the disclaimer that "I wrote this book with my hand, but not my heart . . . my mouth uttered that in my fury, which my heart never thought," suggest an effort by author and bookseller to start a profitable controversy.[5] Swetnam needed no second book: this one proved popular enough to go through ten editions by 1634.

Two years later Rachel Speght published *A Mouzell* [muzzle] *for Melastomus* [black mouth] (1617), identifying herself by name on the title page. She presents herself as a serious, intelligent, religious young woman, not yet twenty, unmarried, with a sound education in those usually male subjects of grammar, rhetoric, logic, and Latin, who is doing battle as a female David with a polemic Goliath.[6] In the same year a second answer appeared—*Ester hath hang'd Haman*—under a female pseudonym, "Ester Sowernam" (punning on Swe[e]tnam); it is a lively and vigorous "arraignment" of Swetnam, turning his own legal metaphor against him. Adopting the persona of a mature, experienced woman "neither Maide, Wife nor Widdowe, yet really all, and therefore experienced to defend all," the author makes several condescending remarks about the "maid" Speght's inadequacies in life experience and in polemical argument.[7] A third response appeared later that year under the pseudonym "Constantia Munda," *The Worming of a mad Dogge: Or a Soppe for Cerberus the Jaylor of Hell;* as the title page asserts, this is not a defense of women but a "sharpe Redargution," or vigorous reproof, of Swetnam in the manner of Juvenalian invective. Whoever the author is, the tract offers a knowledgeable insider's comment on the ubiquitous libels about women produced by the debased popular press and the theater:

The itching desire of oppressing the presse with many sottish and illiterate Libels, stuft with all manner of ribaldry, and sordid inventions, when every foule-mouthed male-content may disgorge his *Licambaean* poyson in the face of all the world, hath broken out into such a dismall contagion in these our dayes, that every scandalous tongue and opprobrious witte, like the Italian Mountebankes will advance their pedling wares of detracting virulance in the publique *Piatza* of every Stationers shoppe . . . Every fantasticke Poetaster which thinkes he hath lickt the vomit of his *Coriphaeus* and can but patch a hobbling verse together, will strive to represent unsemmely figments imputed to our sex (as a pleasing theme to the vulgar) on the publique Theatre.[8]

In 1618 or 1619 an anonymous comedy (perhaps by Thomas Heywood), *Swetnam the Woman-hater, Arraigned by Women* (1620), alludes to and stages the entire controversy as a legal trial with judicial orations, and also as a battle. Misogynos (Swetnam) brings charges against women; the Amazon Atlanta (really the male soldier Lorenzo in disguise) defends them but loses the day, denouncing the partiality of the all-male judge and jury. Subsequently Misogynos is tricked and turned over to a court of women who reveal his identity, convict him, muzzle and torment him.[9] The drama highlights that aspect of the controversy in which men devise female characters or personae to defend women, and also the moment at which women take their defense into their own hands; it also develops the theme of effeminate men bested by aggressive women.

The motif of aggressive women and gender ambiguity was explored in a related series of tracts in these years, focusing on what seems to have become a fad of female cross-dressing in the City of London, one adopted by highborn ladies as well as by legendary lower-class "roaring girls" such as Long Meg of Westminster and Moll Cutpurse.[10] Thomas Adams wrote in 1615 that it was becoming difficult to tell men from women on the streets, "for if they had not more evident distinction of sexe, then they have to shape, they would be all man, or rather all woman: for the *Amazons* beare away the Bell . . . *Hic Mulier* will soon be good latine, if this transmigration hold."[11] Early in 1620 King James, reacting to what he perceived as a veritable epidemic of female cross-dressing threatening all order, unleashed a barrage of denunciation from the pulpit, as Chamberlain reported to Carleton on January 25, 1620:

Yesterday the bishop of London called together all his Clergie about this towne, and told them he had expresse commaundment from the King to will them to inveigh vehemently and bitterly in theyre sermons against the insolencie of our women, and theyre wearing of brode brimd hats, pointed dublets, theyre haire cut short or shorne,

and some of them stillettaes or poinards, and such other trinckets of
like moment, adding withall that yf pulpit admonitions will not reforme them he wold proceed by another course; the truth is the world
is very far out of order, but whether this will mend yt God knowes.[12]

In addition to numerous ballads and sermons sparked by the women's
rebellious gesture or by the King's complaint,[13] three polemical tracts appeared in 1620, all anonymous but more likely than not all written by men.
Hic Mulier: or, the Man-Woman is an oration denouncing cross-dressing,
and the aggressive and impudent actions that accompany it, as a practice
both of great ladies and of City women alike.[14] *Haec-Vir: or, The Womanish
Man* (published one week later by the same bookseller) is a dialogue in
which *Hic Mulier* vigorously denounces the slavery of custom in the matter of female dress and behavior, denounces *Haec-Vir*—the foppish and
effeminate male courtier who has taken over women's garb and activities—and proclaims female freedom of choice: "We are as free-borne as
Men, have as free election." At length both agree that when men are again
manly, women will be womanly.[15] The third tract, *Muld Sacke,* attempts a
summary, criticizing all forms of masculine behavior by women and effeminate behavior by men.[16]

These tracts and circumstances supply the immediate context for
Speght's treatise, suggesting that women's challenge to gender hierarchy
had become a prominent locus of interest and anxiety during James's second decade. Some women were demonstrating in the streets what some
tracts were arguing: that gender definition rests largely on external signs
and social custom. It is the case, however, that Speght's is the first defense
of women in this exchange, and the only one certainly written by a
woman.[17] Though "Anonymous" and "Pseudonymous" may be female
more often than we can know, the use of a female allegorical persona is
not enough to indicate female authorship. It is likely, as both Woodbridge
and Simon Shepherd have argued, that booksellers commissioned the
Sowernam and Munda tracts to get in on a lucrative controversy and keep
it going. They may well have devised the strategy of having those respon-
dents represent themselves as women rushing to improve upon Speght's
answer to Swetnam. Or the booksellers may have sought out, or been
presented with, tracts which in fact were written by women. Present evidence cannot decide these cases, or even whether a woman wrote the 1589
Protection for Women attributed to one "Jane Anger"—though Speght may
have seen Anger's female persona as providing some precedent for herself.[18]

Speght is then the first self-proclaimed and positively identified female
polemicist in England. She either initiated the challenge to Swetnam or
was approached for the purpose (at the tender age of nineteen) by Swet-

nam's bookseller, Thomas Archer, who evidently wanted to reawaken the controversy two years later so as to sell more books. But for all its timeliness, Speght's tract stands at some remove from the formal controversy and its rhetorical gamesmanship.[19] Speght is chiefly concerned to reinterpret biblical texts to make them accommodate women's egalitarian desires. If her language and argument are in some ways less daring than those of Sowernam or Munda (or *Haec-Vir*), her undertaking is more serious: to make the prevailing Protestant discourse yield a more expansive and equitable concept of gender. One evidence of this is the fact that she alone of all the contributors to the Swetnam and cross-dressing controversies of 1615–1620 not only reveals but insists on her authorial identity. Her title page declares her full name; and in 1621 she published a poetic dream-vision and meditation on death, *Mortalities Memorandum,* in part to reassert her authorship of the *Mouzell.*

The epistle to her 1621 poems indicates that she is not much troubled by the anxieties about authorship and especially publication which contemporary noblewomen often exhibit. This London daughter does not share the aristocracy's sense that publishing is déclassé, and she disposes of gender constraints (here and elsewhere) on unimpeachable religious grounds—the desire to benefit others by leading them to prepare for death, and the biblical command to use and not hide a God-given talent:

> Amongst diversitie of motives to induce the divulging of that to publique view, which was devoted to private Contemplation, none is worthy to precede desire of common benefit. Corne kept close in a garner feeds not the hungry; A candle put under a bushell doth not illuminate an house; None but unprofitable servants knit up Gods talent in a Napkin. These premises have caused the Printing presse to expresse the subsequent *Memorandum of Mortalitie.*[20]

This rationale is couched in curiously passive terms, as if these good motives caused the printing press to operate quite apart from Speght's own actions. But this is less female self-abnegation or hesitation to publish than it is a modest way for Speght to position herself among those whose talents must not be wasted and who have the ability to benefit others by publishing their private thoughts. That formula may also imply some initiative from the bookseller—Jacob Bloome this time, not Archer. Her second, and highly personal, reason for publishing is to claim her authorship rights against those who (refusing to credit female achievement) have attributed her tract to her father:

> Having bin toucht with the censures of [critical readers] . . . by occasion of my *mouzeling Melastomus,* I am now, as by a strong motive induced (for my rights sake) to produce and divulge this of-spring of

my indevour, to prove them further futurely who have formerly deprived me of my due, imposing my abortive upon the father of me,
but not of it. Their variety of verdicts have verified the adagie *quot
hominem tot sententiae* [there are as many opinions as there are men]
and made my experience confirme that apothegme which doth af-
firme Censure to be inevitable to a publique act.   (sig. A 2v)

This statement also exhibits a rather remarkable equanimity in the face of
criticism.

Whatever criticism may have emanated from friends and family is not
on record, but Speght and her tract received a good deal of public notice.
Her title *Melastomus* is used to taunt Swetnam in the play *Swetnam the
Woman-hater,* and the comic résumé of his history contains a pun on her
name:

> He put his Booke i'the Presse, and publisht it,
> And made a thousand men and wives fall out.
> Till two or three good wenches, in meere spight [speght ?],
> Laid their heads together, and rail'd him out of th'Land.[21]

The diversity of opinion Speght refers to is especially evident in the tracts
ascribed to women. Sowernam condescends to the youth and inexperience
of "the minister's daughter," and justifies "her" own endeavor by the inadequacy of the "maid's" answer: "I did observe, that whereas the Maide
doth many times excuse her tendernesse of yeares, I found it to be true in
the slendernesse of her answer, for she undertaking to defend women,
doth rather charge and condemne women."[22] Munda by contrast claims
to have written her tract before Sowernam's was published, and her evaluation of Speght is quite respectful:

> You see your blacke grinning mouth hath been muzled by a modest
> and powerfull hand, who hath judiciously bewrayed, and wisely layed
> open your singular ignorance, couched under incredible impudence,
> who hath most gravely (to speake in your owne language) *unfoulded
> every pleat, and shewed every rinckle* of a prophane and brutish dispo-
> sition, so that tis a doubt whether shee hath shewed more modesty
> or gravity, more learning or prudence in the religious confutation of
> your undecent raylings. But as shee hath beene the first Champion of
> our sexe that would encounter with the barbarous bloudhound, and
> wisely dammed up your mouth, and sealed up your jawes lest your
> venomed teeth like madde dogges should damage the credit of many,
> nay all innocent damosels . . . I heare you foame at mouth and groule
> against the Author with another head like the triple dog of hell;
> wherefore I have provided this sop for *Cerberus.*[23]

Biographical information about Rachel Speght is scarce: a few known facts, and some reasonable inferences that can be drawn from them. Born, it would seem, in 1597, she was the daughter of the clergyman James Speght, a rigorous Calvinist and rector of two London churches, St. Mary Magdalen, Milk Street (1592–1637), and St. Clement, Eastcheap (1611–1637).[24] His 1613 tract, *A Briefe demonstration, who have, and of the certainty of their salvation, that have the spirit of Jesus Christ,* argues Calvinist positions on justifying faith and the final perseverance of the elect, using the classic proof texts from Romans 8. Its dedication, "To the Right Worshipful Knights, and Aldermen, to the Wardens and Assistants of the Society of Goldsmiths" in testimony of their "kind linking of me in brotherhood," indicates his incorporation in that London guild. Further evidence of his standing with the City establishment is supplied by his Epiphany sermon, *The Day-spring of Comfort* (on Christ as the only source of the Christian's salvation), preached on January 6, 1611, before the Lord Mayor and aldermen of London.[25] Published in 1615, it is dedicated to the London alderman who appointed him to deliver it, "To the Right Worshipfull Sir Baptiste Hicks, Knight, the Lady Elizabeth his Wife, and to their vertuous of-spring," identified as long-time parishioners, friends, and patrons at St. Mary Magdalen.[26] That Rachel's mother was an important influence in her life is suggested by the fact that she identifies her mother's death as the stimulus for her 1621 poems; but neither Rachel nor any other source provides the mother's name, date of death, or other biographical facts. Thomas Speght, the editor of Chaucer (1598, 1602), may have been a kinsman.

Rachel Speght's classical education must have been approved by, and may have been supervised by, her father; he evidently also approved (and may have encouraged) her tract, given that she wrote it under his roof and makes no reference to family difficulties. It is fair to assume that this nineteen-year-old was somehow empowered to write and publish by her parents and her education. If she was solicited by Swetnam's bookseller, she must have been proposed to him by family or friends; or else she had already acquired some reputation in City circles as a learned young woman.

An important influence on Speght's education, aspirations, and sense of self seems to have been her connection with the Moundfords. *Mortalities Memorandum* was dedicated to her godmother Mary, wife of Thomas Moundford, the renowned London physician who was president six times of the College of Physicians. After his education at Cambridge, he and his wife lived in Milk Street as neighbors and also parishioners of James Speght.[27] Rachel's dedication claims a close relationship with her godmother, to whom she offers the poem "as a testimonie of my true thankefulnesse for your fruitfull love, ever since my beeing, manifested toward me," proposing her as a "paradigma to others" for the performance of religious duties.[28] Dr. Moundford was also a writer: his Latin tract *Vir Bonus* (1622) treats the cardinal virtues of temperance, prudence, fortitude, and justice, emphasizing how his experience as a doctor has fitted him to comment on the conduct of life. The dedications—to James I, to the Bishop of London, and to four judges—indicate the circle of his acquaintance.[29] As Arbella Stuart's physician, he showed himself sympathetic with her situation, colluded with her efforts to prevent exile to Durham by pleading illness, interceded for her with James, and was briefly imprisoned on suspicion of aiding her escape to France with Seymour.[30] Whether or not Moundford's sympathy for the learned Lady Arbella led him to encourage the good education of his wife's goddaughter, the child Rachel may have heard from this source stories about Arbella which reinforced her belief in female intellectual potential and incited her emulation. The Moundford connections may also have encouraged her to invite patronage as male writers do—though she targets female patrons and highlights her special vulnerability as a young woman writer. She dedicates her *Mouzell* "to all vertuous Ladies Honourable or Worshipfull" (noble and City ladies), claiming that her youth and the danger of her enterprise require her to "impetrate patronage from some of power."[31]

Speght's later life is a virtual blank. She tells us that the 1621 *Mortalities Memorandum* was occasioned by her mother's death; her father died in 1637.[32] Seven months after *Mortalities Memorandum* was entered in the Stationers' Register, there is a record of marriage between "Procter, William, gent ['clerk' in the Vicar-General's book], bachelor, 29, and Rachel Speight, spinster, 24, daughter of Mr. James Speight, clerk, parson of St. Mary Magdalen, Milk Street, London, who consents," at St. Mary Woolchurch Haw, London, August 6, 1621.[33] The marriage did not take place at her father's church nor yet at her own (and William's) parish church, St. Botolph's, Aldersgate;[34] it is not clear why, though all these churches were within a few blocks of one another. The legal phrase indicating paternal consent often meant that the couple had a special license dispensing with the three-week reading of the banns.[35]

Rachel's husband was probably the "Procter, William of Somerset (plebs)," who matriculated at Oriel College in October 1609 at age sixteen.[36] There are lots of Procters and Proctors (though no William) in the parish records of St. Mary Magdalen, including the churchwarden Jacob Proctor who regularly signed the register entries. It seems likely that this was a marriage arranged between closely connected families, providing Rachel with a minister husband allied in theology and connections to her minister father. Baptismal records of two children, Rachel (February 26,

1627) and William (December 15, 1630) at St. Giles, Cripplegate, specify that William Procter is a minister and suggest that they then lived in that parish.[37] As these children bear their parents' names, it is likely they were the first two born alive; I found no record of other children. In 1625 the Procters were probably living at Upminster in Essex, just outside London, from which place one William Procter dated a published sermon, *The Watchman warning*. We cannot be sure this is the same William Procter, but his Calvinist theology and City connections resemble those of Speght's father. The sermon was first preached at Paul's Cross, September 26, 1624, and addressed to the "whole Honorable Corporation" of City officers; it is dedicated to the "Right Worshipfull Master Ralph Freeman, Alderman."[38] William Procter died in 1653 and was buried at All Hallows, Lombard Street; I found no record of Rachel Speght's death and burial.[39]

A Mouzell for Melastomus

Speght's *Mouzell* eschews many of the tired formulaic gestures of the *querelle* defenses: citing lists of good women to balance the evil examples adduced, citing authorities who praise women to counter the defamers, overstating claims for female superiority to counter outrageous claims for male superiority. Her first accomplishment was to devise a structure that would allow her to attack Swetnam on particular points (as the genre and readership of such works required) but also to develop her own argument. That structure comprises a dedicatory epistle to all virtuous women; a "Preface" addressed to Swetnam; the tract proper; and an appended small tract, *Certaine Quaeres to the Bayter of Women* (with separate title page, epistle "To the Reader," and preface), in which Speght projects a suitable persona and inveighs against Swetnam's logic and style. In the tract proper she virtually ignores Swetnam in order to mount a serious, coherent, liberalizing critique of gender ideology couched in terms of the dominant discourse: Protestant biblical exegesis, especially of Genesis, chapters 1 and 2. That strategy immediately sets her apart from Swetnam, who indeed begins his tract with a few misogynist jokes grounded upon Scripture— woman as crooked rib, woman no sooner made than procuring man's fall by her aspiring mind and wanton will, woman as "a woe unto man," David and Solomon denouncing women, Saint Paul saying it is better not to marry—but does not develop any serious argument or extended exegesis from his biblical texts.[40] Speght condemns him roundly for thus dallying with "the two-edged Sword of the Eternall" (sig. F 2). With her extended examination of the relevant biblical texts (supported by many cross-references in the margins in the approved manner of Protestant theological argument), Speght looks past Swetnam to engage worthier antagonists—all those ministers or other commentators who find in Scripture some basis to devalue and wholly subjugate women. By the readings she gives to her texts, especially the Creation-Fall story, Speght redefines gender norms and participates in the process of transforming a restrictive ideology: the first stage of such transformation normally involves making received formulas (religious dogma, Marxist theory, constitutional laws, or whatever) bear more generous and expansive meanings.

Speght's various epistles, prefaces, and *Quaeres* offer an especially effective rejoinder to Swetnam in the rhetorical category of ethical proof: the creation of a suitable persona. She presents herself as the living refutation of Swetnam's charges against women: religious, learned, eminently rational, engagingly modest, unassuming, justifiably angry yet self-controlled, truthful, courageous in defending wronged women and their Creator.[41] Against this persona she poses her character of Swetnam from the evidence of his tract: "the very embleme of a monster" (sig. A 4), a blustering, scandal-mongering, indeed blasphemous bully who is "irreligious and illiterate," whose grammatical faults and stylistic errors reveal his abysmal ignorance, and whose disjointed and contradictory arguments reveal his intellectual, moral, and spiritual chaos. Her governing metaphor for her encounter with him is unequal combat, a David battling Goliath, or a Saint George with the dragon. She is "yong and the unworthiest of thousands" doing battle with a "furious enemy to our sexe," and venturing to "fling this stone at vaunting *Goliah*" (sigs. A 3–A 3v). She seeks the shelter of honorable patronesses "against the persecuting heate of this fierie and furious Dragon" (sig. A 4v). She is fearless because "armed with the truth" and the "Word of Gods Spirit" (sig. A 4). Three commendatory poems (possibly by Rachel herself) reinforce the David–Saint George analogues: "Philalethes" praises the "young encombatant" for giving "this *Goliah* . . . the foyle"; "Favour B" commends her "wit and learning" and her "magnanimitie . . . / In ventring with a fierie foe to fight"; and "Philomathes" praises her for doing combat "by force of Learnings Art, / (in which she hath had education)."[42] The prefatory matter also includes Speght's witty acrostic poem on Swetnam's name, which satirically reveals his identity and further displays her own talents.

Speght also engages her reader's sympathy and trust by her unassuming stance and skillful use of the modesty topos: she admits the limitations of her knowledge and experience (owing to her youth and the restrictions imposed upon her sex), but yet demonstrates that she has more than enough of both to reveal the folly of a misogynist like Swetnam. The epistle to her *Quaeres* assures the reader that she would answer Swetnam's points in order if his chaotic tract allowed it:

Although (courteous Reader) I am young in yeares, and more defective in knowledge, that little smattering in Learning which I have obtained, being only the fruit of such vacant houres as I could spare from affaires befitting my Sex, yet am I not altogether ignorant of that Analogie which ought to be used in a literate Responsarie. But [his tract] . . . is altogether without methode, irregular, without Grammaticall Concordance, and a promiscuous mingle mangle.

(sig. F)

She has not studied formal logic—"I have not read *Seaton* or *Ramus,* nor so much as seene (though heard of) Aristotle's *Arganox* [Organon]"—but she can do a better syllogism than Swetnam and one that proves him damnable: "To fasten a lie upon God is blasphemy; But the *Bayter of women* fastens a lie upon God [in falsely claiming what is nowhere in Scripture, that God called women necessary evils]: *ergo,* the *Bayter* is a blasphemer" (33). Her refusal to answer Swetnam's attacks on widows— "in that I am ignorant of their dispositions, accounting it a follie for me to talke of *Robin-hood,* as many doe, that never shot in his Bowe"—effectively convicts Swetnam of the highest presumption in daring to comment on women's lives, with which he has no experience whatever (37).

Speght alludes to and appears to accept without demur the ways in which gender has restricted her access to learning. But her statements hold a barely concealed and quite subversive subtext: if Rachel's "vacant hours" of study have made her so much more learned than Swetnam with all his masculine advantages, then her example makes the case for women's equal intelligence and equal capacity for education. She does not press that conclusion herself but invites the reader to draw it as she displays throughout the tract her logical arguments, her lucid style, her knowledge of rhetoric, her ease with Latin quotations and word play (it may be "small Latin," but she seems in good control of it), and her range of reference beyond the Bible to the Fathers and classical moral philosophers: Lactantius, Seneca, Aristotle, Zoilus, Livy, Pliny, Cicero, Saint Augustine, Plutarch.

Speght's dedicatory epistles evidence some conflict as regards audience and purpose: on the one hand she proposes to speak for and to "all of Hevah's sexe," and on the other she limits her agency and address to a group defined by class, education, or virtue. Her first epistle identifies as her primary audience "all vertuous Ladies Honourable or Worshipfull," the virtuous noblewomen and City gentry from whom she craves patronage and protection. But she then reaches out to all virtuous and God-fearing women of every rank and class, "rich and poore, learned and unlearned," inviting them to see themselves as the common target of the malevolent Swetnam. Here and elsewhere she comes close to recognizing the common plight of all "Hevahs sex" as an oppressed gender in a misogynist, patriarchal society. But then she typically draws back, making herself the defender not of all women but of all good women. These tensions are further in evidence as she explains her reasons for writing: to answer Swetnam (since no other woman has) lest he "insult and account himself a victor" and produce the second "more deadly" book he has promised; to prevent the "vulgar ignorant" from supposing his "Diabolicall infamies to be infallible truths"; and to comfort all good women with the knowledge of Christ's esteem for them (sig. A 3v). In the epistle to the *Quaeres* she reaches out as well to "gentle," "well affected," and "judicious" male readers, making an effective rhetorical distinction between such readers who will readily discredit Swetnam and the unlearned "vulgar sort" who will likely applaud him (sigs. F 2–F 2v).

The preface to Swetnam proposes a double-pronged attack on him as both illiterate and irreligious: Speght's railing style here is sometimes witty, sometimes heavyhanded. She uses his own formula of address to women to effective deflationary purpose—"Not unto the veriest Ideot that ever set Pen to Paper, but to the Cynicall Bayter of Women, or metamorphosed Misogunes, Joseph Swetnam" (sig. A 2)[43]—implying that he cannot even claim primacy in idiocy. By his own bearbaiting metaphor he labels himself a dog (and thereby a cynic in Latin). He uses "such irregularities touching concordance" and "so disordered a methode" that a mere grammar-school student could catch him out (sigs. Bv–B 2). His failures in logic match those in grammar. He draws absurd conclusions, seeking to comprehend any woman who answers him in the proverb "Rub a galled horse and he will kick" (though of course a horse might kick or a woman write for many other reasons). He also contradicts himself, promising to distinguish between good and bad women but in fact denigrating all women. More important, he has put himself beyond the pale of Christianity: he blasphemes God by wresting and perverting Scripture; he dishonors God by disparaging woman, "that excellent worke of Gods hands"; and he looks to "heathenish" authorities for his misogynist ideas (sig. B 2v). She concludes by giving short shrift to his tongue-in-cheek claim that he wrote with his hand, not his heart: "Then are you an hypocrite in Print" (sig. B 3).

In *Certaine Quaeres* she condescends to instance a few specific examples of Swetnam's grammatical errors and illogic, spicing them with invective and puns. He counts women's changes of mood "wonderful," but she thinks him "far more *wonder-fool*" for his failures in grammatical concordance—for example, joining "'women' plural and 'she' singular" (31). She also puns regularly on "as"/ "ass," pointing to Swetnam: "And where-asse you say" (29); "such a monster in nature *Asse* your selfe"; "*Asse* you . . . have done" (29–30).[44] Swetnam cannot recognize the figure of speech "sarcasmus" in the words of Job's wife, nor the biblical counterexamples to his generalizations about women's ingratitude or the cruelty of fair women, nor Ovid's error about the properties of rue. And she catches him up on his occasional, inexplicable repetition of statements from the defenses of women and marriage which contradict the thrust of his treatise.

Speght's tract proper develops an argument grounded in Scripture for the spiritual worth and equality of women: it proceeds without direct reference to Swetnam, as if the proper reading of these texts provides the only really needful answer to him. Although many of Speght's points are commonplaces of liberal Protestant marriage doctrine and earlier defenses of women, she opens the door to a rethinking of gender hierarchy by highlighting contradictions in the biblical-Christian discourse invoked to support it. On the one hand, she insists that the dominant thrust of that discourse affirms the moral and spiritual equality of women (thereby removing any essential ground for their subordination to men); on the other hand, she admits (as she has to) those biblical texts proclaiming woman the weaker vessel (1 Peter 3:7) and the man the "head" of the wife in marriage (1 Corinthians 11:3). Accordingly, she does not directly challenge gender hierarchy as a social arrangement supported by these texts, but she interprets them in such a way as to deny any real basis for gender hierarchy in female nature itself, as created or as redeemed. Speght may not fully recognize the contradiction her analysis points to, given the assumptions of the age about the all-pervasive hierarchical structure of nature and society. Yet her argument has considerable subversive potential precisely because it presses the dominant biblical-Christian discourse so far toward the affirmation of gender equality. Two decades later some radical sects would be ready to make that affirmation without qualification.

Speght's exordium begins with Proverbs 18.22, "He that findeth a wife, findeth a good thing, and receiveth favour of the Lord," expounding that text from Genesis, chapters 1 and 2. To provide Adam with "an helpe meete for him," God "made or built Woman" from Adam's rib, "shewing thereby, that man was as an unperfect building afore woman was made." Not man's worthiness but God's love and mercy led God to grant Adam "this great favour . . . before hee saw his owne want" (2). She concludes the exordium with her formal proposition—"Of the excellencie of this Structure, I meane of Women, whose foundation and original of creation, was Gods love, do I intend to dilate"—offering as her first evidence God's pronouncement that all his Creation (necessarily including woman) was very good (3).

But before developing that thesis, she takes up four objections, grounded upon scriptural texts, which have caused "some" to stumble (9); this gesture elides Swetnam and offers help to the worthy but confused reader. Speght treats at greatest length the first objection: that woman sinned first by giving ear to Satan's temptation and thereby brought death and misery upon humankind. Her strategy here is to admit the narrative facts of Genesis, but to empty them of damaging significance for women. She admits that Satan attacked woman first, as the weaker vessel, but here and elsewhere she explains that "weakness" in purely physical terms, developed through the familiar simile of the man as stone pot and and the woman as crystal glass. She also flatly denies that Eve's primacy in sinning means preponderance of guilt. Adam's sin parallels hers at every point: Adam had free will to resist, and as the stronger was more blameworthy; Eve's sin brought punishment only to the female sex (pain in childbearing), whereas his resulted in the curse on the earth and the punishments of spiritual nakedness and death (6). Speght indeed quotes and appears to accept Augustine's statement that Adam sinned against God and himself, Eve against God, herself, and her husband; but in fact she counters it by referring (as Aemilia Lanyer also does) to the category of intention. Theologians agree that evil intent is required for sin and Eve intended no harm to Adam: "In her giving of the fruit to eate had she no malicious intent towardes him, but did therein shew a desire to make her husband partaker of that happinesse, which she thought by their eating they should both have enjoyed" (6). She ends with her strongest point: God promised in Paradise that the Savior would spring from the woman's seed, so that in the order of grace (Galatians 3:28) "male and female are all one in Christ Jesus" (7).

The other biblical texts are handled briefly and their universal relevance denied by a shrewd analysis of context and circumstances. The statement in 1 Timothy 2:1 that the woman was deceived and in the transgression simply specifies that she was so first; it does not imply Adam's exclusion from deception or guilt. Paul's statement (1 Corinthians 7:1) that "it is good for a man not to touch a woman" refers only to the times and conditions of persecution, evidenced by the fact that Paul himself later married—an impressive and potentially radical claim that culture and historical circumstances are determinants even of sacred texts. Solomon's statement (Ecclesiastes 7:30) that he has not found an upright woman among a thousand is referred, plausibly enough, to context: he was talking about his own experience with his thousand concubines, not about women generally.

Speght argues her central proposition about women's excellence briskly and effectively, on the basis of Aristotle's four causes. The efficient cause of woman's creation is God himself, and so "the work cannot chuse but be good, yea very good, which is wrought by so excellent a workeman" (9). As for the material cause, Adam's rib is more refined matter than the dust from which Adam himself was made. Speght quotes the hoary axiom—Eve was taken not from Adam's foot to signify inferiority, or from his head to signify superiority, but "from his side, neare his heart, to be his equall"—and she offers no qualifications to that conclusion: "God . . .

makes their authority equall, and all creatures to be in subjection unto them both" (10). The formal cause also argues gender equality, eliding all reference to women's supposedly cold humors or imperfect bodies:

> For as God gave man a lofty countenance, that hee might looke up toward Heaven, so did he likewise give unto women. And as the temperature of mans body is excellent, so is womans . . . And (that more is) in the Image of God were they both created; yea and to be briefe, all the parts of their bodies, both externall and internall, were correspondent and meete each for other.   (11)

The final cause or end of woman's creation is formulated conventionally: to glorify God and give good counsel and companionship to her husband. The meaning is partly explicated from biblical examples—Miriam, Sarah, Leah and Rachel, Mary Magdalen. But Speght pushes this formula to unconventional conclusions, basing them on the parable of the talents: "No power externall or internall ought woman to keep idle, but to imploy it in some service of God" (12). This opens the way to an argument, not spelled out here but clearly implied by Speght's own act of writing this tract, about the proper utilization of women's talents well beyond the domestic sphere. A concomitant argument, set forth explicitly, challenges the notion emphasized in most treatises on marriage and marital duties of separate spheres for men and women: he tending to affairs and earning a livelihood abroad, she keeping the house and managing thriftily.[45] Swetnam had heartily approved such separation, casting scorn on those men who meddle with women's domestic concerns when they should tend only to their proper manly business.[46] Speght's counterargument invokes the commonplace that the man is the stronger vessel in order to derive the potentially radical conclusion that he should therefore help his wife with the domestic burdens. Citing examples from nature, she then draws the yet more radical conclusion that husband and wife should share all the offices and duties of life:

> Nature hath taught senselesse creatures to helpe one another; as the Male Pigeon, when his Hen is weary with sitting on her egges, and comes off from them, supplies her place . . . Of small Birds the Cocke alwaies helpes his Hen to build her nest . . . The crowing Cockrell helpes his Hen to defend her Chickens from perill . . . much more should man and woman, which are reasonable creatures, be helpers to one another in all things lawfull . . . excited to a farre more mutual participation of each others burthen, then other creatures.   (13)

The first conclusion is spelled out: that men should help with all domestic duties. The second is left implicit but follows logically: that women should help with nondomestic (public) duties and affairs.

Rachel now turns to a celebration of marriage as a joyful union, an estate far more excellent than the single life. Invoking the familiar pun "merri-age," and appealing to the imagery of Canticles, she concludes her paean with a forthright assertion of women's spiritual equality:

> With God *is no respect of persons,* Nations, or Sexes: For whosoever, whether it be man or woman, that doth *beleeve in the Lord Jesus,* such *shall be saved.* And if Gods love even from the beginning, had not beene as great toward woman as to man, then would hee not have preserved from the deluge of the old world as many women as men; nor would Christ after his Resurrection have appeared unto a woman first of all other, had it not beene to declare thereby, that the benefites of his death and resurrection, are as available, by beleefe, for women as for men; for he indifferently died for the one sex as well as the other. (16)

Speght recognizes a stumbling block to her analysis in the text from 1 Corinthians 11:3: "Yet a truth ungainesayable is it, that the *Man is the Womans Head*"; this text prevents her from concluding that natural and spiritual equality should mandate social equality. She cannot appeal here to particular historical circumstances (as with Paul's recommendation of the unmarried state) since the ideology of hierarchy is firmly in place in her own society. What she does instead is to subject the term "head" to an exegesis which removes every sanction for the husband's arbitrary authority on grounds of natural or spiritual superiority. Her tract contains no statements justifying the husband's headship on the usual grounds of women's natural inferiority—spelled out in detail in the officially promulgated "Homilie of the State of Matrimonie":

> For the woman is a weake creature, not indued with like strength and constancy of minde, therefore, they bee the sooner disquieted, and they bee the more prone to all weake affections and dispositions of minde, more then men bee, and lighter they bee, and more vaine in their fantisies and opinions . . . The woman ought to have a certain honour attributed to her, that is to say, shee must bee spared and borne with, the rather for that she is the weaker vessel, of a frail heart inconstant, and with a word soon stirred to wrath . . . To obey, is an other thing then to controle or command, which yet they [women] may doe, to their children, and to their family: but as for their husbandes, them they must obey, and cease from commanding, and performe subjection . . . By the apparell of her head . . . is signified, that she is under covert or obedience of her husband.[47]

This point of natural female inferiority is reiterated constantly in contemporary marriage sermons and tracts: the wife must obey her husband "because he is her better"; the wife must "acknowledge her inferiorities" and "carry her selfe as an inferior"; the husband is "as it were a little God in the family."[48]

Speght, however, defines the husband's role as "head" wholly in terms of his mandated duties of protection, love, sacrifice, honor, and instruction, not female need or lack. Moreover, she defies the often-articulated precept that wives owe total obedience even to evil husbands (if they are Christians)[49] by appealing to the central tenet of Protestantism—the primacy of the individual conscience:

> If men would remember the duties they are to performe in being heads, some would not stand a tip toe as they doe, thinking themselves Lords & Rulers, and account every omission of performing whatsoever they command, whether lawfull or not, to be matter of great disparagement, and indignity done them; whereas they should consider, that women are injoyed to submit themselves unto their husbands no otherwaies then as to *the Lord;* so that from hence, for man, ariseth a lesson not to bee forgotten, that as the Lord commandeth nothing to be done, but that which is right and good, no more must the husband; for if a wife fulfill the evill command of her husband, shee obeies him as a tempter, *as Saphira* did *Ananias.*   (17–18)

Her epilogue concludes this argument with a stern warning. Men who speak and write against women are guilty of that most odious vice ingratitude in its superlative form, ingratitude toward God. In doing so they invite God's certain revenge, for they revile his best gift and handiwork, "women I meane, whom God hath made equall with themselves in dignity, both temporally and eternally."

Mortalities Memorandum

Mortalities Memorandum (1621) contains two poems: a long meditation on death in six-line stanzas of undistinguished verse, preceded by a much more interesting dream-vision poem in the same stanzaic form, which allegorizes the author's search for knowledge. By describing her dream as "imaginarie in manner, *reall in matter,*" Speght confirms its autobiographical ground: its fictions thereby provide some insight into Speght's sense of self, of her role as author, and of the conditions which empowered her to write and publish. The work reflects some sense of a female community, in that it is conceived as a tribute to the women most important to her. The *memento mori* poem is set forth as a response to the trauma of her mother's death: "Her sodeine losse hath cut my feeble heart, / So deepe, that daily I indure the smart. / The roote is kil'd, how can the boughs but fade?" (10–11). The work is dedicated to her godmother, Mary Moundford, in gratitude for her love and her contribution to Rachel's religious nurture—though she does not credit her godmother with major responsibility for her education. Speght presents herself here as a woman writing both to benefit others and to claim her authorial rights against her own father, who has unintentionally had her anti-Swetnam tract fathered on him. The readership of the poetic work is not gendered, though in the verse address "To the Reader" Speght makes her familiar distinction between the ignorant, censorious reader and the "courteous Reader" who respects art and "learnings fruit" (sig. A 3v).

The longer poem, *Mortalities Memorandum,* marshals religious commonplaces to provide an example of meditation on death, and to urge such meditation. The chief topics are the origins of death in the Fall; the three kinds of death mentioned in Scripture; the benefits to the faithful by death; the comparison of this world's pains with heaven's delights; the evils of human life in this world in all ages, conditions, and stages; the comfort the godly can find in death; the motives we have to meditate on death; and finally, the special benefits of such meditation. The verse (756 lines, in six-line iambic pentameter stanzas, rhymed *a b c b d d*) is pedestrian. Although there are a few sharp images, effective figures, and arresting rhetorical questions, the language is usually flat and the rhymes sometimes awkward and strained. This stanza is one of Speght's better efforts:

> Mans life on earth is like a Ship at Sea,
> Tost on the waves of troubles to and fro,
> Assayl'd by pirates, crost by blustring windes,
> Where rockes of ruine menace overthrow.
> Where stormes molest, and hunger pincheth sore,
> Where *Death* doth lurke at every Cabbin dore.
>
> (23)

Speght argues with some wit and vigor in prose, but she evidently found no models (like Samuel Daniel's verse epistles or John Davies's *Nosce Teipsum*) to teach her how to do so in verse.

The interest of this poem lies in the fact that she here proposes to share in the work of her minister-father and minister-husband, offering her poem as a sanctioned way for a woman to instruct a Christian audience. Speght may also have been aware of the large middle-class market for all sorts of books on piety, devotion, and self-analysis, and may have hoped to earn money by writing for that market.[50] The opening stanzas reveal that Speght, like her father and husband, was a Calvinist: occasional references to election, reprobation, God's "chosen" or "destinate" (13–14) indicate as much, though the poem does not argue controversial issues. At the end of the poem Speght rather amusingly reveals her bourgeois

concern with wills and the disposing of property, listing such arrangements as one major benefit of meditation on death:

> Lastly, premeditation of our *Death,*
> Induceth us to commendable care,
> For setling and disposing our estate
> To those, whom we intend shall have a share,
> That when we are departed from this life,
> Our goods may prove no coales to kindle strife.
> · · · · ·
> Neglect of which disturbs us at our end,
> When we should be exempt from worldly care,
> When doubt of who shall reape what we have sowne
> Distracts our thoughts, and doth our peace impaire;
> Withdrawing our affections from above,
> Where we and no where els should fixe our love.

The first poem, "The Dreame" (fifty stanzas, three hundred lines in all),
uses the same stanzaic form; the verse is sometimes pedestrian, and the
first few stanzas are also marred by awkward poetic diction. But this work
is much enlivened by the allegorical fiction, by the dialogue of the speaker
with allegorical characters, by the author's emotional engagement with
sensitive autobiographical concerns, and especially by the fictional representation of a woman's obstacle-laden path to education. Rachel the
speaker recounts a dream which leads her "into a place most pleasant to
the eye" named *Cosmos,* where, "wanting wisdom," she is amazed and dis-
consolate—a sudden revelation, it seems, of her impaired condition. Approached by Thought, who inquires the reason for her grief and promises
aid, she names her problem as "Ignorance"—defined very generally:

> I feele disease, yet know not what I ayle,
> I finde a sore, but can no salve provide;
> I hungry am, yet cannot seeke for food;
> Because I know not what is bad or good.
> · · · · ·
> And sometimes when I seeke the golden meane,
> My weaknesse makes me faile of mine intent,
> Then suddenly I fall into extremes,
> Nor can I see a mischiefe to prevent;
> But feele the paine when I the perill finde,
> Because my maladie doth make me blinde.
>
> (2–3)

This Ignorance has reduced her to a brutish reliance on instinct, and to
solipsism: "I measure all mens feet by mine owne shooe" (3). Thought

sends her to Age, who directs her to Experience as the best agent to work her cure. Experience recommends Knowledge as "the onely medicine for your maladie," locating it "in *Eruditions* garden" and promising that Industry will serve as her guide (4). The allegory suggests that some persons of age and experience (Rachel's father? or mother? the Moundfords? other friends?) helped her acquire an education and realize its benefits. The assisting allegorical figures are chiefly gendered female, constructing for Rachel a supportive female society.

A dialogue follows, in which Dissuasion sets forth the many difficulties in her way—"As dulnesse, and my memories defect; / The difficultie of attaining lore, / My time, and sex, with many others more" (4)—and is then answered by Desire, Truth, and Industry. Industry promises to "cut away / All obstacles, that in her way can grow," then claims that Speght's "friends" will oppose Dissuasion's efforts, and at last predicts sure victory: "by the issue of her owne attempt, / I'll make thee *labor omnia vincet* know" (5). This clever play on Ovid's "Amor vincet omnia" makes woman's province not love but intellectual labor, and shows Speght taking considerable credit for her own industry and achievements. Truth speaks to the gender issue, claiming that the natures of men and women are alike suited to education on precisely the same basis—the equality of their intellect and the fact that God himself requires from both the use of all talents:

> Both man and woman of three parts consist,
> Which *Paul* doth bodie, soule, and spirit call:
> And from the soule three faculties arise,
> The mind, the will, the power; then wherefore shall
> A woman have her intellect in vaine,
> Or not endeavour *Knowledge* to attaine.
>
> The talent, God doth give, must be imploy'd,
> His owne with vantage he must have againe:
> All parts and faculties were made for use;
> The God of *Knowledge* nothing gave in vaine.
> 'Twas *Maries* choyce our Saviour did approve,
> Because that she the better part did love.
>
> (5)

Speght used this argument from the talents in the *Mouzell* also, evidently recognizing that it is unassailable on biblical grounds, and also of special force with a bourgeois audience. Truth then cites the standard classical examples of learned women (Demophila and Telefilla for poetry, Cornelia for prose style, Hypatia for astronomy, Aspatia for rhetoric, Areta for art, others for science). Speght chose to omit such examples from her biblical indictment of Swetnam, but they are entirely appropriate to this poem's defense of women's general education. Truth concludes by urging Rachel to display courage, withstand Dissuasion, and hold fast to her good purpose—and Desire moves her to follow that advice.

She is then led by Industry to "*Instructions* pleasant ayre" where she delights in the "taste of science . . . / To augment *Theorie* of things above," and desires to "reape this pleasure more and more." In a daring reversal of the usual romance trope, this young virgin finds her right place in a garden of learning, not a garden of love. Wandering with Desire she meets Truth again, who delivers a paean to knowledge and reassures her that she does well to seek more and more of it. Truth's speech forcefully counters the familiar arguments for limiting woman's education to what is of practical use in her life: the Bible, religious treatises, grammar, handwriting, domestic skills (and, for aristocrats, music, dancing, and possibly modern languages). By this utilitarian argument, women are quite properly denied the classical humanist education which prepares young men for public life. Truth, however, takes the high line that all knowledge is useful for all humans by their very nature. It is Speght's most progressive argument, buttressed by numerous scriptural citations in the margins (Colossians 3:10, Proverbs 19:2, John 17:3). Its urgency suggests that she was deeply invested in opposing the restrictive view of women's education—as she perhaps had to do in her own life:

> . . . by it [knowledge] Gods image man doth beare,
> Without it he is but a humane shape,
> Worse then the Devill; for he knoweth much;
> Without it who can any ill escape?
> By vertue of it evils are withstood;
> *The minde without it is not counted good.*

> Who wanteth *Knowledge* is a Scripture foole,
> Against the *Ignorant* the Prophets pray;
> And *Hosea* threatens judgement unto those,
> Whom want of *Knowledge* made to runne astray.
> Without it thou no practique good canst show,
> More then by hap, as blind men hit a Crow.

> True *Knowledge* is the Window of the soule,
> Through which her objects she doth speculate;
> It is the mother of faith, hope, and love;
> Without it who can vertue estimate?
> By it, in grace thou shalt desire to grow;
> 'Tis life eternall God and Christ to *Know.*

Great *Alexander* made so great account,
Of *Knowledge,* that he oftentimes would say,
That he to *Aristotle* was more bound
For *Knowledge,* upon which *Death* could not pray,
Then to his Father *Phillip* for his life,
Which was uncertaine, irkesome, full of strife.

This true report put edge unto *Desire,*
Who did incite me to increase my store,
And told me 'twas a lawfull avarice,
To covet *Knowledge* daily more and more.
This counsell I did willingly obey,
Till some occurence called me away.

And made me rest content with that I had,
Which was but little, as effect doth show;
And quenched hope for gaining any more,
For I my time must other-wayes bestow.
I therefore to that place return'd againe,
From whence I came, and where I must remaine.

(8–9)

Speght does not specify what "occurence" disrupted her education. Did her father terminate whatever arrangements were in place for it, recalling her to household responsibilities? Were there preparations in train for her marriage (which occurred a few months after this work was published)? Whatever the case, her plaintive report of and reluctant acceptance of that "occurence" and its consequences link it to the duties and the obedience demanded of women in the era. She obeys, but makes her dismay evident, indicating that she has not internalized this construction of woman's role.

If the chronology of the allegory conforms to Rachel's life, shortly after being recalled by the "occurence" to her own place she saw the "full fed Beast" (Swetnam) attacking women, and was prompted to muzzle him. She was then nineteen, and by that age her formal education would surely have ended. Her comments on Sowernam and Munda incorporate their allegorical personae into her own allegorical fiction:[51] Sowernam's condescension to her prompts Speght to describe her as a "selfe-conceited Creature"; and she repays Munda's praises by crediting her tract with effectively stopping Swetnam. Speght allegorizes the stimulus for her new book as another monster, an all-devouring Spenserian beast (Death) who is a "fierce insatiable foe, / Depopulating Countries." Suddenly she sees it slay her mother: that event startles her awake, and she finds it true. As in the tract against Swetnam, she again takes up the posture of a courageous romance heroine daring to encounter and seek revenge on a cruel and terrible foe:

But since that *Death* this cruell deed hath done,
I'll blaze the nature of this mortall foe,
And shew how it to tyranize begun.
The sequell then with judgement view aright,
The profit may and will the paines requite.

(II)

In the *Mouzell* Speght does not attack patriarchy as a social arrangement, but she does deny any essential basis for it in nature or in the spiritual order. She also represents the family in terms very different from those of King James, who saw it as an analogue of the absolutist state. Speght's allegorical "Dreame" offers an uncompromising defense of woman's education on the same basis as man's education; and she also represents herself as enjoying, and then forced to give over, that pleasure owing to some unspecified circumstance of a woman's life. Speght's serious effort to rethink the implications of the dominant biblical discourse in regard to women was provoked by Swetnam, but as the "Dreame" indicates, it was also provoked by her own situation as a learned young woman hedged about by restrictions. Both tract and poem strongly, cogently, and subversively argue her own, and all good women's, worth and substantial equality.

III

LITERARY RE-VISIONS

Elizabeth, Lady Falkland, by Athow from a painting by Paul Van Somer.

7 ❧

Resisting Tyrants: Elizabeth Cary's Tragedy and History

Elizabeth (Tanfield) Cary, Viscountess Falkland (1585 1639), was the first Englishwoman to write a tragedy, the Senecan *Tragedie of Mariam* (1613).[1] She was also the first Englishwoman to write a full-scale history, the Taci-tean *History of the Life, Reign, and Death of Edward II* (c. 1627–28).[2] Those works engage issues important in her own life and also in the Jacobean state: the claims of conscience, the analogy of domestic and state tyranny, the powers of kings and husbands, the rights and duties of subjects and wives, the justifications for resistance to tyrants, the role of counselors and favorites, and, most interesting, the possibility and power of nonviolent or passive resistance. Some critics find *Mariam* distressingly (or at its cultural moment necessarily) contradictory, especially in regard to the issue of women's silence; others interpret it from the chorus's vantage point, as denying to wives and subjects any right of resistance (even internal) to their lords.[3] But though the work's contradictions reflect gender anxieties, they find close parallels in contemporary Senecan dramas and histories written in the Tacitean mode—genres often perceived as dangerous by Elizabethan and Jacobean censors precisely because they allow for the clash of ideological positions and for the sympathetic representation of resistance and rebellion. Cary, like Samuel Daniel and Fulke Greville, chose genres and took over generic strategies which allowed her to explore dangerous political issues, focused in her case by the situation of queen-wives subjected at once to domestic and state tyranny.

Most of Cary's other writing does not, apparently, survive. We have her childhood translation of Abraham Ortelius' *Mirroir du Monde*.[4] Also, there is a late epitaph on Buckingham (c. 1628), and a translation of Cardinal Perron's *Reply* to King James, published at Douay in 1630.[5] Apparently lost, however, are other works mentioned in an anonymous *Life* written by one of her daughters:[6] early translations of Seneca's epistles; a verse "Life of Tamurlane" (said to be her best early work); a manual of moral precepts for her children written during a life-threatening illness; several hymns and poems to the Virgin; saints' lives in verse (Mary Magdalene, Agnes the Martyr, and Elizabeth of Portugal); translations of all the works of Cardinal Perron (intended as a help for Oxford scholars who knew no French); and translations of other French divines, including the Flemish Benedictine monk Louis de Blois (*Life*, 9, 13, 39, 109). The memoir also mentions an essay "which was thought the best thing she ever penned," answering a Protestant controversial tract by her son Lucius (*Life*, 114).[7] The most serious loss is another tragedy that both she and her tutor, John Davies of Hereford, refer to as predating *Mariam;* it was apparently set in Sicily and dedicated to her husband.[8]

Cary's tragedy and history may be usefully contextualized with reference to the circumstances of her own life. A major factor was the clash of authorities claiming her obedience, which led her to develop a strong if conflicted sense of self. Throughout her life, parents, family, husband, and the English Church and court establishment urged their various demands, to which Elizabeth opposed her own needs—a powerful attraction to learning and to Roman Catholicism, the latter culminating in her formal conversion in 1626. Constructing Elizabeth Cary's life is complicated by the fact that the major source, a memoir by her daughter written about 1655, is conceived as hagiography and exemplary biography—a providential narrative of conversion, patient endurance of persecution by family and society, and final triumph over oppressors. That unsigned work was probably but not certainly written by her eldest living daughter, Anne, who became a Benedictine nun, Dame Clementina.[9] It was revised by her son Patrick, who, the nineteenth-century editor notes in his preface, "erased several passages which he considered too feminine, and added a few notes and sentences of his own." We have to allow for the author's strong sympathy for her mother, for the revising son's interest in deleting or modifying what seemed to him indecorous, for the probable exaggeration of Cary's accomplishments and religious virtues, for the fact that Cary herself must have been the sole source of information about her early life, for the fitting of fact to the hagiographic paradigm, and for the general unreliability of family gossip and anecdote. Fortunately, other contemporary records can supplement and counterbalance this memoir.[10] Read critically, the biography often registers Cary's sense of her own life, albeit through a distorting filter. It also reveals, as Elaine Beilin notes, Cary's reputation as a deviant or disorderly woman, refusing her assigned role and mounting strong resistance to patriarchal control.[11]

All her life Cary seems to have been caught up in conflict between social and ideological pressures to conform and submit and an inner imperative to resist and challenge authority. Her father, Sir Lawrence Tanfield, was an able and highly successful lawyer, judge, and (after 1607) Chief Baron of the Exchequer; her mother, Elizabeth Symondes, was descended from country gentry and may have felt her marriage to a lawyer involved a descent in the social scale.[12] In their county seat, Burford in Oxfordshire, both were greatly resented for harshness and arrogance, for revoking rights guaranteed to the town under its charter, and later for bribe taking.[13] A precocious only child, Elizabeth Cary grew up at Burford Priory, Oxfordshire (and later Great Tew), reading omnivorously, learning languages, translating, and writing verses. The *Life* underscores her filial reverence—she always addressed the mother "who was never kind to her" on her knees (*Life*, 21–23); but it also reveals her independence and resistance to parental authority in intellectual matters. She learned to read very young and often read all night, bribing the servants to supply the candles her mother refused; and at age twelve, upon receiving a copy of Calvin's *Institutes* from her father, she regaled him with arguments about the work's inconsistencies (*Life*, 7).[14] Stories about her early language learning (obviously originating with her) portray her as an autodidact and proud of it. She reportedly resisted early tuition in French but soon learned it on her own, as well as Spanish, Italian "very perfectly," and Latin; she also learned Hebrew "with very little teaching" and Transylvanian from some native speaker, but forgot this last and also some of her Latin and Hebrew from lack of use (*Life*, 4–5). Despite the disclaimers, she may have had some language tuition from John Davies of Hereford, who refers to her as his "Pupill."[15]

In 1602 she married Sir Henry Cary. As Nancy Cotton Pearse observes, the union "raised Tanfield from the upper middle class into the gentry, and the Tanfield fortune raised Henry Cary from the gentry into the peerage."[16] Elizabeth was seventeen and Henry about twenty-six. The *Life* states bluntly that he married her "only for being an heir, for he had no acquaintance with her (she scarce even having spoken to him) and she was nothing handsome, though then very fair."[17] Henry Cary studied at Gray's Inn and Oxford, was knighted by Essex at Dublin Castle in 1599, and went to fight in the Low Countries in 1603; he was captured by the Spanish at Ostend in 1605, and returned in 1606 after paying an exorbitant ransom that greatly damaged his estate.[18] While he was away Elizabeth lived first at home and then with her mother-in-law, Lady Katherine Cary, adopting a stance of solitary independence and quiet resistance to family expectations and authority. Her mother reportedly had her letters to Henry Cary ghost-written by others, leading him to think that the first genuine letters from her were forgeries (*Life*, 8–9). Did she refuse to write? Or were her letters expected to display learning or sentiments Cary would find disturbing? Reportedly also her mother-in-law found her lacking in proper deference and so used her "very hardly," confining her to her chamber and removing her books, at which point she began writing verses (*Life*, 7–8).

At his return Henry Cary began his successful career as a courtier—Gentleman of the Bedchamber, Master of the Jewel House, then Knight of the Bath (1608), Comptroller of the Household and Privy Councillor (1618), Viscount Falkland in the Scottish peerage (1620), and Lord Deputy of Ireland (1622). The *Life* portrays Elizabeth as struggling continually to conform her own inclinations and "strong will" to that of her "very absolute" husband (14): she learned to ride though she feared horses; she took "care of her house in all things"; she came to live at court when Cary became Comptroller (19); she dressed well though she found it a "torture" (allowing others to tend her "while she writ or read"). She bore eleven children between 1609 and 1624, nursed them all except for Lucius (who was brought up from infancy with his grandfather Tanfield), and took great care of their education, especially in moral and religious matters (11–12). The observation that she was constantly "either with child or giving suck" is crossed through in the manuscript, presumably by Patrick.[19] Reportedly, she taught her children to love their father more than herself, and they did so (14).

Yet the *Life* also testifies to an ongoing process of self-definition. Elizabeth read very widely—especially history, poetry, moral philosophy, and the Church Fathers:

> She had read very exceeding much; poetry of all kinds, ancient and modern, in several languages, all that ever she could meet with; history very universally, especially ancient Greek and Roman historians; all chroniclers whatsoever of her own country, and the French histories very thoroughly; of most other countries something, though not so universally; of the ecclesiastical history very much, most especially concerning its chief Pastors. Of books treating of moral virtue or wisdom, (such as Seneca, Plutarch's Morals, and natural knowledge, as Pliny, and of late ones such as French, Mountaine, and English, Bacon), she had read very many when she was young, not without making her profit of them all. Of the fathers she had read much, particularly the works of St. Justin Martyr, St. Jerome, very much of St. Augustine and of St. Gregory. (113)

She also read "most that has been written" in religious controversy—Luther and Calvin, Latimer, Jewel, and "all English writers of name," especially Thomas More. She contined writing verses "for her private recreation, on several subjects" (*Life*, 9). She also continued her Rome-ward journey, rejecting Hooker's defense of the English church in his *Ecclesiastical Polity* and disputing with various learned clerics.[20] And she began to play a role at court, associating herself with a coterie of Romanizing ladies: Katherine Manners (the future Duchess of Buckingham) and the Countesses of Arundel and Derby.

Recognition of Cary's intellectual and literary gifts came early, from several would-be clients. Drayton dedicated a pair of poems in his *Englands Heroicall Epistles* (1597) to the very young Elizabeth Tanfield, proclaiming her a fourth Grace and a tenth Muse, adorned by nature and education with "many rare perfections," among them her excellent French and Italian, and her precocious "judgment and reading."[21] Her one-time tutor Davies of Hereford associates her with Mary, Dowager Countess of Pembroke, and Lucy, Countess of Bedford, as dedicatees of *The Muses Sacrifice* (1612); he proclaims them the three Graces, "as well Darlings as Patronesses of the Muses" and rulers "of ARTS whole Monarchie, and WITS Empire."[22] He describes Elizabeth Cary as a writer of tragedies (one set in Sicily, one in Palestine), as a famous linguist knowledgeable in abstruse tongues (Hebrew is hinted), and as a poet who far surpasses her sex in wit and art:

> CARY (of whom Minerva stands in feare,
>   lest she, from her, should get ARTS Regencie)
> Of ART so moves the great-all-moving Spheare,
>   that ev'ry Orbe of Science moves thereby.
>
> Thou mak'st Melpomen proud, and my Heart great
>   Of such a Pupill, who, in Buskin fine,
> With Feet of State, dost make thy Muse to mete
>   the Scenes of Syracuse and Palastine.
>
> Art, Language; yea, abstruse and holy Tones,
>   thy Wit and Grace acquir'd thy Fame to raise;
> And still to fill thine owne, and others Songs;
>   thine, with thy Parts, and others, with thy praise.
>
> Such nervy Limbes of Art, and Straines of Wit
>   Times past ne'er knew the weaker Sexe to have;
> And Times to come, will hardly credit it,
>   if thus thou give thy Workes both Birth and Grave.

Davies's tribute, and his comment that these three ladies have regrettably though understandably withheld most of their fine poetry from the debased press,[23] may have prompted Cary to publish *Mariam* shortly thereafter. In the wake of that publication the bookseller Richard More dedicated his new edition of *Englands Helicon* to her as "Englands happy Muse, / Learnings delight."[24]

An inner conflict between domestic subservience and intellectual independence offers itself readily enough as an explanation for her periods of depression, manifested in long spells of sleeping and even, during two pregnancies, loss of "the perfect use of her reason" (*Life,* 16). Such conflicts would only be intensified by her reported conviction that innocence of conscience ought always to be manifested in external behavior—avoiding "all that might have the least show or suspicion of uncomeliness or unfitness" (*Life,* 16). The *Life* interprets the motto she had engraved on her daughter's wedding ring, "Be and Seem," as a demand for decorous behavior, but it points rather to a higher ideal, relevant both to Cary's drama and to her own life choices: personal integrity. She reportedly advised that daughter, Catherine, married at age thirteen to Lord Home, that "whersoever conscience and reason would permit her, she should prefer the will of another to her own" (*Life,* 13). But this apparent proposal of abject wifely submission in fact makes the wife's reason and conscience absolute judge in all cases.

In 1622 Falkland prevailed upon his wife to mortgage her jointure properties to help raise the large sums he needed to take up his appointment in Ireland as Lord Deputy. That imprudence so incensed Tanfield that he disinherited his daughter and left his fortune and estates (Burford and Great Tew) to his grandson Lucius (*Life,* 15–16). Falkland's harshly repressive policies toward the Catholics in Ireland, together with his bigotry, vacillation, political obtuseness, and financial folly, no doubt distressed his wife and certainly irritated the Privy Council. His 1623 and 1624 proclamations banishing Jesuits and other priests made trouble during the negotiations for Prince Charles's Spanish marriage; and his mismanagement, quarrels with the Irish nobles, and illegal seizure of lands led to his recall in 1629.[25]

Elizabeth Cary took her own direction in Ireland. She learned to read Gaelic from a Bible, and she started up ambitious trade school–cum–factories to train Irish children ("more than eight score prentices") in the cloth trades (*Life,* 18–19). That project collapsed after two years, owing in part to her credulity and financial ineptitude but chiefly to a disastrous fire and flood.[26] She also took on the role of literary patron: Richard Belling dedicated his *Sixth Booke to the Countesse of Pembrokes Arcadia* to her with thanks for her favors and encouragement.[27]

During Falkland's tenure in Ireland the marriage foundered. In 1625 he sent Elizabeth to England to be relieved of her uncomfortable presence, embarrassing Romanizing sympathies, and expensive projects. At first he seems also to have hoped she could help him at court by answering his

critics. But from the outset his letters disparage his wife and women generally, expressing a barely concealed desire to be rid of her and at the same
time to control her actions. His notion was that she and the children ac-
companying her (the three youngest) should stay with and be supported
by her mother at Burford Priory while he was in Ireland; the eldest unmarried daughter, Anne, was at court, a maid of honor to Queen Henrietta Maria, and the rest were with him. Writing to the Secretary of State
Sir Edward Conway in January 1626, Falkland takes ungracious note of his
wife's efforts on his behalf:

> By all my wives letters I understand . . . that she beginns to conceive
> hir selfe some able body in courte, by your countenance to doe me
> courtesies, if she had the wit as she hath the wyll. She makes it ap-
> peare she hath donn me sum good offices . . . I must thanke hir much
> for hir carefull paynes in it though it was but an act of duty in hir, to
> see me righted when she knew me wronged . . . I beseech your Lord-
> ship still to continue that favour to us boath . . . giving hir good
> counsell and good countenance within a niew World and Courte, att
> such a Distance from hir husband, a poore weake woman stands in
> the greatest neede of: to despatch hir suits.[28]

April 5 he disdainfully repudiates her apparently unproductive diplomacy,
tries hard to silence her, and urges Conway to effect her return to her
mother's house:

> For hir abilitys in agencye of affayres, as I was never taken with opin-
> ion of them, soe I was never desirous to imploy them if she had them,
> for I conceyve woemen to be noe fitt sollicitors of state affaires, for
> though it sometymes happen that they have good witts, it then com-
> monly falls out that they have over-busye Natures withall: for my part
> I should take much more comefort to hear that she weare quiettly
> retyred to hir Mother's into the country, then that she had obtayned
> a greate suite in the courte . . . If your Lordship will trye your skyll
> to persuade hir with content to that retraite, I shalbe bound to you
> for yt . . . Yf not, I must have yt donn an other way.[29]

But Lady Tanfield flatly refused to take on such a charge for a daughter
she had never understood or much liked.

When Elizabeth Cary openly professed Roman Catholicism in November 1626, she found herself isolated, attacked, cast off by husband and
family, and in acute financial distress. Her daughter attributes her decision
to an apparition of the Virgin Mary to her eldest daughter, Catherine, as
she was dying in childbirth at age seventeen (*Life*, 18). A more mundane
impetus was the example of Queen Henrietta Maria and the recusant and

crypto-Catholic ladies of her court. Roman Catholicism may have afforded these ladies some self-validation through the honors it accorded the Virgin and numerous female saints, and it certainly offered them a heady mix of danger, power, and importance.[30] Undercover priests courted them assiduously as a fifth column which could win back the nation for the true religion; and Laudian bishops such as Dr. John Cosin of Durham worked as assiduously to retain them within an Anglo-Catholic community. Elizabeth Cary was urged, and at one point forcibly constrained, to delay her conversion by her good friend Lady Denby (Buckingham's sister), who was also dallying with Rome (*Life*, 27–29).[31] Cary had evidently planned a covert profession, which could have been accommodated in that court without trouble. But when Lady Denby and Buckingham informed King Charles that she had been received into the Roman Church, he ordered a formal inquiry, which made the affair public and scandalous.[32]

The King had Cary confined to her rooms for six weeks while concerted efforts were made to reconvert her (*Life*, 29–30). Falkland immediately stopped her allowance, had her children and all but one of the servants removed, and left her without coal, wine, food, or money to buy provisions, in an effort to starve her into submission; she survived on crusts of bread and tidbits brought by her servant, Bessie Poulter (*Life*, 31–33). Falkland's letters to the King and court officials display the fury of a thwarted patriarch and Protestant zealot. He denounces his "Apostate" wife and those in the Queen's court who subverted her, decries the danger to himself "to nourish that serpent in my bosom" (alluding injudiciously to the King's similar danger), and demands vehemently that she be sent home to her mother in Burford as the "onely way for her recovery and Reclamation."[33] The King so ordered, but the Duchess of Buckingham won a stay for Elizabeth by raising doubts as to whether her mother would receive her.[34] In furious response, Falkland denounced his wife's "feminine wily pretences . . . assisted by feminine mediation" and refused any support to her until she followed his wishes. He demanded passionately that his orders for his wife be enforced, or else that he be given a legal separation, so as to avoid further dishonor and ruin:

> Surely her residency ought to be according her husbands election and not her owne. Soe *our* religion teacheth, And if *hir* newe Profession teach contrary points of doctrine in that as abhominable as in other things, let me first obtaine an utter and absolute divorce, That I may be separated from all interest in hir person and wayes, soe that dishonour and confusion of face, with ruine of fortune may not thereby assayle me and overwhelme me; and I shalbe contented then to quitt my clayme of superioritye, and being made free, leave hir free.[35]

His letter of July 5, 1627, accuses her of contriving her mother's refusal with "serpentyne subtelty . . . conjoined with Roman hypocrisy" so
that she might stay with her popish friends, and insistently but implausi-
bly denies any responsibility for the loss of her jointure and her father's
inheritance. He also vents his outrage at the notoriety he expects to suffer "over all the Christian world" owing to "this defection of his wives
and her violent contestation with him, against duty and the Lawe Matrimoniall."[36]

Some collusion between mother and daughter is possible, given their
common interest in preventing Elizabeth's return home. But, in sharp
contrast to Anne Clifford's supportive mother, Lady Tanfield seems to
have been only too sincere in her harsh denunciation of her daughter's
ungodly, unfilial, and unwifely conduct:

> Bes— I parcayve by your last letors . . . that I shall never have hope
> to have any comfort from you . . . My desiers was . . . to have you to
> lyve with your husband, and to lyve in that relegeon wherin yow war
> bred . . . to me, he [Falkland] cannot comand you I will not exsept
> [accept] of you, and if by any exterordenary devise he cold compell
> you, you shall fynd the worst of it . . . For my part, you may lyve
> wher you ples. if in essexe, then shall you have som such pore stuf
> from London as I can spar, and if you shold live at Cote [Coates, a
> small family estate in Oxfordshire] ther is yet some stuf, that may
> sarve your turn . . . bes, all your resons are grounded out of your own
> will and your fauteses [faults] . . . Now I see with a hevey sowel an
> utter ruin and over throw of you all, though I shall leve to wryt to
> you or desiere to heere from you.[37]

Cary's formal conversion was a gesture of opposition and resistance,
pitting her private conscience against the massed authority and pressure
of family and society. Reduced to extreme want and acute misery, she no
doubt found some models in the female saints and martyrs whose lives she
versified, but she did not suffer in silence, as her daughter's memoir suggests (*Life,* 36). Rather, she kept up a barrage of forceful, sharply worded,
and rhetorically effective letters and petitions to King Charles, Coke, Conway, and the Buckingham ladies, seeking to avoid being sent to her
mother, and asking that Falkland be required to supply her with food,
house rent, apparel, household staff, and a settled allowance. The substance and style of these letters display an assertive self claiming the rights
of conscience and common humanity. Her petition to the King on May 18
(sent with a copy of her mother's repudiating letter) vigorously urges the
dire consequences of the King's decree and the plausibility of her own
plan. She shrewdly presses her legal and moral claims against Falkland

without directly blaming him, and graphically portrays her deprivations and sufferings:

> Upon my lords goinge into Ireland, I was drawne, by seeinge his occasions, to offer my joynter into his handes, that he might sell, or morgage it, for his supply, which accordingly was done, and that beinge gone from mee, I have nothinge to trust to, hereafter, but my mothers bounty, at her death, for my father disinherited mee, onely, for resigninge my joynter . . . She vowes, if ever I come to hir, either willingly, or by comand . . . shee will never, neither in her life nor at her death, either give mee any thinge, or take any care for mee. Therefore I must humbly importune your majesty to call back a comand so prejudiciall to mee . . . I heard by a person of quality, that your majesty was pleased to beleeve that I altered my profession of religion upon some court hopes, but I beseech you, how wicked soever you may censure mee, to bee, (as it is no lesse, to make religion a ladder to clime by) yet judge me not so foolish, as to understand so little, the state of this time, as to think promotion, likely, to come that way . . . (If my lord woulde allow mee meanes competent, in any indifferent bodys judgement) I woulde take a little house, in essex, neere a sister of my lords, and a deere frend of mine, the lady Barrett . . . I desire nothynge but a quiet life, and to reobtaine my lords favour, which I have done nothynge to loose, but what I coulde not with a safe conscience, leave undone . . . I beseech your majesty, to comand one of your secretarys, to send for [my lord's] agent, and to comand him . . . [to] supply me weekely with [what is] . . . necessary to support mee for victualls, houserent, and apparell . . . Consider how pressant my wants are, that have not meanes, for one meale.[38]

Adjudicating the matter, a Privy Council commission determined that she should go to Coates (the house her mother agreed to lend her in Oxfordshire) and receive £500 a year from Falkland's estate; also, that her "great want" should be supplied with "immediate means." Falkland, however, delayed payment, and Elizabeth remained in a little house outside London, in dire need and wholly dependent on the charity of friends and the Queen (*Life*, 37–38). On August 27 she wrote with wry irony to Conway (who had hesitated to enforce an order attaching Falkland's funds): "None is lother to have my Lord Deputy, discontented, then I, but alas! where the question is, whither hee shoulde bee displeased, or I sterved, it will admit no dispute."[39] In October 1627 the Privy Council commission handed down a formal order: Falkland was to provide her a suitable establishment and maintenance at Coates, including "meat, drink, and all necessaries," nine servants, furniture and horses "to take the air," clothing, and

£100 a year for her private expenses, and also to pay her accrued debts of £272. Failing this, he was to pay her £500 a year.[40] Months later, however, the resistant Falkland still had not paid, and she had to keep up constant pressure.[41] In any event she did not go to Coates but stayed in and near London, close to her Catholic friends; in 1632 or thereabouts she was officially listed as a recusant in the county of Middlesex, lodging in Drury Lane.[42] Henrietta Maria seems to have effected some kind of reconciliation between Henry and Elizabeth in 1631, and in 1633 they were together for a few months at Falkland's country estate, Berkhamstead, in Hertfordshire. That year Falkland broke his leg in a fall from a horse, aggravated the wound when he dutifully rose to his feet in the presence of the King, had to have the leg amputated, and subsequently bled to death.[43]

As a widow, Elizabeth Cary was even more dramatically embroiled in struggles with family, civil, and religious authorities as she undertook to convert her many children and to find money to live on.[44] The eldest daughter, Catherine, had died in 1626 in childbirth. The two eldest sons often stayed with her while at Oxford, but they eluded her proselytizing efforts, carried on through dinnertime discussions with priests and other Catholics and through formal religious disputations (*Life*, 52–56). Lucius, the Falkland and Tanfield heir celebrated by Jonson and Clarendon as the embodiment of Cavalier virtues, came under the influence of the erstwhile Catholic-turned-rationalist William Chillingworth, who had disguised his defection from Rome while a tutor in Cary's household.[45] Lorenzo left England in 1634 to take up a military commission in Ireland. By that date the elder daughters, Anne and Elizabeth, were known Catholics: Archbishop Laud complained to King Charles of the "practice of the Ladye their Mother," who had failed to send them as directed to live with Lucius at Great Tew; and he proposed to call her before the High Commission.[46] Lucius took the younger children to Tew and, when his mother dismissed the deceiving Chillingworth, brought him there as tutor for Patrick and Henry (*Life*, 83).[47] This prompted Elizabeth Cary to mount a daring rescue in 1636 with the connivance of her daughters Mary and Lucy; they spirited the boys away at night, by coach and ship, to be educated in France by the Benedictines.[48] The report of a Privy Council inquiry portrays Elizabeth adopting a shrewd posture of vagueness about the whole affair:

> She saith, that shee did knowe of their cominge awaye from the Lorde Faulklande their brother, and shee did appointe horses to bee sente to them for that purpose, they both havinge beene verie desirous to bee sente for awaye: but shee doth not knowe where they are now, but doth assuredlie beleeve they are well and in saefeteye, for shee hath hearde soe much. Beeinge further demanded whether they

are now about London or in Englande, or sente beyonde the seas, shee saith shee knoweth not where they are, nor whether they be in Englande or out of Englande.[49]

Infuriated by these "uncertaine and illusorie Answers," the Council of the Star Chamber took order for her continued questioning "to answer the charge against her for sending over into forraigne parts twoe of her Sonnes, without Lycence, to be educated there . . . in the Romish Religion," and provided that "in case she shall in her answer use the like subterfuge & evasion as heretofore . . . she is to stand Committed prisoner to the Tower."[50] They let the matter drop, however, apparently recognizing the fait accompli. The boys became Benedictine monks, though both at length returned to England and renounced Catholicism. Four of Cary's daughters—Anne, Elizabeth, Lucy, and Mary—became and remained nuns in the Benedictine convent of Cambray. The fifth, Victoria, married Sir William Uvedale in Wickham in 1640.[51] Commenting on Lucius's heritage from Elizabeth, the historian Clarendon paid reluctant tribute to her "most masculine understanding," though allied as he saw it with the "passion and infirmities of her own sex."[52] She died in October 1639 at the age of fifty-four, needy to the last.[53]

Mariam and the Linkage of Domestic and Political Tyranny

Cary's tragedy *Mariam* explored the issue of domestic tyranny long before Cary herself felt the full force of such tyranny as a result of her conversion. Nonetheless, Falkland's arbitrary nature and low opinion of women make it likely that she experienced often enough the married woman's vulnerability to abuses of power. One terminus for the drama's composition is 1602, the publication date for her principal source, Thomas Lodge's translation of Josephus.[54] The other is suggested but not proved by the dedication to her "worthy Sister, Mistris Elizabeth Carye"—evidently Elizabeth Bland Cary, wife of her husband's brother, Philip, who could not properly have been addressed as "Mistris" after 1605, when her husband was knighted.[55] References in that dedicatory verse epistle to Henry's absence (like Phoebus' nocturnal sojourn in the Antipodes) point to the period of his military adventures and imprisonment (1602–1606). *Mariam* was probably written toward the end of that period, since Elizabeth also claims authorship of an earlier drama set in Sicily and dedicated to her husband.[56] She could of course have revised or even rewritten the drama extensively after Davies's 1612 poem urged its publication. An anecdote in the *Life* about a work pirated from the chamber of her sister-in-law and then published is recognizably a version of the common aristocratic excuse

for stooping to publication, but (along with the dedication) it may suggest some collaboration between the two women in having the drama
published. The daughter's statement that Cary recalled this pirated work
from the press may refer, as Beilin suggests, to the dedicatory poem,
which was in fact removed from most copies of the drama.[57]

Cary is not likely to have encountered, and does not seem to be indebted to, earlier Herod and Mariam plays.[58] Rather, her tragedy finds its
place in the line of French Senecan tragedies inaugurated in England by
the Countess of Pembroke's translation of Robert Garnier's *Marc-
Antoine*.[59] In addition to this influential precedent by an aristocratic
woman, the closest analogues for *Mariam* are other tragedies written by
members of the Countess's circle: Samuel Daniel's *Cleopatra* and *Philotas,*
and Fulke Greville's *Mustapha*.[60] These classicizing dramas stand apart
from the popular stage drama of the period, and also eschew the trappings
of Italianate Senecanism—ghosts, stage violence, horrors and atrocities,
vendettas, gruesome effects, marvels.[61] But they are not mere academic
exercises, as is evident from their authors' fears and the censors' inquiries.
Rather, they were a recognized vehicle for the exploration of dangerous
political topics—the wickedness of tyranny, the dangers of absolutism, the
modes of and justifications for resistance, the folly of princes, the corruption of royal favorites, the responsibilities of counselors.[62] Though these
topics pervade English tragedy of the late Elizabethan and Jacobean periods, they received elaborate intellectual analysis in French Senecan drama,
as did conflicting theories of monarchy, tyranny, and rebellion. Several
generic features promoted such analysis: the primacy of speech over action; long rhetorical monologues; the prominence of women as heroines
and villains; and a chorus which speaks from a limited rather than an authorized vantage point. These dramas often make a strong case for aristocrats and magistrates who resist tyranny on the ground of their own rights
and responsibilities to the state, recalling positions developed by Calvin,
the Jesuit Robert Parsons, and the *Vindiciae Contra Tyrannos,* among others.[63] The dramas do not overtly sanction or encourage rebellion; their
perceived danger resides in the complexity and ambiguity with which issues of tyranny and rebellion are treated. We do not know whether Cary
read any or all of them in manuscript or print before publishing *Mariam,*
but her interests, her reading habits, and her tutor Davies's connections
make that plausible.

The Garnier–Countess of Pembroke *Antonie* (1592) shows Antony and
Cleopatra and their confidants analyzing issues of fate and guilt, shameful
life versus suicide, in the wake of the Actium debacle. The political issue,
explored in multiple perspectives, is Caesar's absolutism, given free rein
by Antony's defeat. In a debate on the sources of the absolute ruler's

strength and resemblance to God, Agrippa locates it in mercy and the people's love, Augustus in severity and the people's fear. A chorus of Roman soldiers finds hope of peace but also intimations of danger in Augustus' absolute rule, while an Egyptian chorus sees that it portends Egypt's slavery to Rome, prepared for by Cleopatra's (and Egypt's) weakness, folly, and licentiousness.

Daniel offered his *Cleopatra* as a companion piece to the Countess's *Antonie,* focusing on Cleopatra after Antony's death. In the first (Elizabethan) version (1594) Cleopatra is an aging, weak, indecisive, and passive woman, evoking pity but little admiration—a "sweet distressed Lady" in the words of her Roman admirer Dolabella, but in the view of the Egyptian chorus a licentious, pleasure-seeking Queen who has infected Egypt with vice and servility. Augustus' tyranny is explored, but at some remove: through a pathetic report of the murder he ordered of the boy Cesario (Cleopatra's son by Julius Caesar); and through a debate by Augustus' counselors setting the inhumanity of killing an innocent against the necessities of the state. In the much-revised Jacobean version (1607)—with Essex's rebellion and execution, Ralegh's imprisonment, and James's absolutist claims in the background—the critique of tyranny is much more forceful. Cesario, now a speaking character, takes on himself the duty to return someday to rule Egypt, and just before his murder portrays himself in pathetic and powerful terms as an innocent sacrificed to Augustus' desire for sole power. Cleopatra is now forceful and resolute, her fault not licentiousness but pride. Her dramatized death scene displays her "great mind" withstanding a barrage of arguments to save herself and staging her death as a triumph over tyranny: "Witnes my soule parts free to Antony, / And thou prowd tyrant Caesar doe thy Worst" (V, ii).

Between these two versions came Daniel's *Philotas,* staged at Blackfriars and published in 1605, with a dedication to Prince Henry urging the analogy of past times to present.[64] It brought Daniel before the Star Chamber to answer charges that the work alludes to the Essex affair, shadowing Cecil as the vindictive and manipulative Craterus. His defense was a claim that much of the drama predated the rebellion and that its themes of ambition and envy are universal.[65] The drama invites sympathy for Philotas, an attractive, valiant, bountiful young general beloved by the people and presumably loyal to Alexander, but imprudent in scorning the King's powerful counselors and in openly disputing Alexander's claims to divine descent and powers. Craterus, suborning witnesses by terror and playing on the King's fears, has Philotas falsely accused of treasonous plots and horribly tortured. He maintains his innocence long and stoically, seeming to speak for the rights of Englishmen at risk from monarchical absolutism, Star Chamber courts, and exaggerated claims of divine right.[66] At length he confesses to conspiring to overthrow Alexander, but the Nuntius who reports the scene questions whether that confession was simply the product of torture. The chorus of three Greeks and one Persian debate their forms of government, the Persian plausibly terming them both tyrannies, since Grecian laws are merely a stalking horse for the monarch to do what he will. Daniel affixed an "Argument" and an "Apology" to the published work, as a sop to the censors with Essex and Cecil on their minds; they are patently at odds with the drama's general tenor, and thereby underscore the interpretive openness and danger of these Senecan dramas. In a transparent gesture to Cecil, the "Apology" declares that Philotas' guilt was "providentially discerned" by Craterus, "one of the most honest men that ever followed Alexander," who thereby prevented the "imbroyling" of the state, or its transformation into "a monstrous body with many heads."[67]

Fulke Greville's *Mustapha* is an even more complex exploration of responses to tyranny.[68] An Elizabethan version written in the mid–1590s highlights the dangers of factions warring over the succession; the Jacobean versions (a 1609 truncated edition, and another written around 1607–1610) highlight the monarch's tyrannical suspicions of his subjects, the danger of rule by favorites, and the destruction of the state caused by political evils—a not so covert warning, as Ronald Rebholz notes, of incipient tyranny in England.[69] In all the versions Mustapha is the worthy, honorable, and universally beloved son of the aging Soliman the Magnificent, who envies his popularity (as James envied Prince Henry) and fears him as a possible usurper. Soliman's second wife, Rossa, is a type of the ambitious courtier who manipulates and dominates the monarch, at length persuading him that security and public order require Mustapha's death, on the mere suspicion of treason. Other positions represented include a chorus of Bashas, court sycophants who promote tyranny by flattering kings, subverting laws, and undermining people's rights; Camena, daughter to Rossa and Soliman, who argues for and acts upon the higher claims of reason and natural law and for that is executed by her own mother; a chorus of priests, who argue various theological positions (humble obedience to tyrants, self-preservation as a mandate of divine law, and even the use of force against oppressive tyrants); and a chorus of Tartars, who speak for nature and reason against theological mystification. The hero, Mustapha, speaks for and enacts absolute obedience to kings— "Our gods they are, their God remains above. / To thinke against annoynted Power is death" (IV, iv)—but his portrayal as a Christ-like martyr positions this response to tyranny above nature.

Achmat, the good counselor, is in some degree normative: he recognizes a duty to his Prince's honor rather than his humors, and also a higher duty—"I first am Natures subject, then my Princes / . . . My God is not the God of subtill murther" (II, i). He first thinks to support the popular uprising provoked by Mustapha's death, as justified by the people's "old equalities of Nature" and the establishment of kings "for the good of all"; but at length he determines to quell it on the pragmatic ground that the state's "prosperity" is better preserved by tyranny than anarchy, which destroys all order, power, and right (V, iii). Yet his decision and justification are put in question since they leave Rossa in absolute control, promising to rule with unfettered cruelty. At the end, the famous "Chorus Sacerdotum" descants on humankind's bondage to the contradictory laws of nature and religion, with the latter itself contradicted by conscience: "Yet, when each of us, in his owne heart lookes, / He findes the God there, farre unlike his bookes."

In Cary's *Mariam* political and domestic tyranny are fused in Herod the Great, a ruthless Idumaean usurper of Israel's throne; his name also evokes the various biblical Herods associated with the Massacre of the Innocents, the trial of Jesus, and the martyrdoms of John the Baptist and various apostles.[70] Issues of obedience and resistance in both the state and the family are explored with the genre's typical complexity and ambiguity. The drama is conspicuously well made: the first half (to the turning point at Act III, scene ii) presents the gains in liberty, happiness, and moral good brought about by the presumed death of the tyrant; the last half portrays the manifold evils unleashed at his return. Observing the unity of time, Cary condenses events and incorporates materials from other parts of the Herod story to heighten the dramatic tension around Herod's supposed death and return, and also to provide apt foils for and conflicting perspectives on Mariam.

Early soliloquies and dialogues bring the pressure of antecedent events to bear on present action. With the aid of Rome, Herod has supplanted Hircanus, the hereditary King and priest in Israel, divorced his Idumaean first wife, Doris, disinherited their son Antipater, and married Hircanus' granddaughter, the singularly beautiful Mariam, whom he loves with fierce intensity and jealous passion. To secure his throne—to which his only legitimate claim comes through Mariam's line—he had old Hircanus murdered, and arranged a drowning accident to remove the new high priest, Mariam's brother Aristabolus. Called to Rome to answer murder charges leveled by Alexandra (mother to Mariam and Aristabolus and daughter to Hircanus), he left orders with his sister Salome's husband, Josephus, to kill Mariam in the event of his death so no other man could possess her. Reinstated as King, he had Josephus killed for telling Mariam about the decree for her death, taking that as evidence supporting Salome's false charge that they were lovers. Just before the play begins,

Herod is again called to Rome and is in grave danger of death as a partisan of the defeated and recently deceased Antony; he leaves another order for Mariam's death with his officer Sohemus, who again reveals it to her.

Cary's drama opens with reports of the tyrant's death, which produce general relief, liberation, and a sense of new beginnings. Mariam is torn between grief and joy—grief for the ardent husband she once loved, joy that the tyrant who murdered her kin, imprisoned her out of jealousy, and twice decreed her death will not return. Her mother, Alexandra, rejoices in the death of the usurper—*"Esaus* Issue, heyre of hell"—who killed her father and son (I, ii). Mariam's son ascends the throne, and in his minority Mariam and Alexandra wield power. Herod's brother Pheroras, forced by Herod to agree to a dynastic marriage with his infant niece, rejoices that he may now marry his beloved but lowborn Graphina: "This blessed houre, till now implord in vaine, / Which hath my wished libertie restor'd, / And made my subject selfe my owne againe" (II, i). Salome's second husband, Constabarus, has for twelve years at great personal peril concealed the two sons of Babus (who were under decree of death from Herod as kin of Hircanus); now neither he nor they are any longer at risk, and they joyfully embrace their liberty, planning to serve the state with merit and valor.[71] Sohemus no longer need fear the tyrant's wrath for disobeying and revealing his order to kill Mariam. Even those who regret Herod's death inadvertently benefit from it. Salome had planned to provoke Herod to execute Constabarus by telling him about Babus' sons, but now she intends to clear her way to a new marriage by divorcing her husband—a scandalously illegal act for a woman in Israel but hardly as wicked as murder. And Herod's rejected wife, Doris, will no longer be able to indulge her groundless hopes that Herod might return to her or at least make Antipater his heir—so she will likely give over her murderous plots to forward that cause.

At Herod's return (IV, i) all the hopeful new beginnings (launched under female rule) are crushed. Pheroras, suborned by Salome with a promise to help preserve his marriage to Graphina, reveals the story of Constabarus and Babus' sons—and they are all led off to death. Sohemus is executed for presumed adultery with Mariam and the revelation of Herod's decree. Mariam refuses Herod's sexual advances and berates him for decreeing her death and killing her kin, reinforcing his jealous conviction that she has been unfaithful with Sohemus. Salome bribes Mariam's servant to offer (as if from Mariam) a cup of poison to Herod, after which the servant hangs himself in remorse for his treachery. Salome extorts a decree for the death of Mariam from the desperate, vacillating Herod. Mariam's mother, Alexandra, denounces her daughter, en route to execution, for wronging "noble Herod"—a blatantly hypocritical and in the event fruitless effort to placate him. A messenger recounts the details of Mariam's noble death, and Herod runs mad with grief and remorse, persuaded at last of her innocence and inestimable worth.

In the political realm Salome plays the role of evil courtier and counselor, encouraging the tyrant's passions and wickedness so as to advance her own interests and desires. The power of tyranny to corrupt is made manifest in the treachery of Pheroras and Mariam's servant, and in Alexandra's hypocrisy. Gestures of political resistance are limited: Alexandra's initial denunciation of Herod's crimes to Rome; Constabarus' valiant efforts to save Babus' sons; the principled disobedience of the "good counselor" Sohemus. At the end of Act II the chorus points out the "weake uncertaine ground" for the report of Herod's death, so eagerly believed by most because it sorts with their desires. The chorus's stated moral warns against self-deception and credulity, but the inference may be drawn that wishes and chance are hardly enough to destroy a tyrant.

Like the other English Senecan dramas, Cary's *Mariam* intertwines the spheres of public life and private desire, but here issues of love and domestic tyranny are central. Mariam's tragic choice—to reject Herod's love and bed as a gesture of conscientious resistance and personal integrity— is read from a number of perspectives, as the dramatic structure sets Mariam against several foils. First there is Graphina, whose true love for Pheroras reprises Mariam's earlier love for Herod, while her silence and humility seem to embody stereotypical feminine ideals.[72] Those ideals are problematized, however, by the class disparity between Graphina and Mariam: they suit with Graphina's lowly station, whereas the highborn Mariam (whose family are the legitimate Kings and priests of Israel) has some right to exhibit family pride and self-regard. The Graphina-Pheroras love match evokes sympathy, but we also know that because of it Pheroras betrays Constabarus and Babus' sons. Another foil is Mariam's mother, Alexandra, whose single-minded hatred of Herod contrasts with the complexity of Mariam's feelings, even as her later hypocrisy in disguising that hatred constrasts with Mariam's integrity. There is also Doris, Herod's divorced wife, who responds to her marital wrongs in a manner very different from Mariam—by cursing her rival's children and devising poison plots against them.

Salome is the chief foil. She repeatedly and maliciously slanders the innocent Mariam for marital infidelity while she herself flaunts her illicit affairs and has two husbands killed when she is ready to replace them. Thoroughly wicked, she will do anything to compass her own will: "I meane not to be led by president, / My will shall be to me in stead of Law" (I, vi). Most readers of the age would share Constabarus' view that his wife's "private conference" with her new lover Silleus is shameful, and

that her proposal to divorce her husband is shocking—a gender confusion
that threatens order in nature and society:

> Are Hebrew women now transform'd to men?
> Why do you not as well our battels fight,
> And wear our armour? suffer this, and then
> Let all the world be topsie turved quite.
> Let fishes graze, beastes, swime, and birds descend,
> Let fire burne downewards whilst the earth aspires:
> Let Winters heat and Summers cold offend,
> Let Thistels growe on Vines, and Grapes on Briers,
> Set us to Spinne or Sowe, or at the best
> Make us Wood-hewers, Waters-bearing wights:
> . . . . .
> You are the first, and will I hope be last,
> That ever sought her husband to divorce.
>
> (I, vi)

Yet for all that, her argument for women's right to divorce is given full
and forceful airing, as it proposes a kind of evenhanded justice for unhappy wives:

> If he [Constabarus] to me did beare as Earnest hate,
> As I to him, for him there were an ease,
> A separating bill might free his fate:
> From such a yoke that did so much displease.
> Why should such priviledge to man be given?
> Or given to them, why bard from women then?
> Are men then we in greater grace with Heaven?
> Or cannot women hate as well as men?
> Ile be the custome-breaker: and beginne
> To shew my Sexe the way to freedomes doore.
> And with an offring will I purge my sinne,
> The lawe was made for none but who are poore.
>
> (I, iii)

Mariam's claims to personal integrity set her apart from all these women,
and her assertion of rights within marriage contrast sharply with Salome's
move from radical social disruption to murder.

The drama offers several formulations of the tragic flaw that precipitates
Mariam's tragedy. The chorus, a company of Jews, construes it variously
in their several odes, judging Mariam according to their very conservative
notion of a wife's duty. They claim that Mariam seeks to be free of Herod
"for expectation of variety"; that she has invited suspicion by her too free

conversation with others; that she seeks public glory; and that she exhibits an ignoble vengefulness of mind (I, vi; III, iii; IV, viii). But these positions are undermined by the drama as a whole. We soon realize that Mariam seeks no other lover, that she loved Herod devotedly until his wrongdoing destroyed that love, and that the qualities the chorus ascribes to her pertain rather to Salome, Alexandra, and Doris. Obviously the chorus sees women as interchangeable entities. The drama especially problematizes the chorus's notion that Mariam's "public" speech has undone her, for, as Margaret Ferguson observes, Mariam's trouble stems rather from the one kind of speech they allow—private speech to her own husband.[73]

Mariam clearly does not fulfill the standard the chorus sets for proper wifely behavior—the entire subjection of mind as well as body to her husband:

> Do they not wholy give themselves away?
> Or give they but their body not their mind,
> Reserving that though best, for others pray?
>> No sure, their thoghts no more can be their owne,
>> And therefore should to none but one be knowne.
>>> (III, iii)

In this genre, however, the chorus is expected to speak from a partial, not an authoritative, vantage point. Their standard does not square with the principle Cary herself enunciated and tried to live by, since it makes no provision for "reason and conscience" in dealing with evil. It also ignores the distinction, so important to this genre and to the age, between rightful authority and tyrannical power. The chorus appeals to a higher and more universal Stoic standard at the end of Act IV, concluding that Mariam was swayed by "sullen passion" to refuse Herod, when she should have been led by a virtuous pride to rise above her injuries and to pay him the due marital debt.[74] But their final definition of Stoic virtue—"To scorne a freeborne heart slave-like to binde"—intimates that subjection to Herod's loathed bed might well amount to spiritual slavery for a freeborn Queen (IV, viii).

Sohemus identifies Mariam's tragic flaw more reliably, as imprudent speech: "Unbridled speech is *Mariam's* worst disgrace, / And will indanger her without desart" (III, iii). She exhibits this trait when she enrages Salome by referring to her base birth, and infuriates Herod by casting up to him all the old wrongs and flatly refusing his love and his bed. This characterization derives from Josephus, whose Mariam is a woman of unparalleled courage, nobility, beauty, and chastity, marred only by a "natural frowardness" and "a great and intemperate libertie in her discourse" with Herod and others.[75] Sohemus, ready to die for disobeying Herod and preserving Mariam's life, praises her pure heart and "grave majestie," which elicit admiration even as they prohibit love (III, iii). The Nuntius who describes to Herod her noble, courageous death laments that with her die "beautie, chastitie and wit" (V, i). Herod, who in life doted on her beauty and understood nothing of her mind or her feelings, celebrates her after death for all these qualities: the beauty of Venus, the chastity of Diana, the wit of Mercury (V, i). And now that he has silenced her forever, he ironically values her every word, demanding of the messenger, "Oh say, what said she more? each word she sed / Shall be the food whereon my heart is fed" (V, i).[76]

As she goes to her death, Mariam herself attributes her plight to imprudence, pride, and the presumption that her innocence and Herod's love would protect her. Throughout, however, she insists on preserving the integrity of her own thoughts and feelings, and this insistence subverts conventional formulations of wifely duty and male idealization. The motif begins in her opening soliloquy as she admits the complexity of her feelings: grief for the death of the husband she once loved; relief that his jealous tyranny is past. Upon hearing of Herod's return, she at once explains to Sohemus the impossibility of pretending love in the face of such wrongs: unable "to live with him I so profoundly hate," she has, she declares, "with solemne vowes . . . forsworne his Bed" (III, iii). She recognizes her sexual power over him but scorns hypocritical pretense in the interests of prudent self-preservation:

> I Know I could inchaine him with a smile:
> And lead him captive with a gentle word,
> I Scorne my looke should ever man beguile,
> Or other speech, then meaning to afford.
> (III, iii)

She looks to her innocence as a shield, not so much from outward danger as from "the pangs of inward griefe," and refuses to sully her spirit "to be commandresse of the triple earth" (III, iii). To Herod, who calls constantly for her, urges her to love him, promises her ever more gifts and power, and insists that she accept his explanations for the death of her kin, she maintains her right to her own judgments and feelings: "My Lord, I suit my garment to my minde, / And there no cheerfull colours can I finde"; "No, had you wisht the wretched *Mariam* glad, / . . . My brother nor my Grandsyre had not dide"; "I cannot frame disguise, nor never taught / My face a looke dissenting from my thought" (IV, iii). When Salome puts her plot in place—the poison cup and the suggestion that Mariam and Sohemus are lovers—Mariam is almost speechless with amazement: "Is this a dream?" At length she manages a dignified denial— "they can tell / That say I lov'd him. *Mariam* saies not so"—but finds it useless (IV, iv).

At the end, Mariam recognizes that prudent humility would have saved her, and admits that the conjunction of chastity and humility is the feminine ideal. But she shows little chagrin over her lack of humility, and certainly no new accession of it, as she projects her triumph over earthly tyrants and imagines an appropriately female heavenly reward—not in Abraham's bosom but in Sarah's lap:

> And I had singly one, but tis my joy,
> That I was ever innocent, though sower:
> And therefore can they but my life destroy,
> My Soule is free from adversaires power.
> You Princes great in power, and high in birth,
> Be great and high, I envy not your hap:
> Your birth must be from dust: your power on earth,
> In heav'n shall *Mariam* sit in *Saraes* lap.
>
> (IV, viii)

Indeed, the drama goes some distance toward disjoining the triad of virtues that constitute the era's feminine ideal, inviting sympathetic identification with a heroine who is chaste but manifestly neither silent nor obedient. Reinforcing that sympathy, several analogies associate Mariam's innocent, noble, unjust death with Christ's crucifixion: the betraying servant who hangs himself upon a tree; Mariam's prediction that Herod "three daies hence" will wish to revive her. Moreover, Mariam's resistance to domestic tyranny has as a direct result the potential overthrow of the tyrant's political power. Herod runs mad, and he explicitly admits that rebellion against him would be justified:

> You dwellers in the now deprived land,
> Wherein the matchles *Mariam* was bred:
> Why graspe not each of you a sword in hand,
> To ayme at me your cruell Soveraignes head.
> . . . . .
> Tis I have overthrowne your royall line.
>
> (V, i)

Historically Herod was not deposed, but Cary's drama ends by holding forth that possibility.

Mariam is the last published in a series of closet Senecan dramas concerned with forms of tyranny, and should perhaps be seen as the first of a series of tragedies (1610–1614) that focus on female resistance to tyrants in the domestic sphere—women who seek to control their own sexual choices, challenging the orthodox ideal of submission.[77] Cary's heroine does not rise to the high eloquence of the Duchess of Malfi, and whereas the Duchess acts to realize her own sexual desire, Mariam's sexual self-assertion takes the form of refusing to have her love commanded. Nevertheless, *Mariam*'s challenge to patriarchal control within the institution of marriage is revolutionary, as the heroine claims a wife's right to her own speech—public and private—as well as to the integrity of her own emotional life and her own self-definition. Cary's *Mariam* intimates that such integrity is the foundation for resistance to tyranny in every sphere.

The History of Edward II: Rebellion and the Queen's Part

Elizabeth Cary was the first Englishwoman to write political, as opposed to family, history. Her work, written around 1627–28 and first published in 1680 (in folio), is entitled *The History of the Life, Reign, and Death of Edward II. King of England, and Lord of Ireland. With the Rise and Fall of his Great Favourites, Gaveston and the Spencers.* Its extended, complex, and sympathetic portrait of Queen Isabel as an intelligent, forceful woman is unparalleled in other accounts of Edward's reign; it also invites continued, pointed comparisons between the reigns of Edward II and James I.

Both external and internal evidence dictate confident attribution of this work to Elizabeth Cary, then Lady Falkland, despite the fact that at first publication, and often afterwards, it was attributed to her husband.[78] The title page bears the information "Written by E.F. in the year 1627, and Printed verbatim from the Original"; the preface to the reader is also signed "E.F." A rewritten and much shortened octavo version of this work was put out by a different bookseller in the same year (1680) and probably also redacted then, judging from the plain style and timely political reference to the Exclusion Crisis (1679–1681). The tentative attribution on the title page of the octavo makes clear the lack of foundation for the authorship assignment: "Found among the Papers of, and (supposed to be) Writ by the Right Honourable Henry Viscount Faulkland, Sometime Lord Deputy of Ireland." This statement evidently accounts for the assignment of the much longer work to Falkland also, and for the handwritten change of "E" to "H" (for Henry) in some copies of the folio. The initials "E.F." on both the title page and the preface in the folio—as well as the style, the invented dramatic speeches, the sympathetic references to the Pope and Catholic clerics, and the remarkable portrait of Queen Isabel—all point to Elizabeth, Lady Falkland, as author. Some of her known writings were also found among the Falkland family papers, including her translation of Cardinal Perron's answer to King James (1630), always attributed to her, though English censorship necessitated its anonymous publication in the Netherlands.[79] That book was seized and burned upon entry into England by order of the Archbishop of Canterbury, George Abbot.

The Perron translation also casts light on Cary's authorship of *Edward*

II. Perron attempted to allay English Protestant suspicions about Roman Catholics as traitors, in the wake of papal depositions of monarchs and assassination plots in France and England.[80] Some issues are akin to those in *Mariam*—the grounds of allegiance, theoretical limitations on royal power, the claims of conscience. Cary employs a terse and forceful prose style appropriate to the subject, and addresses her (unsigned) dedication to Queen Henrietta Maria as the best patron for a Catholic woman's English translation of a French work addressed to King James.[81] The "Epistle to the Reader" presents Cary as a confident and capable scholar and author who recognizes that her gender will affect the reception of her work but who scorns the excuse of unwilling publication, so often employed by aristocrats of both sexes:

> I desire to have noe more guest at of me, but that I am a *Catholique* and a Woman: the first serves for mine honor, and the second, for my excuse, since if the worke be but meanely done, it is noe wonder, for my Sexe can raise noe great expectation of anie thing that shall come from me: yet were it a great follie in me, if I would expose to the view of the world, a worke of this kinde, except I judged it, to want nothing fitt, for a *Translation*. Therefore I will confesse, I thinke it well done, and so had I confest sufficientlie in printing it . . . I will not make use of that worne-out forme of saying, I printed it against my will, mooved by the importunitie of Friends: I was mooved to it by my beleefe, that it might make those English that understand not French . . . reade *Perron*.   (sig. a 2v)

Directly relevant to the authorship question in *Edward II* is the assertion in two commendatory epistles that she translated Perron in a month's time—an assertion for which she was the obvious source.[82] The preface to *Edward II* (signed "E.F.") evidences a similar confidence as to scholarly competence and procedures. And the analogous claim to have written the work in a month's time seems incredible as a coincidence.

> To out-run those weary hours of a deep and sad Passion, my melancholy Pen fell accidentally on this Historical Relation; which speaks a King, our own, though one of the most Unfortunate; and shews the Pride and Fall of his Inglorious Minions.
>
> I have not herein followed the dull Character of our Historians, nor amplified more than they infer, by Circumstance. I strive to please the Truth, not Time; nor fear I censure, since at the worst, 'twas but one Month mis-spended; which cannot promise ought in right Perfection.
>
> If so you hap to view it, tax not my Errours; I my selfe confess them.

The misattribution of *Edward II* seems a clear case of gender expectations suppressing convincing evidence for Elizabeth Cary's authorship.

Cary's brief preface refers to her history as therapy—needful enough in 1627–28, when she was struggling to survive and to resist her husband's plans for her. By this time her reading and her life at court and in Ireland had given her access to the kinds of experience Natalie Davis deems essential for the would-be historian: access to materials and to the genres of historical writing; a deeply felt connection with public concerns such as politics and religion; and also "enough public life . . . to observe intrigue, conflict, and debate."[83] The preface also points to historiographic principles which she in fact follows. She eschews as "dull" the sort of chronicle history written by Holinshed, Speed, and Stow, and defends her methods of amplification. In practice this means that she looks to the classical historians recently made available in good translations—Thucydides, Livy, Sallust, and especially Tacitus[84]—for warrant to clarify motives and causes by creating appropriate speeches and imagining scenes. She also claims allegiance to "Truth"—not factual accuracy but (judging from her practice) the truth of moral exemplum and character as well as the political insights emphasized by the new Tacitean "politic" history in the vein of Machiavelli and Guicciardini. Her work displays most of the characteristics F. J. Levy finds in that mode: treating limited historical periods or reigns, pointing parallels to the present, focusing on specific issues (such as the reasons for a rebellion), and employing a style replete with maxims and (often) elaborate political orations.[85] The chief English examples were Sir John Hayward's *King Henrie the IIII* (1599), which was prosecuted as treasonous; Daniel's *Collection of the Historie of England* (1618); and Francis Bacon's *Henry the Seventh* (1621).[86] In classifying Edward II with these works, Levy notes its pervasive contemporary reference and ambiguous stance toward rebellion.

The reign of Edward II invited a great deal of attention from Elizabethan and Jacobean historians and poets, and much diversity of interpretation; Cary surely knew several versions of the story, and the variety forced choices in emphasis and explanation. In Holinshed's *Chronicles* (1577) the focus is on Edward's "misgovernance": at first he was given over to riot and voluptuous pleasures with his favorite Gaveston, and then wholly controlled by the ambitious Spencers. The Barons' uprisings are condemned but largely excused by the King's complete alienation of his subjects. The Queen's character is not brought into focus, but she is presented with some sympathy as a much-abused wife and an effective leader, along with Mortimer, of the invasion and revolt against Edward. Yet both are strongly condemned for usurping power and for the regicide.[87] Marlowe's drama *Edward II* (1591) dwells chiefly on the King's passionate love for Gaveston; it presents Mortimer as the sinister directing force in the revolt, with Isabel at first a modest, wronged woman but then a villain wholly under his control.[88] The 1610 addition to the *Mirrour for Magistrates* blames the tragedy on Edward's flattering, parasitical courtiers and Isabel's lust for Mortimer.[89] Drayton treated the story in several genres, with different interpretive emphases. The epyllion-like *Piers Gaveston* (1593) focuses sympathetically on Edward's erotic relationship with Gaveston and desperate grief over his death. *Mortimeriados* (1596), replete with romance elements, centers on the love between a brave Mortimer and a wronged yet strong and courageous Isabel, though it also deplores civil war and invites sympathy for Edward's suffering. The Ovidian *Englands Heroicall Epistles* (1597) presents the love complaints of Isabel and Mortimer in epistolary interchange. The epic-like *Barons Warres* (1603) focuses on politics and warfare: it eschews criticism of the King and denounces rebellion, but also emphasizes Mortimer's heroic leadership and Isabel's strength of mind and craft.[90] Daniel's politic history assigns blame to all sides and underscores several political lessons. Edward's behavior shows the danger of riot and disorder and advancing unworthy minions. The justifications offered for the rebellion are "execrable doctrine." Isabella is at first an able and greatly wronged Queen but then "an impotent woman led with passion, and abused by wicked counsell"; she is finally responsible for "the infamy of all what was acted," setting the worst example of any English Queen.[91] Daniel reads this history as a cautionary tale, making the world "wary" to run again into the violence of revolution.

Almost contemporaneous with Cary's history, and possibly available to her in manuscript, is Francis Hubert's poem *The Deplorable Life and Death of Edward the Second* (1628), in the form of a complaint spoken by the King.[92] Urging the need for kings to take lessons from the past, it draws pointed parallels between Buckingham and Gaveston (and Spencer)—one among many indications of the political resonance this history was seen to have in the 1620s.[93] Hubert does almost nothing with the figure of Isabel: she is a weak woman, a pawn of Mortimer who tempts her and wins her love.

Elizabeth Cary's history also highlights parallels between the reigns of Edward II and James I, pointing up lessons through maxims and commentary, and more subtly through the invention of lively scenes and speeches, well-drawn characters, and striking figurative language. In her reading blame attaches to many, but chiefly to the King, whose "degenerate corruption" led him to foster "Parasitical Minions" and flattering sycophants, thereby promoting "a general Subversion of all Law and Goodness" (10–11). Here, as in Marlowe, Edward is weak, querulous, neglectful of state affairs and of his nobles. At first he is utterly besotted with the sensuous and reckless Gaveston; then he is wholly under the control of the shrewd Machiavellian diplomat Spencer and his train of relatives. In an impressive deathbed scene Edward I urges the true kingly ideal, warning his son to elicit love rather than fear from his people and to cherish and heed the ancient nobility. But Edward II insists on his absolute power and will, and gives over the "sway and manage" of state affairs to his minions (159). After his overthrow, Edward's complaints against his false wife and Mortimer evoke pathos but do not rise to tragic dignity. Cary identifies several causes for Edward's fall: his own "Disorder and Improvidence"; the "treacherous Infidelity of his Wife, Servants, and Subjects"; and especially the general defection, prompted by his "oppression of the whole Kingdom" (137). She sees Edward's deposition as a special moral and political case in English history, in that he himself is the root cause of all his wrongs:

> So great a Fall these latter times produce not; a King in a potent Kingdome of his own, deposed by a handful of Strangers, who principally occasioned it, without so much as any Kinsman, Friend, or Subject that either with his Tongue or Sword declar'd himself in his Quarrel. But you may object, He fell by Infidelity and Treason, as have many other that went before and followed him. 'Tis true; but yet withal observe, here was no second Pretendents, but those of his own, A Wife, and a Son, which were the greatest Traytors: had he not indeed been a Traytor to himself, they could not all have wronged him.   (160)

Approximately the first half of Cary's history is given over to the Edward-Gaveston relationship (inviting comparisons with James and Somerset). Gaveston is portrayed as a foreigner (Gascon or, as Cary thinks more likely, Italian),[94] without wealth, noble birth, or much intelligence, but with great physical beauty and "above measure ambitious and aspiring":

> *Gaveston* his Ganymede [was] . . . in shape and Beauty . . . too much for a man, and Perfection enough to have equal'd the fairest Female splendour that breath'd within the Confines of this Kingdom. Though in the abilities of the Brain he were short of a deep and solid Knowledge, yet he had Understanding enough to manage his ways to best advantage; having a smooth Tongue, an humble Look, and a winning Behaviour.   (4)

By pandering to all the King's pleasures, vices, and whims, he soon became the channel for all power and patronage:

> A short time invests in his person or disposure all the principal Offices and Dignities of the Kingdom . . . This Pageant, too weak a Jade for

so weighty a burden, had not a brain in it self able enough to manage such great Actions; neither would he entertain those of ability to guide him . . . This made him chuse his Servants as his Master chose him, of a smooth, fawning temper . . . Hence flew a world of wilde disorder; the sacred Rules of Justice were subverted, the Laws integrity abused, the Judge corrupted or inforc'd, and all the Types of Honour due to Vertue, Valour, Goodness, were like the Pedlers pack, made Ware for Chapmen.   (20–21)

A contemporary would surely think of King James selling titles, Somerset's rise, and the Overbury scandal.

The several banishments of Gaveston forced by the Barons, and his recalls at the King's command, prompt Cary to a trenchant and insightful analysis of the problems of courtiership, with obvious contemporary parallels:

A Champion-Conscience without bound or limit, a Tongue as smooth as Jet that sings in season, a bloudless Face that buries guilt in boldness; these Ornaments are fit to cloath a Courtier: he that wants these, still wants a means to live, if he must make his Service his Revenue . . . if you cast your eye upon the gross body of the Court, and examine the ordinary course of their gradation, it will plainly appear, that twenty creep in by the backgate, while one walks up by the street-door.   (31–32)

Cary censures the entire corrupt court: courtier-"Caterpillers," who urge the King to assert his arbitrary power and will; the timid Council, who fear to oppose him to serve the state's needs; Gaveston, who exhausted the royal treasure and pawned the crown jewels; the King, who is most blameworthy for advancing "such Sycophants" (9). She recognizes the danger and futility of individual opposition, and so holds blameless the Barons who join together in arms to execute Gaveston, this "Blazing-star . . . that liv'd and died, nor lov'd, excus'd, or pitied" (30). She defines Parliament's proper role in terms that directly challenge Stuart absolutism: "The gravest Senate of the Kingdom, that had an over-ruling Power to limit the King, and command the Subject" (36). The impotence of the King's supporters against the warring Barons and the invading Scots is vividly rendered, as in this description of the Archbishop of York's defeat: "The News . . . like the voice of a Night-raven, had no sooner croakt his sad eccho in the King's ear, but he straight raiseth his Army, weaken'd with Famine, and lessen'd with Sickness" (47).

The second half of Cary's history is given over to the machinations of the new favorite, Spencer, and the activities of the Queen, Mortimer, and the Barons, culminating in the regicide. Her fine portrait of Spencer as a

Machiavellian schemer who clothes himself in humility and obsequiousness but "understands the plain-Song of the State, and her progressions"
(51) invites parallels with Buckingham in many details.[95] This narrative
(unlike most others) implies that Spencer is the King's new lover; at one
point he is termed "this Gipsie," with a possible allusion to Buckingham's
starring role in Jonson's *Gypsies Metamorphosed* (1621). Spencer exalts all his
kin to places of favor and rules over all grants (75), exhausting the royal
treasury "to water the *drought* of himself, his herd of hungry Kindred, and
the swarm of Flesh-flies that became his creatures" (80). Forced to flee
abroad by the Barons' revolt and Parliament's formal charge of "*Insolency,
Injustice, Corruption, Oppression, neglect of the publick and immoderate advancement of his own particular*" (61), he returns when Edward puts down
the revolt, binding the King yet more closely to him.

This segment of Cary's history is unique among the various accounts in
that it is structured as a power struggle between Isabel and Spencer. Mortimer plays only an ancillary role. He is "a piece of masculine Bravery
without exception," one among several leaders of the Barons' revolt who
was saved from death at the Queen's intercession, and who responds with
a "Courtly, brave respect" to her initiating "Glances" of love (89). But
Cary gives scant attention to his actions or to the love relationship. He
attends the Queen in France and during the invasion but comes into
prominence only after the King's deposition, sharing power with her during Edward III's minority.

The most unusual feature of Cary's history is the portrayal of Isabel as
a tragic protagonist, an intelligent, forceful woman whose role is central
while her guilt is minimal. In the Gaveston segment she is treated briefly
but sympathetically as a "rare beauty" who was made the victim of an
impossible marriage that was contrived (in vain) to reclaim the King's
affections from Gaveston and to put down his "swelling greatness" (18).
She also plays a minor but positive role in trying to make peace between
the King and his nobles. With Spencer's rise she adopts a course of politic
accommodation—very much as Queen Anne did with Buckingham:

> The *Queen,* that had no great cause to like those Syrens, that caus'd
> her grief, and did seduce her Husband, he yet presumes to court with
> strong professions, vowing to serve her as a faithful Servant. She
> seeing into the quality of the time, where he was powerful, and she
> in name a Wife, in truth a Hand-maid, doth not oppose, but more
> increase his Greatness, by letting all men know that she receiv'd
> him.   (52)

Isabel's love for Mortimer is represented as the almost inevitable result of
her impossible situation, so that she is at once the first mover in that affair
and yet all but guiltless in it:

> She saw the King a stranger to her bed, and revelling in the wanton
> embraces of his stoln pleasures, without a glance on her deserving
> Beauty. This contempt had begot a like change in her, though in a
> more modest nature, her youthful Affections wanting a fit subject to
> work on . . . she had cast her wandering eye upon the gallant
> *Mortimer.*   (89)

Cary's vivid narrative of Isabel's ventures in France and subsequent leadership of the invasion of England departs significantly from most of the
sources, and suggests parallels with Cary's own later life. Spencer proposes
that Isabel go to France to negotiate with the King, her brother, over
contested English territory there, hinting that if she fails, she might simply
remain (the situation recalls Cary's own dispatch to England in 1625). His
true motive is fear of her: "He knew her to be a Woman of a strong Brain,
and stout Stomack, apt on all occasions to trip up his heels, if once she
found him reeling," so he sought "to pare her nails before she scratcht
him" (86–87). In most histories of the reign, Isabel executes her diplomatic mission successfully, the Crown Prince is later sent over to sign papers, and Mortimer joins her there after escaping from the Tower. But in
Cary's account Isabel's mission to France is long delayed, so that she uses
the cover of a pilgrimage to Canterbury to make a daring escape to France
with the Prince and some other partisans—including Mortimer, who by
her direction has escaped from the Tower.[96] Cary's dramatic story of this
escape concludes with gleeful emphasis on Isabel's triumph over Spencer,
who is chagrined that she has control of the Prince:

> Thus did our Pilgrims scape the pride and malice of him which little
> dream'd of this Adventure: his Craft and Care, that taught him all
> those lessons of Cunning Greatness, here fell apparent short of all
> Discretion, to be thus over-reach'd by one weak Woman. For her
> Escape, it skill'd not, nor could hurt him: it was the rising Son with
> cause he feared; which who would have trusted with a Mother, justly
> mov'd by their disorder?   (92)

In Cary's reading, Isabel's mission in France is of her own devising—
an attempt to mount an invasion to oust Spencer as the sole cause of her
troubles and the realm's disorders. Imagining her strategy, Cary creates for
her an affecting rhetorical plea to the King her brother:

> Behold in me (dear Sir) your most unhappie Sister, the true picture
> of a dejected Greatness, that bears the grief of a despised Wedlock,
> which makes me flie to you for help and succour. I have, with a suf-
> ferance beyond the belief of my Sex, outrun a world of tryals . . . my
> tears speak those of a distressed Kingdom, which, long time glorious,

now is almost ruin'd. My blushing cheek may give a silent knowledge, I too much love and honour the cause of my afflictions, to express it. Yet this in modestie I may discover; my Royal Husband is too much abused . . . he still must wander, while such bewitching Syrens are his leaders. But why do I include them as a number? 'tis onely one; the rest are but his creatures . . . besides the Justice of my Cause, the strongest motive, I bring the hearts of a distressed Kingdom, that, if you set me right, will fight my Quarrel. (96–97)

Denied aid, she hopes at least for refuge and resists the demands of Edward (urged on by the "Serpent" Spencer) that she return or at least send back the Prince. Spencer's gold spread broadcast in France and Rome, together with Edward's complaints of her desertion and infidelity, result in her expulsion from France on command from the Pope. But Cary shows her outwitting the "Machiavel," pretending tearfully to leave for England but in fact fleeing to the Duchy of Hainaut. The French officials have then to admit to Spencer that "the Queen had gone beyond them with their Cunning . . . Thus Womens Wit sometimes can cozen Statesmen" (109). Cary emphasizes as well the unwavering devotion and allegiance Isabel inspired in several worthy noblemen who fought in her cause.[97] The narrative elicits sympathy for Isabel's vulnerability, as she is abandoned by her kin and in great danger. It also invites belief in the justice of her cause and admiration for her political skills, as well as for her effective use of the rhetoric of petition to win help from strangers—a skill Cary evidently understands well enough from her own experience.

Humble Sweetnes, cloath'd in truth and plainness, invites the ear to hear, the heart to pity. Who by a crooked fortune is forced to try and to implore the help of Strangers, must file his words to such a winning Smoothness, that they betray not him that hears or speaks them; yet must they not be varnisht o'er with Falshood, or painted with the terms of Art or Rhetorick; this bait may catch some Gudgeons, but hardly him that hath a solid Judgment. (110)

The account of the invasion is briskly told, its success attributed to fortuitous (or providential) storms and also to Isabel's leadership in rallying the Barons and clergy and especially the City of London to her cause.[98]

At this juncture Cary shows the Queen giving way to ambition and "incensed Passion" against Spencer—her tragic fall. She wreaks vengeance on Spencer in a humiliating public progress (recalling that of Shakespeare's Richard II). Cary's extended analysis pronounces that punishment just, but finds in its gratuitous cruelty evidence of the Queen's moral decline:

She thus passeth on with a kinde of insulting Tyranny, far short of the belief of her former Vertue and Goodness, she makes this poor unhappy man attend her Progress . . . merely for Revenge, Despite, and private Rancour; mounted on a poor, lean, ugly Jade, as basely furnisht; cloath'd in a painted Taberd, which was then a Garment worn by Condemned Thieves alone; and tatter'd rascally, he is led through each Town behinde the Carriage . . . Certainly this man was infinitely vicious, and deserv'd as much as could be laid upon him, for those many great and insolent Oppressions, acted with Injustice, Cruel[t]y, and Blood, yet it had been much more to the Queens Honour, if she had given him a quicker Death, and a more honourable Tryal, free from these opprobrious and barbarous Disgraces, which savour'd more of a savage, tyrannical disposition, than a judgment fit to command, or sway the Sword of Justice . . . It was at best too great and deep a blemish to suit a Queen, a Woman, and a Victor.   (128–129)

Yet unlike most other accounts, Cary's narrative distances Isabel from the wrongs done to the King. Parliament is made responsible for Edward's deposition, an act Cary carefully distinguishes from the earlier allowable and even commendable resistance (including armed resistance) to an iniquitous monarch:

It ne're was toucht or exprest by what Law, Divine or Humane, the Subject might Depose, not an Elective King, but one that Lineally and Justly had inherited, and so long enjoy'd it . . . In a true construction [it] was no more than a mere Politick Treason, not more dangerous in the Act than in the Example . . . they had just cause to restrain [the king] from his Errours, but no ground or colour to deprive him of his Kingdom.   (131)

Mortimer alone orchestrates the regicide in order to secure the realm and the usurpers' safety; the protesting Isabel agrees to it only when he threatens to flee the country otherwise, and promises to manage the entire affair himself.[99] Three years later Mortimer is executed for that deed, and Cary narrowly defines the legal limits of the Queen's responsibility for it. She alludes to Isabel's last years as a penitent but elides the usual report of her forced incarceration in a convent: "The Queen, who was guilty but in circumstance, and but an Accessory to the Intention, not the Fact, tasted with a bitter time of Repentance, what it was but to be quoted in the Margent of such a Story" (155).[100]

But if Isabel is located in the margins of the regicide event, she is not marginalized in Cary's history. Rather, she is portrayed with much sympathy as a strong, noble, intelligent woman who is a match for and finally victorious over her principal antagonist, Spencer; whose marital infidelity is entirely understandable and scarcely culpable; who can and does act effectively in the public arena as rhetorician, military commander, and reforming ruler; and whose guilt is recognized but largely deflected. She is treated as a tragic heroine in a very different mold from Mariam, one whose resistance culminates in open rebellion.

On the stage of the imagination, as in her own life, Cary advanced some distance in projecting the possibilities for female self-definition and resistance to tyranny in both the private and the public spheres. Her Senecan tragedy and Tacitean history are remarkable contributions to those dangerous genres, exploring the passions and the politics central to them from a woman's vantage point.

SALVE DEVS
REX IVDÆORVM.

Containing,

1 The Paſſion of Chriſt.
2 Eues Apologie in defence of Women.
3 The Teares of the Daughters of Ieruſalem.
4 The Salutation and Sorrow of the Virgine
   Marie.

With diuers other things not vnfit to be read.

Written by Miſtris *Æmilia Lanyer*, Wife to Captaine
Alfonſo Lanyer Seruant to the
Kings Majeſtie.

At London
Printed by *Valentine Simmes* for *Richard Bonian*, and
are to be ſold at his Shop in Paules Churchyard. *Anno* 1611.

Title page, Aemilia Lanyer, Salve Deus Rex Judaeorum *(1611).*

8

Imagining Female Community:
Aemilia Lanyer's Poems

Aemilia Lanyer (1569–1645) was the first Englishwoman to publish a substantial volume of original poems, and to make an overt bid for patronage as a male poet of the era might, though in distinctively female terms. Her volume of (ostensibly) religious poems, published in 1611, was entitled *Salve Deus Rex Judaeorum*.[1] The author identifies herself on the title page as a married gentlewoman whose status is defined through her husband's position as an officer and court musician: "Mistris *Aemilia Lanyer,* Wife to Captaine Alfonso Lanyer Servant to the Kings Majestie." Besides containing some good poems and passages, the volume is of particular interest for its feminist conceptual frame: it is a defense and celebration of the enduring community of good women that reaches from Eve to contemporary Jacobean patronesses. Lanyer imagines that community as distinctively separate from male society and its evils, and proclaims herself its poet.

We know very little about Aemilia Lanyer, but enough to recognize her as a marginal figure at Elizabeth's, and still more at James's, court. Her family connections were with the circle of court musicians dependent upon patronage, and she had virtually no prospects beyond what she could win for herself. A. L. Rowse's edition of the *Salve Deus* (1978) marshals some of the known facts about her life, chiefly drawn from the casebooks and diary of Simon Forman, the astrologer, in the service of his highly tenuous argument that she was the "Dark Lady" of Shakespeare's sonnets.[2] But the links to Shakespeare suggested by the few records we have are much too weak to support Rowse's confident claim, even if we grant his very questionable assumption that Shakespeare's sonnets are to be read as straightforward autobiography.[3] A more complete and reliable account of the biographical facts and the documents supporting them is supplied in Susanne Woods's edition of Lanyer's poems.[4]

Aemilia was descended from an Italian family, probably of Jewish origin and involved (as their crest suggests) with silk farming.[5] Her father was Baptist Bassano, one of the Queen's Italian musicians, as was also her uncle Anthony Bassano; her mother was Baptist's common-law wife, Margaret Johnson; and she had at least one sibling, an older sister, Angela.[6] Aemilia was christened at St. Botolph, Bishopsgate, on January 27, 1569.[7] Her father died in 1576, when she was seven years old; she told Simon Forman that "the welth of her father failed before he died & he began to be miserable in his estate."[8] He did, however, leave her £100 and some residual rights after her mother's death (1587) in three properties in the suburb of the Spital.[9] A dedicatory poem to Susan (Bertie) Wingfield, Countess of Kent, names her "the Mistris of my youth, / The noble guide of my ungovern'd dayes" (sig. c 2), indicating that as a young girl she lived with and waited upon the Countess, receiving some part of her education in a noble household, as did many children of the nobility and gentry. There are no formal records of her education, but her poems and their sources admit the inference that in her own family or with the Berties she learned Italian, at least a smattering of Latin and classical literature, the Bible, the principles of rhetoric and poetics, and (no doubt) music.

She was for some years the mistress of Elizabeth's Lord Chamberlain, Henry Cary, Lord Hunsdon, forty-five years her senior and a notable patron of the arts (including Shakespeare's company); and she was maintained by him in some wealth and style. On October 18, 1592, she was married at St. Botolph's, Aldgate, to Captain Alfonso Lanyer, one of Queen Elizabeth's (and later King James's) musicians;[10] she was then twenty-three years old. He also came from a distinguished family of musicians, including Nicholas, John, and Innocent Lanier.[11] The marriage was apparently to cover a pregnancy by Hunsdon; her son by him was named Henry. She also had a daughter, Odillya (presumably by Lanyer) who lived less than a year; she was baptized in December 1598 and buried on September 6, 1599, at St. Botolph's, Bishopsgate.[12]

Much of our information about Lanyer's early life and our sense of her as a person derive from Simon Forman's notes, based on several visits she made to him from 1597 to 1600. His notes on her visits reveal something of the way she represented herself to him. She visited him first on May 13, 1597, identified in his casebook as "Millia Lanier of 29 [actually 28] yeares in Longditch at Westmenster"—indicating that she then lived in the City of Westminster.[13] On May 17 she returned for a longer session and a full casting of her horoscope, at which time Forman recorded the facts of her early life: "She hath had hard fortune in her youth . . . She was pa[ra]mour to my old L. of hunsDean that was L. Chamberline and was maintanit in great pride and yt seemes that being with child she was for collour maried to A minstrell [Alfonso Lanyer]."[14] On June 3 he filled in the picture somewhat:

She was brought up with the Countes of Kent and hath bin maried 4 years / The old Lord Chamberlaine kept her longue She was maintaned in great pomp. She is high-minded . . . She hath 40£ a yere and was welthy to him that maried her in moni and Jewells. She can hardly kepe secret. She was very brave in youth / She hath manie fals conceptions. She hath a sonne his name is Henri.[15]

From this it seems clear that Lanyer looked back longingly to her early life in the aristocratic household of the Countess of Kent and in court circles, to which her musician family and especially Hunsdon gave her access; that she gained a considerable estate in money and jewels through her liaison with the great man; that whatever scandal attached to that liaison had been hushed up by a convenient marriage; that she bore Hunsdon's child but then had several miscarriages. Forman's notes on September 2 indicate that her husband was then at sea as a gentleman volunteer with Essex on the 1597 Azores expedition "in hope to be knighted" and that she wanted to know "whether she shall be a Ladi & how she shall speed."[16] He also suggests that her nostalgia for her former life, her present reduced circumstances, and her resentment against her husband for squandering her fortune may induce her to accept new lovers, specifically himself:

She hath been favored much of her mati [majesty, Queen Elizabeth] and of mani noblemen & hath had gret giftes and bin moch made of . . . but her husband hath delt hardly with her and spent and consumed her goods and she is nowe very needy and in debt & it seems for lucrese sake wilbe a good fellowe for necessity doth compell.
She hath a wart or moulle in the pit of the throat or ner yt.[17]

Though Forman predicted in the same entry that Alfonso would be knighted, that Aemilia would be "a Ladie or attain to som further dignitie," and that some additional good fortune would soon fall upon her, he proved a poor prophet. Lanier was not knighted on this voyage or in consequence of his other military engagements in Ireland; nor was he wealthy enough to buy a knighthood from James, as so many did. And Aemilia did not attain the social status or fortune she craved.

In several entries Forman alludes to encounters with Aemilia, from which Rowse unwarrantably concludes that Forman's comment about her loose morals is accurate and that they had an affair which Forman at length found degrading. Forman's casebooks give ample evidence of his disposition to dramatize himself as a Don Juan: he makes a point of recording with pride the variety and frequency of his sexual encounters. In the case of Lanyer, however, his entries indicate that he was attracted to her and attempted to initiate a sexual relationship but that he was frustrated of his expected conquest and finally became furious about that. On September 20, 1597, he recorded (under an astrological chart labeled "Lanier") his first attempted seduction:

> The presente sent his servaunte by who she sente word that if his mr [master] came he shouldbe welcom. & he wente and supped wth her and staid all night. and she was familiar & friendlie to him in all thinges. But only she wold not halek [Forman's personal euphemism for sexual intercourse]. Yet he tolde all parts of her body wilingly. & kyssed her often but she wold not doe in any wise. Wherupon . . . he departed friendes.[18]

Under his own chart he noted "she would not . . . [do] it not / he had great trouble about yt and it confused him." In what seems to be a later entry he wrote, "They were frendes again afterward but he never obteyned his purpose & she was a hore and delt evill with him after." If the episode happened in Lanyer's house and not in Forman's active imagination, it seems to indicate that Lanyer was willing to flirt and have some physical contact with Forman but not to have sex with him. A few other entries in late September record social or professional visits, but none of them indicate that he ever did succeed in seducing her.[19] His disparaging comments about her reflect, it seems, his chagrin and frustration over her continued refusal to succumb. They are reiterated in the last entry about her (January 7, 1600), in which Forman cast his own horoscope to determine "whi Mrs. Laniere sent for me et quid a sequiter / wh[eth]er she Entends Any mor Villani or noe."[20]

Sometime during the early 1600s, and before Anne Clifford's marriage in 1609, Lanyer spent a period of time (how long is not clear) with Margaret and Anne Clifford at Cookham, a royal manor held by Margaret's brother, William Russell of Thornhaugh, and evidently occupied by her on occasion during her separation from her husband and (perhaps) her early widowhood.[21] Lanyer's poem "The Description of Cooke-ham" claims that this sojourn led to her religious conversion and confirmed her in a poet's vocation. It is hard to know how much and what kind of patronage stands behind this claim. None of the records or letters we have identify Lanyer as a client or a member of Margaret Clifford's household, but there are few records to consult. Lanyer alludes knowledgeably to the Countess's domestic unhappiness with her profligate adventurer-husband, George Clifford, and to Anne Clifford's lawsuits over her lands.[22] At the least, Lanyer seems to have received some encouragement in learning, piety, and poetry in the bookish and cultivated household of the Countess of Cumberland, and may have been supported by the Countess in the unusual venture of offering her poems for publication. Her volume of poems, published in 1611, makes a clear bid for continued patronage from the Countess of Cumberland in the first instance, and invites it from eight other noblewomen dedicatees. It did not, however, win for her a permanent association with any of these prospective patrons, nor any niche at the Jacobean court.

These few facts suggest Lanyer's vulnerability, given her insecure social and economic status, to ill usage by fortune and by the men in her life. They also suggest that she was a woman of considerable daring, independence of mind, and resource, especially in her self-definition as a poet worthy of patronage and publication. Her later life displays a similar enterprise as she undertook to provide for herself in difficult circumstances. In 1604 Alfonso Lanyer was awarded a patent to take revenue from the weighing of hay and grain in London; after his death in 1613 Aemilia sought her share of the profits through numerous petitions and lawsuits against his relatives, mounted periodically until 1637.[23] In 1617 she set up a school in the wealthy district of St. Giles in the Fields "for the education of noblemen and gentlemen's children of great worth," as she described it; how many children, of what ages and sexes, and whether they boarded or not is not known. Soon, however, she was mired in controversy with her landlord, the attorney Edward Smith of Middle Temple, about rent arrears and repairs. In November 1620 she brought a chancery case against him[24] in which "Emelia Lanier widdow late wife of captayne *Alphonsoe Lanyer* his ma[jes]ties servante deceased" deposed that "by the death of the said husband beinge left in verry poore estate hee havinge spente a great parte of his estate in the service of the Late Queene in her warres of Ireland and other places she . . . for her maynetaynaunce and releefe was compelled to teach and educate the children of divers persons of worth and understandinge." Smith, she claimed, "found a better Tennaunte who would give him more rente" and so tried to force her out. He "greatlie . . . disinabled disgraced and hindered" her in her enterprise with "continuall trouble and molestation" and finally legal action, as he tried to collect rents that were in arrears. She claimed that Smith was indebted to her "for the some of ten pounds and upwards for repairs," and requested a stay of all suits until she could receive a hearing in the chancery courts. Smith responded that he had wanted to accept the better offer from a new tenant because he doubted her ability to make her school pay; and that she had left his house in a state of "great decay" in August 1619 without paying her midsummer rent or giving a quarter's notice.

She kept her school for two years (1617–1619). After 1620 she drops from view, save for the periodic lawsuits over the hay and grain patent. Her son, Henry, also became a court musician, a flautist, and had two children; he died in 1633, and her later petitions claim that she had responsibility for these grandchildren.[25] She remained in London, and at some point took up residence in the parish of St. James, Clerkenwell (where her son's family lived); her burial from that church is recorded on August 3, 1645. She is listed as a "pensioner"—and so ended her seventy-six years with at least some settled income.[26]

The title of Lanyer's volume of poems promises, somewhat misleadingly, a collection of religious poetry—a genre thought especially appropriate for women writers: *Salve Deus Rex Judaeorum. Containing, 1. The Passion of Christ. 2. Eves Apologie in defence of Women. 3. The Teares of the Daughters of Jerusalem. 4. The Salutation and Sorrow of the Virgine Marie. With divers other things not unfit to be read.* In a postscript to the volume addressed "To the doubtfull Reader," she claims that the Latin title was delivered to her in a dream long before she conceived of the work, but that she later read that dream as a God-given sign appointing her to it:

> Gentle Reader, if thou desire to be resolved, why I give this Title, *Salve Deus Rex Judaeorum,* know for certaine, that it was delivered unto me in sleepe many yeares before I had any intent to write in this maner, and was quite out of my memory, untill I had written the passion of Christ, when immediately it came into my remembrance, what I had dreamed long before; and thinking it a significant token, that I was appointed to performe this Worke, I gave the very same words I received in sleepe as the fittest Title I could devise for this Booke.

Lanyer's statement at once claims a divine sanction for her work, and at the same time asserts complete responsibility for it since she remembered the dream only after she finished the book. But despite the title and the dream, the volume in fact contains several kinds of poems on subjects not exclusively religious, in various poetic genres and verse forms. As a whole, the work is devised as a comprehensive Book of Good Women, fusing religious devotion and feminism so as to assert the essential harmony of those two impulses. Lanyer does not imitate (though she might conceivably have read) Boccaccio or Christine de Pisan or Chaucer;[27] her volume offers in a quite unexpected form a feminist defense and celebration of women and of Lanyer as woman poet.

The volume was entered in the Stationers' Register on October 2, 1610, by the bookseller Richard Bonian, and the poems were probably written within a year or two of that date.[28] It was issued twice in 1611, with a minor change in the printer's imprint, and is now very rare; possibly only a few copies were printed, chiefly for presentation purposes, though the epistle "To the Vertuous Reader" implies a larger intended audience.[29] In at least two copies (and perhaps more) certain dedications were omitted to tailor the volume for the recipient. Lanyer's husband seems to have taken some pride in her work, as he presented a copy to Thomas Jones, Lord Chancellor of Ireland and Archbishop of Dublin, whom he knew from his Irish service.[30]

The book is in three parts. The first section contains nine dedicatory poems in a variety of genres addressed to royal and noble ladies, a prose dedication to the Countess of Cumberland, and a prose epistle "To the Vertuous Reader," which is a vigorous apologia for women's equality or superiority to men in spiritual and moral matters. The title poem is a long meditation on the Passion and death of Christ (1,056 lines) which in fact incorporates the three other items listed as separate poems on the title page. But while that table of contents is misleading, it properly registers the title poem's emphasis on the good women associated with the Passion story. The Passion narrative is itself contained within a frame of 776 lines (more than a third of the whole), comprising elaborate tributes to Margaret Clifford as virtuous follower of the suffering Christ. The volume concludes with a country-house poem, "The Description of Cooke-ham," celebrating an estate that was occupied on occasion by Margaret Clifford, as a lost female paradise. This poem may or may not have been written before Jonson's "To Penshurst" (commonly thought to have inaugurated the genre in English literature), but it can certainly claim priority in publication.[31]

Given Lanyer's dubious past, her evident concern to find patronage, and her focus on women, contemporary and biblical, we might be tempted to discount the Passion subject as a thin veneer for a subversive feminist statement. But Lanyer was a woman of her age, and her imagination was governed by its terms. At the time of this writing, she appears to have been sincerely, if not very profoundly, religious, and she presents Christ's Passion as the focus for all the forms of female goodness (and masculine evil) her poems treat. Her good women meditate upon and imitate this model, and as poet she interprets her experience of life in religious categories. Her feminist perceptions can be rendered only in terms of the discourse of Scripture, but they force a radical imaginative rewriting of its patriarchal norms to place women at the center.

Salve Deus: The Dedications

The nine dedications make a bold bid for patronage on a very wide front: they are obviously intended to call Lanyer to the attention of past patrons or acquaintances from her better Elizabethan days, and to attract new ones. She has chosen her targets very carefully, reaching out to all the obvious female power brokers of the court. In the opening dedication to Queen Anne, Lanyer laments that she does not now enjoy the associations and favors of that earlier time, when "great *Elizaes* favour blest my youth" (sig. a 4v), intimating that the present Queen might like to renew that happy condition. She next addresses Princess Elizabeth, whom she does not claim to know personally, as heir to all the virtues of her great name-sake.[32] Then she reaches out "to all vertuous Ladies in generall" who at-tend on "Queen" Virtue and with the Muses wait on Pallas (Queen Anne's chosen personification in masques and addresses);[33] these allusions direct this long poem to all of Queen Anne's female entourage, suggesting that those about to be singled out are particularly worthy examples of that large community of female virtue. Next, Lanyer addresses the ladies she does know from happier Elizabethan days. First, as rank dictates, Arbella Stuart: "Great learned Ladie, whom I long have knowne, / And yet not knowne so much as I desired";[34] then her former mistress and patron, the Dowager Countess of Kent, Susan (Bertie) Wingfield, "the Mistris of my youth."[35] Then, though she cannot claim acquaintance with either of them, she appeals to the greatest literary patronesses (respectively) of the Elizabethan era and of the Jacobean court: Mary (Sidney) Herbert, Dow-ager Countess of Pembroke, and Lucy (Harrington) Russell, Countess of Bedford.[36] A prose dedication follows, identifying Margaret (Russell) Clifford, Dowager Countess of Cumberland, as the major dedicatee of the volume; she is honored throughout as Lanyer's past patron and best pre-sent hope.[37] The poem that follows, to the Countess of Suffolk, Katherine (Knevet) Howard,[38] is an effort to reach out to the powerful Howard faction, though Lanyer admits that she is a "stranger" to that lady. She concludes with the address to Anne Clifford, now Countess of Dorset, whom she claims as a close former acquaintance, inviting her to take up her mother's legacy of virtue and generosity as Lanyer's patron.

These dedications reveal something about Lanyer's actual associations; though hyperbolical like most of their kind, they would fail of their pur-pose if they were to falsify too outrageously the terms of a relationship. Offering multiple dedications was tricky though not uncommon; it was perhaps easiest to bring off when (as in Spenser's *Faerie Queene*) the mon-arch was the principal dedicatee, and the others (seventeen in Spenser's case) were ancillary. Lanyer devises a comparable strategy, making the sev-eral ladies an ideal version of Queen Anne's own court and entourage. More than that, however, she comprehends all the dedications within the thematic unity of her volume, addressing these ladies as a contemporary community of good women who are spiritual heirs to the biblical and historical good women her title poem celebrates.

Whatever actual patronage Lanyer may have enjoyed, her dedications rewrite the institution of patronage in female terms, transforming the relationships assumed in the male patronage system into an ideal community. Here the patrons' virtue descends through the female line, from mothers to daughters—Queen Anne and Princess Elizabeth, Margaret and Anne Clifford, Catherine and Susan Bertie, Katherine Howard and her daughters—and it redounds upon their female poet-client and celebrant, Lanyer. Many though not all of the dedicatees were linked through kinship or marriage with the Sidney-Leicester faction, which promoted resistance to Spain, active support of Protestantism on the Continent, continued reform in the English Church, and patronage of the arts, especially Christian poetry. The author describes her book as the glass which shows their several virtues, and she invites them to receive and meditate upon Christ their Bridegroom, here depicted.

The qualities Lanyer associates with her gallery of good women—heroic virtue, extraordinary learning, devotion to the Muses, and high poetic achievement—implicitly challenge patriarchal ideology and help to justify her own undertaking. Although Lanyer often excuses her poems as faulty and unlearned by reason of her sex, her several apologias seem closer to the *humilitas* topos than to genuine angst. She appeals to her subject matter itself as justification for attempting what is "seldome seene, / A Womans writing of divinest things."[39] Since religious poetry is often considered the highest genre,[40] this claim gives an honorific, rather than a restrictive, value to the widespread assumption that women, if they write at all, should treat religious subjects. Lanyer continually proclaims her poems worthy of attention for their divine, and their female, subject, implying that a woman poet may write worthily since all these women are seen to be so worthy.

The dedication to Queen Anne, in six-line pentameter stanzas rhymed *a b a b c c,* establishes the contemporary community of good women. Its Queen is another Juno, Venus, Pallas, and Cynthia, attracting Muses and artists to her throne. With some sense, it seems, of the Queen's oppositional politics and subversive masques, Lanyer calls her particular attention to "*Eves* Apologie, / Which I have writ in honour of your sexe" (sig. a 4). As self-appointed female poet of this community of women, Lanyer claims to derive her poetics not from classical learning but from "Mother" Nature, source of all the arts:

> Not that I Learning to my selfe assume,
> Or that I would compare with any man:
> > But as they are Scholers, and by Art do write,
> > So Nature yeelds my Soule a sad delight.

And since all Arts at first from Nature came,
That goodly Creature, Mother of perfection,
Whom *Joves* almighty hand at first did frame,
Taking both her and hers in his protection:
    Why should not She now grace my barren Muse,
    And in a Woman all defects excuse.

                                 (sig. a 4v)

    The other dedications elaborate the ladies' qualities and Lanyer's poetics. The sonnet-like poems to Princess Elizabeth and Arbella Stuart[41] emphasize their learning: Lanyer offers her own "first fruits of a womans wit" to Elizabeth, whose "faire eyes farre better Bookes have seene," and she apostrophizes Arbella as "Great learned Ladie . . . / so well accompan'ed / With *Pallas,* and the Muses." The third poem (in seven-line pentameter stanzas rhymed *a b a b a c c*), "To all vertuous Ladies in generall," praises all who are ladies-in-waiting to Queen Virtue, companions of the Muses in attending on Pallas, and Virgins waiting for the Bridegroom. The fifth dedication (in the same verse form as that to the Queen) praises the Countess of Kent as a glass displaying all virtues to the young Aemilia, and as a heroic follower of Christ even in infancy, when her staunchly Protestant mother, Catherine Bertie, Countess of Suffolk, fled England with her family during Queen Mary's reign:[42]

Whose Faith did undertake in Infancie,
All dang'rous travells by devouring Seas
To flie to Christ from vaine Idolatry,
Not seeking there this worthlesse world to please,
    By your most famous Mother so directed,
    That noble Dutchesse, who liv'd unsubjected.

From *Romes* ridiculous prier and tyranny,
That mighty Monarchs kept in awfull feare;
Leaving here her lands, her state, dignitie;
Nay more, vouchsaft disguised weedes to weare:
    When with Christ Jesus she did meane to goe,
    From sweet delights to taste part of his woe.

                         (sigs. c 2–c 2v)

    The next dedication is given special importance by its central position, its length (224 lines), its verse form unique in this volume (four-line pentameter stanzas rhymed *a b a b*), and its genre: it is a dream-vision narrative entitled "The Authors Dreame to the Ladie Marie, the Countesse Dowager of Pembroke." The poem is well made and graceful, with the dream-vision journey serving admirably to mark the Countess's unique status as a paradigm of female worth, as well as her absence from the present court—both because she remained for the most part on her country estates and because she belonged in spirit to the Elizabethan era. The poem recounts Lanyer's dream journey under the conduct of Morpheus to the Idalian groves, where she finds the Countess of Pembroke enthroned in Honor's chair, crowned by eternal Fame and receiving tribute from various classical representatives of Art, Beauty, and Wisdom: the Graces, Bellona, Dictina, Aurora, and Flora. Under the Countess's aegis the strife between Art and Nature is resolved, and all the company join to sing the Countess's Psalm versions:

> Those holy Sonnets they did all agree,
> With this most lovely Lady here to sing;
> That by her noble breasts sweet harmony,
> Their musicke might in eares of Angels ring.
>
> While saints like Swans about this silver brook
> Should *Hallalu-iah* sing continually,
> Writing her praises in th'eternall booke
> Of endlesse honour, true fames memorie.
>
> (sig. d v)

Morpheus then reveals the lady's name, indicates that she spends all her time "in virtuous studies of Divinitie," and (continuing Lanyer's argument for the equality or superiority of women in moral and spiritual matters) ranks the Countess "far before" her brother Sir Philip Sidney "for virtue, wisedome, learning, dignity" (sig. d 2).

Upon awakening from her vision, Lanyer resolves to present her own "unlearned lines" to that lady, expecting that she will value these "flowres that spring from virtues ground" even though she herself reads and writes worthier and more profound books:

> Thogh many Books she writes that are more rare,
> Yet there is hony in the meanest flowres:
>
> Which is both wholesome, and delights the taste:
> Though sugar be more finer, higher priz'd,
> Yet is the painefull Bee no whit disgrac'd,
> Nor her faire wax, or hony more despiz'd.
>
> (sig. d 3)

The Countess of Pembroke, as learned lady and poet, is hereby asked to recognize Lanyer as her successor in a female poetic line. And Lanyer points to the Countess as her model by the length, art, and extended personal reference of the dream-vision poem.

The later dedications are again epistolary in form. That to the Countess of Bedford (in seven-line pentameter stanzas rhymed *a b a b b c c*) identifies

Knowledge, wielded by Virtue, as the key to her heart, and emphasizes (as does Jonson's epigram) her "cleare Judgement" (sig. d 3).[43] The unique prose dedication to the Countess of Cumberland marks her as Lanyer's primary patron and audience; it offers the Passion poem as a worthy text for the Countess's meditations, at once a mirror of her "most worthy minde" and a subject certain to grace "the meanest & most unworthy hand that will undertake to write thereof." Lanyer here claims for herself and her patron-subject the conventional eternizing power of poetry, asserting that these poems "may remaine in the world many yeares longer than your Honour, or my selfe can live, to be a light unto those that come after" (sig. c–c v). The dedication to the Countess of Suffolk (in six-line pentameter stanzas rhymed *a b a b c c*) takes note of the power and honor her Howard husband wields, but (true to the female focus) identifies the Countess as the "fountaine" of his chief delights and honors, and urges her to guide her "noble daughters" in meditations based on Lanyer's Passion poem (sig. e 2v). At this point Lanyer claims forthrightly that her poetic vocation and poetic achievement are God-given: she was led by her birth star "to frame this worke of grace," and enabled to do so by God, whose "powre hath given me powre to write, / A subject fit for you to looke upon" (sig. e 2).

The final long dedication to Anne, Countess of Dorset (116 lines in eight-line pentameter stanzas rhymed *a b a b a b c c*), presents her as the worthy heir and successor to her mother's excellences, virtues, and stewardship of the poor. Here, uniquely, Lanyer presumes to teach proper moral attitudes and conduct to her subject, as if privileged to do so by former familiarity. For one thing, in praising Anne's inheritance of Margaret's "Crowne / Of goodness, bountie, grace, love, pietie," she urges Anne to practice these virtues, including "stewardship" toward Lanyer herself:

> To you, as to Gods Steward I doe write,
> In whom the seeds of virtue have bin sowne,
> By your most worthy mother, in whose right,
> All her faire parts you challenge as your owne;
> . . . . .
> You are the Heire apparent of this Crowne
> Of goodnesse, bountie, grace, love, pietie,
> By birth its yours, then keepe it as your owne,
> Defend it from all base indignitie;
> The right your Mother hath to it, is knowne
> Best unto you, who reapt such fruit thereby:
>   This Monument of her faire worth retaine
>   In your pure mind, and keepe it from al staine.
>   (sig. e 4v)

More boldly, she makes their former association and the present gulf between them, owing to rank and class, the basis for a trenchant critique of hierarchy founded upon patriarchal values. Alluding both to Anne's loss of her lands and to her own loss of contact with Anne, now Countess of Dorset, Lanyer contrasts male succession through aristocratic titles with a female succession grounded on virtue and holiness, drawing radical egalitarian conclusions:

> What difference was there when the world began,
> Was it not Virtue that distinguisht all?
> All sprang but from one woman and one man,
> Then how doth Gentry come to rise and fall?
> Or who is he that very rightly can
> Distinguish of his birth, or tell at all,
>> In what meane state his Ancestors have bin,
>> Before some one of worth did honour win.
>>   (sig. e 4v)

This first part of Lanyer's volume concludes with a prose epistle "To the Vertuous Reader" which extends the idealized community of learned and virtuous women to a broader readership, offering the book "for the generall use of all virtuous Ladies and Gentlewomen of this kingdome" (sig. f 3). The imagined presence of male readers as well prompts a switch to polemics: the epistle makes a brief but forceful contribution to the *querelle des femmes,* that centuries-old controversy over women's inherent worthiness or faultiness which Rachel Speght was soon to address in her polemic against Swetnam.[44] Lanyer first lectures those women who "forgetting they are women themselves . . . speake unadvisedly against the rest of their sexe," urging them to leave such "folly" to "evill disposed men" (sig. f 3). With considerable passion she then denounces those men "who forgetting they were borne of women, nourished of women, and that if it were not by the means of women, they would be quite extinguished out of the world, and a finall ende of them all, doe like Vipers deface the wombes wherein they were bred"—associating such men with those who "dishonoured Christ his Apostles and Prophets, putting them to shamefull deaths" (sig. f 3). Marshaling biblical examples with rhetorical force and flair, she argues that God himself has affirmed women's moral and spiritual equality with or superiority to men, and more than that, their call to exercise military and political power:

> God . . . gave power to wise and virtuous women, to bring down their pride and arrogancie. As was cruell *Cesarus* by the discreet counsell of noble *Deborah,* Judge and Prophetesse of Israel: and resolution of *Jael* wife of *Heber* the Kenite: wicked *Haman,* by the divine prayers and prudent proceedings of beautifull *Hester:* blasphemous *Holo-*

fernes, by the invincible courage, rare wisdome, and confident carriage of *Judeth:* & the unjust Judges, by the innocency of chast *Susanna:* with infinite others, which for brevitie sake I will omit.

(sig. f 3v)

In clipped, forceful phrases, she also details the singular honors accorded
to women by Christ, and their fidelity to him:

It pleased our Lord and Saviour Jesus Christ, without the assistance
of man . . . to be begotten of a woman, borne of a woman, nourished
of a woman, obedient to a woman; and that he healed woman, pardoned women, comforted women: yea, even when he was in his
greatest agonie and bloodie sweat, going to be crucified, and also in
the last houre of his death, tooke care to dispose of a woman: after
his resurrection, appeared first to a woman, sent a woman to declare
his most glorious resurrection to the rest of his Disciples. Many other
examples I could alleadge of divers faithfull and virtuous women,
who have in all ages, not onely beene Confessors, but also indured
most cruel martyrdome for their faith in Jesus Christ.   (sig. f 3v)

In Lanyer's imaginative vision, as in Anne Clifford's and Rachel
Speght's, God testifies for women and takes their part. This prose address
delivers a hard-hitting defense of women, and of Lanyer herself as author.
By defining the attitudes toward women which well-disposed men ought
to hold, she undertakes to reclaim some segment of the male sex from the
evil mass, and so ends by offering her book to good Christians of both
sexes.

The Title Poem

Lanyer's Passion poem, the *Salve Deus* (in eight-line pentameter stanzas,
rhymed *a b a b a b c c*) proposes Christ as the standard that validates the
various kinds of female goodness her poems treat, and condemns the multiple forms of masculine evil. The poem also undermines some fundamental assumptions of patriarchy, in that it presents Christ's Passion from the
vantage point of good women, past and present. Lanyer as woman poet
recounts and interprets the story. The Countess of Cumberland is the subject of the extended frame, as chief reader and meditator on the Passion,
as well as exemplary image and imitator of her suffering Savior. And the
Passion narrative itself emphasizes the good women who played a major
role in that event, setting them in striking contrast to the weak and evil
men: the cowardly apostles, the traitor Judas, the wicked Hebrew and
Roman judges, the tormenting soldiers, the jeering crowds.

As poet-narrator, Lanyer treats her material variously, sometimes relating events, sometimes elaborating them in the style of biblical commentary, sometimes meditating upon images or scenes, often apostrophizing participants as if she herself were present with them at these events. She uses rhetorical schemes—especially figures of sound, parallelism, and repetition—with considerable skill; her apostrophes often convey strength of feeling; she describes and sometimes dramatizes a scene effectively. And the inset rhetorical speeches such as "Eves Apologie" are forceful and effective. There are few striking images or metaphors, but Lanyer's allusions are usually appropriate and her language straightforward, taking on at times colloquial directness. Her greatest fault is a tendency to pad lines and stanzas to fill out the metrical pattern.

The poem has some generic precedents, whose elements are here well mixed. One strain is the religious complaint poem—the tears of the Magdalen, of Christ himself, of penitent sinners—usually focused on the Passion and Crucifixion. This was often, though not exclusively, a Counter-Reformation genre: the best-known English example was probably Robert Southwell's *Saint Peters Complaynt,* in which Peter laments Christ's Passion and his own denial of Christ, bitterly berating himself and the woman who questioned him.[45] Lanyer incorporates elements of this genre in the stanzas on the tears of the Daughters of Jerusalem and on the grief of the Virgin, though she apostrophizes those personages rather than having them voice their own complaints, as was more usual. The segment called "Eves Apologie" mixes complaint and rhetorical argument; it might well be a direct response to the frequent outbursts of misogyny in Southwell's poem, as Peter lays his and all men's sins at woman's door:

> O Women, woe to men: traps for their falls,
> Still actors in all tragicall mischances:
> Earths Necessarie evils, captivating thralls,
> Now murdring with your toungs, now with your glances.[46]

The other important genre is the meditation on the Passion, mixed with lamentation; often, as here, it incorporated erotic elements from the Song of Songs. In this kind perhaps the closest analogue for Lanyer is the almost contemporary "Christ's Triumph over Death" (1610) by Giles Fletcher.[47] Other suggestive Protestant analogues for Lanyer are a series of poems Nicolas Breton addressed to his patron, the Countess of Pembroke, in which he associates Mary Sidney with his meditative subjects by devising various kinds of frames. In *The Ravisht Soule,* an ecstatic meditation on Christ's works and glory, he invites the Countess to be the ravished soul that so meditates; in *The Blessed Weeper* he takes on the persona of the Magdalen meditating on the Passion and urges the Countess to become such a weeper; in *The Pilgrimage to Paradise* he invites her to identify with the travails of the Christian pilgrim he describes. Closest of all, perhaps, is the *Countess of Pembrookes Love,* in which Breton directly associates the Countess with the poem's speaker, who is undertaking a meditation on Christ in a *contemptus mundi* vein. His prefatory epistle explicitly describes the work as hers: "The heavenly Meditations, of an honourable Lady, the weake discourse whereof, far short of her worthiness . . . I have here [set forth]."[48] Another of Mary Sidney's clients, Abraham Fraunce, also associated his patron directly with his subject in poetic meditations on Christ which he entitled *The Countesse of Pembrokes Emanuell.*[49] Lanyer's demonstrated interest in the Countess of Pembroke as both patron and poet makes it likely she knew these works and that they provided some basis for the extended frame in which she positions the Countess of Cumberland as part of her subject: Margaret Clifford both reprises her savior's sufferings and is the chief meditator on them. Visual analogues for this device are those Renaissance religious paintings with the patron prominently portrayed within the scene as a worshipper.

The long preface (stanzas 1–33) addresses Margaret Clifford and sets up the frame. The first nine stanzas propose to immortalize her in verse and recall the solace she has found for her many sorrows in the beauties of Cookham and the love of God. Stanzas 10–18 comprise an embedded psalmic passage praising God as the strong support of the just and the mighty destroyer of all their enemies, with obvious (and later overt) application to the much-wronged Margaret Clifford. The passage echoes or paraphrases a melange of Psalm texts—chiefly Psalms 18, 84, 89, and 104— in what seems to be a gesture of discipleship to the Countess of Pembroke:

> With Majestie and Honour is He clad,
> And deck'd with light, as with a garment faire;
> . . . . .
> He of the watry Cloudes his Chariot frames,
> And makes his blessed Angels powrefull Spirits,
> His Ministers are fearefull fiery flames,
> Rewarding all according to their merits;
> The Righteous for an heritage he claimes,
> And registers the wrongs of humble spirits:
>   Hills melt like wax, in presence of the Lord,
>   So do all sinners, in his sight abhorr'd.
>   (sigs. A 2–A 2v)[50]

Stanzas 19–33 identify Margaret Clifford as one of those just who are specially beloved and protected by God, and praise her for abandoning the delights of the court to serve her heavenly King in rural retirement. This section includes a dispraise of the most notable beauties of history—Helen, Cleopatra, Rosamund, Lucretia, Matilda—all women whose beauty led them or their lovers to sin or ruin. By contrast, the Countess's inner beauty of grace and virtue made Christ the husband of her soul, and his death "made her Dowager of all" (sig. B).

This statement leads into the Passion narrative proper (stanzas 34–165). First, however, Lanyer invokes and admonishes her "lowely Muse" for risking the fate of Icarus or Phaeton by flying so far above her "appointed straine":

> Thinke when the eye of Wisdom shall discover
> Thy weakling Muse to flie, that scarce could creepe,
> And in the Ayre above the Clowdes to hover,
> When better 'twere mued up, and fast asleepe;
> They'l thinke with *Phaeton,* thou canst ne'r recover,
> But helplesse with that poore yong Lad to weepe:
>   The little World of thy weake Wit on fire,
>   Where thou wilt perish in thine owne desire.
>   (sigs. B–Bv)

But she takes courage from the story of the Widow's Mite, and the conviction that God's glory will shine the more "the Weaker thou doest seeme to be / In Sexe, or Sence" (sig. Bv). Proposing, like many Protestant poets of her era, to render sacred matter "in plainest Words" so as not to distort it,[51] she prays God to "guide my Hand and Quill" (sig. B 2).

Her account of the Passion is part commentary or meditation on the biblical story and part apostrophe, a figure she uses to intensify emotion and create an effect of immediacy. The first section (stanzas 42–79) begins with Christ's prayers and subsequent capture in the Garden of Gethsemane. Using apostrophe to poignant effect, Lanyer conveys Christ's profound isolation even from his beloved apostles:

> Sweet Lord, how couldst thou thus to flesh and blood
> Communicate thy griefe? tell of thy woes?
> Thou knew'st they had no powre to doe thee good,
> But were the cause thou must endure these blowes.
>   (sig. B 3)

In this section the primary emphasis is on the sins and failures of Christ's own (male) apostles. Peter declared that his faith would never fail, but Christ knew Peter would deny him three times. Christ implored the apostles to wait and watch with him, but they slept. The apostle Judas proved to be "a trothlesse traytor, and a mortall foe" (sig. B 4v). Peter offended Christ and the law by drawing his sword against Christ's enemies. Then, with a fine flourish of parallelism and antithesis Lanyer castigates the "accursed crew" of scribes and Pharisees who apprehended Christ:

> How blinde were they could not discerne the Light!
> How dull! if not to understand the truth,
> How weake! if meekenesse overcame their might;
> How stony hearted, if not mov'd to ruth:
> How void of Pitie, and how full of Spight,
> Gainst him that was the Lord of Light and Truth:
>   Here insolent Boldnesse checkt by Love and Grace,
>   Retires, and falls before our Makers face.
> . . . . .
>
> Here Falshood beares the shew of formall Right,
> Base Treacherie hath gote a guard of men;
> Tyranny attends, with all his strength and might,
> To leade this siely Lamb to Lyons denne.
>
> (sigs. C, C 2)

This section ends by reverting to the disciples' failures: "Though they protest they never will forsake him, / They do like men, when dangers overtake them" (sig. C 2v). That formulation prepares for Lanyer's sharply drawn contrast between the weak and evil men in the Passion story and the good women.

The second section (stanzas 80–118) treats the torment Christ suffered from yet more wicked men, the several judges: wicked Caiphas, proud Pontius Pilate, scoffing Herod. It begins by describing Christ through a series of epithets—Herbert's technique in "Prayer I":

> The beauty of the World, Heavens chiefest Glory;
> The mirrour of Martyrs, Crowne of holy Saints;
> Love of th'Almighty, blessed Angels story;
> Water of Life, which none that drinks it, faints;
> Guide of the Just, where all our Light we borrow;
> Mercy of Mercies; Hearer of Complaints;
>   Triumpher over Death; Ransomer of Sinne;
>   Falsely accused; now his paines begin.
>
> (sig. C 3)[52]

Caiphas is summed up in a nice metaphor, "Thy Owly eies are blind, and cannot see," and Pilate in another, "A golden Sepulcher with rotten bones" (sigs. C 4, D 3v).

Then Lanyer addresses a lengthy apostrophe to Pilate (stanzas 94–105), contrasting good women with all these evil men. Associating herself with Pilate's wife, Lanyer pleads with Pilate to spare Christ, relating that plea to a remarkable apologia pronouncing Eve innocent of any evil intention

in the Fall. This part—"Eves Apologie"—takes Eve and Pilate's wife as
representatives of women, while Adam and Pilate represent men:

> O noble Governour, make thou yet a pause,
> Doe not in innocent blood imbrue thy hands;
>> But heare the words of thy most worthy wife,
>> Who sends to thee, to beg her Saviours life.
> . . . . .
>> Let not us Women glory in Mens fall,
>> Who had power given to over-rule us all.
>
> Till now your indiscretion sets us free,
> And makes our former fault much less appeare;
> Our Mother *Eve,* who tasted of the Tree,
> Giving to *Adam* what shee held most deare,
> Was simply good, and had no powre to see,
> The after-comming harme did not appeare:
>> The subtile Serpent that our Sex betraide,
>> Before our fall so sure a plot had laide.
>>> (sigs. C 4v–D)

She presses that argument hard, using the Fall and Passion stories to weigh
the characteristic sin of women (excessive love) against that of men (violence). Her argument is that Eve's "harmeless Heart" intended no evil at
all, that her fault was only "too much love, / Which made her give this
present to her Deare, / That what shee tasted, he likewise might prove, /
Whereby his knowledge might become more cleare" (sig. Dv). By taking
the name of the Tree of Knowledge literally, Lanyer makes knowledge the
gift of Eve or woman: "Yet Men will boast of Knowledge, which he
tooke / From *Eves* faire hand, as from a learned Booke." In Lanyer's argument, all the guilt of the Fall belongs to Adam, who was strong, wise,
and undeceived. Moreover, any faults which women might have inherited
from Eve are far outweighed by the guilt, malice, and violence of men,
epitomized in Pilate:

> Her weakenesse did the Serpents words obay,
> But you in malice Gods deare Sonne betray.
>
> Whom, if unjustly you condemne to die,
> Her sinne was small, to what you doe commit.
>> (sig. Dv)

Lanyer's biblical exegesis would have been outrageous (by contemporary standards), and she may have intended the shock to underscore the
susceptibility of the biblical narratives to very different interpretations,
depending on the interests involved. They had been hitherto constrained

to patriarchal power, so she by a neat reversal wrenches them to women's interests. She concludes with a forthright declaration of gender equality, denouncing hierarchy and men's unjust claim to rule:

> Then let us have our Libertie againe,
> And challendge to your selves no Sov'raigntie;
> You came not in the world without our paine,
> Make that a barre against your crueltie;
> Your fault being greater, why should you disdaine
> Our beeing your equals, free from tyranny?
>   If one weake woman simply did offend,
>   This sinne of yours, hath no excuse, nor end.
>
> To which (poore soules) we never gave consent,
> Witnesse thy wife (O *Pilate*) speakes for all.
> (sig. D 2)

The third section (stanzas 119–165) presents the procession to Calvary, the Crucifixion, and the Resurrection, again contrasting the responses of good women and evil men to these events. The journey scene is described with considerable dramatic effectiveness:

> First went the Crier with open mouth proclayming
> The heavy sentence of Iniquitie,
> The Hangman next, by his base office clayming
> His right in Hell, where sinners never die,
> Carrying the nayles, the people still blaspheming
> Their maker, using all impiety;
>   The Thieves attending him on either side,
>   The Serjeants watching, while the women cri'd.
> (sig. D 4)

A lengthy apostrophe to the Daughters of Jerusalem follows (stanzas 122–126), offering them as examples of women's pity and mercy, as opposed to men's fierce cruelty:

> When spightfull men with torments did oppresse
> Th'afflicted body of this innocent Dove,
> Poore women seeing how much they did transgresse,
> By teares, by sighes, by cries intreat, nay prove,
> What may be done among the thickest presse,
> They labour still these tyrants hearts to move;
>   In pitie and compassion to forbeare
>   Their whipping, spurning, tearing of his haire.
>
> But all in vaine, their malice hath no end,
> Their hearts more hard than flint, or marble stone.
> (sig. D 4v)

Then, in another long apostrophe, Lanyer locates herself with the mother of Jesus as observer and grief-stricken mourner at the Crucifixion, meditating as well on Mary's wondrous role in the Redemption and her exaltation as "Queene of Woman-kind" (stanzas 127–142):

> How canst thou choose (faire Virgin) then but mourne,
> When this sweet of-spring of thy body dies,
> When thy faire eies beholds his bodie torne,
> The peoples fury, heares the womens cries.
>
> (sig. E 2v)

Lanyer's baroque description of the Crucifixion itself (somewhat reminiscent of Giles Fletcher)[53] is not without poetic force and religious feeling:

> His joynts dis-joynted, and his legges hang downe,
> His alablaster breast, his bloody side,
> His members torne, and on his head a Crowne
> Of sharpest Thorns, to satisfie for pride:
> Anguish and Paine doe all his Sences drowne,
> While they his holy garments do divide:
>   His bowells drie, his heart full fraught with griefe,
>   Crying to him that yeelds him no reliefe.
>
> (sig. E 3)

But the emphasis on good women continues. This icon of the Crucifixion is presented as an object of meditation to the Countess of Cumberland, who is apostrophized as "Deere Spouse of Christ" (sig. E 3) and urged to judge "if ever Lover were so true" (sig. E 4v). Finally, the precious balms brought by still other good women to annoint the dead Christ are interpreted as a figure of the precious ointments "of Mercie, Charitie, and Faith" brought to the risen Christ (the Bridegroom of Canticles) "by his faithfull Wife / The holy Church" (sig. F).

A long coda (166–230) completes the frame begun with the long prologue; it recounts the many forms in which Christ appears to Margaret Clifford as she practices the works of mercy, and portrays her in Canticles imagery as Christ's spouse. It also proclaims her superiority to the various worthy women of history, reworking here that familiar topos of the *querelle* defenses of women, the review of female worthies from classical antiquity and the Bible. She is more noble and more beloved by her spouse than Cleopatra was, since she does not flee from him in his troubles, and she dies not one death for love but a thousand, every day (sig. F 3v). The Countess also surpasses the famous female warriors—the Scythian women who put Darius to flight; Deborah, who judged Israel; valiant Judith, who defeated Holofernes—in that she wages "farre greater warre . . . / Against that many headed monster Sinne" (sig. F 4). Esther, who fasted and prayed three days to free her people from Haman, gives way to Margaret Clifford, who for "dayes, weekes, months, and yeares" (sig. F 4v) has worn the sackcloth of worldly troubles. She overmatches the chaste Susanna's single trial of chastity since she subdues all base affections in her own breast. And the journey of the noble Queen of Sheba to find the greatest earthly king, Solomon, is but a figure of the Countess's love and service to an almighty and everlasting King.

This section concludes with a sensuous baroque passage expatiating upon the sweetness of Christ's grace and love:

> Sweet holy rivers, pure celestiall springs,
> Proceeding from the fountaine of our life;
> Swift sugred currents that salvation brings,
> Cleare christall streames, purging all sinne and strife.
> Faire floods, where souls do bathe their snow-white wings,
> Before they flie to true eternall life:
>   Sweet Nectar and Ambrosia, food of Saints,
>   Which, whoso tasteth, never after faints.
>
> (sig. G 4)

This sweetness "sweet'ned all the sowre of death" (sig. G 4) to the first martyrs—Saint Stephen, Saint Lawrence, the apostles Andrew and Peter, and John the Baptist. The praise of these male saints (stanzas 219–228) provides some small counterweight to the massive wickedness Lanyer lays to men's charge throughout the poem. She concludes the poem by declaring that the Countess of Cumberland treads in the footsteps of these martyrs and folds up "all their Beauties" in her breast (sig. Hv).

The Country-House Poem: "Cooke-ham"

"The Description of Cooke-ham," in 210 lines of pentameter couplets, presumably executes the Countess of Cumberland's charge, referred to in *Salve Deus* as not yet fulfilled, to write "praisefull lines of that delightfull place," the "*Paradice*" of Cookham (sig. A). Although the house and estate do not survive, the area is still a beauty spot. Located in Berkshire a few miles from Maidenhead, it has extensive frontages on the Thames, rich woodlands, lush meadows, picturesque scattered hamlets, and high hills in the west.[54] The poem sustains a gentle elegiac tone throughout, since this is a valediction by author and residents to an Edenic pastoral life and place.

"Cooke-ham" may have been written before Jonson's "To Penshurst," published in 1616 but from the reference to Prince Henry (l. 77) obviously written before his death in November 1612. Jonson's poem, usually identified as the first English country-house poem, establishes the terms of a genre that celebrates patriarchy: Robert Sidney's Penshurst is a quasi-Edenic place whose beauty and harmony are centered on and preserved by its Lord, who "dwells" permanently within it. In sharpest contrast, Lanyer's country-house poem describes a paradise inhabited solely by women: Margaret Clifford, who is the center and sustainer of its beauties and delights; her young virgin daughter, Anne; and Aemilia Lanyer. "Cooke-ham" portrays the destruction of this Edenic place when its lady departs—presumably to her widow's dower residences.[55]

Lanyer's poem looks back to several classical and Renaissance poems which contributed to the development of the country-house genre. One is the *beatus ille* tradition praising a happy rural retirement from city business or courtly corruption, with its origins in Horace's Epode II, and Martial's Epigram III.58 on the Baian villa.[56] In Lanyer's version the male speaker and the virtuous happy man are replaced by women. Another strand contains landscape or topographical descriptive poetry, such as Michael Drayton's *Polyolbion*, and, more generally, classical and Renaissance pastoral and Golden Age poetry. Closest of all are poems built upon the controlling topos of the valediction to a place, the best-known example of which was Virgil's First Eclogue.[57] Read against that model, Lanyer's poem makes the pastoral departure a matter of social and domestic rather than state politics.

Whichever poem came first, it is instructive to compare Lanyer's poem with Jonson's, as they draw upon the same generic resources and are so nearly of a date; they offer, as it were, a male and a female conception of an idealized social order, which respond to contemporary ideology and which are epitomized in the life of a specific country house. Jonson's poem is cast in the form of an ode celebrating the estate of Sir Robert Sidney as a *locus amoenus* which perfectly harmonizes pastoral and providential abundance with georgic cultivation, associating the course of life at Penshurst with the permanence and stability of nature. It begins by contrasting the house itself with more recent and much more ostentatious "prodigy" houses (such as Knole and Longleat) built chiefly for show. Jonson then describes the estate and its life: the woods inhabited by nature gods; the fish, fowl, and beasts eagerly offering themselves for the lord's table; the tenants tendering their produce out of love rather than need; the generous and egalitarian hospitality of the hall (which the poet describes from his own experience); the "high huswifery," virtue, fruitfulness, and maternal devotion of Barbara Sidney; the presence of Robert Sidney as the moral center who gives order and stability to the entire estate and social community.[58]

However false to social reality, the social ideals projected by the poem are clear: a benevolent and virtuous patriarchal governor; a house characterized by simplicity and usefulness; a large extended family with lord, lady, children, servants, and retainers all fulfilling their specific, useful functions and coming together for prayer and for dinner in the Great Hall; the harmony of man and nature; a working agricultural community of interdependent classes linked together in harmony, generosity, and love; ready hospitality to guests of all stations, from poets to kings; and stability ensured by the religion and virtue passed on from the lord and lady to their progeny.[59] Jonson presents Penshurst as an integral part of the larger society as well as an idealized microcosm of it.

Jonson's extended praise of Barbara (Gamage) Sidney focuses on her role as helpmeet, housewife, and mother, offering an idealized traditional version of the aristocratic lady's role. The reality behind the idealization can be glimpsed in the more than 320 extant letters from Robert Sidney to his wife, which voice great affection and tenderness, but also complaints about their separations, worries about the children, and constant anxieties about money.[60] Like many of his contemporaries, Sidney had to rely heavily on his wife to manage family, household, and estate during his frequent and prolonged absences on the Continent and at court.[61] Jonson's poem portrays Lady Sidney in that responsible domestic role, and also gives her mythic significance as embodying the estate's ideal fusion of nature and culture. The ready and liberal hospitality of the hall is founded upon her "high huswifery"; her fruitfulness has produced a flourishing progeny; and her chastity and careful religious education of her children guarantee that they will be fit heirs to Penshurst's culture:

> what praise was heap'd
> On thy good lady, then! who, therein, reap'd
> The just reward of her high huswifery;
> To have her linnen, plate, and all things nigh,
> When shee was farre: and not a roome, but drest,
> As if it had expected such a guest!
> These, PENSHURST, are thy praise, and yet not all.
> Thy lady's noble, fruitfull, chaste withall,
> His children thy great lord may call his owne:
> A fortune, in this age, but rarely knowne.
> They are, and have been taught religion: Thence
> Their gentler spirits have suck'd innocence.
> Each morne, and even, they are taught to pray,
> With the whole household, and may, every day,
> Reade, in their vertuous parents noble parts,
> The mysteries of manners, armes, and arts.
> Now, *Penshurst,* they that will proportion thee
> With other edifices, when they see

> Those proud, ambitious heaps, and nothing else,
> May say, their lords have built, but thy lord dwells.
>
> (ll. 83–102)[62]

Lanyer's poem, by contrast, displays the real superimposed upon the ideal, affording a very different representation of the lady's situation. In this country-house poem the house itself is barely mentioned: it belonged, after all, to the crown, not to the Countess. But the estate is described in evocative pastoral imagery as a *locus amoenus;* it enacts the pathetic fallacy continually as it responds to Margaret Clifford's presence according to the seasonal round. No lord dwells here, but three ladies prepare to leave, forever. Moreover, there is no larger society here: no extended family, no servants, no villagers, no visitors, no men at all. This poem gives mythic dimension to Lanyer's dominant concerns throughout the volume: this lost Eden was a female paradise and as such an ageless, classless society in which three women lived together in happy intimacy.

The elegiac tone is established in the opening lines, as Lanyer bids farewell to the place she associates with her religious conversion and the confirmation of her vocation as poet:

> Farewell (sweet *Cooke-ham*) where I first obtain'd
> Grace from that Grace where perfit Grace remain'd;
> And where the Muses gave their full consent,
> I should have powre the virtuous to content:
> . . . . .
> Never shall my sad eies againe behold
> Those pleasures which my thoughts did then unfold.
>
> (sig. H 2)

She represents Margaret Clifford as sharing these elegiac sentiments, and advises her to regard those "pleasures past" as "dimme shadowes of celestiall pleasures."

Then begins the description of the estate as it responds to the arrival and departure of its mistress. It becomes a *locus amoenus* as each part decks itself out in all its spring and summer loveliness for her arrival:

> The Walkes put on their summer Liveries,
> And all things else did hold like similies:
> The Trees with leaves, with fruits, with flowers clad,
> Embrac'd each other, seeming to be glad,
> Turning themselves to beauteous Canopies,
> To shade the bright Sunne from your brighter eies:
> The cristall Streames with silver spangles graced,
> While by the glorious Sunne they were embraced:

> The little Birds in chirping notes did sing,
> To entertain both You and that sweet Spring.
>
> (sig. H 2–H 2v)

Other aspects of nature contribute to the welcome with an obsequiousness like that of the Penshurst fish and game offering themselves to capture, but Lanyer's tone carries no hint of Jonson's amused exaggeration.[63] The hills descend humbly that the Countess may tread on them. The gentle winds enhance her pleasure in the woods by their "sad murmure." "The swelling Bankes deliver'd all their pride" (their fish) upon seeing this "Phoenix." The birds and animals sport before her—only slightly more timorous than they would have been with Eve:

> The pretty Birds would oft come to attend thee,
> Yet flie away for feare they should offend thee:
> The little creatures in the Burrough by
> Would come abroad to sport them in your eye;
> Yet fearefull of the Bowe in your faire Hand,
> Would runne away when you did make a stand.
>
> (sig. H 2v)

Although at Cookham most aspects of nature are ungendered, the female personifications Philomela and Echo are prominent exceptions: in the Edenic phase their voices bring praise and delight, but at the ladies' departure they sound again their familiar tones of grief and woe—associating their sad stories with this new example of women's wrongs and sorrows. As in that other Eden, the focus of interest in this place is a "stately Tree" (sig. H 2v), which is somehow an entire forest, incorporating the qualities of many trees. This tree is almost the only element of nature gendered male: it is an oak which surpasses all its fellows in height; it is straight and tall "much like a comely Cedar"; and it has outspread arms and broad leaves "like a Palme tree" (sigs. H 2v–3). The tree serves the Countess as a kind of ideal lover, more dependable than her own husband as it shelters and protects her against the too fierce onslaughts of the (also male) sun, Phoebus; and she implants on it her last farewell kiss before departing. Seated by this tree the Countess enjoys regal honors and delights. "Hills, vales, and woods, as if on bended knee" salute her, and she has a view of "thirteene shires" (not actually possible but here a substitute for Adam and Eve's view of all the world from their paradise): "A Prospect fit to please the eyes of Kings" (sig. H 3). This tree offers no temptation, sexual or otherwise, only contentment and incitement to meditate upon the creatures as they reflect their Creator's beauty, wisdom, love, and majesty. Elsewhere in the woods the Countess meditates on the Scriptures "with Christ and his Apostles there to talke; / Placing his holy

Writ in some faire tree"; and she daily follows in the spiritual footsteps of the greatest Old Testament saints:

> With *Moyses* you did mount his holy Hill,
> To know his pleasure, and performe his Will.
> With lovely *David* you did often sing,
> His holy Hymnes to Heavens Eternall King.
> . . . . .
> With blessed *Joseph* you did often feed
> Your pined brethren when they stood in need.
>
> (sig. H 3)

As a counterpart to the oak in the realm of nature, these biblical figures supply spiritual male companionship in Cookham's Edenic world.

The next passage is a complaint that Lanyer can no longer associate with Anne Clifford, now Countess of Dorset, because "Unconstant Fortune" (sig. H 3v) has placed too great a social divide between them. While the passage gives vent to Lanyer's discontent with her station and makes a transparent bid for further attention from Anne, it is thematically appropriate. In Edenic Cookham, Lanyer (who is twenty years older than Anne Clifford) can describe herself nostalgically but improbably as a constant participant in the young Anne's "sports." But now the social constraints which accompany Anne's aristocratic rank by birth and marriage are set off against those natural associations dictated solely by virtue and pleasure, "Whereof depriv'd, I evermore must grieve" (sig H 3v).

Then, Cookham's grief at the ladies' preparations for departure is described in a notably effective passage in which pathetic fallacy fuses with the seasonal change from autumn to winter:

> Me thought each thing did unto sorrow frame:
> The trees that were so glorious in our view,
> Forsooke both floures and fruit, when once they knew
> Of your depart, their very leaves did wither,
> Changing their colours as they grewe together.
> But when they saw this had no powre to stay you,
> They often wept, though speechlesse, could not pray you;
> Letting their teares in your faire bosoms fall:
> . . . . .
> Their frozen tops, like Ages hoarie haires,
> Showes their disasters, languishing in feares:
> A swarthy riveld ryne all over spread,
> Their dying bodies halfe alive, halfe dead.
>
> (sig. H 4)

The Countess's gracious leave-taking of all the beloved creatures and places on the estate culminates in her charge to Lanyer to preserve them in poetry. Then the scene turns sentimental as Lanyer portrays herself stealing the farewell kiss the Countess bestows on the noble oak.

The final passage echoes the imagery of the opening passage, as all the elements of the *locus amoenus* transform themselves from beauty to desolation:

> And those sweet Brookes that ranne so faire and cleare,
> With griefe and trouble wrinckled did appeare.
> Those pretty Birds that wonted were to sing,
> Now neither sing, nor chirp, nor use their wing;
> But with their tender feet on some bare spray,
> Warble forth sorrow, and their owne dismay.
> Faire *Philomela* leaves her mournfull Ditty,
> Drownd in dead sleepe, yet can procure no pittie:
> Each arbour, banke, each seate, each stately tree,
> Lookes bare and desolate now for want of thee;
> Turning greene tresses into frostie gray,
> While in cold griefe they wither all away.
> The Sunne grew weake, his beames no comfort gave,
> While all greene things did make the earth their grave:
> Each brier, each bramble, when you went away,
> Caught fast your clothes, thinking to make you stay:
> Delightful Eccho wonted to reply
> To our last words, did now for sorrow die:
> The house cast off each garment that might grace it,
> Putting on Dust and Cobwebs to deface it.
> All desolation then there did appeare,
> When you were going whom they held so deare.
>
> (sigs. H 4–I 1)

In sharpest contrast to Jonson's "Penshurst," whose lord "dwells" permanently within it and thereby preserves its quasi-Edenic beauty and harmony, Lanyer's "Cooke-ham" portrays the destruction of an idyllic place when its lady departs. Cookham takes on the appearance of a ravaged Eden after the first human couple is expelled. But here it is a female pair— or rather trio—who depart: the Countess called away by the "occasions" attendant upon her widowhood; the virgin daughter to her conflict-ridden marriage; Lanyer to social decline. Offering her poem as "this last farewell to *Cooke-ham*" (sig. I 1), Lanyer suggests that none of them will return to this happy garden state in which women lived without mates but found contentment and delight in nature, God, and female companionship.

As yet we can only speculate about the factors—education, female patronage, ambiguous social status, somewhat unusual sexual freedom, life experiences—that led Lanyer to write and especially to publish poetry. Nor
can we explain the remarkable feminist conceptual frame that unifies her
Salve Deus, with its egalitarian challenge to sexual and class hierarchy and
its insistent contrast of good women and evil men, past and present.
Whatever Lanyer's actual experience in the households of Margaret Clifford and Susan, Countess of Kent, her book projects an imaginative vision
of an enduring female community. The patronage poems present a female
lineage of virtue from mother to daughter, a community of good women
extending from Catherine Bertie, Protestant fugitive in Mary Tudor's
reign, to the young Anne Clifford. They also rewrite patronage in female
terms, imagining for the poet Lanyer a family of maternal and sisterly
patronesses who will honor and reward her celebrations of them and of
the female sex. The Passion poem extends this community back to biblical
times and even to Eve, portraying women as Christ's truest apostles and
followers. In "Cooke-ham" a female Eden suffers a new Fall when the
structures of a male social order force its women inhabitants to abandon
it. Lanyer's poems boldly reimagine and rewrite the fundamental Christian myths—Eden, the Passion, the Community of Saints—with women
at their center.

Lady Mary Wroth with archlute, artist unknown.

Revising Genres and Claiming the Woman's Part: Mary Wroth's Oeuvre

Lady Mary Wroth (1587?–1651?) was the most prolific, most self-conscious, and most impressive female author of the Jacobean era. Her published work (1621) includes the first prose romance and the first sonnet sequence by an Englishwoman: the 558-page prose romance *The Countesse of Mountgomeries Urania* (which includes more than fifty poems); and appended to it a lyric sequence of 103 sonnets and songs, *Pamphilia to Amphilanthus*.[1] Her unpublished work includes several letters, a few poems omitted from the 1621 *Pamphilia to Amphilanthus*, a very long but unfinished continuation of the *Urania*, and a pastoral drama, *Love's Victory*, also a first for an Englishwoman.[2] Making this remarkable achievement possible is Wroth's strong sense of identity as a Sidney author, heir to the talent and cultural role of her famous uncle Sir Philip Sidney; her famous aunt Mary Sidney Herbert, Countess of Pembroke; and her own father, Robert Sidney, Viscount Lisle of Penshurst, whose poems (thirty-five sonnets, eighteen songs, five pastorals, and a few other pieces) have recently been discovered and published.[3] As Margaret Hannay persuasively argues, the recognized cultural status of the Countess of Pembroke was of special importance to Wroth's self-definition: though the male Sidneys supplied her with major generic models, her aunt offered a precedent for female authorship and may also have served as mentor.[4] As a girl, Wroth knew about, and may have had some contact with, the Countess's literary and intellectual coterie at Wilton. Later she evidently exchanged poems with the Countess's son, her first cousin and lover William Herbert, who was himself a poet and who succeeded to the Pembroke title in 1601.[5]

Wroth's romance and lyric sequence often echo works by the Sidney authors,[6] and often allude to family members—Sidneys, Herberts, and especially Pembroke (Amphilanthus in the romance and lyric sequence). Gary Waller sees this as Wroth's response to the pressures of male patriarchal dominance, her construction in terms of "the Sidney family romance."[7] But that reading misses the boldness of her rewriting. She used her heritage transgressively to replace heroes with heroines at the center of several major genres employed by the male Sidney authors, transforming their values and gender politics and exploring the poetics and situation of women writers. Wroth's works are not throwbacks to the past, or pale imitations of Philip Sidney's *Countess of Pembroke's Arcadia, Astrophil to Stella,* and *The Lady of May,* but a self-conscious reworking of genres commonly addressed by male authors to a female readership, often with claims that they were "inspired" or evoked or partly produced by those addressees. An obvious starting point for a woman writer is to make actual such pretenses of female agency and authorship. Wroth's originality resides in claiming the romance, the lyric sequence, and the pastoral drama as vehicles for exploring women's rather than men's consciousness and fantasies, and making all of those genres resonate against a Jacobean rather than an Elizabethan milieu.[8]

Since Wroth's texts often allude to the circumstances of her life and family relationships, biography provides one important context for them. Mary Wroth, probably born October 18, 1587, was the eldest daughter and eldest surviving child of Sir Robert Sidney and the Welsh heiress Barbara Gamage.[9] Their wedding (on September 23, 1584, fifteen days after the death of Barbara's father) was a successful coup on the part of Sidney and his friends in stealing a march on her numerous other suitors and beating by barely two hours Queen Elizabeth's letter forbidding the match.[10] As Governor of Flushing, Robert Sidney spent most of the decade from 1588 to 1598 in the Netherlands, but his frequent letters to his wife testify to his affection for her and for Mary, to whom he referred often and fondly as "little Mall."[11] As Hannay shows, Sidney's letters also document the frequent visits between his family and that of his sister, the Countess of Pembroke[12]—visits which provided opportunities for the Countess to influence her niece (and probable namesake), as well as for the growth of affection between the cousins Mary and William.

Some information about Mary Wroth's education can be gleaned from letters to Robert Sidney by his friend and estate manager Roland Whyte. On October 23, 1595, Whyte reported, "She is very forward in her learning, writing, and other excercises she is put to, as dawncing and the virginals";[13] and on December 28, 1602, he noted that "upon St Stevens Day" (December 26) she danced galliards and corantes at court and was "much comended by her Majestie."[14] With her mother and other siblings Mary made at least three visits of several months' duration to the Continent to visit her father (1590, 1592, and again in 1597)—visits which brought to the fore disagreements between Robert and Barbara Sidney over the girls' education, which he thought would be better advanced in the household of the Countesses of Huntingdon and Warwick. Barbara insisted on keeping them at home and bringing them to the Continent with her, gaining support from Lady Huntingdon, who suggested that a visit to the Hague would improve Mary's French.[15] Mary Wroth's writings give evidence of wide reading in English and Continental romances and pastoral dramas, and in English poetry and drama.

On September 27, 1604, at age seventeen, she was married to Sir Robert Wroth, descendant of an ancient and staunchly Protestant family. At his father's death in 1606 he inherited large estates—Durrance in Enfield and the leasehold of Loughton Hall near the royal forest of Essex—as well as his father's office of Riding Forester, charged with protecting the game and facilitating the royal hunt.[16] The marriage was entirely a matter of patriarchal arrangement; there was no hint of affection between the young people, and they had almost nothing in common. Strapped for funds, Robert Sidney borrowed £1,000 from his nephew Pembroke to make up the first installment of the wedding settlement—a nice irony, given Mary Wroth's later extramarital relationship with Pembroke. Sidney was also hard-pressed to make the other payments due Wroth.[17] Robert Sidney's letter of October 10, 1604, to his wife notes early evidence of marital trouble—probably related to these financial matters but perhaps also to signs of temperamental incompatibility, or of Mary's affections placed elsewhere, or of the jealousy later alluded to in Ben Jonson's cryptic comment that "my Lady Wroth is unworthily maried on a Jealous husband."[18] Sidney's expressed concern is rather for his reputation than for Mary's happiness:

> I found my son Wroth come up [to court] as hee tels mee to despatch some busines: and wil bee againe at Penshurst on Fryday. I finde by him that there was somewhat that doth discontent him: but the particulars I could not get out from him: onely that hee protests that hee cannot take any exceptions to his wife nor her carriage towards him . . . It were very soon for any unkindnesses to begin: and therfore whatsoever the matters bee, I pray you let all things bee carried in the best maner til wee all doe meet. For mine ennimies would be very glad for such an occasion to make themselves merry at mee.[19]

As a young wife Mary Wroth attended the court, but she was not one of Queen Anne's inner circle: she danced in *Blacknesse* (1604) in the role of Baryte, but not in *Beautie* or *Queenes,* nor do the often incomplete records identify her as a participant in any other masque.[20] Over the years she often played hostess to the King and his hunting parties at Lough-ton.[21] In 1612 she made a personal appeal to Queen Anne to request her support for Robert Wroth's (successful) petition for an extension of his leasehold on Loughton Manor: that letter alludes to "the infinite favours which from you I have reseaved," and underscores her own interest in Loughton, promised by Wroth as an addition to her jointure.[22] But for all that, Mary Wroth remained securely embedded in the Sidney family net-work. Robert Sidney's letters to Barbara over the next decade report the frequent visits exchanged between Mary Wroth, Robert Sidney, and Mary's cousins—Pembroke, Elizabeth, Countess of Rutland (Philip Sid-ney's daughter), and Susan, Countess of Montgomery (Philip Herbert's wife and Mary Wroth's closest friend).[23] Moreover, Mary retained the Sid-ney Phaon as her seal rather than her husband's device, and followed her aunt's practice in using an *S* fermé ($) in her letters.[24]

In the years 1606–1613 several dedications and literary praises addressed her as a likely patron. They inevitably praise her Sidney heritage—as epit-ome of virtue and true religion, as patron, and (occasionally) as poet; almost as often they pun on her married name (Wroth/worth). Among Nicholas Breton's addresses to the Sidney-Pembroke ladies is one to her as "M. Agape Wrotha," honoring her heritage of heroic love and virtue from "Arcadian *Sydney.*"[25] In one of the dedicatory sonnets appended to his *Iliades of Homer,* Chapman apostrophizes her as "the Happy Starre, discovered in our Sydneian Asterisme, comfort of learning, Sphere of all the vertues, the Lady Wrothe."[26] George Wither (1613) puns on Wroth/worth to commend her (Sidneian) patronage: *"Arts sweeet Lover;* (unto whom I know / There is no happie *Muse* this day remaines; / That doth not for your *Worth* and bounty owe / Even himselfe, his best and sweetest straines."[27] In a rather heavy-handed epigram William Gamage (1613) of-fers to correct the title she has from her husband: "For R the O; then justly Lady Worth / I might thee stile, worth what? hie honours Grace."[28]

Jonson's tributes also emphasize the Sidney connection: he dedicated *The Alchemist* (1612) to her as "the Lady, most aequall with vertue, *and her Blood:* The Grace, and Glory of Women," declaring it safe "in your judge-ment (which is a SIDNEYS)"; and his Epigram 103 turns explicitly on the conceit that to name her a Sidney is sufficient praise. More extravagantly, Epigram 105 claims that all the classical virtues pertaining to Ceres, Oen-one, Flora, May, Venus, Diana, Pallas and Juno could, if lost, be recreated from her.[29] Jonson's verse epistle "To Sir Robert Wroth" praises his delight in country life as opposed to courtly pleasures—masques, extravagant din-ners, and jeweled displays; but that tribute is problematized by praises of Wroth's "noblest spouse" for her magnanimity in providing entertain-ments for his rustic society. Mary Wroth's entertainments, where "Apollo's harpe and Hermes lyre resound" and the Muses are welcomed, as well as her virtues and "the great *Heroes,* of her race,"[30] provide a nobler standard against which to measure Wroth's rural virtues and interests.

Some tributes indicate that Mary Wroth was recognized as a poet and that her poems had some currency beyond the family circle long before their publication. Josuah Sylvester's sonnet to her, appended to his funeral elegy for her brother William Sidney (1613), refers to her as *"Al-Worth* [anagram for "La Wroth"], Sidneides, / In whom, Her Uncle's noble Veine renewes."[31] Jonson addressed his only sonnet to her (*Underwood* 28), a deft compliment to her preferred form; his claim that he wrote out or "excribed" her sonnets suggests that he encountered them in manuscript. Jonson's poem offers the most attentive comment on Wroth's poetic artistry and the erotic power of her poetry before the twentieth century:

> I That have beene a lover, and could shew it,
> Though not in these, in rithmes not wholly dumbe,
>   Since I excribe your Sonnets, am become
> A better lover, and much better Poët.
> Nor is my Muse, or I asham'd to owe it
>   To those true numerous Graces; whereof some,
>   But charme the Senses, others over-come
> Both braines and hearts; and mine now best doe know it:
> For in your verse all *Cupids* Armorie,
>   His flames, his shafts, his Quiver, and his Bow,
>   His very eyes are yours to overthrow.
> But then his Mothers sweets you so apply,
>   Her joyes, her smiles, her loves, as readers take
> For *Venus Ceston,* every line you make.[32]

In an undated ode Jonson's friend William Drummond also praises Wroth's love sonnets: "Your spacious thoughts with choice inventiones free, / Show passiones power, affectiones severall straines" (ll. 5–6).[33] And Wroth's 1619 letter to Dudley Carleton indicates that she presented some manuscript verses ("rude lines") to him.[34] She was also spectacularly and unequivocally defined as a poet-singer in the splendid Penshurst portrait of her with a giant archlute.[35]

In March 1614 Robert Wroth died, leaving (as Chamberlain noted) "a younge widow with 1200ˡⁱ joynter, and a young sonne not a moneth old: and his estate charged with 23000ˡⁱ debt."[36] Whatever their differences, Wroth in his will praised his wife's "sincere love, loyaltie, virtuous conversation," lamented his inability to do more for her, and made a point of bequeathing her "all her books and furniture of her studdye and closett."[37] Their son, James, died two years later (July 5, 1616), leaving the estate to a

distant relative and Mary Wroth plagued by debts. At some point the affection between Mary Wroth and her cousin Pembroke developed into a
love affair and produced two children. Pembroke had been briefly imprisoned in 1601 for getting Queen Elizabeth's maid of honor Mary Fitton
with child and refusing to marry her; in 1604 he married Lady Mary Talbot, daughter to the Earl of Shrewsbury and cousin to Arbella Stuart, who
helped make the match. Pembroke continued, Clarendon observes, to be
"immoderately given up to women," though attracted less by physical
beauty than by such intellectual gifts as Mary Wroth evidently possessed:
"extraordinary wit, and spirit, and knowledge."[38] Pembroke's own talents
and interests—as poet, as patron of theater, music, literature and art, as
powerful courtier, and as James's Lord Chamberlain after 1615—no doubt
enhanced his attractiveness for Wroth.[39]

A genealogical manuscript by Pembroke's cousin, Sir Thomas Herbert
of Tintern, supplies the names of the Wroth-Pembroke children—William
and Catherine—but does not list their birth dates; it records the army
career of the son and the marriage of the daughter to one "Mr. Lovel neare
Oxford."[40] A poem by Sir Edward Herbert of Cherbury, "Sent to Lady
Mary Wroth upon the birth of my Lord of Pembroke's Child. Born in the
Spring," alludes wittily to her poetry, her scandal-mongering enemies, and
her new baby:

> Madam, though I'm one of those,
> That every spring use to compose,
> That is, add feet unto round prose.
> Yet you a further art disclose,
> You can, as everybody knows,
> Add to those feet fine dainty toes,
> Satyrs add nails, but they are shrews,
> My muse therefore no further goes
> But for her feet craves shoes and hose,
> Let a fair season add a Rose
> While thus attir'd we'll oppose,
> The tragic buskins of our foes.[41]

The illicit relationship and its offspring were obviously not secret, but also
not notorious: those egregious gossips Chamberlain and Carleton say
nothing about it, nor does Lord Denny in his denunciations of Wroth's
Urania. Evidently, as several critics have supposed, the powerful Sidneys
and Herberts rallied 'round to shield Wroth and foster the natural children, as was often the case in aristocratic families.[42] Some episodes in the
Urania suggest that Wroth was disgraced at court over the Pembroke relationship, but ascribe the fall from grace to the Queen's jealousy rather

than to bastard children. In any case, if the disgrace occurred, it was not total or permanent. Wroth took part in the grand funeral procession for Queen Anne (1619), and in 1621 received a present of deer from the King's forest as a mark of royal favor.[43] And her several petitions to the court to relieve her financial distress and give her protection from her creditors were always successful.[44]

However fraught with anxiety, Wroth's love affair of some duration with a kinsman who was also a courtier-poet connected her yet more securely to her Sidney-Herbert family and heritage, and probably encouraged her to write and publish. Her *Urania*, widely assumed by contemporaries to be a *roman à clef*, alludes to her own and her family's affairs and also at times to notable scandals and personages of the Jacobean court, as Chamberlain reports to Carleton:

> The other paper [I send] are certain bitter verses of the Lord Dennies upon the Lady Marie Wroth, for that in her booke of Urania she doth palpablie and grossely play upon him and his late daughter the Lady Hayes, besides many others she makes bold with, and they say takes great libertie or rather license to traduce whom she please, and thincks she daunces in a net: I have seen an aunswer of hers to these rimes, but I thought yt not worth the writing out.[45]

Wroth seems to have had warning soon after publication that a fire storm was about to break, for in a letter to Buckingham on December 15, 1621, she denies any covert allusions, claims she never intended to publish, and promises to do everything possible to stop the sales and call in the copies. But the letter reads more like a conventional pro forma disclaimer to avoid trouble than like true angst: Wroth indicates with some pride that she expects real difficulty in getting people to relinquish their copies, and asks Buckingham to set a good example by returning the presentation copy she sent to him. Pretty clearly she expected (and expects) him to enjoy the work.[46] There is no record of any formal procedures to stop sales or recall the book.

The only courtier to vent his rage publicly was Lord Edward Denny. He saw himself and his family barely concealed in the story of Sirelius (Sir James Hay), whose violent jealousy of his wife (Denny's daughter Honoria) led him to torment her but then to rescue her when her own father (Denny) attempted to kill her:

> Her father a phantastical thing, vaine as Courtiers, rash as mad-men, and ignorant as women, would needs (out of folly, ill nature, and waywardnesse, which he cald care of his honour, and his friends quiet) kill his daughter, and so cut off the blame, or spot, this her offence might lay upon his noble bloud, as he termed it, which by

any other men must with much curiositie have been sought for, and as rarely found, as Pearles in ordinary Oysters . . . It was a strange sight to behold a father incensed for a husbands sake against an onely child, & that husband to be the shield of her defence.   (Part I, 4, 439)

It is wicked satire and evidently came close to the mark. In response, Denny produced a scurrilous satirical poem (as from Sirelius' father-in-law to Pamphilia), and Wroth with fine satirical panache turned it back on Denny line for line:

To Pamphilia from the father-in-law of Seralius

Hermophradite in show, in deed a monster
  As by thy words and works all men may conster
Thy wrathfull sprite conceived an Idell book
  Brought forth a foole which like the damme doth look
Wherein thou strikes at some mans noble blood
  Of kinne to thine if thine be counted good
. . . . .

Thus hast thou made thy self a lying wonder
  Fooles and their Bables seldome part asunder
Work o th'Workes leave idle bookes alone
  For wise and worthyer women have writte none.

Railing Rimes Returned upon the Author
by Mistress Mary Wrothe

Hirmophradite in sense in Art a monster
  As by your railing rimes the world may conster
Your spitefull words against a harmless booke
  Shows that an ass much like the sire doth looke
Men truly noble fear no touch of blood
  Nor question make of others much more good
. . . . .

Thus you have made your self a lying wonder
  Fooles and their pastimes should not part asunder
Take this then now lett railing rimes alone
  For wise and worthier men have written none.[47]

Wroth enclosed her poem in a letter fathering Denny's poem on some "drunken poett" and claiming that she never intended "one word of that book to his Lordships person or disgrace." He responded that "the whole wor[l]d conceves me to be ment" and rages that she has made him "to be the onely chosen foole for a May-game, before all the World and especially before a Wise King and Prince, with all the nobility." He then prays "that you may repent you of so many ill spent yeares of so vaine a booke," and may follow "the rare and pious example of your vertuous and learned Aunt" in translating holy books and Psalms rather than writing lascivious tales.[48] He intimates by this that Wroth has disgraced her noble family by writing and publishing matter unfit for a woman. Her response is a romancelike challenge, affirming that both she and they will boldly defend her book and her innocence:

> Not now with words or submission (which I scorne) goe about to give sattisfaction, but [with] true and loyall faith prove and justifie what I have said: wherefore if you desire truth; knowledg of truth; or use of truth, let mee know my accusers; bring us together, and be assured you shall find mee; what my blood calls mee to be, and what my words have said mee to be. Feare not to saie what you please, for beleeve it my noble allies will not thank you for forbearing mee; nor [when] the tyme shall serve spare you for what you have done.[49]

Denny declined further exchange since "the truth is too apparant," affirming with some irony that he would ever honor and serve her "noble allies."[50] Wroth played out the game with panache, relying on the Sidney-Pembroke power base, though she also found it expedient to send the entire correspondence to the Earl of Denbigh with a plea that he "make all well with his Majestie."[51]

As an attempt to silence Wroth the maneuver was partly successful in that the contretemps probably discouraged her from attempting further publication. But it did not stop her from writing, and no doubt circulating, a second part of the *Urania* nearly as long as the first, as well as her pastoral drama *Love's Victory*—works probably written during the 1620s. Facts about Wroth's later life are sparse: according to a chancery deposition she held title to some property at Loughton and at Woodford, and lived on these estates until her death, recorded as approximately 1651. She was then sixty-four.[52]

Pamphilia to Amphilanthus (1621)

The poems of the lyric sequence *Pamphilia to Amphilanthus* were written and circulated over several years and some were known before 1613.[53] Here, however, I focus on the sequence in Wroth's final conception, revision, and arrangement—the 103 sonnets and songs appended to the *Urania*, Part I. The *Urania* context assimilates to the titular lovers of the sequence the characterizations and name significations developed in the romance: the constant, "all-loving" Pamphilia (associated with Wroth) and the unfaithful Amphilanthus, "lover of two" (associated with Pembroke). The first fifty-five poems constitute a very regular Petrarchan sequence—forty-eight sonnets (numbered sequentially) arranged in groups of six, with each set followed by a song. In context we are perhaps to identify them as the poems Amphilanthus finds and reads in Pamphilia's closet (2, 266), in an episode that leads to their mutual declaration of love. The last poem of this sequence (sonnet 48) is signed "Pamphilia," and the Amphilanthus/William Herbert identification is signaled by puns on *will*/Will (ll. 6, 14). The remaining forty-eight poems are numbered discretely and arranged in several shorter sequences loosely related through the speaker, Pamphilia: they include a carefully executed corona of fourteen interlinked sonnets as well as elegant songs in a variety of meters and tones.

The initial fifty-five-poem sequence claims the Petrarchan tradition for an English woman poet and gives voice and subjectivity to a sonnet lady, normally the silent object of the sonneteer's desire. Women's appropriation of the available discourses of love occurred much earlier on the Continent, with the sixteenth-century French and Italian poets Louise Labé, Catherine des Roches, Tullia D'Aragona, Vittoria Colonna, and Gaspara Stampa. But Wroth's rewriting differs markedly from theirs, and there is no evidence that she knew their work.[54] As is usual in Petrarchan sequences, Wroth's poems present particular moments, emotional crises, and vacillating passions over the course of a love relationship; and they trace a slight narrative beginning with the awakening to love and ending with separation (typically in such sequences by death, absence, or renunciation of love). But Wroth is not simply imitating, belatedly, a now passé genre. Since the Petrarchan sequence had become the preeminent genre for analyzing the male lover's desire, passions, frustrations, and fantasies (while also reflecting cultural and sometimes career anxieties), it is the obvious beginning point for a woman poet undertaking the construction of subjectivity in a female lover-speaker.

Wroth's specific allusions to her uncle's *Astrophil* and her father's unnamed sequence indicate her concern to embed herself within the Sidney literary heritage.[55] Still more important, however, is Wroth's reach back to the beginnings of the love sequence tradition (Dante's *Vita Nuova;* Petrarch's *Rime* and *Trionfi*) to rewrite those originary moments. Nona Fienberg calls attention to an important precedent for Pamphilia and Wroth in Petrarch's *Triumph of Death,* translated by the Countess of Pembroke, in which Laura's desire found voice as it did not in the *Rime.*[56] Also, Wroth's first sonnet revises Dante's first sonnet, in which the speaker dreams that his flaming heart is offered to and devoured by the lady. Pamphilia by contrast dreams that Venus and Cupid implant a flaming heart in her breast—her awakening to love.[57] In Petrarchan (and Ovidian) convention

Cupid exercises his power through the lady's wounding eyes, typically the instigators of love as they flash fiery darts into the lover's heart, and also by residing in, ruling, and tormenting the lover's heart. In Wroth's second sonnet the (male) beloved's eyes are sparkling and gently wounding (they are suns of "Aprills sweetest morne" and "Two starrs of Heaven, sent downe to grace the Earthe"). They conquer her heart (sonnet 3), but they do not initiate love, since that is already burning in her heart. These revisions represent the awakening to love as grounded in the desires of the woman, not the physical charms of the (male) beloved.

Pamphilia addresses very few sonnets to Amphilanthus, and seldom assumes the Petrarchan lover's position as an abject servant begging pity from a cold and cruel beloved. That note is sounded in sonnet 6, where she complains that his "disdaine" and "cruelty" cause her to despair and desire death; elsewhere (sonnet 13) she claims that the sight of him is her necessary life-sustaining food; or she cites his apparition to her in sleep as an argument that he should pity her "in whom thy self doth live" (sonnet 21); or (invoking the familiar Petrarchan motif of the exchange of hearts) she begs his heart in return for hers, which has fled to him (sonnet 26). It is probably no accident that three of these sonnets pun on *will*—the last one twice: "Dear cherish this and with itt my soules will," / "Butt if you will bee kind, and just indeed, / Send mee your hart" (sonnet 26).

Normally, however, Wroth avoids a direct role reversal. A female lover's overt, passionate solicitation of her male beloved would violate cultural norms too egregiously; but also, her assumption of the Petrarchan lover's subservient posture would approximate contemporary patriarchal structures all too closely, and could not empower her to construct her own identity and story. By virtually excising this conventional Petrarchan relationship, and by eschewing related Petrarchan motifs, Wroth's sequence displaces and silences the male beloved even more completely than is usually the case with the Petrarchan lady. There are no praises of his overpowering physical beauty or charms, no narratives of kisses or other favors received or denied, no reports of his words or actions, no blazons scattering his parts as a gesture of aggrandizement or control, no promises to eternize him through the poet's songs, no palinodes or renunciations of love.

Instead, Wroth makes central the Petrarchan (and Ovidian) motif of subjection or slavery to Cupid, who is usually identified here with the force of the female lover's desire. Always blind, Cupid is most often figured as he is in Petrarch (and Ovid)—a powerful boy-king tyrannizing over his subjects. Pamphilia proclaims Cupid's, rather than Amphilanthus', conquest—"I ame thy subject, conquer'd, bound to stand." She locates the sources of Cupid's awesome power in her own desire while disavowing his blindness and mischief: "Yett this Sir God, your boyship I dispise; / Your charmes I obey, butt love not want of eyes" (sonnet 7). Often she struggles against his charms but fails to regain her liberty:

> Why should wee nott loves purblind charmes resist?
>   Must wee bee servile, doing what hee list?
>   Noe, seeke some hoste to harbour thee: I fly
>
> Thy babish trickes, and freedome doe profess;
>   Butt O my hurt, makes my lost hart confess
>   I love, and must: So farwell liberty.
>
> (sonnet 14)

Sonnet 22 may allude to Wroth's role in Queen Anne's subversive masque *Blackness,* as Pamphilia associates herself with the Indians whose dark skin marks their devotion to their sun god, even as she wears the mark of her deity, Cupid, in her heart. At length she recognizes that lovers project their own blindness and folly upon Cupid, and so can honor and internalize the essential Cupid as the principle of desire: "for admire / Thee sure wee must, or bee borne without fire" (sonnet 33).

Wroth's sequence represents other Petrarchan motifs and personifications—Night, Grief, Time, Absence, Hope, Joy—as acting upon or located within the psyche of the female lover-poet. Both terms of the classic fire-ice paradox reside in her:

> Heat in desire, while frosts of care I prove,
>   Wanting my love, yett surfett doe with love
>   Burne, and yett freeze, better in hell to bee.
>
> (sonnet 17)

At times she has some sense of renewal from the dark night of grief— "Forbeare darke night, my joyes now budd againe" (sonnet 4)—but those joys soon dissolve into doubt and despair (sonnets 5, 6). Often she welcomes Night and its qualities—blackness, coldness, absence, grief—as valued female companions, identifying Night especially as her alter ego:[58]

> My thoughts are sad; her face as sad doth seeme:
>   My paines are long; her houers taedious are:
>   My griefe is great, and endles is my care:
>   Her face, her force, and all of woes esteeme:
>
> Then wellcome Night, and farwell flattring day
> Which all hopes breed, and yett our joyes delay.
>
> (sonnet 12)

In other sonnets she reiterates her affinity for Night's "grave, and saddest lookes," and "sober pace" (sonnet 15); or seeks out a dark place ("Sweet shades") consonant with her own "night / of griefe" (sonnet 17); or finds day and night alike miserable in that both display her wrongs, griefs, doubts, and jealousy (sonnet 18); or rejects light and day (appropriate to the joys of the loved one's presence) for night, consonant with the grief of absence (sonnets 19, 20). Elsewhere she calls the false flatterer Hope to the bar of justice, urging her to "prove true at last, and gaine your liberty" (sonnet 27); and she invites Grief as a welcome guest, banishing Joy (sonnets 28, 29). In sonnet 31 a blind female Fortune embraces her, "colde with griefe," dispelling her clouds of fears and urging her to depend on Love and Fortune. But she links herself in closest comradeship with the female triad of Night, Silence, and Grief: "And from you three, I know I can nott move, / Then lett us live companions without strife" (sonnet 37).

As the sequence develops, the woman lover-poet claims for herself powers and Petrarchan motifs usually (but here only occasionally) associated with the loved one. At moments of joy and hope his eyes are the sun and the stars which bring light (song 6, sonnet 41); but in sonnet 25 she asserts the power of her own eyes at once to wound like a Petrarchan lady's, and to weep blinding tear-floods like a Petrarchan lover's. More remarkably, she adjures her own eyes to "bee true unto your selves" and blind others by their self-control—a gesture to free herself from the male and the societal gaze and claim for herself its pleasures and power:

> Soe you kept safe, lett them themselves looke blinde
> Watch, gaze, and marke till they to madnes runn,
>
> While you, mine eyes injoye full sight of love
> Contented that such hapinesses move.
>
> (sonnet 34)

But she continues to suffer from Cupid's (and Amphilanthus') blindness, which ironically exposes her publicly, making her a "stage of woe," and an "open showe" of disasters: "None ever felt the truth of loves great miss / Of eyes, till I deprived was of bliss; / For had hee seene, hee must have pitty show'd" (sonnet 42).

The final set of sonnets (43–48) explores absence, one conventional endpoint for a Petrarchan sequence. Read in terms of the romance, this motif carries allusions to Amphilanthus' inconstancy while avoiding direct treatment of a topic hardly decorous in a Petrarchan sequence. The major Petrarchan motifs—eyes, tears, Cupid—are here reprised. The beloved's eyes are again "the lights, and guides of love" so that darkness envelops Pamphilia in his absence (sonnet 43). Sonnet 44 apostrophizes a spring flowing swiftly in an effort to escape innundation by her tears; and sonnet 47 continues that motif as she urges her eyes to forgo futile weeping until their overflow can drown her, bringing the dubious freedom of death. In a dramatic monologue (sonnet 45) Pamphilia seeks to repel some unwelcome interlocutor (like the one in Donne's "Canonization") whose "multitudes of questions" amount to a "toungue torture." Representing herself as driven "senceles" by absence, she attempts to "fright / That Divell speach," and begs to be spared till that absence ends, "till I ame my self, and blest." But as this sequence concludes, she again draws all love's potency and agency into herself. Seeking to quench her flames of passion at a well, she plays wittily with the Petrarchan mirror conceit, recognizing herself and the (female) water as mirror within mirror to contain love: "Drinke I could nott, butt in itt I did see / My self a living glass as well as shee / For love to see him self in truly plac'd" (sonnet 46). Sonnet 48 affords stronger closure than is usual in a Petrarchan sequence, as both lover and Love are made wholly subject to the female speaker. Punning on *will*/Will, Pamphilia admits that her steadily increasing fires of love outreach her capacity for expression through eyes or breath (poems), but she insists on the power of her free choice and her constancy: "Yet love I wil till I butt ashes prove. Pamphilia."

In locating the drama of love and desire in the consciousness of the woman lover-poet, Wroth reverses (and exaggerates) the customary Petrarchan focus on the male speaker's psyche. The Petrarchists, however, define the male lover-poet's subjectivity by constructing the female beloved as object, while Wroth deliberately eschews this move. Amphilanthus is virtually elided from the sequence, and Pamphilia defines herself and her determined, constant love by direct and persistent introspection and self-analysis. This is neither narcissism nor solipsism but a creative response to the dilemma posed by the conflict between Petrarchan generic norms and the dramatic circumstances here inscribed. The male Petrarchan lover finds supreme beauty and worth in the beloved lady, and he is not disempowered by her cruelty, rejection, or sovereignty over him; indeed his texts exhibit his power as poet and his privilege as a male to make her his object. By contrast, Pamphilia's beloved is flawed by infidelity; and her inferior social status as a woman puts her at risk of disempowerment were she to praise his supreme worth, enact subjection to his power, or endure his rejection. Accordingly Wroth makes the love experience itself—not the beloved—the locus of value and the stimulus to poetry: the female lover-speaker's experience of love as constancy is represented, paradoxically, as the fulfillment of her own desire and determination. From that position the woman lover can claim the Petrarchan poet's power of self-definition.

This sequence articulates an expressive Petrarchan poetics, in which poetry is seen to be prompted by the powerful emotions attendant upon unfulfilled love. The song ending the first set of six sonnets looks back to the romance, reprising Pamphilia's situation in that of a shepherdess who laments her inconstant lover, affirms her constancy, decries the disproportion between the spring season and the cold dark winter of her griefs, and determines to "write / The tale of haples mee" on a tree's bark, to be read by some other understanding lover.[59] In sonnet 8 Pamphilia claims that grief has led her to write, but that "griefe is nott cur'd by art." In sonnet 23 she rejects the courtly pastimes—hunting, hawking, gaming, conversation, music—as mere vanity, finding their perfected forms in her own thoughts and poems. Elsewhere she contrasts the courtiers' poetic games to her own heartfelt poems, which neither bring her pleasure nor adequately embody her emotions:

> Nor can I as those pleasant witts injoy
> > My owne fram'd words, which I account the dross
> > Of purer thoughts, or recken them as moss
> > While they (witt sick) them selves to breath imploy,
>
> Alas, think I, your plenty shewes your want
> > For wher most feeling is, words are more scant.
> > > > > (sonnet 39)

Song 5 makes the eternizing claim the Petrarchan poet normally directs to the lady. Reversing Petrarch's *Trionfi*, where Time conquers Fame, she paradoxically offers to eternize Time if it will slow down and allow her to enjoy love's pleasures: "On fames wings I'le rayse thee: / Never shall thy glory dying / Bee untill thine owne untying."

   These sonnets, and especially Wroth's elegant and various songs, display the power of the female speaker to order emotion into art, and the power of the female author to enter into dialogue with both Petrarchan and contemporary love poetry, voicing the woman's part. Song 4 exemplifies both dialogues, providing what we might see as Wroth's answer to Donne's song "Sweetest love, I do not goe,"[60] in the persona of the female lover. Both poems develop the Petrarchan conceit of exchanged hearts and souls, but the witty turn of Wroth's song exposes the inadequacy of that consolation:

> Sweetest love returne againe
> > Make nott too long stay:
> Killing mirthe, and forceing paine
> > Sorrow leading way:
> Lett us nott thus parted bee
> Love, and absence ne're agree;
>
> Butt since you must needs depart,
> > And mee haples leave,

In your journey take my hart
  Which will nott deseave
Yours itt is, to you itt flyes
Joying in those loved eyes,

Soe in part, wee shall nott part
  Though wee absent bee;
Time, nor place, nor greatest smart
  Shall my bands make free
Ty'de I ame, yett thinke itt gaine;
In such knotts I feele noe paine.

Butt can I live having lost
  Chiefest part of mee
Hart is fled, and sight is crost
  These my fortunes bee
Yett deere hart goe, soone return
As good there, as heere to burne.

The remaining forty-eight sonnets and songs are organized into shorter sequences loosely linked by a slight narrative in which Pamphilia struggles to move from a Petrarchan to a revised Neoplatonic conception of love and poetics; she engages with Cupid in several guises, falls prey to jealousy, and at last attains a settled content. In these sequences (which I see disposed into four segments)[61] the speaker sees her distresses as more transitory, her prospects as more hopeful, her situation as closer to that of other lovers—whose voices she ventriloquizes in several love songs. Here the Petrarchan motifs of absence, grief, longing, wounding eyes, love's tyranny, disdain, and cruelty are much less in evidence. But the figure of Cupid remains dominant, embodying competing images of love's nature and power: the mischievous Anacreontic child, the Ovidian boy-tyrant, the powerful young monarch of Petrarch's *Triumph of Love,* the Neoplatonic higher Eros.

The first segment centers thematically on constancy and Pamphilia's struggle to hold fast to that self-definition. An unnumbered sonnet is followed by six songs—reversing the structure of Wroth's Petrarchan sequence.[62] In the sonnet the lady speaker renounces Petrarchan motives and behavior: she desires only content and pleasure for her loved one, wishing unrest, disdain, and despite upon any Petrarchan "she" that shows him "least scorne" (115). The songs voice several love predicaments: a lament for an impending absence; an address to Venus, "Goddess of desire," to rule her wayward child, Cupid; the complaint of the love-crossed speaker kept from her true love by "an other ruler" (perhaps alluding to Wroth's husband): "I, that must nott taste the best / Fed must sterve, and restles

rest" (116–117). Next, Pamphilia voices a shepherd's song, a fervent declaration of constancy despite rejection, and follows it with one reaffirming
her own constancy. The final song seems at first a conventional Petrarchan
apostrophe to the beloved's eyes as instruments of love—"Fairest, and still
truest eyes / Can you the lights bee, and the spies / Of my desires?"—but
the terms are soon seen to apply as well or better to her own eyes, bringing
the power of the gaze and the power of choice back to the female speaker.
She recalls those eyes from jealousy, distrust, and suspicion, and urges art
and interiority upon them: "Learne to guide your course by art / Chang
your eyes into your hart, / And patient bee . . . / That you injoy what all
joy is / Happy to love" (119).

   The next segment comprises ten sonnets, three songs, and a concluding
(unnumbered) sonnet, exploring diverse perspectives on love as emblem-
atized in the Anacreontic and Ovidian Cupid. In the sonnets the woman
lover often speaks for all lovers caught in the throes of foolish passions
and tormented by Cupid. Love is like the Moon and Fortune's wheel in
its fickle changeableness (sonnet 1); the child Cupid is a wanton trickster,
abusing lovers ("wee fooles") who share his qualities: "Yett childlike wee
can nott his sports refuse" (sonnet 2). Some sonnets emphasize the personal: Pamphilia laments her imprisonment in a strange "cage" of suspicion, grief and "bace jealousie" (sonnets 4, 7); she seeks to avoid the fore-
knowledge of absence so as to preserve present joys (sonnet 9); she appeals
wittily to the other theological virtues when hope is shipwrecked: "Yett
faith still cries, Love will nott falsefy" (sonnet 6). The last sonnet offers a
retrospective on this sequence: the speaker was led by Folly (personified
as a false female friend) into "slaverie" to blind Cupid, but knows now
that love has quite another nature and character: "When love came blind-
fold, and did chaleng mee / Indeed I lov'd butt wanton boy, not hee"
(sonnet 10). The songs that follow include two palinodes. One berates
Love, figured as the Anacreontic Cupid, a spoiled and wayward child:

> Feathers are as firme in staying
> Woulves noe fiercer in theyr preying.
> As a child then leave him crying
> Nor seeke him soe giv'n to flying.
>   (125)

The second figures Love as the Ovidian boy-tyrant; spoken in the persona
of "Freedome," it advises taking love lightly and escaping quickly (126). A
concluding sonnet offers Pamphilia's formal apologia to Cupid for this
"treason," proposing to make amends by offering a "crowne unto thy endless prayse" (126).

   That crown, a corona of fourteen interlinked sonnets, constitutes the
third segment. It redefines the nature of love by replacing the Anacreontic

wanton child and the Ovidian boy-tyrant with the monarch figure of Petrarch's *Trionfi,* conceived as an honored and powerful King ruling a court
of noble Love. To that image Wroth assimilates the refining and ennobling
power of the Neoplatonic Eros, radically revised to locate love's transformative power not in the beloved but in the female speaker's inner experience of a worthy, constant love, figured as service to the mighty monarch,
Cupid. Wroth's lady embodies Constancy, not the Chastity of the *Trionfi*
who triumphs over Love; chastity is sometimes linked to constancy in the
corona, but in the sense of fidelity to one, not the renunciation of desire.
As the corona form dictates, the final line of each sonnet is repeated in the
first line of the next, and the last line of the concluding sonnet repeats the
opening line of the first: "In this strange labourinth how shall I turne?"

In the first sonnet Pamphilia locates herself in the labyrinth, hedged all
about with the Petrarchan love torments—suspicion, fear, shame, doubts,
danger—yet ready to take Theseus' "thread of love" and so escape. In
several subsequent sonnets she speaks for all true lovers ("us"), advising
them of Love's greatness and ennobling power: he is the "soules content,"
"the roote of peace," the "Image of fayth, and wombe for joyes increase"
(sonnet 2); his essence is constancy and truth, and service in his "brave
court" is noble (sonnets 3, 4). As a Neoplatonic "Tuter" he, though blind,
opens our eyes to "true desire" and happiness, and inspires our "Soules
with devine love" (sonnet 5)—not the Neoplatonic Good, or God,[63] but
the faithful, constant love which ennobles the female poet-lover, enhancing her "witts" and talents:

> Itt doth inrich the witts, and make you see
>   That in your self, which you knew nott before,
>   Forcing you to admire such guifts showld bee
>   Hid from your knowledg, yett in you the store.
>   (sonnet 6)

Unlike the traditional Neoplatonic ladder of love, which leads the lover
away from the particular object to the eternal form of Love, Wroth's Neoplatonism leads back to the eyes of the loved one, "which kindle Cupids
fire" and make the lover an artist in the Petrarchan mode:

> Love will a painter make you, such, as you
>   Shall able bee to drawe your only deere
>   More lively, parfett, lasting, and more true
>   Then rarest woorkman, and to you more neere,
>
> Thes be the least, then all must needs confess
> Hee that shunns love doth love him self the less.
>   (sonnet 7)

Subsequent sonnets continue the redefinition of love. The Petrarchan fire-ice oxymoron is reworked to advise lovers not to eschew ardent desire "like one longe frozen in a sea of ise," but instead to achieve a love both passionate and chaste, "maintaind by heavnly fires / Made of vertu, join'de by truth, blowne by desires / Strengthned by worth, renued by care-fullnes, / Flaming in never changing thoughts" (sonnet 8). Repudiating Venus as a figure for lascivious sensuality and lust, the speaker turns instead to the redefined Cupid, "her sunn; where sinn / Never did dwell" (sonnet 9). Sonnets 10 and 11 describe the rightly ordered internal state: Love as (male) ruler, Reason as (female) adviser, the two as the parents of "Desert, and liking." This order banishes "wantones" and unruly desires, permitting the proper Triumph of Love, defined as constancy: "Lett love his glory have and might / Bee given to him who triumphs in his right" (sonnet 11). This noble love makes the lover "pale with loving care"; its clear light banishes Venus' night and fogs; it produces joys, "treasures of content," and "holly friendship" (sonnets 12, 13). In sonnet 13 the speaker formally offers herself and her poetic crown to the great monarch Love:

> To thee then lord commander of all harts,
>   Ruller of owr affections kinde, and just
>   Great King of Love, my soule from fained smarts
>   Or thought of change I offer to your trust
>
> This crowne, my self, and all that I have more
> Except my hart which you beestow'd beefore.
> (sonnet 13)

The conceit of Love bestowing the speaker's heart on the loved one allows the final sonnet to end as the form demands. Despite Pamphilia's exalted concept of love as constancy, she is still vulnerable to Love's foe, "Curst jealousie," and so turns back into the labyrinth:

> So though in Love I fervently doe burne,
> In this strange labourinth how shall I turne?

We know from the romance that Pamphilia's jealousy is provoked by Amphilanthus' inconstancy, but she treats it here as the single remaining flaw in her own love. Wroth thereby keeps the focus securely on her female speaker's subjectivity.

The fourth segment begins with an interlude of four love songs incorporating several voices and attitudes. One pleads for an end to absence, "Sweet lett mee injoye thy sight"; another offers a lighthearted narrative of the Ovidian Cupid's conquest of a scoffing nymph and her companions (135–136); next, a reverde celebrates spring's delights but interjects into the scene the "luckles payning" of the nightingale, and with it remembrance of Philomela's sad story (136–137). The last song chides deceiving male lovers who lie to win their lady's favor, urging them to "returne, / Unto truth in love" (138–139). Then comes a sequence of nine sonnets analyzing the course of a love threatened by jealousy. Pamphilia begins in distress— "My hart is lost"—but she immediately repudiates "looce desires" stemming from Venus, "Queene of lust," and turns to Cupid, "God of love" (sonnet 1). The next sonnet reports the beginnings of love as an encounter with the Anacreontic lost child Cupid, "Colde, wett, and crying," who ungratefully repaid the speaker's help by "burning my hart who had him kindly warmd" (sonnet 2). Another reports an amusing dialogue between Pamphilia and the jealous goddess Juno seeking her philandering husband—an encounter which replays the issue of male infidelity and female jealousy in universal, even divine, terms (sonnet 3). The "poyson" of Pamphilia's own jealousy gives rise to a conflict between fear and desire, but she holds fast to the heart's truer vision: "Yett in my hart unseene of jealous eye / The truer Image shall in triumph lye" (sonnet 4). Lamenting the "clowds of smoke" (sonnet 5), the darkness and thick mists that attend her "wounding jealousie," she yet insists that in her own thoughts the "true forme of love shall live" (sonnet 6). Reaffirming her Petrarchan poetics, Pamphilia sees her pain as the stimulus for writing, which cannot "give rest, or quiett to my loving hart"; but she adjures Love to continue his "art" in her so that her passions may continue to "rule, wounde, and please" (sonnet 7). Then, shifting to her (revised) Neoplatonic perspective, she apostrophizes Love as educative, ennobling, and eternal:[64]

> How thou doest traveile owr best selves to gaine:
> Then howerly thy lessons I doe learne,
>
> Think on thy glory which shall still assend
> Untill the world come to a finall end,
> And then shall wee thy lasting powre deserne.
>
> (sonnet 7)

The last sonnet affords a strong resolution,[65] but it is not the palinode or repudiation of earthly love we expect at the close of a Petrarchan sequence. Rather, Pamphilia now unequivocally gives over Petrarch for a revised Neoplatonism, claiming that she has moved beyond the love fostered by Venus and Cupid to a higher love, defined by her inner constancy. She also turns toward a Neoplatonic poetics. Bidding not love but the Petrarchan love sequence farewell, as the proper exercise of "young lovers" still enmeshed in the turmoil of changeable passions, she expects her achieved constancy and personal integrity to lead her to a higher poetic mode. Her new subject must be truth (perhaps though not necessarily religious truth), which brings true joy and endless gain:

> My muse now hapy, lay thy selfe to rest,
>   Sleepe in the quiett of a faithfull love,
>   Write you noe more, butt lett thes phant'sies move
>   Some other harts, wake nott to new unrest,
>
> Butt if you study, bee those thoughts adrest
>   To truth, which shall eternall goodnes prove;
>   Injoying of true joye, the most, and best,
>   The endles gaine which never will remove;
>
> Leave the discource of Venus, and her sunn
>   To young beeginers, and theyr brains inspire
>   With storys of great love, and from that fire
>   Gett heat to write the fortunes they have wunn,
>
> And thus leave off, what's past showes you can love,
> Now lett your constancy your honor prove.
>
> (sonnet 9)

In claiming the Petrarchan love sequence for the female lover-poet, Wroth did not use it as male courtiers often did, for overt political purposes. She may have hoped that her romance and lyric sequence would interest Buckingham and the court, helping her to overcome whatever "disgrace" she may have suffered from the now deceased Queen. She may also have supposed that the gender politics of her radically revised Petrarchan sequence would speak for and to the women of the court. That politics identifies female desire as the source and center of the love sequence, and the impetus for the woman lover's movement from the bondage of chaotic passion to the "freedom" of self-chosen constancy. On the surface that ideal seems close to contemporary patriarchal ideology—close enough, perhaps, to afford Wroth some cover by soothing readers likely to be threatened by the challenge to patriarchy it actually inscribes. In these poetic sequences Pamphilia (and Wroth) affirm constancy not chastity, to a lover not a husband, as a matter of choice not cultural imposition, and as a means to personal and artistic growth.

Urania, Part I (1621)

The romance *Urania* has the expected generic markers—a multitude of characters; interwoven and interpolated tales; knights fighting giants, pirates, monsters, and usurping Kings; Spenserian symbolic places. The two parts of the *Urania* make a continuum, with prophecies about the protagonists Pamphilia and Amphilanthus in the published Part I fulfilled in Part II. Part I begins with several young royal scions taking over from an older generation: some are about to inherit a throne (Amphilanthus, Pamphilia, Rosindy); others must win back their sovereign rights from usurpers (Antissius, Dolorindus, Steriamus, the Queen of Hungary); others have been raised as shepherdesses and must find out their true royal identity (Urania, Veralinda); all are enmeshed in love adventures. The unpublished Part II begins with the children of these and other principals preparing to take over the challenges of love and rule from their parents. Both parts signal their incompletion by ending in midsentence (in imitation of the *Arcadia*); Wroth may have intended further installments, in the manner of the popular Continental romances *Amadis de Gaule, Diana,* and *L'Astrée*.[66] Despite such conceptual links, however, it is useful to treat the two parts separately, to highlight the large differences in the worlds portrayed and in the literary strategies that register Wroth's development as a writer of fiction.

Despite Wroth's conventional disclaimer, much evidence indicates that she intended Part I for publication: the elegant folio format, the elaborate title-page engraving illustrating a central episode (the Palace of Love), the careful positioning of Wroth on the title page as heir to all the Sidneys, the fact that she sent a copy to Buckingham, the formal registration of the book with the Stationers, the absence of any recorded effort to stop publication or recall the work.[67] Part II was not prepared for publication, as is evident from the blanks left for later insertion of poems.

The published *Urania* claims the Sidney mantle immediately and ostentatiously by structural, thematic, and verbal allusions to *The Countesse of Pembrokes Arcadia*. These include the title (*The Countesse of Mountgomeries Urania*); the interspersed songs and complaint poems assigned to characters at moments of special emotional crisis; the eclogues ending book one; the opening *locus ameonus* passage; the first episode focusing on a shepherdess, Urania (1, 1–4); a knight who cross-dresses as a nymph to woo a shepherdess (Leonius and Veralinda, 3, 362–372, 387–390); the counterfeit death of a captive lady staged to deceive her lover (1, 130–133).[68] Wroth also positions her work within Renaissance romance generally by the use of many romance topoi: lists or barriers in which knights defend their ladies' beauties (1, 136–139; 2, 196–200) or display their own prowess (1, 62–63; 3, 394; 4, 434); single combats to rescue a heroine or restore her kingdom (4, 431–433); knights adventuring incognito and undergoing tests of love (1, 89–91, 130–133); numerous spells, enchantments, and oblique prophecies. Several symbolic places recall Spenser—the Tower of Love, the Theatre of Love, the Lady of Rhodes's Bower of Bliss, the Hell of Deceit; and the Veralinda story reprises Perdita in *The Winter's Tale*.[69]

But Wroth revises these generic topoi as she rewrites the major concerns of the male romance world—love, heroism, virtue, friendship, adventure, celebration of dynasty or nation—from a Jacobean woman's position and consciousness.

In Wroth's romance an idealizing fantasy of female desire only partially overlies a dark image of the Jacobean world. At the level of fantasy all Wroth's principal characters are Kings, Queens, and Emperors, with the power (and comparative freedom) incident to those positions. The landscape, however, is not Arcadia or Fairyland: the action takes place all over Europe and Asia—not only Peloponnesus (Morea) and Turkey (Pamphilia) but also Romania, Albania, Germany, Hungary, Phrygia, Slavonia, Tartary, Britain, and Naples; at times the wars in the Germanies and central Europe evoke the Thirty Years' War. This world is rife with rape, incest, tortured women, endangered children. The male heroes are courageous fighters and attractive lovers, but all are flawed by inconstancy or worse. The higher heroism belongs to a few women, and involves the preservation of personal integrity and agency amid intense social and psychological pressures and constraints.

The work only occasionally behaves like a true roman à clef, but it points insistently to Jacobean England and its ethos—not only to Hay, Honoria, and Lord Denny (4, 438–440) but more generally to hunting kings, masques (1, 34; 2, 155; 3, 424), "Dancings and all Court sports" (3, 392), and the Somerset–Frances Howard–Overbury scandal.[70] Names, family relationships, and personal qualities also associate several characters with Sidney-Pembroke family members.[71] Wroth and Pembroke are figured in the faithful poet-Queen Pamphilia and her inconstant lover and cousin, Amphilanthus; Wroth's brother Robert Sidney seems to be shadowed in Pamphilia's brother Rosindy; the Countess of Pembroke is figured in the Queen of Naples (Pamphilia's aunt and Amphilanthus' mother), "who was as perfect in Poetry, and all other Princely vertues as any woman that ever liv'd" (3, 320), and the "most incomparable Queene, or Lady of her time" (3, 416). The Lindamira story (3, 423–425), narrated by Pamphilia and judged by its audience to be "some thing more exactly related then a fixion" (3, 429), also shadows Sidney affairs. The courtier Lindamira (Ladi Mari) has a father, Bersindor (Robert Sidney), who married "a great Heyre in little Brittany" (Barbara Gamage), a jealous husband (Wroth), and an unfaithful lover (Pembroke); she serves a jealous Queen who covets her lover and so dismisses her from court; and Pamphilia turns her complaints into sonnets.

The world of Wroth's romance is defined in large part through the numerous interpolated stories which reiterate again and again, with a few changes in detail and dramatis personae, the dangers and social constraints affecting women, from shepherdesses to Queens. This world is rigorously patriarchal in its institutional arrangements: "Lord the husband is in all estates from Shepheards unto Kings" (3, 296), the narrator observes. Arranged or forced marriages are the norm, usually resulting in a triangle of husband, wife, and true lover, with the husband sometimes complaisant (2, 154–155; 4, 463) but often murderously jealous. Limena's husband subjects his wife to cruelty, torture, and attempted murder (1, 1–12, 68–72); and a bride who flees with her lover on her wedding day is pursued and killed (1, 34–36). Queens are often forced to wed for reasons of state (Melisinda of Hungary, 2, 245–246). Other women may be given in marriage by fathers or brothers for wealth or property (3, 350) or out of sheer arbitrariness (the very young Lisea wed to a churlish lord with "unsufferable passions," 4, 474). Still others are threatened by and barely escape rape or incest (1, 31–32; 4, 442–446). In romance fashion, many stories tell of courageous women who resist the tricks and torments used to force their submission to unwanted mates (Liana, 2, 206–212; Sedelia, 2, 229–240; the Princess of Lycia, 4, 495–498) until they are rescued by one or another of the work's heroes; at great cost these ladies remain faithful to lovers who often prove unfaithful to them. Violence abounds, as does corruption, jealousy, and betrayal—especially at court. Several stories (Lindamira, 3, 423–427; Lisea, 4, 474–476; Elena, 4, 506–509) reprise Wroth's own situation as a court lady with an unworthy husband and an unfaithful courtier-lover; Wroth's situation may also be hinted obliquely in the disgrace these ladies suffer at court because the Queens they serve are jealous of their lovers. The diatribe on the Queen's court in the Lisea story may well allude to Queen Anne's court during her declining years:

> These [ladies] served to fill up places, and adorne a chamber of state, like ill Pictures, yet bravely guilt and set forth . . . an noise they also made of mirth, banqueting and inviting company . . . Dance they did, and all ridiculous things that ancient, but young made women could invent to do. I came again, having liberty to behold them, but never any more to serve in ordinary. Lord how I admird the alteration, and the place, being changd from what it was, as much as from a Court to a Playhouse.   (4, 476)

Also, the stories that Pelarina (4, 449–454) and Bellamira (3, 326–337) tell of themselves and their writing closely parallel Wroth's case. The reprise of Wroth's story in that of so many others—unfaithful lover, unhappy arranged marriage, psychic suffering, arbitrary censure, disgrace, writing—offers it as (almost) Everywoman's story, at least in the higher social ranks.

The special psychological pressures this world produces are explored under two motifs: the tyranny of love, and the ubiquity of male inconstancy. No one, male or female, escapes the tyranny of love: there are no Belphoebes here, and the shepherdess Allarina (Silviana), who took up a chaste nymph's life when rejected in love, at length marries her repentant lover (3, 410). Urania in the first throes of love for Parselius is sleepless, "love commanding her soule to take no advantage of restfull houres" (1, 38). Pamphilia in love with Amphilanthus complains of love's "tormenting passion" and "tyrannies" (1, 204), and at one point cries out, "O love, thou dost master me" (1, 52). Desiring Pamphilia, Steriamus curses "the time I ever suffered the unrightfull Monarchy of love to governe me, & thus to soveraignize over me" (2, 153).

The power of love is allegorized in the Spenserian Palace of Love and Temple of Love, where most of the principal characters are at one time or another held captive. The chief symbolic place of book one is the magnificent Palace of Love on Venus' island (Cypris), whose marble pillars are carved with figures of the "brave, and mighty men, and sweet and delicate Ladies . . . conquer'd by loves power" (1, 39). The bridge approaching it has three towers: on the first stands Cupid with bow and arrow, figuring Desire, and open to false, merely sensual lovers who "endure torments fit for such a fault." The second is surmounted by Venus, figuring Love; it is open to all lovers, who "suffer unexpressable tortures, in severall kindes as their affections are most incident to; as Jealousie, Despaire, Feare, Hope, Longings." On the third tower stands the figure of Constancy holding the keys of the palace, which "can bee entred by none, till the valiantest Knight, with the loyallest Lady come together" (1, 40). Sclarina is held captive in the Tower of Desire, Urania in the Tower of Love, along with such later adventurers as Limena, Perissus, Leonius, Antissius, and Ollorandus. The prisoners are released when Amphilanthus and Pamphilia fulfill the conditions of the enchantment: he opens the gate of Desire, as one who "had as much strength in desire as any"; both together open that of Love; but only Pamphilia can take the keys from the figure of Constancy, which then "vanished, as metamorphising her self into her breast" (1, 141). The emblematic episode figures the several lovers' situation at this early stage, identifying Constancy as the highest mode of love and the essence of Pamphilia's self-definition.

The marble Temple of Love, the chief symbolic place of book three, encloses four ladies—Pamphilia, Urania, Philistella, Selerina—who adventured themselves needlessly on the sea (figuring turbulent passions), and also many knights who tried to rescue them (3, 321–322). It is also a theater, "as magnificent a Theater, as Art could frame" (3, 322), where the ladies are transfixed on golden thrones, charmed by sweet music, and deluded with blissful but false fantasies of fulfilled love. The enchantment can be broken only by "the man most loving, and most beloved" (Amphilanthus); he will himself be held captive until all are freed by "the sweetest and loveliest creature [Veralinda], that poore habits had disguised greatnesse in" (3, 322). After Amphilanthus restores the ladies to their perfect senses, Pamphilia discovers in dismay Amphilanthus' renewed attraction to his former lover, Musalina (3, 377). When Veralinda completes the rescue, the theater vanishes, leaving behind a book recounting the whole story of Urania and Veralinda, supposed shepherdesses but in fact Princesses (3, 388–389). This emblematic episode highlights lovers' propensity to deception, disguise, and self-delusion, implying that love must be based on truth.

But while men and women alike suffer the tyranny of love and desire, women are subjected to the further psychic torment of male inconstancy. There are a few stories of fickle or promiscuous women—a lady who deceives two friends by offering her favors to both (4, 516–517); a woman who loves two suitors equally and cannot choose (3, 385–387); the Queen of Bulgaria, who loves only herself, abuses her husband, and collects lovers to satisfy her pride (3, 342–343; 4, 463, 469–470); the lascivious Lady of Rhodes (3, 344–450), who captivates men with sensual pleasure. This last episode is a delightfully ironic reworking of the Bower of Bliss in which the Guyon-figure, Polarchus, makes love to the lady in order to rescue his friend but then regrets leaving her, "more delight lodging by halfe in this sort than in twenty marriages" (3, 348). These cases, however, are exceptional, included to show that "if men be faulty . . . women can be so likewise" (4, 469), whereas among men infidelity is ubiquitous. Indeed, in a direct reversal of the common stereotype of female changeableness, inconstancy is taken to be a defining characteristic of men. Urania advises Pamphilia that inconstancy "is a thing familiar with men" (3, 398); Limena comments, "Mens words are onely breath, their oathes winde, and vowes water" (2, 190); Bellamira, like Wroth a courtier, a poet, and a faithful lover, tells Amphilanthus that her lover loved "no more constantly then your sex useth, not meaning to bee a Phaenix among men-lovers, for feare of envy" (3, 327). And a female courtier turned country lass after being rejected in love urges the point strongly in her irony-laden advice to Musalina:

> Trust not too much; for believe it, the kindest, lovingst, passionatest, worthiest, loveliest, valliantest, sweetest, and best man, will, and must change, not that he, it may bee, doth it purposely, but tis their naturall infirmitie, and cannot be helped. It was laid to our charge in times passed to be false, and changing, but they who excell us in all perfections, would not for their honours sake, let us surpasse them in any one thing, though that, and now are much more perfect, and excel-

lent in that then wee, so there is nothing left us, that they excell us
not in, although in our greatest fault.   (3, 375)

Amphilanthus is the very embodiment of male inconstancy: loved by
and by turns loving many (Musalina, Luciana, Antissia, Pamphilia), he is
confessed by all women the "fittest to bee beloved" (2, 242). Before loving
Pamphilia he always found his greatest delight in variety: "Left I till now
any wherein change brought not unspeakable content?" (1, 111). A shepherd who serves as a kind of alter ego for Amphilanthus recounts his many
conquests since age fourteen, concluding, "I thinke varietie the sweetest
pleasure under Heaven, and constancy the foolishest unprofitable whining
vertue" (4, 484). Wroth's narrator apostrophizes Amphilanthus as "match-
lesse in all vertues, except thy love," ironically concluding that he is in fact
"constant to love; for never art thou out of love, but variety is thy staine"
(3, 312–313). His very name points to his nature, signifying "the lover of
two" (2, 250).

The Hell of Deceit, the chief symbolic place of book four, rewrites the
Amoret-Busyrane episode in *Faerie Queene* (III, 12). In an illusion devised
by Musalina, Pamphilia sees Amphilanthus in a cave surrounded by
flames, his heart ripped open, and Musalina about to raze her name out of
it with a sword; but unlike Britomart, she cannot pass the flames to save
him since this Hell is only for false lovers. Amphilanthus later thinks he
sees Pamphilia dead in the same place, with her breast open and his name
in her heart; when he attempts to revive her, he is cast from the cave and
displays his inconstancy by promptly following Musalina (4, 554). When
he later returns to Pamphilia with renewed and intensified love, he destroys the entry to that Hell, "resolving nothing should remaine as witnesses of his former ficklenes" (4, 558).

This romance explores female rather than male heroism, the challenges
of love rather than of war. There are battles, but they do not test character:
love does. In the harsh social and psychological world of this romance,
women must balance the claims of personal desire and duty (to parents or
husband or nation), of surrender to passion and self-control, of constancy
and change, of display and concealment of emotion. The principal heroines—Pamphilia, Urania, and Veralinda—meet these challenges differ-
ently, validating a range of female attitudes, values, and lives. But they and
many other heroines all insist on making their own choices in love—op-
timally in marriages based on choice but also by resisting arranged marriages or within them maintaining a faithful though (usually) chaste relationship with the chosen lover. The norm of female heroism involves
self-definition, preserving personal integrity (especially in regard to love),
and exercising various forms of agency—as rulers, counselors, lovers, storytellers, poets, seers.[72] Appropriately, the primary supernatural agent is a

woman: the astrologer, magician, and seer Melissea (based on Ariosto's
female mage, Melissa) makes obscure predictions about the principal characters (2, 159–160) which are later realized, and intervenes at times to cause
enchantments or release those captivated by them.

One aspect of this work's fantasy of resistance to patriarchal norms involves Queens who are rulers in their own right, though as the genre
dictates Queens and Kings alike are more concerned with issues of love
than with governance and rule. Wroth treats female rule itself as natural,
usual, and worthy, the Queens no more prone to passion, and rather less
prone to tyranny, than the Kings. As Josephine Roberts notes, however,
those Queens who are tyrants or usurpers are usually driven by power lust
or sexual passion.[73] The usurping Queen of Romania, "that devill of
women," dominates and then murders her husband after having him expel
his own son and advance hers (1, 59–61). Ramiletta, daughter of the King
of Negroponte, imprisons her own father, who has disinherited his son to
set her on the throne (1, 97–98). The virgin Queen Olixia of Epirus rules
her people aggressively and well until she is smitten by (unrequited) love
for Selarinus and dies in a violent, self-induced fever (2, 255–261). The case
of the strong-willed Queen Nereana is more complex: she defies cultural
norms by her forthright love pursuit of the unwilling Steriamus; then she
is driven frantic as a would-be lover strips her, dresses her, and forces her
to play out roles he fantasizes for her; finally she is abandoned and deposed
for overweening pride and apparent lunacy, but after being humbled by
suffering she regains her throne (2, 161–168, 277–291; 3, 421). This cautionary tale underscores the dangers of female pride and passion, and, as Carolyn Swift notes, it also starkly displays the cultural construction of
women by men.[74]

Despite their power, Wroth's Queens must usually call upon male heroes to fight for them and help repel aggressors. There are no martial
heroines—no Britomarts or Bradamantes or Clorindas—and only one
cross-dressed lady who puts on page's garb to follow and serve her beloved
(3, 380–381).[75] Yet the text reaches toward androgyny as, despite the labels
employed, stereotypical qualities normally assigned to men or women are
seen to be the property of both genders. Pamphilia is praised for her
"brave and manlike spirit" (4, 483), as is Lucenea for her "masculine" courage (1, 134); Amphilanthus and Philarchos, by contrast, are said to have
soft white hands and to weep readily, intimating female delicacy in the
emotions (1, 102; 2, 222). Many women ride and hunt;[76] and Ramiletta's
castle is defended by women who, though evil, are skillful in shooting
(1, 108).

Pamphilia is the primary example of a good Queen, the legitimate, designated successor to an uncle who had no male heir (1, 140); by taking the
country's name (Pamphilia) as her own, she symbolically espouses it.[77]

More than any other Queen, she attends to the responsibilities of rule—visiting her people, repelling invasions (2, 161; 3, 429)—but her love problems with Amphilanthus take up most of her attention. As Queen in her own right she is free to choose for herself in love and marriage, yet she sees herself bound by public duty and familial bonds. While she can invoke those bonds for her own purposes—to dissuade an unwelcome suitor—she recognizes social constraints which deny complete autonomy even to reigning Queens. While the choice of love is always in her hands, choice in marriage might not be:

> My Lord (said she) I cannot but thanke you for your princely offer; but it must bee my fathers liking, with the consent of my nearest and dearest friends that can set any other Crowne on my head, then that which my people have already setled there; and the consent of so great a people, and so loving to me, must not be neglected . . . Why? are you not (cryd *Leandrus*) soveraigne of your selfe by Judgement, yeares and authoritie unlimited by fortunes, by government, and the love of your Parence . . . These still are but the thread that tie my dutie, replide the Queene.   (2, 179–180)

Her father properly limits his role to persuasion, but in pressing the case for Leandrus, he slights Pamphilia's status and role as an independent Queen: assuming paternal authority, he refers to her country simply as a marriage portion to be offered her husband. She counters adroitly, declaring herself married to her country (like Queen Elizabeth) and also asserting the claims of love:

> She confessed . . . that he [Leandrus] was worthy of the greatest fortune the world had in a wife: but his Majestie had once married her before, which was to the Kingdome of *Pamphilia*, from which Husband shee could not bee divorced, nor ever would have other, if it might please him to give her leave to enjoy that happinesse; and besides, besought his permission, for my Lord (said shee) my people looke for me, and I must needs be with them. Why, said the King, that is but as if it were a portion given you to your marriage! Not to *Leandrus* my Lord (said shee) I beseech you, for I cannot love him; nor can I believe he loves in me ought besides my kingdome, and my honour in being your daughter . . . The King knew she had reason for what she said, and so assuring her, that he would not force her to any thing against her mind, though he should be glad of the match.
>
>   (2, 218–219)

The romance focus on love permits exploration of the conflict between private desire and public duty (the Queen's two bodies) in the several Queens and especially Pamphilia. But the work looks to unite rather than to separate those roles. Urania voices the ideal of the integrated self as she challenges Pamphilia to conquer her despair over Amphilanthus's infidelity and to exercise both in private and public life the self-control proper to a Queen:

> Where is that judgment, and discreet govern'd spirit . . . hath made you famous? . . . call your powers together, you that have been admired for a Masculine spirit, will you descend below the poorest Femenine in love? . . . if your people knew this, how can they hope of your government, that can no better governe one poore passion? how can you command others, that cannot master your selfe; or make laws, that cannot counsel, or soveraignise over a poor thought? . . . I love Love, as he should be loved, & so deare Lady do you . . . it is our want of courage and judgement makes us his slaves.   (3, 398–399)

The interconnection of private and public domains is highlighted by a shepherd subject of Pamphilia's, who is comically unaware of her presence when he comments on her worthiness as Queen and the political danger from her love troubles:

> She is (said he) a Lady loved, and well thought on by all that ever I heard speake of her, curteous, affable, no pride dwells in her, to the meanest she will speake; yet the greatest feare her, which is her judgement and goodnesse that breedes that respect to her; shee is upright and just, in her government mild, and loving to her subjects, shee loves all good exercises as well abroad, as at home; shee hath indeed they say, a brave and manlike spirit, and wondrous wise shee is; yet for all these good parts, shee could not keepe out of *Cupids* clawes, but was mightily in love, and is still as it is mutterd about with a gallant man, a brave fighting man, for whose sake shee refused all others, and lately the King of Celicia her next neighbour; but for all her wisdome, there I believe she was ill advised to refuse him, for he came with such an Army against her, to have her by force, as had like to have marrd all . . . yet at last hither came that brave man her love . . . [who] did gallantly to release her, yet hee dwells so farr off, and having as it is said, a prety humour of changing, wee doe not wish him to her, least wee should loose her.   (4, 483–484)

Pamphilia, the protagonist of the romance, is the heroine of constancy. While Amphilanthus attracts and returns the love of many women, Pamphilia attracts the love of many men (Steriamus, Leandrus, Amphilanthus, the King of Sicily), but loves only Amphilanthus. Her love is at first tormented and passionate, expressed through numerous complaints of suffering, jealousy, and love's power, but she brings it under some control by her self-chosen and self-defining values of constancy and discretion. Discretion prompts her to keep the object of her love secret from all except her confidant Urania and Amphilanthus himself:

> Soft said she [addressing Echo, who might betray her], shall I turne blabb? no Echo, excuse me, my love and choyce more precious, and more deere, then thy proud youth must not be named by any but my selfe . . . nor yet hath any eare (except his owne) heard me confesse who governs me . . . As none but we doe truely love, so none but our owne hearts shall know we love.   (2, 264)

Not only is such discretion appropriate to her profound love, as she says, but also it allows her to maintain her self-respect and to avoid being defined by others' jealousy or pity. So discreet is she that she can remain, albeit at considerable emotional cost, a confidant and friend to Antissa, who is violently in love with Amphilanthus (1, 50–53, 75–79, 120–123). But this discretion robs her of the relief other lovers derive from open complaint: the narrator observes that her love was "most painefull to endure, as being haunted with two hellish Spirits of keeping it secret, and bearing the waight it selfe" (3, 314).

Pamphilia defines and vigorously defends her ideal of constancy in response to Urania's argument for reasonable limits to that virtue, in the light of Amphilanthus' infidelity:

> To leave him for being false, would shew my love was not for his sake, but mine owne, that because he loved me, I therefore loved him, but when he leaves I can doe so to. O no deere Cousen I loved him for himselfe, and would have loved him had hee not loved mee, and will love though he dispise me; this is true love . . . *Pamphilia* must be of a new composition before she can let such thoughts fall into her constant breast, which is a Sanctuary of zealous affection, and so well hath love instructed me, as I can never leave my master nor his precepts, but still maintaine a vertuous constancy. Tis pittie said *Urania,* that ever that fruitlesse thing Constance was taught you as a vertue, since for vertues sake you will love it, as having true possession of your soule, but understand, this vertue hath limits to hold it in . . . those with whom it is broken, are by the breach free to leave or choose againe where more staidnes may be found.   (3, 400)

Urania implies that Pamphilia has been indoctrinated to accept female passivity and the inequities of the double standard, but Pamphilia insists that her constancy is a conscious choice, emanating from her own nature and emotional imperative. Constancy and discretion are her route to personal integrity and agency: whatever the cost, she will define the terms of her love, not have them defined for her by society or by her unreliable lover.[78] Part I of the *Urania* breaks off with Amphilanthus apparently reformed, protesting that Pamphilia's tears have "infused constancy and perfect truth of love" in him. Reunited, the lovers anticipate a joyous life together: "all now merry, contented, nothing amisse; greife forsaken, sadnes cast off, *Pamphilia* is the Queene of all content; *Amphilanthus* joying worthily in her; And" (4, 558). But that tantalizing last word breaks the closure, denying us a sentimental "happily ever after" romance ending.

Urania embodies a different model of female heroism, founded upon a different kind of self-definition, personal integrity, and agency. For Urania, stolen away as an infant, raised as a shepherdess, and at length revealed to be a Princess (daughter to the King of Naples and sister to Amphilanthus), self-discovery requires a search for origins: she claims that without embeddedness in a family and without knowing her social status and rank, a woman cannot know herself. Wroth's romance begins with generic allusion to, and reversal of, the opening of Sidney's *Arcadia,* where two shepherds lament the absence of their beloved Urania; here Urania is present but absent to herself, lamenting a loss of identity that she sees as especially threatening for women:

> Of any miserie that can befall woman, is not this the most and greatest which thou art falne into? Can there be any neare the unhappinesse of being ignorant, and that in the highest kind, not being certaine of mine owne estate or birth? . . . What torments do I then suffer, which never knew my mother? (1, 16)

Urania attains integrity by discovering her royal origins and by embracing an appropriate and worthy second love. She is a model of good change, a contrast to Pamphilia's fierce constancy and also to Amphilanthus' casual profligacy. First mildly attracted to Perissus and then to Steriamus, she soon falls suddenly and passionately in love with Parselius even before she knows who she is (1, 21). Parselius is as suddenly smitten, vowing to marry her "whoever she was," regardless of what "Father, Country, Friend" might say (1, 22). Their untempered passion leads to Urania's captivity in the Tower of Love and to Parselius' overwhelming attraction to Dalinea, whom he promptly marries (1, 102–105). At this juncture, Urania's now hopeless love is cured by Melissea's enchantment: she instructs Amphilanthus to cast Urania into the sea, then Parselius and Steriamus rescue her and the water cleanses all of them of their former passions, nurturing better ones. Urania no longer loves Parselius but Steriamus; Parselius is released from his lingering love for and guilt over Urania; Steriamus no longer loves Pamphilia but Urania. This focal symbolic episode of book two may register (as Maureen Quilligan argues) the traffic in sisters by brothers,[79] but in the text it figures a baptismal "new birth" to a better life and love for all the participants, male and female. By freely giving herself up to this adventure, Urania relinquishes her old self, and so can rise from the psychic depths with a new perspective, a new maturity, and, appropriately, a new love. She explains the experience to Philistella in just such terms:

> It was mee thought a wonderfull odde change, and passing different affection I did feele, when I did alter: for though I were freed from my first love, and had a power to choose againe, yet was I not so amply cured from memorie, but that I did resemble one newly come out of a vision, distracted, scarce able to tell whether it were a fixion, or the truth: yet I resolved, and so by force of heavenly providence lost the first, and live in second choice . . . Oft did I study, how I might compasse my blessing, when for my most, and future happinesse, hee was as much engaged unto me, and so was *Melisseas* Prophecy performed, for wee from death in shew rose unto a new love.
>
> (2, 275–276)

Though Urania becomes a Queen, her chief mode of agency is as an effective counselor to others. She rescues the despairing Perissus by showing him that he might and should revenge his beloved Limena, supposedly murdered by her jealous husband. Perissus discounts her aid at first, with a put-down based on gender: "But now I see you are a woman; and therefore not much to be marked, and lesse resisted" (1, 4). But he soon recognizes her as a counselor of great judgment, wisdom, and reason (1, 13). Later she advises her cousin Philistella (2, 275–277) in love matters, and "by her excellent wit" (3, 400) overcomes Pamphilia's despair over Amphilanthus' inconstancy.

Veralinda's story begins as a pastoral interlude (3, 362–372, 388–390), with allusions to Perdita, Philoclea, and Wroth's Urania. Daughter and prophesied heir to the Phygian King, she was as an infant the target of her brothers' murderous plots, then was rescued and raised as a shepherdess in Arcadia. She loves and is loved by Urania's brother Leonius, but their mutual love at first sight seems threatened by disparity of class. To overcome her fears and his own timidity, Leonius takes on the role and garb of a love-smitten nymph (Leonia). The specter of lesbian love is briefly raised by scenes in which Veralinda is persuaded to embrace the nymph as she would her lover; more centrally, the cross-dressing grounds the love relationship in friendship and empathy, as Leonius willingly if temporarily embraces the female role and experience. When Veralinda's story is revealed in the Temple of Love, Leonius also reveals himself, the class bar now removed:

I am the Knight you loved as a Knight, I am the man, who for feare you lov'd me not, to move your love made my selfe a woman, and the same man that loves if you cheerish, else dies if you forsake. I am (my Lord) said shee, the woman that loves you as much, or more, if possible, then I did, having so many more bonds to tye me unto it; my life I owe you, I will pay it you, by spending it in being yours, and now I know my selfe to be a Princesse, the freelyer will I say this, being the fitter for you.   (3, 389)

Veralinda's story of mutual love based on choice ends in a marriage blessed by paternal approval. That model of love is repeated with other happy couples, wedded after harsher trials: Urania and Steriamus, Philistella and Selarinus, Parselius and Dalinea, Limena and Perissus, Rosindy and Meriana, Philarchos and Orelina, Melisinda and Ollorandus. Against the norm of arranged or forced marriages in this romance, Wroth sets the ideal of a marriage meeting both the societal requisites of equal rank and parental sanction, and the personal demands of mutual love and free choice. As Paul Salzman notes, Wroth breaks the romance convention of a plot centered on courtship, portraying instead married heroines and their love relationships—both inside and outside of marriage.[80]

Antissia is, as her name suggests, the antiheroine, Pamphilia's chief rival for Amphilanthus' love. Buffetted by external forces and internal passions, she is unable to attain self-direction, agency, or self-protective discretion: "Rage now outgoing judgement . . . she was a meere *Chaos,* where unfram'd, and unorder'd troubles had tumbled themselves together without light of Judgement" (1, 95). Her early life is emblematic of her nature: she is captured by pirates; her arranged marriage is disrupted; courtiers attempt to rape her. She is torn between friendship for Pamphilia, whose virtues she admires, and fierce jealousy of her as a suspected rival for Amphilanthus' love (1, 92–94). Utterly lacking in discretion, she displays her love for Amphilanthus openly to him and to others (1, 76–78; 2, 267). At one point, driven by passion and jealousy, she commissions her nephew and her lover to kill Amphilanthus (3, 308–311), but is promptly torn between revenge and regret:

Antissia after shee had fedde her selfe with this fury, was more then satisfied, for Envy being a little appeas'd, shee came to her good nature againe, or love, or feare, or, and indeed all passions, whirling about like a wheele they draw wyer out with all: so drew shee painefull thoughts, longer then before, lengthned, with dispaire.   (3, 311)

Her lack of self-control subjects her to the control of others, and to an arranged marriage with her lover Dolorindus, which Amphilanthus makes a condition of his forgiveness (3, 341).

Through the romance's many interpolated tales and poems, Wroth explores issues of poetics, reading, and women's writing. Some episodes represent romances as proper vehicles for women's self-discovery, thereby valorizing the kind of reading long denounced as characteristic of, but very dangerous to, women.[81] Both Urania and Veralinda find their stories written for them in the Temple of Love, and they then adventure to open the book and "author" themselves in terms of those stories (3, 387–389). By contrast, Pamphilia angrily rejects a book of romances that contains an analogue of her own sad story, seeking to deny its evident applicability:

> The subject was Love, and the story she then was reading, the affection of a Lady to a brave Gentleman, who equally loved, but being a man, it was necessary for him to exceede a woman in all things, so much as inconstancie was found fit for him to excell her in, hee left her for a new. Poor love said the Queene, how doth all storyes, and every writer use thee at their pleasure . . . punish such Traytors and cherrish mee thy loyall subject who will not so much as keepe thy injuries neere me; then threw she away the booke.   (2, 264)

At times the stories provide foils for the principal characters. A country lady's story told to Musalina is an analogue of Musalina's own love triangle with Lucenia and Amphilanthus—a discourse covered, the lady observes, "with the third person" (3, 375–376). Bellamira's story, recounted to Amphilanthus (3, 326–337), should (but does not) prepare him for the parallel deceptions he and Pamphilia encounter in Part II. These narratives also explore issues in Wroth's poetics: the relation of literature and life, the conditions making for literary creation, the uses of stories and poems, the nature and value of women's writing.

A major means of self-definition and agency for Wroth's heroines is literary composition—the telling of tales about themselves and others, and the making of poems. These stories allow the narrators to shape their lives artfully, giving them meaning and rhetorical power. Syderia wins Amphilanthus' support through her tale, "related . . . with as much passion, and fine expression of witty sorrow as could be" (2, 229–236). The pilgrim Pelarina, whose love story (4, 449–454) closely parallels that of Pamphilia and Wroth, highlights the problems women writers may face in making fictions of their own experience. Denying that her pilgrimage is a penance for yielding to her inconstant lover, she explains it rather as a response to his apparent (though silent) disapproval of her writing, as coming too near the truth. Conceivably, the incident alludes to Pembroke's response to Wroth's romance:

> This [love] I repent not, but a vanity I had about mee, which because once liked by him, and admired by our Sexe, or those, of them that I

durst make my follies seene unto, a fond humour of writing, I had
set downe some things in an idle Booke I had written, which when
hee saw, hee thought touched, or came too neere, or I imagine so,
because in some places he had turnd downe leaves, and onely at such
as he might if hee would dislike, and were those I thought hee would
take notice of, yet he neither did by word nor writing, not honouring
me so much, who was his slave, as to finde fault, or to seeme pleasd.
I was me thought left to conjecture, and the further I went in such
conjecture I runne into feare and sorrow that I had offended, yet I
can cleare my selfe if I might come to answere, but I cannot, nor
could, so as finding my selfe thus miserable, I tooke my Pilgrymage
willingly.   (4, 454)

For Wroth's storytellers inside the text, the implied fictional ideal is to
attain enough aesthetic distance to give artful shape to life experience. The
antiheroine Antissia can neither control her own life nor make an artful
tale of it: she baldly recounts how she was "betraid, sold, stolne, almost
dishonored," then was rescued by Amphilanthus, and now is passionately
in love with him (2, 267). Immediately thereafter, she tells of a British lady
whose character and story so closely approximate her own that the fiction
collapses: her audience smiles knowingly as she herself says, "Pray God
. . . I doe not play the Brittaine Lady now" (2, 269). By contrast, Pamphilia succeeds with her tale of Lindamira (3, 423–429), "faigning it to be
written in a French Story" (3, 423). The names mark this as a version of
Wroth's (and Pamphilia's) story, as does the allusion to the quasi-
autobiographical tale in the *Old Arcadia* by Sidney's persona, Philisides,
followed by songs to "Mira." Pamphilia's tale is followed by her sonnets
based on Linda*mira*'s complaint—"which complaint, because I lik'd it, or
rather found her estate so neere agree with mine, I put into Sonnets" (3,
425). But unlike Antissia, Pamphilia is artful, not obvious: she hints, and
her audience suspects, that the story "was some thing more exactly related
then a fixion" (4, 429), but its truth claims remain ambiguous. Such narrative strategies invite us to read Wroth's own narrative as an adroit fiction
grounded on truth, rather than as a close topical allegory.

Following romance precedent (notably that of the *Arcadia*), Wroth incorporates some fifty-six poems within the published *Urania,* showing
herself a skillful poet in many genres and verse forms. Included are nineteen sonnets, fourteen of them assigned to Pamphilia: she engraves one,
with an added quatrain, on an ash tree (1, 75–76), recalling Pamela's similar
inscription of her verses in a tree;[82] and she devises a short sequence of
seven sonnets based on her fictional character Lindamira's complaint (3,
426–428). An unusual sonnet assigned to Philarchos is monorhymed on
the words *anguish/languish* (2, 166–167). Three eclogic dialogues and

songs by Cyprian shepherds conclude book one (143–145), recalling the eclogues following each book of the *Old Arcadia*. In addition there are three inscriptions (4, 494–495, 498, 554); a witty dialogic exchange between an old man and a young woman (4, 515–516); several madrigals and songs in a variety of meters and stanzaic forms, one of them imitating Sapphics (4, 512); a long pastoral narrative in thirty-nine stanzas of eight-line ballad meter (4, 520–529); a comic aubade by a Florentine knight (4, 538–539); and a verse epistle in couplets (imitating Ovid's *Heroides*), in which Dorolina likens her situation to that of several abandoned but constant classical heroines—Dido, Ariadne, Medea, Calypso, Penelope (3, 418–420). Thematically most of the poems are love complaints on standard topics: the moon, by Steriamus (2, 152); a lady's eyes, by a shepherd (2, 212); absence, by Pamphilia (2, 178); Cupid, by "a country swain" who is in fact "third sonne to an Earle" (3, 294–295); a solitary place with woods and a mount, by Dolorindus (1, 111–112).[83]

Wroth uses the poems to help develop theme and character, as in the first poem in the romance, a sonnet in which Urania identifies herself with the nymph Echo, who voices the complaints of them both for loss of self.[84] She uses the poems also to continue her metacommentary on poetics and women writers. One central issue concerns the quality and quantity of women poets. When Amphilanthus asks to see Bellamira's poems, he voices the condescending male view that poetic accomplishment is "rare in women, and yet I have seene some excellent things of their writings" (3, 336). Upon hearing the poems, he places her among those rare women: "Perfect are you sweet *Bellamira,* said the King in this Art, pittie it is that you should hide, or darken so rare a gift" (3, 337). But Wroth's assignment of poems in the romance acts to discredit Amphilanthus' assumption about the scarcity of women poets: seventeen are assigned to male speakers, twice as many (thirty-four) to female speakers. Most of the women characters and storytellers—Urania, Bellamira, the Queen of Naples, Musalina, Antissia, Dorolina, Pelarina, Melasinda, Emilena, Lycencia, Lemnia, the daughter of Plamergus, the wife of Polydorus, a shepherdess, a female angler—voice at least one poem and so assume the status of amateur poets. Moreover, poetry is described as an expected accomplishment of lovers, women as well as men: the previously unpoetic Musalina, when in love, "was grown likewise a Poet as being a necessary thing, and as unseparable from a witty lover as love from youth" (3, 422–423). Wroth's management of this issue makes an oblique argument for the pervasiveness of female poetic talent, and may intend to claim the status of amateur poet for many Jacobean aristocratic ladies.

Pamphilia, Wroth's surrogate as poet and storyteller, is singled out as a poet by vocation by the number and declared excellence of the poems attributed to her. Her first poem elicits the narrator's tribute proclaiming her "excellent in writing" as well as prolific (1, 51); later Meriana testifies to her reputation: "I heare deare Sister, you are excellent in Poetry" (3, 392). The Queen of Naples (Amphilanthus' mother), who almost certainly figures the Countess of Pembroke, receives similar commendation—"as perfect in Poetry, and all other Princely vertues as any woman that ever lived" (3, 320). Her elegant poem on a nightingale makes an artful song of Philomela's (and woman's) woes (3, 416).

The implicit Petrarchist poetics in Part I locates the stimulus to worthy poetry in deeply felt emotions and conflicting passions; accordingly, the poems occur at, or are reports of, moments of emotional turmoil and self-analysis. This issue is addressed directly during an episode on shipboard, as Pamphilia and Orilena pass the time by making verses on standard topics: "Comparing the evening to the coolnesse of absence, the day break, to the hope of sight, and the warmth to the enjoying, the waves to the swelling sorrowes their brests indured" (3, 314). Pamphilia's ability to make fine poems while discreetly hiding her love "made some eroniously say, that counterfeting was more excellent then true suffering, because judgment governs where passions are free" (3, 314); but that view is labeled "erroneous" since Pamphilia is in fact deeply in love. Counterfeit emotions give rise to superficial or counterfeit poetry, the chief examples being assigned to men: the Florentine knight's foolish aubade is described as an exercise of conceited wit little better than "babling" (4, 538–39); and the plagiarized sonnet the inconstant Duke of Brunswick offers to his lady "was liker a Lovers present, counterfeite as his vowes" (4, 513–514).

In this romance good poets (female and male) experience deep emotions but manage to control them in their lives and their verse; bad poets do not. Pamphilia and Antissia are the chief examples. Pamphilia finds in poetry some means of relief, control, and agency. Carving a sonnet in an ash tree, she can "make others in part taste my paine, and make them dumbe partakers of my griefe" (1, 75–76). As she walks quietly in her garden after Amphilanthus' departure, "her inward thoughts more busie were, and wrought, while this Song came into her mind" (2, 177–178). Later, fearing that Amphilanthus has left her for Musalina, she "cast some Verses Sonnet-waies in her thoughts" (3, 390). Uttering "many sorrowfull sighs, and deepe groanes" over Amphilanthus' desertion, she finds her thoughts "more perfectly setting them selves before her eyes" and composes a sonnet (3, 409). That her verses are products both of her inner emotional state and her choice of a suitable genre (the Petrarchan sonnet) is clear from her response to Meriana's request for a poem:

> I have written something, said *Pamphilia,* but so sad they are, as onely
> fit me to heare, and keepe . . . I seldome make any but Sonnets, and
> they are not so sweet in rehearsing as others that come more roundly

off; but if you will heare some, I that can denye you nothing, will say one to you which I made not long since, and so is the freshest in my minde.   (3, 392)

This interconnection of life and art, love and poetry, is underscored in a climactic scene in Pamphilia's study, when Amphilanthus asks to see her poems and, as he recognizes her excellence as a poet, also perceives that she is a lover, and of him.[85] Her art, and his ability to read it, makes possible the first declaration of love between them:

> When they were there [in her study], she tooke a deske, wherein her papers lay, and kissing them, delivered all shee had saved from the fire, being in her owne hand unto him, yet blushing told him, she was ashamed, so much of her folly should present her selfe unto his eyes.
>   He told her, that for any other, they might speake for their excellencies, yet in comparison of her excelling vertues, they were but shadowes to set the others forth withall, and yet the best he had seene made by a woman: but one thing (said he) I must find fault with, that you counterfeit loving so well, as if you were a lover, and as we are, yet you are free; pitie it is you suffer not, that can faigne so well. She smild, and blusht, and softly said (fearing that he or her selfe should heare her say so much) Alas my Lord, you are deceived in this for I doe love. He caught her in his armes, she chid him not, nor did so much as frowne, which shewed she was betrayd.   (2, 266)

Antissia by contrast cannot order either her emotional life or her poems. Believing herself rejected by Amphilanthus, she first attempts a sonnet prompted "either by her own passion, or the imitation" of Pamphilia's sonnet in the ash tree, but she can only "put some of her thoughts in some kind of measure" (1, 94). Her next effort is either incomplete or so imperfect as to seem so: "Assuredly more there was of this Song, or else she had with her unframed and unfashioned thoughts, as unfashionably framd these lines" (1, 122). She herself burns her last poems, composed in despair when Amphilanthus abandons her for Pamphilia, prompting the narrator's speculation: "Whether judgment of seeing them but poore ones, or humble love telling her she had committed treason to that throne moved her, I cannot justly tell" (2, 271–272). In *Urania*, Part I, she writes no more poems.

Although sonnets are Pamphilia's chosen form for the analysis of love and for self-definition, Mary Wroth's finest poems, here as in the lyric sequence, are her songs—a talent probably nourished by her lute playing. An example is this song assigned to a shepherdess, a definition poem which displays both Wroth's lyrical gift and her wit:

Love what art thou? A vaine thought,
  In our mindes by fancy wrought,
  Idle smiles did thee beget,
  While fond wishes made the nett
  Which soe many fooles have caught.

Love what art thou? light, and faire,
  Fresh as morning, cleere as th'ayre:
  But too soone thy evening change,
  Makes thy worth with coldenesse range,
  Still thy joy is mixt with care.

Love what art thou? A sweet flowre,
  Once full blowne, dead in an howre.
  Dust in winde as stayd remaines
  As thy pleasure, or our gaines,
  If thy humour change to lowre.

Love what art thou? childish, vaine,
  Firme as bubbles made by raine:
  Wantonesse thy greatest pride,
  These foule faults thy vertues hide,
  But babes can no staydnesse gaine.

Love what art thou? Causeles curst,
  Yet alas thes nott the worst,
  Much more of thee may bee said,
  Butt thy Law I once obay'd,
  Therfor say no more at first.

                  (1, 144)

Urania, Part II

The variety of inks and pens used in the Newberry manuscript of *Urania,* Part II, suggests that it may have been written over several years. It begins with the "And" that ends Part I, and itself ends in midsentence: "Amphilanthus was extreamly" (2, f. 62). Some blanks allow for the later insertion of poems, and still more poems may have been planned, but their minimal use here accords with the more novelistic quality of this text. As before, interpolated tales are recounted by peripheral personages—knights, ladies, pastoral figures—but most of the stories are by and about the new major characters: the children of the principals in Part I. In this text Wroth recounts much more of the action directly, as omniscient narrator, and often employs a tone of irony and bantering wit. Also, the stories themselves are more diverse: instead of almost obsessive variations on the theme of men's inconstancy, women's fidelity, marital triangles, and a jealous

Queen's punishment of a faithful female courtier, they often recount obstacles overcome and end with happy relationships and marriages.

Here the major battles are fought to rescue the children of the various monarchies from enchantments and imprisonments (1, ff. 65–67, 35v–37), and to defend Pamphilia from threats of invasion and forced marriage (2, ff. 18–19v, 36–37v, 39). Part II has many more romance motifs—lost children, supernatural protectors, multiple enchantments, fierce giants, devilish spirits, mythical monsters—but no Spenserian symbolic places. Instead there are masques and dialogues whose significance is a matter of textual interpretation. Some romance topoi are replayed in a comic vein: in a Bower of Bliss episode (1, ff. 58–58v) the seductress is a rather ugly, heavily painted court lady; in a pastoral episode in the Vale of Tempe not one but all the pastoral characters turn out to be lords and ladies (2, ff. 2v–4, 5v–6v).[86]

Even more than Part I, this text evokes Jacobean court society: there are theatrical performances, court entertainments, grand banquets, dances and song, triumphs and lists, hunting parties, elaborate court weddings—and a homosexual attraction hinted as the recently widowed Selarinus "lay close by Amphilanthus, the Emperour beeing then his love, now Philistella was nott" (1, f. 11). Two complete masques are included: the King of Tartaria's masque of Honor triumphing over Cupid (1, ff. 14v–15v), and Melissea's masque in dispraise of love's idolatry (1, ff. 41–41v). Registering the heightened concern with female cross-dressing in the 1620s,[87] the character Isabella is cross-dressed and knighted: in the role of Polarchus' squire Lisio she reforms her erring lover Drusio as she sleeps (chastely) with him and subjects him to a Rosalind-like inquisition on love (2, ff. 48–49v). A new character, the Merry Marquis, is a comic portrait of a frivolous Jacobean court lady—perhaps readily identifiable by contemporaries. "Merry-minded" and "freely harmeles" (2, ff. 32), she is full of witty advice to the newly married Pamphilia about how to handle a husband and how to distinguish between the duties owed to a husband and to a lover:

> I would never have a wife cry and whine for her husband, butt keepe her hart merry, and Joviall . . . For husbands are strange things if nott discreetly handled, they will bee in such commaunding hiegth, if they may have ther owne swinge, as wee must bee even wreched vassalls, Noe Madame, Noe, obay your husband with discresion, and noe farder, and that will make him soe discreete as nott to tirannise which els they will doe fiercly when they have the raines, like horses gett the bitt beetweene their teeth, and runn the full race or course of their owne humour and the wives slaverye. Love itt self is nott to bee commaunded, hee is Emperiall, and all soverainlye governing. butt as a Monarchy hath many lawes to bee governed by, soe is this a part,

therfor heere the lawe binds you only discreetly to respect, and love your husband, nott to abound as lovers doe, united wholy butt to Loves sweetest tiranny.   (2, ff. 24–24v)

Later, when she flees in fear as Pamphilia is visited by a water nymph, she excuses herself with a witty but quite complacent self-analysis:

Itt is butt a Court witt, and spiritt which possesses mee, sollidnes I finde I have non, I ame butt flashes, noe true fire, a pretty light, butt nott a pure, steddy day light, I see I ame a vearie woeman, without the true mixtur of the masculin power, and rare temper.   (2, ff. 33–33v)

The restricted circulation of Part II perhaps accounts for its more numerous and more explicit allusions to the Sidney-Pembroke family circle by comparison with Part I. In confirmation of the Amphilanthus-Pembroke identification, Pamphilia sings a poem ascribed to Amphilanthus which is known to be by Pembroke.[88] Further details reinforce the association of the Queen of Naples with the Countess of Pembroke and of Rosindy with Wroth's brother, Robert Sidney.[89] Also, in the Vale of Tempe episode (2, ff. 3v–4), the brother and sister Bellario and Clorina seem to shadow Philip Sidney and the Countess. Bellario's perfections include unparalleled beauty, strength, valor, and musical gifts: "For Musick hee might have binn a new Orpheus, soe rarely did hee play on all instruments, calling all harts to give eare and attend him" (2, f. 3v). Clorina's name probably alludes to Clorinda, the pastoral name Spenser assigned the Countess of Pembroke as he introduced her funeral elegy for Sidney into his *Astrophil*.[90] An elaborate prose blazon describes her as a paragon of beauty[91] and a "true Efigiea of all excellencies," remarkable especially for learning and poetic gifts:

If all spiritt, witt, and poetrie had binn laine aside, and lost, yett thes tow had binn sufficient to bring them to light againe . . . The Nimphe was called Clorina, and often for her skill in all arts, and siences, as well of the letters, as other the choisest knowledges in the cheifest of Natures workes was called Sophia, a name most proper for her since itt portendeth wisdome, and exquisitt understanding in all things both in nature, and the highest deserned, or with presumption to bee knowne in the heavens, nor in the seaes, or any sort of hearts, and the proper uses of them.   (2, f. 4)

Less certainly, Queen Candia (C-*an*-dia) may allude to Anne of Denmark and her close friendship with Pembroke:[92] Candia lures Amphilanthus "in the sweet delights of an infectious Queene, and more of a furious ill natur'd Queene if nott observ'd as she pleased"; wearying of him, she arranges his marriage with the Princess of Slavonia as a means to make "the all deserving Pamphilia likewise suffer" (1, f. 48v). It sounds like another version of the jealous Queen motif from Part I, alluding here to Pembroke's marriage to Mary Talbot.

The romance elements of Part II overlie a more realistic world than that of Part I, one closer to the generational novel than to the *Arcadia*. As Naomi Miller observes,[93] Wroth's heightened concern with family relations, generational transmission, and the problems of growing up and growing older transform this romance, making it register from a woman's vantage point the chances and changes of ordinary life. In a family gathering at the Court of Morea, the chief personages of Part I (now middle-aged) recall the "Olde passions" of their youth, the love torments and griefs which have now mellowed into the contentment of happy marriages (1, f. 11). Urania and Steriamus have now spent "som yeers in hapines unparaleld, blessed with many children" (1, f. 8), as have Parselius and Dalinea, Rosindy and Meriana, Antissius and Selarina, Leonius and Veralinda. But the passage of time also brings the ordinary family griefs: parents grow old and die (the Queen of Morea, 2, f. 58); wives die in childbirth (Philistella, 1, f. 1; Dalinea and her infant, 2, f. 34v); knights die not on the battlefield but from genetic disease (Parselius, 2, f. 57); children die in infancy (the unnamed child of Pamphilia and Rhodomandro, 2, f. 58); children resent parental control (Rosindy's son Mirrosindo, 2, f. 43); children disappoint their parents (the Queen of Hungary's son, "degenerating from his peerles father," has become a painted courtier, "a glimering of a golden substance, nott the thing itt self," 2, f. 57).

Male inconstancy remains a fact of psychic life, though some heroes now have it under control. Steriamus is briefly tempted by memories of his early love for Pamphilia, but (owing to Melissea's oversight) his settled love for Urania is not threatened (1, ff. 55v–56v). Rosindy is slightly tempted by the wonderfully beautiful and learned Sophia, but remains loyal to Meriana (1, f. 60v). Polarchus begins to succumb to the seductions of a lovely Princess, but at length denounces the courtly romance ethos she exemplifies, to exalt marriage and female chastity:

> I ame nott in any way fitt for you to thinke of in that kinde, in the best way you can nott, for I ame maried, and you knowe itt, in the other what butt dishoner[?] I ame an others, and soe justly tide in untying bands of golden hapines, as noe linck shall ever slip, ore open to unty, ore lesson the band, and chaine of perfectest love, and Zealous affection to her deerest she and my onely unfained love . . . Correct thes sinfull and firy sparckes in time, least they flame, and blace to your destruction . . . for without modestie, and sincere living, a woman is butt a beast of the hansommer sort; when chaste and modest an Angell, and in thes latter times of loosnes to bee adored.
>
> (1, ff. 47v–48)

Leonius, however, is besotted by a painted and frivolous court lady, not beautiful but "the greatest libertine the world had of female flesh . . . winning by matchless intising . . . more like a play boy dressed gawdely up to shew a fond loving woemans part, then a great Lady" (1, f. 58v). In a generic allusion to both Spenser's Bower of Bliss and Virgil's Dido, Leonius is rescued by Steriamus, who shames him into reclaiming his arms and his honor: his cure is so complete that he remains unmoved by reports of the lady's impending death by fire or by drowning (1, ff. 58v–59v). More tragically, when Selarinus' beloved wife, Philistella, dies in childbirth, he is plagued by evil spells, devilish faeries, and degrading sexual subjection to a "deadly Hellhound . . . being constraind by force, nott by will to bee ill" (2, f. 31; cf. 1, ff. 4–4v, 2, f. 55v).

As before, Amphilanthus is the primary exemplar of inconstancy, and the Pamphilia-Amphilanthus relationship remains the central narrative focus. The ongoing discourse about love and marriage is conducted primarily through this story, in counterpoint with the several happy marriages for love and with the diverse views on love and marriage advanced by various characters: the Merry Marquis, Veralinda, the Nymph of the Fountain, the shepherdess Fancy (who speaks for female liberty against the bondage of marriage), the faithful husband Rosindy.

The narrative begins with Pamphilia and Amphilanthus happily reunited and on a visit to her parents' Court of Morea. A comic scene rather like a contemporary Court of Love shows them secure enough with each other to engage in witty banter on the subject of male inconstancy:

> [The King of Morea:] Deerest Nephew, then this very staydnes is a change, for itt is I beeleeve butt lately come to you.
>
> Noe, sayd Amphilanthus. What say you deerest Lady, this is nott your opinion of mee, too[?] I hope you have a better conceipt of mee your servant then your father hath;
>
> Truly my Lord sayd Pamphilia, I have the honor nott to degenerate much from my father and many have favour mee above my meritt to say I was much of his minde in most things, therefor in this I can nott but aske pardon, and nott answer, onely I knowe you are most excellent in all things,
>
> And yett you most excellently condemne mee, well, I fear onely that I shall sett you all such a patterne of Constancy as the wourke will bee soe hard noe woeman can learne itt, pick itt out[.]
>
> I hope wee may in time sayd Pamphilia and then growne cunning in that wourck, sett a new way to express our learning for men, who have nott the art to desifer the true Caracter of Constancy, which beeleeve itt my Lord would bee quickly learnte if you would sett your minde to itt, butt I feare yett you have nott that perfectnes, though

in all things els, all parfections save in this dull thinge (as most men call) Constancye;

And deere Brother sayd Urania I must commend you yett, for truly I thinke you are the Constantest man breathing, for you have nott soe much alltered from your first maner of loving, as to change one Jot from change, and thus, are nott you the very patterne itt self of Constantcy[?] . . .

Soe sayd the Emperour, butt in this I will defend my self, and will putt my self onely to the sensure (though I knowe her a severe Judg) of this all-knowing Queene Pamphilia, that since my often change hath wholy proceeded from desire to knowe the best, now I have found that, and heere fixe, is my former inconstancy, beeing without affection to varietie to bee remember'd as punnishable[?]

Pamphilia satt still yett as kindly looking on him as her hart would afford, and that was the kindliest, and lovingest of any lookes, onely smiled, butt making noe answere.[94]   (1, ff. 9v)

This exchange is placed in some perspective by the confession (or boast) of the King of Morea that in his youth he was another Amphilanthus for inconstancy; the implication is that all young men are thus, and that Amphilanthus will also settle down in due course.[95]

Soon after this, Amphilanthus, jealous of Pamphilia's admirer Rhodomandro, King of Tartary, begs Pamphilia to tie "the knott never to bee untide" (1, f. 14v). They contract a form of private marriage before witnesses—a contract *di praesenti,* described "nott as an absolute mariage though as perfect as that, beeing onely an outward serimony of the church, this as absolute beefore God and as fast a tiing, for such a contract can nott bee broken by any lawe whatsoever" (1, f. 14v). The ambiguities surrounding such forms of marriage in English law are played out in this text: they can be considered "before God" fully binding; but they might also be later renounced or ignored, as not "absolute" public and legal marriages.[96]

When Amphilanthus falls to his old ways again and succumbs to Queen Candia, that infidelity makes him vulnerable to the treachery of an old tutor who convinces him that Pamphilia has already married Rhodomandro. Angry, despairing, and almost devoid of volition, he allows Queen Candia to arrange his marriage to the Princess of Slavonia, and playacts his role in the wedding, "soe afflicted as he seemed rather the representer of a bridegroome then one indeed" (1, f. 49v). He flees in remorse before consummation, but later accedes to demands from the bride's parents for a solemn, public wedding (2, f. 36). When Amphilanthus discovers his mistake about Pamphilia, he attempts suicide, but is prevented by Urania's good counsel. The lovers' agony and the seemingly irreparable breach between them is slowly overcome as Amphilanthus endures a long and often amusing trial resulting from Pamphilia's vow to speak to him only through intermediaries (2, ff. 2–2v).

Later, Pamphilia does in fact marry Rhodomandro, her principal defender in Amphilanthus' absence. Her motives are not spelled out but can be inferred: the political need to secure the kingdom by providing a male champion, and the dynastic need for progeny. Rather like a seventeenth-century Virginia Woolf, Wroth projects in the circumstances of Pamphilia's marriage a woman writer's fantasy of what a supportive marriage might be. Pamphilia's father gives his consent readily, but cannot force her choice: the marriage will occur only "if she liked" (2, f. 21). Coming to propose, Rhodomandro finds "boockes about her, which she ever extreamly loved and she writing" (2, f. 21). She turns him away at first, explaining that "a booke, and solitarines" are the only companions she desires (2, f. 21v). But he then defines a most unusual role for himself, to support her as a writer and an intellectual:

> Love your booke, butt love mee soe farr as that I may hold itt to you that while you peruse that, I may Joye in beeholding you, and som times gaine a looke from you, if but to chide mee for soe carelessly parforming my office, when love will by chance make my hand shake, purposely to obtaine a sweet looke . . . Bee solitarie, yett favour mee soe much as that I may butt attend you, when you waulke in deserts, and woods, I will serve you as a guard to keepe you from all harmes may proceed from serpents and venimous beasts. I will keepe att what distance you please, butt still in your sight els how shall I serve you[?]   (2, f. 21v)

Deeply conflicted, she refuses to accept such subservience, but agrees to the marriage "against her owne minde, yett nott constrain'd, for non durst attempt that . . . though nott in soule contented" (2, f. 22).

Her wedding rites inscribe the ambiguities of her situation: the Queen of Naples, who helps to dress her, leaves her hair bound up, not loose and flowing as was customary for virgin brides; by that gesture both aunt and niece imply that the earlier private marriage to Amphilanthus was consummated.[97] Amphilanthus proposes himself as a bride-knight, an office reserved for unmarried men; his claim that he is "yett unmaried" (2, f. 22v) reveals a desperate desire to rewrite history, founded on the fact that his Slavonian marriage is as yet unconsummated. As the narrative proceeds, Pamphilia begins to relax her vow of silence,[98] and at length the tutor's deathbed confession allows for a complete reconciliation (2, ff. 52v–53v). With Amphilanthus presumably truly reformed, Rhodomandro and the (supposedly chaste) lovers settle into a happy *ménage à trois,* associating together at one or another of their courts:

Now how can wee leave them better then thus contentedly together, Urania with her dearest freind Pamphilia, and Steriamus her more deere with them, Amphilanthus with his deerest sister, and his yett deerer part, in the Court of his true and loyall freind the Great Cham [Rhodomandro], who lived butt in ther sights.   (2, f. 55)

Rhodomandro's impending death is foretold (2, f. 58), but the text breaks off before it occurs.

A second major narrative focus is the capture of several royal children from the various courts, as they travel to Naples to be educated by that realm's Queen. Over several years, many knights undertake their rescue from giants and enchantments, during which time Melissea protects them, engineers rescues, and causes new enchantments (1, ff. 24, 64v–66; 2, ff. 6v, 35v–36, 43v–44). Shadowed here perhaps is the breakdown of the old educational system in the noble household or court: Amphilanthus reminisces happily about his breeding at the Court of Morea (2, f. 18v), but the new generation never reaches the Queen of Naples's court. Melissea's much-enhanced role in Part II substitutes in the supernatural realm for the powerful female protectors children are seen to need in the dangerous passage to adulthood but may no longer readily find. Melissea presents a fantasy of female agency exercising beneficial control.

This text tells of the new generation losing their identities in childhood and finding them through assorted adventures: being knighted, fighting monsters, falling in love, resisting tyrants and rapists, preparing for rule. The important new principals include Claribella and Floristello (the Knight of Venus), who are children of Urania and Steriamus; Lindavera, Verolindo (the Knight of Love), and Amphilonius, who are children of Veralinda and Leonius; Antidorindo, the son of Antissia and Dolorindus; and Trebisound and Candiana, the children of Parselius and Dalinea (known as Bellario and Clorina during their enchantment in the Vale of Tempe, 2, ff. 3v–6). Interestingly enough, given Wroth's own history, there are several illegitimate children, all readily accepted by their families: Perissus rejoices in his natural nephew (1, ff. 4v–5) and Polarchus in his natural son, Andromarko (2, f. 26v). Also, the text hints strongly that the "poore, unknowne" Knight of the Fair Designe will be revealed and readily accepted as Amphilanthus' natural son.[99]

Although romance figures abound in this text, they often represent forces in the contemporary world. Several giants, griffons, and other monsters serve villains who embody the Pagan (Muslim) threat: Lamarandus the Tirible, who seeks to subvert the Christian monarchs by cutting off their progeny (1, ff. 21v–24, 66v–67), and the usurping Persian Soldan, who seeks marriage with Pamphilia and also tries to force his niece, the rightful Christian heir, into an incestuous marriage (1, ff. 60v–61; 2, ff. 39–

40v). Behind them and their allies we should probably recognize Christian Europe's fear of the Ottoman Turks. Other monsters are or serve usurpers of thrones or instigators of popular rebellion: the fiends who torment and hold in bondage the King of Denmark and Queen of Norway (2, ff. 36–38); the giant Tortullo, who leads an attack on Urania's court, inciting her own servants to treachery (2, ff. 44v–46). Their symbolism is interpreted by the metaphorical description of the rebels who rose against the Queen of Hungary as "monsterous beasts" (1, f. 64). These figures allegorize threats to Christian monarchy, seen in the conservative politics of Part II to emanate from "perverse" notions of liberty (2, ff. 30, 49). On this topic the King of Denmark echoes James I:

> Malice, an emminent ennimie to greatnes, joined with much ambi-
> tion to allter governments; when they can nott make probable titles
> to monarchye, then libertie must bee made the sweete motive to
> change, and make kings, and subjects all alike . . . They cry slavery,
> and bondage, and take the free libertie due unto us. Libertie of the
> subject, which most times brings a farr greater bondage, since sure
> service is more pleasing, and contentfull to serve one, then bee tied
> in dutie to many.[100]   (2, f. 37v)

The numerous enchantments often enact fate, described as immutable: "Destinie must prevaile" (2, ff. 6v, 20v). At other times they represent desperate psychological states: for example, the Hell hounds who plague Selarinus (2, ff. 30v–31, 55v), or the grief-induced immobility of Parselius after Dalina's death in childbirth (2, ff. 33v–36). Most enchantments are either dispelled by Melissea or engineered by her to aid the principal char-acters: her extensive but not unlimited powers represent female agency undertaking to cure psychic trauma and to redirect "fate" through reason, self-knowledge, moral reformation, and mature wisdom. To Selarinus, Melissea sends a potion which dispels the charms, together with dreams of Philistella "bitterly correcting him for his fault twise with spiritts, and faeries, and yett still expressing forgivnes" (2, ff. 55v–56). To Parselius she shows two young people about to be devoured by harpies, propelling him to the rescue; then she reconnects him to the future by revealing that the young people he has saved are his son, Trebisound, and the Sophia of Babylon, who are fated to wed (2, ff. 35v–36). On her island of Delos, Melissea cures Antissia of raving madness and mad poetry with calming hot baths, darkness, and rest (1, ff. 16–16v); and she rescues Amphilanthus from one of his bouts of despair by shipwrecking him there and proffering good advice (1, ff. 62–62v). Her interventions also offer Pamphilia advice and help her attain emotional stability (1, ff. 41–42; 2, ff. 31–31v, 59–59v, 61v). Throughout, Melissea's powers are engaged to protect the lost children[101] and to further the love of Pamphilia and Amphilanthus.

The fantasy world of this text is more hopeful than that of Part I, primarily because the now mature heroines play a larger and more public role, seeking to bring its most agonizing problems under some control. Several women participate with Melissea in the duties of advice and counsel—for one another, for decisions of state, and especially for the young. Urania's special role as counselor is more fully developed here, so that in some ways she becomes Melissea's counterpart. Twice she saves her brother Amphilanthus from suicide by sharply reproving his faults and advising him to seek Pamphilia's forgiveness by confessing his faults and seeking her pardon. On the first occasion (1, ff. 51v–52) she alludes to her past successes as counselor:

> Lett me truly understand all your sorrow, and the true cause of itt, and you shall see my fortune wilbee to serve you to all blessednes againe. did nott I say thus much to Perissus, and did itt nott fall out soe[?] did nott I for my everlasting blis redeeme, and save my deerest Lord Steriamus, and his brave brother, and most worthy sister Selarina[?]   (1, f. 52)

On the second occasion (1, ff. 61v–62) Amphilanthus pays highest tribute to Urania's "discreet and devine counsell," which has led him, at least temporarily, to see his situation "with the cleere eyes of understanding" (1, f. 62). Steriamus also extols his wife's wisdom in counsel: "How did her counsell ravish our eares, more Judiciall, more exquisite then the whole great counsells of the greatest Monarchies" (1, f. 57).

Many women take on the reponsibility of counsel for Pamphilia. The Queen of Naples was "the true Secretary of her thoughts" (2, f. 23) during the agonizing time of her wedding to Rhodomandro; and Veralinda, Urania, and the Nymph of the Fountain all help her find a satisfactory if not ideal resolution of her love problems. Responding to Pamphilia's (true) foreboding dream that Amphilanthus is married to another, Veralinda advises her to accept male inconstancy as a fact of life (drawing no doubt on her own experience with Leonius) and to assert her own worth—either by refusing to be bound by the double standard, or by maintaining a stoic self-sufficiency:

> You were and are the discreetest of your sex, yett you would have impossibilities, you say Amphilanthus is a man, why did you ever knowe any man, especially any brave man, continue constant to the end[?] if then Amphilanthus might have binn such an one, ore that man alone, butt all men are faulty. I would nott my self have my Lord Constant for feare of a miracle. beesids you have seene Amphilanthus in several slips allreddy, yett still hath come back wholy to you againe, and soe will now when hee beeholds you againe . . . If hee bee faulce,

lett faulshood Joye him, if hee marry, marry, too, lett nott him have a
hapines beeyound you, butt if hee bee just, accuse him nott wrong-
fully, Iff hee sue to you receave him . . . Hee did love you, soe did as
good, as great as hee, butt say hee hath left you, let him goe in his
owne pathe, tread nott in itt, an other is more straite: follow that and
bee the Emperess of the world, commaunding the Empire of your
owne minde.   (1, ff. 40–40v)

Later Urania, at Melissea's prompting, brings Pamphilia to her court to
help cure her melancholy (2, ff. 31–33v). There, the Nymph of the Fountain (Leatissia) helps Pamphilia put her problems in some perspective by
telling how she witnessed a vicious scene of attempted rapes, incest, and
multiple family murders, herself escaping rape and death only by being
transformed into a nymph of Diana (2, ff. 32–33). The encounter provides
Pamphilia with a measure of chaste constancy outside herself: "Pamphilia,
who till then thought her self the onely patterne of love, found she was
heerin surpassed," and was moved to "blush att her pretty falacies, and
extoll the Nimphe" (2, f. 33). Accordingly, she is receptive to the nymph's
advice to cease tormenting herself and Amphilanthus, and to welcome him
as friend and chaste lover into a happy marital triangle:

Butt deere Madame, why doe you torment your self[?] you grieve for
his griefe, and soe their is noe hope of amendment butt by death and
what love doe you show in that[?] You will kill your self purposely to
kill him certainly . . . Bee nott guilty of such a sinn, and save your
soule from hasarde . . . You have a brave kinge to your husband, who
is soe much yours as you can nott please him better then to com-
maunde him, and bring your freinds to him, and you. What then can
hinder you from contedly [contentedly] and chastely to beeholde
your deerest, safely and gloriously, unless you doe nott trust your
owne power in having absolute commaundness of your self, Therfor
thinck of somm such course which may bring you thus together, for
Love is happy, by ten times more hapy when injoyde with Chastetie,
and pure innocent affections.   (2, ff. 50–50v)

Pamphilia herself takes over the role of her aunt the Queen of Naples in
offering aid and counsel to the young: she helps to reunite her niece Candiana with the lover who knows her only in shepherdess disguise (2, f.
44v), and helps her nephew Stervanius obtain knighthood when his father
declares him too young. (The new knight immediately proves his worth
by saving his parents from attackers; 2, ff. 46v–47).[102] Such intergenera-
tional bonds, fostered especially by the sympathy and agency of women,
seems to augur greater happiness for the younger generation in their lives
and loves.

Learned women, and specifically wise women rulers, are also more prominent in Part II, exhibiting another mode of female agency. The norm of female education is described by one young lady (bred in a noble house) as "musick, learning, languages, and all things fitt any brave woeman to have" (2, f. 51v). But a much higher standard, involving excellence in poetry, science, and all learning, is set by the shepherdess Clorina (really Candiana and known sometimes as Sophia in tribute to her wisdom, 2, f. 4), as well as by the Queen of Naples. The young Persian Sophia is another paragon of beauty, wit, and profound learning:

> Her librearie was ther, and the most sumptious in the world for a woeman to have and the rarest, since non butt the rarest of bookes were permitted to bee ther; all chosen ones, and as choisely chosen, and as truly used, and imployed by ther owner; she beeing exactly, and parfectly learned in all siences, and learning well beestowed on her, who honored learning for the truth of learnings sake, perfect knowledg.   (1, f. 61v)

In Part II Pamphilia busies herself with state affairs more often than in Part I, notably in marshaling a coalition of Kings and Queens to defend her against the usurping Sophy of Persia: in council she accepts their recommendations for prosecuting the war, and is acknowledged by them as their "sole comaunderess" (1, ff. 39–42v). Another noble lady is herself a military strategist, advising Steriamus how to direct his forces against the Sophy and how to resue his love-besotted friend Leonius (1, ff. 57v–59). The narrator describes her in androgynous terms: she "had soe great a spiritt, as might be called Masculine" (1, f. 57v), as well as great "knowledg and judiciall counsell" (1, f. 58).

The interpolated stories in Part II are quite various in content and narrative strategy; unlike those of Part I, they do not deal repetitively with constant women as suffering victims. A long pastoral episode in the Vale of Tempe is narrated by Wroth from the vantage point of Parselius, and includes a remarkable page-long prose blazon of the shepherdess Clorina (2, f. 4). A quasi-allegory of Fancy and Love—part dialogue, part argument, part song—shows Fancy renouncing the bondage of marriage in favor of liberty and variety, but beginning to worry about how she will fare in old age (1, ff. 12–13). Parselius draws out the *applicatio* for the audience of now mature royal couples: "Soe have wee had our shares in this note att times . . . Butt itt is past with us" (1, f. 13). The uxorious King of Bulgaria recounts in unintentionally humorous hyperbole the story of his wife (there present) who deigned to marry him against her father's wishes (2, ff. 14v–15v). The continuing saga of the mad Antissia is set forth in terms of dark comedy: her nephew Rosindy recounts her antic behavior during his visit to her court (1, ff. 11–11v); then the narrator describes her journey to Delos, during which she and her brain-sick tutor inflicted "fustian poetry" and "jarring discords" on all the company (1, ff. 15v–16v). After her cure by Melissea she narrates her own story of capture and torment at the hands of a monster (2, ff. 16–16v), concluding with a newly self-critical perspective on her life and her verse:

> Thus itt was idlenes, with a unsteddy braine, mixt with mulltitude of phansies, led mee to a studdy able to unsettle a more serious braine then ever mine was, and soe I learnt Poetrie and grew soe high in the search of the Gods as I fell lowe inough in my sences . . . For perfectly I was possest with poettical raptures, and fixions able to turne a world of such like woemens heads into the mist of noe sence, and such learned furies, as have their title of poetticall furie, which in true sence is distraction.   (2, f. 16)

In Part II Antissia is a more obvious foil for Pamphilia (and Wroth), a scapegoat created to deflect from those good poets society's cautionary tale of the psychic dangers that threaten female authors.

The eighteen poems of Part II are also more diverse in theme and function than those of Part I, and their disposition accords with the final poem in *Pamphilia to Amphilanthus,* in which Pamphilia gives over Petrarchan poetry of passionate love to "young lovers" and looks toward higher poetic kinds. Several expressive love poems representing poetry as the outpouring of passion are voiced by the new generation of young lovers: the Prince of Corinth's complaint against his tormenting mistress (1, f. 8v); the sad laments of the (supposed) shepherdess Lindavera, who fears she has lost her Prince Floristello (1, f. 36v); the "mournful" song of the young Princess of Tartary voicing her hesitant, budding desires (1, f. 24v); Licandro's enraptured "free verse" celebration of that Princess's eyes. Licandro thrusts his poem—"a strange measure, beeing a new unmeasurd way, and yett serv'd att that time to give a little respite to his overflowing passions"—into the fire as an unsuccessful product of an uncontrolled imagination, but his friend Ollymander rescues it (1, ff. 26–26v). Older lovers still caught in this stage, or else recalling their former loves, also produce such poems: Amphilanthus' despairing complaint over Pamphilia's supposed marriage to Rhodomandro, which "rent his very hart in sunder" (1, ff. 50v–51); Steriamus' sonnet to memory, product of the "prety little frency" evoked by the thought of his old love for Pamphilia (1, f. 56v). Antissia's antic state licenses Wroth to create for her a remarkable, frankly sensual praise of Venus' pleasures from the woman's perspective, and then to pronounce it (with tongue in cheek) a "tedious ditty, onely noiseworthy, butt noe way senceble"; Antissia's husband finds it shockingly immodest and unchaste (1, ff. 15v–16). Her second mad poem is an extravagant greeting to Melissea delivered as she stirs "up and downe like a new broke colte in a haulter" (1, f. 16), but it also hints of her impending cure. The second book of Part II contains only one poem and its revision: the Duke of Sabbro's daughter, who seeks in verse to "choke up" her "millions of phantisies, and wandering thoughts" and to find "a little scope of expression," voices a deprecation of Cupid (2, ff. 59v–60); then Andromarko, breaking "into a passion," rewrites it as a love song to her (2, f. 61v).

Other poems indicate Wroth's development of a more comprehensive poetics, one that recognizes the multiple sources and uses of poetry and makes place for public poems. Several are artful performance pieces, appropriate to the circumstances but not directly expressive of the speakers' emotions; in them speakers often adopt other personae, or perform other poets' verses. Pamphilia's songs to the lute are said to show the superiority of "naturall parfections" over skill, demonstrating "how truly Nature excelleth arte" (1, f. 10), but the song so commended is by Amphilanthus (the Pembroke poem), intended for her though in pretense addressed to Antissia (1, ff. 10–10v). In a similar exchange between quasi-allegorical Petrarchan personages, (female) Fancy sings (male) Love's complaint of her cruelty to him (1, f. 13). On another occasion, a pair of youths indifferent to love are awakened to it by overhearing a part-song about passion's fires performed by ladies (1, ff. 27–27v). After an entertainment put on by rustics at Urania's court, with rebec music, dancing apes, and sonnet gifts to Urania and Selarina (blanks are left for them in the text), Amphilanthus with unconscious irony voices a woman's complaint that her lover's hair is more constant than his heart (1, f. 53v–54). It is a song Pamphilia might have written, though it is not formally credited to her, and Amphilanthus sees it as "fild with hope."

Two complete masques serve as focal points of meaning in this work.[103] The men's masque, presented at the Morean court by Rhodomandro's elaborately costumed Tartarian company, is a kind of wedding masque (anticipating his marriage to Pamphilia). It stages the triumph of Honor over Cupid, making Cupid "a new creature . . . a servant to honor, and a page to truthe" (2, ff. 14v–15v). At length Cupid celebrates "Honors purest throne," and leads the merry ditty for the final masque dance:

This is Honor's holly day:
Now sheapheard swaines, neatheards play,
    Cupid wills itt soe.
Kings and princes come alonge
You shall safely pass from wronge
    Desire was your foe.

                    (1, f. 15)

As an embodiment of Rhodomandro's hopes, the masque stages the sub-ordination of (Pamphilia's) desire. But it also anticipates the marriage–chaste love triangle which at last resolves the plight of Amphilanthus, Pamphilia, and Rhodomandro. The second masque—"a verie pretty show"—is Melissea's production, designed "only to please the Queene," Pamphilia (1, f. 41–41v); it is a comic dispraise of love, and serves to tem-per Pamphilia's overwrought emotions when she hears of Amphilanthus' marriage. A young seafaring lad complains despairingly of his love for a sea nymph, but she (identified with Venus, "the Goddess sole of Love") will have nothing to do with him. An aged shepherd intervenes with sober advice: "Learne of age, and the best mother of learning experience, never to follow the sea-borne Queenes phansies, much less her power, and least of all her instructions" (1, f. 41v); he concludes with a song: "Love butt a phantesie light and vaine, / Fluttering butt in poorest braine." At the end, all three join together "in a conting maner" to renounce the "bace idolatrie of love." This masque demands subtlety in interpretation. Pamphilia resists the facile equation of her situation with that of the easily converted sea lad, and Melissea concurs: "You are non of thes, madame, nor is this butt a phansie, for love indeed hath a more steddy place and throne of abiding when in such Royall harts" (1, f. 41v). Pamphilia may, however, find some use in the warnings against "bace idolatrie" in love.

Several other characters—Pamphilia (2, f. 23v), Philarchos (1, f. 45), Lamprino (2, f. 5v), Arcas (2, f. 6), Rustick (2, f. 7v)—allude to but do not show their poems (2, f. 139; 1, ff. 197–198; 2, f. 31): some of them might have been included had the work been prepared for publication. It is clear, however, that this text does not showcase Pamphilia's and women's poetry. The reason seems to be that the female claim to the status of poet has already been established, that Pamphilia herself has moved beyond the private, expressive poetics of love, and that Wroth no longer wishes to associate herself so closely with Pamphilia's situation and voice. These more public songs and poems are seen to be transferable between genders, obliterating the special category "woman poet." The songs, masques, and entertainments of Part II show Wroth taking up the poet's public role of providing many kinds of poems and songs for many voices and many occasions.

Love's Victory

Wroth's unpublished pastoral tragicomedy, *Love's Victory,* was probably known only to a small coterie readership and audience.[104] The date of composition is uncertain, though a few parallels to the Vale of Tempe episode in *Urania,* Part II (book two) suggest that it postdates that work.[105] This drama may have been written for performance at private theatricals at the Wroths' country estate at Durrants in Enfield (or perhaps at Penshurst), but there is no record of such performance.[106] Wroth here appropriates another genre—pastoral—which was prominently associated with women but which traditionally served as a vehicle for male desire, nostalgia, and political commentary. As Richard Cody observes: "The pastoral is as much a man's world as the heroic. Nymph and shepherdess are not personalities but images of women."[107] Wroth makes pastoral a vehicle for women's voices, values, and vision. Her pastoral drama challenges the norms both of the genre and of Jacobean society by its emphasis on female agency, egalitarianism, female friendships, and community.[108]

The few parallels between *Love's Victory* and the Vale of Tempe episode (*Urania*, Part II, 2, ff. 3a v–8) highlight the difference in genre. Both have a band of shepherds smitten with love, but in the romance they are royalty and nobility in shepherd guise, led by a brother and sister famed for poetry; in the drama they are true shepherds who share alike in poetry and leadership. There are a few parallel characters—Rustick, Dalinea/Magdalaine, Arcas—though Arcas is a faithful knight in the romance and in the drama a mean-spirited, slander-mongering shepherd.[109] *Love's Victory* is most usefully contextualized in relation to pastoral tragicomedy, a mixed genre especially popular at the Renaissance courts of Italy, France, and England.[110] The politics of pastoral has been much studied recently—by Louis Montrose as a vehicle for Elizabethan courtiership; by Stephen Orgel as a *locus amoenus* myth for the Stuart court; by Annabel Patterson as a means to negotiate multiple and complex stances toward ideology, especially through Virgil's First Eclogue.[111] In *Love's Victory,* I suggest, pastoral is adapted to a species of feminist politics.

Tragicomedy emerged into prominence with Tasso's *Aminta* (1580) and Guarini's *Pastor Fido* (1590), touching off a storm of controversy over issues of artistic unity and decorum.[112] Guarini, the chief defender and analyst of the new form,[113] declared it to be natural (since nature is full of mixtures), and praised its comprehensiveness in portraying gods, kings, and shepherds of several ranks and classes. He pronounced it a unified and perfect "third thing" using only those elements of comedy and tragedy that can blend together:

> He who composes tragicomedy takes from tragedy its great persons but not its great action, its verisimilar plot but not its true one, its movement of the feelings but not its disturbance of them, its pleasure but not its sadness, its danger but not its death; from comedy it takes laughter that is not excessive, modest amusement, feigned difficulty, happy reversal, and above all the comic order . . . [Yet] it is still not

impossible for the plot to have more of one quality than of another, according to the wish of him who composes it.[114]

In England, Sidney repeated the Italian critics' charges against "mongrell Tragicomedie" that mixes kings and clowns, "horne Pipes and Funeralls," though his target seems to be the use of comic scenes in tragedy rather than the new mixed kind, which he explicitly allowed: "Some *Poesies* have coupled togither two or three kindes, as the *Tragicall* and *Comicall,* whereupon is risen the *Tragicomicall* . . . if severed they be good, the coniunction cannot be hurtfull."[115] In 1610 Fletcher provided a much simplified definition of the kind: "It wants deaths, which is inough to make it no tragedie, yet brings some neere it, which is inough to make it no comedie."[116]

When Lady Mary Wroth wrote *Love's Victory,* she may have had only a general awareness of these definitions and controversies. But she certainly looked to the canon of the new kind—Tasso, Guarini, Daniel, Fletcher— to provide what Hans Robert Jauss terms the horizon of generic expectations,[117] and to suggest a range of generic possibilities and identifying topics. The major works all have a five-act structure. Except for Daniel's *Queen's Arcadia,* all contain lyrical songs and choruses. All contain stock characters: a shepherdess sworn to chastity, a lustful satyr, a libertine or worldly-wise nymph. All contain thwarted lovers, shepherdesses threatened with rape and slander, wounds and apparent deaths, miraculous escapes. All use the device of a narrator to describe the final turns of the plot. And all present an Arcadia that has declined some distance (small or great) from its Golden Age perfection.

Tasso's *Aminta* and Guarini's *Pastor Fido* were the chief Italian canonical texts. The *Aminta* was produced for the court at Ferrara in 1573–74 and first published in 1580; it became instantly popular throughout Europe.[118] If Wroth did not know it in Italian, an English translation was readily accessible in *The Countess of Pembroke's Ivychurch* (1591) by her aunt's client Abraham Fraunce. Tasso's style is lyrical throughout, heightened by songs, poignant love complaints, and choruses, the most famous of them extolling the lost Golden Age when love was free and unhampered by notions of chastity and honor. Here the source of trouble is the psyche of the nymph Silvia, whose dedication to chastity and the chase leads her to scorn the devoted love of the hero, Aminta. Silvia is saved by Aminta from rape by a lustful Satyr but then is (mistakenly) reported to have been killed by wolves, prompting Aminta to cast himself off a cliff; he miraculously survives, Silvia repents, and the lovers are at last united.[119] *Il Pastor Fido* (1590) was devised for court occasions in Turin and Mantua.[120] By 1602 twenty Italian editions had appeared, as well as an anonymous English translation set forth with commendatory verses by Samuel Daniel, who may have introduced Guarini's drama to Wroth.[121] Guarini offers a darker alternative for tragicomedy, an Arcadia which has declined much further than Tasso's from the Golden Age, as his parallel "Golden Age" chorus indicates. The plot is much more complex than Tasso's, as the lovers Amarillis and Mirtillo are threatened by violence and death from many sources—the gods, society, human evil and perversity—though they are at last saved and united.

In England Samuel Daniel and John Fletcher continued this vein of pastoral tragicomedy. Wroth may have read or even seen Daniel's *Queen's Arcadia* (1606), presented to Queen Anne and her ladies by the University of Oxford in August 1605.[122] Daniel further darkens Guarini's vision with an Arcadia marred by manifold evils and lacking the usual lyrical songs and choruses. A licentious traveler, Colax, imports into Arcadia the mores of foreign lands (with allusion to the new mores of James's court): Colax seduces and slanders nymphs while his female associate unsettles them with city fashions, cosmetics, and wanton attitudes. At the end the foreigners—and also the lawyer who promotes litigation, the doctor who promotes illness, and the religious imposter—are revealed and expelled, and the lovers are united. Wroth may also have known Fletcher's *Faithful Shepherdess* (1610), though its brief run at a private theater was evidently a disaster.[123] The title and several episodes suggest a response to Guarini, lighter in tone but with more overt violence, arising chiefly from the unrestrained passions of many lovers. Here the restoration of Arcadia is accomplished by a shepherdess dedicated to chastity, who cures the lovers' physical wounds and unchaste desires and joins them in virtuous love. Daniel's *Hymen's Triumph* (1615), a wedding entertainment at the Queen's court,[124] is closer in tone to Tasso than Guarini, with many songs and many comic mischances (but also dangers) arising from the heroine's cross-dressing. Here the chief source of trouble is paternal avarice, which leads the heroine's father to promise her to a wealthy swain instead of to her true love; but after she survives capture by pirates and a sword wound, he relents and blesses the union.

Wroth's *Love's Victory* appears to draw upon and respond to this entire tradition. In tone it is closest to Tasso, but even more lyrical, with songs and choruses resounding throughout; on Guarini's scale it stands much closer to comedy than tragedy. Also, Wroth's Arcadia is even closer than Tasso's to the Golden Age. Here, troubles arise chiefly from love's natural anxieties—jealousy, misapprehensions, suspicions, and fears—rather than treacherous plots and violence: there are no near-rapes or near-murders. Moreover, Wroth's drama portrays (beyond anything else in this genre) an egalitarian community without gender or class hierarchy, bound together by friendships within and across gender that are strong enough to survive even rivalries in love. It is a community in which friends aid, console, and sacrifice themselves for one another.

There are four pairs of lovers. Philisses loves Musella but believes she loves his friend Lissius and so prepares to relinquish her and die of grief; he is restored when Musella confesses her love to him. Lissius begins as a scorner of women and love but soon comes to love Simeana (Philisses' sister); their love is threatened by Arcas' slander and Simeana's jealousy, but they are reunited by Musella's good counsel. Silvesta loves Philisses but devotes herself to a life of chastity when she realizes that he loves her friend Musella; accordingly she rejects (until the end) the Forester's faithful love for her—though their names predict their final union. And the fickle but not unchaste coquette Dalina is finally matched with the boorish Rustick—both of them seeking comfort and convenience rather than high passion or an ideal union. Other characters exemplify misguided or unrequited love: the foreigner Climeana, who is (by Arcadian standards) too bold in wooing Lissius; the hopeless lovers Fillis (who loves Philisses) and Lacon (who loves Musella). Arcas is the lone villain: rejected by Musella, he takes malicious delight in crossing true love by slander.

In the fifth act Arcas sets in train Guarini-like complications, but the expected marvelous escapes are contrived by human wit and natural means. Musella's mother, for "bace gaine" (V, l. 14) arranges her daughter's immediate marriage to Rustick, spurred on by his lies about Musella's wanton pursuit of Philisses. Repairing to the Temple of Love to pray, Philisses and Musella are about to stab themselves in a mutual suicide pact when Silvesta urges them instead to drink the poison potion she offers, which (apparently) causes their death. Venus' priests then condemn Silvesta to be burned at the stake for the murder, but the Forester offers himself in her stead, and (as in Guarini) such substitutions must by law be accepted. Rustick then formally disclaims all right in Musella, and her mother repents the hasty wedding arrangements. At this point the potion wears off, the seeming dead are called forth by Venus and her priests, Silvesta promises to love the Forester (whether other than chastely is left unclear), Rustick matches with the fickle Dalina, and Arcas is punished by public shame.

Love's Victory is marked by conceptual and structural innovations that emphasize female agency. In the supernatural realm Venus, not Cupid, is the dominant presence. Tasso's prologue has Cupid (escaped from Venus) claiming credit for the love complications, whereas in Wroth, Venus masterminds the entire enterprise. In the prologue she sends Cupid to foment trials and troubles so as to subject all these lovers more completely to love's power, and he agrees to serve "your will and minde" (I, l. 31). At the end of Act I she complains that he still spares half the lovers—"I wowld have all to waile, and all to weepe" (l. 387)—and he promises to effect that, so as to do her honor. At the end of Act II Venus and Cupid appear together in glory, as in a Triumph. At the end of Act III Cupid brags of his conquests, but Venus is still unsatisfied—"Tis pretty, butt tis nott enough; some are / To slightly wounded" (ll. 355–356)—and Cupid promises to cause the lovers still more grief. At the end of Act IV Venus pities the now humble lovers, and (with her priests) urges Cupid to cease the torments. But now Cupid resists, determined to inflict more pain on some before saving them. It is probably significant that when Cupid departs from Venus' wishes, the Guarini-like complications come into play: Arcas' treachery, the apparent suicide, the threat of a burning at the stake.

At the end of Act V Venus again takes firm charge, managing the entire resolution. She commends the Forester's offer to die for Silvesta; she claims that the "resurrection" of the lovers was "my deed, / Who could nott suffer your deere harts to bleed"; she terms Silvesta "my instrument ordain'd / To kill, and save her freinds" (V, ll. 487–488); and she directs her priests to celebrate these events with joyful songs. At the very end Cupid asks her to pass judgment on Arcas and she does so, imposing what Arcas sees as a sentence worse than death—to live on in this society bearing the marks of shame, infamy, and a gnawing conscience.

The emphasis on female agency is also evident in the human sphere—causing as well as resolving problems. As Musella's father is dead, her mother is the family authority who decides to enforce the marriage arrangement with Rustick. And as in the *Urania,* it is chiefly the women who act to resolve problems and to foster friendships and community. To be sure, most of the Arcadian shepherds, male and female, do the offices of friendship for one another—proffering aid and good advice in the tribulations of love; generously giving way to others' better love claims; maintaining friendship despite rivalries in love. They are committed to the principle Philisses enunciates: "Yett when the paine is greatest, 'tis some ease / To lett a freind partake his freind's disease" (I, ll. 295–296). Only a few are excluded from this noble ethos: the villain Arcas, and to a lesser degree the insensitive farmer Rustick and the foreigner Climeana, who boldly pursues Lissius despite the better claims of her friend Simeana. Male friendship is important in *Love's Victory,* but is somewhat more exclusive in its objects and more limited in its scope than female friendship. Philisses and Lissius are a typical pair of male friends, rather like Pyrocles and Musidorus in the *Arcadia,* who after some attempts at secrecy share confidences and provide mutual help.[125] But other male friends—the Forester, Lissius, Rustick—are so at odds about love philosophy that their exchange of advice is unhelpful.[126]

The principal female characters are more nearly agreed on the nature

and claims of love, more unstinting in the offices of friendship to both
women and men, and more active in problem solving. Silvesta is the most
eminent exemplar of all these traits. Conquering her unrequited love for
Philisses by embracing a life devoted to chastity and the chase, she rejoices
in her new freedom and independence but also remains a true friend to
both Philisses and Musella. When Musella confides to Sylvesta her love
for Philisses and his failure to declare himself to her, Silvesta finds a solu-
tion: she hides Musella where she will hear Philisses' plaints and can respond, reassuring him of her love. Later, Silvesta puts herself at risk of
death to rescue her friends. When she hears of Musella's impending marriage to Rustick, she immediately declares: "It showld nott bee, nor shall
bee; noe, noe, I / Will rescue her, or for her sake will dy" (V, ll. 176–178).
When she offers the lovers the supposed poison draught, Philisses praises
her as the embodiment of noble friendship:

> Freindship, what greater blessing then thou art,
> Can once desend into a mortall hart.
> Silvesta, freind and priest, doth now apeere,
> And as our loves, lett this thy deed shine cleere.
>
> (V, ll. 250–253)

Venus grants "immortall fame" to her deed of friendship, and Musella
declares: "In you only was true freindship found" (V, ll. 493, 506). At the
end, when the Forester matches Silvesta's self-sacrifice by his own offer to
die in her stead, she recognizes him as her true soul mate. Though Venus
uses her as instrument, Silvesta herself produces the happy resolution—
not by magical or supernatural powers (like Fletcher's chaste shepherdess),
but by her wit, her skill in potions, and her high ideal of friendship.

The other women are also ready to counsel their friends in trouble. The
coquette Dalina is Simeana's first confidant, advising her not to be won
too soon by lovers' protestations. But when they overhear Simeana's lover
Lissius complain of his miseries, she counsels pity and a trial of his affections—advice Simeana promptly acts on. Musella is friend and confidant
to men and women alike—Lissius, Fillis, Simeana, even Rustick—and she
always offers warm sympathy and sensible advice. Her most notable accomplishment is the reuniting of Lissius and Simeana, parted by Arcas'
slanderous tales about Lissius' infidelity. After exposing the truth with
cool reason, she urges Simeana to conquer "this vild humour of bace jealousie" (IV, l. 263), after which the reunited lovers praise her as "sole re-
storer of this joy" (IV, l. 330).

Musella is not so wise in her own affairs and has need of her friends'
help. Like Pamphilia she was arguably too discreet in hiding her love for
Philisses, and she clearly misjudged his feelings for her. Distraught upon

hearing that she must marry Rustick at once, Musella is aided by Simeana's counsels of patience to think through her duties and her options. She sees herself bound to the marriage by her dead father's will and by her mother's commands, "beeing in her hands" (V, l. 45). At length, however, she identifies as the principal bond her own formal consent to the contract, given when she despaired of Philisses' love. She thereby accepts responsibility for her choices and actions despite the social constraints and the tyranny of Cupid, and this acceptance empowers her to act. She proposes a visit to the Temple of Venus, looking to find some means to live or die with her lover.

Wroth's representation of a tight-knit, nonhierarchical community linked by bonds of friendship and love is advanced by certain structural innovations in the genre. The most important is a reach back to the origins of pastoral, to the eclogues which present shepherds' dialogues and singing matches during their noontime repose. Each of Wroth's first four acts has at its structural center an ecloguelike game or contest engaging several members of the community (sometimes called the troop, or the flock), when they withdraw at noon into a shady grove. Female agency is again underscored, since on each occasion Dalina initiates the discussion about game playing.[127] Each exercise comments on the nature and circumstances of the participants, highlighting thematic and plot issues as well as enhancing the drama's lyrical quality.

In Act I the game is that most eclogic of activities, a singing match in which the characters sing of their own love experiences.[128] The game in Act II (proposed by Arcas) is fortune-telling: and the characters' chosen fortunes closely anticipate their own futures. Rustick extends the book of fortunes first to Musella, hinting his claim on her: "What shalbee you need nott feare, / Rustick doth thy fortune beare" (II, ll. 150–151). Her fortune, read out by Philisses, affirms that though her patience will be much tried, "Fortune can nott cross your will" (l. 161). Philisses' fortune, read out by Dalina, promises that he will suffer much but then obtain his bliss (l. 179). Dalina's lot predicts that her choices in love have conformed to her nature and will continue to do so: "Fickle people, fickly chuse, / Slightly like, and soe refuse" (ll. 194–195). In Act III the game, played only by women, is confessions of past loves and passions.[129] The game in Act IV is riddles, which the characters decide not to expound: in each case they allude to the nature and circumstances of the speaker. Musella begins with a riddle about shunning what is easy but does not please (Rustick), and desiring what can only be gained with pain (Philisses). Dalina's riddle is about seeking what she cannot find in herself (constancy). Philisses riddles about a star whose light he thought to be his own (Musella) and which, though clouded, is still visible. Here, amusingly, Rustick betrays his bluntness by repudiating the pastoral wit game altogether and insisting on the superiority of his low georgic interests and talents:

> Truly, I can nott ridle, I'was not taught
> Thes tricks of witt; my thoughts ne're higher wrought
> Then how to marck a beast, or drive a cowe
> To feed, or els with art to hold a plowe,
> Which if you knew, you surely soone would find
> A matter of more worth then thes od things,
> Which never profitt, butt some laughter brings.
> Thes others bee of body, and of mind.
>
> (IV, ll. 391–398)

Lissius follows with a riddle alluding to a fog (jealousy) and an unwanted light (Climeana), and then two suns (himself and Simeana) who "without envy hold each deere" (IV, l. 424). Fillis' riddle alludes to her disappointment (over Philisses' love) in spring, summer, and autumn.

In Act V the emphasis on community is heightened by another structural change. Generic convention calls for the final resolutions—the lovers' miraculous escape from danger and their reunion—to be narrated in the classical manner, not dramatized. Wroth partly follows this convention as Simeana and Silvesta report Musella's impending marriage, the suicide attempt in the Temple, Sylvesta's potion, and the lovers' "deaths." But she follows this with a dramatic scene assembling all the company in the Temple of Venus for a Kommos-like finale. Here in sight of all, the supposedly dead lovers arise, all the pairs of lovers are properly matched, true friendship is honored, and villainy is punished by public shame.

Seen in its generic context Wroth's drama is conceptually and structurally innovative. Stylistically it is competent and often charming, especially when we imagine (as I think we should) a performance in which the all-pervasive songs and choruses are set to music. The dialogue, rendered in heroic couplets, is usually natural and easy. It also manages nice distinctions—as in the exchange in which Rustick's lowness of mind is reflected in his low diction, and the power of Philisses' passion in his high rhetoric:

Philisses	Rustick, faith tell mee, hast thou ever lov'd[?]
Rustick	What call you love? I'have bin to trouble mov'd
	As when my best cloke hath by chance bin torne.
	I have liv'd wishing till itt mended were,
	And butt soe lovers doe; nor cowld forbeare
	To cry if I my bag, or bottle lost,
	As lovers doe who by theyr loves ar crost,
	And grieve as much for thes, as they for scorne.

Philisses   Call you this love? Why love is noe such thing,
              Love is a paine which yett doth pleasure bring.
              A passion which alone in harts doe move
              And they that feele nott this they cannott love.
              'Twill make one joyfull, merry, pleasant, sad,
              Cry, weepe, sigh, fast, mourne, nay somtims stark mad.

(II, ll. 85–98)

Woven into the texture of the heroic couplet dialogue are several set pieces
with their own distinctive metrical patterns. The hymns of Venus' priests
(II, ll. 311–342), the prayers of Musella and Philisses to Venus and Cupid
(V, ll. 188–225), the chantlike fortunes and riddles of Acts II and IV, Philisses' song celebrating Reason guiding Love (II, ll. 213–224), and Lacon's
love complaint (I, ll. 358–374) are all in octosyllabic couplets.[130] Also, several kinds of love songs in many different stanzaic patterns are scattered
throughout: Philisses' love complaint (I, ll. 38–62); Lissius' spring song
(I, ll. 75–80, 85–90); the Forester's complaint sonnet (I, ll. 185–198); Climeana's love complaint (I, ll. 311–322); Rustick's comic blazon of Musella
(I, ll. 335–352); Lissius' song defying Cupid (II, ll. 79–85); the paragone of
Chastity and Love spoken by Silvesta and Musella (III, ll. 1–24); the
spring-winter duet of Lissius and Simeana (IV, ll. 153–158). These extracts
may serve as examples:

 I. Climeana's love lament:

> O mine eyes, why doe you lead
> My poore hart thus forth to rang
> From the wounted course, to strange
> Unknowne ways, and pathes to tread?
> Lett itt home returne againe,
> Free, untouch'd of gadding thought,
> And your forces back bee brought
> To the ridding of my paine.
> Butt mine eyes if you deny
> This small favor to my hart,
> And will force my thoughts to fly
> Know yett you governe butt your part.

(I, ll. 311–322)

 II. The Silvesta-Musella paragone of chastity and love:

Silvesta   Silent Woods with desart's shade,
         Giving peace.
  Where all pleasures first ar made
         To increase.

> Give you favor to my mone
> Now my loving time is gone.
> Chastity my pleasure is.
> > Folly fled
>
> From hence, now I seeke my blis.
> > Cross love dead,
> In your shadowes I repose
> You then love I rather chose.
>
> Musella   Choice ill made were better left,
> > Being cross.
> Of such choice to bee bereft
> > Were no loss.
> Chastitie, you thus commend,
> Doth proceed butt from love's end.
>
> And if Love the fountaine was
> > Of your fire,
> Love must chastitite surpass
> > In desire.
> Love lost bred your chastest thought,
> Chastitie by love is wrought.

> > > > (III, ll. 1–24)

This variety (like that of the *Urania* songs) seems intended in part to display Wroth's technical skill.

What of the political resonance of Wroth's pastoral tragicomedy? Like the *Urania* it may contain allusions to particular court personages, though the family allusions are more obvious. Carolyn Swift finds an allusion in the Musella-Philisses-Rustick plot to Penelope Devereaux, Sir Philip Sidney, and Sir Robert Rich; and that plot seems also to allude to Wroth herself, Pembroke, and Sir Robert Wroth.[131] Jonson's portrait of Sir Robert Wroth repudiating the entertainments and ethos of the court to devote himself to country affairs (husbandry, sheep, rude country festivals)[132] seems to be shadowed in Rustick's repudiation of the witty riddle game to follow his country pursuits. The contrast honors pastoral over georgic, but a pastoral associated less with the court than with the Sidneys of Penshurst and the Herberts of Wilton. Here the values of love, leisure, harmonious community, wit, artful play are set in opposition to the rude tastes of King James's Riding Forester.

More important, Wroth's pastoral drama repudiates the patriarchal ethos of Jacobean society to develop an ideal community centered on women. Wroth's generic alterations evidence a sophisticated knowledge of literary tradition and appear to be used deliberately to project a female pastoral fantasy whose elements are a nonhierarchical community, close female and cross-gender friendships, and strong women—Venus, Silvesta, Musella, and even Dalina—who solve problems and make life better for themselves and others. In this work female agency is pervasive and positive, as it is in Wroth's Petrarchan sequence and in the *Urania;* but here it is attended with much less pain and societal danger. One reason for this is generic—the idealizing ethos of pastoral—yet Wroth's pastoral tragicomedy goes far beyond its generic antecedents in such idealization. Another reason may be the greater comfort and security Wroth felt in writing for a coterie audience of family and friends. But it may also be the case that Wroth here carries further the poetics and gender politics of *Urania*, Part II, evidencing a more secure sense of authorial power and self-confidence.

Wroth reinvented the Petrarchan lyric sequence, the romance, and the pastoral drama, claiming those genres for women's voices and values. In doing so she produced works of great historical interest and often impressive aesthetic quality. By any measure that is a remarkable achievement.

Afterword: The Politics of Jacobean Women's Writing

As individuals, the women of this study made specific and significant contributions to Jacobean culture. As authors, they produced texts in a wide variety of genres—letter, funeral elegy, diary, biography, autobiography, family history, polemic tract, Petrarchan lyric sequence, sonnet, song, romance, pastoral tragicomedy, tragedy, history, dream-vision poem, religious meditative poem, didactic poem, country-house poem, dedicatory poems of various kinds. These texts are only beginning to accumulate the kind of scholarship and criticism that will enable us to assess and properly value their often considerable aesthetic merit. Nevertheless, by studying women writers in early modern England as they contextualize one another and as they interact with contemporary cultural forces and literary traditions, we can take some measure of their important role in literary history and cultural politics. As we have seen, in their lives and works these Jacobean women collectively challenged patriarchal ideology, resisting the construct of women as chaste, silent, obedient, and subordinate; and they rewrote the major discourses of their era in strikingly oppositional terms.

Some challenged patriarchy on the domestic front by displacing the hierarchical authority of fathers and husbands. Elizabeth, Electress Palatine, was widely recognized as the dominant partner in her marriage. The Countess of Bedford lived the life of a courtier and major patron in virtual independence of her exiled and disabled husband, forming her closest bonds with her mother and her good friend Lady Cornwallis. Rachel Speght honored her mother and godmother as the dominant influences in her life. Anne Clifford's lawsuits (in partnership with her mother) contested the authority of her father, male relatives, husband, and monarch to determine her property rights, and at length she herself assumed the patriarchal role of estate owner and Sheriff of the county. Her diary and family memoirs record domestic trials and persecution but discount the importance of her two husbands to her sense of self: she defines that self through the property and offices she claimed from her father and, even more important, through the female line—as heir to her mother's strength of character and as protector of her daughter's rights. Aemilia Lanyer gave literary representation to these displacements. Her dedicatory poems emphasize the legacy of virtue from mothers to daughters, and one of them protests, in strikingly egalitarian terms, the class distinctions and privileges produced by male structures of inheritance. Lanyer's country-house poem "Cooke-ham" celebrates an estate without a lord—or indeed any male inhabitants—but with a virtuous mother and daughter as its defining and ordering principle.

Some of these women challenged patriarchy and absolutism as they were interlinked in family and nation. Queen Anne set herself in opposition to her King-husband by her pro-Spanish diplomacy, her court politics, and her association with Roman Catholicism; the masques she acted in and helped produce (probably aided by the Countess of Bedford) undermine the symbolism of Jacobean absolutism by emphasizing the worth and power of women—Anne as Pallas, exotic black beauties, militant Queens. Arbella Stuart openly defied James as King and head of her family by her forbidden marriage and daring escape from the Tower; her letters implore his pardon but refuse to give over the marriage or her justifications for it. Elizabeth Cary was at odds with family authorities all her life, and especially after her conversion to Catholicism; her writings recast discourses often used to explore political tyranny, so as to link that to domestic tyranny. Her Senecan tragedy *Mariam* focuses on a much-wronged wife and Queen who refuses her tyrant-husband's bed, claiming the integrity of her own emotional life; it also contrasts a halcyon period under female rule when the tyrant is believed dead with the murderous abuses of power that follow upon his return. Her Tacitean history of Edward II comments none too obliquely on abuses of power in the Jacobean court, paralleling Edward's homosexual favorites with Somerset and Buckingham; it also makes Edward's much-wronged Queen, Isabel, into a major character—an effective military leader and ruler whose armed rebellion against her King-husband is all but sanctioned. Mary Wroth's *Urania* also alludes to evils in Jacobean England—infidelity, rape, incest, forced marriages, violence against women and children—but they are countered in her romance world by mutually supportive Queens and a powerful female seer. Wroth's pastoral drama, *Love's Victory,* portrays an ideal pastoral community where men and women are bound together by ties of friendship, love, and song—in contrast to the entirely female ideal household described in Lanyer's country-house poem. In Wroth's pastoral society, however, women are the leaders; it is they who maintain its idyllic ethos and overcome threats to it.

Several Jacobean women rewrote cultural and literary discourses pertaining to courtiership and patronage, creating coteries and communities with women at the center. Queen Anne established her own separate court and sphere of activities, gathering an entourage of female and male courtiers around her, with the Countess of Bedford chief among them. Lucy Bedford had her own circle of female and male courtiers and clients at her Twickenham estate, including several of the era's finest poets and wits; she transformed the patron-client relationship into coterie participation, exchanging her own poems and letters with Donne and perhaps others. Rachel Speght invited the protection of noble ladies and city gentlewomen for her polemic defense of women. Aemilia Lanyer evidently enjoyed some actual patronage from the Countess of Cumberland—the first English instance of female patron and female client—and her dedicatory poems envision a community of patronesses ready to encourage and support a female poet who celebrates them and all womankind.

Romance, identified for a century as a literary discourse especially attractive to and dangerous for women, was in this period preempted by them. Elizabeth, Electress Palatine, enacted in her life and letters the romance roles of Queen of Hearts, Warrior Queen, and Woman in the Wilderness (symbol of Ecclesia in the Apocalypse). Arbella Stuart lived out a bold romance escapade, making a forbidden marriage which enhanced her claim to the throne, and then fleeing England (cross-dressed) in an unsuccessful bid for a life with her husband on the Continent. Rachel Speght cast herself as a David defying Goliath and a Saint George battling the dragon in her polemic defense of women against the black-mouthed "monster" Swetnam. Her dream-vision poem allegorizing her education revises the romance topos of the knight in a garden of love to present the young Rachel overcoming many obstacles in order to enter and enjoy the flowers of "Erudition's Garden." Revising Ovid, she takes as her motto *Labor Omnia Vincit*. Mary Wroth's massive romance *Urania* categorically claims the genre for women. Several heroines find their own stories written in books of romance, and then see their lives fitted to those stories. Wroth replaces the usual romance emphasis on knightly adventures, quests, battles, and courtship by a focus on female integrity in love, female agency (rulers, counselors, the seer Melissea), and enduring female friendships. In Part II Wroth moves the romance some distance toward the generational novel by emphasizing women's domestic concerns—marriage problems, births and deaths, the crises of middle age, the new generation taking over from the old.

Women also appropriated and redirected genres and discourses associated with self-definition and self-fashioning, claiming in them the position of subject, not object. Their texts reached out as well from the purely private to the public sphere. Private letters had long been the province of both women and men, but we find a remarkably complex fusion of personal, rhetorical, and political strategies in Jacobean women's letters: the Electress Palatine's political self-presentations; Arbella Stuart's and Lucy Bedford's trenchant commentaries on court life; Arbella's rhetoric of concealment and self-justification; Anne Clifford's exchanges with her mother about legal strategies and domestic difficulties; Elizabeth Cary's cogent and poignant arguments seeking, in defiance of her enraged husband, to gain a settled allowance and the right to live where she chooses. The diary is also a personal genre, used (almost for the first time) by Anne Clifford to probe and express personal feelings and attitudes about nonreligious experience; her diary helped her develop a sense of self, but at some point she supplemented its record of her legal and domestic struggles with cross-references to the public sphere, apparently with a view to placing it in the Clifford family "Chronicles." Mary Wroth's lyric sequence *Pamphilia to Amphilanthus* appropriates Petrarchan discourse and reconstitutes it to analyze the desire, the love philosophy, and the sources of poetic inspiration of a female poet-lover. Wroth's heroine, Pamphilia, defines her subjectivity in relation to love itself in its various guises. Virtually eliding the male beloved, she finds the sources of her consciousness and her art in her own desire and willed constancy. As poet, Pamphilia creates not only personal, Petrarchan love poetry but also artful songs for various voices.

Religious and devotional writing, long identified as safe and perhaps even laudable genres for women, underwent a sea change as Jacobean women dared to invoke for themselves the common Protestant privilege of individual interpretation of Scripture. They openly challenged the authoritative exegesis of biblical texts constantly cited to support patriarchy, laying some groundwork for the female preachers and prophets of the Civil War period. Rachel Speght used biblical exegesis as the principal weapon in her polemic defense of women: she interprets the Genesis Creation story as evidence of women's natural and spiritual equality to men, and reads the parable of the talents as a divine command that women as well as men use all their gifts in God's service. Her most daring exegetical move is to read the Pauline definition of marital roles, with the husband as head and the wife as weaker vessel, as a charge to husbands to help their wives with burdensome domestic duties. Aemilia Lanyer went further, making her long poem on the Passion the vehicle for a vigorous assertion of women's moral and spiritual superiority to men throughout biblical history, and their greater favor from God. Her most daring exegetical move is to rewrite the Adam and Eve story, ascribing to Eve only loving intentions in offering the apple to Adam, and identifying woman as, through that gift, the source of men's knowledge. This exegesis culminates in a forthright demand that men give over their false claims of gender hierarchy and the unjust social structures based on them. It is probably no accident that these most direct challenges to patriarchy came from non-aristocrats—the daughter of a London minister (Speght), and an ambitious gentlewoman in decline (Lanyer). It is also no accident that they grounded those challenges on a radical rewriting of the dominant discourse of the age, Protestant biblical exegesis.

Finally, several Jacobean women intervened in the era's developing discourse about authorship, so as to claim authority for themselves as women writers. And several underscored their quest for learning amid culturally imposed restrictions. Anne Clifford attributed her excellent education to her mother, claimed that her father had forbidden her to learn languages, and all her life kept careful record of the books she read—classical and modern, in many genres and subjects. Elizabeth Cary read omnivorously as a child, and (chiefly as an autodidact) learned several languages: Latin and Hebrew as well as French, Spanish, and Italian. Both Clifford and Cary were said to be especially fond of history: Clifford drew on such reading as she compiled her massive family history; Cary did so more directly as she took up the distinctively male genre of political history. Rachel Speght's remarkable dream-vision poem allegorizes her personal quest for learning and makes a powerful argument for the appropriateness of any and all subjects to a woman's education.

While the Countess of Bedford circulated her poems in manuscript to a coterie audience, and Elizabeth Cary retained some anonymity by publishing under her initials, Rachel Speght, Aemilia Lanyer, and Mary Wroth published their works under their own names. Speght claimed her ultimate authority to write from God, who requires from all men and women the exercise of all their talents; she may have had a more immediate commission from a bookseller, taking on the role of a professional writer in her polemic against Swetnam. She insisted on public recognition as an author, asserting that she published her second book in part to establish her authorship of the first, wrongly attributed by some readers to her father.

Aemilia Lanyer appealed to several sources of authority to validate her self-proclaimed role as poet. Although her poems display considerable knowledge of classical rhetoric, the Bible, and poetic traditions, Lanyer assigns learned poetry to men, and to women a (perhaps superior) poetry based on experience and on Nature, mother of all the arts. She authorizes her writing also by the excellence of her subject—Christ's Passion, and all the worthy women she celebrates. She claims further that she was given the title (and by implication divine sanction) for her Passion poem in a dream. Moreover, Lanyer placed herself directly in a female poetic line: in a dream-vision poem she imagines herself being accepted by the Countess of Pembroke as her poetic heir.

Mary Wroth presented herself as literary heir to all the Sidneys, male and female; and her several works analyze the poetics of women's writing. The interpolated stories and poems of the *Urania* assert the quality and quantity of women's texts: in Part I fully twice as many poems are penned by women as by men; the heroine Pamphilia is generally proclaimed as excellent in both kinds; and only Pamphilia claims the office of poet by vocation. The experience of love is the initial stimulus to poetry for women and men, but poetic art is seen to require control of the emotions in life and in poetry. At length, both in Wroth's lyric sequence and in her romance, a Petrarchan expressive poetics gives way to a revised Neoplatonism in which the educative experience of love as willed constancy frees the poet-heroine to undertake more comprehensive and public kinds of poetry. Likewise, many of the interpolated stories in the *Urania* are versions of Wroth's own experiences in life and love; and the poetics of fiction defined through them involves making true experience into an artful story. In her pastoral drama *Love's Victory,* Wroth portrays a community in which artful songs of all kinds are voiced by many characters, women and men, who turn private experience into matter of public delight.

It seems obvious that these texts are profoundly concerned with the politics of gender. I have avoided terming their authors feminists, not only to sidestep controversy as to what set of attitudes warrants that modern label, but also, and more important, to focus attention on the stances possible at an earlier historical moment. No one can stand outside language or outside culture, and it is of little use to consider what such an Archimedean point for women might be. But, as this study shows, the dominant ideology does not always define women's place and women's speech with the rigid determinism seen by some theorists—at least it does not when women take up the pen and write their own texts. In the Jacobean era women appropriated and rewrote available literary and cultural discourses to serve their own needs and interests, placing women at the center and exploring the consequences of that move. They seem to have approached those discourses not as an exclusively male preserve but as common human property, ready to be reclaimed for women. While these women writers could not change the external circumstances of Jacobean women's lives, or even of their own lives, they nonetheless challenged Jacobean patriarchal ideology in their own consciousnesses and in the public forum. If we can move beyond deterministic formulas of containment and control, we will hear these new voices sounding new themes.

APPENDIX A

Elizabeth, Lady Falkland, and the Authorship of Edward II

The title page of the folio reads *The History of the Life, Reign, and Death of Edward II. King of England, and Lord of Ireland. With the Rise and Fall of his Great Favourites, Gaveston and the Spencers.* Written by E. F. in the year 1627, and printed verbatim from the Original. London: J. C. for Charles Harper, 1680. The link with Henry, Lord Falkland, comes not from this text, but from the much shorter octavo abridgment of it entitled *The History of the Most Unfortunate Prince King Edward II. With Choice Political Observations on Him and his Unhappy Favourites, Gaveston & Spencer.* Containing some rare passages of those Times, not found in other historians. Found among the papers of, and (supposed to be) Writ by the Right Honourable Henry Viscount Faulkland, Sometime Lord Deputy of Ireland. London: Printed by A. G. and J. P. for John Playford, 1680. The attribution offered in the abridgment is probably based on the discovery of the longer version among Falkland's papers; the abridgment was clearly devised to comment on the Exclusion Crisis (1679–1681), and contains a long preface from the bookseller, John Playford, underscoring its relevance to present occasions. This text also elaborates much more than the folio on the fate of the regicides and their punishment.

The longer folio version appeared with no attempt at attribution, only the letters *E.F.* on the title page and as signature to the preface (dated February 20, 1627 [1628]). It contains only a short preface by the bookseller, Charles Harper, which does not emphasize contemporary applications. Ironically—but perhaps deliberately, if Harper knew the real identity of the author and wanted to reassure a readership that regarded history as a male genre—Harper wrote: "As for the Gentleman that wrote this History . . . he was every way qualified for an Historian. And 'bating

a few obsolete words, (which shew the Antiquity of the Work) we are apt
to believe those days produced very few who were able to express their
Conceptions in so Masculine a Stile." The handwritten change of *E. F* to
H. F. in some copies of the folio is evidently based on the octavo's attribution. A genuine printer's mistake in the folio's initials would be unlikely
enough the first time, but quite impossible twice—on both the title page
and the author's preface. In this regard it is significant that *Mariam* appeared under the initials *E. C.* (for Elizabeth Cary), and this text bears the
initials *E. F.* (for Elizabeth Falkland, as she then was).

The most likely scenario is that the longer manuscript from 1627–28 was
found among Falkland's papers, seen to have general relevance to present
problems, and published in folio by the bookseller Harper in 1680. It then
became available for various political uses. In the same year another bookseller, John Playford, commissioned or had presented to him a truncated
version of it, intended as an attractive and timely volume suited to the
stylistic canons and political interests of the time. The speeches, the rhetorical figures and flourishes, and the dramatic scenes which locate the
folio text in the earlier seventeenth century are mostly eliminated; the political moralizing is flattened, reduced to simple statement. It seems impossible that Elizabeth Cary could or would have produced this version,
and highly unlikely (given the 1680s aura) that Viscount Falkland or anyone else from that era abridged Elizabeth's longer text. Some years later
another edition of the folio version was printed (for a different bookseller,
R. Baldwin); it omits the epistle from the publisher and the author's preface to the reader, as well as the initials *E.F.* Baldwin's new title and title
page represses the earlier date of writing (and the authorship issue) so as
to invite contemporary (1689) application: *The Parallel: or, the History of
the Life, Reign, Deposition and Death of King Edward the Second, With an
Account of his Favourites, P. Gaveston and the Spencers. Wherein also The In-
trigues of his Queen Isabel and Roger Mortimer are Discovered.* By a Person
of Quality (London: R. Baldwin, 1689).

The gender bias dictating the attribution to Viscount Falkland persists
in library entries. At times it has led to other suppositions about authorship. F. W. Levy's fine discussion of Tacitean history in the period (*Tudor
Historical Thought* [San Marino, Calif.: Huntington Library, 1967], 270–
271) attributes this work on the strength of the initials and the usual gender expectations to a nonexistent Edward, Lord Falkland. The seventeenth-century Falklands were: 1. Henry, 2. Lucius, 3. Lucius, 4. Harry, 5.
Anthony, 6. Lucius Henry (1687–1730); there was an Edward Cary in a
collateral line, but he was never Lord Falkland, so not possibly E. F.

Donald A. Stauffer ventured a hesitant attribution to Elizabeth Cary on
grounds of dramatic scenic elements and style, "A Deep and Sad Passion,"

in *Essays in Dramatic Literature: The Parrott Presentation Volume,* ed. Hardin Craig (Princeton: Princeton University Press, 1935), 289–314. Douglas Bush, *English Literature in the Earlier Seventeenth Century* (Oxford: Clarendon, 1945), 22, thought the history was "perhaps" by her. More recent essays on Cary chiefly treat *Mariam* and do not address the issue of attribution of this text. But Tina Krontiris ("Style and Gender in Elizabeth Cary's *Edward II,*" in Haselkorn and Travitsky, *Renaissance Englishwoman,* 137–153) accepts Stauffer's argument and adduces some of the evidence summarized here.

D. R. Woolf, "The True Date and Authorship of Henry, Viscount Falkland's *History of the Life, Reign, and Death of King Edward II,*" *Bodleian Library Record,* 12, no. 6 (1988), 440–452, accepts that neither work is by Viscount Falkland, but dates both works from 1680, assuming (unwarrantably) that both the folio and its abridgment must belong to the same historical moment. He also cites a few passages to argue a late date for the folio—a reference to the rarity of men of true religion "in the wars of late years" and a reference to the "engines of the adverse Party." Isobel Grundy answers Woolf's objections and defends the attribution to Elizabeth Cary in "Falkland's *History of . . . King Edward II,*" *Bodleian Library Record,* 13, no. 1 (1988), 82–83. She notes that in context the "party" reference calls up not post-Restoration national parties but the struggles of groups and factions—country lords against insidious courtiers at the close of Buckingham's career. And the "war" passage, with its contrast between a justifiable invasion motivated by true religion and "our" unlawful "Plantations" and "Purchase" seems to refer not to the Civil War but to the continuous bloody battles in Ireland, of which Elizabeth Cary was very much aware. The passage in question describes the Isabel-Mortimer invasion as

> one of the most memorable Passages of our time, since it was merely guided by pity and compassion . . . rich in purchase; not gained by pillage, robbery, or unjust rapine . . . Men that were vertuously inclin'd, and aw'd with the true sense of Religion (in the Wars of late years become a mere stranger) where no Victory is esteem'd dishonourable, no Purchase unlawful. Certainly our Wars and our Plantations nearly resemble, being both used as a Broom to sweep the Kingdome, rather than an enterprize to adorn it. (145–146)

Internal evidence pointing toward Elizabeth Cary's authorship of the folio includes the dramatic scenes and speeches, the feminist portrait of Queen Isabel, and the sympathetic treatment of the Pope and the Catholic clergy—inconceivable from the rabidly antipapist Falkland. For example, at the Scots uprising after the death of Gaveston, the Pope "with a pious and truly compassionate eye beheld the misery of this Dissention, and the

unnatural effusion of so much Christian Blood" (42) and sent two Cardi-
nals to act as mediators. Most striking, and virtually impossible as a coincidence, is the author's claim, both here and in the translation of Perron
known to be by her, that each of these works was produced in a month's
time.

APPENDIX B

Presentation Copies of Lanyer's
Salve Deus Rex Judaeorum

The Dyce copy in the Victoria and Albert was at one point a presentation copy for Prince Henry: it is bound in vellum with the encircled ostrich-feather emblem of Prince Henry in gilt in the center of the front and back bindings. It also has the signature "Cumberland" in what looks like the hand of Margaret Clifford, Countess of Cumberland, on the recto of the page preceding the title page, suggesting that the volume was initially presented to her as the principal dedicatee (she may have been given more than one copy) and perhaps by her presented to the Prince in an effort to do Lanyer some good at court. Dyce has tipped into this copy from another with slightly smaller pages the signatures initially omitted in the presentation copy, as his letter to his friend Bliss (now inserted in the Huntington Library copy) indicates. The Cumberland–Prince Henry copy initially had dedications to the Queen, Princess Elizabeth, "All Virtuous Ladies," the Countess of Bedford, the Countess of Cumberland, and the Countess of Dorset, as well as the Epistle "To the Vertuous Reader." The omissions make sense for these recipients: Arbella was in disgrace in 1610 and in March 1611 was sent to the Tower; the Countess of Suffolk was a member of the Catholic Howard family (the opposing faction to Henry's); the Countess of Pembroke and the Countess of Kent would deflect the praise from the primary targets. With these omissions, the dedications address the obvious court patrons as well as the principal dedicatee, the Countess of Cumberland, and her daughter.

The Chapin Library copy is inscribed "The guift of Mr. Alfonso Lanyer 8 No: 1610" with the signature of "Tho: Jones." This means that the gift was made only a month after the work was entered in the Stationers' Register (October 2, 1610). For this recipient most of the dedications and the blatantly feminist epistle "To the Vertuous Reader" have been removed; all that remain are the royal dedicatees and the primary patrons: the Queen, Princess Elizabeth, "All Vertuous Ladies," the Countess of Cumberland, and the Countess of Dorset.

The British Library copy lacks the dedications to Arbella Stuart and to the Countesses of Kent, Pembroke, and Suffolk, as well as the epistle "To the Vertuous Reader"; it also lacks all but the first seven stanzas of the Dorset dedication. (The front matter is not reset: signature c is eliminated, as are all but the final leaf of signature d–d 4—the Bedford dedication— and also all of signature f). The dedications appear in the following order: the Queen, Princess Elizabeth, "All Virtuous Ladies," the Countess of Bedford, the Countess of Dorset (seven stanzas), the Countess of Cumberland. This may also have been a presentation copy, but there is no evidence as to the recipient. In the Bodleian copy "Cooke-ham" is missing; it is not clear why.

Notes

Abbreviations

BL	British Library
CBEL	*The New Cambridge Bibliography of English Literature*, vol. 1, *600–1660*, ed. George Watson (Cambridge: Cambridge University Press, 1974)
Cal. SP	*Calendar of State Papers, Domestic Series, of the Reigns of Edward VI, Mary, Elizabeth, and James I, preserved in the Public Record Office*, 12 vols., ed. Robert Lemon and Mary Anne Everett Green (London, 1856–1872)
Cal. SP Venetian	*Calendar of Letters and State Papers relating to English Affairs, preserved in archives and collections of Venice and in other libraries of northern Italy*, 38 vols., ed. Rawdon Brown et al. (London, 1864–1947)
Chamberlain	John Chamberlain, *Letters*, ed. N. E. McClure, 3 vols. (Philadelphia: American Philosophical Society, 1939)
Carleton, *Letters*	*Dudley Carleton to John Chamberlain, 1602–1624: Jacobean Letters*, ed. Maurice Lee (New Brunswick: Rutgers University Press, 1972)
DNB	*Dictionary of National Biography*
ELH	*English Literary History*
ELR	*English Literary Renaissance*
JEGP	*Journal of English and Germanic Philology*
H&S	C. H. Herford and Percy and Evelyn Simpson, eds., *Ben Jonson*, 11 vols. (Oxford: Clarendon, 1941)
MLQ	*Modern Language Quarterly*
N&Q	*Notes and Queries*
Nichols	John Nichols, ed., *The Progresses, Processions, and Magnificent Festivities of King James the First, His Royal Consort, Family, and Court*, 4 vols. (London, 1828)

PRO	Public Record Office, Chancery Lane, London
RES	*Review of English Studies*
RQ	*Renaissance Quarterly*
SEL	*Studies in English Literature*
SQ	*Shakespeare Quarterly*
SP	State Papers, Domestic, Public Record Office, London
STC	*A Short Title Catalogue . . . 1475–1640,* ed. A. W. Pollard and G. R. Redgrave, 2nd ed., rev. W. A. Jackson et al., 3 vols. (London: Bibliographical Society, 1986–1991)

Introduction

1. See, for example, Joan Kelly-Gadol, "Did Women Have a Renaissance?" in *Becoming Visible: Women in European History,* ed. Renate Bridenthal and Claudia Koonz (Boston: Houghton Mifflin, 1977), 137–164; Linda T. Fitz [Woodbridge], "'What Says the Married Woman?': Marriage Theory and Feminism in the English Renaissance," *Mosaic,* 13 (1980), 1–22; Ian Maclean, *The Renaissance Notion of Women: A Study in the Fortunes of Scholasticism and Medical Science in European Intellectual Life* (Cambridge: Cambridge University Press, 1980); Constance Jordan, *Renaissance Feminism: Literary Texts and Political Models* (Ithaca: Cornell University Press, 1990); Michel Foucault, introduction to *The History of Sexuality,* vol. 1 (New York: Pantheon, 1978); Thomas Laqueur, *Body and Gender from the Greeks to Freud* (Cambridge, Mass.: Harvard University Press, 1990); Susan Dwyer Amussen, *An Ordered Society: Gender and Class in Early Modern England* (Oxford: Blackwell, 1988); and Margaret Ferguson, Maureen Quilligan, and Nancy J. Vickers, eds., *Rewriting the Renaissance: The Discourses of Sexual Difference in Early Modern Europe* (Chicago: University of Chicago Press, 1986).

2. See Arthur F. Marotti, "'Love is not Love': Elizabethan Sonnet Sequences and the Social Order," *ELH,* 49 (1982), 396–428; Marotti, *John Donne: Coterie Poet* (Madison: University of Wisconsin Press, 1986); Louis Montrose, "'Shaping Fantasies': Figurations of Gender and Power in Elizabethan Culture," *Representations,* 2 (1983), 61–94; Patricia Parker and David Quint, eds., *Literary Theory/Renaissance Texts* (Baltimore: Johns Hopkins University Press, 1987); Heather Dubrow and Richard Strier, eds., *The Historical Renaissance: New Essays on Tudor and Stuart Literature and Culture* (Chicago: University of Chicago Press, 1988); Sheila Fisher and Janet Halley, *Seeking the Woman in Late Medieval and Renaissance Writings* (Knoxville: University of Tennessee Press, 1989); Catherine Belsey, *The Subject of Tragedy: Identity and Difference in Renaissance Drama* (London: Methuen, 1985); Stephen Greenblatt, "Fiction and Friction," in *Shakespearean Negotiations* (Berkeley: University of California Press, 1988), 66–93; Lisa Jardine, *Still Harping on Daughters: Women and Drama in the Age of Shakespeare* (Totowa, N.J.: Barnes & Noble, 1983); Mary Nyquist and Margaret Ferguson, eds., *Re-Membering Milton: Essays on the Texts and Traditions* (New York: Methuen, 1987).

3. Margaret Ezell argues persuasively in *The Patriarch's Wife: Literary Evidence and the History of the Family* (Chapel Hill: University of North Carolina Press, 1987), 62–100, that the processes of canon making have prompted us to ignore much women's writing that received "publication" through manuscript circulation.

4. Some valuable collections of essays include *Beyond Their Sex: Learned Women of the European Past,* ed. Patricia H. Labalme (New York: New York University Press, 1980); *Women in English Society: 1500–1800,* ed. Mary Prior (London: Methuen, 1985); *Silent But for the Word: Tudor Women as Patrons, Translators, and Writers of Religious Works,* ed. Margaret P. Hannay (Kent, Ohio: Kent State University Press, 1985); *Women in the Middle Ages and the Renaissance: Literary and Historical Perspectives,* ed. Mary Beth Rose (Syracuse: Syracuse University Press, 1986); Carol Levin and Jeanie Watson, eds., *Ambiguous Realities: Women in the Middle Ages and the Renaissance* (Detroit: Wayne State University Press, 1987); Anne M. Haselkorn and Betty S. Travitsky, *The Renaissance Englishwoman in Print: Counterbalancing the Canon* (Amherst: University of Massachusetts Press, 1990). Some overviews include: Retha M. Warnke, *Women of the English Renaissance and Reformation* (Westport, Conn.: Greenwood, 1983); and Elaine Beilin, *Redeeming Eve: Women Writers of the English Renaissance* (Princeton: Princeton University Press, 1987). For some anthologies, see Betty Travitsky, ed., *The Paradise of Women: Writings by Englishwomen of the Renaissance* (Westport, Conn.: Greenwood, 1981); Moira Ferguson, ed., *First Feminists: British Women Writers, 1578–1799* (Bloomington: University of Indiana Press, 1985); Angeline Goreau, *The Whole Duty of Woman: Female Writers in Seventeenth-Century England* (New York: Dial, 1985); and *Kissing the Rod: An Anthology of Seventeenth-Century Women's Verse,* ed. Germaine Greer et al. (New York: Noonday, 1988).

5. Josephine Roberts has edited Mary Wroth's complete poems, *The Poems of Lady Mary Wroth* (Baton Rouge: Louisiana State University Press, 1983); she is also preparing an edition of Wroth's *Urania,* both the rare Part I (1621) and the unpublished manuscript of Part II. Margaret Ferguson and Barry Weller are editing Elizabeth Cary's *Mariam* (Berkeley: University of California Press, forthcoming). Susanne Woods is general editor and Elizabeth Hageman is Renaissance section editor for a series of women writers to be published jointly by the Oxford University Press and the Brown Women Writers Project. Elaine Beilin is editing Anne Askew's polemical writing; Sara Jayne Steen, Arbella Stuart's letters; Susanne Woods, Aemilia Lanyer; Barbara Lewalski, Rachel Speght's polemic and poetry. Margaret P. Hannay has published a critical biography of the Countess of Pembroke, *Philip's Phoenix: Mary Sidney, Countess of Pembroke* (New York: Oxford University Press, 1990), and is preparing a complete edition of her works.

6. Some studies in this vein are Stephen Greenblatt, *Renaissance Self-Fashioning* (Chicago: University of Chicago Press, 1980), and Greenblatt, ed., *Representing the English Renaissance* (Berkeley: University of California Press, 1988); Jonathan Dollimore and Alan Sinfield, eds., *Political Shakespeare: New Essays in Cultural Materialism* (Ithaca: Cornell University Press, 1985); Dollimore, *Radical Tragedy: Religion, Ideology, and Power in the Drama of Shakespeare and His Contemporaries* (Chicago: University of Chicago Press, 1986); Frank Whigham, *Ambition and Privilege: The Social Tropes of Elizabethan Courtesy Theory* (Berkeley: University of California Press, 1984); and Peter Stallybrass and Allon White, *The Politics and Poetics of Transgression* (Ithaca: Cornell University Press, 1986).

7. Carol Thomas Neely, "Constructing the Subject: Feminist Practice and the New Renaissance Discourse," *ELR,* 18 (1988), 5–18. For a related critique, see Lynda E. Boose, "The Family in Shakespeare Studies; or—Studies in the Family of Shakespeareans, or—the Politics of Politics," *RQ,* 40 (1987), 707–742; and Jean

E. Howard, "The New Historicism in Renaissance Studies," *ELR*, 16 (1986), 13–43.

8. This phrase, underscoring the ideal continually held forth in treatises on women's domestic and spiritual duties, serves as the title for Suzanne W. Hull's useful survey of books directed to a female audience, *Chaste, Silent, and Obedient: English Books for Women, 1475–1640* (San Marino: Huntington Library, 1982).

9. On the Jacobean patriarchal ethos, see Gordon J. Schochet, *Patriarchalism in Political Thought: The Authoritarian Family and Political Speculation and Attitudes Especially in Seventeenth-Century England* (New York: Basic Books, 1975); and Jonathan Goldberg, *James I and the Politics of Literature* (Baltimore: Johns Hopkins University Press, 1983).

10. James I, *The Trew Lawe of Free Monarchie* (Edinburgh, 1598), and *Basilikon Doron, Or, His Majesties Instructions to his Dearest Sonne, Henry the Prince* (London, 1603), both reprinted in *The Workes of the Most High and Mighty Prince, James* (London, 1616).

11. See, for example, Myra Reynolds, *The Learned Lady in England, 1650–1760* (Boston: Houghton Mifflin, 1920), 23–37; Katherine Henderson and Barbara McManus, *Half Humankind: Contexts and Texts of the Controversy about Women in England, 1540–1640* (Urbana: University of Illinois Press, 1985), 82–98; Dorothy Gardiner, *English Girlhood at School* (Oxford: Oxford University Press, 1929); J. R. Brink, *Female Scholars: A Tradition of Learned Women before 1800* (Montreal: Eden, 1984).

12. See Linda Woodbridge, *Women and the English Renaissance: Literature and the Nature of Womankind, 1540–1640* (Chicago: University of Chicago Press, 1984).

13. Most of these Continental women writers are analyzed by Ann Rosalind Jones in *The Currency of Eros: Women's Love Lyric in Europe, 1540–1620* (Bloomington: Indiana University Press, 1990). For accounts of the translation activities of Tudor women, see Hannay, *Silent But for the Word*. Besides translations, we have a few original poems and prose meditations by Mary Sidney, Isabella Whitney, Elizabeth Grymston, Queen Elizabeth, Mary Queen of Scots, Anne Lok, and (possibly) Anne Cecil de Vere, Countess of Oxford.

14. Natalie Zemon Davis, "Boundaries and the Sense of Self in Sixteenth-Century France," in *Reconstructing Individualism: Autonomy, Individuality, and the Self in Western Thought* (Stanford: Stanford University Press, 1986), 53–63, emphasizes the emergence of the sense of self as a member of a group, especially the family. See also Davis, "Women on Top: Symbolic Sexual Inversion and Political Disorder in Early Modern Europe," in *The Reversible World: Symbolic Inversion and Political Disorder in Art and Society*, ed. Barbara Babcock (Ithaca: Cornell University Press, 1978), 147–190; and Davis, *Society and Culture in Early Modern France* (Stanford: Stanford University Press, 1979).

15. Antonio Gramsci, *Selections from the Prison Notebooks* (Q. 25), ed. Quintin Hoare and Geoffrey Nowell-Smith (London: Lawrence and Wishart, 1971), 52–55. Jones, *Currency of Eros*, 1–10, develops three models of such negotiation to analyze the women she treats: empowerment through the use of a dominant discourse; modification in the service of a different group; and openly oppositional strategies.

16. See, for example, Alice Clark, *Working Life of Women in the Seventeenth Century* (London: Routledge, 1919; rpt. 1982); Lawrence Stone, *The Family, Sex, and*

Marriage in England, 1500–1800 (New York: Harpers, 1977); Keith Wrightson, *English Society, 1580–1680* (New Brunswick, N.J.: Rutgers University Press, 1982); David Underdown, *Revel, Riot, and Rebellion: Popular Politics and Culture in England, 1603–1660* (Oxford: Clarendon, 1985); Martin Ingram, *Church Courts, Sex, and Marriage in England, 1571–1640* (Cambridge: Cambridge University Press, 1987); Alan Macfarlane, *Marriage and Love in England: Modes of Reproduction, 1300–1840* (Oxford: Oxford University Press, 1986); Susan Cahn, *Industry of Devotion: The Transformation of Women's Work in England, 1500–1600* (New York: Columbia University Press, 1987); Margaret George, *Women in the First Capitalist Society: Experiences in Seventeenth-Century England* (Urbana: University of Illinois Press, 1988).

17. Elizabeth Jocelin, *The Mothers Legacie to her unborn Childe* (London, 1624); Dorothy Leigh, *The Mothers Blessing: Or, The godly Counsaile of a Gentle-woman* (London, 1616); Elizabeth Clinton, *The Countess of Lincolnes Nurserie* (Oxford, 1622). Cf. Betty Travitsky, "The New Mother of the English Renaissance: Her Writings on Motherhood," in *The Lost Tradition: Mothers and Daughters in Literature,* ed. Cathy N. Davidson and E. M. Broner (New York: Ungar, 1980), 33–43.

18. *The Diary of Lady Margaret Hoby, 1599–1605,* ed. Dorothy M. Meads (London: Routledge, 1930). Grace [Sherrington] Mildmay, *Journal* (almost 1,000 pages, in the public library of Northampton, England); excerpt in Rachel Weigall, "An Elizabethan Gentlewoman: The Journal of Lady Mildmay," *Quarterly Review,* 215 (1911), 119–138.

19. Elizabeth Melville, *Ane Godlie Dreame* (Edinburgh, 1603); English version, *A Godlie Dreame* (Edinburgh, 1606).

20. The only competitor I can think of is Simon Forman's much shorter "Autobiography," Bodleian, MS Ashmole, 208.

21. We cannot be sure on present evidence whether a woman wrote the earlier tract entitled *Jane Anger her Protection for Women* (London, 1589), or if so, who she is. Speght might, however, have seen Anger's female persona as providing some precedent for herself.

22. See Jones, *Currency of Eros,* 36–52.

23. For the recognition of Senecan tragedy and Tacitean history as dangerous genres, see M. F. Tenney, "Tacitus in the Politics of Early Stuart England," *Classical Journal,* 27 (1941), 152–163; and Albert Tricomi, *Anticourt Drama in England, 1603–1642* (Charlottesville: University of Virginia Press, 1989), 53–79.

24. For Lanyer's tribute to Mary Sidney as model, see Barbara Lewalski, "Of God and Good Women: The Poems of Aemilia Lanyer," in Hannay, *Silent But for the Word,* 209–210; and for Wroth's, see Hannay, "'Your vertuous and learned Aunt': The Countess of Pembroke as a Mentor to Mary Wroth," in *Reading Mary Wroth: Representing Alternatives in Early Modern England,* ed. Naomi Miller and Gary Waller (Nashville: University of Tennessee Press, 1991), 15–34.

25. Karl J. Weintraub, "Autobiography and Historical Consciousness," *Critical Inquiry,* 1 (1975), 841–842.

26. Among many formulations of the containment thesis, Stephen Greenblatt's essay "Invisible Bullets" (1981) has become classic: it is revised and reprinted in his *Shakespearean Negotiations,* 21–65.

27. The subversive impact of the drama is explored in Woodbridge, *Women and the English Renaissance,* 244–268; Simon Shepherd, *Amazons and Warrior Women:*

Varieties of Feminism in Seventeenth-Century Drama (Brighton: Harvester, 1981), 67–218; and in more qualified terms by Jean E. Howard, "Crossdressing, the Theatre, and Gender Struggle in Early Modern England," *SQ,* 39 (1988), 418–440.

28. In E. K. Chambers, *The Elizabethan Stage,* 4 vols. (Oxford: Clarendon, 1923), I, 325. Women's presence in the audience at the public as well as the private theaters (aristocrats, citizens' wives, artisans, vagrants, and whores) is documented in Andrew Gurr's study *Playgoing in Shakespeare's London* (Cambridge: Cambridge University Press, 1987), 54–63. For Queen Anne's playgoing, see chapter 1 of this book. Some sense of women's reading in the period is provided in Margaret Spufford, *Small Books and Pleasant Histories: Popular Fiction and Its Readership in Seventeenth-Century England* (Athens: University of Georgia Press, 1981).

29. Ezell, *The Patriarch's Wife,* 9–61.

30. Antonia Fraser, *The Weaker Vessel* (New York: Knopf, 1982), 12–16, 292.

31. For an analysis of actual cross-dressing in the period and its implications, see Howard, "Crossdressing, the Theatre, and Gender Struggle." For discussion of transvestism in the theater and its ideological implications, see Laura Levine, "Men in Women's Clothing: Antitheatricality and Effeminization from 1579 to 1642," *Criticism,* 28 (1986), 121–143; Phyllis Rankin, "Androgyny, Mimesis, and the Marriage of the Boy Heroine on the Elizabethan Stage, *PMLA,* 102 (1987), 29–41; and Catherine Belsey, "Disrupting Sexual Difference: Meaning and Gender in the Comedies," *Alternative Shakespeares,* ed. John Drakakis (London: Methuen, 1985), 166–190. For a stimulating theoretical analysis of the phenomenon of cross-dressing at various historical moments, see Marjorie Garber, *Vested Interests: Cross-Dressing and Cultural Anxiety* (London: Routledge, 1991). See chapter 6 of this book for discussion of the transvestism tracts of the 1620s.

32. For a penetrating study of various kinds of literary coding, see Annabel Patterson, *Censorship and Interpretation: The Conditions of Reading and Writing in Early Modern England* (Madison: University of Wisconsin Press, 1984).

1. Enacting Opposition: Queen Anne

1. *Letters to King James the Sixth from the Queen . . . From the Originals in the Library of Advocates* (Edinburgh, 1835). Queen Anne's life is treated in Ethel Carleton Williams, *Anne of Denmark: Wife of James VI of Scotland, James I of England* (London: Longman, 1970); and David M. Bergeron, *Royal Family, Royal Lovers* (Columbia: University of Missouri Press, 1991).

2. John Harington, *The Letters and Epigrams of Sir John Harington,* ed. Norman E. McClure (Philadelphia: University of Pennsylvania Press, 1930), 120.

3. James I, *Basilikon Doron,* 173.

4. Thomas Playfere, *The Power of Prayer* (Cambridge, 1603).

5. Andrew Willet, *Ecclesia Triumphans: that is, The Joy of the English Church, for the Happy Coronation of the Most vertuous and Pious Prince James* (Cambridge, 1603), sig. # 4v. In a more positive vein, John Hopkins (one of the King's Chaplains in Ordinary who sought the Queen's patronage) held her forth as a Protestant exemplar—attentive at sermons, a frequenter of divine services, and a daily and affectionate reader of godly books—as well as "the most worthie and famous Queene of Europe." *A Sermon Preached Before the Queenes Majestie at Hampton Court* (London, 1609).

6. William Cowper, *Heaven Opened. Wherein the Counsell of God Concerning Man's Salvation is further Manifested* (London, 1611). The tract is dedicated to Anne.

7. Leeds Barroll, "The Court of the First Stuart Queen," in *The Mental World of the Jacobean Court,* ed. Linda Levy Peck (Cambridge: Cambridge University Press, 1991), 191–208.

8. [Frances Erskine], *Memoirs Relating to the Queen of Bohemia by one of her Ladies* (privately printed, n.p., n.d.), 13–18. The ascription is almost certainly spurious: diction and stylistic features place it as an eighteenth-century work, evidently written by one Frances Erskine (1715–1776), daughter of the eleventh Earl of Mar. The sketch is probably based on materials handed down in the family of the Erskines, Earls of Mar, who had the care of King James and later Prince Henry in their youth and were on intimate terms with the royal family.

9. She was entertained at York, Grimston, Worksop (by the Earl of Shrewsbury), Ashby-de-la-Zouch (by the Earl of Huntington), Wollaton Hall, the city of Leicester, Dingley Hall, and Althorpe (by Sir Robert Spencer), among other places. The contemporary historian Arthur Wilson reports James's disaffection from the multitude: "In his publick Appearances . . . the Accesses of the People made him so impatient, that he often dispersed them with Frowns." The Venetian Ambassador Nicolò Molin reported in 1607 that the King's open "contempt and dislike" for the multitude made him "despised and almost hated." Quoted in Robert Ashton, *James I by His Contemporaries* (London: Hutchinson, 1969), 63–64, 10.

10. Grant Dugdale, *The Time Triumphant* (London, 1604), Nichols, I, 415–416. Dudley Carleton reported to Sir Thomas Parry on June 28, 1603, that the Queen gave "great contentment to the world in her fashion and courteous behaviour to the people." Nichols, I, 190.

11. Hugh Holland, *Pancharis* (London, 1603).

12. Alexander Craigie, *Poetical Essayes* (London, 1604), sig. C 3; also *The Amorose Songes, Sonets, and Elegies,* (London, 1606), which contains poems celebrating several pseudonymous ladies—Idea, Cynthia, Kala, Pandora, Penelope. Craigie claims that Anne bestowed on him "munificens and frequent benefites" and that it was her "Princely pleasure" to protect his verses.

13. *A Particular Entertainment of the Queene and Prince their Highnesse to Althorpe, at the Right Honourable the Lord Spencers, on Saterday being the 25. of June 1603* (London, 1604), in H&S, VII, 121–131. The speakers are satyrs and fairies of the local forest personated by Spencer's and other sons of the county nobility. Both Queen and Prince (and the attendant ladies) are offered entertainments of hunting and morris dancing. The title "Oriana" had been earlier (and less felicitously) applied to Queen Elizabeth in a book of madrigals, *The Triumphs of Oriana,* in 1601.

14. *A Private Entertainment of the King and Queene, on Mayday in the Morning, at Sir William Cornwalleis his house, at High-gate, 1604,* in H&S, VII, 136–144. The mix of panegyric and jest indicates that Jonson is now comfortable taking such a tone with both his royal patrons. Later, Campion's entertainment for the Queen at Caversham House has woodsmen and gardeners in their speeches and songs paying tribute to Anne as Venus and Flora.

15. Nichols, I, 386–387. Most of the elaborate coronation ceremonies were deferred until March 1604 because of the plague.

16. Dugdale, *Time Triumphant,* in Nichols, I, 408–419.

17. George Chapman, *Homer Prince of Poets* (London, 1611), sig. A 7. The work

is dedicated to Prince Henry but includes a verse epistle to Anne extending all Henry's praises to her as their source.

18. The sonnet is included in his translation of Montaigne's *Essays* (London, 1613), dedicated to the Queen. The epistle dedicatory transfers to her this and other works originally dedicated to other ladies: "Seeing with me, all of me, is in your Royall possession, and whatsoever pieces of mine have heertofore, under other starres, passed the publike view, come now of right to be under the predomination of a power, that both contains all their perfections, and hath influences of a more sublime nature." Similar tributes are offered (though with less appropriateness) in certain Latin poems addressed to Anne in books of panegyrics for the royal family; A.D.D.'s *Xenia Regia ad Jacobum* (1607) honors her for piety, virtue, mercy, grace, charity; Thomas Rosa (another Scot) praises her in her ancestry, her progeny, and her marital love, as an Artemisia, a Julia, and a Portia.

19. George Wither, *Abuses Stript and Whipt. Or, Satirical Essayes* (London, 1613), "Epigram 3," sigs. V 8v–X.

20. Aemilia Lanyer, *Salve Deus Rex Judaeorum* (London, 1611), sigs. A 3–A 4.

21. James could scarcely believe the Queen innocent of complicity when her Scottish maid of honor Margaret managed the escape of Bothwell and her own lover from the castle. Balladeers made a love story of the Queen's admiration for Bothwell's friend, the handsome Earl of Moray (slain by the King's friend, the Earl of Huntley, some said at the jealous King's behest). Some of the ballads are reprinted in Agnes Strickland, *Lives of the Queens of England,* 12 vols. (London, 1840–1848), VII, 354–355. Sir Henry Wotton testified to the rumors in his letter to Lord Zouche on August 14, 1592: "We hear the Queen of Scots, with a Scottish Earl (of whom she was enamoured) conspired the King's death, which proceeded so far to execution, as to slay some of his court." *Life and Letters of Sir Henry Wotton,* 2 vols. (Oxford, 1907; rpt. 1966), I, 284–285. In 1600 she publicly signaled her disbelief in James's implausible story about the treason (and subsequent killing) of the Ruthven brothers by heaping gifts upon their sister, her maid of honor Beatrice Ruthven, and at length forcing the unwilling King to grant her a pension. Williams, *Anne of Denmark,* 38–45, 61–65. John Colville reported to Cecil in 1594 that the King repented his elaborate arrangements for Prince Henry's baptism because he had begun to doubt his paternity. Bergeron, *Royal Family,* 55.

22. *Letters . . . from the Queen,* no. 3. For an account of the incident, see Dudley Carleton's letter to Sir Thomas Parry, July 3, 1603, in Nichols, I, 197–198. The nobles were Lords Grey and Southampton, the latter recently pardoned by James for his part in Essex's rebellion; the quarrel arose over the Queen's provocative question about the ease with which that rebellion had been quelled.

23. From a report of their quarrel sent to England on May 25, 1595, cited in Strickland, *Lives of the Queens of England,* VII, 363–364. Princess Elizabeth, born 1596, was also given into fosterage, to Lord and Lady Livingstone.

24. Quoted in preface to *Letters . . . from the Queen,* xxxi–xxxiii. The original is in the Ferdinand Dreer Autograph Collection, vol. 173, Historical Society of Pennsylvania, Philadelphia.

25. A. W. Ward, "Review," *English Historical Review,* 3 (1888), 795–986; Leo Hicks, "The Embassy of Sir Anthony Standen in 1603," *Recusant History,* 5 (1959–1960), 205–206; 6 (1961–1962), 164; 7 (1963–1964), 60, 76. Hicks cites a 1602 report on the State of Scotland by the Jesuit Abercrombie to the effect that Anne had

been received into the Church three years earlier, and also the testimony of Count Alfonso Montecuccoli (1603) of Tuscany and George Conn (1604) that the Queen had told them she was a Catholic. He reports as well that the Pope sent a rosary to the Queen in 1604, with a message urging her to promote the safety of Catholics in the realm and the conversion of her husband, to which "God, *qui facit salutem in manu feminae,* will vouchsafe his aid, as already he has given her the courage at the coronation not to participate with the heretics in their pseudo-communion" (VI, 164).

26. John Fynett to Mr. Trumbull, October 23, 1612, in Sir Ralph Winwood, *Memorials of the Affairs of State in the Reigns of Queen Elizabeth & James I,* ed. E. Sawyer, 3 vols. (London, 1725), III, 403; Chamberlain to Winwood, January 9, 1613, ibid., 421. See also A. Le Fèvre de la Boderie, *Ambassades en Angleterre,* 5 vols. (Paris, 1750), III, 10.

27. R. W., *The Dialogues of S. Gregorie, Surnamed the Greate: Pope of Rome and the First of that name* (Paris, 1608), sig. A 2–A 8v.

28. Michael Walpole, *English Catholikes, Concerning a late Proclamation set forth against them* (n.p., 1610), sigs. 2v–3. Less welcome, we might suppose, was R.B.P.'s blatant insistence on the necessary subservience of Anne and her Catholic ladies to the authority of the Church's male magisterium, and their essentially passive role as messengers: "The cause why I principally dedicate it to you, is not to make you patrons of the prayers of Sainctes, and their holie faith, but to make them Patrones unto you . . . not to make your unlearned sexe unpeare over the whole Church of God, but to procure you to be true members of that holie companie, forth of which there is no salvation; not because I would exclude your Lordes . . . but to have it presented to them by you." *A Manual of Praiers used by the Fathers of the Primitive Church* (n.p., 1618), 7–8.

29. They included the King's choice for her Lord Chamberlain (Sir George Carew), the Earls of Sussex and Lincoln, the Countesses of Worcester and Kildare, and the Ladies Scope, Rich, Anne Herbert, and Walsingham, who at the King's behest brought with them some of Queen Elizabeth's personal jewels and dresses for Anne's use.

30. Sir Thomas Edmonds to the Earl of Shrewsbury, June 15, 1603, in Edmund Lodge, *Illustrations of British History,* 3 vols. (London, 1838), III, 164.

31. Edward Somerset, Earl of Worcester, to Gilbert Talbot, Earl of Shrewsbury, February 2, 1604, in Lodge, *Illustrations,* III, 227–228. The Countess of Derby was formerly Elizabeth de Vere, daughter of the Earl of Oxford; the Countess of Suffolk was Catherine Howard; Lady Rich was Penelope Devereaux, Sidney's "Stella"; the Countess of Nottingham was Margaret (Stuart) Howard, daughter of the Earl of Moray; Susan de Vere was soon to marry Philip Herbert and become Countess of Montgomery; Lady Ethelreda Walsingham and her husband, Sir Thomas, were made chief Keepers of the Queen's Wardrobe; Lady Southwell was also a Howard by birth. Sir Robert Carey reports in his memoirs that at Windsor his wife was sworn of the Queen's Privy Chamber and made mistress of her "Sweet Coffers," or robes. Nichols, I, 247.

32. Anne Clifford observes in her diary that "my Lady of *Bedford* was so great a woman with the Queen as everybody much respected her"; that at Althorpe "we saw the Queen's favour to Lady *Hatton* and Lady *Cecil,* for she shewed no favour to the elderly ladies, but to Lady *Rich* and such like company." *The Diary of Lady*

Anne Clifford, ed. V. Sackville-West (London: Westminster, 1923), 8–9. Later she notes a temporary reassignment of first place: "Now was my Lady *Rich* grown great with the Queen, in so much as my Lady of *Bedford* was something out with her, and when she came to *Hampton Court* was entertained, but even indifferently, and yet continued to be of the bedchamber" (13). Cf. Carleton, *Letters,* 34–35.

33. Stewardships over the Queen's various properties and lands were shared out among Robert Sidney (General Surveyor of the Queen's Possessions and High Steward of Snave, Neots, Northborne); the Earl of Rutland (High Steward of Grantham); Lord Cecil (High Steward of her Courts and Keeper of Somerset House); Lord Compton (High Steward of Henly, Hampton, St. Needs); George Carew (General Receiver of her Revenues); and the Earl of Southampton—Essex's close associate—(Master of her Forests, Chases, Parks, and Warrens). Nichols, I, 281. A full list of the properties in the Queen's jointure (in England), together with a list of her officers, is in Lodge, *Illustrations,* III, 206–213.

34. Lady Rich was also the longtime mistress of another member of that circle, Charles Blount, Lord Mountjoy.

35. The Countess of Bedford's brother, John Harington, and Essex's son (the young Earl of Essex) were Prince Henry's closest friends. Sir Robert and Lady Carey were guardians to the sickly Prince Charles; Carey's *Memoirs* (London, 1759, 164–169) report that his wife and the Queen strongly and successfully opposed the King's proposals to treat Charles's speech impediment by cutting the tendon under his tongue and the weakness in his legs by putting him in iron boots.

36. See Tricomi, *Anticourt Drama in England,* 3–50. Tricomi notes that these audacious plays appealed to a disenchanted audience of younger sons of the nobility, students at the Inns of Court, literary men associated with noble households, and other sophisticates; they appealed as well, it seems, to the Queen and her ladies.

37. Ibid., 43, 63–71. At the beginning of James's reign the general licensing authority, the Master of the Revels, was in some confusion, with Edmund Tillney, Sir Lewis Leuknor, and Sir George Buc all having some responsibilities—one reason why several daring works found production. Daniel retained his salaried post despite the controversy over *Philotas* (1605), until the Children's Company was stripped of its royal patronage in the wake of the *Isle of Gulls* production. For *Philotas,* see chapter 7.

38. The document is reprinted in Chambers, *Elizabethan Stage,* I, 325. Also see the letter from Samuel Calvert to Ralph Winwood (March 28, 1605) confirming the atmosphere of license and satire on the stage: "The play[ers] do not forbear to represent upon their stage the whole course of this present time, not sparing either King, state, or religion, in so great absurdity and with such liberty, that any would be afraid to hear them." Winwood, *Memorials,* II, 54.

39. Carr was aided in his assorted governmental duties by his friend Sir Thomas Overbury. In letters to the King and Robert Cecil in 1611, the Queen complained about their insults to her (BL, Additional MS 4160, f. 3); she also protested Carr's appointment as Lord Chamberlain, insisting that the office had been promised to her friend the Earl of Pembroke.

40. George Abbot, quoted in Nichols, III, 80–81. Abbot further reports that the Queen guided James's shaking hand as he conferred the knighthood.

41. Queen Anne addressed several notes to Buckingham as "my kind dog,"

commending him for "lugging the sow's ear" (that is, bringing her desires to the King's notice), thanking him for his "carefulness" about the paling of her deer park, and seeking through him the wardship and lands of George Saville. BL, Harleian MS 6986, ff. 190, 192, 134.

42. Bodleian, Tanner MS 74, f. 138. After Raleigh's debacle in Guiana, the umbrage of Spain and the Spanish ambassador Gondomar landed Raleigh again in the Tower with the ancient death sentence against him reinstated. In 1618 he appealed to the Queen in a poetic address:

> Then unto whom shall I unfold my wrong,
> Cast downe my teares or hold up folded hands?
> To her to whom remorse doth most belong.
> . . . . .
>
> To her who is the first and maye alone
> Be justlie called the empresse of the Britainnes:
> Who should have mercye if a Queen have none?
> . . . . .
>
> Then cast your eyes on undeserved woe.
> That I and myne maye never murne the misse
> Of her wee had, but praise our living Queene,
> Who brings us equall, if not greater, Blisse.

Drummond MS (Edinburgh); rpt. in *The Poems of Sir Walter Ralegh*, ed. Alice Latham (London: Routledge, 1929), 98–99.

43. SP 14 (James I) 98/97.

44. John Chamberlain to Dudley Carleton (January 4, 1617), Nichols, III, 232.

45. Chamberlain to Carleton, March 8, 1616, SP 14 (James I) 90/105.

46. Carleton to Sir Ralph Winwood (January 1605), Winwood, *Memorials,* II, 44.

47. August 5, 1608, Nichols, II, 203–204. He continues with coded allusions (but in jesting tone) to the Queen's possible attraction to these courtiers: "For youre pairt, maister 10, quho is wanton and uyfeles [wifeless] I can not but be ialous of youre greatnes with my uyfe; but most of all ame I suspicious of 3, quho is so laitelie fallen in aquaintance uith my uyfe . . . his face is so amiabill as it is able to intyse, and his fortune hath ever bene to be great with Sho-saintis [she-saints]."

48. Chamberlain, I, 468: "At theyre last beeing at Tiballs which was about a fortnight since, the Quene shooting at a deere mistooke her marke and killed Jewell the Kings most principall and speciall hound, at which he stormed excedingly a while, but after he knew who did yt, he was soone pacified, and with much kindnes wisht her not to be troubled with yt, for he shold love her never the worse, and the next day sent her a diamond worth 2000 £ as a legacie from his dead dogge. Love and kindnes increases dayly between them, and yt is thought they were never in better termes." On November 25, 1613, Chamberlain wrote to Carleton that "the Quene by the late pacification hath gained Greenwich into her joynter" (I, 487).

49. Chamberlain, II, 32. Also, when the King and Prince Charles visited Cambridge University in March 1615, the Queen did not attend. On March 16 Chamberlain commented on the reasons for her absence in a letter to Carleton, intimating a Howard slight to the Queen under color of the ladies' lack of Latin: "The

Prince came along with him, but not the Quene, by reason (as yt is saide, that she was not invited, which error is rather imputed to theyre chancellor [the Earl of Suffolk, Thomas Howard] then to the scholars that understand not these courses . . . But the absence of women may be the better excused for default of language, there beeing few or none present but of the Howards or that alliance" (I, 586).

50. On this progress she was accompanied by Lord Chancellor Ellesmere; his wife, Alice; the Dowager Countess of Derby; Edward Somerset, Earl of Worcester, who was Master of her Household; Lady Anne Clifford; and Lady Jane Drummond, her friend and attendant from Scotland and now first Lady of her Bedchamber.

51. Thomas Campion, *A Relation of the Late Royal Entertainment, Given by the Right Honorable the Lord Knowles, at Cawsome House Near Redding, to our Most Gracious Queene, Queene Anne* (London, 1613); rpt. in Nichols, II, 638. This was a Howard affair: the hostess was Suffolk's daughter, and the principal masque dances were executed by four of his sons. The appearances of hospitality clearly had to be preserved on both sides.

52. Chamberlain to Carleton (June 10, 1613), Chamberlain, I, 457. Her entertainment at Wells in early August was chiefly pageants performed by the various trades and occupations.

53. She began laying the brickwork and foundations sometime after she received the property in jointure in 1613. Chamberlain wrote Carleton on June 21, 1617, "She is building somwhat at Greenwich . . . some curious devise of Inigo Jones, and will cost about 4000^{li} [pounds]." Chamberlain, II, 83.

54. Mounting anxiety about her gout, dropsy, and hemorrhages is mentioned in several letters and reports through November and December 1618. Nichols, III, 492–499. See Williams, *Anne of Denmark,* 201.

55. On March 6, 1619, Chamberlain wrote to Carleton his information about her death (Chamberlain, II, 219): "The reports ran at first that she had made a will (according to the privilege of our Quenes who as our lawiers say have *potestatem testandi,* and may dispose of all they have saving lands or jewells belonging to the crowne), that she had written a letter and set apart a casket of jewells for the Lady Elizabeth, that she made a very Christian confession and excellent end. But for ought I can learne yet, she made none other then a nuncupative will, or by word of mouth, geving all she had to the Prince . . . as likewise the maner of her will was rather in aunswering questions and sayeng yea to any thing that was demaunded of her, then in disposing ought of herselfe . . . She was earnestly moved by the archbishop of Caunterburie, the Lord Privie Seale and the bishop of London to prepare herself and set all things in order, but she could not be perswaded that her end was so neere, and so wold needs defer yt till the next day."

A supposed eyewitness account (in Scots dialect), purporting to be by one of the Queen's Scots attendants, provides more details and quotes snatches of conversation. But some fictionalizing seems evident here, in the interests of confirming the Queen's good Protestant sentiments, notably in the quoted answer she supposedly gave to the Archbishop: "I do, scho answeres, and withall, scho says, I renonce the mediation of all santes, and my awin mereits, and does only rely upone my Saviour Chryst, who hes redeamed my saull with his bloode. This being said, gaif a great satisfactioun to the Bischopes, and to the few number that hard hir." "Madame the Quein's Death, and Maner thairof," in *Miscellany of the Abbotsford Club* (Edinburgh, 1837), I, 81.

56. The funeral was postponed more than once "for want of money to buy the blacks," wrote Thomas Larkin to Sir Thomas Puckering, April 17, 1619, in Thomas Birch, *The Court and Times of James I*, 2 vols. (London, 1849), II, 153. Chamberlain wrote to Carleton to the same effect on March 27, 1619 (Chamberlain, II, 224–225): "The Quenes funerall is put of till the 29th of Aprill, and perhaps longer unles they can find out monie faster, for the master of the ward-robe [Cranfield] is loth to weare his owne credit thread-bare . . . In the meane time the Ladies grow wearie of watching at Denmarke House, though all day long there is more concourse then when she was living. Her obsequies (they say) shalbe very solemne and well may they be so, yf she left such an estate behind her as is reported . . . as for the speach of a will yt is like to prove nothing, and perhaps yt fell out for the best, for yt is verely thought she meant to have made the king of Denmarke her executor yf she had had time and leysure." On April 24, 1619, Chamberlain reported the contest between the Countess of Arundel and the Countess of Nottingham for the place of chief mourner (Chamberlain, II, 232–233), an office pertaining to rank, not personal friendship.

57. The ceremonial funeral procession from Denmark House to Westminster Abbey (together with all the noble participants) is reported in BL, Harleian MS 5176, ff. 50–55, and printed in full in Nichols, III, 538–543. Chamberlain found it less than impressive: "The funerall . . . was but a drawling tedious sight, more remarqueable for number then for any other singularitie, there beeing 280 poore women besides an army of meane fellowes that were servants to the Lordes and others of the traine, and though the number of Lordes and Ladies were very great, yet me thought altogether they made but a poore shew, which perhaps was because they were apparelled all alike, or that they came laggering all along even tired with the length of the way and waight of theyre clothes, every Lady having twelve yardes of broade cloth about her and the countesses sixteen." Chamberlain, II, 237.

58. Bergeron, *Royal Family*, 143.

59. The Neoplatonic dimensions of the masques are emphasized in Stephen Orgel and Roy Strong, *Inigo Jones: The Theatre of the Stuart Court*, 2 vols. (Berkeley: University of California Press, 1973), a magnificent collection of the texts, costume sketches, and sets for the masques which Inigo Jones mounted. The Neoplatonic emphasis is developed further in Stephen Kogan, *The Hieroglyphic King: Wisdom and Idolatry in the Seventeenth-Century Masque* (London: Associated University Presses, 1986). Orgel's *Illusion of Power: Political Theater in the English Renaissance* (Berkeley: University of California Press, 1975) analyzes the masque as instrument of Stuart political ideology.

60. Orgel and Strong, *Inigo Jones*, I, 7; Goldberg, *James I and the Politics of Literature*, 57.

61. Strains evident in the masques for Prince Henry are noted in Orgel, *Illusions of Power;* Roy Strong, *Henry, Prince of Wales, and England's Lost Renaissance* (New York: Thames & Hudson, 1986); David Norbrook, "The Reformation of the Masque," in David Lindley, ed., *The Court Masque* (Manchester: Manchester University Press, 1984), 94–110; David Norbrook, *Poetry and Politics in the English Renaissance* (London: Routledge, 1984); Goldberg, *James I and the Politics of Literature*, 122–126.

62. This issue is broached in David Riggs, *Ben Jonson: A Life* (Cambridge, Mass.: Harvard University Press, 1989), 179; Hardin Aasand, "'To blanch an

Ethiope, and revive a corse': Queen Anne and *The Masque of Blackness*," *SEL* 32 (1992), 271–285; and Leeds Barroll, "A New History for Shakespeare and His Time," *SQ*, 39 (1988), 441–464. Suzanne Gossett, in "'Man-maid, begone!': Women in Masques," *ELR* 18 (1988), 96–113, argues to the contrary that the masques display Ben Jonson's antipathy to women. I am indebted to Kate Schwarz for the suggestion that the Amazonian allusions in these masques are one locus for their subversion, given the cultural anxiety evoked by Amazons in early modern England.

63. Samuel Daniel, *The Vision of the 12. Goddesses, presented in a Maske the 8. of January, at Hampton Court* (London, 1604); rpt. in *The Whole Workes of Samuel Daniel Esquire in Poetrie* (London, 1623), 403–420; the latter is the edition I cite. Daniel purports in this text to correct a pirated and truncated version published under the title *The True Description of a Royall Masque* (London, 1604).

64. *Vision*, 411–412. The Countess of Bedford brought Daniel to the attention of the King and Queen at Burleigh Harrington in Rutlandshire, where he presented his *Panegyrike Congratulatory* to the King, a plainspoken instruction to James to "teach him how to live." Published in 1603, it also contained verse epistles to several court ladies—Margaret Clifford, Countess of Cumberland; Lucy Russell, Countess of Bedford; and Lady Anne Clifford (whose tutor he had been)—as well as to Sir Thomas Egerton (Keeper of the Great Seal) and the Earl of Southampton. The volume also contained Daniel's *Defence of Ryme*, dedicated to William, Earl of Pembroke (another former pupil). Several of these dedicatees were closely associated with the Essex faction.

65. Carleton to Chamberlain, January 15, 1604, Carleton, *Letters*, 55.

66. In the British Library copy of *The True Description*, the names of all the performers are penned in by a contemporary hand. Venus was Lady Rich (Sidney's "Stella"); Juno was personated by Catherine Howard, Countess of Suffolk; Diana by the Countess of Hertford; Proserpina by Elizabeth Stanley, Countess of Derby; Corcordia by Margaret Howard, Countess of Nottingham; Astraea by Ethelreda, Lady Walsingham; Flora by Lady Susan de Vere; Ceres by Lady Dorothy Hastings; and Tethis by Lady Elizabeth Howard, the Earl of Suffolk's daughter.

67. Kogan, *Hieroglyphic King*, 51–69, emphasizes the allegorical elements. Some political aspects are noted in Pierre Spriet, "Samuel Daniel (1563–1619). Sa Vie—Sa Oeuvre," *Etudes Anglaises*, 29 (1968), 134–175.

68. Carleton, *Letters*, 55. No costume sketches for this masque survive; it was not designed by Inigo Jones. Simon Shepherd, *Amazons and Warrior Women: Varieties of Feminism in Seventeenth-Century Drama* (London: Harvester, 1981), 139, calls attention to the "warrior women" motif in *Queenes*, but it was also present in this early masque.

69. Carleton, *Letters*, 55; Daniel, *Vision*, 411–412.

70. H&S, VII, 178. Jonson masque texts are cited in text and notes from this edition.

71. According to Chamberlain (December 18, 1604, to Winwood) a lesser sum was first projected: "The Queen hath likewise a great Mask in hand against Twelfth-tide, for which there was 3000^li [pounds] delivered a month ago." Winwood, *Memorials*, II, 43. But on January 10, 1605, Ambassador Vincent reported the much higher actual costs. SP 14 (James I) 12/16.

72. Winwood, *Memorials*, II, 44.

73. H&S, VII, 169.

74. Winwood, *Memorials,* II, 44. To Chamberlain, Carleton's critique was harsher: "Theyr black faces, and hands wch were painted and bare up to the elbowes was a very lothsome sight, and I am sory that strangers should see owr court so strangely disguised," H&S, X, 448. The Venetian ambassador, Nicolò Molin, had kinder words for it, terming it "very beautiful and sumptuous." January 27, 1605, *Cal. SP Venetian,* X (1603–1607), 213.

75. See sketches in Orgel and Strong, *Inigo Jones,* I, plate 1. Myths about the Amazons emphasized their African or Asian origins, but some contemporary accounts located them in the Americas. They ruled themselves and warred on men—though in the classical stories they were finally subdued by men.

76. On January 5, 1606, Jonson's masque *Hymenaei* (with Inigo Jones) celebrated the ill-starred wedding of Robert Devereaux, Earl of Essex (Essex's son), and Frances Howard. Though presented at Whitehall, this was not a royal masque but was at the charge of the bride's and groom's friends, and the Queen did not take part. Several of her ladies did, however—the Countesses of Montgomery, Bedford, and Rutland; the Ladies Knollys, Berkeley, Dorothy Hastings, and Blanche Somerset; and Mistress Cecily Sackville. Their presence again had a subtly subversive influence in that the female figures—Reason, Juno Pronuba and the masquers representing her eight powers—control the male masquers who represent the four humors and four affections, subjecting them to the higher ends of wedlock and union. The following year, on Twelfth Night 1607, Thomas Campion's *Masque* (for nine male dancers) was presented at Whitehall, celebrating the wedding of Lord James Hay and Honora Denny.

77. Chamberlain to Carleton (January 5, 8) reported the hall in the new Banqueting House not ready. Chamberlain, I, 250, 252. But see M. de la Boderie's dispatches of January 1 and 14, 1608, to M. de Villeroy, *Ambassades,* III, 8–31. He was skeptical of the public excuse and refused to be mollified by reports that the King was "greatly grieved" at the Queen's "lightness" in this matter.

78. December 27, 1607, *Cal. SP Venetian,* XI (1607–1610), 76. See account in Chambers, *Elizabethan Stage,* III, 380–381.

79. H&S, VII, 181.

80. The daughters of Edward Somerset, Earl of Worcester—Ladies Elizabeth Guildford, Katherine Petre, Anne Winter, and Catherine Windsor—were known Catholics; the Countess of Arundel was so regarded because her husband was a Howard. The French ambassador La Boderie commented on the Queen's choice of cast as signaling a better feeling toward Catholics in England. *Ambassades,* II, 490. The other younger ladies who danced are Frances, Lady Chichester (daughter to Lord Harington of Exton and sister to the Countess of Bedford), Lady Mary Nevill (daughter to the Earl of Dorset), and Lady Elizabeth Gerard.

81. January 24, 1608, *Cal. SP Venetian,* XI (1607–1610), 86.

82. Chamberlain to Winwood, October 12, 1605, Chamberlain, I, 208. A long contemporary account tells of the King's delight in the several disputations, various poetic addresses to the King in Latin and the Queen in English, a Sunday church service with no women present "save the Queen and about eight or ten ladies that attended her Majesty," and the success of Daniel's English play after several dull Latin offerings: "There was an Englisyh play acted in the same place before the Queen and young Prince, with all the Ladies and Gallants attending

the Court. It was penned by Mr. Daniel, and drawn out of Fidus Pastor [Guarini's *Pastor Fido*] . . . I was not there present, but by report it was well acted and generally applauded." Nichols, I, 530–553.

83. Samuel Daniel, *The Queenes Arcadia. A Pastorall Trage-Comedie presented to her Majestie and her Ladies, by the Universitie of Oxford in Christs Church, in August last 1605* (London, 1606), Act I, scene i, sig. B.

84. Suzanne Gossett speculates ("Man-maid, begone!") that the invention of the antimasque, with men or boy actors playing the hags or witches, intends a sharp separation between distorted images of women and true ones (the Queens), in an effort to obviate the problems created by presenting the ladies in blackface in *Blacknesse*. This may be so, given Jonson's prefatory comment about seeking to preserve the ladies' due dignity. But I do not agree with Gossett that the Queens are portrayed as delicate and passive rather than the active agents their stories present (97–101). They are explicitly said to participate in the "heroic and martial virtue" figured in Perseus, and on that score to deserve their place in the House of Fame.

85. Donne, *Letters to Severall Persons of Honour* (London, 1651), 143. The King's warrant is dated December 1, 1608, quoted in H&S, X, 492. *Queenes* was supposed to cost no more than £1,000, but the various recorded payments amount to more than £3,000.

86. Report of Marc'Antonio Correr, January 22, 1609; rpt. in H&S, X, 494, along with a description of the House of Fame when it was set up in the Banqueting House.

87. Chamberlain to Carleton, January 10, 1609, Chamberlain, I, 281.

88. January 8, to M. de Villeroy, *Ambassades,* IV, 144–155.

89. February 20, 1609, *Cal. SP Venetian,* XI (1607–1610), 233.

90. H&S, VII, 282.

91. I am indebted to Kate Schwarz for this insight.

92. Orgel and Strong, *Inigo Jones,* I, 140–153, reproduces from Jones's Chatsworth drawings eight full-length costume sketches and some headpieces. Each Queen was given a distinctive costume: the Amazon Penthesilea wears a classical helmet and close-fitting lorica, and rests her hand on a sword hilt; the Scythian Thomyris displays a barbaric richness of ornament and carries a baton; Candace, Queen of Ethiopia, wears a lorica with armorlike pieces over sleevetops and skirt and a spiked headdress. The other Queens' costumes, though not martial, are imposing.

93. The passage reads:

Who, *Virtue,* can thy power forget,
That sees these live, and triumph yet?
The *Assyrian* pompe, the *Persian* pride,
Greekes glory, and the *Romanes* dy'de:
  And who yet imitate
Theyr noyses, tary the same fate.
Force Greatnesse, all the glorious wayes
    You can, it soone decayes,
  But so *good Fame* shall, never:
Her triumphs, as thryr Causes, are for ever.
(ll. 764–773)

94. *Tethys Festival: Or, The Queenes Wake. Celebrated at Whitehall, the fifth day of June, 1610* (London, 1610). Daniel's defensive preface to the published text indicates that he again expects "detraction and opposition"—evidently from the partisans of Jonson. The masque is notably static and pageantlike, but Daniel asserts, in direct contradiction to Jonson, that he regards the masque as essentially spectacle: "The arte and invention of the Architect [Inigo Jones] gives the greatest grace, and is of most importance; ours, the least part." John Pilcher offers a persuasive defense of Daniel's complex masque aesthetics, "'In those figures which they seeme': Samuel Daniel's *Tethys' Festival*," in Lindley, *Court Masque,* 33–46.

95. John Fynett to Mr. Trumbull, Winwood, *Memorials,* III, 179–180. In his printed text Daniel opposed his kind of antimasque to Jonson's: "And in all these shewes, this is to be noted, that there were none of inferiour sort, mixed amongst these great Personages of State and Honour (as usually there have beene) but all was performed by themselves with a due reservation of their dignity." Even the speaking parts were performed by gentlemen, not actors. Nichols, II, 357–358.

96. The Countess of Arundel was Nymph of Arun, the Countess of Derby Nymph of Derwent, the Countess of Essex Nymph of Lee, the Countess of Dorset Nymph of Ayr, the Countess of Montgomery Nymph of Severn, the Viscountess Haddington Nymph of Rother, the Lady Elizabeth Gray Nymph of Medway, and the four daughters of the Earl of Worcester—Ladies Elizabeth Guildford, Katherine Petre, Anne Winter, and Catherine Windsor—the Nymphs respectively of the rivers Dulesse, Olwy, Wye, and Usk in Monmouthshire.

97. Correr's report is dated January 21, 1611, *Cal. SP Venetian,* XII (1610–1613), 110. The published text, *A Masque of Her Majesties. Love Freed from Ignorance and Folly,* appeared first in Jonson's *Folio* of 1616.

98. Thomas Campion, *The Description of a Maske: Presented in the Banqueting roome at Whitehall, on Saint Stephens night last, at the Mariage of the Right Honourable the Earle of Somerset. And the right noble the Lady Frances Howard* (London, 1614). In order to marry the King's favorite, Somerset, Frances Howard obtained a divorce from her husband, Essex, claiming him impotent and herself still a virgin and suborning witnesses to support those claims (Essex admitted himself impotent, though only with her). Somerset's friend Overbury, who opposed the marriage, was imprisoned, and subsequently poisoned, in the Tower by the Somersets' machinations. The affair culminated in their notorious trial, conviction, and imprisonment.

99. The Buckingham-Jonson-Jones dominance in producing court masques was fixed after 1614. Apparently there was an abortive ladies' masque planned by Lady Hay and eight others for the Twelfth Night ceremonies of 1618, but as Chamberlain wrote Carleton on January 3, "They had taken great pains in continual practising, and were almost perfect, and all their implements provided; but, whatsoever the cause was, neither the Queen nor King did like or allow of it,—and so all is dashed." Nichols, III, 454.

100. *Hymens Triumph. A Pastorall Tragicomaedie. Presented at the Queenes Court in the Strand at her Maiesties magnificent intertainement of the Kings most excellent Maiestie, being at the Nuptials of the Lord Roxborough* (London, 1615).

101. Chamberlain to Carleton, November 25, 1613: "The Queen will [make] . . . a maske of maides, yf they may be found; and that is all the charge she meanes to be at, saving the brides wedding gowne and the marriage bed, wherin she will not

exceed 500[li], for she saith her maide Drummond is rich enough otherwise, as well in wealth as in virtue and favor." Chamberlain, I, 487.

102. Nichols, III, 246.

103. Published in Nichols, III, 283–296. The conceit is that Occasion, Diana, Hymen, and others affirm the values of Chastity and display the young maids conquering the lustful Cupid. The dedication to the Countess of Bedford thanks her for "the honorable furtherance and noble encouragement your Ladyship gave us in presentinge our Maske to her Majesty." The Queen's goddaughters are Anne Sandelands and Anne Chaloner. On the evidence of the masque, music, dancing, and needlework were major activities at the school.

104. Ibid., 285, 296.

2. Scripting a Heroine's Role: Princess Elizabeth

1. H. S. Bennett, *English Books and Readers* (Cambridge: Cambridge University Press, 1970); Louis B. Wright, *Middle-Class Culture in Elizabethan England* (Chapel Hill: University of North Carolina Press, 1935). John Lyly claims to address a female readership in *Euphues;* Sidney addresses the *Arcadia* to the Countess of Pembroke; Spenser identifies Queen Elizabeth as primary reader of the *Faerie Queene.*

2. The very popular Continental romances were all available in English translation in the Jacobean era. The *Amadís de Gaula* (originally published 1508) went through hundreds of editions in many languages; the first four books were translated by Anthony Munday as *The Ancient, Famous and Honourable History of Amadis de Gaule* (London, 1619). Jorge de Montemayor's *Diana* (Valencia, 1559) was translated by B. Yong (London, 1598), with a second part by A. Perez and also a continuation entitled *Enamoured Diana* by G. Gil Polo. The first part of Honoré D'Urfé's *L'Astrée* (Paris, 1607) was translated anonymously as *The History of Astrea* (London, 1620). On May 11, 1622, Chamberlain wrote to Carleton that James had asked Ben Jonson to translate Barclay's *Argenis* (Paris, 1621). Chamberlain, II, 435–436. An English version was published in 1625 by Kingsmill Long and another (with a key) in 1629 by Sir Robert Le Grys.

3. "Mes pensées sont bien a mon cher Astre qui j'aymeray jusques a la mort parfaictment." August 1622, SP 81 (Germany States) 26/179v. "Continuez toujours à aimer votre pouvre Celedon, & assurez-vous que ses pensees sont continuelles à son astre." September 1622, in *Collection of Original Royal Letters,* ed. Sir George Bromley (London, 1837), 22. Frederick wrote hundreds of letters to Elizabeth ("Mon cher unique coeur"), usually signing himself "votre très-fidele amie, & tres-affectionné serviteur."

4. September 13, 1638; April 12, 1638; May 28, 1639, in *The Letters of Elizabeth, Queen of Bohemia,* ed. L. M. Baker (London: Bodley Head, 1953), 106, 101, 130. This edition contains many, but by no means all, of Elizabeth's letters.

5. SP 16 (Charles I) 352/41; cf. SP 16, 317/12.

6. *Letters of Elizabeth* (from 1655), 210, 248–249, 264, 272–273. Queen Candace of Ethiopia figures in the classical historians Dio Cassius and Josephus; Elizabeth may also have remembered her from Jonson's *Masque of Queens.* Artaxerxes may have been taken from Xenophon's *Cyropaedia* or from Plutarch. The story of Berenice (Queen of Palestine), Titus, and Arsace is told in Josephus and Dio Cassius,

but Elizabeth may have had the Berenice story from Mme. de Scudéry's popular *Les Femmes Illustres* (1642).

7. For discussion of this Spenserian fusion and its influence, see Norbrook, *Poetry and Politics in the English Renaissance,* 121–124, 195–234.

8. Northrop Frye, *The Secular Scripture: A Study of the Structure of Romance* (Cambridge, Mass.: Harvard University Press, 1976), 172.

9. The chief biographies of Elizabeth are Elizabeth Benger, *Memoirs of Elizabeth Stuart, Queen of Bohemia* (London, 1825); Mary Anne Everett [Wood] Green, *Elizabeth Electress Palatine and Queen of Bohemia;* rev. S. C. Lomas (London: Methuen, 1901); Carola Oman, *Elizabeth of Bohemia* (London: Hodder & Stoughton, 1938); Josephine Ross, *The Winter Queen* (New York: St. Martin's Press, 1979). She is treated at some length also in her daughter Sophie's memoir, *Memoiren der Herzogin Sophie Nachmals Kurfürstin von Hannover,* ed. A. Kocher (Leipzig, 1879), and in Bergeron, *Royal Family.*

10. The young Elizabeth's letters to James are filled with conventional sentiments of duty and obedience; those to Henry beg to spend more time with him. Several letters to Prince Henry (chiefly in French) are in BL, Harleian MS 6986, ff. 80–152; some to James in the early years of her marriage are in *Letters to King James the Sixth . . . From the Originals in the Library of the Faculty of Advocates* (Edinburgh: Maitland Club, 1835).

11. Lord Harington (of Exton) to Sir John Harington, January 6, 1607, in *Nugae Antiquae: Being a Miscellaneous Collection of Original Papers . . . by Sir John Harington, Knt. and by others,* ed. Henry Harington; rev. Thomas Park, 2 vols. (London, 1804), II, 375; Harington of Exton, *Accounts Book, Exchequer of Receipt, Miscellanea,* cited in Green, *Elizabeth Electress Palatine,* 24.

12. BL, Harleian MS. 6989, f. 24.

13. January 1, 1608, "Pour Madame la Princesse, je vous assure qu'il me tiendra jamais à elle qu'elle me soit Dauphine . . . Elle est belle, de bonne grace, fort bien nourrie, & parle très-bien Francais, beaucoup mieux que son frere." La Boderie, *Ambassades,* III, 6.

14. James is quoted as saying "that even a Man who was vain and foolish, was made more so by Learning, and as for Women, who he said were all naturally addicted to Vanity, where it did one good, it did harm to twenty." [Erskine], *Memoirs,* 109. Samuel de Sorbiere (June 3, 1652) states that Elizabeth taught her daughters "les six languages qu'elle parle fort eloquement," specifying among them Latin. *Lettres et Discours* (Paris, 1660), 74. Elizabeth was evidently good at languages and may have learned Latin later; there are no schoolgirl letters in Latin.

15. In *Nugae Antiquae,* II, 411–416.

16. Sir Edward Hoby reported her near escape to Sir Thomas Edmonds, ambassador to Brussels (November 19, 1605), in Thomas Birch, *Court and Times of James the First,* 2 vols. (London, 1849), I, 39.

17. *Nugae Antiquae,* II, 373–334. Elizabeth expressed her sentiments further in a letter to Prince Henry, thanking God for his deliverance (Nichols, III, 1068): "Je ne doubte pas que vous n'ayez rendu graces a nostre bon Dieu, de la delivrance qu'il nous a donnée, comme j'ay aussy fait et fais en mon particulier; mais je veux joindre mes voeuz auls vostre, et dire avec vous, 'Si le Seigneur est pour nous, qui sera contre nous? en sa garde je ne craindray rien que l'homme puisse faire.'"

18. Thomas Rosa [Scoto-Britanna], *Idaea, Sive de Jacobi Magnae Britanniae, Galliae et Hyberniae* (London, 1608), 322–323:

Huic ingenium acutum, memoria tenax, iudicium supra aetatulam acre. Pie-
tate *Flavium Clementii* Romani Consulis filiam, *Faustam & Eulaliam* adae-
quat . . . Linguarum cognitione & varietate *Zenobiae* Palmirianorum Reginae,
Aretiae & Corneliae comparanda est, aut anteponenda. Musicam etiam dili-
genter ex coluit, qua in arte plurimum profecit . . . Huic morum suavitas,
liberalium mentis corporisque exercitationum quae Regiam decent virginem,
haud vulgaris peritia: denique quicquid excellens excelsumque in *Elizabetha*
Angliae Regina, id omne in una hac virgine Principe pro aetate compactum,
& si illam nobis superstitem servaverit Deus, accumulatum reperietur.

19. Lanyer, *Salve Deus,* sigs. a 4v, b

20. H&S, VII, 323–336, ll. 431–435; cf. X, 508–517.

21. La Boderie, *Ambassades,* III, 6–7. Prince Henry wanted such an alliance,
and hoped to join Henry IV in an anti-Hapsburg campaign. He reportedly prom-
ised Elizabeth not to consent to a French princess for himself unless she became
Dauphiness. But the new regent, Marie de Medici, looked to alliances with Spain.
See Roy Strong, *Henry, Prince of Wales, and England's Lost Renaissance* (London:
Thames and Hudson, 1986), 76.

22. The Swedish Prince Gustavus Adolphus was at odds with Queen Anne's
brother the King of Denmark; Frederick Ulric, Duke of Brunswick, Maurice of
Nassau, and Otto of Hesse (kin to Queen Anne) were thought too inferior in
rank; and two English suitors of the Howard family, Henry, Earl of Northampton,
and Theophilus, Lord Howard of Walden, were summarily dismissed. Strong,
Henry, Prince of Wales, 77–79, calls attention to the cultural and diplomatic inter-
play between England and the small German states whose rulers were the Queen's
kinfolk. See also Oman, *Elizabeth of Bohemia,*

23. Chamberlain to Carleton, December 18, 1611, SP 14 (James I) 67/42; Beaulieu to Trumbull, February 21, 1611, Winwood, *Memorials,* III, 341.

24. *The Life and Letters of Sir Henry Wotton,* ed. Logan Pearsall Smith, 2 vols.
(Oxford, 1907), I, 113ff.; Winwood, *Memorials,* III, 27. Ralegh, responding to
Prince Henry's request for his opinion, marshaled the case against Savoy: Elizabeth's perfections, both of body and mind, make her a "worthy spouse for the
greatest monarch in Christendom"; the Savoy Prince "could neither stead us in
time of war nor trade with us in time of peace"; she would be isolated in a strange
place; and her children "must all be bred and brought up contrary to her conscience." *Works,* 8 vols. (Oxford, 1829), VIII, 234–235. A match for Henry with the
Savoy princess was under consideration at the time of Henry's death. Strong,
Henry, Prince of Wales, 82–83.

25. Strong, *Henry, Prince of Wales,* 78–79; Winwood, *Memorials,* III, 410, 420,
489.

26. Fynett to Trumbull, October 23, 1612, Winwood, *Memorials,* III, 403. Cf.
Antonio Foscarini's account, November 9, 1612, *Cal. SP Venetian,* XII (1610–1613),
443–444.

27. Chamberlain to Carleton, October 22, 1612, Chamberlain, I, 380–382;
Chamberlain to Winwood, November 3, 1612, Winwood, *Memorials,* III, 406.

28. R. Coke, *Detection of the Court and State of England* (London, 1719), I, 73;
G. P. V. Akrigg, *Jacobean Pageant* (Cambridge, Mass.: Harvard University Press,
1962), 143; Winwood, *Memorials,* III, 421.

29. Contemporary reports blamed a "tertian ague" or a fever brought on by

eating grapes or overmuch exercise in the night air; some even suspected poison at the hands of the King's favorite, Somerset, perhaps with the connivance of the King himself to remove his too popular and often antagonistic son and rival. See Sir Charles Cornwallis's account in Nichols, II, 451–453, 470–487, and Birch, *Court and Times of James*, I, 201–205, for the various speculations, as well as the macabre regime of bloodlettings, pigeons, cordials, and purges the frantic physicians tried. Ralegh sent a concoction, but said it was tried too late. For the typhoid diagnosis, see Norman Moore, *Illness & Death of Henry, Prince of Wales in 1612, an Historical Case of Typhoid Fever* (London, 1882).

30. Chamberlain to Carleton, November 12, 1612, Chamberlain, I, 390.

31. See the long (but partial) list in Nichols, II, 504–512, and in E. C. Wilson, *Prince Henry and English Literature* (Ithaca: Cornell University Press, 1946).

32. Frank Kermode, in the introduction to the Arden *Tempest* (Cambridge, Mass.: Harvard University Press, 1954), xxii, summarizes this tradition as well as contemporary reports that Elizabeth, Prince Charles, and the Elector attended "fowerteene severall playes" at Whitehall around this time, six of them by Shakespeare: *Much Ado, The Tempest, The Winter's Tale, Merry Wives, Othello,* and *Julius Caesar.*

33. Chamberlain, I, 418. For other reports of her opposition and change of attitude, see Chamberlain to Winwood, January 9 and February 23, 1613, Winwood, *Memorials*, III, 421, 434; Chamberlain to Carleton, December 31, 1612, and February 11, 1613, Chamberlain, I, 399, 404, 421, 427.

34. *The Magnificent Marriage of the Two Great Princes Frederick Count Palatine, &c. and the Lady Elizabeth, Daughter to the Imperial Majesties of King James and Queen Anne, to the Comfort of All Great Britain* (London, 1613), in Nichols, II, 542–544. James valued Elizabeth's coronet at £1 million and jewels worn by other family members at £900,000. Arthur Wilson's account emphasized the emblematic aspects: "Her vestments were White, the Emblem of Innocency"; her train was supported by young ladies, "in White Garments so adorned with Jewels, that her Passage looked like a Milky-Way." Quoted in Oman, *Elizabeth of Bohemia*, 82.

35. Chamberlain to Alice Carleton (February 18, 1613), Chamberlain, I, 424.

36. Cited in Oman, *Elizabeth of Bohemia*, 83.

37. "An Epithalamion, or Mariage Song on the Lady Elizabeth, and Count Palatine being married on St. Valentines Day," in *John Donne: The Epithalamions, Anniversaries, and Epicedes,* ed. W. Milgate (Oxford: Clarendon, 1978), 6–10. The two-line reference to progeny occurs in stanza two: Elizabeth and Frederick, as two phoenixes, are said to be nests for each other "Where motion kindles such fires, as shall give / Yong Phoenixes, and yet the old shall live" (ll. 24–25). In the final stanzas, where we expect wishes for progeny, we find none. A temporary gender reversal compliments Elizabeth and her higher rank by making her a "shee Sunne" to his "hee Moone," but then equalizes them—"each is both." For an extended analysis of the poem, see Heather Dubrow, "Tradition and the Individualistic Talent: Donne's 'An Epithalamion, or Mariage Song on the Lady Elizabeth,'" in Claude Summers and Ted-Larry Pebworth, eds., *The Eagle and the Dove: Reassessing John Donne* (Columbia: University of Missouri Press, 1986); also Dubrow, *The Happier Eden: The Politics of Marriage in the Stuart Epithalamion* (Ithaca: Cornell University Press, 1990), 164–177. George Herbert's brief Latin epithalamium for the couple, presented to Frederick at his visit to Cambridge University,

focuses on the bride's beauty and the wedding day; it makes no reference whatever to progeny. Leicester Bradner, "New Poems by George Herbert: The Cambridge Latin Gratulatory Anthology of 1613," *Renaissance News*, 15 (1962), 208–211.

38. Thomas Campion, *A Relation of the Late Royall Entertainment . . . Whereunto is annexed the Description, Speeches, and Songs of the Lords Maske, presented in the Banquetting-house on the Marriage night of the High and Mightie, Count Palatine, and the royally descended the Ladie Elizabeth* (London, 1613), sig. D.

39. The Latin reads:

Quam pulchra pulchro sponsa respondet viro!
Quam plena numinis? Patrem vultu exprimit,
Parens futura masculae prolis, Parens
Regum, imperatorum: Additur Germaniae
Robur Britannicum. ecquid esse par potest?
Utramque junget una mens gentem, fides,
Deique Cultus unus, & simplex amor.
Idem erit utrique hostis, sodalis idem, idem
Votum periclitantium, atque eadem manus.
Favebit illis Pax, favebit bellica
Fortuna, semper aderit Adjutor Deus.

(sig. D 3)

40. Strong, *Henry, Prince of Wales*, 176–177.

41. Antonio Foscarini's dispatch of November 9, 1612, *Cal. SP Venetian*, XII (1610–1613), 444.

42. The most complete of the several contemporary tracts describing these spectacles was by John Taylor (the Water Poet), *Heavens Blessing and Earths Joy, or A true relation, of the supposed Sea-Fights & Fire-workes, as were accomplished, before the Royall Celebration, of the al-beloved Mariage, of the two peerlesse Paragons of Christendome, Fredericke & Elizabeth. With Triumphall Encomiasticke Verses* (London, 1613).

43. On February 18, 1613, Chamberlain wrote to Carleton: "The King and all the companie took so little delight to see no other activitie but shooting and potting of gunnes, that yt is quite geven over, and the navie unrigged, and the castle pulled downe, the rather for that there were divers hurt in the former fight (as one lost both his eyes, another both his handes, another one hande, with divers others maymed and hurt." Chamberlain, I, 423.

44. George Chapman, *The Memorable Maske of the Two Honorable Houses or Inns of Court, The Middle Temple and Lyncoln's Inne; as it was performed before the King at Whitehall on Shrove Monday at Night, being the 15th of February, 1612–1613* (London, 1613). The designer was Inigo Jones. See Strong, *Henry, Prince of Wales*, 178.

45. Francis Beaumont, *The Masque of the Inner Temple and Gray's Inne; Presented before His Majesty, the Queen's Majesty, The Prince Count Palatine, and the Lady Elizabeth their Highnesses, in the Banqueting-House at Whitehall on Saturday the 20th day of February 1612–1613*, in Nichols, II, 591–600. Strong, *Henry, Prince of Wales*, 180, speculates plausibly that a barriers (jousts of knights on horseback) would have made a more satisfactory conclusion. Chamberlain's letter to Carleton of February 18 describes the contretemps over this performance, as the masquers were not allowed to perform as scheduled on the sixteenth, partly because the room was so crowded that the masquers themselves could not get in, but chiefly because "the

King was so wearied and sleepie with setting up almost two whole nights before, that he had no edge to yt." Chamberlain, I, 426. On that same Saturday, Marston's *Dutch Courtesan* was presented by the bride's own players, the Lady Elizabeth's Company—a curious choice, it would seem.

46. This masque, summarized and partly translated in D. Joquet, *Les Triomphes, Entrees, Cartels, Journois, Ceremonies, et Aultres Magnificences, Faites en Angleterre, & au Palatinat* (Heidelberg, 1613), sigs. H–H 4v, was mistakenly described by Joquet as the Tuesday entertainment. Strong argues the probability of the substitution after Henry's death, of which Joquet was unaware. *Henry, Prince of Wales,* 181. This masque is also discussed in David Norbrook, "The Reformation of the Masque," in Lindley, *Court Masque,* 99.

47. Thomas Heywood, *A Marriage Triumphe Solemnized in an Epithalamium, In Memorie of the happie Nuptials betwixt the High and Mightie Prince Count Palatine. And the Most Excellent Princesse the Lady Elizabeth* (London, 1613), sig. Ev. See the partial listing of celebratory works in English and Latin in Nichols, II, 624–626. Oxford University produced 238 Latin epithalamia.

48. Henry Peacham, *Minerva Britanna, or a Garden of Heroical Devises* (London, [1612]), sig. P 4; Peacham, *The Period of Mourning. Disposed into Six Visions. In Memorie of the late Prince. Together with Nuptiall Hymnes, in Honour of this Happy Marriage between the Great Princes, Frederick, Count Palatine of the Rhine, and The Most Excellent and Aboundant President of all Virtue and Goodness, Elizabeth* (London, 1613). Many texts, like this one, combine mourning for Henry with epithalamic celebrations.

49. Joannis Maria de Franchis, *De Auspicatissimis Nuptiis.* (London, 1613); *Of the Most Auspicatious Marriage; Betwixt the High and Mightie Prince Frederick . . . And the Most Illustrious Princesse, the Ladie Elizabeth Her Grace . . . In Three Bookes* (London, 1613), 15, 21.

50. George Webb, *The Bride Royall, or The Spirituall Marriage betweene Christ and his Church Delivered by way of congratulation upon the happy and hopefull marriage betweene the two incomparable Princes, the Palsgrave and the Ladie Elizabeth* (London, 1613). The tract notes that Frederick's ancestors were the first of all the European Princes to set themselves against the Pope and bring in the name of Protestantism.

51. George Wither, *Epithalamia: Or, Nuptiall Poems upon the most blessed and happie mariage betweene the High and Mightie Prince Frederick . . . and the most gracious and thrice excellent Princesse, Elizabeth* (London, 1612 [1613]), sigs. B 2v–B 3, D 2.

52. See, for example, [Anon.], *The Magnificent, Princely, and most Royall Entertainments given to the High and Mightie Prince and Princesse, Frederick, Count Palatine, Palsgrave of the Rhyne: and Elizabeth, sole Daughter to the High and Mighty King of England, James, our Soveraigne Lord. Together with a true relation of all the Gifts, Presentations, Showes, Fire-workes, and other sumptuous Triumphs in every place where the said Princes were lodged, and received, after their landing upon the Coasts of Germany* (London, 1613); James Maxwell, *A Monument of Remembrance Erected in Albion in Honor of the Magnificent Departure from Britannie, and Honorable Receiving in Germany, Namely at Heidelberge, of the Two Most Noble Princes Fredericke . . . & Elizabeth* (London, 1613).

53. Elizabeth's crossbow invited much comment, since the Palatine custom was

to use lances: "Her Grace shot twelve deer with her cross-bow, and at last, from her horse, she shot at a stag of the second head, struck it in the ham and brought it to the ground; whereat the Elector and the princes were much surprised." Quoted in Oman, *Elizabeth of Bohemia,* 116; cf. ibid., 122, 125. Salomon de Caus, *Hortus Palatinus* (Frankfurt, 1620); cf. Frances B. Yates, *The Rosicrucian Enlightenment* (London: Routledge, 1972), 11–13, and ills. 5 and 6.

54. Reports of the pregnancy, confirmed by the physicians and all the usual "tokens and probabilities," were reported by correspondents in Brussels and London; see Winwood, *Memorials,* III, 407. After the birth, writing to the Duchess de la Tremoille on February 14, 1614, Elizabeth attributes her "petite dissimulation" to her "inexperience," her unwillingness to raise "des vaines esperances," and her wish to avoid "de payer d'apparence où je doibs des effects." *Letters of Elizabeth,* 35. Much later, her daughter Sophie commented caustically that Elizabeth cared more for her monkeys and little dogs than for her children; however exaggerated, the remark probably points to less-than-intense maternal feelings; see *Memoiren,* 34.

55. SP 81 (Germany States) 14/205; Wotton, *Life and Letters,* II, 89. James settled £2,000 per annum on his daughter to testify his delight; bells rang; bonfires and fireworks were set off in London and Edinburgh. Among the congratulatory tracts and poems was Josuah Sylvester's *Little Bartas* (London, 1614), offered to Elizabeth to congratulate "your little PALATINE."

56. Chamberlain to Winwood, March 10, 1612, Winwood, *Memorials,* III, 441. He notes that the prodigiously expensive wedding forced immediate retrenchments, including the dispersal of the Elector's separate household, "which the Lady Elizabeth's Highness took very grievously, and not without Cause, but that necessity hath no Law." The only companions of her journey who were close to her were her guardians, Lord and Lady Harington, who soon returned to England, and Anne Dudley, who remained as her chief maid of honor. Her permanent household in Heidelberg numbered ninety-seven persons by one account, though none of rank. Her letter of April 20, 1613, to Sir Julius Caesar asks payment to her jeweler for rings given as gifts. *Letters of Elizabeth,* 33.

57. Schomberg was given a salary by James to serve as Elizabeth's adviser and steward. He explains the basic problem in several letters to King James and to Somerset (now Rochester): "Madame allows herself to be led by anyone, and is almost afraid to speak for fear of giving offence." SP 81 (Germany States) 12/175; cf. ibid., 12/223. He had her subscribe to various common-sense rules: Never grant anything on the first request; never be teased into countermanding an order; be more severe with servants; "let it be known that you will be ruled by Reason, that you abhor disobedience, flattery, and lying." SP 81 (Germany States) 14/221–223. Winwood, *Memorials,* II, 90.

58. SP 81 (Germany States) 14/93: "Jay nourry le Prince, reforme cest cour, installe Madam, maintenu la balance propre a la conformation de leurs HH ay offence un chacun pour servir bien a sa Majestie & a Madame & tellement que sa Majestie vente vere jamais avec verite reproche ny representation avec gens si jeunes maries assister se peu delaisser d'un chacun flatter cest moy seul qui ay ce fardeau ny sur les epaules."

59. Frederick's melancholy and the Dowager's pressures are the subject of a letter from Elizabeth to Sir Ralph Winwood in October 1614, SP 81 (Germany

States) 13/242: "He is verie heavie and so extremlie melancholie as I never saw in my life so great an alteration in anie. I cannot tell what to say to it, but I think he hath so much bussiness at this time as troubles his mind too much, but if I may say truth I think there is some that doth trouble him too much, for I find they desire he should bring me to be all dutch and to theyre fashions . . . I think they doe the Prince wrong, in putting into his head at this time when he is but too malincholie."

60. Wotton supplied James (April 23, 1616) with a lengthy report on the problems over Elizabeth's precedence—the pressures on Frederick from the Dowager Electress and other German princes, and Frederick's own sense that he would be "diminished" if he defied Germanic custom. Wotton, *Life and Letters,* II, 90. At length the matter of precedence was settled by default, as Frederick made a practice of visiting other German princes without his consort.

61. In June 1616 James wrote to Frederick, "Vous vous pouvez asseurer que jamais pere ne s'esvertuera plus que moy de faire sa fille humblement obeissante á son mary, mais en ce qui concerne sa qualité et l'honneur de sa naissaine, ell seroit indigne de vivre si elle quitteroit sa place sans mon sçeu et advis"; to Elizabeth he wrote, "Je vous remerecie de tout mon coeur que vous, n'avez voulu ceder en ce qui concerne la qualité de vostre naissance sans mon consentement." *The Fortescue Papers,* ed. S. R. Gardiner (London: Camden Society, 1871), 13–14.

62. Elizabeth wrote to James several times in 1615 explaining her need to pawn jewels to cover the gift giving en route to Heidelberg and her gift of jeweled buttons to a faithful, long-serving maid of honor at her departure, actions James objected to. In both cases she explains with some spirit her need to behave properly and her lack of adequate resources. SP 81 (Germany States) 14/17, 73, 105.

63. For recognition of this and some other "romance" elements of Princess Elizabeth's early life, I am indebted to Nick Halpern. James seems to have worried that the couple would have too much sway over Elizabeth, but her letters firmly insist on the fidelity and value of them both. To Winwood (May 19, 1614) she reiterates that Schomberg's service is necessary "for my good as well as the Princes" and that the only way to keep him in her service is to allow the marriage. On April 16, 1615, she wrote to James: "Your majesty desired to know what Dudley hath in charge she hath nothing but some plate that was given me since my coming hither though I assure your majesty I have nothing to keepe that I should not put sooner into her care and trust than anie creatures." On May 28 she wrote to him again: "I . . . am well contented with both theire service, and must confess that none in this state hath had care or done so much for me, my good ranke, reputation and profitt as Schonberg." SP 81 (Germany States) 14/73, 105.

64. SP 81 (Germany States) 14/258; Oman, *Elizabeth of Bohemia,* 152.

65. Letters sent by the various ambassadors to London—Julian Sanchez de Ulloa (Spain), Pietro Marioni (Venice), and Noel de Caron (United Provinces)—in September 1619 agree on the details: James's irritation at the news of the crown offered to Frederick; his postponement of an answer to Frederick's messenger, Baron Dohna; his vacillation after Frederick accepted the crown and asked for aid; and the contradictory pressures affecting him: desire to keep well with Spain; pleasure in seeing his daughter a Queen; anger at Frederick's decision taken before he sent his advice; awareness of widespread support for the Bohemian venture in his Council and throughout Protestant Europe. See *Letters and Other Documents*

Illustrating the Relations Between England and Germany at the Commencement of the Thirty Years' War, ed. S. R. Gardiner (London: Camden Society, 1868), 24–27, 35–38, 139–142.

66. Frederick's letter to the Elector of Saxony was reported in *Mercure Francais,* 6 (Paris, 1619), 137: "Quel blasme on in impureroit d'avoir refusé la legitime & ordinaire vocation de Dieu."

67. An often-reported but unsupported tale has it that she told her husband she "would sooner eat sauerkraut at a king's table than feast on delicacies with an Elector." Oman, *Elizabeth of Bohemia,* 172. Hapsburg caricatures of the defeated Elizabeth and Frederick often depict the Winter King as a fugitive or a menial with his socks falling down, in allusion to the loss of his much-treasured Garter Knight's emblem during his hasty departure from Prague.

68. F. von Moser, *Patriotisches Archiv* (Mannheim, 1787), VII, 47. See discussion in Oman, *Elizabeth of Bohemia,* 172–173.

69. See the letter of the English ambassador in France, Sir Edward Herbert (of Cherbury), to Sir Robert Naunton on September 19, 1619: "God forbid he [Frederick] should refuse yt [the offer of Bohemia], being the apparent way His providence hath opened to the ruine of the Papacie. I hope therfore his Majestie will assist in this great work." *Letters and Other Documents,* 13.

70. Chamberlain, II, 284–287.

71. Lord Doncaster, sent by James to Heidelberg and Frankfurt to try to settle the Bohemian problem, reported enthusiastically on the Palatine rulers in June 1619. He praised Frederick's "worth beyond his years" and his valiant courage as leader of the armies of the Union; Elizabeth he extolled as the "same devoute good sweet princess" the King's daughter should be, "obliging all hearts that come neere her by her courtesy." SP 81 (Germany States) 16/52. Donne accompanied Doncaster on that visit, preaching before Frederick and Elizabeth on June 16 on the apposite text (Rom. 13:11), "For now is our salvation nearer than when we believed." *The Sermons of John Donne,* ed. George R. Potter and Evelyn M. Simpson, 10 vols. (Berkeley: University of California Press, 1953–1962), II, 250–268. His second sermon for them does not survive.

72. Frederick consulted Doncaster in October about the safe disposition of Elizabeth in England; James did not want her there, and Doncaster (happily for him) was able to report "her owne vehement inclination and almost inexorableness to the contrary." Oman, *Elizabeth of Bohemia,* 176–177.

73. [John Harrison], *A Short relation of the Departure of the High and Mightie Prince Frederick King Elect of Bohemia; with his Royall & Virtuous Ladie Elizabeth . . . to receive the Crowne of that Kingdome. Whereunto is annexed the Solemnpnitie or maner of that coronation* (Dort, 1619), sigs. A iii v–A iv. At the borders of Bohemia, Baron Rupa thanked Elizabeth for her part in Frederick's decision, to which she responded in French that she did what she did "for the honor of God and the good of our religion," and promised her continued support.

74. "Relation of the Coronation of the King of Bohemia, etc., with the Ceremonies and Prayers," *Mercurius Gallo-Belgicus,* xiii (Cologne, 1619), 97–104.

75. See Nethersole's dispatches on September 5, 1620, SP 81 (Germany States) 18/27, 33; 19/132–133.

76. Chamberlain to Alice Carleton, February 4, 1613, Chamberlain, I, 416.

77. Quoted in Oman, *Elizabeth of Bohemia,* 277.

78. Bromley, *Royal Letters,* 10–11. Frederick refers constantly to Elizabeth's welcome letters, but evidently he, or she, did not preserve them. His many letters to her continually proclaim his love and devotion; that she reciprocated is evident in a letter to Sir Thomas Roe (April 12, 1633) some months after his death: "Though I make a good show in company, yet I can never have any more contentment in this world, for God knows I had none but that which I took in his company, and he did the same in mine; for since he went from hence, he never failed writing me twice a week, and ever wished either me with him, or he with me." *Letters of Elizabeth,* 88.

79. SP 81 (Germany States) 19/193v, Nethersole to the Secretary of State, November 20, 1620. Cf. Oman, *Elizabeth of Bohemia,* 230, 241.

80. *Letters of Elizabeth,* 50.

81. *Letters and Other Documents,* 144: "Le Roy est party adjourd'hui vers la Moravie, et Silesie, et les autres provinces, pour recevoir leur serment et hommage. Je supplie trèshumblément V. M. d'avoir soing de son beaux fis et moy icy et de nous assister en ceste guerre; j'espère que le Baron de Dona aura desja satisfait V. M. touchant la bonne cause de ce pais icy."

82. *Fortescue Papers,* 138.

83. *Letters of Elizabeth,* 54.

84. SP 84 (Holland) 98/85.

85. *Letters of Elizabeth,* 57–58.

86. SP 81 (Germany States) 20/313, 329, 342; 21/155; 27/72; 30/16, 29, 216.

87. SP 81 (Germany States) 27/192; 29/120; cf. 21/30, 216.

88. James conveyed his wishes bluntly in a letter to Carleton: "If our daughter also do come into those parts, with any intention to transport herself hither, you do use all possible means at this time to divert her; and rather than fail, to charge her, in our name and upon our blessing, that she do not come, without our good liking and pleasure first signified unto her." *Fortescue Papers,* 151; Bergeron, *Royal Family,* 150.

89. Chamberlain, II, 295–296, 300, 328, 410, 414. An account of the expeditionary forces is set forth by John Taylor (the Water Poet), *An English-mans Love to Bohemia: With a friendly Farewell to all the noble Souldiers that goe from Great Britaine to that honorable Expedition* (London, 1620). James refused to allow Southampton (a former supporter of Essex's rebellion) to go with a volunteer force.

90. Historical Manuscripts Commission, 21, *Hamilton MSS, Supplementary Report* (London: HM Stationery Office, 1932), 9 (undated).

91. Girolando Lando to the Doge, April 30, 1621, *Cal. SP Venetian,* XVII (1621–1623), 37–38.

92. SP 81 (Germany States) 17/94.

93. SP 81 (Germany States) 17/62. Elizabeth evoked such sentiment on the Continent as well and made political use of it. Prince Christian of Brunswick, her cousin, adored her in courtly-love fashion, wore her glove in his hat, had as his motto "for God and for her," swore to be her "constant, faithful, affectionate, and obedient slave" till death—and, more important, raised a 10,000-strong army to defend her rights. Oman, *Elizabeth of Bohemia,* 212–213.

94. *Reliquiae Wottonianae* (London, 1651), 518. Two poems, probably by George Herbert, were addressed to Elizabeth at the Hague shortly after the Bohemian fiasco. They proffer consolation in the apocalyptic mode, prophesying that

God and Elizabeth's children will defeat her enemies and restore her kingdoms. The poems are published in Ted-Larry Pebworth, "George Herbert's Poems to the Queen of Bohemia: A Rediscovered Text and a New Edition," *ELR,* 9 (1979), 108–120.

95. Mr. Meade to Sir Martin Stuteville, January 25, 1622, in Nichols, III, 751.

96. See [Thomas Scott], *Vox Populi, or Newes from Spayne, translated according to the Spanish coppie. Which may serve to forewarn both England and the United Provinces how farre to trust the Spanish pretences* (London, 1620); [Scott], *The Second Part of Vox Populi, or Gondomar appearing in the likenes of Matchiavell in a Spanish Parliament* (London, 1620); [Anon.], *Vox Regis* (London, [1622–1623?]); [Anon.], *Certaine Reasons and Arguments of Policie, Why the King of England should hereafter give over all further Treatie, and enter into Warre with the Spaniard* (n.p., 1624).

97. George Wither, *Wither's Motto. Nec Habeo, nec Careo, nec Curo* (London, 1621); see John Reynolds, *Vox Coeli* (Elisium [London], 1624). Ben Jonson satirized Wither's poem in his masque *Time Vindicated* (1623).

98. [Anon.], *Tom Tell-Troath: Or, A Free Discourse touching the Manners of the Time. Directed to his Majestie by Waye of humble Advertisement* [1622], in *Harleian Miscellany,* 10 vols. (London, 1809), II, 420–423.

99. March 28, 1623, SP 14 (James I) 140/57.

100. The firstborn son, Frederick Henry, had died on a military expedition at sea at age fifteen. If the Queen of Bohemia was not noted for maternal tenderness, her children (male and female) turned out to be quite remarkable. Her second son, Charles Lewis, was notably effective in restoring his war-ravaged country to prosperity, and was a discriminating patron of men of learning. Rupert (Prince Rupert of the Rhine) was a formidable soldier under Charles I, and a founding Fellow of the Royal Academy. Her daughter Elizabeth was a friend of Descartes, thought by him to possess one of the most remarkable minds in Europe. Louise was a talented painter, and Sophie was a philosopher and a patron of Leibnitz.

101. Historical Manuscripts Commission, 21, *Hamilton MSS, Supplementary Report,* 26.

102. July 27, 1636, *Letters of Elizabeth,* 94; in an earlier letter (June 1, 1636) she explains that she does not believe her son can be restored except by arms: "Sixteen years makes me believe it" (93).

103. H. R. Trevor-Roper, *Religion, the Reformation, and Social Change* (London: Macmillan, 1967), 256, points to this patronage and argues the need for a careful study of Elizabeth's court-in-exile. Yates, *Rosicrucian Enlightenment,* 174–178, supplies a few more facts. Elizabeth later turned against Dury for his support of Cromwell and the Regicide.

104. Sorbiere, *Lettres et Discours,* 74. A few other writings by Elizabeth are extant. Green notes (*Elizabeth Electress Palatine,* 95) that the library at Heidelberg has a small manuscript prayerbook in Elizabeth's handwriting, containing some prayers of her composition (MS 661, 690, 694).

105. After his restoration, Elizabeth's frequent letters to him often criticize and reproach him for his support for Parliament in the English Civil War, his ungrateful refusal to supply her needs from her jointure lands, and his open immorality in throwing over his wife for a mistress.

3. Writing Resistance in Letters: Arbella Stuart

1. The major biographies of Arbella Stuart are Elizabeth Cooper, *The Life and Letters of Lady Arabella Stuart*, 2 vols. (London, 1866); E. T. Bradley, *Life of the Lady Arabella Stuart*, 2 vols. (London, 1889); P. M. Handover, *Arbella Stuart: Royal Lady of Hardwick and Cousin to King James* (London: Eyre & Spottiswoode, 1957); David N. Durant, *Arbella Stuart: A Rival to the Queen* (London: Weidenfeld, 1978); and Ian McInnes, *Arabella: The Life and Times of Lady Arabella Seymour, 1575–1615* (London: W. H. Allen, 1968).

2. Many letters and relevant documents are printed in Bradley, *Life of Lady Arabella Stuart*, vol. 2, and Cooper, *Life and Letters*, vol. 2; the most important manuscript sources are BL, Harleian MSS 7003 and 6986; BL, Sloane MSS 4161 and 4164; and Hatfield House, Cecil Papers 135. BL, Additional MS 22,563 contains copies of her letters to her Aunt and Uncle Shrewsbury. Sara Jayne Steen, "Fashioning an Acceptable Self: Arbella Stuart," *ELR*, 18 (1988), 78–95, discusses revisions in drafts of the letters; Steen is preparing an edition of the letters of Arbella Stuart for the Oxford series of women writers.

3. Handover, *Arbella Stuart*, 17–26, 40–47. Arbella's royal pension was £200. Her mother's pension of £400 reverted to the crown at her death, despite Bess's efforts to retain it for Arbella. Bess of Hardwick was said to be the wealthiest woman in England after the Queen.

4. Ibid., 57.

5. SP 12 (Elizabeth) 153/39.

6. Burghley's words, reported by Arbella's uncle Charles Cavendish, were supposedly addressed to Ralegh in 1587 at court; he concluded by wishing her already fifteen, as if in reference to a desirable marriage. Quoted in Durant, *Arbella Stuart*, 45.

7. John Harington, *Tract on the Succession to the Crown* [1602?] (London: Roxburghe Club, 1880), 40–45. Ariosto's Drusilla uses skillful deception to revenge her murdered husband and at last joins him by taking a poison draught. The story offers interesting analogues to Arbella's later strategies of deception. Ariosto, *Orlando Furioso*, trans. James Harington (London, 1591), book 37, cantos 41–64.

8. The Venetian ambassador Nicoló Molin reported in 1607 that Arbella speaks "fluently Latin, Italian, French, Spanish, reads Greek and Hebrew, and is always studying." *Cal. SP Venetian*, X (1603–1607), 514.

9. Durant, *Arbella Stuart*, 50–73.

10. Among them Ludovic Stuart, son of Esmé and now Duke of Lennox (proposed by James); Henry Percy, Earl of Northumberland ("the wizard Earl"); Cardinal Farnese, the brother of Rainutio (proposed by the Pope, who would release him from his vows); Duke Mathias, brother to Archduke Albert, the Spanish ruler in the Netherlands; and the Prince of Condé, nephew to Henry IV. Durant, *Arbella Stuart*, 50–73.

11. Arbella to Sir Henry Brounker, Cecil Papers 135, f. 131v.

12. Ibid.

13. Cecil Papers 135, ff. 131v–134. Many years later Scaramelli attributed the banishment to her haughtiness in claiming precedence over the other royal prin-

cesses—but there were no other such princesses. February 27, 1603, *Cal. SP Venetian,* IX (1592–1603), 541.

14. In 1597 there was a report from Munich of another kidnapping plot by recusants and English exiles. Trouble was also caused by the publication of *A Conference About the Next Succession to the Crown of England* [Antwerp, 1594] ostensibly by R. Doleman (the Jesuit Robert Parsons), though in fact he only revised Richard Verstegan's text. The book purports to evaluate the claims of the various possible successors, and while it discounts Arbella's claim and presses those of the Spanish Infanta, it names Burghley as one who especially favored Arbella. While Doleman did not hold her chances very high, he suggested that she might well be malleable as to religion: "It may be supposed to be as tender green and flexible yet . . . to be wrought hereafter and settled according to future events and times" (141, 249). The English Cardinal Allen was also known to favor her. By 1602 Cecil had a report that Catholics on the Continent would be less likely to support her in future, having determined that she was a "notable Puritan" and therefore unlikely to convert or favor Catholic toleration. Bishop of London to Cecil, April 27, 1602, SP 12 (Elizabeth) 283A/86.

15. BL, Lansdowne MS 71, f. 2.

16. The Queens, Admirals, and Pembroke's Players visited Chatsworth and Hardwick during the period 1593–1600, as did many companies of musicians. Durant, *Arbella Stuart,* 82–83.

17. Edward Seymour, Earl of Hertford, secretly married Catherine Grey, sister of the tragic Lady Jane Grey, conjoining their independent claims to the throne; both were imprisoned in the Tower for life (Hertford was released eight years later, after the death of Catherine). The marriage was declared illegal, and the two sons were (for a time) illegitimate. It was to the son (Edward Seymour) of one of the sons of this marriage (Edward, Lord Beauchamp) that Arbella proposed herself.

18. Arbella's elaborate plan called for the young Seymour to visit Hardwick in the company of some older man pretending to have property to sell, and to bring with them some letter or memento of Lady Jane Grey "whose hand I know," or of Catherine Grey or Queen Jane Seymour. Some of Arbella's bold and precise, if wildly optimistic, directions to John Dodderidge are in Cecil Papers 135, f. 107. Her emissary Dodderidge (known also as John Good) was apprehended by Hertford, imprisoned, and often questioned. A clergyman at Hardwick, James Starkey, was also questioned at length about an earlier plot Arbella initiated with him; even though he had refused to become involved, he committed suicide in prison. His confession is in Cecil Papers 135, f. 175.

19. This is the position taken by Handover (*Arbella Stuart*) and Durant (*Arbella Stuart*); McInnes (*Arabella*) considers her derangement possibly feigned.

20. Cecil Papers 135, f. 114.

21. Ibid., f. 146.

22. Ibid., f. 128. Bess, furious with Arbella and at her wits' end as to how to cope with her, wrote to the Queen on January 9 urging that Arbella "may be placed elswhere, to lerne to be more considerate, and after that it may pleas your majestie eyther to accept of hir service about your majesties most Royall person, or to bestoe hir in mariage" (ibid., f. 112). She wrote again on January 29, lamenting the actions of "this unadvised yong woman" and urging that she be married,

declaring that she would not care "howe meanly soever she were bestowed, so as it were not offensive to your Highnes" (ibid., f. 127).

23. Ibid., ff. 144–144v.

24. Ibid., ff. 140v–141v.

25. Ibid., ff. 139–140.

26. Ibid., ff. 140–141v.

27. Ibid., ff. 147–147v.

28. Ibid., f. 150.

29. Ibid., ff. 153–155; another copy, 156–158. "The Examination of the Lady Arbella, the seconde of March, 1602 [1603]." The Council's concern was no doubt whetted by the spread of rampant and disconcerting rumors. At the end of February the Venetian ambassador had heard gossip about a match in hand between Seymour (he wrongly supposed it to be Thomas Seymour) and this beautiful, accomplished, and unhappy lady who "has lived so many years buried." February 27, 1603, *Cal. SP Venetian*, IX (1592–1603), 541.

30. Cecil Papers 135, ff. 142–142v.

31. Ibid.

32. Cecil Papers 92, f. 1. To Sir J. Stanhope (Vice-Chamberlain) and Sir R. Cecil, March 3, 1603: "I most earnestly beseech you both to be a mean to hir gratious Majestie for hir speedie remove, yt maye be the change of place will work some alteration in hir . . . She is so wilfully bent, and there is so little reason in moste of her doings that I can not tell what to make of yt. A fewe more such weekes as I have suffred of late will make an end of mee."

33. March 9, 1603, Cecil Papers 135, f. 130v: "Hir Majesties favour . . . I do not doubt of if it would please hir Majesty to take that course which hir Royall inclination would take with those of her own bloud, if it weare not to my great astonishment diverted from them, to those 2. counseller's kinred. They favour theyr kinred against hir Majesties, hir Majestie defendeth not hir innocent, unstained bloud against theyr mallice."

34. Ibid., ff. 138v, 166.

35. Ibid., ff. 159–160, 131v.

36. Ibid., ff. 134v, 163.

37. March 9, 1603, ibid., ff. 135, 165.

38. March 9, 1603, ibid., ff. 133v–136. Essex was executed February 25, 1601, Ash Wednesday.

39. Ibid., ff. 130, 136v–137v. Arbella also alludes (f. 159) to James's "unprincely and unchristian giving ear to the slanderous and unlikely surmise of the Earl of Essex and me"—a reference, it seems, to the speculation John Harington points to (*Succession*, 40): "The Earl of Essex, in some glancing speeches, gave occasion to have both himself and her honourable friends to be suspected of that which I suppose was no part of their meaning"—that is, to join in with Spanish plots to marry Arbella to a Catholic and support her title to the crown.

40. Ibid., ff. 167, 171–174; Bradley, *Life of Lady Arabella Stuart*, II, 172–175.

41. Cecil Papers 135, f. 177. The letter begins: "Forasmuch as we are desirous to free our cosin the Lady Arbella Stuart from that unpleasant life which she hath ledd in the howse of her grandmother with whose severity and age she being a younge Lady could hardly agree." Kent's nephew had married Arbella's cousin.

42. *Cal. SP Venetian,* X (1603–1607), 3.

43. Quoted in Handover, *Arbella Stuart,* 173. See "Certain Observations concerning the Life and Reign of Elizabeth of England," Sloane MS 718, f. 39.

44. Bodleian, MS Ashmole 1729, f. 80, and BL, Additional MS 22,563, f. 41. See also her letters to Cecil of June 14 (Cecil Papers 135, f. 176), and her thanks for the first grant, June 26, 1603 (Cecil Papers 100, f. 134) and June 30 (Cecil Papers 134, f. 39). Later she complained to her aunt of Cecil's actions in the matter (August 23, 1603, Sloane MS 4164, ff. 177v–178). In 1606 and 1609 she petitioned Cecil for patents for wines in Ireland (Cecil Papers 134, f. 94); and in December 1609 she asked that in lieu of these patents and her allowance for food she might have her debts paid and an additional £1,000—apparently to allow her more freedom to choose her residence. SP 14 (James I) 47/108.

45. Arbella to Mary Talbot, Countess of Shrewsbury, December 8, 1603, Additional MS 22,563, f. 45v; cf. ff. 41–41v.

46. An impost on oats was granted her in July 1608. Lodge, *Illustrations,* III, 354–355.

47. The prosecution of those involved in the "Main" Plot was engineered by Cecil to entrap Ralegh. The associated Bye Plot involved two Catholic priests who, together with the Puritan Lord Grey of Wilton, intended to kidnap James and Prince Henry until they agreed to a general pardon for the conspirators and greater religious toleration. The priests were found guilty and executed. Durant, *Arbella Stuart,* 126–129; Handover, *Arbella Stuart,* 179–191. Details of the trials are chiefly taken from BL, Harleian MS 39, ff. 275–278, and D. Jardine, *Criminal Trials* (London, 1832), I, 389–476.

48. Reported by Carleton to Chamberlain, November 27, 1603, Carleton, *Letters,* 39–40. See also Jardine, *Criminal Trials,* I, 408, 434, 466, and Nichols, I, 297. The Lord Admiral Nottingham, who was in the gallery with her, also rose in her defense, declaring: "The Lady doth here protest upon her salvation, that she never dealt in any of these things, and so she willed me to tell the Court." Jardine, *Criminal Trials,* I, 434.

49. To the Countess of Shrewsbury, December 8, 1603, Additional MS 22,563, f. 45; see also Sloane MS 4164, f. 184. In a letter dated December 18, 1603, to her uncle (Additional MS 22,563, f. 47) she also comments gratefully on Cecil's eloquence in defending a wronged lady (herself).

50. Fowler reported to Shrewsbury on October 3, 1604, about the overtures on behalf of Count Maurice of the Netherlands, and that the Polish ambassador intended to negotiate for Arbella's marriage to the King of Poland. Lodge, *Illustrations,* III, 236. William Pembroke wrote to Shrewsbury on the same day about the Polish King's suit. Additional MS 22,563, f. 46. Arbella herself reported to her uncle the arrival and audience of the Polonian ambassador, but says nothing about marriage negotiations. December 18, 1603, Additional MS 22,563, f. 47v.

51. To the Countess, August 23, 1603, Sloane MS 4164, f. 178. Arbella's letters are frequent; she promises at times to write weekly, but if she did so most of the letters are lost. Unfortunately, we do not have the Shrewsburys' side of the correspondence.

52. To Shrewsbury, September 16, 1603. Lodge, *Illustrations,* III, 177–178.

53. December 8, 1603, Additional MS 22,563, f. 44.

54. Ibid., f. 43.

55. From Hampton Court, December 18, 1603, Additional MS 22,563, f. 47.

56. To the Countess, n.d., Sloane MS 4164, f. 195. To the Countess, October 6, 1603, from Winchester, Sloane MS 4164, f. 179.

57. William Fowler to Shrewsbury, October 3, 1603, Lodge, *Illustrations,* III, 256.

58. August 14, 1603, to Shrewsbury, Additional MS 22,563, f. 46. In other letters to the Earl and Countess she takes notice of (but does not comment on) several masques and plays at court, often complains of her "bad eyes" and a raging toothache, reports gifts given and received, chides Shrewsbury for putting her in an awkward position by his secrecy, makes self-deprecating comments about her "unhandsome carving." See her letters to Shrewsbury from court, Sloane MS 6164, ff. 188–191.

59. The peerage was sold for £2,000, which no doubt Bess had to pay, along with gifts to Arbella as the agent. Arbella had been dropped from Bess's will in 1603, but was now reinstated, to receive the £1,000 initially provided.

60. March 15, 1607, Harleian MS 6896, f. 78. The Queen's brief note is in the same manuscript (f. 74). Queen Anne also had Prince Henry write, and Arbella reponds to similar effect: "Although I may have some cause to be sorry to have lost the contentment of a good Lute, yet I confesse that I am right glad to have found any occasion whearby to expresse to her Majesty and your Highnesse the humble respect which I ow you." Harleian MS 7003, f. 38. To King Christian she wrote about the same date, in Latin, observing that few lutenists please her as Cutting does, that he was sent to the best masters and trained in the art to her pleasure, that the King would have no difficulty finding a host of such, but that she is nonetheless happy to send him, and would send, if possible, Orpheus or Apollo. Harleian MS 7003, f. 37. She received, as did several other ladies, a gift of jewels from Christian. Other letters exchanged between Arbella and the Danish court in Latin and English date from October 1606 to July 1607; drafts are in Harleian MS 7003, ff. 49–54b.

61. Chamberlain to Carleton, January 8, 1608, Chamberlain, I, 252–253.

62. Michael Cavendish, *14 Ayers in Tabletorie* (London, 1598), quoted in Handover, *Arbella Stuart,* 134.

63. In Nichols, I, 261. Fowler's letters to Shrewsbury hint obliquely of his interest in marrying the lady—a proposal that would of course have been scorned by all parties.

64. Holland, *Pancharis,* 5, a work planned for dedication to Queen Elizabeth and revamped for the new regime; David Hume, *Lusus Poetici* (London, 1605), 3–4; John Owen, *Epigrammata* (London, 1607), sig. E 8.

65. John Wilbye, *Cantus* (London, 1609), cited in Handover, *Arbella Stuart,* 250.

66. Chapman, *Homer Prince of Poets* [1609?], sig. E c v. The work was dedicated to Prince Henry, with a shorter dedication to Queen Anne; among the presentation verses were poems to the Countesses of Bedford and Montgomery and Lady Mary Wroth. Chapman removed the verses to Arbella in the 1611 edition, after Arbella's disgrace.

67. Sig. C. Lanyer's dedication to Arbella is fourth, following those to Queen Anne, Princess Elizabeth, and "All Virtuous Ladies." In some copies it has been removed, evidently in response to Arbella's disgrace.

68. *Cal. SP Venetian*, X (1603–1607), 514.

69. To Shrewsbury, December 8, 1608, in Cooper, *Life and Letters*, II, 90–91.

70. June 17, 1609, in Lodge, *Illustrations*, III, 372.

71. Handover, *Arbella Stuart*, 244–249. Details of Arbella's finances and expenses for the journey appear in Hugh Crompton's accounts; extracts are published in Bradley, *Life of Lady Arabella Stuart*, II, 227–237. A letter from Isabel Bowes, December 5, 1609, reports that she has written to her brother to seek out a suitable house for Arbella (Harleian MS 7003, f. 55); soon after Bowes reports that one has been found.

72. See James Beaulieu, December 29, 1609, Historical Manuscripts Commission (Downshire) II, 211. H&S, V, 217–219, summarizes details about Janiculo, also called Bogdan: he was one of three pretenders to the Moldavian crown, and Wotton reported to Cecil from Venice (February 22, 1608) that he was bragging about his engagement to Arbella though he was already married to a Venetian.

73. Act V, scene i, ll. 24–25, in H&S, V, 251.

74. On February 8, 1610, the Venetian ambassadors report that the play has been suppressed: "Her Excellency is very ill pleased and shows a determination in this coming Parliament to secure the punishment of certain persons, we dont know who." *Cal. SP Venetian*, XI (1607–1610), 427. As David Riggs notes, it is not clear whether the play was formally suppressed (*Ben Jonson*, 156) but effectively it was: after the first performance(s) there were none for half a century, and no 1612 quarto is extant.

75. January 15, 1610, *Cal. SP Venetian*, XI (1607–1610), 410.

76. Winwood, *Memorials*, III, 117. Arbella had a household of twenty-two servants, costing £156 a year. The "diet," or dishes supplied for the household by the King, was essential and had the effect of tying Arbella to the court. Her letter of December 17, 1609, petitions to have her debts paid, to renounce her Irish patent for wines, and to be given £1,000 in lieu of the diet. Cooper, *Life and Letters*, II, 96–97.

77. The Privy Council records for this period burned in the fire of 1666, so we are dependent on other reports and rumors for what transpired.

78. She had been staying at a Seymour residence in late December 1609 when she was first taken into custody and brought before the Council—possibly that of the recently married Edward, or the Beauchamp townhouse. Handover, *Arbella Stuart*, 256.

79. Seymour was called before the Council and signed his confession on February 20. Harleian MS 7003, f. 59.

80. March 4, 1610, *Cal. SP Venetian*, XI (1607–1610), 439. Beaulieu wrote to Trumbull at Brussels on February 15 (Winwood, *Memorials*, III, 119) fixing Arbella's Council appearance as February 14: "The Lady *Arabella*, who as you know, was not long ago *censured for having without the King's Privity entertained a Motion of Marriage*, was again within these few Days *deprehended* in the like Treaty with the Lord of Beauchamp's second Sonne, and both were called and examined yesterday at the Court about it. What the Matter will prove I know not; but these *Affectations of Marriage in her*, do give some Advantage to the World of impairing the Reputation of her constant and vertuous Disposition."

81. Carleton to Edmondes, July 13, 1610, Winwood, *Memorials*, III, 124.

82. Many are in Harleian 7003 and Sloane 4164, as well as SP 14 (James I). She

probably sent many more which are not extant. There are several drafts to unspec-ified recipients, suggesting that versions of them may have been sent broadcast to various influential Lords, for example, Harleian MS 7003, f. 104, and Bodleian, Cotton Vespasian F. 3, f. 35. Steen ("Fashioning," 90–91) discusses several ex-amples of revisions from draft to draft, as Arbella works to get the tone of defer-ence right, to emphasize her guiltlessness, or to show herself properly humble.

83. Two letters in July to Shrewsbury beg his help with the disposing of her servants (whom she can no longer maintain, and cannot make decisions about "till I know how his Majesty is inclined towards me"). She asks Shrewsbury to try to find out. Harleian MS 7003, ff. 71, 74. A petition in August to the Lords of the Council asks that Reeves and Crompton be moved from the dangerously un-healthful Marshalsea prison "to some other healthfull Aire." Harleian MS 7003, f. 92.

84. Harleian MS 7003, ff. 90, 91; for another version, see Sloane MS 4161, f. 38.

85. Harleian MS 7003, f. 57.

86. July 22, 1610, BL, Lansdowne MS 1236, f. 62.

87. Harleian MS 7003, f. 61 (draft). For other letters to Drummond, see Sloane MS 4161, f. 47.

88. "To the Queen, with the Petition to the King's Majesty Enclosed," October 1610, SP 14 (James I) 57/118. This draft has curious fragmentary notes on the back.

89. Harleian MS 7003, f. 87. As the petition to the King is undated, we cannot be sure this is the one enclosed in October, but it seems tonally apt.

90. Ibid., f. 70.

91. Ibid., f. 64; cf. Sloane MS 4161, f. 48.

92. Emphasis added. Harleian MS 7003, f. 66; cf. Sloane MS 4161, f. 49.

93. Harleian MS 7003, f. 78; Steen ("Fashioning") notes the revision from an (apparently) earlier draft (f. 82v) to remove the suggestion that the King has faults needing forgiveness: "When the rather I am sure his Majesty forgiveth greater offences as freely as he desires to be forgiven by him whose Sacrament he is to receive."

94. Harleian MS 7003, f. 85, n.d., but thematically consonant with the letter to the Queen; for another version, see Sloane MS 4161, f. 35.

95. Durant, *Arbella Stuart*, 186–187. Her single surviving letter to William is filled with solicitous concern for his health, and fears that they will not survive long enough to enjoy a restoration to favor: "No separation but that [death] de-prives me of the comfort of you. for whearsoever you be or in what state so ever you are it suffiseth me that you are mine . . . I assure you nothing the State can do with me can trouble me so much as this newes of your being ill doth." N.d., Harleian MS 7003, f. 150.

96. *Cal. SP Venetian*, XII (1610–1613), 110.

97. Dated from Royston, March 13 [1611], Harleian MS, 7003, ff. 94–97: Whereas our cousin the Lady Arbella hath highlie offended us in seekinge to marry her self without our knowledge (to whom shee had the honor to be neere in blood) and in proceedinge afterwarde to a full conclusion of a Mar-iage with the selfe same person, whom (for manie juste causes) we had ex-presslie forbidden to marrie . . . itt is more necessarie for us to make some such demonstration nowe of the juste sense and feelinge we have after so

greate an Indignitie offered unto us, as may make others knowe by her example, that no respect of personall affection, can make us neglect those con-
sideratons, wherein both the honor and order of the governemente is interested . . . This beinge the difference as you see betweene us and her—that
whereas she hath abounded towards us in disobedience, and ingratitude, we
are (on the contrarie) still apt to temper the severitie of our Justice with grace
and favor towards her, as may well appeare by the course wee have taken to
committ her onely to your custodie.

Cf. Sloane 4161, f. 51. As a member of the Privy Council, Arbella's uncle Shrewsbury was forced to put his hand to the Council order to this effect on March 15.

98. Harleian MS 7003, f. 152; for another version, see Sloane MS 4161, f. 46.
N.d., but probably March 1611.

99. Gilbert to Moundford, March 29, 1611, Harleian MS 7003, f. 116. A report
by the Bishop of Durham describes Arbella's weak and ailing state, and her refusal
to proceed further on her journey. March 16, 1611, SP 14 (James I), 62/30.

100. In an undated petition Arbella portrays herself "in so weake case, as I verily
thinck it would be the cause of my deathe to be removed anie whither att this time
. . . I trust your Lordships will not looke I should be so unchristian as to be cause
of my owne death, and I leave itt to your Lordships' wisdom to consider what the
world would conceive if I should be violentlie enforced to doe it." Harleian MS
7003, f. 149.

101. Ibid., f. 89.

102. Moundford to the Bishop of Durham, May 1611, Sloane MS 4161, f. 61v.

103. Harleian 7003, f. 80. An earlier, much-corrected draft is f. 79.

104. This draft with the corrections is Harleian MS 7003, ff. 83–83v. The changes
are pointed out in Steen, "Fashioning," 92.

105. Handover, *Arbella Stuart,* 191–194. At Leigh they at first failed to find the
arranged-for French bark and attempted to persuade John Bright, captain of the
Thomas bound for Berwick, to take them. He refused but took careful note of
the party, imagining Ann Bradshaw to be the notorious cross-dressing thief Moll
Cutpurse. His statement is in SP 14 (James I) 64/30.

106. Handover, *Arbella Stuart,* 275–280. The account of Arbella's capture is in
Harleian MS 7003, ff. 128, 130; the list of prisoners is in f. 140.

107. Durant, *Arbella Stuart,* 195–201. Upon landing, William tried to find Arbella, and after learning of her capture petitioned Cecil to be allowed to live quietly
abroad with her. He was refused, but told that he would be left alone. He went
on to Paris later that year. After Arbella's death he returned to England and married a daughter of the Earl of Essex; one of their daughters was named Arabella.

108. More to Winwood, June 28, 1611, Winwood, *Memorials,* III, 281.

109. James Spedding et al., *The Works of Francis Bacon,* 14 vols. (London, 1861–
1872), IX, 297–298.

110. Harleian MS 7003, f. 153; for another version, see Sloan MS 4161, ff. 63–64.
See also Lady Arbella Seymaure to Lord [Salisbury], Harleian MS 7003, ff. 104,
107, Sloane MS 4161, f. 54; Lady Arbella Seymaure to ———— [someone with an
interest in Northampton], Bodleian, Cotton Vespasian MS. F. 3, f. 35.

111. Harleian MS 7003, f. 146. That such abject self-presentation is by no means
unusual is evident from a letter of Donne's to Buckingham, August 8, 1621, *Fortescue Papers,* 158:

I ame so far from dependinge upon the assistance of any but your Lordship, as that I do not assist myselfe so far as with a wishe that my Lord Keeper would have left a hole for so poore a worme as I ame to have crept in at. All that I meane in usinge thys boldnes, of puttinge myselfe into your Lordship's presence by thys ragge of paper, ys to tell your Lordship that I ly in a corner, as a clodd of clay, attendinge what kinde of vessell yt shall please you to make of Your Lordship's humblest and thankfullest and devotedst servant.

112. Durant, *Arbella Stuart*, 205.

113. On July 7, 1614, Chamberlain reported to Carleton the arrest of Crompton and a clergyman, Dr. Palmer, "for some business about the Lady Arbella, who, they say, is far out of frame this midsummer moon." Handover, *Arbella Stuart*, 292. Reeves was arrested later in July for "some new complot" for her escape. Rev. Thomas Larkin to Sir T. Puckering, July 21, 1614, Birch, *Court and Times of James*, I, 338. Also, see Chamberlain to Carleton, April 29, 1613, Chamberlain, I, 443.

114. The report of the postmortem is in Historical Manuscript Commission, *8th Report and Appendix*, Part I (London, 1881), 229a.

4. Exercising Power: The Countess of Bedford

1. See Franklin B. Williams, Jr., *Index of Dedications and Commendatory Verses in English Books before 1641* (London: Bibliographical Society, 1962). Excluding royal ladies, the entry for the Countess of Bedford is matched only by that for the Countess of Pembroke. Such power as the female nobility under Queen Elizabeth could wield was shared among many: female courtiers such as the Russell sisters (the Countesses of Warwick, Bath, and Cumberland); learned ladies such as the Cooke sisters, whose influence depended chiefly on their marriages; and the most notable patroness of the age, the Countess of Pembroke, whose center of activity was her country estate (Wilton) rather than the court.

2. Some biographical information about the Countess of Bedford and her family is supplied by Margaret M. Byard, "The Trade of Courtiership: The Countess of Bedford and the Bedford Memorials; A Family History from 1585 to 1607," *History Today* (January 1979), 20–28; J. H. Wiffen, *Historical Memoirs of the House of Russell*, 2 vols. (London: Longman, 1833), II, 74–123; Ian Grimble, *The Harington Family* (London: Jonathan Cape, 1957), 165–176; Barbara Lewalski, "Lucy, Countess of Bedford: Images of a Jacobean Courtier and Patroness," in *Politics of Discourse: The Literature and History of Seventeenth-Century England*, ed. Kevin Sharpe and Steven N. Zwicker (Berkeley: University of California Press, 1987), 52–77. See also R. C. Bald, *John Donne: A Life* (New York: Oxford University Press, 1970), 170–179, 275–276; and Helen Gardner, ed. *The Elegies and The Songs and Sonnets* (Oxford: Clarendon, 1978), 248–251.

3. *The Letters and Epigrams of Sir John Harington*, ed. Norman E. McClure (Philadelphia: University of Pennsylvania Press, 1930), 320.

4. The familiar story is reviewed and supplemented by Byard from family records. The Earl's statement disclaiming any treasonous activity is in BL, Additional MS 4160, f. 70. Lady Bedford and her father were active in pleading his case; see Lord Harington's letter to Robert Cecil, March 11, 1600. Hatfield, Cecil Papers 180, f. 37.

5. The Chamberlain-Carleton letters and other reports in the State Papers Domestic and Venetian for the reign of James I provide some record of her activities, role at court, and influence during these years. Her letters to Jane Cornwallis were published in *The Private Correspondence of Jane Lady Cornwallis, 1613–1644* (London, 1842). Other important sources of letters by and about her are Donne's correspondence; BL, Additional MS 4160; Hatfield, Cecil Papers III, 180; and Maidstone, Kent, De L'Isle MSS U 1475.

6. Byard, "Trade of Courtiership," 26. The contributions of several friends and relatives (including Lord Harington) and Lady Bedford's sale of part of her jointure for £2,000 enabled him to pay almost £7,000. Shortly after his succession James I forgave Bedford the remaining £3,000. The growing impoverishment of the aristocracy in these years is documented by Lawrence Stone, *The Crisis of the Aristocracy, 1558–1641* (Oxford: Oxford University Press, 1965).

7. Recounted in chapters 1 and 2.

8. Wiffen, *Memoirs*, II, 66–68, 102–103.

9. For the Goodyere relationshipship, see Lady Bedford's letter to Cecil, June 1605, Hatfield, Cecil Papers III, f. 96. For Gorges, see the epistle dedicatory to his translation of *Lucan's Pharsalia* (London, 1614). For discussion of her relations with John Burges, see Patricia Thomson, "John Donne and the Countess of Bedford," *Modern Language Review*, 44 (1949), 329–340. See also Bald, *John Donne*, 172–179.

10. Donne's correspondence mentions various visits to Twickenham; see *Letters to Severall Persons of Honour* (London, 1651), 53–54, 117, 139, 143. Drayton was no longer Lady Bedford's client during the Twickenham years.

11. John Chamberlain to Dudley Carleton, August 1, 1613, Chamberlain, I, 470. Cf. SP 14 (James I) 74/49, 109/80, 89. See also Thomson, "Donne and the Countess of Bedford," 333–334.

12. *Works of Sir William Temple*, 2 vols. (London, 1720), I, 170. Temple credits Lucy Bedford with designing the gardens.

13. SP 14 (James I) 109/133. Chamberlain wrote to Carleton on June 19, 1619, "The worst is they say the masterpocks hath setled in one of her eyes, wherby she is like to lose it." Chamberlain, II, 244–245, 250.

14. John Russell, born on January 19, 1602, was buried at Chenies on February 19, 1602. Byard, "Trade of Courtiership," 26. Robert Sidney wrote his wife on September 5, 1610, of another such tragedy: "Upon Monday my Lady of Bedforde was brought to bed of a daughter, but it dyed with in twoe howers. Shee herself is very weake and much greeved for the loss of the childe." Maidstone, Kent, De L'Isle MS U 1475 C 81/205. Rowland Whyte reports the rumor of an earlier pregnancy in his letter to Sir Robert Sidney on November 5, 1595. De L'Isle MS U1475 C 12/19.

15. Clifford, *Diary*, 8; Chamberlain to Carleton, August 1, 1613, Chamberlain, I, 306.

16. Hatfield, Cecil Papers 114, f. 130.

17. Chamberlain to Carleton, February 22, 1617, identified Lucy Bedford as mistress "of his [Hay's] love to the Earl of Northumberland's youngest daughter, with whom he is far engaged in affection" (Chamberlain, II, 551); the Earl strongly opposed the marriage. The collaboration of Pembroke, Lucy Bedford, and Southampton in orchestrating the Sir John Smith–Isabella Rich union is described by Reverend Thomas Lorkin to Sir John Puckering on January 5, 1619:

Sir Thomas Smith's only son and Mrs. Isabella Rich . . . finding themselves both together at Sir . . . Udals, some few days since, and liking well enough either the other, my lord chamberlain, who was there present, sent for his own chaplain, to Barnard Castle, to make the matter sure by marrying them; who making some difficulty, for that they had no licence, his lordship encouraged him, upon assurance of saving him harmless. So they were presently married; and from thence conducted to my Lord of Southampton's to dinner, and to my Lady Bedford's to bed, where all was consummate. But the father is a heavy man to see his son bestowed without his privity and consent. Birch, *Court and Times of James,* II, 122.

18. John Pory to Carleton, November 28, 1618, SP 14 (James I) 103/111.

19. Daniel, *Whole Workes,* 405–412. See chapter 1 and notes 63–64. Carleton wrote to Chamberlain on December 21, 1603: "We shall have a merry Christmas at Hampton Court, for both male and female maskes are all ready bespoken, whereof the Duke [of Lenox] is *rector chori* of th'one side, and the La: Bedford of the other." SP 14 (James I) 5/20.

20. Edmund Gosse, *The Life and Letters of John Donne,* 2 vols. (New York: Dodd, Mead, 1899), I, 199: "The King . . . hath left with the Queen a commandment to meditate upon a masque for Christmas, so that they grow serious about that already; that will hasten my Lady Bedford's journey."

21. SP 14 (James I) 90/79.

22. See discussion at the end of chapter 1.

23. Daniel, *Whole Workes,* 407, 413. Andrew Sabol notes in *Four Hundred Songs and Dances from the Stuart Masques* (Providence: Brown University Press, 1978), 231, 580, that a musical score for one of the dances for this masque (BL, Additional MS 10444, ff. 39, 89v) is entitled "The Lady Lucies Masque," in reference to her role as *rector chori.*

24. H&S, X, 448.

25. Ibid., VII, 186–187.

26. Ibid., VII, 218.

27. Ibid., VII, 230. The illustration at the beginning of this chapter is reproduced from the portrait at Woburn Abbey. Cf. Roy Strong, *The Elizabethan Image* (London: Tate Gallery, 1970), 78. The Countess is not portrayed as a masquer in Isaac Oliver's miniature (c. 1605), at the Fitzwilliam Museum, Cambridge, but the gauzy veils, rich floral gown, curled hair, and large jewels project much the same aura of fantasy and magnificence.

28. Orgel and Strong, *Inigo Jones,* I, 135–136. See also H&S, VII, 306.

29. Orgel and Strong, *Inigo Jones,* I, 140, fig. 16.

30. She does not appear in the cast for Daniel's masque *Tethys Festival,* danced by the Queen and thirteen ladies on June 5, 1610. She may have been one of the ten unnamed ladies who danced in *Love Freed from Ignorance and Folly* (February 3, 1611), but her serious and disabling illness in the winter of 1612–13 makes it unlikely that she took part in *The Lord's Masque* at the wedding of Princess Elizabeth (February 14, 1613).

31. H&S, I, 143. Jonson told Drummond of Hawthornden "that the half of his comedies were not in Print, he heth a Pastorall intitled the May Lord, his own name is Alkin Ethra the Countess of Bedfoords Mogibell overberry, the old Countess of suffolk ane inchanteress other names are given to somersets Lady, Pembrook the Countess of rutland, Lady Wroth."

32. See chapter 1.

33. Claudius Desainliens, alias Holyband, *Campo di Fior, or else The Flourie Field of Foure Languages* (London, 1583).

34. John Florio, *A Worlde of Wordes, or Most copious, and exact Dictionarie in Italian and English* (London, 1598), sig. A 3v.

35. John Florio, trans., *The Essays or Morall, Politike and Millitarie Discourses of Lo: Michaell de Montaigne* ([London], 1603), sigs. A 2–A 4. Florio dedicated book one of the *Essays* to the Countess of Bedford and her mother, Lady Harington; book two to the Countess of Rutland and Lady Penelope Rich; and book three to the Ladies Elizabeth Grey and Marie Nevill.

36. Chapman, *Homer Prince of Poets,* sig. Ee 2; epistle dedicatory, Arthur Gorges, *Pharsalia,* (London, 1614) sigs. A 3–A 3v. In the epistle, Carew Gorges describes himself as a young attendant upon the Countess and the agent for presenting his father's text to her. He claims to have found this text in his father's study and won his permission to amend and print it with the aid of his schoolmaster. In presenting it to her he emphasizes the Sidney blood "wherewith you do so neerely participate."

37. John Dowland, preface to *The Second Booke of Songs or Ayers* (London, 1598). See discussion in Diana Poulton, *John Dowland* (London: Faber, 1972), 56, 245–249.

38. Arthur Saul, *Famous Game of Chesse-Play* (London, 1614).

39. Letter of John Harington to the Countess of Bedford, Inner Temple, Petyt MS 538.43.14, f. 303.

40. John Davies of Hereford, *The Muses Sacrifice or Divine Meditations* (London, 1612), sigs. ✳✳✳ 2–2v. He also appended a sonnet to his *Scourge of Folly* (1611), observing that the Countess is celebrated by all the poets, "Apollos most refulgent sonnes."

41. Lanyer, *Salve Deus,* sigs. d 4–d 4v.

42. See epistles dedicatory by William Perkins, *A Salve for a Sicke Man* (Cambridge, 1595) and Thomas Draxe, *The Worldes Resurrection, or The Generall Calling of the Jewes* (London, 1608). Richard Stock, in his funeral sermon for John Harington, *The Churches Lamentation for the Losse of the Godly* (London, 1614), urges Harington's mother and sisters to emulate his "worthy graces and practise of godliness."

43. Clement Cotton, *The Mirror of Martyrs* (London, 1615); John Calvin, *Two and Twenty Lectures Upon the Five First Chapters of Jeremiah,* trans. Clement Cotton (London, 1620). Cotton was the most prolific English translator of Calvin.

44. N. Byfield, Epistle dedicatory, *Sermons upon the first chapter of the first epistle general of Peter* (London, 1617).

45. John Reading, *A Faire Warning, Declaring the Comfortable Use both of Sicknesse and Health* (London, 1621).

46. This image was copied in later portraits, including one attributed to Gerard Honthorst in 1628, now at Woburn Abbey. It is reproduced in H&S, VIII, 60; cf. x–xi of that volume.

47. John Carey, *John Donne: Life, Mind, and Art* (New York: Oxford University Press, 1981), 78.

48. Bernard H. Newdigate, *Michael Drayton and His Circle* (Oxford: Basil Blackwell, 1941), 25–39, 56–69; Epistle dedicatory, *Matilda. The Faire and Chaste*

Daughter of the Lord Robert Fitzwater (London, 1594); Dedicatory sonnet, *Endimion and Phoebe. Ideas Latmus* (London, [1595]). This sonnet was reprinted as no. 57 of his sonnet sequence *Idea* in 1599.

49. Epistle dedicatory, *The Tragicall Legend of Robert, Duke of Normandy . . .* (London, 1596). This dedication is followed by a dedicatory sonnet to Lucy's mother, Anne Harington, later reprinted as no. 58 of *Idea*.

50. Dedicatory poem, *Mortimeriados. The Lamentable civill warres of Edward the second and the Barrons* (London, 1596). The invocations are at ll. 260–267, and ll. 2080–87.

51. *England's Heroicall Epistles* (London, 1597) has no general dedication. The first pair, Rosamond and King Henry II, is addressed to the Countess of Bedford; another pair, Queen Isabel and Mortimer, is addressed to Lucy's mother, Anne Harington; and those of Queen Isabel and Richard II to her husband the Earl of Bedford. Other pairs are addressed to other patrons. The fact that the dedications to Lady Bedford were retained when some of these poems were reprinted is plausibly explained by Dick Taylor, Jr., as an accommodation to the printer's wishes, in "Drayton and the Countess of Bedford," *Studies in Philology*, 49 (1952), 214–228. They were removed in the collected *Poems* of 1619.

52. Included in *Poemes Lyrick and Pastorall* (London, [1606]), sigs. F 8–F 8v. The four stanzas are added to the "Eighth Eglog," but omitted in the 1619 *Poems*. On Cerberus, see Jonson's references to a rival poet in his "Epistle" to the Countess of Rutland, pp. 106-107.

53. See discussion in Newdigate, *Michael Drayton*, 124–135, of the difficulties Drayton created for himself at court by his satire on several ministers in *The Owle*, his tactlessness in failing to take any poetic notice of Queen Elizabeth's death, and his reiterated complaints of neglect from all and sundry. Jean R. Brink, *Michael Drayton Revisited* (Boston: Twayne, 1990), 8–12, emphasizes the political folly in his choice of subjects (deposed kings, rebels) and several of the dedicatees of the *Heroicall Epistles*.

54. Daniel's primary patrons were the Pembrokes, the Cliffords, and later Queen Anne. He was for some years resident at Wilton as tutor to William Herbert; subsequently he was tutor to Anne Clifford in the household of the Countess of Cumberland. Other patrons were Fulke Greville, Lord Mountjoy, and the Earl of Hertford. See Joan Rees, *Samuel Daniel* (Liverpool: University Press, 1964), 43–88, 122–146; and Margaret Maurer, "Samuel Daniel's Poetical Epistles, Especially Those to Sir Thomas Egerton and Lucy, Countess of Bedford," *Studies in Philology*, 74 (1977), 418–444.

55. See discussion in Spriet, "Samuel Daniel," 134–137. The first installment of the *Civile Warres betweene the two houses of Lancaster and Yorke* was published in 1594.

56. *Vision of the 12. Goddesses*, in *Whole Workes*, 412.

57. "To the Lady Lucie, Countesse of Bedford," in *A Panegyrike Congratulatory Delivered to the Kings Most Excellent Majesty . . . Also Certaine Epistles. With a Defence of Ryme* (London, 1603), sigs. E 3v–E 4v. The stanza form, terza rima, is the first extended use of that form in English poetry. For Lucy Bedford's patron-client relationships with Jonson, see Riggs, *Ben Jonson*, 118–162; and Robert C. Evans, *Ben Jonson and the Poetics of Patronage* (Lewisburg, Pa.: Bucknell University Press, 1990), 48–51.

58. Chiefly William Herbert, Earl of Pembroke (the Countess of Pembroke's son); Elizabeth, Countess of Rutland (Sir Philip Sidney's daughter); Sir Robert Sidney (Viscount Lisle, later Lord Leicester); and Lady Mary Wroth (daughter of Sir Robert) and her husband.

59. H&S, VIII, 115. For dating, see H&S, XI, 41.

60. The letter is reprinted in H&S, I, 197–198. The addressee is not identified in the MS, but the Countess of Bedford's position at court makes it likely that she (rather than the Countess of Rutland) was the addressee. Vigorously protesting his innocence, Jonson compliments the Countess by the suggestion that she both can and will respond to this injustice: "I wolde intreate some little of your Ayde, to the defence of my Innocence . . . The cause we understand to be the Kinges indignation, for which we are hartelye sorie, and the more, by how much the less we have deserv'd it."

61. The three poems to the Countess included in Jonson's *Epigrammes* cannot be precisely dated. Probably they all predate 1612, the date that volume was registered for publication.

62. The manuscript version, headed "To: L: C: off: B:," is in Bodleian, Rawlinson Poets MS 31, ff. 20v–21. It was published in very slightly revised form as "Ode enthousiastike," along with three other poems which made up Jonson's contribution to the lyric collection *The Phoenix and Turtle*, to which Shakespeare, Marston, and Chapman also contributed. The dedication was removed in the collection, evidently to generalize the poem. See H&S, VIII, 364–365; XI, 40–41.

63. H&S, VIII, 54–55. Drummond of Hawthornden reports that this epigram was one of the five which Jonson best liked to recite. H&S, I, 134–135. In inscribing his gift copy of *Cynthia's Revells* (1601) to Lucy as "CYNTHIAS fayrest Nymph," he also presumes her delight in witty, epigrammatic turns. He directs the book to claim as reward "a Kisse (if thou canst dare it) / of her white Hand: or [if] she can spare it." H&S, VIII, 662.

64. Ibid., VIII, 60–61.

65. George Rowe, *Distinguishing Jonson: Imitation, Rivalry, and the Direction of a Dramatic Career* (Lincoln: University of Nebraska Press, 1988), 8–9.

66. H&S, VIII, 52.

67. Riggs, *Ben Jonson*, 122–126, 152–163.

68. "Under-wood," no. 49, in H&S, VIII, 222–223. For the "News" game and the composition of aphoristic essays and poems on themes of "State, Religion, Bawdrie," see *The "Conceited Newes" of Sir Thomas Overbury and his Friends, 1616* facsimile of *Sir Thomas Overbury His Wife*, ed. James E. Savage (Gainesville: Scholars' Facsimiles & Reprints, 1968). The first edition, *A Wife: Now The Widdow of Sir Tho. Overburye . . . whereunto are added many witty Characters, and conceited Newes, written by himselfe and other learned Gentlemen his friends* (London, 1614), contains an entry signed "Mris. B," evidently Mistress Bulstrode; it is reprinted in subsequent editions. The short essay, entitled "Newes of my morning worke," contains a potpourri of cynical aphorisms about the court, including: "That most fear the worlds opinion more then Gods displeasure. That a Court friend seldom goes further then the first degree of charitie. That the divell is the perfectest Courtier . . . That constancy in women and love in men is alike rare. That Art is truth's Jugler. . . . That womens fortunes aspire but by others powers. That a man with a female wit is the worst *Hermaphrodite* . . . That the worst part of ignorance is

making good and ill seem alike. That all this is newes onely to fooles" (sigs. H 2–H 2v).

69. H&S, I, 150. For further discussion of the "News" game and of this affair, see Marotti, *John Donne: Coterie Poet*, 204–206; Evans, *Ben Jonson*, 75–80; and Jongsook Lee, "Who Is Cecilia, What Was She? Cecilia Bulstrode and Jonson's Epideictics," *JEGP*, 85 (1986), 20–34.

70. H&S, VIII, 371–372. In the covering letter to George Gerrard, which he no doubt expected the Countess to see, Jonson voices a wish that he had earlier known of Bulstrode's illness: "Would God I had seene her before that some yt live might have corrected some prejudices they have had injuriously of mee."

71. *Epicoene Or The Silent Woman*, Act II, scene ii, ll. 91–123, in H&S, V, 181–182. See also chapter 3.

72. Gosse, *Life and Letters of Donne*, I, 188–189, 198–199, 216–217, 220, 230; II, 42–43. Studies focusing especially on her patron-client relationship with Donne include Thomson, "John Donne and the Countess of Bedford," 329–340; Margaret Maurer, "John Donne's Verse Letters," *MLQ*, 37 (1976), 234–259; Maurer, "The Real Presence of Lucy Russell, Countess of Bedford, and the Terms of John Donne's 'Honour is so Sublime Perfection,'" *ELH*, 47 (1980), 205–234; Marotti, *John Donne: Coterie Poet*; and Claude J. Summers, "Donne's 1609 Sequence of Grief and Comfort," *Studies in Philology* (in press).

73. The verse letters were probably written in the years 1608–1610; he also addressed an "Epitaph on Himself" to the Countess (perhaps on the occasion of his departure for France with Sir Robert Drury), and an unfinished verse letter sometime after the publication of the *First Anniversary* (1611). See W. Milgate, ed., *John Donne: The Satires, Epigrams, and Verse Letters* (Oxford: Clarendon, 1967), 90–104, 252–274. For discussion of the elegies, see Milgate, ed., *John Donne: The Epithalamions, Anniversaries, and Epicedes of John Donne* (Oxford: Clarendon, 1978), 57–63, 66–74. My citations are from these editions.

74. Unavailing because James I determined that he would advance Donne only in the Church. For discussion of Donne's relation to his various patrons, see Bald, *John Donne*, 155–301; Arthur F. Marotti, "John Donne and the Rewards of Patronage," in *Patronage in the Renaissance*, ed. Guy F. Lytle and Stephen Orgel (Princeton: Princeton University Press, 1981), 207–234; and Marotti, *John Donne: Coterie Poet*; also Goldberg, *James I and the Politics of Literature*, 210–239.

75. Gosse, *Life and Letters*, I, 293–295, 314. The anxiety about the *Anniversaries* found poetic expression in a verse letter, "Begun in France but never perfected":

> First I confesse I have to others lent
> Your stock, and over prodigally spent
> Your treasure, for since I had never knowne
> Vertue or beautie, but as they are growne
> In you, I should not thinke or say they shine,
> (So as I have) in any other Mine.

(ll. 11–16)

He proceeds to explain that his praises of others are only "copies" of the original (which she is) for "low Spirits" to read, but he evidently did not complete (or send) this wire-drawn apology. Milgate, *Satires and Verse Letters*, 104.

76. Gosse, *Life and Letters*, I, 213, 220.

77. Ibid., I, 217–218.

78. Both major editors of the *Songs and Sonnets* identify "Twicknam Garden" and "A Nocturnall" as poems for the Countess. See H. J. C. Grierson, *The Poems of John Donne,* 2 vols. (Oxford: Clarendon, 1912), II, 22, and Gardner, *Elegies and Songs and Sonnets,* 249–251. C. M. Armitage, "Donne's Poems in the Huntington Manuscript 198: New Light on 'The Funerall,'" *Studies in Philology,* 63 (1966), 697–707, argues on the basis of some manuscript evidence that "The Funerall" may also have been addressed to her. See also Marotti, *John Donne: Coterie Poet,* 211.

79. "To the Countesse of Bedford: Honour is so sublime perfection," ll. 44–45, in Milgate, *John Donne: The Satires, Epigrams and Verse Letters,* 102.

80. See discussion in Barbara K. Lewalski, *Donne's Anniversaries and the Poetry of Praise: The Creation of a Symbolic Mode* (Princeton: Princeton University Press, 1973), 42–70.

81. David Aers and Gunther Kress, "'Darke Texts Needs Notes': Versions of Self in Donne's Verse Epistles," in David Aers, Bob Hodge, and Gunther Kress, eds., *Literature, Language, and Society in England, 1580–1680* (Totowa, N.J.: Barnes & Noble, 1981), 23–48.

82. Marotti, *John Donne: Coterie Poet,* 202–232.

83. Ibid., 209.

84. Maurer, "Real Presence." See also Maurer, "John Donne's Verse Letters," 234–259.

85. For a reading focused on Donne's frustrations with clientage and subversive relativizing of values, grounded in class identity, see Aers and Kress, "'Darke Texts Needs Notes,'" 23–48.

86. Ll. 21–26. The final line is hardly evidence, as Marotti claims, of "Donne's latent antifeminism" (*John Donne: Coterie Poet,* 225), since the other sex is presumably not ransomed at all, and it is James's court that needs preserving. But the poem does intimate, as he notes, that Donne knew "his patroness's courtly maneuverings—from which he desperately wished to profit"—were sometimes less than virtuous.

87. See the extended reading of this poem in Maurer, "Real Presence," 223–228. Donne also coauthored a verse letter with Henry Goodyere, "A Letter Written by Sir. H. G. and J. D. *alternis vicibus,*" in which the two friends in alternate stanzas profess their Petrarchan devotion to two women (Bedford and perhaps Markham). Milgate, *Satires and Verse Letters,* 76–78.

88. I discuss this exchange at the end of this chapter.

89. Gosse, *Life and Letters of Donne,* II, 44.

90. See the plausible argument to this effect developed by Thomson, "Donne and the Countess of Bedford," 331–335.

91. Gosse, *Life and Letters of Donne,* II, 73.

92. Ibid., II, 127; *The Sermons of John Donne,* ed. George R. Potter and Evelyn Simpson, 10 vols. (Berkeley: University of California Press, 1953–1962), III, 187–205.

93. Jane, Lady Cornwallis (the former Jane Meutys, who was in the Countess's entourage at Twickenham), married Sir William Cornwallis in 1608; he died three years later, and in 1614 she married the painter Nathaniel Bacon. As he was untitled at the time of the marriage (in 1625 he was created Knight of the Bath), she kept her former style.

94. *Cornwallis Correspondence,* 62, 25–26, January 20, 1619; September 9, 1614.

95. SP 14 (James I) 122/99, August 30, 1621; SP 14 (James I) 103/41, October 18, 1621; SP 14 (James I) 130/67, May 13, 1622; *Cornwallis Correspondence*, 57–58, 126, October 1618, April 12, 1625.

96. *Cornwallis Correspondence*, 24–25, September, 1614.

97. SP 14 (James I) 143/569, April 24, 1623.

98. *Cornwallis Correspondence*, 86, November 1623. In the same vein she conveys the general anxiety about new court appointments after Charles's coronation: "It is thought he will imploye his owne and dismisse his fathers . . . he makes his owne determinacions and is very stiff in them; having already changed the whole face of the court very near to the same forme itt had in Queene Elizabeth's tyme." Ibid., 125, April 12, 1625.

99. SP 14 (James I) 74/49, August 1, 1613.

100. See Thomson, "Donne and the Countess of Bedford," 334–335; Birch, *Court and Times of James*, I, 262. Writing to recommend a preacher to the Queen of Bohemia, she referred to his "good aprobacion from Doctor Burges & Mr Preston." SP 14 (James I) 203/127, April 23, 1622.

101. *Cornwallis Correspondence*, 44–45, May 1617. Lady Roxborough was dismissed from the Queen's service for failing to consult her before seeking her husband's appointment as Prince Charles's Chamberlain. A little later Lady Bedford reports, "The noble Lady Roxbrough is in Scotland, which makes me perfectly hate the court." Ibid., 48, October 22, 1617.

102. See chapter 2.

103. Oman, *Elizabeth of Bohemia*, 201–203, 296–297.

104. SP 14 (James I) 130/15, May 4, 1622.

105. SP 14 (James I) 140/57, March 28, 1623. Her enclosed letter to the Queen apparently has not survived. In another letter she urges the Queen of Bohemia to write to Charles about the good reports of him reaching her from England, as a means to calm suspicions and enlist his support; BL, Additional MS 5503. f. 126. She also wrote to Carleton urging such a move; SP 14 (James I) 130/15, May 4, 1622.

106. Historical Manuscripts Commission, vol. 21, *Hamilton MSS, Supplementary Report* (London: HM Stationery Office, 1932), 9. See also chapter 2.

107. *Cornwallis Correspondence*, 28–29, October 27, 1614.

108. Ibid., 61–62, 71–72.

109. SP 14 (James I) 109/102, June 19, 1619. See Thomson, "Donne and the Countess of Bedford," 335–340.

110. *Cornwallis Correspondence*, 76.

111. Ibid., 73, 144. The Countess was especially grateful to her friend for gifts of hunting dogs.

112. Ibid., 59–61, January 20, 1619. These letters of consolation customarily end with an invitation to visit the Countess for a change of scene and air.

113. Ibid., 65–67, June 1, 1620.

114. Ibid., 118–119, March 23, 1625. A little later she voices her indignation at the rumors that the Marquis died a Roman Catholic, and her willingness at least to entertain the idea that he may have been poisoned. She recounts the physical evidence in graphic detail but weighs it judiciously:

> Being att first . . . as fayer a corse as ever their eyes beheld, in the space of three owres his hoole body, head, and every part swelled so strangely and

gangrened so generally as it astonished them all . . . God only knows the truth, who, if he had any wrong, I trust will in his justice declare it. It is true that, when he was opened in his stomack and head, there appeared nothing to confirm this jealousie, which makes the phisicians confident it could be no poison they are in these parts acquainted with; yett both myselfe and many other of his friends rest not clear of doubt, though, but upon some farder evidence, it is not to be stirred in.

Ibid., 128–129, April 12, 1625.

115. Ibid., 88–90, February 28, 1624.

116. Ibid., 57, 47, October 4, 1618; October 22, 1617.

117. Ibid., 50–51, March 7, 1618.

118. The elegy is attributed to the Countess in several manuscripts, and both Grierson and Milgate argue the plausibility of the attribution. The poem and the evidence for the Countess's authorship are set forth in Milgate, *John Donne: Epithalamions, Anniversaries, and Epicedes,* Appendix B, 235–237.

119. Ibid., 59–61. Summers, "Donne's 1609 Sequence," argues the close connections to the elegy on Markham.

120. Milgate, *John Donne: Epithalamions, Anniversaries, and Epicedes,* 61–63.

5. Claiming Patrimony and Constructing a Self: Anne Clifford

1. I cite Vita Sackville-West's edition of the *Diary* (1923). It is based on what is probably a nineteenth-century copy of the lost original (MS Sackville of Knole, U269/F48, now at the Center for Kentish Studies, Maidstone, Kent); the manuscript is in three volumes, without pagination, folio, or signature numbers. D. J. H. Clifford, ed., *The Diaries of Lady Anne Clifford* (Wolfeboro Falls, NH: Alan Sutton, 1991) contains the Knole *Diary* and also Anne's later memoirs; this edition appeared too late for me to use. An eighteenth-century copy of the lost *Diary,* made by Elizabeth Harley Bentinck, Duchess of Portland (1715–1785), contains some additional material; it is in the Portland Papers (vol. 23, ff. 74–118v), at Longleat House, Wiltshire. I am indebted to Katherine Acheson for a description of this manuscript, which forms the basis of her edition of the *Diary,* now in preparation.

2. *The Lawes Resolutions of Womens Rights: or, The Lawes Provision for Woemen. A Methodicall Collection of Such Statutes and Customes, with the Cases, Opinions, Arguments and points of Learning in the Law, as doe properly concerne Women* (London, 1632), 30. This work, by one T.E., revises and updates an earlier (anonymous) Elizabethan text.

3. The major biographical accounts of Anne Clifford are George C. Williamson, *Lady Anne Clifford, Countess of Dorset, Pembroke & Montgomery, 1590–1676: Her Life, Letters, and Work* (Kendal: T. Wilson, 1922), which supplies generous extracts from letters and other documents; and Martin Holmes, *Proud Northern Lady: Lady Anne Clifford, 1590–1676* (Chichester: Phillimore, 1975). Other studies include Wallace Notestein, *Four Worthies* (London: Jonathan Cape, 1956), 123–166; and R. T. Spence, "Lady Anne Clifford, Countess of Dorset, Pembroke, and Montgomery (1590–1676): A Reappraisal," *Northern History,* 15–16 (1979–1980), 43–65. For Margaret Clifford, the best account remains chapter 21 in George Williamson's *George, Third Earl of Cumberland (1558–1605): His Life and His Voyages* (Cambridge: Cambridge University Press, 1920).

4. For documents or references to legal proceedings, see Oxford, Clifford MS; Lincoln's Inn, Hales MSS 83 and 94; also SP 14 (James I) 17/85, May 30, 1608; 89/405, November 14, 1616; Grant Book, March 14, 1617, March 21, 1620, December 10, 1620, March 29, 1624; SP 14 (James I) 162/212, April 10, 1624; SP 16 (Charles I) 169/4, June 17, 1630. Many personal letters of Anne and Margaret Clifford are at Kendal, Cumbria Record Office, WD/Hoth/Box 44; other letters and papers are in WD/Hoth/Box 71/6; WD/Hoth/Boxes 33, 46, 47, 49; WD/Hoth/Additional Records 6, 7, 9, 14, 16, 17, 21. Cf. Appendix, Williamson, *Anne Clifford,* 456–520; and *Collectanea Cliffordiana,* ed. Arthur Clifford (Paris, 1819). Contemporary references are in John Chamberlain to Dudley Carleton, Chamberlain, I, 214, 280, 287, 446 (November 7, 1605, January 10, 1609, March 3, 1609, April 29, 1613); Chamberlain, II, 63, 198, 288 (March 15, 1617, January 2, 1619, February 12, 1620).

5. Three large volumes, called the "Great Books of the Records of Skipton Castle," were compiled under Lady Anne's direction; a copy of the entire set is at Kendal, Cumbria Record Office, WD/Hoth/Great Books.

6. An eighteenth-century copy of Anne's lives of her parents and herself (from the third volume of the "Great Books") is in BL, Harleian MS 6177; it is the basis of an edition by J. P. Gilson, *Lives of Lady Anne Clifford and of Her Parents* (London: Roxburghe Club, 1916). Her own autobiographical account is entitled *A Summary of the Records and a true memorial of the life of me the Lady Anne Clifford* . . . ; hereafter cited as *Life of Me,* with page number. The memoir of her father is entitled *A Summary of the Records of George, Lord and Baron of Clifford . . . 3rd Earl of Cumberland;* the memoir of her mother is called *A Summary of Records and also a memorial of that religious and blessed lady, Margaret Russell, Countess of Cumberland.* I cite them from the Roxburghe edition (*Records of George, Memorial of Margaret*), with page number.

7. *Life of Me,* 33–34; *Records of George;* Williamson, *George, Third Earl of Cumberland.*

8. *Lawes Resolutions,* 9–10.

9. He may also have thought that his brother could best manage the estate and arrange for the payment of his massive debts. See Williamson, *Anne Clifford,* 31–36, 456–457; Holmes, *Proud Northern Lady,* 1–20; Spence, "Reappraisal," 43–47.

10. Jointure properties were ceded by the husband to the wife, to guarantee her a fixed income in widowhood. The author of the *Lawes Resolutions* strongly urges this arrangement as far preferable to the common-law guarantee of dower (one-third of the income for her lifetime), as that right was subject to many contingencies and might have to be sought through litigation (182–192).

11. Williamson, *Anne Clifford,* 79–83; *Life of Me,* 37–41. A letter of Richard, Archbishop of Canterbury, to Dorset on March 14, 1608, certifies that the marriage took place "in the private house of the Dowager" in London on February 25, 1608, between 8 and 11 A.M., "without banns and without faculty or license obtained by the said Geoffrey Amherst, clerk"; it absolves all participants from danger of excommunication for these irregularities. Historical Manuscripts Commission, *Fourth Report and Appendix* (London, 1874), 310.

12. See chapter 1; Orgel and Strong, *Inigo Jones,* I, 146. The Berenice role may have paid tribute to Anne's long hair (to midcalf), in which she took great pride.

13. See John Aubrey, *Brief Lives,* ed. Oliver Lawson Dick (Ann Arbor: University of Michgan Press, 1962), 100; Clifford, *Diary.*

14. *Lawes Resolutions,* 125, 139: "A woman as soone as she is married is called *covert,* in Latine *nupta,* that is, veiled, as it were clouded and over shadowed . . . she is continually *sub potestate viri.* Bracton terms her under the scepter of her husband . . . Every Feme Covert is quodammodo an infant . . . even in that which is most her owne."

15. Clifford, *Life of Me; Diary.* Chamberlain to Carleton, March 29, 1624; April 10, 1624, Chamberlain, II, 288.

16. A consolatory letter from her old tutor Samuel Daniel refers to her many afflictions as trials sent by God "that you may be numbred amongst the examples of patience and substancy to other ages." *Whole Works,* sig. N 1. Henry Peacham's funeral elegy for Dorset called for her soul, like the emblematic palm tree, to grow stronger under its many burdens—"Father, Mother, Sonne, now Husbands losse,"—in *An Aprill Shower, Shed in Abundance of Teares, for . . . Richard Sacville* (London, 1624).

17. Philip Herbert's first wife was Lady Susan Vere, the Countess of Montgomery, to whom Lady Mary Wroth dedicated her *Urania* (see chapter 9). He engaged King James's interest by his good looks and his passion for hunting.

18. For Philip's character, see Williamson, *Anne Clifford,* 160–185; *DNB,* IX, 659–660; Tresham Lever, *The Herberts of Wilton* (London: John Murray, 1967), 76–117. John Aubrey (*Brief Lives,* 146) credits him with aesthetic judgment, based on his commissions to Inigo Jones and other artists for the remodeling of Wilton.

19. George Sedgwick, *Memoirs,* reprinted in Joseph Nicolson and Richard Burn, *The History and Antiquities of the Counties of Westmoreland and Cumberland,* 2 vols. (London, 1777), 294–303. Sedgwick's original is not extant, except for the segments published here. Sedgwick records Anne's resolution "if God ordained a second marriage for her, never to have one that had children, and was a courtier, a curser and swearer (I, 299). And it was her fortune to light on one with all these qualifications in the extreme." He also underscores the irony of Philip's appointment as Chancellor of Oxford University since "[he] could scarce either write or read" (I, 297).

20. *Life of Me,* 47–49; Williamson, *Anne Clifford,* 162–163.

21. Williamson, *Anne Clifford,* 160–197; *Life of Me,* 49–55. While at Wilton, Anne received one letter from George Herbert (December 10, 1631) expressing gratitude for some "goodness" from her. George Herbert, *Works,* ed. F. E. Hutchinson (Oxford: Clarendon, 1941), 376–377. Aubrey (*Brief Lives,* 157) states that Herbert was chaplain to his kinsman Philip Herbert, and Arthur Woodnoth claims that Herbert paid Anne an hour's visit at Wilton in October 1631. *The Ferrar Papers,* ed. B. Blackstone (Cambridge: Cambridge University Press, 1938), 267. If she had further contacts with the poet, no records survive.

22. Anne notes that her cousin and friend Francis, Earl of Bedford (who assumed the duties of her nearest male relative), was instrumental in drawing up the jointure arrangements. She comments that Baynard's Castle was "full of riches, and was the more secured by my lying there," while recognizing as well that it was "a place of refuge for me to hide myself in, till those troubles were over passed." Her six-years' stay there was "the longest time that ever I continwed to lye in one Howse in all my Life." *Life of Me,* 51.

23. *Lawes Resolutions,* 232.

24. Sedgwick may exaggerate the boldness of her reply to Cromwell's offer of

help in resolving disputes with her tenants over rents, but the appeal to law rather than the judgment of rulers is quite in her style: "She . . . told them plainly she would never refer any of her concerns in that kind to the protector or any other person living, but leave it wholly to the discretion of the law; adding further, that she had refused to submit to king James on the like account, and would never do it to the protector, whatever hazard or danger she incurred thereby." *Memoirs,* 301.

25. Edward Rainbowe, *A Sermon Preached at the Interrment of Anne, Countess of Pembroke, Dorset, and Montgomery* (London, [1676]), 47–49.

26. Rainbowe, *Sermon,* 13, 23–28. Anne Clifford restored the almshouse at Beamsley founded by her mother, and founded another herself, at Appleby; both are designed for thirteen impoverished widows. Sedgwick notes (*Memoirs,* 300–301) that she was willing to incur a "vast charge in law-suits to vindicate her rights" vis-à-vis her tenants—rights thrown into confusion by some of Francis Clifford's arrangements. To illustrate, he tells the possibly apocryphal story that she spent £200 for the recovery of a single tributary hen, and then invited the tenant to dine upon it with her. Sedgwick insists that her building and local purchases were "a great help and support for those parts" (*Memoirs,* 302) in stimulating the local economy, though Spence in "Reappraisal" argues that the high rents her tenants paid to support those policies may have outweighed the benefits.

27. Williamson, *Anne Clifford,* 226–284, 393–403. Anne's "Day by Day Book" for January 1 to March 21, 1676, is the only extant diary from the later years. It is printed verbatim in Williamson, *Anne Clifford,* 265–284, 226–284, 393–403.

28. Rainbowe, *Sermon,* 51. Rainbowe reads her later life against the paradigm provided by Proverbs 14:1, "Every wise Woman buildeth her House," expanding the metaphor of house building from the very appropriate architectural to the intellectual and spiritual realm. After asserting the spiritual equality of women and men ("Souls know no Sexes"), he details how Anne Clifford fulfilled women's special responsibility for house building by her numerous material edifices but also her nonmaterial ones: a prudent and well-governed family; free and open hospitality to friends, clients, and "all of Quality"; personal oversight of her estates and exact accounts kept weekly "in Books of her own Method"; and a soul furnished with "all Virtues belonging to her Sex and Condition," notably humility, modesty, temperance, justice, courage, courtesy, beneficence, and piety.

29. Anne directed the enterprise (notable among family histories for its completeness and accuracy), annotated the volumes, and wrote the memorials of her immediate family and herself. The project had its origin (the title pages proclaim) in Margaret Clifford's "great and painful industry" in collecting records "out of the several offices and courts of this kingdom" to begin the lawsuits in Anne's behalf.

30. *Records of George,* 1.

31. See discussion and record of inscriptions in Williamson, *Anne Clifford,* 334–345, 489–507.

32. *Life of Me,* 36.

33. *Records of George,* 6.

34. Anne's collection of his voyages is entitled "A Brief Relation of the Severall Voyages undertaken and performed by the Right Honourable George, Earle of Cumberland in his own person and at his owne charge . . . faithfully collected out of the Relations Observations and Journals of Severall Credible and Worthie Per-

sons Actors and Commanders under the said Noble Earle." The original is at Kendal, Cumbria Record Office, WD/Hoth/Additional Records, 70; the Lambeth Palace Library has a copy, MS 2688.

35. *Records of George,* 7–8.

36. The tombstone identifies George Clifford as the "last heir male of the Cliffords that rightfully enjoyed those ancient lands of inheritance in Westmoreland and in Craven, with the Baronies and Honours appertaining to them," and herself as his only surviving "legitimate" child. Williamson, *Anne Clifford,* 405.

37. *Life of Me,* 40. Cf. *The Countess of Pembroke's Arcadia* [The Old Arcadia], ed. Jean Robertson (Oxford: Oxford University Press, 1973), 85. The passage echoes verses sung by Dorus in "The First Eclogues": "Come from marble bowers, many times the gay harbour of anguish." In the Van Dyke painting at Wilton of Philip Herbert, his first and second wives, and his children, Anne is shown curiously detached from the rest of the family, in a sober black dress, gazing straight forward.

38. In retrospect she counts Dorset and Pembroke (for their nobility) among the many blessings Providence bestowed on her (*Life of Me,* 39): "I must confess with unexpressible thankfullness, that . . . I was born a happy creature in mind, body, and fortune, and that those two lords of mine, to whom I was afterwards by the Divine providence marryed, were in their several kinds worthy noblemen as any then were in this kingdom; yet was it my misfortune to have contradictions and crosses with them both." She says nothing about the profligacy of either.

39. *Life of Me,* 44. Her "character" of Dorset portrayed him as "of a just mynde, of a sweete Disposition, and verie valiant in his own person"; as "so good a scholar in all manner of learning" that he surpassed all the young nobility at Oxford; and as a generous patron "to scholars, soldiers, and all worthy men." His chief fault was diminishing his estate through "excessive bounty" and "excessive prodigality in house-keeping, and other noble ways at court, as tilting, masquing, and the like." To Dorset's brother Edward, who succeeded to the title, she ascribed "malitious hatred" and constant machinations, deflected by the usual providential protection: "By the cuningness of his witt he was a great practiser against me, from the time that I marryed his brother till his own death . . . but I, whose destiny was guided by a mercyfull and divine Providence, escaped the subtilty of all his practices, and the evils which he plotted against me." *Life of Me,* 45–46.

40. *Life of Me,* 49. Her "character" of Pembroke (Philip Herbert) points with pride to his heritage—his mother was "only sister to the renowned Sir Philip Sidney." But she implies his failure to live up to it: he was "no scholar at all," having left the university after only a few months to become a courtier, "as judging himself fit for that kind of life when he was not passing fifteen or sixteen years of age." Again she sits in judgment, offering a balanced evaluation of his qualities: "He was of a very quick apprehension, a sharp understanding, very crafty withal, and of a discerning spirit, but extreamly cholerick by nature" and "generally throughout the realm very well beloved." *Life of Me,* 55. Anne evidently wanted (and achieved with Northampton) a much better match for her daughter, but she describes herself simply as supporting her daughter's wishes and interests against her stepfather. The terms again suggest mother and daughter united in opposition to the patriarchy: "A great cause of anger and falling out between my lord and me, because he desired to have one of his younger sons marryed with my daughter

Isabella, which I could no way remedie, my daughter being herself extreamly averse from that match, though he believed it was in my power to have brought it to pass." *Life of Me,* 52.

41. See "A Summary by way of digression, concerning Francis Clifford, who came to be 4th Earl of Cumberland" (Gilson, *Lives,* 11–14), and "A Summary, by way of digression, concerning Henry, Lord Clifford, fifth and last heir male of the Cliffords that were Earls of Cumberland" (Gilson, *Lives,* 15–17). She describes her usurping uncle Francis as "an honorable gentleman, and of a good, noble, sweet, and courteous nature," displacing her resentment onto his son and heir, Henry, whom she identifies as the prime mover against her in that he "did absolutely govern both him [Francis] and his estate." She also claims (improbably) that his marriage to the daughter of Robert Cecil, "the greatest man of power then in the kingdom . . . was made purposely on his side to maintain those suits of law more powerfully" against her. Gilson, *Lives,* 15.

42. *Life of Me,* 36. She reaffirmed this point in her *Memorial* of Margaret Clifford (30), citing a "great divine" who said that Margaret was like a seraph in her "ardent love and affection toward the most Divine Trinity, towards all goodness and good folks, and that she had the virtue of the bowells of compassion in her in more perfection than any he ever knew; and therefore he thought it much more happiness to be descended from so blessed a woman, than to be born heir to a great kingdom."

43. *Memorial of Margaret,* 19–23. Her interests are underscored in the Great Picture, which depicts Margaret holding the Psalms of David; the Bible, an English translation of Seneca, and (her own) handwritten book of alchemical distillations and medicines are on a shelf over her head. See the illustration at the beginning of this chapter, and Williamson, *Anne Clifford,* 339. Her "high spirit" is both alluded to and demonstrated in several letters from Margaret to her husband in 1603–4 protesting his account of their separation as owing to her "extreme high spiritt, that your Lordshipp cannot endure to live withall, nor to afford such allowance, as in honour you have promised." Portland Papers, vol. 23, ff. 25–26; cf. ff. 17, 35.

44. *Memorial of Margaret,* 26.

45. These letters between Anne Clifford and her mother are from the period June 16, 1614–April 26, 1616, and are in Kendal, Cumbria Record Office, WD/Hoth/Box 44. I have modernized orthography in Margaret's letters, as it is very eccentric and marked with northern dialect elements. A copy by Anne in the Portland Papers, vol. 23, ff. 65–66, is much condensed.

46. Ibid. Cf. Williamson, *Anne Clifford,* 146, 151–153.

47. WD/Hoth/Box 44. Cf. Williamson, *Anne Clifford,* 154.

48. WD/Hoth/Box 44.

49. *Memorial of Margaret,* 18.

50. Anne Clifford's letters of May 3, 1615, and April 26, 1616, to her mother, WD/Hoth/Box 44. See also Williamson, *Anne Clifford,* 149, 154.

51. *Memorial of Margaret,* 23–24. She also found a quasi-typological meaning in the "remarkable" destiny whereby "those countries where my mother lived a stranger and a pilgrim and in some discontents are now the setled abode and habitation of both her [married] grandchildren." *Life of Me,* 53.

52. Reprinted in Williamson, *George, Third Earl of Cumberland,* 285–288.

53. The monument, known locally as "The Countess's Pillar," is inscribed:
THIS PILLAR WAS ERECTED IN ANNO DOMINI JANUARY, 1654 BY YE RIGHT
HONOBLE ANNE, COUNTESS DOWAGER OF PEMBROKE, ETC. DAUGHTER AND
SOLE HEIRE OF YE RIGHT HONOBLE GEORGE EARL OF CUMBERLAND, ETC.
FOR A MEMORIAL OF HER LAST PARTING IN THIS PLACE WITH HER GOOD
AND PIOUS MOTHER, YE RIGHT HONOBLE MARGARET, COUNTESS DOWAGER
OF CUMBERLAND, YE 2ND OF APRIL 1616, IN MEMORIAL WHEREOF SHE ALSO
LEFT AN ANNUITY OF FOUR POUNDS TO BE DISTRIBUTED TO YE POOR
WITHIN THIS PARISH OF BROUGHAM EVERY 2ND DAY OF APRIL FOR EVER,
UPON YE STONE TABLE HERE HARD BY. LAUS DEO.
The epitaph inscribed on the tomb was possibly written by Anne:
WHO, FAYTH, LOVE, MERCY, NOBLE CONSTANCIE,
TO GOD, TO VIRTUE, TO DISTRESS, TO RIGHT,
OBSERV'D, EXPRESS'T, SHOW'D, HELD RELIGIOUSLIE
HATH HERE THE MONUMENT THOU SEEST IN SIGHT.
THE COVER OF HER EARTHLY PART, BUT, PASSENGER,
KNOW HEAVEN AND FAME CONTAYN THE BEST OF HER.

54. *Memorial of Margaret,* 24. She made large claims for her aunt's influence:
"This Countess of Warwick . . . was no less generally esteemed and honored
through the whole court and all the said Queen's dominions; which indeed she
deserved, for she was a great friend to virtue and a helper to many petitioners and
others that were in distress, that came to court for relief of their wrongs."

55. *Life of Me,* 36, 38.

56. Anne Clifford, *Life of Me,* 35–36. Daniel had formerly served as tutor to
William Herbert, son to the Earl of Pembroke and Mary Sidney. For the account
books, see T. D. Whitaker, *The History and Antiquities of the Deanery of Craven*
(London, 1878), 388. Also see Williamson, *Anne Clifford,* 58–67.

57. *Memorial of Margaret,* 28.

58. See illustration at beginning of chapter. Williamson, *Anne Clifford,* 498–
500, provides a listing of the books.

59. Among the literary works addressed to Margaret Clifford as patron are
Spenser's *Fowre Hymnes* (1596), Daniel's *Poetical Essayes* (1599) and *Whole Workes*
(1601, 1604, 1607); Henry Lok, *Ecclesiastes* (1597); Robert Greene, *Penelope's Web*
(1587); Thomas Lodge, *Prosopopeia: Containing the Teares of the holy Marie* (1596);
and Lanyer, *Salve Deus* (1611). Also works by Henry Peacham, Henry Constable,
and Francis Davison. See Williams, *Index of Dedications.*

60. Theological works addressed to Margaret Clifford as patron include Wil-
liam Perkins, *Salve for a Sicke man* (1611), and *Workes* (1600); Samuel Hieron, *Cer-
tain Meditations* (1615) and *Sermons* (1620); Richard Greenham, *Works* (1599);
Thomas Saville, *The Raising of Them that are Fallen* (1606); Peter Muffett, *The
Excellencie of the Mysterie of Christ Jesus* (1590); Richard Vennor, *The Right Way to
Heaven* (1602). Also works by James Balmford, Thomas Tymme, H. Graie, and
Christopher Shutte. See Williams, *Index of Dedications.*

61. Samuel Daniel, "To the Lady Anne Clifford," in *A Panegyrike Congratulatory . . . Also Certaine Epistles,* sigs. E 5–6.

62. "To the right noble Lady Anne Clifford," in *Certaine Small Works* (London,
1607) [sig. A 7]; "To the Lady Anne, Countesse of Dorcet," in *Salve Deus,* sigs. e

4-f 2. Lanyer's country-house poem "The Description of Cooke-Ham" contains a much idealized and perhaps wholly fanciful description of Anne's youthful sports and recreations.

63. Anthony Stafford, *Staffords Niobe*, pt. 2 (London, 1611), rpt. in Williamson, *Anne Clifford*, 516–517; cf. ibid., 329–333.

64. Williamson, *Anne Clifford*, 63.

65. Rainbowe, *Sermon*, 39.

66. Both comment on her readiness to quote Scripture, and her special fondness for the Psalms and Romans 8, Sedgwick observing also that "she could give a good account of most histories that are extant in the English tongue." Both comment as well on her lifelong inattention to food and clothing: Sedgwick notes that "she wore in her latter days, always very plain and mean apparel; indeed far too mean for her quality." Rainbowe, *Sermon*, 39–40; Sedgwick, *Memoirs*, 302–303.

67. Rainbowe, *Sermon*, 40.

68. BL, Additional MS 15,232.

69. See *Faerie Queene* VI, stanza 36, ll. 6–7: "Through infusion sweete / Of thine own spirit, which doth in me survive / I follow here the footing of thy feete."

70. For some theoretical treatments of autobiographical writing, and the special features of women's autobiography, see James Olney, ed., *Autobiography: Essays Theoretical and Critical* (Princeton: Princeton University Press, 1980); Elizabeth W. Bruss, *Autobiographical Acts: The Changing Situation of a Literary Genre* (Baltimore: Johns Hopkins University Press, 1976); Wayne Shumaker, *English Autobiography: Its Emergence, Materials, and Forms* (Berkeley: University of California Press, 1954); Karl J. Weintraub, *The Value of the Individual: Self and Circumstance in Autobiography* (Chicago: University of Chicago Press, 1978); Domna C. Stanton, ed., *The Female Autograph* (New York: Literary Forum, 1984; rpt. Chicago: University of Chicago Press, 1987); and Sidonie Smith, *A Poetics of Women's Autobiography: Marginality and the Fictions of Self-Representation* (Bloomington: Indiana University Press, 1987). Some historical treatments of autobiographical writing in early modern England include Paul Delany, *British Autobiography in the Seventeenth Century* (London: Routledge, 1969); Sara Heller Mendelson, "Stuart Women's Diaries and Occasional Memoirs," in *Women in English Society, 1500–1800*, ed. Mary Prior (London: Methuen, 1985), 181–210; Harriet Blodgett, *Centuries of Female Days: Englishwomen's Private Diaries* (New Brunswick: Rutgers University Press, 1988). Extracts are reprinted in Elspeth Graham et al., eds. *Her Own Life: Autobiographical Writing by Seventeenth-Century Englishwomen* (London: Routledge, 1989). Delany accounts for the upsurge of autobiographies by both men and women in the later seventeenth century by pointing to the increased self-awareness and self-importance promoted by Puritan methods of introspection and also the widespread consciousness of changes in social roles (*British Autobiography*, 1–23).

71. See list in *CBEL*, I, 2259–64; also W. Matthews, ed., *British Diaries: An Annotated Bibliography of British Diaries Written between 1442 and 1942* (Berkeley: University of California Press, 1950). Both of the domestic diaries were products of a Puritan upbringing, and probably undertaken as exercises in spiritual account keeping. Lady Margaret Hoby's *Diary* records Hoby's daily prayers and medita-

tions, her constant attention to household management and accounts, and her frequent medical and surgical attentions to the sick of the community, but displays little introspection or self-analysis. Grace Sherrington Mildmay's lengthy memoir of her life (c. 1570–1617) as child and wife (written in her old age, as a contribution to the education of her daughter and other young people of her class) contains much lively description of daily activities and family life.

72. Simon Forman, "Autobiography," Bodleian, MS Ashmole 208.

73. Sackville-West's edition obscures the effect of the format by placing Anne's marginalia, together with her own explanatory notes, at the bottom of the pages. Two hands at least are identifiable in the marginal notes, though the voice is Anne Clifford's.

74. That some marginal notations were added much later is clear from that for December 15, 1616: "Upon the 15th was Mr. *John Tufton* just 8 years, being he that was afterwards married to my 1st Child in the Church of *St. Bartholomew*" (*Diary,* 44). That marriage took place in 1629. There is some attention to public matters in the *Diary* proper, but the large number of such references in the marginalia suggest that Anne felt called upon to fill in that aspect of the record, so as to fit her diary for a wider audience—including at least her descendants.

75. *Diary,* 12. Anne conveys a sense of the plague as a fact of daily life:
From *Windsor* the Court removed to *Hampton Court,* where my mother and I lay at *Hampton Court,* in one of the round towers, round about which were tents where they died two or three in a day of the plague. There I fell extremely sick of a fever, so as my Mother was in some doubt it might turn to the plague, but within two or three days I grew reasonably well, and was sent away to my cousin *Stiddolph's,* for Mrs. *Taylor* was put from me, her husband dying of the plague shortly after . . . The next day Mr. *Menerill* as he went abroad fell down suddenly and died, so as most thought it was the plague, which was then very rife; it put us all in great fear and amazement.

76. *Diary,* 7–17. Anne records her particular excitement over the ceremonies surrounding the Feast of Saint George at Windsor: "I stood with my Lady *Elizabeth's* Grace in the shrine of the great hall at Windsor, to see the King and all the knights set at dinner. Thither came the Archduke's Ambassador, who was received by the King and Queen in the great hall, where there was such an infinite company of lords and ladies and so great a Court, as I think I shall never see the like again" (11).

77. *Diary,* 18–19. On the same day, she notes, Lady Grantham warned her of the impending visit of the Archbishop of Canterbury and "persuaded me very earnestly to agree to this business which I took as a great argument of her love."

78. Kendal, Cumbria Record Office, WD/Hoth/44. The paper, duly witnessed by nine men's signatures and also her mother's, reads:
Memoranda that I *Anne* Countesse of dorsett, soale daughter and heire to George late Earle of Cumberland, doth take witnesse of all these gentlemen present: that I both desier and offer my selfe to goe up to *London,* with my men and horses, but they having Received a Contrary Commandment, from my Lord my husband will by no meanes Consent nor permitt me to goe with them, Now my desire is, that all the world may know that this stay of myne, percedes onely from my husbands Command, Contrary to my Consent or

agreement, whereof I have gotten these names underwritten to testefye the same.

79. *Diary*, 45. Specifically, she reports that Lady Arundel "had much talk with me about the business and persuaded me to yield to the King in all things"; and that "Lady D[erby?], my Lady *Montgomery*, my Lord *Burleigh*, persuaded me to refer these businesses to the King" (*Diary*, 46, 49).

80. One was Lady Selby (Dorset's cousin and daughter to the Lord Treasurer), who told her "she had heard some folks say that I have done well in not consenting to the composition" (*Diary*, 31–32).

81. Banished to the country, she was especially anxious when Dorset reported in late February "how bitter the King stood against me," and that he would disallow even her rights of reversion if she held out (*Diary*, 56).

82. Ibid., 80–81. She notes that the King "bid me to go to his attorney, who should inform him more of my desires," suggesting some gesture to secure the rights of reversion; she records also that on this occasion "King *James* kissed me when I was with him, and that was the first time I was so near King *James* as to touch him."

83. Ibid., 91–92. The "thirds" were her general dowry rights as a widow to one-third of her husband's estate; she had agreed (reluctantly) to the revocation of the previous jointure settlement securing those rights.

84. Ibid., 106. Earlier, as Aubrey notes (*Brief Lives*, 100) Dorset was said to be the "greatest gallant" of Venetia Stanley (later Digby) and to have had "one, if not more children by her." Aubrey reports also that Dorset settled on her an annuity of £500.

85. *Diary*, 102. He responded by promising her a jointure of £4,000 a year, though that was to be derived in part from funds that would be forfeited to Cumberland if she renewed her lawsuits.

86. Williamson, *Anne Clifford*, 149.

87. Her second daughter, Isabella, was born in 1622, after the period covered by the *Diary*.

88. Lawrence Stone, among others, has speculated that the high rate of infant mortality contributed to the disposition of early modern era parents to hold their young children at some emotional distance. *Family, Sex, and Marriage*, 37–66. The youngest infants were at greatest risk, and by age five the worst hazards had been survived. The *Diary* shows that Anne kept no such distance from the infant Margaret, but the naming at age five recognizes the place in society she might now live to fill. On that birthday also Dorset "caused her health to be drank throughout the house," and in the same month she began to sit for her portrait by Van Somer (*Diary*, 104–105).

89. *Diary*, 36, 46, 80, 83–84. Besides Lady Bedford (her kinswoman and the Queen's favorite), she sought out Lady Ruthven, Lady Wotton, Lady Verulam (wife of Francis Bacon, the Lord Chancellor), and Lady Pembroke (wife of the Lord Chamberlain).

90. She visited Penshurst with some frequency, associating with Lady Lisle (Barbara Sidney), Lady Mary Wroth, and Lady Dorothy Sidney (75–77). On one occasion, however, after a quarrel (August 4, 1617) Dorset went off to Penshurst without her, "although my Lord and Lady *Lisle* sent a man on purpose to desire

me to come." She also cultivated Dorset's sisters, the Ladies Sackville, Compton, and Beauchamp, and his niece Cecily Neville, endeavoring "to win the love of my Lord's kindred by all the fair means I could" (*Diary*, 69).

91. Ibid., 74. She also records visits (January 1619) from "my old Lady Donne and my young Lady Donne, with whom I had much talk about religion" (85).

92. This book, belonging to her mother, is a treatise inspired by Petrarch's *De Vita Solitaria;* it has been attributed to Sir John Harington, and is included in *The Letters and Epigrams of Sir John Harington Together with The Prayse of Private Life*, ed. Norman McClure (Philadelphia: University of Pennsylvania Press, 1930), 323–378. The manuscript was presented to Margaret Clifford by Samuel Daniel.

6. Defending Women's Essential Equality: Rachel Speght

1. For an excellent survey of the English Renaissance phase of the *querelle*, see Woodbridge, *Women of the English Renaissance*. For a survey of the English controversy from the beginnings to 1568, see Francis Utley, *The Crooked Rib: An Analytical Index to the Argument about Women in English and Scots Literature to the End of the Year 1568* (New York: Octagon, 1970; 1st. ed., 1944). For the social context and readership, see Wright, *Middle-Class Culture*, 465–507. See also Katherine Rogers, *The Troublesome Helpmate: A History of Misogyny in Literature* (Seattle: University of Washington Press, 1966). Some tracts from the controversy and a survey of the social and literary contexts appear in Katherine U. Henderson and Barbara F. McManus, eds., *Half Humankind: Contexts and Texts of the Controversy about Women in England, 1540–1640* (Urbana: University of Illinois Press, 1985), and Simon Shepherd, ed., *The Women's Sharp Revenge* (London: Fourth Estate, 1985).

2. Joan Kelly, "Early Feminist Theory and the *Querelle des Femmes*, 1400–1789," *Signs: Journal of Women in Culture and Society*, 8 (1982), 4–28. Christine de Pisan (1364–1430), *The Boke of the Cyte of Ladys*, trans. Brian Anslay (London, 1521); Henry Cornelius Agrippa, *De Nobilitate et Praecellentia Foemenei Sexus, Opera* (Lyons, 1531), trans. David Clapham, *A Treatise of the Nobilitie and excellencye of woman kynde* (London, 1542); Baldassare Castiglione, *Il Cortegiano* (1528), trans. Sir Thomas Hoby (London, 1561).

3. Woodbridge usefully distinguishes the formal genre, with its distinctive rhetorical features, from general literary attacks on women. Those features include positing an opponent, real or imagined; use of the dialogue or judicial oration forms; arguing a thesis about the nature of women; employing logical and rhetorical methods; using exempla (historical and literary, biblical and classical); cataloguing women's faults and virtues. Contemporary English defenses of women, some of them possibly known to Speght, include Lodowick Lloyd, *The Choyce of Jewels* (London, 1607); I.G., *An Apologie for Women-Kinde* (London, 1605); and Daniel Tuvil, *Asylum Veneris; or, A Sanctuary for Ladies* (London, 1616). Later important defenses include Christopher Newstead, *An Apology for Women; or, Womens Defence* (London, 1620); and Thomas Heywood, *Gynaikeion: or, Nine Bookes of Various History Concerninge Women* (London, 1624).

4. Thomas Tel-troth [Joseph Swetnam], *The Araignment of Lewde, idle, froward, and unconstant women: Or the vanitie of them, choose you whether* (London: E. Allde for T. Archer, 1615). In later editions, his cover blown, Swetnam signed his epistle with his full name. Swetnam's only other known book deals with fencing,

The Schoole of the Noble and Worthy Science of Defence (London, 1617). Swetnam draws heavily upon, indeed virtually plagiarizes from, John Lyly's "Cooling Carde for Phalautus and all Fond Lovers," appended to *Euphues* (London, 1578), as well as from Antonio de Guevara, *The golden boke of Marcus Aurelius*, trans. Thomas North (London, 1557). Other contemporary attacks on women include Thomas Nashe, *The Anatomie of Absurdity: Contayning a breefe confutation of the slender prayses to feminine perfection* (London, 1589), and *The Bachelars Banquet* (London, 1603).

5. Swetnam, *Araignment*, sigs. A 2v–A 4. The tone of jesting disclaimer recurs at the end of the tract, as Swetnam advises readers already involved with women "to take it merrily, and to esteeme of this booke onely as the toyes of an idle head." And he again seems to invite a woman respondent, saying, "I would not have women murmur against me for that I have not written more bitterly against men . . . a most unkinde part it were for one man to speake ill of another" (sig. I 4v, 64).

6. Rachel Speght, *A Mouzell for Melastomus, The Cynical Bayter of, and foul mouthed Barker against* EVAHS SEX. *Or an Apologeticall Answere to that Irreligious and Illiterate Pamphlet made by Jo. Sw. and by him Intituled, The Arraignment of Women* (London: Nicholas Oakes for Thomas Archer, 1617).

7. Ester Sowernam, *Ester hath hang'd Haman: or, An Answere to a lewd Pamphlet, entituled The Arraignment of Women. With the arraignment of lewd, idle froward, and unconstant men, and Husbands. Divided into two Parts. The first proveth the dignity and worthinesse of Women, out of divine Testimonies. The second shewing the estimation of the Foeminine Sexe, in ancient and Pagan times . . . Written by Ester Sowernam, neither Maide, Wife nor Widdowe, yet really all and therefore experienced to defend all* (London: Nicholas Bourne, 1617).

8. Constantia Munda, *The Worming of a mad Dogge: Or, a Soppe for Cerberus the Jaylor of Hell. No Confutation but a sharpe Redargution of the bayter of Women* (London: Laurence Hayes, 1617), 1, 3.

9. *Swetnam the Woman-hater, Arraigned by Women. A new Comedie, Acted at the Red Bull by the late Queenes Servants* (London, 1620). Cf. *Swetnam the Woman-Hater: The Controversy and the Play*, ed. Coryl Crandall (Lafayette: Purdue University Studies, 1969); Crandall, "The Cultural Implications of the Swetnam Anti-Feminist Controversy in the Seventeenth Century," *Journal of Popular Culture*, 2 (1968–1969), 136–148. Crandall argues that making Swetnam a figure of fun indicates that theater audiences (with their large female component) were in sympathy with the notion of a rough equality of the sexes.

10. Their legends as lower-class warrior women, and literary treatments of them in popular ballads and news reports as well as in Middleton and Dekker's comedy *The Roaring Girl* (1611), are treated in Shepherd, *Amazons and Warrior Women*, 65–106.

11. *Mystical Bedlam. Or the World of Mad-Men* (London, 1615), 50.

12. Chamberlain, II, 286–287.

13. On February 12 Chamberlain again wrote to Carleton (ibid., II, 289): "Our pulpits ring continually of the insolence and impudence of women: and to helpe the matter forward the players have likewise taken them to taske, and so the ballades and ballad-singers, so that they can come no where but theyre eares tingle: and yf all this will not serve the King threatens to fall upon theyre husbands,

parents, or frends that have or shold have powre over them and make them pay for yt."

14. *Hic Mulier: Or, the Man-Woman: Being a Medicine to cure the coltish disease of the Staggers in the Masculine-Feminine of our Times. Exprest in a breif Declamation* (London: J.T., 1620).

15. *Haec-Vir; Or, the Womanish-Man: Being an Answere to a late Booke intituled Hic-Mulier. Exprest in a brief Dialogue betweene Haec-Vir the Womanish-Man, and Hic-Mulier the Man-Woman* (London: J.T., 1620).

16. *Muld Sacke: Or the Apologie of Hic Mulier: to the late Declamation against her* (London: R. Meighen, 1620).

17. Woodbridge and also Henderson and McManus assume that Sowernam and Munda are women; Shepherd and Ann Jones suspect Munda is not. Both may well be men: Sowernam's claim that "she" is neither maid, wife, nor widow would of course be true of a man, though it alludes to Swetnam's use of the formula to designate a harlot; that formula also allows Sowernam to condescend to the "maid" Rachel, and to allude to the hoary (male) literary genre of debates between virgins and wives (and sometimes widows) as to which is the best estate. Also, Sowernam's description of her activities in relation to the terms of the law courts—"my repair to London this last Michaelmas Term"—might hint that the writer is a law student or law clerk. Jones argues that Munda's learned patchwork of Juvenalian invective and breathless rage replete with technical jargon suggests male professional training. Ann Jones, "Counterattacks on 'the Bayter of Women': Three Pamphleteers of the Early Seventeenth Century," in Haselkorn and Travitsky, *Renaissance Englishwoman*, 45–62.

18. *Jane Anger her Protection for Women* (London, 1589).

19. Woodbridge, *Women of the English Renaissance*, 88–89.

20. Rachel Speght, *Mortalities Memorandum with a Dream Prefixed, imaginarie in manner; reall in matter* (London: Jacob Bloome, 1621), sig. A 2.

21. *Swetnam the Woman-hater*, sigs. I 4v–Kv.

22. Sowernam, *Ester*, sig. A 2v. This may smack somewhat of male condescension to the woman who cannot really bring off the intellectual enterprise she attempts. The comment that Speght charges and condemns women is unjustified; she merely makes the usual distinction between good and bad women to underscore Swetnam's failure to fulfill his promise to do so. Speght insists that there are good and bad of both sexes.

23. Munda, *Soppe for Cerberus*, 16.

24. Shepherd, *The Women's Sharp Revenge*, 58. Parish registers—Guildhall, microfilm 6984; *The Registers of St. Mary Magdalen, Milk Street (1558–1666)*, transcribed by A. W. Hughes Clarke, 2 vols. (London, 1942)—show each year's entries of baptisms, marriages, and deaths from 1558 on subscribed "per me Jacobum Speght sacrae Theologiae Bacchalaurum." Either the James Speght who was ordained in 1591 took over the parish from a father or relative of the same name; or, more likely, he brought into order and subscribed the parish records back to the beginning of Elizabeth's reign. There are numerous Speghts among the entries, but no record of Rachel's baptism; the only Rachel was buried May 21, 1595 (*Registers of St. Mary Magdalen*, I, 42). Rachel's birth date is calculated on the basis of her statement that she had "not yet seen twenty years" when she wrote her *Mouzell* (1617).

25. James Speght, *A Briefe Demonstration, who have, and of the certainty of their*

salvation, that have the Spirit of Christ. Published at the instant desire of some godly affected, for the setling of their hope, that are shaken with temptations (London, 1613). *The Day-spring of Comfort. A Sermon Preached before the Lord Maior and Aldermen of London on Sunday the 6. of January, Anno 1610.* [*1611*] *being also the Feast of the Epiphanie* (London, 1615), reprinted as *The Christian's Comfort. A Sermon Preached before the Lord Maior and Aldermen of London* (London, 1616).

26. The epistle to Hicks and his wife thanks them for "that continued love on your part, and undeserved kindness to me-wards (more like the kindnesse of Parents, then meere friends) which ever since my first comming to have Pastorall charge, where God cast your lot of habitation, and on your selves a lot of many and great blessings, hath not suffered Eclypse . . . but dayly increase." He later identifies their offspring as "that pair of elect Ladies." The parish registers of St. Mary Magdalen record births, marriages, and deaths for numerous members of the Hicks family.

27. *DNB.* The Moundford family is also conspicuous in the parish records of St. Mary Magdalen. "Mr Doctor Moundeford, Phitision" was buried in the church on December 13, 1630, his wife on November 9, 1655.

28. *Mortalities Memorandum*, sigs. A 2v–A 3.

29. Thomas Moundford, *Vir Bonus* (London, 1622). The first impression carries a dedication to James alone; the next (also 1622) adds the other dedicatees. The judges are Sir James Lee, Sir Julius Caesar, Sir Henry Hobart (married to a daughter of Robert Sidney), and Sir Lawrence Tanfield (Elizabeth Cary's father). Moundford also translated from French to Latin André de Laurens, *De Morbis Melancholis, & eorum cura Tractatus* (London, 1599).

30. See chapter 3.

31. *Mouzell*, sigs. A 3, A 4v.

32. Guildhall, microfilm 4783; *The Register of St. Clement, Eastcheap*, transcribed by A. W. Hughes Clarke, 2 vols. (London, 1937), I, 87, records the marriage of "Mr. James Speght, parson of this parish & Elizabeth Smyth, widdow, of Newington Butts" on February 13, 1620. The parish registers of St. Mary Magdalen record the burial "within the Rail" on April 7, 1637, of "James Speght, Doctor in Divinity and Rector of this Parish."

33. Joseph Foster, ed., *London Marriage Licenses, 1521–1869* (London: Bernard Quaritch, 1887), 1098.

34. There is a record of marriage at St. Mary Woolchurch Haw, on August 6, 1621, between "Mr. Willliam Proctor and Rachel Spight, both of St. Buttals [Botolphs] Aldersgate," Guildhall, microfilm 7644; *The Transcript of the Records of the United Parishes of S. Mary Woolnoth and S. Mary Woolchurch haw*, transcribed by J. M. S. Brooke and A. H. Hallen (London, 1886), 351.

35. *Kissing the Rod*, 68.

36. *Alumni Oxoniensis*, ed. Joseph Foster (Oxford, 1891), III, 1215. See *Registers of St. Mary Magdalen*, passim, for the Procter entries.

37. The parish registers of St. Giles, Cripplegate (Guildhall, microfilm 6419/2), record the baptisms: "Rachell dau: of William Procter Minister" (February 26, 1626 [1627]); and "William, sonne of Mr. William Procter Minister" (December 15, 1630). The mother's name is not given (in these records it sometimes is and sometimes is not). William might, of course, be the son of a second marriage; on present evidence we cannot be sure.

38. William Procter, *The Watchman warning. A Sermon Preached at Pauls Crosse*

the 26. of September, 1624 (London, 1625). Procter identifies himself as "Master of Arts and Minister of Gods Word," and dates his sermon "From my house at Up-minster in Essex, this 20, of October, 1624." The sermon is offered as a "forewarn-ing of this famous Citie especially, and whole kingdome also" as inviting destruc-tion for their sins; it develops the metaphor of ministers as watchmen, and justifies God's decree of reprobation against sinners.

39. Guildhall, microfilm 17,614, parish registers of All Hallows, Lombard Street, record the burial of one William Proctor in 1653. The Guildhall burial index, 1538–1853, compiled by Percival Boyd, records only men's burials. Parish records regularly enter women's burials, but for the period in question records for many City churches were destroyed by the great fire of 1666.

40. Swetnam, *Araignment*, 1–5.

41. For a similar argument, see Jones, "Counterattacks," 49–50.

42. Sigs. B 4–B 4v. The chief basis for this suspicion is the use in "Philo-mathes" of one of Speght's favorite terms, "obtrectation," together with the simi-larity of the verse in all three to Speght's own.

43. Swetnam's first epistle is addressed "Neither to the best nor yet to the worst, but to the common sort of Women"; his second, "To the Reader," is ad-dressed "Neyther to the wisest Clarke, nor yet to the starkest Foole, but unto the ordinary sort of giddy-headed young men" (sigs. A 2, A 4).

44. Speght's (or the printer's) italics point to the pun.

45. See Robert Cleaver, *A Godlie Forme of Household Government* (London, 1598), 170: "The dutie of the husband is, to travell abroad to seeke living: and the wives dutie is to keep the house"; and William Whately, *A Bride-Bush. Or, A Di-rection for Married Persons* (London, 1616), 84: "He without doores, she within: he abroad, she at home." For further discussion, see Fitz [Woodbridge], "'What Says the Married Woman?'"

46. Swetnam, *Araignment*, 56.

47. "A Homilie of the State of Matrimonie," in *The Seconde Tome of Homilies* (London, 1595). The homilies were appointed to be read regularly in the churches in Elizabeth's reign, and the practice continued under James.

48. Henry Smith, *A Preparative to Marriage* (London, 1591), 62; Whately, *Bride-Bush*, 189, 113.

49. William Gouge, *Of Domesticall Duties: Eight Treatises* (London, 1622), 317–318.

50. Wright, *Middle-Class Culture*, 228–296.

51. Since it suits Speght's allegory to accept the names and female identities of these writers, her doing so is not a persuasive argument for female authorship. She may or may not have known the authors' identities.

7. Resisting Tyrants: Elizabeth Cary

1. *The Tragedie of Mariam, the Faire Queene of Jewry. Written by that learned, vertuous, and truly noble Ladie, E.C.* (London, 1613); rpt., Malone Society (Oxford: Oxford University Press, 1914). I cite the 1613 edition by act and scene. One of the three copies in the British Library has a near-contemporary manuscript note on the title page, "Lady Eliz. Carew only piece [play]." Margaret Ferguson and Barry Weller are editing *Mariam*, together with the *Life* of Cary written by her daughter (see note 6 and Introduction, note 5).

2. *The History of the Life, Reign, and Death of Edward II. King of England, and Lord of Ireland. With the Rise and Fall of His Great Favourites, Gaveston and the Spencers. Written by E.[lizabeth] F.[alkland] in the year 1627, and printed verbatim from the Original* (London, 1680); cited in text by page number. The author's preface is dated "20 February 1627 [1628]." The grounds for this attribution are summarized in this chapter and discussed in detail in Appendix A.

3. Among those who read the work as espousing total wifely submission are Betty S. Travitsky, "The *Feme Covert* in Elizabeth Cary's *Mariam*," in Levin and Watson, *Ambiguous Realities*, 184–196; Maurice J. Valency, *The Tragedies of Herod & Marianne* (New York: Columbia University Press, 1940), 88–91; Nancy Cotton Pearse, "Elizabeth Cary, Elizabethan Playwright," *Texas Studies in Literature and Language*, 18 (1976–77), 601–608, and Nancy Cotton, *Women Playwrights in England, c. 1363–1750* (Lewisburg, PA: Bucknell University Press, 1980), 31–39. Catherine Belsey's reading emphasizes contradictions in the text which at once affirm and deny subjectivity to Mariam in *The Subject of Tragedy: Identity and Difference in Renaissance Drama* (New York: Methuen, 1985), 164–175. Readings closer to my own in recognizing some subversive elements in the work are Sandra K. Fischer, "Elizabeth Cary and Tyranny, Domestic and Religious," in Hannay, *Silent But for the Word*, 225–237; and especially Margaret W. Ferguson, "Running On with Almost Public Voice: The Case of 'E.C.,'" in *Tradition and the Talent of Women*, ed. Florence Howe (Urbana: University of Illinois Press, 1991), 37–67. Elaine Beilin reads Mariam as attaining to the role of Christlike martyr-heroine in *Redeeming Eve*, 157–176.

4. The MS is at the vicarage, Burford, Oxfordshire; based on the abridged edition of Ortelius (Amsterdam, 1598), it is without maps. The hand is very different from Elizabeth's later cursive writing: it is evidently a schoolgirl exercise in careful printing as well as in translation. The dedication (to her uncle Sir Henry Lee) is signed E. Tanfelde.

5. The witty, tonally ambivalent epitaph is BL, Egerton MS 2725, f. 60, headed "An Epitaph upon the death of the Duke of Buckingham by the Countesse of Faukland." The speaker is Buckingham:

Reader stand still and see, loe, here I am
Who was of late the mighty Buckingham;
God gave to me my being, and my breath;
Two kings their favourers, and a slave my death;
Now for my Fame I challenge, and not crave
That thou beleeve two kings before one slave.

The Perron translation (always attributed to Elizabeth Cary) is *The Reply of the Most Illustrious Cardinall of Perron, to the Answeare of the Most Excellent King of Great Britaine* (Douay, 1630).

6. *The Lady Falkland, Her Life,* ed. R.[ichard] S.[impson], from a manuscript in the Imperial Archives at Lille (London: Catholic Publishing Co., 1861); cited as *Life,* with page number. The work is noted in Donald Stauffer, *English Biography before 1700* (Cambridge, Mass.: Harvard University Press, 1930), 148–150. Georgiana Fullerton's biography *The Life of Elizabeth, Lady Falkland*, Quarterly Series, 43 (London, 1872), follows the daughter's account very closely.

7. The *Life* reports that Lucius Cary had answered a *Defence of the Church of Rome,* by Elizabeth's friend, Mr. Montague; Lucius charged Catholics with the divisions occasioned in families by conversions. Her essay answered his.

8. See p. 183.

9. The work is usually ascribed to Anne, the eldest surviving daughter and the one with widest experience: she was a maid of honor at court and led a group of nuns to Paris to establish a community. But Lucy, also a Benedictine, is another possibility, given that the text characterizes her more fully than the other children.

10. They include personal and public letters in the State Papers Domestic, State Papers (Ireland), and Carew Manuscripts (Lambeth Palace); BL, Additional MSS 11,033 and 3827, and BL, Harleian MSS 1581 and 2305; and contemporary dedications and praises from clients or would-be clients. See also T. Langueville, *Falklands* (London, 1897), 1–94; Kenneth B. Murdock, *The Sun at Noon: Three Biographical Sketches* (New York: Macmillan, 1939), 6–40; Kurt Weber, *Lucius Cary, Second Viscount Falkland* (New York: Columbia University Press, 1940).

11. Although the *Life* emphasizes Elizabeth's humility, it also portrays her "heedlessness" and lack of social decorum, testifying to a deep-rooted indifference to conformity and custom. She often forgot where she was and whom she was with or whom she had met; she neglected her dress and social expectations; she would kneel down in public to ask a blessing of priests. Her carelessness about money is writ large—notably her disposition to give largess when she had no notion of her own financial resources. Beilin argued a similar case in a paper at the Modern Language Association, Washington, D.C., December 28, 1989.

12. Her attitudes are discussed in Ferguson, "Running On," 41, 62–63, n. 21.

13. Weber, *Lucius Cary*, 8–10. Lady Tanfield seems to have been especially resented.

14. She was said to owe the servants £100 for candles, and £200 more, probably for books and writing materials. One (perhaps apocryphal) anecdote in the *Life* tells of the ten-year-old Elizabeth visiting her father's court and saving a woman accused of witchcraft, who had confessed (after interrogation and torture) to causing sickness and death to many persons. Elizabeth reportedly whispered to her father to ask the woman if she had bewitched her uncle (present in court and obviously healthy); when the woman said yes, her confession was seen to be the result of fear, and was dismissed. *Life*, 5–6.

15. John Davies of Hereford, *The Muses Sacrifice* (London, 1612), sig. ✳✳✳3v.

16. Pearse, "Elizabeth Cary," 602.

17. *Life*, 7. She was elsewhere described as rather short and fat. On June 27, 1602, Chamberlain wrote to Carleton the precise sums involved: "Sir Henry Carey [is to marry] Mr. Tanfeild's daughter with 2,000^{li} presently, 2,000^{li} at two years, and 3,000^{li} at his death, yf he chaunce to have more children, otherwise to be his heir." Chamberlain, I, 153. As this letter reveals, the *Life* is mistaken in dating the marriage two years earlier, in 1600.

18. *DNB*, "Henry Cary," III, 1149–50; Weber, *Lucius Cary*, 15–16; *The Scots Peerage*, ed. James Balfour (Edinburgh, 1906), III, 609–612.

19. *Life*, 15. Her eleven children born alive were Catherine, b. 1609, m. Lord Home 1622, d. 1626 (in childbirth); Lucius, b. 1610, d. 1643 (in the Battle of Newbury); Lorenzo, b. 1613, d. 1642 (in battle in Ireland); Anne, b. 1614, professed as Dame Clementina 1639, d. (?); Edward, b. (?), d. 1616; Elizabeth, b. 1617, professed as Sister Augustina 1638, d. 1683; Lucy, b. 1619, professed as Sister Magdalena 1638, d. (?); Victoria, b. 1620, m. Sir William Uvedale 1640, d. (?); Mary, b. 1622, professed as Sister Maria 1638, d. 1693; Patrick, b. 1624 in Ireland, d. 1656; Henry, b.

1625(?), professed as Father Placid, d. 1656. See Balfour, *Scots Peerage,* 609–612, and Weber, *Lucius Cary,* passim.

20. She met with clerics frequenting the house of Richard Neale, Bishop of Durham and later Archbishop of York, and was persuaded by them that she might safely remain in the English Church at present. *Life,* 9–10.

21. Michael Drayton, *Englands Heroicall Epistles* (London, 1597); rpt. 1598, 1599, 1600, 1602, with *The Barons Warres* (1603), *Poems* (1605, 1623). The epistles for the young Elizabeth—an exchange between William de la Pole, Duke of Suffolk, and Queen Margaret—fittingly portray Petrarchan devotion and admiring friendship rather than amorous passion. Drayton adopts a Petrarchan stance himself, claiming that Petrarch's praises of Laura have not evoked in him such admiration of women as has his own observation of Elizabeth.

22. Davies, *Muses Sacrifice,* sig. ✳✳✳2, identifies Elizabeth Cary as "Wife of Sr. Henry Cary," suggesting her relative obscurity compared to the others, but also the need to distinguish her from several other Elizabeth Carys with whom she might be (and has been) confused: Elizabeth Bland Cary, her sister-in-law and the dedicatee of *Mariam;* Elizabeth Spencer Cary, second Lady Hunsdon; and Elizabeth, wife of Sir Robert Carey, who was the guardian of Prince Charles.

23. Ibid., sigs. ✳✳✳3v, A–Av. Ferguson, "Running On," 44–45, unpacks the contradictory messages in Davies's poem, which on the one hand urges the noble ladies to publish, but on the other reinforces the cultural construct of publication as a debasement of noble status and a likely indicator of a woman's sexual license.

24. *Englands Helicon. Or, The Muses Harmony* (London, 1614).

25. "A Proclamation . . . for Banishing of Jesuits and Priests from Ireland," in *Catalogue of the Carew MSS (Lambeth) 1603–1624* (London, 1873), 432–433. *DNB;* Weber, *Lucius Cary,* 30–34.

26. *DNB,* "Elizabeth Cary," III, 1151; *Life,* 19–21. Falkland at first seems to have tolerated the enterprise as possibly good for public relations, though he offered no support or financial assistance, and allowed it to collapse entirely after Elizabeth left Ireland.

27. Richard Belling [or Beling], *A Sixth Booke to the Countesse of Pembrokes Arcadia* (Dublin, 1624). Later, the bookseller William Sheares sought her patronage for his edition of Marston, as one "well acquainted with the Muses." John Marston, *The Workes* (London, 1633).

28. SP 63 (Ireland) 242/213, Lord Falkland to Lord Conway, January 26, 1626.

29. SP 63 (Ireland) 242/280, Falkland to Conway, April 5, 1626. The *Life,* 36, asserts that a servant poisoned Falkland's mind against his wife, claiming that she worked to block his affairs at court. Conway's answer, commending Elizabeth's "good sollicitation" for Falkland, elicits further truculence and blame shifting: "I rather wishe she weare at home with hir Mother . . . then travayling to procure Court favour for me . . . from whence I have never receyved other [than] . . . diminutions." SP 63 (Ireland) 242/284.

30. A few years earlier, King James had charged his judges "to have a special care of the papists, and likewise of their wives; for he said, the women were the nourishers of papistry in this kingdom . . . which our Catholic ladies take very ill." Sir Thomas Wynne to Sir Dudley Carleton, February 14, 1618–19, Nichols, II, 136. See chapter 1 for Catholic appeals to Queen Anne and her ladies. Noted recusant (or crypto-Catholic) women of the Caroline court include Queen Henrietta

Maria; Buckingham's mother; Buckingham's wife, Katherine (Manners), who was persuaded to conform outwardly after he married her; Lady Jane Weston; and Lady Jane Clifford.

31. Lady Denby (or Denbigh), to whom Crashaw addressed a famous verse epistle urging her to convert, did not finally make that move and tried hard to restrain Elizabeth from doing so—at one point even locking her in her chambers. Elizabeth escaped, and was promptly received into the Roman Church by one Father Dunstan (Pettinger).

32. Had the conversion remained private—a matter of rumor only—Falkland would have hated it on principle but would not have felt himself shamed and his prospects threatened. Lady Denby probably felt she had to reveal Cary's action lest she be charged with complicity; and the King evidently thought he had to inquire once the affair was public. Cary's letter to her husband, abstracted and enclosed in his letter to Coke on December 29, 1626, claims she is not placing him in jeopardy by entertaining priests illegally and at his expense. She also lays all the unwelcome publicity to the King's charge:

> You chardge me with feedeing Priests and Jesuists; for Jesuists, to my knowl-edge, I never saw the face of any one in my leif, nor intend not to doe. For Priests, it is true I must have conversed with some, els I could not have bene what for no death I will deny my self to be. For feeding them, it is possible some one man may have sum tymes, dined or supped heere, but yf there weare a bitt the more, or yf I ever appointed any thing, but only satt down to such as they provided, I wilbe subject to your displeasure. *And since it pleased his Majesty, to make me wheather I would or not, declare my self Catholike, which is on Tuesdaye last a Month, there is not one of that function ever entred within this howse.*

SP 63 (Ireland) 243/515. Falkland's cover letter to Coke declares: "If I cannot pre-vayle by the assistance of his Majestys just Power, I must Resorte to a separat[i]on *a mensa et thoro,* which I intend for a Last Refudge yf I despayre of her recovery . . . that deales soe treasonablye with me." SP 63 (Ireland) 243/515.

33. SP 63 (Ireland) 243/503, December 8, 1626, Falkland to the King:

> Howe cann your Throne be long well established, or your sacred Person safe in it, whilest these Locusts of Rome, whose Doctrines are as full of horrid treasons, as many of their lives full of horrible Impieties, be permitted to pass at Liberty . . . Some of these Priests as I am informed, expect to receive speedy preferment in hir Majesty's household . . . For the Apostate hir selfe, since I was not so happie to obtain her Confinement at the first to her Mothers, which possibly might have prevented this falling away; yet I most humbly beseech your Majestie that shee may bee nowe committed thither, with Com-mandment to her Mother to receive hir, and to keep hir safe and free from any Communication by word or letter with . . . those Inchanters.

34. Katherine, Duchess of Buckingham, wrote to Conway on Elizabeth's be-half on March 24, 1627, and again on June 20, 1627. SP 16 (Charles I) 58/17, 71/55.

35. SP 63 (Ireland) 244/630, April 4, 1627, Falkland to Conway.

36. SP 63 (Ireland) 245/726, Falkland to Conway (now Viscount Killultagh). He explains his failure to relieve Elizabeth's needs on two grounds:

> First, of an impossibility for my estate to affoord that which the wealth of both the Indiaes cannot supply . . . Next, for that she is and lives, that, there, and as I would not have hir: & will never allow hir penny to be such and

thereas and where she is . . . That hir father disinherited hir for hir obedience to mee is much misrepresented by hir; he foresawe in hir that bade condition which she hath since manifested to the world which made him do that he did against hir and me for hir sake. If hir joynture be sould, it is she that hath the benefitt of the sale, and hath spent treble of the valliew of yt out of my purse . . . If hir mother refuse to receyve hir and doe conjure hir stay, yt is hir self that hath sued for these rejections, to have the better collor still to remayn wheare she is . . . Lawe Matrimoniall, notwithstanding hir specious pretences, doth require that he [the King] should remove hir, and settle hir with her Mother, where she shall receyve such allowance from mee as is fitt for hir: but nothinge for hir Popelinges that depends uppon hir.

37. SP 16 (Charles I) 62/62, May 6, 1627.

38. SP 16 (Charles I) 63/89, May 18, 1627. The cover letter to Conway (ibid., 63/102) enclosed her mother's letter and urges that her petition to the King be presented "when my lord steward and my lord chamberlaine are by, in whose good wishes, I have much confidence." She also hopes for the support of Buckingham: "If you can, I pray you let the duke of Buckingham bee present, for I know, hee will second so just and necessary, a request." She has most confidence in the Romanizing Buckingham ladies, promising Conway, "If you second it strongly . . . I dare bee bound, you shall receave extraordinary thankes from all the three great ladyes of my Lord of Buckinghams family." An earlier letter to Conway on March 24, SP 16 (Charles I) 58/19, vigorously protests the King's order

to comand me to my mothers in the nature of a prisoner . . . I have committed no fault that I know of, and though I had, sure I beleeve the kinge would take some other way for my punishment, then so unusuall a one, as to sterve mee to death. My mother hath exprest to mee, that if ever I come downe to her (which she beleeves his majesty will never inforce mee to doe), she will never give mee the least releefe now, or at her death . . . I have nor meat, drinke, nor clothes, nor mony to purchase any of them, and longe, have I bene, in this misery. I ly in a lodgynge, where I have no meanes to pay for it.

39. On August 13 she had appealed to Conway to preserve her from starvation by getting an order to pay her out of money due Falkland from a grant for pipe staves. SP 16 (Charles I) 73/81. Conway responded (ibid., 75/29, August 27) that the grant of the pipe staves was already a matter of much discontentment to Falkland, and to give part of the award to her would further embroil the matter. Her response, quoted in the text, concludes by urging him to find some other means, if not this, to meet her needs (ibid., 75/85, August).

40. On September 8, 1627, Conway reported to Sir Richard Weston, Chancellor of the Exchequer, that the King "hath been pressed with infinite importunity from the Lady Falkland" and directed him to take some course to provide for her. SP 16 (Charles I) 77/24. The formal provision, dated October 4, 1627, is reported in a letter to Falkland dated October 31, SP 63 (Ireland) 245/822. The Council further provided for changes in attendants or places of residence if necessary, reserving to themselves the right to arbitrate any difficulties.

41. In May 1628 the King directed the Privy Council to subtract from Lord Falkland's salary the allowance for Lady Falkland mandated by their decree of October 4, 1627, SP 63 (Ireland) 246/1021. On June 27, 1628, Falkland proposed in a letter to the King (ibid., 246/1050) to pay £300 rather than the £500 stipulated, claiming straitened circumstances and declaring truculently that it should be

enough, though the Indies could not supply her humors. He also begs she be forbidden to come within ten miles of the court or the City of London, to "silence the scandal and shame" she has brought upon him.

42. SP 16 (Charles I) 229/131. The report is undated; the *Calendar* supplies the date, 1632, but queries it. A deleted sentence in the *Life* indicates Cary's involvement at this time in several unsuccessful suits and projects to get free from debt.

43. *Life*, 46; Murdock, *Sun at Noon*, 8.

44. She assigned the small part of her jointure that she still retained to the payment of her debts, and also £100 of the £200 she had from her parents; this left her only £100 for living expenses (*Life*, 51). She remained dependent upon the charity of friends and occasional grants from the King and Queen. Lucius, now Lord Falkland, was apparently a dutiful son, but he complained with some justice of her imprudence in managing her finances (*Life*, 83–84, records her constant outlays for charity and support of priests). Lucius resisted the Council's recommendation of December 9, 1636, that he settle an allowance on her, and proposed instead "not [to] ty my selfe to give her any certaine allowance" but rather to supply her wants as he can. SP 16 (Charles I) 337/40. He claimed not to have known how dire her situation was.

45. Ben Jonson, "To the Immortal Memory and Friendship of that Noble Pair, Sir Lucius Cary and Sir H. Morison," *Underwood* no. 70, H&S, VIII, 242–247. Edward Hyde, Earl of Clarendon, *The History of the Rebellion and Civil Wars in England, begun in the year 1641*, ed. W. Dunn Macray, 6 vols. (Oxford: Clarendon, 1888), III, 178–190. Weber, *Lucius Cary*, 167–170.

46. SP 16 (Charles I) 272/29, July 20, 1634. Laud holds out hope that the daughters may yet be reclaimed: "But the greatest thinge I feare is that the Mother will still be practisinge, and doe all shee can to hinder."

47. Anne, the maid of honor, soon returned to her mother and court life, her maintenance provided by the Duchess of Buckingham; Elizabeth also returned. This left Mary and Lucy with Patrick and Henry at Tew. See *Life*, 84.

48. On pretense of a holiday trip, the children arose at an early hour and set off together. The boys ran off to a waiting coach, then were taken by boat (in the charge of very drunken boatmen) to London and thence abroad. Weber, *Lucius Cary*, 176–180; Murdock, *Sun at Noon*, 33–37. See SP 16 (Charles I) 337/230 for the testimony of the coachman, Henry Auxley.

49. SP 16 (Charles I) 321/29, May 16, 1636. This report, and that of May 28 (at which she indicated that she thought her sons were in France, probably Paris), are signed by Elizabeth and the Chief Justice, John Bramston.

50. SP 16 (Charles I) 322/6, Star Chamber, Order of Council, May 25, 1636.

51. *Life*, 111–112; Weber, *Lucius Cary*, 301–326.

52. Clarendon, *History of the Rebellion*, III, 180.

53. She was buried in the burial ground of Henrietta Maria's private chapel at St. James's Palace—now covered by a road.

54. Thomas Lodge, trans., *The Famous and Memorable Workes of Josephus* (London, 1602).

55. Philip Cary (Carew) was knighted at Greenwich in 1605. William A. Shaw, *The Knights of England*, 2 vols. (London, 1906), II, 137.

56. I cite the Huntington copy of *Mariam* (STC 4613) by act and scene number. The dedicatory poem (present in that copy) reads:

When cheerfull *Phoebus* his full course hath run,
His sisters fainter beams our harts doth cheere:
So your faire Brother is to mee the Sunne,
And you his Sister as my Moone appeere.

You are my next belov'd, my second Friend,
For when my *Phoebus* absence makes it Night,
Whilst to th'*Antipodes* his beames do bend,
From you my *Phoebe,* shines my second Light.

Hee like to *SOL,* cleare-sighted, constant, free,
You *Luna*-like, unspotted, chaste, divine:
Hee shone on *Sicily,* you destin'd bee,
T'illumine the now obscurde *Palestine.*
My first was consecrated to *Apollo,*
My second to *Diana* now shall follow.

57. Cary's play was entered on the Stationers' Register in December 1612, and published the following year. The anecdote specifically mentioning the sister-in-law, along with the warm dedication to her in the drama, points to *Mariam* as the work in question. The dedicatory poem may have been removed because the dedicatee (now Lady Carew) did not want her name associated with the publication, or perhaps because it would identify the author publicly, as the initials alone did not. For Davies's poem alluding to a "Sicily" tragedy, see p. 183.

58. Valency, *Tragedies of Herod,* 291, lists the following as predating Cary's drama: the Herod mystery plays; Hans Sachs, *Tragedia der Wütrich König Herodes* (MS, 1552); Lodovico Dolce, *Marianna* (1565); L. L. de Argensola, *La Alejandra* (1772), performed c. 1585; Alexandre Hardy, *Mariamne* (1625), performed c. 1600; and two Latin plays at Cambridge University by William Goldingham (1567) and Patrick Adamson (1572).

59. Robert Garnier, *M. Antoine* (Paris, 1578). *Discourse of Life and Death written in French by Ph. Mornay. Antonius A Tragedie written also in French by Ro. Garnier. Both done in English by the Countess of Pembroke* (London, 1592); Mary Sidney, Countess of Pembroke, *The Tragedie of Antonie* (London, 1595); ed. Alice Luce (Weimar, 1897).

60. Samuel Daniel, *The Tragedie of Cleopatra* (London, 1594; rpt., 1599, 1601, 1602, 1605; rev. ed., 1607, 1609, 1611). I cite the 1599 and 1611 versions. Daniel, *Certaine Small Poems Lately Printed: With the Tragedie of Philotas* (London, 1605; rpt., 1607, 1611, 1623). I cite by act and scene number in the 1623 edition. Fulke Greville, Lord Brooke, *Mustapha,* MS C, 1594–1596; London, 1609; rev., MS W, 1607–1610; and in *Certaine Learned and Elegant Workes of the Right Honorable Fulke Lord Brooke* (London, 1633). I cite by act and scene number in the 1633 edition. Other works in the Countess of Pembroke's line of French Senecan tragedies include Thomas Kyd's translation of Garnier's *Cornelia* (London, 1594); Samuel Brandon, *The Tragicomeodi of the Vertuous Octavia* (London, 1598); Fulke Greville, *Alaham* (1599–1604, rev., MS. W, 1607–1610), in *Certaine Learned . . . Workes;* Sir William Alexander, *Darius* (1603), *Croesus* (1604), *The Alexandrian* (1607), and *Julius Caesar* (1607). In *Sejanus* (1603–4) and *Cataline* (1611), Jonson attempts (unsuccessfully) to revise the genre to make it viable on the stage.

61. For an illuminating discussion of the two strains, Italian and French Sene-

canism, see H. B. Charlton, ed., *The Poetical Works of Sir William Alexander*, 2 vols. (London, 1921), I, introduction.

62. Responses to the Daniel and Greville plays suggest that contemporary analogues were widely recognized: to Essex and Elizabeth; to the Burleigh faction versus Essex and the Protestant war party; to James I's theories of absolutism, his corrupt court, and notorious favorites; to assassination attempts and rumored conspiracies—Essex's rebellion (1602), Guy Fawkes (1605), Arbella Stuart's royal claims and elopement (1609). Greville also composed an *Antony and Cleopatra* sometime before 1601, and committed it to the fire at the time of Essex's rebellion, claiming that it might be "construed, or strained to a personating of vices in the present Governers, and government." *Sir Fulke Greville's Life of Sir Philip Sidney*, ed. Nowell Smith (Oxford: Clarendon, 1907), 156. See also notes 64–68.

63. Junius Brutus [Hugh Languet], *Vindiciae Contra Tyrannos, sive, de principis in populum, populique in Primcipem, legitima potestat* (Frankfurt, 1608), also attributed to Du Plessis Mornay, whose works were translated by Philip Sidney and his sister. The argument of the tract is that any group of nobles or magistrates (or even one such) in whom is vested some measure of governing authority devolved from the people may resist or overthrow by force a tyrant who threatens ruin to God's Church or to the Commonwealth. R. Doleman [Robert Parsons], *A Conference about the Next Succession to the Crowne of Ingland* (n.p., 1594), questions the notion of automatic succession, and argues the right of those empowered to act for the people to depose a ruler, especially if the Pope sanctions it.

64. The drama was staged on January 3, 1605, by the Children of the Queen's Revels, the company and theater for which Daniel was special licenser and which were becoming a locus for audacious plays. See chapter 1. Daniel's troubles seem to have stemmed more from the production than the publication.

65. Daniel's letter to his patron Devonshire (Mountjoy) reiterates his testimony: "First I tolde the Lordes I had written 3 Acts of this tragedie the Christmas before my L. of Essex troubles, as divers in the cittie could witnes." Grosart, *Works of Samuel Daniel*, III, xxii–xxiii. His letter to Cecil (Cranbourne) explains the supposed contemporary analogies by the "universall notions of the affayres of men . . . No tyme but brought forth the like concurrencies, the like interstriving for place and dignitie, the like supplantations, rysings & overthrows." He offers, however, "yf it shall seeme skandalous to any by misconceiveing it," to withdraw "the booke & mee to my poore home, pretending some other occasion, so that the suppressing it by authoritie might not make the world to ymagin other matters in it then there is." Hatfield, Cecil Papers 191/123. No penalty was imposed, but his career was damaged; he had no court commissions until the Queen commissioned *Tethys Festival* from him in 1610.

66. The "Argument" to *Philotas* notes that Alexander's claim of divinity "withdrew many the hearts of the nobilitie and people from him."

67. "Apology," Grosart, *Works of Samuel Daniel*, III, 180–181. The "Apology" appeared for the first time in the 1623 edition, though it was obviously written much earlier; since Daniel managed to deflect official trouble, he perhaps thought publishing it at the time would simply call attention to the problem. The "Argument" provided sufficient cover by offering a somewhat similar misreading of the drama (sigs. A 6–A 6v).

68. After the death of Sidney, Greville's closest literary relationship was with

Daniel, whom he probably introduced to the Countess of Pembroke's Wilton circle and to other literary women.

69. Ronald A. Rebholz, *The Life of Fulke Greville, First Lord Brooke* (Oxford: Clarendon, 1971), 200–205.

70. Valency, *Tragedies of Herod*, 23. Herod the Great massacred the Innocents; Herod Antipas condemned John the Baptist and interrogated Jesus; Herod Agrippa sat in judgment on Paul and other apostles.

71. This episode occurred much later in Josephus' account of Herod, but Cary incorporates it here to reinforce the motif of liberation and new beginnings.

72. Ferguson, "Running On," 47–48, makes the plausible argument that Graphina (the only character not present in Josephus or in the Lodge translation, though the name is perhaps suggested by Glaphyra, wife to a certain Alexander) is purposively named as a play on *graphesis* (writing). She seems to represent a safe, nontransgressive discourse in compliance with her husband's wishes, which is rewarded with Pheroras' devoted love. It is, however, a love that overpowers his moral sense.

73. Ibid., 52–53.

74. This is substantially the recommendation of Fulke Greville in his *Letter to an Honorable Lady*, in *The Prose Works of Fulke Greville, Lord Brooke*, ed. John Gouws (Oxford: Clarendon, 1986), 138–176. Citing the opinions of "worthie men, borne under Tyrants," he draws an explicit parallel to the case of a lady matched with a tyrannous husband: "the comparison holdinge in some affinitie betweene a wives subjection to a husband and a subjects obedience to his soveraign" (154). But Greville, unlike the chorus of *Mariam*, would not imprison the lady in her domestic sphere; instead he comforts her with liberation from that realm to "newe *Ideas*, larger ends, and nobler wayes," whereby she may win fame in all the world and finally with God (172). Joan Rees, *Fulke Greville, Lord Brooke, 1554–1628: A Critical Biography* (London, 1971), 175–177, and Mark Caldwell, "The Prose Works of Fulke Greville, Lord Brooke" (Ph.D. diss., Harvard University, 1973), xxiv–xxvi, argue that the letter was probably addressed to Margaret Clifford, Countess of Cumberland.

75. Lodge, *Workes of Josephus*, 398–399.

76. Cf. Ferguson, "Running On," 56–57.

77. Shepherd, *Amazons and Warrior Women*, 107–128, points to a group of such plays staged in the years 1610–1614: Chapman's *Bussy D'Ambois* (1610–1611) and *Second Maiden's Tragedy* (1611); Dekker's *Meet Me in London* (1611–1612); Tourneur's *Atheist's Tragedy* (1611); and Webster's *Duchess of Malfi* (1612). Among the circumstances promoting the treatment of such themes, Shepherd cites Arbella Stuart's love match in defiance of James's restrictions and his harsh and arbitrary response, and also James's wrangles with the Parliament of 1610 over his absolutist claims and prerogative.

78. For a summary and analysis of the authorship issue, see Appendix A.

79. Cary's daughter makes clear that the translation was generally known to be hers (*Life*, 39). Also, one of the commendatory poems prefacing it is by Cary's friend and admirer Peter Clayton, who helped supply her needs after her conversion.

80. The exchange between Cardinal Perron and James I began with Perron's *Lettre de Monseigneur le Cardinal du Perron, envoyée au Sieur Casaubon en Angleterre*

(Paris, 1612), dated July 15, 1611, and intended to be shown to James I; Perron upholds the general right of the Pope to depose kings, but denies charges that Rome fosters rebellion and regicide and harbors traitors. The work was translated into English by Thomas Owen in 1612. Casaubon answered in Latin in the same year, *Isaaci Casauboni ad Epistolam . . . Cardinalis Perronii, responsio,* also translated into English in 1612. James responded with his *Remonstrance for the Right of Kings, and the Independence of Their Crowns. Against an Oration of the Most Illustrious Cardinall of Perron,* dated January 15, 1615, and published in his *Workes* (1616). This reply Perron answered with the tract Cary translated, first published as *Replique à la Response du Serenissime Roy de la Grande Bretagne* (Paris, 1620), and the next year in a Latin version. James was notably anxious about arguments justifying deposition of monarchs and regicide, especially after the Gunpowder Plot, the murder of Henry IV of France (1610), and the various plots surrounding Arbella Stuart.

81. She develops this claim through a series of crisp, parallel assertions: "You are a daughter of France . . . You are the Queene of England . . . You are King James his Sonns wife . . . And for the honor of my Sexe, let me saie it, you are a woeman, though farr above other wemen, therefore fittest to protect a womans worke. And last . . . you are a Catholicke, and a zealous one" (sig. a 2).

82. Cary asserts that the copier spent "fower times as long in transcribing, as it was in translating" (sig. a 2v); one commendatory poem describes the male sex's amazement "that a Womans hand alone should raise / So vast a monument in thirty dayes." The other exclaims, "One woman in one Month, so large a booke."

83. Natalie Zemon Davis, "Gender and Genre: Women as Historical Writers, 1400–1820," in Labalme, *Beyond Their Sex,* 153–157.

84. Tacitus, *The Ende of Nero and Beginning of Galba,* trans. H. Savile (Oxford, 1591); Livy, *The Romane Historie,* trans. Philamon Holland (London, 1600); Thucydides, *The Hystory,* trans. Thomas Nicholls (London, 1550); Sallust, *The Two Most Worthy and Notable Histories,* trans. Thomas Heywood (London, 1608).

85. F. J. Levy, *Tudor Historical Thought* (San Marino: Huntington Library, 1967), 237–294.

86. Hayward's play, *The First Part of the Life and Raigne of King Henrie the IIII* (London, 1599; rpt. 1610), became a *cause célèbre* and landed him in the Tower. The objectionable elements were a pair of speeches, one opposing but one eloquently defending revolution, as well as an unwise dedication to the Earl of Essex. Francis Bacon, *Historie of the Raign of King Henry the Seventh* (1621), in *Works,* VI, 27–245. Daniel's unfinished *Collection of the Historie of England* (London, 1618) covers the period from William the Conqueror to Edward III; see especially "The Life, and Reigne of Edward the Second," 172–184. Robert Cotton, *King Henry the Third* (London, 1627), is in the same mode.

87. Raphael Holinshed, *The Laste Volume of the Chronicles of England, Scotlande, and Irelande, with their Descriptions* (London, 1577). Other chronicles important for Cary's *Edward II* are Robert Fabyan, *Chronycle* (London, 1533), and John Stow, *The Annales, or Generall Chronicle of England* (London, 1615).

88. Marlowe, *The Troublesome Raigne and Lamentable Death of Edward the Second, King of England: with the Tragicall Fall of Proud Mortimer* (London, 1594); the drama was written in 1591 and first performed in 1592.

89. Richard Niccols's addition to the *Mirrour for Magistrates* was titled *A Winter Nights Vision: Being an Addition of Such Princes Especially Famous, who were ex-*

empted in the former Historie (London, 1610). The speaker is Edward II's ghost. The 1587 *Mirrour* contained a poem by Thomas Churchyard, "The Two Mortimers."

90. Michael Drayton, *Piers Gaveston Earle of Cornwall. His Life, Death, and Fortune* (London, [1593]). This is in the "mirror" form, influenced strongly by the erotic epyllia of the era. *Mortimeriados* (London, 1596), adopts Spenserian romancelike elements—rhyme royal, wall paintings, bowers of bliss, and so on. *The Barons Warres* (London, 1603) revises in the direction of epic, with an emphasis on wars and political affairs; the 1619 revision was still harsher on the rebels and even less critical of Edward.

91. Daniel, *Historie of England,* 172, 182–183.

92. [Francis Hubert], *The Deplorable Life and Death of Edward the Second, King of England. Together with the Downefall of the two Unfortunate Favorits, Gavestone and Spencer* (London, 1628). The following year Hubert published an expanded and corrected edition under his name, *The Historie of Edward the Second. Surnamed Carnarvan, one of our English Kings. Together with the Fatall down-fall of his two unfortunate Favorites Gaveston and Spencer* (London, 1629), claiming that the first edition was printed surreptitiously. He says he began the work in Elizabeth's time, and that it "grew to more maturitie in King JAMES's." Cary may possibly have seen one of the several manuscripts (BL, Additional MSS 28,021 and 3416; also Bodleian MS Rawlinson Poets 98), or even the first edition if her claim of a month's writing time is to be taken seriously.

93. Others in the 1620s (Buckingham's heyday) compared the reigns of James I and Edward II, among them Sir Henry Yelverton (1621), defending himself in the Lords against charges of corruption. Chamberlain wrote to Carleton (Chamberlain, II, 369) that he "cast many aspersions upon the Lord of Buckingham . . . and further comparing these times in some sort to those of Edward the second wherin the Spencers did so tirannize and domineer." Prince Charles interrupted him, "as not able to indure his fathers government to be so paralelled and scandalised."

94. Most accounts make Gaveston a Frenchman, taking his name from his region, Gascoigne; Cary, however, claims that his devious nature leads her to credit an unnamed source labeling him an Italian (4). D. R. Woolf, "The True Date and Authorship of Henry Viscount Falkland's *History of the Life, Reign, and Death of King Edward II,*" *Bodleian Library Record,* 12, no. 6 (1988), 444, identifies that source as the fourteenth-century chronicle *Vita et Mors Edwardi Secundi,* at the time attributed to Thomas de la More but in fact an extract from the chronicle of Geoffrey le Baker.

95. While Cary received a good deal of help from the Buckingham ladies in her troubles, and hoped for help from Buckingham, there is no evidence that he involved himself in her affairs—save to exacerbate them by revealing her conversion to the King. Her tonally ambiguous epitaph for Buckingham was of course a gesture to her friends, the Romanizing women of the family.

96. In Cary's version the King delays the French mission because he has misgivings about it, so Isabel sets off on pilgrimage to Canterbury, sending Mortimer word of the plan. He escapes, plying his captors with drink or a sleeping potion, and meets the Queen's party at Canterbury, where they all take ship together. Conceivably, Cary recalled her imaginative account of this adventure when she later came to plot her sons' escape to France.

97. They include the Frenchman Robert of Artois, "a man both wise and valiant, that loved Goodness for her own sake . . . a well-resolved, steady States-man, not led by Complement, or feign'd professions" (105); also the Earl of Hainaut and his brother Sir John, who raise a small invasion force to accompany the Queen to England.

98. Cary credits the Queen especially for making a bold play for the City of London, calling upon the Mayor to hold it for her and her son. But Cary denounces the London mob who rise to support her, beheading the King's agent Bishop Stapleton: "This same heady monster Multitude never examine the Justice, or the dependance, but are led by Passion and Opinion; which in fury leaves no Disorder unacted, and no Villany unattempted" (122). Cary conveys the uncertainties of the operation—whether the army will hold for her, whether the city will yield and surrender the King's agents, whether the King will escape—and underscores the Queen's good fortune and courage in meeting them. The providential storms first help the invaders escape Spencer's armies, then prevent the King and Spencer from making their escape.

99. Blame is also deflected from Isabel (and lessened for Mortimer) by Cary's refusal to provide the horrendous details of Edward's death recounted in most of the sources: it was caused by a hot iron thrust into his bowels through the anus, so as to leave no outward trace. Cary says simply, "It was one of the most inhumane and barbarous acts that ever fell within the expression of all our *English* Stories; fitter rather to be pass'd over in silence, than to be discours'd" (155).

100. Cary's history also makes little of Mortimer and Isabel as lovers after the King's death, and does not report his capture in her boudoir as do many sources. Rather, the emphasis is political, giving some attention to the reforms they inaugurated in the state. Similarly, Isabel's later life as a penitent in a convent—much elaborated by Drayton and others—is alluded to cryptically in a single phrase.

8. Imagining Female Community: Aemilia Lanyer

1. All citations are from the Huntington Library copy of the first issue (STC 15,227) with the imprint in four lines, "AT LONDON / Printed by *Valentine Simmes* for *Richard Bonian,* and / are to be sold at his Shop in Paules Church- / yard. *Anno* 1611."

2. A. L. Rowse, ed., *The Poems of Shakespeare's Dark Lady: Salve Deus Rex Judaeorum by Emilia Lanier* (London: Jonathan Cape, 1978). This edition is based on the Bodleian copy, complete except for the Cookham poem, which is supplied from the British Library copy. Rowse urges his thesis in an edition of Shakespeare's sonnets and also in *Sex and Society in Shakespeare's Age: Simon Forman the Astrologer* (New York: Scribners, 1974). The relevant Forman casebooks are Bodleian, MSS Ashmole 226 and 354 (his "Geomantica," a book of horoscopes exemplifying answers to particular problems).

3. Rowse notes that Shakespeare's landlady also visited Forman; that the patron of Shakespeare's company was Lord Hunsdon, father of Lanyer's illegitimate son; and that Lanyer's dark Italian beauty, musical family, literary talent, and questionable moral character fit the general description of the sonnet Dark Lady.

4. Susanne Woods, ed., *Salve Deus Rex Judaeorum* (New York: Oxford University Press, 1993).

5. Roger Prior, "More (Moor? Moro?) Light on the Dark Lady," *Financial Times* (London), October 10, 1987, 17, points to the Bassano arms, containing a silkworm moth and mulberry tree, as an indication of their Italian Jewish origins; their town, Bassano del Grappa near Venice, was a center of the silk trade. But Prior's argument that this crest strengthens the identification of Aemilia as the Dark Lady is also tenuous, based on the questionable supposition that when Shakespeare uses the words "moor" and "more," he is usually punning on the Italian for the mulberry (*moro*), and hence alluding to Aemilia.

6. Baptist Bassano's will, dated January 3, 1576, refers to "Emelia Bassany Daughter of the bodie of Margarett Bassany also Margarett Johnson my reputed wieff." PRO, Probate 11/58, f. 153. The sister is described in the will as "Angela Hollande nowe wieff of Joseph Holland gentleman."

7. Guildhall, microfilm 4515/1, Parish Registers of St. Botolph, Bishopsgate, records the baptism on January 17, 1568 [1569], of "Emillia Baptyst"; although the entry is incomplete (the form should have been Emillia, daughter of Baptyst Bassano), the conjunction of names and proper dates almost certainly points to her.

8. Ibid. Baptyst Bassano was buried at St. Botolph, Bishopsgate, on April 11, 1576; Margaret on July 7, 1587. See *The Registers of St. Botolph, Bishopsgate*, trans. A. W. C. Hallam, 2 vols. ([London], 1889), I, 277, 295. Bodleian, MS Ashmole 226, f. 95v.

9. PRO, Probate 11/58, f. 154. See Woods's edition for further information on these properties.

10. Guildhall, microfilm 9221, Register General of St. Botolph's, Aldgate, 1571–1593. The entry under the year 1592 reads: "Alfonso Lanyer one of the Queenes musitions & Emilia bassano Maryed the 18 Daye of october." I am grateful to Susanne Woods for calling this entry to my attention.

11. Roger Prior, "Jewish Musicians at the Tudor Court," *Musical Quarterly*, 69 (1983), 253–265. *DNB*, "Nicholas Lanier." II. C. De Lafontaine, ed., *The King's Musick: A Transcript of Records Relating to Music and Musicians (1460–1700)* (London: Novello, 1909).

12. *The Parish Registers, 1539–1660, of St. Margaret's, Westminster*, ed. A. M. Burke (London: Eyre & Spottiswoode, 1914), 62, record the baptism of "Odilia," daughter of Alphonso Laniere, December 2, 1598. The parish registers of St. Botolph's, Bishopsgate (Guildhall, microfilm 4515/1; Hallam, *Registers of St. Botolph, Bishopsgate*, I, 324), record the burial of "Odillya Lanyer" on September 6, 1599.

13. Bodleian, MS Ashmole 226, f. 93v.

14. Ibid., f. 95v. He casts her horoscope on this occasion, identifying her as "Emilia Bassana" who "also is Lanier." This time he describes her as "of 27 yeares 2 filia Baptista Bassano et Margarete Johnson."

15. Ibid., f. 110v. On this occasion he also notes that she might be pregnant: "She seams to be with child of 12 daies or 12 weakes moch pain in the left syd."

16. Ibid., f. 201; "Geomantica" (Bodleian, MS Ashmole 354, f. 296), also dated September 2, 1597. Earlier, on June 16, she began the inquiries about her husband, "wh[ether] he shall com to Any preferment before he com hom Again or no. & how he shall speed." Bodleian, MS Ashmole 226, f. 122v.

17. Bodleian, MS Ashmole 226, f. 201.

18. Bodleian, MS Ashmole 354, f. 250.

19. Ibid. On September 23 he queries, "Best to goe to Laniere todae or noe,"

and indicates that he did not; the next day he records that some "she" (perhaps Lanyer, perhaps not) sent for him and he went to her. But he does not record that he "did halek" with her, though he regularly reports this with regard to other women. On September 29 he simply records her name, indicating (perhaps) a consultation. Bodleian, MS Ashmole 226, f. 222v.

20. Bodleian, MS Ashmole 236, f. 5. See Woods's edition for a more detailed discussion of these entries, drawing similar conclusions.

21. Cookham, a manor belonging to the crown from before the Conquest until 1818, was annexed to Windsor Castle in 1540. It was evidently granted or leased to Lord Russell and occupied by the Countess of Cumberland at some periods during her estrangement from her husband in the years before his death in 1605, and perhaps just after. During the period September–November 1604 Margaret Clifford dated five letters from "Cookham in Berkshire," all of them seeking to secure a suitable allowance from her husband by complaints to him and various court officials (Longleat, Portland Papers, vol. 23, ff. 24–28). Anne Clifford's *Diary* (15) records one visit to Cookham in 1603, but it has nothing before 1603 and then skips to 1616, so has no occasion to record Lanyer's stay.

22. See chapter 5 for an account of these matters, and of Margaret Clifford's patronage.

23. SP 14 (James I) 9/20, 75/22; SP 16 (Charles I) 283/57, 327/128, 356/95, 391/81.

24. PRO, Chancery Case C2 (James I) L 11/64.

25. SP (Charles I) 283/57. The baptisms of Mary (July 25, 1627) and Henry (January 16, 1629) are recorded in *A True Register of all the Christenings, Mariages, and Burialls in the Parish of St James, Clerkenwell*, ed. R. Hovenden, 6 vols. (London, 1884), I, 105, 113. Henry's death is recorded in October 1633 (ibid., IV, 210).

26. Ibid., IV, 263.

27. Lanyer may or may not have known or known about Boccaccio's *De mulieribus claris*, Chaucer's *Legend of Good Women*, or Christine de Pisan's *Livre de la Cité des Dames*, published in 1521 in an English translation by Brian Anslay.

28. Since the Passion poem contains an apology for the author's delay in fulfilling the Countess of Cumberland's charge to write about Cookham, it was evidently written before the Cookham poem. Since it alludes to the Countess as a widow, it was written sometime after the death of George Clifford, Earl of Cumberland, on October 30, 1605. The several dedications were probably written shortly before publication; the Countess of Dorset's marriage date (1609) supplies a *terminus post quem* for the dedication to her by that name.

29. There are nine known copies but only one (the Huntington copy) of the rare first issue (STC 15,227) with imprint in four lines. Eight carry the imprint in five lines: AT LONDON / Printed by *Valentine Simmes* for *Richard Bonian,* and are / to be sold at his Shop in Paules Churchyard, at the / Signe of the Floure de Luce and / Crowne, 1611 (STC 15,227.5).

30. Only five of the nine extant copies are complete: three presentation copies have had several dedications omitted, and the Bodleian copy is missing "Cookeham." See Appendix B for analysis of the presentation copies and these omissions.

31. From internal evidence it is clear that Jonson's "Penshurst" was written sometime before the death of Prince Henry in November 1612, as a reference to the Prince (l. 77) indicates; but it was first published in *Works* (1616). Lanyer's poem was written sometime after Anne Clifford's marriage to Richard Sackville

on February 25, 1609 (she is referred to as Dorset, the title her husband inherited two days after the marriage), and before the volume was registered with the Stationer's on October 2, 1610. If Jonson's poem was written first, Lanyer might possibly have seen it in manuscript.

32. See chapter 2.

33. See chapter 1.

34. See chapter 3.

35. Susan Bertie's first husband was Reynold Grey of Wrest, de jure Earl of Kent, who died in 1573. In 1581 she married Sir John Wingfield of Withcall, a member of the Leicester-Sidney faction (knighted by Leicester at Zutpen, one of the twelve honor guard at Sidney's funeral, and a participant in the Cádiz expeditions). Lanyer's girlhood residence with the Countess may or may not have taken place before the Countess's second marriage. Lanyer is clearly being disingenuous when she disclaims (ll. 43–48) any thought of "former gaine" or "future profit" from the Countess.

36. Sidney's sister, the Countess of Pembroke, extended hospitality and patronage at her Wilton estate to many writers (Nicholas Breton, Samuel Daniel, Abraham Fraunce, Gervase Babington, Thomas Moffatt) and received dedications from many others (Michael Drayton, Thomas Nashe, Henry Lok, Nathaniel Baxter, Edmund Spenser). The Countess of Bedford was patron and friend to Donne, Daniel, Jonson, and many others (see chapter 4). Williams, *Index of Dedications*, lists more dedications and praises to these two noblewomen than to any other persons except members of the royal family.

37. Margaret Clifford's literary and clerical clients include Robert Greene, Thomas Lodge, Samuel Daniel, Henry Lok, Edmund Spenser, Samuel Hieron, Henry Peacham, William Perkins, Richard Greenham, and Peter Muffett, among others. See Williams, *Index of Dedications*, and chapter 5.

38. Katherine, Countess of Suffolk, was wife to the wealthy and ambitious Lord Admiral and Lord Chamberlain of the Household, Thomas Howard, whose manor, Audley End, was said to have been built on a foundation of Spanish gold. She alone seems wholly out of place in Lanyer's company of good women, though she and her husband were not yet notorious for the rapacity which was to lead in 1618 to their disgrace and imprisonment for extortion and embezzlement.

39. "To the Queenes most Excellent Majestie" (sig. a 3).

40. As, for example, in Sidney's *Defence of Poetry* (London, 1595), sigs. Cv 1–C 2, and [George] Puttenham, *The Arte of English Poesie* (London, 1589), 23–24.

41. These poems, the second and fourth dedications, are in fourteen lines, divided into two stanzas. That to Princess Elizabeth is rhymed *a b a b a c c, d e d e d f f*; that to Arbella Stuart *a b a b b c c, d e d e e f f*.

42. The dedication is entitled "To the Ladie Susan, Countesse Dowager of Kent, and daughter to the Duchesse of Suffolke," associating her at the outset with her famous mother, whose flight and wanderings with her family in Europe—as recorded by her husband, Richard Bertie—were incorporated in Foxe's *Book of Martyrs*. Catherine married Richard Bertie in 1553, after the death of her first husband, Charles Brandon, Earl of Suffolk; Susan was born in 1554, only a few months before the flight. Susan herself accompanied her second husband, Sir John Wingfield, on his military expeditions and was imprisoned with him briefly in Breda after the fall of Gertruydenburg.

43. Cf. Jonson, Epigram 76. See chapter 4, p. 108.

44. See chapter 6, especially notes 1 and 3, for major studies and topics of the *querelle*.

45. [Robert Southwell], *Saint Peters Complaynt* (London, 1595); rpt. with other poems 1595, 1597, 1599, 1602, 1607.

46. *Saint Peters Complaynt* [1607], 14.

47. "Christ's Triumph over Death" is the third part of Giles Fletcher's *Christs victorie and triumph in heaven and earth, over and after death* (Cambridge, 1610).

48. Nicholas Breton, *A Divine Poeme, divided into two Partes: The Ravisht Soule, and the Blessed Weeper* (London, 1601). Breton, *The Pilgrimage to Paradise, Joyned with the Countesse of Pembrookes Love* (Oxford, 1592), sig. ¶ 3.

49. Abraham Fraunce, *The Countesse of Pembrokes Emanuell* (London, 1591). The volume contains a poem on the Nativity of Christ, and another on "The Passion, Buryall, and Resurrection of Christ," together with some metaphrased Psalms.

50. See especially Psalm 104:

2. Who coverest thyself with light as with a garment: who stretchest out the heavens like a curtain:

3. Who layeth the beams of his chambers in the waters: who maketh the clouds his charriot: who walketh upon the wings of the wind.

4. Who maketh his angells spirits; his ministers a flaming fire.

32. He looketh on the earth, and it trembleth: he toucheth the hills, and they smoke.

51. Sig. Bv. See the discussion of this concern in Barbara Lewalski, *Protestant Poetics and the Seventeenth-Century Religious Lyric* (Princeton: Princeton University Press, 1979), 3–13, 213–250.

52. Cf. Herbert, "Prayer I," *Works*, 51, ll. 1–4.
Prayer the Churches banquet, Angels age,
Gods breath in man returning to his birth,
The soul in paraphrase, heart in pilgrimage,
The Christian plummet sounding heav'n and earth.

53. Cf. Fletcher, "Christ's Triumph over Death," *Christs victorie*, 57 (stanza 35):
His radious head, with shamefull thornes they teare,
His tender backe, with bloody whipps they rent,
His side, and heart they furrow with a spear,
His hands, and feete, with riving nayles they tent
And, as to disentrayle his soule they meant,
They jolly at his griefe, and make their game,
His naked body to expose to shame,
That all might come to see, and all might see, who came.

54. Some sense of the area can be gleaned from the *Victoria History of Berkshire*, ed. P. H. Ditchfield and William Page, 4 vols. (London: A. Constable, 1906–1924), III, 124–125.

55. The valedictory mode of this poem suggests a permanent rather than a seasonal departure, probably related to the Countess's permanent departure to her dower residences in Westmoreland after she was widowed in 1605. See chapter 5.

56. For a study of this tradition, see Maren-Sofie Rostvig, *The Happy Man:*

Studies in the Metamorphoses of a Classical Idea, vol. I, 1600–1700 (Oslo: Norwegian Universities Press, 1962); vol. II, 1700–1760 (1971).

57. In his *Peri Epideiktikon,* Menander identifies the valediction to or praise of a place as one of the Epideictic topics for speeches and poems, as does Julius-Caesar Scaliger in his *Poetices libri septem* (Geneva, 1561), chaps. 106, 119.

58. For further discussion of these issues in Jonson's and other seventeenth-century estate poems, see Barbara Lewalski, "The Lady of the Country-House Poem," in *The Fashioning and Functioning of the British Country House,* ed. Gervase Jackson-Stops et al. (Washington, D.C.: National Gallery of Art, 1989), 261–275.

59. For some overview of the changing patterns of life in the country houses of the period, see Mark Girouard, *Life in the English Country House: A Social and Architectural History* (Harmondsworth: Penguin, 1980), 81–118. For the suppression of real social conditions in Jonson's idealization, see Raymond Williams, *The Country and the City* (New York: Oxford University Press, 1973), 26–34, and Don E. Wayne, *Penshurst: The Semiotics of Place and the Poetics of History* (Madison: University of Wisconsin Press, 1984).

60. Barbara Sidney's side of the correspondence did not, apparently, survive: the Penshurst papers contain only a few lines to him in her hand. His letters in the years 1594–1609 project a portrait of Barbara as a highly valued domestic helpmeet, manager of the estate and its hospitality, and devoted mother of his children (she bore twelve in all). Sidney regularly discussed his mounting financial difficulties with his wife, and sought her advice and help in coping with them. Maidstone, Kent, Centre for Kentish Studies, De L'Isle MSS U 1475, C 81/41, 158, 192, 198.

61. For the important range of duties often devolving upon the mistress of the house in seventeenth-century England, see Ezell, *The Patriarch's Wife,* 1–61.

62. H&S, VIII, 95–96.

63. Cf. Jonson, "To Penshurst," ibid., 94, ll. 29–38:
The painted partridge lies in every field,
    And for thy mess is willing to be killd.
And if the high-swoll'n Medway fail thy dish,
    Thou hast thy ponds that pay thee tribute fish:
Fat, aged carps, that run into thy net;
    And pikes, now weary their own kind to eat,
As loath the second draught or cast to stay,
    Officiously, at first, themselves betray;
Bright eels, that emulate them, and leap on land
    Before the fisher, or into his hand.

9. Revising Genres and Claiming the Woman's Part: Mary Wroth

1. Published together in *The Countesse of Mountgomeries Urania. Written by the most honourable the lady Mary Wroath. Daughter to the right Noble Robert Earle of Leicester And Neece to the ever famous and renowned Sr Philips Sidney knight. And to ye most exelent Lady Mary Countesse of Pembroke late deceased* (London, 1621). Josephine Roberts's edition of *The Poems of Lady Mary Wroth* (Baton Rouge: Louisiana State University Press, 1983) collects all the known poems and correspondence, and supplies an extensive biographical and critical introduction. I cite the 1621 *Urania* (Part I) by book and page number, from a personal copy kindly lent me

by my colleague Gwynne Evans. I cite *Pamphilia to Amphilanthus* from Roberts's edition—both for the convenience of readers, and because that edition retains Wroth's orthography and pointing, from manuscript sources.

2. The unpublished Part II exists uniquely as a holograph manuscript in the Newberry Library (Case MS fY 1565. W 95). I cite *Urania* (Part II) by book number and folio page in that manuscript. I retain Wroth's spelling and (very light) punctuation—but on a very few occasions have supplied a full stop where needed for clarity. I am grateful to Josephine Roberts, who is preparing a critical edition of the complete *Urania* for the Renaissance English Text Society, for supplying me with a typescript of *Urania,* Part II. A complete manuscript of Wroth's pastoral comedy in five acts, *Love's Victory,* is at Penshurst; it was edited by Michael G. Brennan (London: Roxburghe Club, 1988). The Huntington Library has an incomplete manuscript, lacking beginning and ending pages (HM 600).

3. See Mary Ellen Lamb, *Gender and Authorship in the Sidney Circle* (Madison: University of Wisconsin Press, 1990). *The Poems of Robert Sidney,* ed. P. J. Croft (Oxford: Clarendon, 1984). His sonnet sequence, *Rosis and Lysa,* was inscribed "For the Countess of Pembroke."

4. Margaret Hannay, "'Your vertuous and learned Aunt': The Countess of Pembroke as a Mentor to Mary Wroth," in *Reading Mary Wroth: Representing Alternatives in Early Modern England,* ed. Naomi Miller and Gary Waller (Knoxville: University of Tennessee Press, 1991), 15–34.

5. *DNB,* "William Herbert," XXVI, 226–231; also Hannay, *Philips Phoenix.*

6. See Roberts, *Poems,* 41–49; Lamb, *Gender and Authorship,* 142–193.

7. Gary Waller, "Mary Wroth and the Sidney Family Romance: Gender Construction in Early Modern England," in Miller and Waller, *Reading Mary Wroth,* 35–63.

8. There is some exploration of generic transformation in Naomi Miller, "Rewriting Lyric Fictions: The Role of the Lady in Lady Mary Wroth's *Pamphilia to Amphilanthus,*" in Haselkorn and Travitsky, *Renaissance Englishwoman,* 295–310; Miller, "'Not much to be marked': Narrative of the Woman's Part in Lady Mary Wroth's *Urania,*" *SEL,* 29 (1989), 121–137; and Maureen Quilligan, "Lady Mary Wroth: Female Authority and the Family Romance," in *Unfolded Tales: Essays on Renaissance Romance,* ed. George Logan and Gordon Teskey (Ithaca: Cornell University Press, 1989).

9. Although there is no record of her birth, a letter by Rowland Whyte designates October 18 as her birthday (Maidstone, Kent, Centre for Kentish Studies, De L'Isle MS U 1475 C 12/286) but does not mention the year; a letter of Robert Sidney's (April 20, 1597) refers to her as almost ten; Arthur Collins, *Letters and Memorials of State,* 2 vols. (London, 1746), II, 43. Cf. Roberts, *Poems,* 6.

10. Roberts, *Poems,* 4–5, cites letters from Sir Walter Ralegh and Barbara's kinsmen to her uncle and guardian Sir Edmund Stradling reaffirming the Queen's demand that her permission be sought for any marriage, and also a later letter from Walsingham testifying that the Queen blamed no one and that the marriage, was "generally well liked of."

11. For example, Robert Sidney to Barbara Sidney, April 26, 1588, De L'Isle MSS U 1475 C 81/2 and C 95/98.

12. Hannay, "Your vertuous and learned Aunt." Hannay notes that Robert's letters are frequently directed to his wife at his sister's various residences (Bay-

nard's Castle, Ivychurch, Wilton), that he expects them to share news, and that there are frequent references to the Countess's visits to Penshurst. See De Lisle MSS U 1475 C 81/3, C 82/4, C 81/7 (written during the Armada scare), C 81/42 (1594), C 12/40 (1595), C 81/113 (1604).

13. De L'Isle MS U 1475 C 12/14.

14. Whyte also noted that her partner was Mr. Palmer, "the admirablest dawncer of this tyme." De L'Isle MS U 1475 C 12/289.

15. On April 2, 1597, Robert Sidney urged Barbara to leave the oldest children behind when she came to Flushing, "For . . . neither can they learne any thing heer especially the twoe girls." De L'Isle MS U 1475 C 81/96. In a letter of April 10, 1597 (Collins, *Letters and Memorials,* II, 43–44), he elaborated his plans for the girls' education:

> I meane for the Girls with my Lady of Huntington, and my Lady of Warwick, with whome also yow told me yow were willing to leave them. They are not so yong now, but that they may wel bee from their Mother. *Mary* is almost ten, and *Kate* almost Eight; and although I cannot find Fault hether unto, with their Bringing up, yet I know now every Day more and more, it wil bee fit for them to be out of their Fathers Hows. For heer they cannot learne, what they may do in other Places . . . I know that these things are nothing pleasing to yow; but yow must remember I have Part in them, as wel as yow, and therfore must have Care of them. I know also, that a better, and more carefull Mother there is not, then you are; and indeed, I doe not feare any thing so much as your to much Fondnes.

Rowland Whyte reported on April 18 that the Countess of Huntington had declared herself unable to take Mary, and had recommended that she come to Flushing and the Hague to improve her French. De Lisle MS U 1475 C 12/84. Also, it seems that Barbara protested vigorously, for in his next letter (April 20, 1597) Sidney leaves the decision about the girls to her, as "I see you wil not be otherwise pleased." But he insists that his son and heir, William, hereafter be educated apart from the girls, "not to have him [the tutor] when hee is to teach him [William] to be trubled with the wemen"—apparently indicating that by Barbara's arrangement the tutor had taught Mary, Katherine, and William together. De Lisle MS U 1475 C 81/97.

16. *Cal. SP* James I, (1603–1610), 285. On February 3, 1606, Wroth was granted his father's office of Forester of Linton Walk, Waltham Forest, and Keeper of Woodford Walk, Essex, for life. He also received various later grants to purchase lands to enlarge royal parks.

17. See De Lisle MSS U 1475 C 81/106 (July 14, 1604), C 81/108 (July 26, 1604). In October 1604 (C 81/114) Robert Sidney writes that he used the £200 sent to Mary as a wedding gift from his regiment to help make up part of the first payment to Wroth and cover the costs of the wedding (£100). He sent Mary £50, "which is as much as I can do, and I doubt not will serve her turn til shee come to London, at which time shee shall not fayle of the rest, and so I doe wryte unto her." On August 25, 1605, he writes: "I have seen my daughter Wrothes letter. If you have let her have any mony or do let her have any I will repay it at my return: and indeed I should bee very loth that shee did want." De L'Isle MS U 1475 C 81/145.

18. H&S, I, 142.

19. De L'Isle MS U 1475 C 81/117.

20. She is sometimes said to have been a dancer in *Beautie,* on the strength of Jonson's comment that the Queen directed him to make a masque for the "same twelve daughters of Niger"; but the cast of dancers is in fact very different. See H&S, VII, 191, and discussion in chapter 1.

21. On July 1, 1607, Robert Sidney wrote to his wife that Mary "must be at home, because the King will be in the [Epping] forest," and again on September 28 that her visit to Penshurst would be delayed till the King's departure. De L'Isle MS U 1475 C 81/170; cf. C 81/150.

22. This holograph letter, SP 14 (James I) 130/174, is undated, but was written before June 30, 1612, when the manor was described as "rebuilt." The petition insists on the need to provide for the King's better comfort on his visits, and alludes to Wroth's losses in allowing the King's deer "to feede in his best grounds, to which by his lease hee is nott bound."

23. See De L'Isle MSS U 1475 C 81/146 (October 7, 1606?); C 81/151 (October 5, 1607). Other letters, C 81/153 and 156 (October 20, 31, 1607), report Susan Herbert at Durrance taking physic; 81/320 (November 1, n.d.) reports the visits of Pembroke and Susan Herbert to Mary Wroth; C 81/162 (September 18, 1608) and 81/166 (October 16, 1608) report family visits to Robert Wroth during a dangerous sickness. Cf. De L'Isle MSS U 1475 C 81/167 (October 20, 1608); C 81/150 (September 28, 1607); C 81/160 (August 28, 1608); 81/210 (October 4, 1610).

24. Hannay, "Your vertuous and learned Aunt," 18. The crest, an arrowhead within a diamond, is described in Henry Peacham, *The Compleat Gentleman* (London, 1622), along with the basis for its use by Mary Wroth:

This forme of bearing is tearmed a Lozenge, and is proper to women never marryed, or to such in courtesie as are borne Ladies; who though they be marryed to Knights, yet they are commonly stiled and called after the Sirname of their fathers, if he be an Earle; for the greater Honour must ever extinguish the lesse: for example, the bearer hereof is the Lady *Mary Sidney,* the late wife of Sir *Robert Wroth* Knight, and daughter of the Right Honourable, *Robert* Lord *Sidney* of *Penshurst,* Viscount *Lisle,* Earle of *Leicester,* and companion of the most noble Order of the Garter, who seemeth by her late published *Urania* an inheritrix of the Divine wit of her Immortall Uncle.

25. N.[icholas] B.[reton], *Sir Philip Sidneys Ourania* (London, 1606), sig. A 4.

26. George Chapman, *The Iliades of Homer* (London, 1611), sig. Gg v.

27. George Wither, *Abuses Stript and Whipt* (London, 1613), sig. X 4.

28. William Gamage, *Linsi-Woolsie, or Two Centuries of Epigrammes* (Oxford, 1613), sig. D 3v. In 1613 also John Davies of Hereford dedicated a sonnet in praise of music to her (alluding to her musical interests), and there are other anonymous praises of her patronage and virtue in manuscript collections, cited in Roberts, *Poems,* 18–22.

29. Jonson, *The Alchemist* (London, 1612); H&S, VIII, 66–68.

30. "To Sir Robert Wroth," in H&S, VIII, 96–100. Gary Waller reads the poem as a backhanded compliment, measuring Wroth as an unsophisticated country gentleman against the courtly standards of his wife and Pembroke. "Mary Wroth and the Sidney Family Romance," 43–44. That is probably too strong; the poem resonates against the long tradition of *beatus ille* poems in which city sophisticates praise rural retirement. More to the point is Waller's suggestion that

this is a delicate exercise in addressing diverse audiences with very different values and interests.

31. Josuah Sylvester, *Lacrymae Lachrymarum* (London, 1613), sig. H 2.

32. H&S, VIII, 182. How much personal contact Wroth had with Jonson is unclear, but he was a long-standing Sidney-Pembroke client, and she may well have shown him her poems in manuscript. Lamb, *Gender and Authorship*, 154–156, finds some sexual innuendo in the poem, and notes the attribution to her verses of the aphrodisiac power of Venus' girdle or ceston, said in the *Iliad* (book 14) to have power to arouse passion in all beholders.

33. L. E. Kastner, ed., *The Poetical Works of William Drummond of Hawthornden*, 2 vols. (Manchester: Manchester University Press, 1913), II, 271. Drummond also praised her in a sonnet, invoking the familiar pun to extol her power of mind and her "worth accomplisht" (II, 277).

34. SP 14 (James I) 108/73.

35. See the illustration at the beginning of this chapter. The artist and date are unknown, but the figure is of an adult Mary Wroth defined by her lute. The picture is in the collection of Viscount De L'Isle, V.C., K.G., at Penshurst Place. See Quilligan, "Lady Mary Wroth," 278–280.

36. Chamberlain to Carleton, March 17, 1614, Chamberlain, I, 519.

37. Quoted in Roberts, *Poems*, 23. During Robert Wroth's earlier illness in 1608, Robert Sidney declared himself much pleased with the arrangements made for Mary, especially the fact that Wroth remitted the £1,200 still due him from the marriage agreement. De L'Isle MS U 1475 C 81/166.

38. Clarendon, *History of the Rebellion*, I, 73.

39. His poems circulated in manuscript but were not published until 1660, as *Poems Written by the Right Honorable William Earl of Pembroke...* (London, 1660). For his arts patronage, see Michael Brennan, *Literary Patronage in the English Renaissance: The Pembroke Family* (London: Routledge, 1988); and Hannay, *Philip's Phoenix*, 210–211. Letters from Mary Wroth and others indicate that she was often at the Pembroke town house, Baynard's Castle. Two were dated from there in 1619, to Dudley Carleton, SP 14 (James I) 108/56, 108/73.

40. The manuscript, a history of the Herbert family entitled "Herbertorum Prosapia," is at the Cardiff Central Library (Phillipps MS 5.7, 92). It records that William Herbert "had two natural children by the Lady Mary Wroth the Earle of Leicester's Daughter, William who was a Captain under Sir Henry Herbert, Collonell under Grave [Count] Maurice, and dyed unmarried and Catherine the wife of Mr. Lovel neare Oxford." Roberts, *Poems*, 24. Roberts also cites a second manuscript at Cardiff that records the children's names (*Poems*, 25). It is possible that Robert Sidney's letter to Barbara (De Lisle MS U 1475 C 81/264) on August 15, 1615, refers to this William ("You have done very well in putting wil away, for it had bin to grete a shame he should have stayed in the house"), but as Hannay notes (*Philip's Phoenix*, 277), the full context of the letter seems to point rather to the child of a servant. Sidney's accounts of 1620 record £20 "paid the mid wife," but there is no indication of who needed the services. De L'Isle MS U 1475 A 41/2.

41. C. G. Moore Smith, ed., *Poems English and Latin of Edward, Lord Herbert of Cherbury* (Oxford: Clarendon, 1932), 42 (undated).

42. Roberts (*Poems*, 25) cites a letter of May 14, 1645, indicating that Philip Herbert had helped Wroth's son to "a brave livinge in Ireland." Also see Roberts, "'The Knott Never to Bee Untide': The Controversy Regarding Marriage in Mary Wroth's *Urania*," in Miller and Waller, *Reading Mary Wroth*, 109–132; and Lamb, *Gender and Authorship*, 145–147.

43. SP 14 (James I) 122/35.

44. SP 14 (James I) 139/53, 158/65; SP 16 (Charles I) 183/Docquet; the dates involved are January 30, 1624; February 12, 1625; and April 12, 1627.

45. March 9, 1622, Chamberlain, II, 427.

46. Bodleian, MS Add. D. 111, ff. 173: "My thoughts [are] free from soe much as thinking of any such thing as I ame censurd for; I have with all care caused the sale of them to bee forbidden, and the books left to be shut up, for thos that are abroad, I will likewise doe my best to gett them in, if itt will please your Lordship to procure mee the kings warrant to that effect, without which non will deliver them to mee, besids that your Lordship wilbe pleased to lett mee have that which I sent you, the example of which will without question make others the willinger to obay."

47. Reprinted in Roberts, *Poems*, 32–35, from contemporary manuscripts on deposit in the University of Nottingham Library. For discussion of the Denny controversy, see John J. O'Connor, "James Hay and *The Countess of Montgomerie's Urania*," N&Q, n.s., 2 (1955), 150–152; Josephine Roberts, "An Unpublished Literary Quarrell Concerning the Suppression of Mary Wroth's *Urania* (1621)," N&Q, n.s., 24 (1977), 532–535; Paul Salzman, "Contemporary References in Mary Wroth's *Urania*," RES, 29 (1978), 178–181.

48. Hatfield, Cecil MSS 130/117 (February 16, 1622); 130/118–119 (February 26, 1622).

49. Cecil MS 130/120.

50. Cecil MS 130/121.

51. Reprinted in Roberts, *Poems*, 242.

52. "Chancery Proceedings before 1714, Whittington" (PRO, C 10, 110/89).

53. A holograph manuscript of an earlier version of Wroth's poems is in the Folger Library (V. a. 104); it contains in somewhat different arrangement each of the songs and sonnets in the published sequence except sonnet 4 from the first set; it also contains nine poems that were later dispersed throughout the prose *Urania*, and six poems not in Wroth's published work. Roberts, *Poems*, 62–64. See my earlier discussion in this chapter for evidence that Wroth's poetry circulated before 1613, the date of Sylvester's tribute.

54. For an illuminating study of these women, see Jones, *Currency of Eros*. Unlike Jones, I do not find pastoral to be a dominant motif in most of Wroth's poems: Pamphilia is a Queen, not a shepherdess, and her activities are centered on various courts more than rural retreats.

55. Roberts, *Poems*, annotates Wroth's many allusions to the Robert and Philip Sidney sequences. See also Miller, "Rewriting Lyric Fictions," 295–310; and Lamb, *Gender and Authorship*, 149–151.

56. Nona Fienberg, "Mary Wroth and the Invention of Female Poetic Subjectivity," in Miller and Waller, *Reading Mary Wroth*, 184–185.

57. Ibid.

58. Naomi Miller discusses this affinity in "Rewriting Lyric Fictions," 299–300.

59. Cf. *Urania*, I, 75–76.

60. Donne's poem, spoken by the male lover, begins and ends as follows (Gardner, *Donne: The Elegies and The Songs and Sonnets*, 31–32):

> Sweetest love, I doe not goe,
> For weariness of thee,
> Nor in hope the world can show
>   A fitter Love for mee;
> . . . . .
>   But think that wee
> Are but turn'd aside to sleepe;
> They who one another keepe
> Alive, ne'r parted bee.

61. Roberts (*Poems*, 44–46) disposes these poems into three segments.

62. In these last sequences the sonnets are numbered but the songs are not. My intertextual references are to sonnet numbers within the respective sequences; but for the two unnumbered sonnets and the songs, I give page numbers in Robert's edition.

63. For the opposite argument, that Pamphilia's constancy comes to involve spiritual virtue and a movement from earthly to divine love, see Elaine V. Beilin, "'The Onely Perfect Vertue': Constancy in Mary Wroth's *Pamphilia to Amphilanthus*," *Spenser Studies*, 2 (1981), 229–245, and *Redeeming Eve*, 232–243.

64. Beilin argues ("Onely Perfect Vertue," 240), that in this sonnet the beloved "is divine, is Christ himself." I suggest rather that the poem has appropriated that Christian redemptive language, applying it to the effects wrought by Pamphilia's experience of love as noble constancy. This ending is consonant with Pamphilia's conviction as *Urania*, Part I, breaks off, that her constancy is now firm and her love relationship with Amphilanthus secure.

65. In the Folger manuscript this sonnet is also signed "Pamphilia," but it is unsigned in the published text.

66. For publication of the Continental romances in parts, see chapter 2, note 2.

67. For a counterargument asserting Wroth's anxieties about publication and claiming that her poems stage a relentless effort to withdraw into a private space, see Jeff Masten, "'Shall I turne blabb?': Circulation, Gender, and Subjectivity in Mary Wroth's Sonnets," in Miller and Waller, *Reading Mary Wroth*, 67–87.

68. In another allusion to Sidney, two knights save the shepherdess-princess Urania from an attack by a wolf.

69. For other close analogues to Shakespeare's comedies and late romances, see Naomi Miller, "Engendering Discourse: Women's Voices in Wroth's *Urania* and Shakespeare's Plays," in Miller and Waller, *Reading Mary Wroth*, 154–172.

70. These allusions are pointed in the story of a lady who claims (like Frances Howard) to have remained a virgin throughout her marriage (4, 478–479), and in the story of a nobleman (Overbury) besotted by a young man (Somerset) who replaces him at court and attempts to murder him (1, 28–29).

71. These allusions are discussed in detail in Roberts, *Poems*, 29–30, 43–44, and Hannay, "Your vertuous and learned Aunt," 15–34.

72. Cf. Carolyn Swift, "Feminine Identity in Lady Mary Wroth's Romance *Urania*," *ELR*, 14 (1984), 328–346.

73. For an argument urging Wroth's "highly ambivalent view of female rule," see Josephine Roberts, "Radigund Revisited: Perspectives on Women Rulers in Lady Mary Wroth's *Urania*," in Haselkorn and Travitsky, *Renaissance Englishwoman*, 187–207.

74. See discussion in Swift, "Feminine Identity," 344–346.

75. More conventionally, Prince Leonius disguises himself as a nymph to court the supposed shepherdess Veralinda, in allusion to Sidney's Pyrocles (3, 362–372, 388–390).

76. Wroth inscribes contemporary controversies about women riding and hunting in this description of an unnamed lady: "The Lady was great, and therefore faire, full of spirit, and intising, pleasing and richly shee was attired, and bravely serv'd, an excellent hors-woman, and hunts-woman she was, though these be no properer commendations, *as some have said,* then to say, a man is a fine Semster, or Needle-man, yet qualities that were, and are commended at this day, allowed of, and admired" (4, 470; emphasis added). The heroines' use of these activities throughout the romance offers Wroth's rebuttal, as when Pamphilia cures her melancholy after parting with Amphilanthus by engaging in "those delights shee was wont to affect, which was, Hunting and Hawking, and such like" (2, 222). During that parting (in further reversal of gender stereotypes) Amphilanthus' tears are readier to fall than Pamphilia's: "*Urania* wept to part with her deare brother, and cosen. *Pamphilia's* heart was pierced with like sorrow, or greater, but stop'd her teares, as having a stronger spirit, till beholding the water in *Amphilanthus* eyes ready to fall, and waite upon the least summons her eyes would give; she then let some few slide, and drop, and so saluted him, love smiling in their teares" (2, 222).

77. Roberts, *Poems,* 42–43, notes that Pamphilia's name may allude to the poet and historian of that name in the reign of Nero, whose works are noted by Suidas, Aulus Gellius, and Edward Phillips. The fragment of her voluminous history (in Greek) which remains is in C. Müller, ed., *Fragmenta Historicorum Graecorum* (Paris: Didot, 1860–1861), III, 520–522.

78. The point is made in somewhat different terms in Quilligan, "Lady Mary Wroth," 273.

79. Ibid., 269–280.

80. Paul Salzman, *English Prose Fiction, 1558–1700: A Critical History* (Oxford: Clarendon, 1985), 141.

81. See Mary Ellen Lamb, "Women Readers in Mary Wroth's *Urania*," and Nona Fienberg, "Mary Wroth and the Invention of Female Poetic Subjectivity," in Miller and Waller, *Reading Mary Wroth*, 175–190, 210–227. Lamb discusses various scenes of reading in the work which respond to warnings over two centuries about the dangers to women in reading romance.

82. Sir Philip Sidney, *The Countess of Pembroke's Arcadia* [The Old Arcadia], ed. Jean Robertson (Oxford: Clarendon, 1973), 198.

83. Roberts notes (*Poems,* 153) that this poem revises an earlier poem entitled "Penshurst Mount," named for a feature of the Penshurst estate; the earlier version is BL, Additional MS 23,229, ff. 91–92.

84. On this point, see Maureen Quilligan, "The Constant Subject: Instability and Female Authority in Wroth's *Urania* Poems," in *Soliciting Interpretation: Literary Theory and Seventeenth-Century Poetry,* ed. Katherine Maus and Elizabeth

Harvey (Chicago: University of Chicago Press, 1990), 311–312. Quilligan suggests that Wroth here stages her own imitation of her uncle's text, identifying with one of the few discursive possibilities this tradition offers a female speaker (Echo), and also commenting through this identification on the lateness of her start. It is important to emphasize, however, that this is Wroth's beginning point only and that Urania voices only this single sonnet (as if in testimony that the poetics of Echo will not carry a female writer far). The major poet and storyteller, Pamphilia, looks to other sources.

85. Fienberg, "Mary Wroth and the Invention of Female Poetic Subjectivity," 179–180, reads this episode as an invasion of Pamphilia's privacy.

86. Other romance motifs include a Squire of Low Degree (2, f. 48v), several ladies rescued from attacks by wild beasts, and a pet lion (like Una's) belonging to Urania (2, f. 31v).

87. See chapter 6.

88. The attribution to Pembroke is discussed in Roberts, *Poems*, 217–218. It is attributed to Pembroke in three manuscripts (BL, Harleian MS 6917, ff. 33v–34; BL, Additional MSS 25,303, f. 130; and 21,433. ff. 119v–120).

89. Hannay, "Your vertuous and learned Aunt," 24–28.

90. "The Doleful Lay of Clorinda." Spenser introduces the poem as the song of Astrophil's sister: "Which least I marre the sweetnesse of the vearse, / In sort as she it sung, I will rehearse." For a review of the substantial evidence for Mary Sidney's authorship, see Hannay, *Philip's Phoenix*, 63–67.

91. The blazon likens her eyes "soe sparckling and bright shining" to those of Amphilanthus (Pembroke) as a further hint that she figures the Countess of Pembroke (2, f. 4).

92. See chapter 1.

93. Miller, "'Not Much to be Marked,'" 121–137.

94. In the MS the several speeches are not set off as dialogue; I present them so here, for clarity.

95. Pamphilia's father, the King of Morea, declares, "This . . . was I crowned in my youth among Ladys with, that I never alltered from my Counstant course of inconstancy" (1, f. 9v).

96. For discussion of this issue, see Roberts, "The Knott Never to Bee Untide," 109–132. For the dangers attending such "irregular" marriages or elopements, see *The Lawes Resolutions of Womens Rights*, 3, 144.

97. Queried by Amphilanthus on the matter, the Queen of Naples protests she does not know why she did it, and Pamphilia argues the appropriateness of the gesture as an expression of mourning for her dead brother Polarchos. But her glance at Amphilanthus makes her meaning clear: "With thos words her eyes hapened (itt may bee) by chance, butt I thinke rather truly ment, on Amphilanthus, who blusht" (2, f. 22v).

98. At the wedding her aunt the Queen of Naples advises Pamphilia that she might speak to Amphilanthus "as the Bride, nott as Pamphilia" without breaking her vow (2, f. 23), and intimates her approval of their continuing love (2, f. 24).

99. Fair Designe bears a cypher on his heart as a key to his identity, which will be revealed only when he discovers his destined beloved, who will bear a similar emblem. He was directed to seek knighthood from Amphilanthus, who confers it readily on the youth, "in whose face hee beelievcd hce sawe more then civile cause

to respect him for" (2, f. 29). Fair Designe's exploits clearly mark him as heir to Amphilanthus' prowess and superlative merit (2, ff. 29–29v). Conceivably, Wroth might have intended to supply hints later that the private marriage of Pamphilia and Amphilanthus resulted in this child, in allusion to the illegitimate son of Pembroke and Wroth.

100. Cf. the argument of James I in *The Trew Lawe of Free Monarchie*.

101. Among other examples, Melissea supplies King Clarimundo with a magic protective shield (2, ff. 16–17), and carries off the Persian Sophia in a magic chariot, to wait until the time is right for her to marry Trebisound and go to her kingdom (2, f. 20v).

102. Later, Pamphilia and Amphilanthus together advise a pair of young lovers and poets rather like themselves when young, Licunia and Andromarko (2, ff. 59–61v).

103. For a different argument about the function of these masques, see Heather Weidemann, "Theatricality and Female Identity in Mary Wroth's *Urania*," in Miller and Waller, *Reading Mary Wroth*, 200–209.

104. My intertextual citations are to act and line number in Brennan's edition of Wroth's *Love's Victory*. Of the two holograph manuscripts the one at Penshurst is complete except for the song of Venus' priests and all the shepherds, which is mentioned but not supplied at the end of Act V. The Huntington manuscript (HM 600) lacks a title page and several passages: the beginning exchange between Venus and Cupid (Act I, ll. 1–38) and most of Act V (ll. 68–74, 76, 103-end). Brennan concludes (17–20) that HM 600 represents an intermediate stage of composition, and is itself the supposedly missing Plymouth manuscript from which James O. Halliwell published some extracts, in *A Brief Description of the Ancient and Modern Manuscripts Preserved in the Public Library Plymouth* (1853), 212–236.

105. The similarities are noted by Roberts (*Poems*, 38). See also Brennan, *Love's Victory*, 22, and Margaret [Witten-Hannah] McLaren, "An Unknown Continent: Lady Mary Wroth's Forgotten Pastoral Drama, 'Loves Victorie,'" in Haselkorn and Travitsky, *Renaissance Englishwoman*, 284.

106. That Wroth took an interest in such theatrical occasions is suggested by the fact that Jonson identified her as a performer in his lost pastoral *The May Lord*, cast chiefly by the Sidney-Herbert family and alliance. H&S, I, 143. See chapter 4, note 31.

107. Richard Cody, *The Landscape of the Mind* (Oxford: Clarendon, 1969), 54.

108. For a different view, see McLaren, "An Unknown Continent," 276–294, which focuses on the intersection and conflict of several discourses in this work: courtly Petrarchanism and Neoplatonism, comedic satire, myth and ritual, and what she calls "a special language of avoidance" papering over the increasing powerlessness of women at James's court. Based only on the incomplete Huntington manuscript, this essay cannot take account of an ending which emphasizes female power rather than powerlessness. Carolyn Ruth Swift, in "Feminine Self-Definition in Lady Mary Wroth's *Love's Victorie* (c. 1621)," *ELR*, 19 (1989), 171–188, reads the drama as a dream of female empowerment and autonomy, compensating for Wroth's own frustrations in love.

109. In the drama the brother is identified as Philisses, in evident allusion to the name under which Sidney shadowed himself in the eclogues to the *Arcadia*, Philisides.

110. At the court of the Estensi in Ferrara a series of literary works gave impetus to the development of pastoral drama: Giraldi Cinthio's *Egle* (1545), Agostino de Beccari's *Il Sacrificio* (1554), Alberto Lollio's *Aretusa* (1563), and Argenti's *Lo Sfortunato* (1567) point the way toward the full realization of the form in Tasso's *Aminta*. See W. W. Greg, *Pastoral Poetry and Pastoral Drama* (London: H. H. Bullen, 1906), 153–176, and Barbara Lewalski, "Mary Wroth's *Love's Victory* and Pastoral Tragicomedy," in Miller and Waller, *Reading Mary Wroth*, 88–108.

111. Louis Adrian Montrose, "Of Gentlemen and Shepherds: The Politics of Elizabethan Pastoral Form," *ELH*, 50 (1983), 415–459, and Montrose, "'Eliza, Queene of shepheardes,' and the Pastoral of Power," *ELR*, 10 (1980), 153–182; Orgel, *The Illusion of Power;* Annabel Patterson, *Pastoral and Ideology: Virgil to Valéry* (Berkeley: University of California Press, 1987), 60–163.

112. Italian critics complained that the mix of comedy and tragedy violates artistic unity, that the mixture of clowns and kings violates decorum, and that stories of rude shepherds could not instruct sophisticated city dwellers. Jason de Nores attacked the tragicomedies of Tasso and Guarini in *Discorso intorno . . . che la commedia, la tragedia, et il poema eroica* (1587), and *Apologia contra l'auttor del Verato* (1590), as did others. See the account of the controversy in Bernard Weinberg, *A History of Literary Criticism in the Italian Renaissance,* 2 vols. (Chicago: University of Chicago Press, 1961), II, 1074–1105.

113. Italian defenses of tragicomedy include: Cecchi, "Prologue," in *La Romanesca* (1554); Torquato Tasso, *Discoursi del poema heroico* (Naples, [1587]); and especially Battista Guarini, *Il Verato* (Ferrara, 1588), *Il Verato secondo* (Florence, 1593), and *Il Compendio della poesia tragicomica* (Venice, 1599). Guarini also defined the genre's specific purpose (to purge melancholy by pleasure) and found some warrant for it in antiquity in Aristotle's double plot and in Plautus' *Amphitryo*. He even proclaimed it the highest kind, best suited to the refined modern age, in that it includes all the good features and rejects the excesses of comedy and tragedy.

114. From *The Compendium of Tragicomic Poetry,* ed. and trans. Allan H. Gilbert, *Literary Criticism: Plato to Dryden* (Detroit: Wayne State University Press, 1962), 511, 524.

115. *The Defence of Poesie* (London, 1595), sigs. Iv, E 3v.

116. *The Faithful Shepherdess by John Fletcher: A Critical Edition,* ed. Florence A. Kirk (New York: Garland, 1980), 15–16, "To the Reader."

117. Hans Robert Jauss, "Literary History as a Challenge to Literary Theory," trans. Elizabeth Bensinger, *New Literary History,* 2 (1970–71), 7–37.

118. The *Aminta* was first acted on July 31, 1573; the first edition (Cremona, 1580) lacked the choruses and epilogue; they first appeared complete in the Venice edition (1590). It was soon translated into French, German, English, and Spanish.

119. Cupid in the prologue claims his agency in these affairs, undertaken to conquer Silvia's cold chastity; and an epilogue by Venus describes her errant son's power over humankind. There is some local allegory in allusions to personages at the Ferrari court, with Tasso himself shadowed in Thyrsis. Some critics think Tasso may also shadow his hopeless passion for Leonora D'Este in the characters of Aminta and Silvia. See discussion in Greg, *Pastoral Poetry,* 176–194; and "Introduction," in *Torquato Tasso's Aminta Englisht,* trans. Henry Reynolds (1628), ed. Clifford Davidson (Fennimore, Wisc.: John Westburg, 1972).

120. The prologue was written for a performance at Turin (which may not have

taken place) celebrating the marriage of Carlo Emanuele I, Duke of Savoy, to Catherine of Austria, daughter of Philip II of Spain, in 1585. The first known performance was at Crema in 1596. The lavish (twentieth) edition (Venice, 1602) contained illustrations and notes, together with a treatise on tragicomedy.

121. The English translation (London, 1602) was by an anonymous relative of Daniel's friend and traveling companion Sir Edward Dymocke; it is much condensed from the original and often inaccurate. Daniel was at one time tutor to the young William Herbert; for his court connections, see chapter 1. See "Introduction," in Walter F. Staton, Jr., and William E. Simeone, eds., *A Critical Edition of Sir Richard Fanshawe's 1647 Translation of Giovanni Battista Guarini's "Il Pastor Fido"* (Oxford: Clarendon, 1964).

122. See chapter 1 and note 83. The work was reprinted in Daniel's *Certaine Small Workes* in 1607, 1609, and 1611, and independently in 1623. The fact that Wroth danced in the Queen's Twelfth Night masque of 1605 places her among the Queen's attendants in that year; so she may have been one of the (unnamed) ladies who visited Oxford with the Queen in August.

123. The play was produced about 1609–10, probably at Blackfriars, since Jonson's commendatory poem refers to a six-pence entrance fee. All the commendatory poems speak of the play's failure, as does Fletcher himself in dedicating the published version to Sir William Aston (ll. 2–3), *The Faithfull Shepheardesse* (London, [1610]).

124. See chapter 1 and notes 100, 101.

125. Believing that his beloved Musella loves Lissius, Philisses tries to hide the cause of his pain from his friend and relinquish his own claims. Lissius at length prevails in his repeated appeals to their bond of friendship (II, ll. 251–310). Lissius reveals his new-found love for Philisses' sister Simeana, and encourages Philisses to declare his love openly to Musella; Philisses in turn pledges his good offices with his sister.

126. Lissius listens to the Forester's complaint that his beloved, Silvesta, has withdrawn to the woods after being rejected by Philisses, but in reply Lissius—as yet untouched by and scornful of love and women—urges the pursuit of sexual pleasure. The Forester is as yet a strict Neoplatonist who desires to love Silvesta "in truest kind" (I, l. 261), simply in the chaste beholding of her. Rustick also invites but cannot gain love confidences from Philisses, because of the wide gulf between them in sensibility.

127. Dalina: "Now we are mett, what sport shall we invent / While the sun's fury somewhat more bee spent?" (I, ll. 300–301); "Mee thinks wee now to silent ar, lett's play / Att something while we yett have pleasing day" (II, ll. 1–2); "Now w'are alone lett every one confess / Truly to other what our lucks have bin, / How often lik'd, and lov'd and soe express / Our passions past" (III, ll. 125–128); "Heere bee owr fellows, now lett us beegin / Some pretty pastime pleasure's sport to winn" (IV, ll. 351–352).

128. Here Climeana breaks through the initial impasse over choice of game by singing a love complaint of her wandering eyes and heart; Philisses and Musella propose themselves as judges since they do not have glad hearts for song; Rustick sings a comic blazon of Musella comparing her parts to farmyard animals and crops; and Lacon sings of initiation into love by Cupid's dart and beauty's sight.

129. Dalina recounts her former coquetry: many lovers wooed her, but she was

too fickle to choose any of them, so all at length abandoned her; she now terms that behavior youthful folly and determines to accept the next man who offers. Simeana, without identifying the man, tells of her constancy despite rejection, and her tentative hopes. Fillis follows with her tale of unrequited love for Philisses. Finally, Climeana tells of leaving home and country for a lover who then rejected her; and of her new love for Lissius. A love debate follows, in which Simeana challenges Climeana's claims to Lissius, charging her with inconstancy and folly but accepting the love contest with good grace: "Take your course, and win him if you can" (III, l. 245).

130. Other set pieces include the little autobiographical narratives and the love debate between Simeana and Climeana in Act III.

131. Swift, "Feminine Self-Definition," 171–188, suggests that the Philisses-Musella story rewrites the Philip Sidney–Penelope Rich relationship with a happy ending. The suggestion gains plausibility from the pastoral name under which Sidney represented himself in the *Arcadia* (Philisides). But that works rather as an allusion than an identification meant to be exclusive.

132. See note 30.

Index

Aasand, Hardin, 336n62

Abbot, George (Archbishop of Canterbury), 24, 27, 51, 52, 56, 126, 143, 201, 332n40, 334n55

Abercrombie, Father, 21, 330n25

Acheson, Katherine, 368n1

A.D.D · *Xenia Regia ad Juvubum,* 330n18

Aers, David, 112, 366nn81,85

Agrippa, Cornelius, 154; *De Nobilitate et Praecellentia Foemenei Sexus,* 378n2; *Vanity of Sciences,* 137

Akrigg, G. P. V., 342n28

Albert, Archeduke, 351n10

Alexander, William: *Darius, Croesus, The Alexandrian, Julius Caesar,* 389n60

Allen, Cardinal, 352n14

Alumni Oxoniensis, 381n36

Amadis de Gaule, 45, 264, 340n2

Amussen, Susan, 324n1

Anger, Jane (pseud.?): *Jane Anger her Protection for Women,* 156, 327n21, 380n18

Angus, Earl of, 68

Anhalt, Prince of, 78

Anna, Infanta of Spain, 21

Anne, Queen, 2, 14, 15–43, 284, 299, 328n28, 329n9, 332n35; and King James, 4–5, 8, 9, 328n1, 332nn39,40, 337n77; and Buckingham, 24–25, 207; tributes to, 18–19, 328n5, 329n17, 330n18, 355n66; modes of resistance of, 18–28; Catholicism of, 20, 21–22, 27, 29, 39, 43, 310, 330n25, 331n28; household of, 22–23, 220, 221, 311,

330n21; death of, 27, 334nn54,55; funeral of, 27–28, 149, 249, 335nn56,57; and Princess Elizabeth, 50, 51; and Arbella Stuart, 77, 78, 79, 80, 86, 87; and the Countess of Bedford, 95, 97, 98, 109, 115, 116, 117, 122; and Anne Clifford, 141, 142, 145; and Aemilia Lanyer, 220, 221; and Mary Wroth, 245, 246, 263, 266, 410n122; and court masques and entertainments, 15, 17, 27–43, 53, 80, 96, 99, 100, 101, 116, 128, 221, 254, 310, 335nn59,61,62; *Letters,* 328n1, 330nn21,24, 332n41

Antonius (Marcus Aurelius): *Meditations,* 138

Archer, Thomas, 157

Ariosto, Ludovico, 69, 97, 351n7

Aristotle, 166, 174, 409n113; *Organon,* 163

Armitage, C. M., 366n78

Arthur, King, 49

Arundel. *See* Howard

Ashton, Robert, 329n9

Askew, Anne, 325n5

Astin, William, 138

Augustine, Saint, 163, 166, 182; *City of God,* 137, 150

Babcock, Barbara, 326n11

Babington, Gervase, 397n36

Bacon, Sir Francis (Lord Verulam), 26, 53, 90, 182; *Henry the Seventh,* 203, 392n86; *Works,* 358n109

413

Bacon, Lady Jane. *See* Cornwallis, Lady Jane

Bacon, Nathaniel, 118, 120, 366n93

Bald, R. C., 359n2, 360n9, 365n74

Barclay, John: *Argenis,* 45, 138, 340n2

Barroll, Leeds, 16, 329n7, 335n62

Bassano, Angela (Holland), 214, 395n6

Bassano, Anthony, 214

Bassano, Baptist (Aemilia Lanyer's father), 214, 395nn5–8,14

Bassano, Margaret Johnson (Aemilia Lanyer's mother), 214, 395n6

Bath, Elizabeth, Countess of, 136, 359n1

Baxter, Nathaniel, 397n36

Beaulieu, James, 336nn72,80

Beaumont, Francis, 53; *Masque of the Inner Temple,* 344n45

Beaumont (French ambassador), 24, 31

Bedford, Countess of. *See* Russell, Lucy Harington

Bedford, Francis Russell, second Earl of, 127

Beilin, Elaine, 180, 191, 325nn4,5, 383n3

Belcamp, Jan van, 124, 131

Belling, Richard: *Sixth Booke to the Countesse of Pembroke's Arcadia,* 184, 385n27

Belsey, Catherine, 324n2, 328n31, 383n3

Benger, Elizabeth, 341n9

Bennett, H. S., 340n1

Bergeron, David M., 328n1, 330n21, 335n58, 341n9, 349n88

Berkeley, Lady, 337n76

Bertie, Catherine, Countess of Suffolk, 221, 222, 241, 397n42

Bertie, Richard, 397n42

Bertie, Susan, Countess of Kent, 214, 215, 220, 221, 222, 241, 397nn35,42

Bess of Hardwick, 68–69, 70–71, 74, 75, 76, 77, 80, 82, 351n3, 352n22, 353n32, 355n59

Bevill, Lady, 31

Bible, 194, 214, 219, 226–227, 230–234; reading of, 137, 138, 150, 173; interpretation of, 161–167, 175, 226–234, 312–314; Psalm 104, 398n50

Birch, Thomas: *Court and Times of James I,* 335n56, 341n16, 343n29, 359n113, 361n17, 367n100

Blodgett, Harriet, 375n70

Blois, Louis de, 180

Blount, Charles, Lord Mountjoy, 332n34, 363n54

Boccaccio, Giovanni: *De mulieribue claris,* 218, 396n27

Boethius: *Consolation of Philosophy,* 137

Boose, Linda, 325n7

Bothwell, Earl of, 20, 330n21

Bradley, E. T., 351nn1,2, 353n40, 356n71

Bradner, Leicester, 344n37

Bradshaw, Ann, 85, 89, 91, 358n105

Brahe, Tycho, 15

Brandon, Charles, Earl of Suffolk, 397n42

Brandon, Samuel: *Octavia,* 389n60

Brennan, Michael, 403n39, 408nn104,105

Breton, Nicholas, 397n36; *The Blessed Weeper,* 227–228, 398n48; *The Countess of Pembrookes Love,* 228, 398n48; "M. Agape Wrotha," 246; *The Pilgrimage to Paradise,* 228, 398n48; *The Ravisht Soule,* 227, 398n48; *Sir Philip Sidneys Ourania,* 402n25

Bridenthal, Renata, 324n1

Brink, Jean R., 326n11, 363n53

Bromley, George: *Collection of Original Royal Letters,* 340n3, 349n78

Broner, E. M., 327n17

Brooke, Lord, 77

Brounker, Sir Henry, 71, 72, 74, 75, 76, 351n11

Bruss, Elizabeth, 375n70

Buc, Sir George, 332n37

Buckingham, George Villiers, Duke of, 24–25, 116, 117, 141, 145, 179, 186, 204, 207, 310, 319, 358n111, 383n5, 386n30, 393n93; and James I, 15, 24–25, 28, 95, 119, 310; and court masques, 41, 101, 339n99; and Queen Anne, 24–25, 332nn40,41; and Princess Elizabeth, 59, 60, 65; and Mary Wroth, 263, 264; and Elizabeth Cary, 387n38, 393n95

Buckingham, Katherine (Manners), Duchess of, 95, 186, 386nn30,34, 387n38, 388n47, 393n95

Buckingham, Mary, Countess of (Buckingham's mother), 95, 186, 387n38, 393n95

Bull, Dr. John, 47

Bulstrode, Cecilia, 96, 97, 109, 110, 114, 120, 121, 122, 364n68, 365nn69,70

Burges, Dr. John, 98, 114–115, 116, 360n9, 367n100

Burghley. *See* Cecil, William

Byard, Margaret, 359nn2,4, 360n6

Byfield, Nicholas, 103; *Sermon upon . . . Peter,* 362n4

Cahn, Susan, 327n16
Caldicott, Matthew, 128, 147
Caldwell, Mark, 391n74
Calvert, Samuel, 332n38
Calvin, John, 57, 182, 191; *Institutes,* 181
Campion, Thomas, 27; *Entertainment . . . at Cawsome House,* 329n14, 334n51; *The Lords Masque,* 52, 344n38, 361n30; *Muske* (for Somerset-Howard wedding), 40–41, 339n98; *Masque* (for Hay-Denny wedding), 337n76
Carew (Carey), Sir George, 22, 23, 331n29, 332n33
Carey, John, 103–104, 362n47
Carey, Lady (wife of Sir Robert), 332n35
Carey, Sir Robert: *Memoirs,* 331n31, 332n35, 385n22
Carleton, Sir Dudley, 42, 57, 60, 116, 117, 155, 247, 248, 249, 333nn44,45,48,49, 335n56, 340n2, 342n23, 349n88, 356n81, 360n5; on Queen Anne, 26, 29, 30, 329n10; on court masques, 31, 80, 336nn65,68, 337n74, 339nn99,101, 361n19; and Countess of Bedford, 99, 100, 116, 117; *Letters,* 332n32, 333n46, 336nn65,68,69, 354n48
Carr. *See* Somerset, Robert Carr, Earl of
Cary, Anne (Dame Clementina; daughter of Elizabeth Cary), 180, 185, 187, 189, 190, 384nn9,19, 388n47
Cary, Catherine, Lady Home (daughter of Elizabeth Cary), 184, 185, 189, 384n19
Cary, Elizabeth (Sister Augustina; daughter of Elizabeth Cary), 189, 190, 384n19
Cary, Elizabeth Bland (Lady Carew; sister-in-law of Elizabeth Cary), 190, 385n22, 389n57
Cary, Elizabeth Spencer (second Lady Hunsdon), 385n22
Cary, Elizabeth Tanfield, Viscountess Falkland, 2, 3, 8, 10, 101, 102, 149, 178, 179–211, 313, 385n26, 388nn42,44, 392n82; *Life,* 180, 181, 182, 183, 184, 190, 383nn6,7, 384nn11,14,17,19, 385nn20,29, 388nn43,44,47,51, 391n77; conversion to Catholicism, 180, 185–190, 310, 386nn31,32,36; children of, 182, 384n19, 388nn48,49, 393n96; death of, 190, 388n53; letters of, 187–

189, 312, 387nn38,39; *Tragedie of Mariam,* 6, 179, 180, 183, 190–201, 202, 211, 310, 325n5, 382n1, 388n56, 389n57, 391nn70,71,74; *History of the Life, Reign, and Death of Edward II,* 179, 201–211, 310, 317–320, 383n2, 393n96, 394nn97–100; translation of Ortelius's *Mirroir,* 179, 383n4; epigram on Buckingham, 179, 383n5; lost works, 179–180, 320, 383n7; translation of *The Reply of the . . . Cardinall of Perron,* 383n5, 392nn80–82
Cary, Henry (Father Placid; son of Elizabeth Cary), 189, 384n19
Cary, Henry, Lord Hunsdon, 214, 215, 394n3
Cary, Henry, Viscount Falkland, 6, 181, 182, 184–185, 186–189, 201, 317–320, 385nn22,26,28,29, 386nn32,35,36, 387n41, 393n94
Cary, Lady Katherine (mother of Henry, Lord Falkland), 181
Cary, Lorenzo (son of Elizabeth Cary), 189, 384n19
Cary, Lucius (second Viscount Falkland; son of Elizabeth Cary), 180, 182, 190, 383n7, 384n19, 388nn44,45
Cary, Lucy (Sister Magdalena; daughter of Elizabeth Cary), 189, 190, 384nn9,19, 388n47
Cary, Mary (Sister Maria; daughter of Elizabeth Cary), 189, 190, 384n19, 388n47
Cary, Patrick (son of Elizabeth Cary), 180, 182, 189, 384n19, 388n47
Cary, Philip (brother of Henry, Lord Falkland), 190, 388n55
Cary, Victoria (Lady Uvedale; daughter of Elizabeth Cary), 190, 384n19
Casaubon, Isaac: *Ad Epistolem . . . Cardinalis Perronii, responsio,* 392n80
Castiglione, Baldassare, 137; *Il Cortegiano,* 378n2
Caus, Solomon, 54; *Hortus Palatinus,* 346n53
Cavendish, Charles, 351n6
Cavendish, Elizabeth (mother of Arbella Stuart), 68, 351n3
Cavendish, Henry, 76
Cavendish, Michael, 81; *14 Ayers in Tabletorie,* 355n62
Cavendish, William, 74

Cecil, Robert, Earl of Salisbury, 192, 193, 330n21, 332nn33, 39, 352n14, 354n47, 390n62; and Queen Anne, 22, 26; and Arbella Stuart, 71, 72, 73, 74, 76, 77, 90, 354n49, 358n107; and the Countess of Bedford, 98–99; and Anne Clifford, 142, 373n41

Cecil, William, Lord Burghley: and Arbella Stuart, 69, 70, 351n6, 352n14

Certaine Reasons and Arguments, 350n96

Cervantes, Miguel de: *Don Quixote,* 137

Chaloner, Anne, 340n103

Chamberlain, John: letters from and to, 26, 29, 50, 98, 128, 155, 247, 248, 249, 331n26, 333nn48,49, 334nn52,53, 340n2, 348n76, 355n61, 359n113, 360nn5,11,13,15,17, 360n5; on entertainments and masques, 35, 36, 42, 50, 99, 336n71, 337nn77,80, 338n87, 339nn99,101, 344nn43,45, 349n89; on Queen Anne's death, 27–28, 334n55, 335nn56,57; on Princess Elizabeth, 52, 55, 57, 58, 342n23, 343nn30,33,35, 348n70, 369n4, 370n15, 379nn12,13

Chambers, E. K., 328n28, 332n38, 337n78

Chapman, George, 19, 53, 98, 107, 329n17, 344n44; *Bussy D'Ambois,* 391n77; *Charles Duke of Byron,* 24; *Homer, Prince of Poets,* 102, 329n17, 355n66; *Iliades of Homer,* 81, 246; *Memorable Maske,* 344n44; *Monsieur D'Olive,* 24; *Second Maid's Tragedy,* 391n77; *Widow's Teares,* 24

Charles, Prince (later King Charles I), 27, 28, 39, 54, 59, 60, 65, 98, 117, 129, 332n35, 333n35, 343n32, 350n100, 367nn98,105, 385n22, 393n93; created Prince of Wales, 141; negotiations for marriage of, 57, 64, 116, 184; and Elizabeth Cary, 186, 187, 189

Charles II, King, 65

Charles Lewis (son of Elizabeth, Electress Palatine), 46, 56, 65, 350nn100,105

Charleton, H. B., 390n61

Charron, Pierre: *Book of Wisdom,* 138

Chaucer, Geoffrey, 137, 140, 150, 159; *Legend of Good Women,* 140, 218, 396n27

Children of the Queen's Revels, 24, 332nn36,37, 390n64

Chillingworth, William, 189

Christian, Prince (of Brunswick), 65, 349n93

Christian IV, King (of Denmark), 17, 27, 80, 342n22, 355n60

Christina, Queen (of Sweden), 46

Christine de Pisan, 153, 218; *Cité des Dames,* 378n2, 396n27

Churchyard, Thomas: "The Two Mortimers," 393n89

Cicero, 163

Clapham, David: translation of Agrippa, *The Nobilitie and excellencye of woman kynde,* 378n2

Clarendon, Edward Hyde, earl of, 189, 190, 248; *History of the Rebellion,* 388nn45,52, 403n38

Clark, Alice, 326n16

Clayton, Peter, 391n79

Cleaver, Robert: *A Godlie Forme of Household Government,* 382n45

Clement VIII, Pope, 21

Clifford, Anne (Countess of Dorset, Pembroke, and Montgomery), 2, 3, 5, 8, 10, 124, 125–151, 220, 221, 224, 226, 235, 309, 313, 336n64, 339n96; marriages of, 127–128, 129, 133, 144–148, 376n78, 377n90, 396nn28,31; management of estates, 130, 370n24, 371nn26,28; monuments to Margaret Clifford, her mother, 136, 374n53; library of, 137–140; "Great Picture," 137–138; intellectual interests of, 139–140, 150, 375n66; and daughter, 148–149; and Cookham, 216, 235, 239, 241, 375n62; and King James, 145–147, 377nn81,82; and Queen Anne, 23, 33, 38, 128, 137, 145, 331n32, 334n50; letters of, 134–136, 312, 369n4, 373nn45–50, 376n78, 386n32; *Diary,* 5–6, 15, 98, 140–151, 331n32, 360n15, 368n1, 376nn74–77, 377nn79–90; "Day by Day Book," 371n27; *Life of Me,* 126, 127, 128, 131, 369nn6,7,11, 370nn15,20,22, 371n32, 372nn37–40, 373nn42,51, 374nn55,56; "Memorial of Margaret" (Clifford), 133–134, 369n6, 371nn30,33, 372n35; "Records of George . . . Clifford," 132, 369nn6–7, 373nn42–44,49,51, 374nn54,57; "Summary" concerning Francis Clifford and Henry, Lord Clifford, 373n41; "Great Books" (Chronicles), 126, 131, 141,

146, 150, 312, 369n5, 371n29; "Severall
Voyages" of George Clifford, 132, 150,
371n34. *See also* Clifford, George;
Clifford, Margaret Russell; Sackville,
Richard
Clifford, D. J. H., 368n1
Clifford, Francis, fourth Earl of Cumber-
land, 127, 128, 129, 132, 133, 134, 146,
371n26, 373n41
Clifford, George, third Earl of Cumberland
(father of Anne Clifford), 126–127,
131–132, 142–143, 216, 369n9,
371n34, 372n36, 376n78, 396n28
Clifford, Henry, fifth Earl of Cumberland,
128, 129, 132, 133, 373n41
Clifford, Lady Jane, 386n30
Clifford, Margaret Russell, Countess of
Cumberland (mother of Anne Clifford):
and Anne Clifford, 125, 127, 133–136,
144, 187, 371n29, 373nn42–51; in
"Great Picture," 131, 373n43; as patroness, 138, 150, 311, 336n64, 340n1,
359n1, 374nn59,60, 378n92, 391n74,
396n22, 397n37; and Aemilia Lanyer,
216–217, 219, 220, 221, 224, 225, 226,
228–229, 233–234, 241, 374n59; and
Cookham, 235, 237, 240, 396nn21,28,
398n55; letters, 134–136; "autobiogra-
phy," 136
Clifford family, 130, 143, 146; "Great Pic-
ture" of, 124, 131, 137, 139, 373n43;
"Chronicles" of, 126, 131, 141, 146,
150, 312, 371n29
Cobham, Lord, 77, 78, 141
Cody, Richard, 297
Coke, Sir Edward, 10, 77, 88, 187, 386n32
Coke, R.: *Detection of the Court,* 342n28
Colonna, Vittoria, 3, 252
Colville, John, 330n21
Comenius, Jan Amos, 65
Comines, Philippe de, 138
Compton, Lord, 332n33
Conde, Prince of, 351n10
Conn, George, 331n25
Constable, Henry, 374n59
Conway, Sir Edward, Viscount Killul-
tagh, 59, 61, 185, 187, 188,
385nn28,29, 387nn38–40
Cooke sisters, 349n1
Cooper, Elizabeth, 351n1, 356n76
Cornwallis, Lady Jane (Meutys; later, Lady
Bacon), 97, 115, 116, 117, 118, 120,

309, 366n93; *Correspondence,* 360n5,
366n94, 367nn95,96,98,101,107, 110–
114, 368nn115–117
Cornwallis, Sir William, 18, 329n14,
366n93
Correr, Marc'Antonio (Venetian ambassa-
dor), 36–37, 40, 88, 338n86, 339n97
Cosin, John, 186
Cotton, Clement, 103; *The Mirror of Mar-
tyrs,* 362n43; translations of Calvin,
362n43
Cotton, Richard: *King Henry the Third,*
392n86
Cowper, William, 16; *Heaven Opened,*
329n6
Craigie, Alexander, 18; *Poetical Essays, Amo-
rose Songes,* 329n12
Cranbourne, Viscountess, 38
Crandall, Caryl, 379n9
Crashaw, Richard, 386n31
Crewe, Sir Randal, 146
Croft, Sir James, 88, 89
Crompton, Hugh, 85, 89, 91, 356n71,
357n83, 359n113
Cromwell, Oliver, 130, 350n103, 370n24
Cuff, Henry: *Age of Man's Life,* 138
Cumberland, Countess of. *See* Clifford,
Margaret Russell
Cutpurse, Moll, 155, 358n105
Cutting, Thomas, 80, 355n60

Damse, Marquis, 141
Daniel, Samuel, 27, 33, 98, 103, 104, 110,
111, 138, 170, 179, 204, 298–299,
390nn62,68, 397nn36,37; as tutor to
Anne Clifford, 137, 138, 139, 336n64,
363n57, 370n16; as tutor to William
Herbert, 336n64, 363n54, 410n121; patrons of, 105, 363n54, 378n92; *Certaine
Epistles with a Defence of Ryme,* 336n64,
363n57; *Certaine Small Works,* 374n62,
389n60; *Civile Warres,* 105, 137,
363n55; *Cleopatra,* 191, 192, 389n60;
Historie of England, 137, 203, 392n86,
393n91; *Hymens Triumph,* 41–42, 299,
339n100; *A Panegyrike Congratulatory,*
105–106, 336n64; *Philotas,* 24, 191,
192–193, 332n37, 389n60, 390nn64–
67; *Poetical Essayes,* 374n59; *Queen's Arcadia,* 35–36, 298, 299, 337n82,
338n83, 410n122; *Tethys Festival,* 39, 80,
84, 128, 339nn94,95, 361n30, 390n65;

Daniel, Samuel (*continued*)
  "To the Lady Anne Clifford," 374n61; *A
  True Description,* 336nn63,66; *Vision of
  Twelve Goddesses,* 29–30, 80, 99–100,
  105, 336nn63,64,69, 363n56; *Whole
  Workes,* 336n63, 361nn19,23, 370n16,
  374n59
Dante: *Vita Nuova,* 252
D'Aragona, Tullia, 252
Davidson, Cathy, 327n17
Davies, John (of Hereford), 98, 180, 181,
  190, 191, 385n23, 389n57, 402n28; *Di-
  vine Meditations,* 102, 362n40; *Muses Sac-
  rifice,* 183, 362n40, 384n15, 385n22;
  Nosce Teipsum, 170; *Scourge of Folly,*
  362n40
Davis, Natalie Zemon, 3, 203, 326n14,
  392n83
Davison, Francis, 374n59
Day, John: *Isle of Gulls,* 24, 332n37
de Franchis, Joannis, 53; *De Auspicatissimis
  Nuptiis,* 345n49
Dekker, Thomas, 9; *Meet Me in London,*
  391n77; *Roaring Girl,* 379n10
De Lafontaine, H. C., 395n11
Delany, Paul, 375n70
de la Tour, Baron (French ambassador), 99
Denbigh, Earl of, 251
Denbigh (Denby), Susan, Countess, 186,
  386nn31,32
Denny, Honoria, 265, 337n76
Denny, Lord Edward, 248, 249–250, 265
de Nores, Jason: *Discorso . . . che la comedia,*
  409n112
Derby, Dowager Countess of, 334n50
de Roy, Loys: *Variety of Things,* 137
Descartes, René, 350n100
de Vere, Anne (Cecil), Countess of Oxford,
  326n13
de Vere, Susan. *See* Herbert, Susan
Devereaux, Penelope. *See* Rich, Penelope
Devereaux, Robert. *See* Essex, Robert Dev-
  ereaux, second Earl of
Dialogues of S. Gregorie (R. W.), 22, 331n27
Digby, Sir John, 141, 146
di Girone, Don Fernandez (Spanish ambassador), 36
Dio Cassius, 340n6
Dodderidge, John (also John Good), 71,
  352n18
Dollimore, Jonathan, 325n6
Dona (Dohna), Baron, 60, 347n65,
  349n81

Doncaster. *See* Hay, James
Donne, John, 1, 138, 139, 149, 311,
  358n111, 360n10, 397n36; and Countess of Bedford, 98, 99, 103, 104, 107,
  110–115, 120–122, 123, 365nn72–75,
  366nn78–92; letters, 338n85, 360n10,
  361n20, 365nn72,75,77, 366nn89,91;
  "Aire and Angels," 111; *Anniversaries,*
  111, 365nn72,73,75; "At New-Yeares
  Tide," 113–114; "Canonization," 256;
  "Death be not Proud," 121; *Devotions,*
  65; elegies on Cecilia Bulstrode, 121–
  122; "Epithalamion" (for Princess Elizabeth), 52, 343n37; "The Feaver," 111;
  "The Funerall," 111; "Honour is so sublime perfection," 114, 366n79; "A Letter
  written by Sir H. G. and J. D.," 366n87;
  "A Nocturnall upon S. Lucies Day," 111;
  "Obsequies to the Lord Harrington,"
  114, 115; "Reason is our Soules left
  hand," 112–113; *Sermons,* 138, 348n71,
  366n92; "Sweetest love, I doe not goe,"
  257, 405n60; "T'have written then,"
  113–114; "Twicknam Garden," 110,
  111, 366n78; verse letters, 111–114,
  365nn72,73,75, 366nn81,84–86; "You
  have refin'd mee," 113; "You that are she
  and you" (elegy for Lady Markham), 114
Dorset. *See* Sackville, Richard
Dowland, John, 98, 102; *Second Book of
  Songs,* 362n37
Downame, John: *Christian Warfare,* 137
Draxe, Thomas, 103; *The Worldes Resurrection,* 362n42
Drayton, Michael, 103, 139, 360n10,
  397n36; *Barons Warres,* 104, 204,
  385n21, 393n90; "Eighth Eclogue,"
  Poems Lyrick and Pastorall, 363n52; *Endi-
  mion and Phoebe,* 104, 363n48; *England's
  Heroicall Epistles,* 104, 183, 204,
  363nn51,53, 385n21; *Idea the
  Shepheard's Garland,* 104; *Matilda,* 104,
  362n48; *Mortimeriados,* 104, 204,
  393n90; *The Owle,* 263n53; *Piers Gaves-
  ton,* 204, 393n90; *Polyolbion,* 235; *Robert,
  Duke of Normandy,* 363n49
Drummond, Lady Jane, 41, 86, 87,
  334n50, 340n101
Drummond, William (of Hawthornden),
  109, 247, 361n31, 364n63, 403n33
Drury, Elizabeth, 111, 112, 114
Drury, Sir Robert, 365n73
Dubrow, Heather, 324n2, 343n37

Dudley, Anne, 55–56, 346n56, 347n63
Dudley, Anne Russell (Countess of War-
wick), 136, 142, 245, 374n54, 401n15
Dudley, Robert, 70
Dugdale, Grant, 19; *The Time Triumphant,*
329nn10,16
Dunstan, Father, 386n31
Durant, David, 351nn1,6,9,10,
352nn16,19, 354n47, 357n95,
358n107, 359n12
D'Urfé, Honoré, *L'Astrée,* 45–46, 264,
340n2
Durham, Bishop of, 88, 89, 358n99,
385n20
Dury, John, 65, 360n103
Dymocke, Sir Edward: translation of
Guarini, *Il Pastor Fido,* 410n121

Edmonds, Sir Thomas, 22, 331n30,
341n16
Edward II, King, 6, 127, 201, 203, 204,
205, 208, 209, 210, 392nn88,89,
393nn92,93
Edward III, King, 49, 68, 207
Egerton, Sir Thomas (Keeper of the Great
Seal), 141, 336n64
Elizabeth, Princess (daughter of Electress
Palatine), 350n100
Elizabeth, Saint (of Hungary), 58
Elizabeth I, Queen, 6, 18, 30, 33, 37, 40,
46, 53, 54, 57, 63, 64, 248, 271,
326n13, 329n13, 331n29, 390n62;
compared with Queen Anne, 4, 16;
death of, 7, 50, 76–77, 97, 142,
363n53; progresses of, 28; and Arbella
Stuart, 68, 69, 70–74, 76–78, 82;
female courtiers of, 107, 136, 359n1;
and Anne Clifford, 126, 127, 137; and
Aemilia Lanyer, 213, 214, 215; and
Sidney-Gamage marriage, 244, 400n10;
and *The Faerie Queene,* 340n1
Elizabeth Stuart, Princess (daughter of
James I, Electress Palatine, Queen of Bohemia), 2, 5, 8, 17, 24, 44, 45–65, 96,
97, 115, 221, 222, 230n23, 343n32; as
romance heroine, 45–65, 67, 311,
347n63, 349n93; marriage of, 21, 26,
49–52, 54, 91, 309, 342n21,
343nn34,37, 344n43, 347nn60–62; celebrations at wedding of, 343nn34–37,
344n38–345n51, 346n56, 361n30; and
Queen Anne, 27, 39, 334n55; education
of, 47, 341n14; Protestantism of, 47, 51,

53, 56, 61, 65; as mother, 54–55,
346nn54,55, 350n100; as Queen of
Bohemia, 58, 116, 117, 346nn56,57,59,
347nn60–64, 348nn67,72,73; children
of, 350n100; and Anne Clifford, 142;
letters of, 46, 55, 59–62, 64–65, 312,
341nn10,17, 347nn62,63, 349nn78,81,
350n102; *Letters,* 340nn4,6, 341n10,
346nn54,56, 349nn80,83,85, 350n102
Ellesmere, Lady Alice, 334n50
Ellesmere, Thomas Egerton, Lord Chancellor, 334n50
Elmes, Alice, 136
England's Helicon, 184, 385n24
Epictetus: *Manual,* 137
Erskine, Frances, 47; *Memoirs,* 329n8,
341n14
Erskine, John (Earl of Mar), 20, 21
Erskine family, 17, 329n8
Essex, Countess of. *See* Howard, Frances
Essex, Robert Devereaux, Earl of, 23, 24,
61, 100, 181, 193, 215, 332n33,
336n64, 349n89, 390n62, 392n86; and
Arbella Stuart, 70, 75–76, 353n39;
rebellion of, 96, 97, 192, 330n22,
390nn62,65; execution of, 75–76, 192,
353n38
Essex, Robert Devereaux, second Earl of,
332n35, 337n76, 339n98
Eusebius of Caesarea: *History of the Church,*
137
Evans, Gwynne, 400n1
Evans, Robert C., 363n57, 365n69
Evelyn, John, 65
Ezell, Margaret, 10, 324n3, 328n29,
399n61

Fabyan, Robert: *Chronicle,* 392n87
Falkland. *See* Cary
Farnese, Cardinal, 351n10
Farnese, Rainutio, 70, 351n10
Fawkes, Guy, 48, 390n62
Fenton, Viscount, 90, 91
Ferdinand, Prince (King of Bohemia; later
Holy Roman Emperor), 56
Ferguson, Margaret, 198, 324nn1,2,
325n5, 382n1, 383n3, 384n12, 385n23,
391nn72,76
Ferguson, Moira, 325n4
Fienberg, Nona, 252, 404nn56,57, 407n85
Fischer, Sandra, 383n3
Fisher, Sheila, 324n2
Fitton, Mary, 248

Fitz, Linda. *See* Woodbridge, Linda

Fletcher, Giles, 233; *Christ's victorie and triumph,* 398nn47,53

Fletcher, John, 9, 298, 299; *The Faithful Shepherdess,* 299, 302, 409n116, 410n123

Florio, John, 19, 105, 330n18; *World of Words,* 102; translation of Montaigne's *Essays,* 330n18, 362n35

Forman, Simon: "Autobiography," 141, 213, 327n20, 376n72; notes on Aemilia Lanyer from his "Casebooks," 213–216, 394nn2,3, 395nn13– 17, 396nn19,20; "Geomantica," 394n2, 395nn18,19

Foscarini, Antonio, 344n41

Foucault, Michel, 2, 9, 324n1

Fowler, William, 78, 79, 81, 354n50, 355n63

Foxe, John, 9, 147; *Book of Martyrs,* 397n42

Franco, Veronica, 3

Fraser, Antonia, 328n30

Fraunce, Abraham, 397n36; *The Countesse of Pembrokes Emanuell,* 228, 398n49; *The Countess of Pembroke's Ivychurch,* 298

Frederic II, King of Denmark, 16

Frederic V, Elector Palatine, 44, 56–59, 60, 61, 117, 346n59, 347n65, 348nn66,72; marriage of, 50–51, 53, 55, 97, 343n34; defeat of, 348n67; death of, 64; letters to Elizabeth, 45–46, 340n3, 343n32, 346n59, 349n78

Frederick Henry, Prince (son of Elizabeth, Electress Palatine), 54, 350n100

Frederick Ulric, Duke of Brunswick, 342n22

Frye, Northrop, 46, 341n8

Fullerton, Georgiana, 383n6

Fynett, John, 39, 331n26, 339n95, 342n26

G., I.: *An Apologie for Women-kinde,* 378n3

Gamage, William, 246; *Linsi-Woolsie,* 402n28

Garber, Marjorie, 328n31

Gardiner, Dorothy, 326n11

Gardner, Helen, 359n2, 366n78

Garnier, Robert: *Marc-Antoine,* 191–192, 389n59

Gaveston, Piers, 201, 203, 204, 205, 206, 207, 393nn92,94

George, Margaret, 327n16

Gerard, Lady Elizabeth, 337n80

Gerard, John: *Herball,* 137

Gerrard, George, 365n70

Girouard, Mark, 399n59

Goldberg, Jonathan, 28, 326n9, 335n61

Gombleton, Will, 115

Gondomar, Count of (Spanish ambassador), 333n42, 350n96

Goodyere, Sir Henry, 36, 97, 99, 104, 110, 114, 360n9, 366n87

Goreau, Angeline, 325n4

Gorges, Arthur, 98, 102, 362n36; translation of Lucan's *Pharsalia,* 360n9

Gorges, Carew, 98, 102, 362n36

Gossett, Suzanne, 336n62, 338n84

Gouge, William: *Of Domesticall Duties,* 382n49

Graham, Elspeth, 375n70

Gramsci, Antonio, 3, 326n15

Gray, Lady Elizabeth, 339n96

Green, Mary Anne Everett (Wood), 341nn9,11, 350n104

Greenblatt, Stephen, 116, 324n2, 325n6, 327n26

Greer, Germaine, 325n4, 381n35

Greg, W. W., 409n110

Gregory, Saint, 182

Greville, Fulke (Lord Brooke), 179, 363n54, 390nn62,68, 391n74; *Antony and Cleopatra,* 390n62; *Letter to an Honorable Lady,* 391n74; *Mustapha,* 191, 193–194, 389n60; *Works,* 138, 389n60

Grey, Lady Catherine, 71, 87, 90; 352nn17,18

Grey, Lady Elizabeth, 362n35

Grey, Henry, Earl of Kent, 76, 330n22, 353n41

Grey, Lady Jane, 352nn17,18

Grey, Lord (of Wilton), 354n47

Grey, Reynold (of Wrest), 397n35

Grierson, H. J. C., 366n78, 368n118

Grimble, Ian, 359n2

Grundy, Isobel, 319

Grymston, Elizabeth, 326n13

Guarini, Giovanni Battista, 297–298, 409n112; *Il compendio della poesia Tragicomica,* 409nn113,114; *Il Pastor Fido,* 297, 298–299, 300, 301, 338n82, 409n120, 410n121; *Il Verato,* 409n113

Guicciardini, Francesco, 138, 203

Guildford, Lady Elizabeth, 38, 337n80, 339n96

Gurr, Andrew, 328n28

Gustavus Adolphus, King of Sweden, 342n22

Haddington, Viscountess, 339n96
Haec-Vir: or, The Womanish Man, 156, 157, 380n15
Hageman, Elizabeth, 325n5
Hakewell, George: *Apologie of the Providence and Power of God,* 138
Hall, Joseph: *Works,* 137
Halley, Janet, 324n2
Halpern, Nick, 347n63
Hamilton, James, Marquis of, 65, 97, 118, 119, 367n114
Handover, P. M., 351nn1,3, 352n19, 354nn43,47, 355n65, 356nn71,78, 358nn105,106, 357n113
Hannay, Margaret, 243, 244, 325nn4,5, 326n13, 327n24, 383n3, 400nn4,12, 402n24, 403nn39,40, 405n71, 407n89
Harington, Lady Anne (mother of Countess of Bedford), 22, 24, 47, 56, 96, 97, 98, 346n56, 362n35, 363n49
Harington, Frances (Lady Chichester, sister of Countess of Bedford), 97, 337n80
Harington, John (first Baron of Exton; father of Countess of Bedford), 24, 47, 96, 97, 98, 337n80, 346n56, 359n4; "Accounts Book," 341n11
Harington, John (second Baron of Exton, brother of Countess of Bedford), 97, 110, 112, 114, 115, 332n35, 362n42
Harington, Sir John (of Kelston, poet), 15–16, 69, 97, 102, 150, 362n39; *Letters and Epigrams,* 328n2, 359n3, 378n92; *Nugae Antiquae,* 341nn11,15,17; *Prayse of a Private Life,* 378n92; *Tract on the Succession to the Crown,* 351n7
Harrison, John, 57; *A Short Relation,* 348n73
Hartlib, Samuel, 65
Haselkorn, Anne, 325n4, 380n17, 400n8, 406n73, 408n105
Hastings, Lady Dorothy, 22, 336n66, 337n32
Hatton, Lady Elizabeth, 10, 22, 23, 30, 33, 141, 331n32
Hay, James, Viscount Doncaster, 15, 59, 141, 265, 337n76, 348nn71,72
Hay, Lady, 249, 339n99

Hayward, Sir John: *King Henrie the IIII,* 203, 292n86
Henderson, Katherine, 326n11, 378n1, 380n17
Henrietta Maria, Queen, 185, 188, 189, 202, 385n30, 388n53, 392n81
Henry, Prince (son of James I), 5, 15, 16, 20, 23, 47, 97, 112, 192, 193, 329nn8,17, 330n21, 332n35, 355n66; and court masques, 18, 19, 28, 37, 39, 40, 41, 52, 53, 80, 101, 128; and marriage negotiations, 21, 342nn21,24; death of, 26, 50, 51, 234, 342n29, 345n48, 351n10, 392n80
Henry IV, King of France, 36, 51, 342n21, 351n10, 392n80
Henry VII, King, 68
Henry VIII, King, 15
Herbert, Lady Anne, 31, 331n29
Herbert, George, 343n37, 349n94; "Prayer I," 398n52; *The Temple,* 138
Herbert, Henry, second Earl of Pembroke, 129, 146
Herbert, Mary (Sidney), Countess of Pembroke. *See* (Sidney), Mary Herbert
Herbert, Mary (Talbot), Countess of Pembroke. *See* (Talbot), Mary Herbert
Herbert, Philip, fourth Earl of Pembroke and Montgomery, 15, 31, 40, 125, 129, 133, 246, 331n31, 370nn17–19,21, 372nn37,38, 404n42
Herbert, Susan (de Vere), Countess of Montgomery, 23, 31, 33, 38, 141, 246, 331n31, 336n66, 337n76, 339n96, 355n66, 370n17, 402n23
Herbert, Sir Thomas (of Tintern), 248
Herbert, William, third Earl of Pembroke, 97, 118, 119, 285, 332n39, 336n64, 354n50, 360n17, 364n58, 374n56, 402n23, 403n39, 407n88; and Queen Anne, 23, 24, 284; and Lady Mary Wroth, 7, 243–244, 245, 246, 248, 251–252, 265, 277, 284, 306, 402n23, 403n40; *Poems,* 403n39, 407n88
Herbert family, 243, 248, 249, 306, 402n23, 403n40
Herbert of Cherbury, Edward, Lord, 56, 65, 348n69; *Poems,* 403n41
Hertford, Countess of, 336n66
Hertford, Edward Seymour, Earl of, 71, 72, 352n17, 363n54

Heywood, Thomas, 9, 155; *Gynaikeion,*
378n3; *A Marriage Triumphe,* 53,
345n47; translation of *Sallust,* 292n84
Hicks, Sir Baptiste (Alderman), 159,
381n26
Hicks, Leo, 330n23
Hic Mulier: or, the Man-Woman, 156,
380n14
Hieron, Samuel, 138, 397n37; *Certain
Meditations,* 374n60
*History of the Most Unfortunate Prince, King
Edward II,* 317–318
Hoby, Sir Edward, 341n25
Hoby, Lady Margaret, 4, 140; *Diary,*
327n18, 375n71
Hodge, Bob, 366n8
Holbein, Hans, 120
Holinshed, Raphael: *Chronicles,* 203,
392n87
Holland, Hugh, 81; *Pancharis,* 18, 329n11,
355n64
Holland, Philamon: translation of *Livy,*
392n84
Holmes, Martin, 368n3, 369n9
Holyband (Claudius DeSainliens), 102;
Campo di Fior, 362n33
Home, Lord, 184
Homer, 38, 69, 81; *Iliad,* 403n32
Homilie of the State of Matrimonie, 382n47
Hooker, Richard: *Ecclesiastical Polity,* 183
Horace: "Epode II," 235
Howard, Alatheia, Countess of Arundel,
27, 33, 38, 149, 183, 335n56, 337n80,
339n96, 377n79
Howard, Charles, Earl of Nottingham
(Lord Admiral), 354n48
Howard, Elizabeth (daughter of Earl of
Suffolk), 31, 336n66
Howard, Frances, Countess of Essex,
Countess of Somerset, 24, 38, 40, 41,
95, 96, 100, 141, 265, 337n76,
339nn96,98, 405n70
Howard, Henry, Earl of Northampton,
129, 372n40
Howard, Jean, 325n7, 328n31
Howard, Katherine (Knevet), Countess of
Suffolk, 23, 31, 95, 96, 141, 220, 221,
331n31, 336n66, 397n38
Howard, Lady, Countess of Northamp-
ton, 95
Howard, Margaret (Stuart), Countess of
Nottingham (daughter of Earl of Mo-
ray), 23, 331n31, 335n56, 336n66

Howard, Thomas, Earl of Arundel, 146
Howard, Thomas, Earl of Suffolk, 27, 141,
334nn49,51, 397n38
Howard, Lord William, 143
Howard family, 23, 40, 41, 95, 117, 129,
142, 220, 224, 333n49, 334n51,
342n22, 372n40, 354n48
Howard of Effingham, Lady, 31
Howe, Florence, 383n3
Hubert, Francis: *The Deplorable Life and
Death of Edward the Second,* 204, 393n92;
Historie of Edward the Second, 393n92
Hull, Suzanne, 326n8
Hume, David, 81
Huntingdon, Countess of, 38, 112, 245,
401n15
Huntingdon, Earl of, 329n9
Huntley, Earl of, 330n21
Huss, John, 57

Ingram, Martin, 327n16
Isabel, Queen (wife of Edward II), 6, 201,
204, 206, 207–210, 310, 319, 393n96,
394nn97–100

James IV, King (of Scotland), 68
James VI and I, King, 2, 15, 17, 18, 47,
68, 108, 112, 115, 116, 118, 122–123,
141, 175, 193, 202, 248, 299, 306,
329nn8,9, 333n49, 337n82, 341n14,
370n17, 385n30, 390n62, 391n77; and
Queen Anne, 15, 17, 18, 20, 21, 22, 24–
26, 29, 43, 59, 60, 113, 330n21,
333nn47,48; coronation of, 19, 105,
142, 329n15; and masques, 28–43 passim, 53, 107; and Gunpowder Plot, 48,
392n80; on cross–dressing, 10, 155–
156, 328n31, 379n13; on learning for
women, 341n14; and Princess Elizabeth,
45, 51, 55, 61, 62, 63, 64, 65, 347n61,
349n88; and Prince Frederick, 56,
347n61; and Arbella Stuart, 68, 71–92
passim, 160, 310, 392n80; and Anne
Clifford, 126, 127, 128, 129, 134, 143,
145, 146, 147, 377n82; and Aemilia
Lanyer, 213, 214, 215; *Basilikon Doron,*
2, 16, 326n10, 328n3; *Remonstrance for
the Right of Kings,* 392n80; *The Trew
Lawe of Free Monarchie,* 2, 326n10,
408n100; *Workes,* 326n10
Janiculo, Stephan (also Bogdan), 83,
356n72
Jansen, Cornelius, 103

Jardine, David, 345nn47,48
Jardine, Lisa, 324n2
Jauss, Hans Robert, 298, 409n117
Jerome, Saint, 182
Jocelin, Elizabeth, 4; *The Mothers Legacie,* 329n17
John of Gaunt, 70
Jones, Ann Rosalind, 326nn13,15, 327n22, 380n17, 382n41, 404n54
Jones, Inigo, 27, 28, 334n53, 370n18; and court masques, 27, 31, 32, 36, 39, 52, 100, 101, 335nn59,60, 337nn75,76, 338n92, 339nn94,99
Jones, Thomas (Lord Chancellor of Ireland; Archbishop of Dublin), 219
Jonson, Ben, 1, 106, 107, 189, 339n99, 364nn58,60, 397n36, 410n123; and Queen Anne, 18, 19, 27, 28, 29, 31, 329n14; and Countess of Bedford, 98, 103, 104, 106–110, 363n57, 364n62; and Mary Wroth, 245, 246, 403n32; *The Alchemist,* 246, 402n29; *Barriers,* 28, 40; *Cataline,* 389n60; *Conversations with Drummond,* 109; "The Court Pucell," 109, 121; *Cynthia's Revells,* 364n63; *Eastward Ho,* 24, 107; *Entertainment . . . at Althorpe,* 329n13; *Entertainment at High-gate,* 329n14; *Epicoene,* 83, 109–110, 356n74, 365n71; "Epigram 76," 108, 398n43; *Epigrammes,* 108, 121, 224, 246, 364n61; "Epistle" to the Countess of Rutland, 106–107, 363n52; *Gypsies Metamorphosed,* 207; *Hymenaei,* 100, 337n76; *Love Freed from Ignorance and Folly,* 40, 339n97, 361n30; *Lovers Made Men,* 99; *Masque of Beautie,* 31, 33–35, 80, 99, 100, 245, 402n20; *Masque of Blacknesse,* 28, 31–33, 35, 37, 80, 100, 245, 254, 336nn62,71, 337n74, 338n84; *Masque of Queenes,* 28, 36, 37, 38, 80, 101, 111, 128, 245, 336n68, 338n85, 340n6; *The May Lord,* 101, 361n31, 408n106; *Oberon,* 28, 40; *Sejanus,* 389n60; *Time Vindicated,* 350n97; "To L: C: off B," 364n62; "To Penshurst," 7, 219, 234, 235–236, 238, 240, 340n2, 396n31, 399nn58,60–63; "To Sir Robert Wroth," 246–247, 306, 402n30; "To the Immortal Memory of . . . Sir Lucius Cary and Sir H. Morrison," 388n45; *Underwood,* 28, 247, 364n68; *Workes,* 138, 396n31
Joquet, D.: *Les Triomphes,* 345n46

Jordan, Constance, 324n1
Josephus, 150, 190, 198, 340n6, 388n54, 391nn72,75
Justin Martyr, Saint, 182
Juvenal, 154

Kelly (Kelly-Gadol), Joan, 153, 324n1, 378n2
Kelway, Anne, 96
Kennedy, Mr., 22
Kent, Countess of. *See* Bertie, Susan
Kent, Dowager Countess of, 140
Kermode, Frank, 343n32
Kildare, Lady, 22, 331n29
King, Bishop Henry: *Sermons,* 138
Knollys, Lady, 27, 337n76
Knollys, Lord William, 27
Kogan, Stephen, 335n59, 336n67
Koonz, Claudia, 324n1
Kress, Gunther, 112, 366nn81,85
Kyd, Thomas: translation of *Cornelia,* 389n60

Labalme, Patricia, 325n4, 392n83
Labé, Louise, 3, 252
La Boderie, Le Fèvre de (French ambassador), 36; *Ambassades en Angleterre,* 331n26, 337nn77,80, 338n88, 341n13, 342n21
Lactantius, 163
Lamb, Mary Ellen, 400n3, 403n32, 404n55
Langueville, T., 384n10
Lanier, Innocent, 214
Lanier, John, 214
Lanier, Nicholas, 214, 395n11
Lanyer, Aemilia, 2, 3, 8, 9, 10, 101, 138, 166, 213–241, 394n3, 395nn5,14,15,16; *Salve Deus Rex Judaeorum,* 6–7, 81, 138, 212, 218–241, 310, 311, 321–322, 325n5, 327n24, 330n20, 394nn1,4, 396nn29,30; presentation copies, 321–322; "Dedications," 219–226, 310; "To the Queenes most Excellent Majestie," 19–20, 220, 221–222, 397n39; "To the Lady Elizabeths Grace [Princess Elizabeth]," 48, 222, 342n19; "To all vertuous Ladies," 222; "To the Ladie Arabella [Stuart]," 81, 222, 355n67; "To the Ladie Susan, Countesse Dowager of Kent [Susan Bertie]," 222, 397nn35,42; "The Authors Dreame to the Ladie Marie, the Countesse Dowager of Pem-

Lanyer, Amelia (*continued*)
    brooke [Mary Sidney Herbert]," 222–
    223, 397n36; "To the Ladie Lucie,
    Countesse of Bedford [Lucy Harington
    Russell]", 102–103, 223–224, 362n41,
    397n36; "To the Ladie Margaret Count-
    esse Dowager of Cumberland [Margaret
    Clifford]," 224, 397n37; "To the Ladie
    Katherine Countesse of Suffolke
    [Katherine Howard]," 224, 397n38;
    "To the Ladie Anne, Countesse of
    Dorcet [Anne Clifford]," 224–225,
    374n62; "To the Vertuous Reader,"
    225–226; The Title Poem, *Salve Deus,*
    226–234, 313; "The Description of
    Cooke-ham," 216, 219, 234–241,
    310, 311, 375n12, 394n2, 396n21,
    398n55
Lanyer, Alphonso, 213, 215, 217, 219,
    321, 395nn10,12,16,19
Lanyer, Henry (son of Aemilia Lanyer),
    214, 218, 396n25
Lanyer, Henry (grandson of Aemilia Lan-
    yer), 396n25
Lanyer, Mary (granddaughter of Aemilia
    Lanyer), 396n25
Lanyer, Odillya (daughter of Aemilia Lan-
    yer), 214, 395n12
Laqueur, Thomas, 324n1
Larkin, Thomas, 335n56, 359n113
Laud, Archbishop William, 65, 186, 189,
    388n46
Laverdin, Marshal (of France), 40
Lawes Resolutions of Womens Rights (T. E.),
    125, 127, 129, 368n2, 369nn8,10,
    370nn14,23, 407n96
Layfield, Dr., 136
Lee, Jongsook, 365n69
Leigh, Dorothy, 4; *The Mothers Blessing,*
    327n17
Lennox, Margaret, 68
Leuknor, Sir Lewis, 332n37
Levin, Carol, 325n3, 383n3
Levine, Laura, 328n31
Levy, F. J., 203, 318, 392n85
Lewalski, Barbara K., 325n5, 327n24,
    359n2, 366n80, 398n51, 399n58,
    409n110
Lincoln, Countess of (Elizabeth Clinton),
    4; *The Countess of Lincolnes Nurserie,*
    327n17
Lincoln, Earl of, 331n29
Lindley, David, 335n61, 339n94, 345n46

Livingstone, Alexander, Earl of Linlithgow,
    47, 330n23
Livingstone, Lady, 47, 330n23
Livy, 163, 203, 392n84
Lloyd, Lodowick: *The Choice of Jewels,*
    278n3
Lodge, Edmund: *Illustrations of British
    History,* 331nn30,31, 332n33, 354n46,
    356n70
Lodge, Thomas, 138, 190, 397n37; *Proso-
    popeia,* 374n59; translation of *Josephus,*
    388n54, 391n75
Lok, Anne, 326n13
Lok, Henry, 138, 397nn36,37; *Ecclesiastes,*
    374n59
London, Bishop of, 27, 160, 334n55,
    352n14
Long Meg of Westminster, 155
Louise, Princess (daughter of Elizabeth,
    Electress Palatine), 350n100
Lowenstein, Countess of, 46
Lucan: *Pharsalia,* 102
Luther, Martin, 57, 182
Lyly, John: *Euphues,* 340n1, 379n4
Lytle, Guy F., 365n74

Macfarlane, Alan, 327n16
Machiavelli, Niccolò, 203, 207
Maclean, Ian, 324n1
*Magnificent Marriage of the Two Great
    Princes,* 343n34
*Magnificent, Princely, and most Royall Enter-
    tainments,* 345n52
Manners, Katherine. *See* Buckingham,
    Katherine (Manners), Duchess of
Manual of Prayers (R. B. P.), 331n28
Margaret, Princess (daughter of Henry
    VII), 68
Marguerite of Navarre, 3
Marie di Medici, 342n21
Markham, Bridget, Lady, 97, 110, 114,
    121, 366n87, 368n119
Marlowe, Christopher: *Edward II,* 203,
    204, 392n88
Marotti, Arthur, 111, 112, 324n2,
    365nn69,72,74, 366nn78,82,83,86
Marston, John, 364n62; *Dutch Courtesan,*
    24, 345n45; *The Silver Mines,* 24; *Workes,*
    385n27
Martial: Epigram III, 235
Mary, Princess (daughter of Henry VII),
    68, 222, 241
Mary, Princess (daughter of James I), 80

Mary I, Queen, 222, 241
Mary Stuart, Queen of Scots, 37, 68, 326n13, 330n21
Masten, Jeff, 405n67
Mathias, Duke, 351n10
Matthews, W., 375n71
Maurer, Margaret, 112, 363n54, 365n72, 366nn84,87
Maurice, Prince (of Orange), 58, 64, 78, 354n50
Maurice, Prince (son of Elizabeth, Electress Palatine), 59
Maxwell, James: *A Monument of Remembrance*, 345n52
McInnis, Ian, 351n1, 352n19
McLaren, Margaret (Witten-Hannah), 408nn105,108
McManus, Barbara, 326n11, 378n1, 380n17
Melville, Elizabeth (Lady Culross), 4; *Ane Godlie Dreame*, 327n19
Menander: *Peri Epideiktikon*, 399n57
Mendelson, Sara, 375n70
Mercure Francais, 348n66
Mercurius Gallo-Belgicus, 348n74
Meutys, Jane. *See* Cornwallis, Lady Jane
Middleton, Thomas, 9; *The Roaring Girl*, 379n10
Mildmay, Lady Grace (Sherrington), 4, 140; *Journal*, 327n18, 376n71
Milgate, Wesley, 365n73, 368nn118,120
Miller, Naomi, 285, 327n24, 400nn4,8, 404nn42,55,58, 405nn67,69, 407n93, 408n103, 409n110
Milton, John, 1
Mirrour for Magistrates, 204, 393n89
Moffett, Thomas, 397n36
Molin, Nicolò (Venetian ambassador), 82, 329n9, 337n74, 351n8
Montague, Lord Chief Justice, 146
Montaigne, Michel de: *Essays*, 102, 137, 150, 182, 330n18, 362n35
Montecuccoli, Alfonso, 331n25
Montemayor, Jorge di: *Diana*, 45, 264, 340n2
Montgomery, Countess of. *See* Herbert, Susan (de Vere)
Montrose, Louis, 297, 324n2, 409n111
Moore, Norman, 343n29
Moray, Earl of, 330n21, 331n31
More, Henry: *Map of Mortalitie*, 138
More, Richard, 183
More, Sir Thomas, 182

Mortimer, Roger, 203–208, 210, 393n96, 394nn99,100
Moundford, Mary, 159–160, 169–170
Moundford, Thomas, 88, 89, 92, 159, 358nn99,102; *Vir Bonus*, 160, 381n29; translation, *De Morbis Melancholis*, 381n29
Muffett, Peter, 138; *The Mysterie of Christ*, 374n60
Muld Sacke, 156, 380n16
Munda, Constantia (pseud.): *The Worming of a mad Dogge*, 154–155, 156, 157, 158, 174, 379n8, 380nn17,23
Murdock, Kenneth, 384n10, 388n43

Nashe, Thomas, 397n36; *The Anatomie of Absurdity*, 379n4; *The Bachelors Banquet*, 379n4
Neely, Carol Thomas, 2, 325n7
Nethersole, Sir Francis, 58, 59, 348n75
Nevill, Lady Mary, 337n80, 362n35
Newdigate, Bernard, 362nn48,53
Newstead, Christopher: *An Apology for Women*, 378n3
Niccols, Richard: addition to *Mirrour for Magistrates*, 392n89
Nichols, Thomas: translation of *Josephus*, 392n84
Norbrook, David, 335n61, 341n7, 345n46
Northampton, Countess of. *See* Howard, Lady
Northampton, Earl of. *See* Howard, Henry
Notestein, Wallace, 368n3
Nottingham, Countess of. *See* Howard, Margaret (Stuart)
Nottingham, Earl of. *See* Howard, Charles
Nyquist, Mary, 324n2

Oliver, St. John, 141
Olney, James, 375n70
Oman, Carola, 341n9, 342n22, 343nn34,36, 346n53, 347n64, 348nn67,68,72,77, 349nn79,93, 367n103
Orgel, Stephen, 28, 29, 297, 335nn59,60,61, 337n75, 338n92, 361nn28,29, 365n74, 369n12
Ortelius, Abraham: *Mirroir du Monde*, 137, 179, 383n4
Overbury, Sir Thomas, 91, 206, 265, 332n39, 339n98, 405n70; *A Wife . . . and Conceited Newes*, 364n68

Ovid, 172, 204, 252, 253, 258, 259, 260, 261, 311; *Heroides,* 279; *Metamorphoses,* 137, 150

Owen, John, 81

Owen, Thomas, 392n80

Oxford, Henry de Vere, Earl of, 61, 331n31

Palma, Duke of, 70

Parallel, The: or the History of . . . Edward the Second, 318

Parker, Patricia, 324n2

Parry, Sir Thomas, 329n10, 330n22

Parsons, Robert (also R. Doleman): *A Conference about the . . . Succession,* 352n14, 390n63; *Resolutions,* 150, 191

Patterson, Annabel, 297, 328n32, 409n111

Paul, Saint, 4, 8, 166, 168, 172, 312

Peacham, Henry, 53, 374n59, 397n37; *An Aprill Shower* (for Richard Sackville), 370n16; *The Compleat Gentleman,* 402n24; *Minerva Britanna,* 345n48; *The Period of Mourning,* 345n48

Pearse, Nancy Cotton, 181, 383n3, 384n16

Pebworth, Ted-Larry, 343n37, 394n94

Peck, Linda Levy, 329n7

Pembroke. *See* Herbert

Penniston, Lady, 128, 148

Percy, Henry, Earl of Northumberland, 99, 351n10, 360n17

Percy, Lady Lucy, 99

Perkins, William, 103, 138, 397n37; *Salve for a Sicke Man,* 362n42, 374n60

Perron, Cardinal, 180, 201–202, 383n5, 391n80; *Lettre,* 391n80; *Replique,* 179, 391nn79,80

Perry, Sir Thomas, 84

Petrarch, 4, 18, 32, 111, 123, 253, 256, 258, 259, 261, 262, 263, 280, 294, 385n21, 408n108; *De Vita Solitaria,* 378n92; *Rime,* 7, 252, 307, 309, 312, 314; *Trionfi,* 252, 257, 258, 260; *Triumph of Death,* 252; *Triumph of Love,* 258

Petre, Lady Katherine, 80, 339n96

Philip III, King of Spain, 21

Phoenix and Turtle, The, 364n62

Pilcher, John 339n94

Pilgrim's Progress, 4

Pisan, Christine de. *See* Christine de Pisan

Plato, 34, 35, 113, 114, 258, 260, 262, 314, 335n59, 408n108

Plautus: *Amphitryo,* 409n113

Playfere, Thomas, 16; *The Power of Prayer,* 328n4

Pliny, 69, 163, 182

Plutarch, 46, 69, 75, 132, 163, 340n6; *Lives,* 126, 138; *Morals,* 138, 182

Poland, King of, 78, 354n50

Poulter, Bessie, 186

Poulton, Diana, 362n37

Prior, Mary, 325n4, 375n70

Prior, Roger, 395nn5,11

Procter, Rachel (daughter of Rachel Speght), 160

Procter, William, 160, 381nn34,37, 382n39; *The Watchman warning,* 381n38

Procter, William (son of Rachel Speght), 161

Proctor, Jacob, 160

Puckering, Sir Thomas, 335n56, 359n113

Puttenham, George: *Arte of English Poesie,* 397n40

Quilligan, Maureen, 274–275, 324n1, 400n8, 403n35, 406n84

Quint, David, 324n2

Rainbowe, Bishop Edward, 130, 139, 371nn25,26,28, 375nn65–67

Ralegh, Lady, 149

Raleigh, Sir Walter, 23, 25, 77, 192, 342n24, 343n29, 354n47, 400n10; *Poems,* 333n42

Rankin, Phyllis, 328n31

Rann, Dr., 147, 150

Reading, John, 103; *A Faire Warning,* 362n45

Rebholz, Robert, 193, 391n69

Rees, Joan, 363n54, 391n74

Reeves, Edward, 85, 91, 357n83, 359n113

Reynolds, John: *Vox Coeli,* 63, 350n97

Reynolds, Myra, 326n11

Rich, Isabella, 99, 141, 149, 360n17

Rich, Penelope (Sidney's "Stella"; sister of Essex), 23, 30, 31, 36, 306, 331nn31,32, 332n34, 411n131

Rich, Sir Robert, 306

Richmond, Lady, 119–120

Riggs, David, 108–109, 335n62, 356n74, 363n57, 364n67

Roberts, Josephine, 270, 325n5, 399n1, 400nn2,9,10, 402n28, 403n40, 404nn42,47,51,53,55, 405nn61,71, 406nn73,77,83, 407nn88,99, 408n105

Roches, Catherine des, 252

Roe, Sir Thomas, 46, 59, 61, 62, 65, 97, 349n78

Rogers, Katherine, 378n1

Rosa, Thomas, 330n18; *Idaea,* 341n18

Rose, Mary Beth, 325n4

Ross, Josephine, 341n9

Rostvig, Maren-Sofie, 399n56

Rous, Lord, 143

Rowe, George, 107, 364n65

Rowse, A. L., 213, 215, 394nn2,3

Roxborough, Lady, 117, 367n101

Roxborough, Lord, 41, 339n100

Rupa, Baron, 348n73

Rupert, Prince (son of Elizabeth, Electress Palatine), 46, 58, 350n100

Russell, Edward (third Earl of Bedford), 95, 96, 97, 98, 115, 117, 359n4, 360n6

Russell, Francis (fourth Earl of Bedford), 132, 143, 370n22

Russell, Lucy Harington (Countess of Bedford), 2, 10, 47, 59, 62, 64, 65, 94, 95–123, 313, 337n80, 360nn13,14; as patroness, 5, 95–96, 101–115, 183, 220, 223, 309, 336n64, 355n66, 397n36; portraits of, 94, 103, 361n27, 362n46; and Queen Anne, 22, 23–24, 29, 30, 31, 33, 38, 42–43, 97, 99, 100, 142, 310, 311, 331n32, 336n64; and court masques, 99–101, 103, 310, 337n76, 340n103, 361nn19,20,23; coterie of, 95, 97–98, 109–111, 114; and Princess Elizabeth, 117, 367n105; and Anne Clifford, 146, 377n89; "Death be not Proud," elegy on Cecilia Bulstrode, 120–122, 368n118; letters of, 115–120, 312, 360nn5,9, 367n105; *Private Correspondence of Jane, Lady Cornwallis,* 360n5

Russell, William (of Thornaugh), 216

Russell family, 131, 142, 143, 147, 149, 359n1, 360n14, 396n21

Ruthven, Lady Beatrice, 146, 320n21, 377n89

Ruthven brothers, 20, 330n21

Rutland, Elizabeth Manners, Countess of (Sir Philip Sidney's daughter), 100, 106, 246, 360n31, 362n35, 364n58

Rutland, Roger Manners, Earl of, 332n33

Sabol, Andrew, 361n23

Sackville, Cecily, 337n76

Sackville, Sir Edward, 141, 143, 372n39

Sackville, Isabella (Anne Clifford's daughter, later Countess of Northampton), 128, 129, 130, 133, 377n87

Sackville, Margaret (Anne Clifford's daughter, later Countess of Thanet), 128, 129, 130, 136, 144, 145, 148, 377n88

Sackville, Richard, third Earl of Dorset, 139, 337n80; and Anne Clifford, 125–135 passim, 143–150 passim, 372nn38,39, 377nn81,84,85

Sackville family, 144, 378n90

Sackville-West, Vita, 368n1, 376n73

Sallust, 203, 392n84

Salzman, Paul, 276, 406n80

Sandelands, Anne, 340n103

Sandys, George, 138; *Government of the Turks,* 150

Saragol: *Supplication of the Saints,* 150

Saul, Arthur, 102; *Famous Game of Chesse-Play,* 362n38

Savile, H.: translation of *Tacitus,* 392n84

Saville, George, 333n41

Saville, Thomas, 138; *The Raising of Them that are Fallen,* 374n60

Scaliger, Julius-Caesar: *Poetices,* 399n57

Scaramelli (Venetian secretary), 70, 351n13

Schochet, Gordon J., 326n9

Schwarz, Kate, 336n62, 338n91

Scope, Lady, 331n29

Scott, Thomas: *Vox Populi,* 63, 350n96

Scudery, Madeleine de: *Les Femmes Illustres,* 341n6

Selden, John, 140

Seneca, 163, 179, 180, 182, 191, 196, 200, 211, 310, 327n23, 373n43, 389n61

Seymour, Edward, 71, 83, 352nn17,18, 353n29, 356n78

Seymour, William, 5, 83–84, 88, 89, 90, 160, 356n79, 357n95, 358n107

Seymour family, 68, 83, 84, 352nn17,18, 353n29, 356n78

Shakespeare, William, 1, 9, 214, 343n32, 364n62, 405n69; Dark Lady of, 213, 394nn2,3, 395n5; *Julius Caesar, Merry Wives, Much Ado, Othello,* 343n32; *Richard II,* 209; *The Tempest,* 51, 343n32; *The Winter's Tale,* 264, 343n32

Sharpe, Kevin, 359n2

Shepherd, Simon, 156, 327n27, 336n68, 378n1, 379n10, 380nn17,24, 391n77

Shrewsbury. *See* Talbot, Gilbert; Talbot, Mary

Shumaker, Wayne, 375n70

Sidney, Barbara Gamage, Viscountess Lisle;

Sidney, Barbara Gamage (*continued*)
  Countess of Leicester (mother of Mary
  Wroth), 235, 236, 238, 244, 245, 246,
  265, 377n90, 399n60, 400n10, 401n15,
  403n40
Sidney, Lady Dorothy, 377n90
Sidney, Lucy, 97
(Sidney), Mary Herbert, Countess of Pembroke, 7, 23, 101, 129, 243, 244, 265,
  280, 284, 314, 326n13, 327n24, 340n1,
  361n31, 391n68, 400n3, 401n12,
  402n24, 407n91; as patroness, 8, 183,
  220, 222–223, 227–228, 359n1,
  397n36; Psalm versions, 223; translation, *The Tragedie of Antonie,* 191–192,
  252, 389n59
Sidney, Sir Philip, 7, 9, 23, 50, 97, 223,
  243, 284, 298, 306, 364n58, 372n40,
  390nn63,68; *Arcadia,* 45, 132, 137, 150,
  244, 246, 264, 274, 278, 279, 285,
  340n1, 372n37, 405n68, 406n75,
  408n109, 411n131; *Astrophil to Stella,*
  244, 252, 284, 331n31; *Defence of
  Poetry,* 397n40, 409n115; *The Lady of
  May,* 244
Sidney, Robert, Viscount Lisle of
  Penshurst, Earl of Leicester (father of
  Mary Wroth), 7, 235, 244, 245, 265,
  332n33, 360n14, 364n58, 400n9,
  402n24, 403n37; and Queen Anne, 23;
  letters to his wife Barbara, 244, 245,
  246, 360n14, 399n60, 400nn9,12,
  401nn15,17, 402n21, 403n40; *Poems,*
  243, 400n3. *See also* Jonson, Ben:
  "To Penshurst"; Sidney, Barbara
  Gamage
Sidney, Robert (brother of Mary Wroth),
  265
Sidney, William (brother of Mary Wroth),
  247
Sidney family, 243–244, 248, 249, 252,
  264, 306, 314, 362n36, 377n90,
  408n106
Sidney-Leicester-Pembroke faction, 106,
  117, 221, 251, 265, 284, 397n35,
  403n32
Sinfield, Alan, 325n6
Skinner, Lady, 83
Smith, Edward, 217
Smith, Henry: *A Preparative to Marriage,*
  382n48
Smith, Sir John, 99, 360n17

Smith, Sidonie, 375n70
Smith, Sir Thomas, 361n17
Somerset, Lady Blanche, 337n76
Somerset, Countess of. *See* Howard,
  Frances
Somerset, Edward, Earl of Worcester, 22–
  23, 77, 95, 114, 265, 310, 334n50,
  405n70; daughters of, 337n80, 339n96
Somerset, Robert Carr, Earl of, 15, 23, 24,
  25, 40, 41, 205, 206, 332n39, 339n98,
  343n29, 405n70
Sophie, Electress Palatine (daughter of Eliz-
  abeth, Electress Palatine), 46, 350n100;
  Memoiren, 341n9, 346n54
Sophie, Queen of Denmark (Queen Anne's
  mother), 17
Sorbière, Samuel de: *Lettres et Discours,*
  341n14, 350n104
Southampton, Earl of, 330n22, 332n33,
  336n64, 349n89, 360n17
Southwell, Lady, 23, 331n31
Southwell, Robert: *Saint Peters Complaynt,*
  227, 398nn45,46
Sowernam, Ester (pseud.): *Ester hath
  hang'd Haman,* 154, 158, 174, 379n7,
  380nn17,22
Speght, James (father of Rachel Speght),
  159, 380n24, 381n32; *A Briefe Demonstration,* 159, 380n25; *The Day-spring of
  Comfort,* 159, 381nn25,26
Speght, Rachel, 2, 3, 6, 9, 153–175, 226,
  309, 311, 312, 313, 325n5, 327n21,
  380n24, 382n51; *Certaine Quaeres to the
  Bayter of Women,* 161, 162, 164; *A Mouzell for Melastomus,* 152, 154, 157, 158,
  160, 161–169, 172, 175, 225, 311,
  379n6, 381n31; *Mortalities Memorandum,* 157, 160, 169–175, 380n20,
  381n28. *See also* Procter, William;
  Speght, James
Speght, Thomas (editor of Chaucer), 159
Spence, R. T., 368n3, 369n9, 370n26
Spencer (Hugh le Despenser), 201, 203,
  204–205, 206–207, 208, 209, 210,
  393n93, 394n98
Spencer, Sir Robert, 329nn9,13
Spenser, Edmund, 1, 9, 53, 105, 110, 137,
  138, 139, 174, 397nn36,37, 407n90;
  Astrophil, 407n90; *The Faerie Queene,* 45,
  46, 150, 220, 263, 264, 267, 269, 286,
  340n1, 375n69, 393n90; *Fowre Hymnes,*
  374n59

Spinola, General Ambrogio di, 60, 61

Spriet, Pierre, 336n67, 364n55

Spufford, Margaret, 328n28

Stafford, Anthony: *Staffords Niobe,* 139, 375n63

Stallybrass, Peter, 325n6

Stampa, Gaspara, 3, 252

Stanhope, Sir John (Vice-Chancellor), 72, 73, 74–75, 353n32

Stanley, Elizabeth (Countess of Derby, née de Vere), 23, 31, 33, 38, 149, 183, 331n31, 336n66, 339n96

Stanley, Lady Venetia, 128

Stanton, Domna C., 375n70

Stapleton, Henry, 76

Starkey, James, 76, 352n18

Stauffer, Donald, 383n6

Steen, Sara Jayne, 67, 325n5, 351n2, 357n93, 358n104

Stock, Richard: *The Churches Lamentation,* 362n42

Stone, Lawrence, 326n16, 360n6, 377n88

Stow, John: *Annales,* 292n87

Stradling, Sir Edmund, 400n10

Strickland, Agnes, 330nn21,23

Strier, Richard, 324n2

Strong, Roy, 335nn59–61, 337n75, 338n92, 342nn21,22,24,25, 344nn40,44,45, 345n46, 361nn27–29, 369n12

Stroude, George: *Book of Death,* 138

Stuart, Arbella, 2, 8, 66, 67–92, 101, 109, 153, 220, 222, 248, 351n3, 354nn44,46, 355n67, 356nn71,76; marriage of, 5, 83–90, 356nn78,80, 357nn95,97, 358n100, 391n77; claim to throne, 37, 68, 72, 352n14, 390n62; education of, 69, 351n6; and Queen Anne, 33, 39, 78–80, 86–87, 357n88; and King James I, 68, 71–92 passim, 310, 357n97, 391n77; escape to France and imprisonment, 89–91, 160, 311, 358nn105,107; death of, 91; letters of, 5, 67, 82, 312, 325n5, 353n33, 354n51, 355nn58,60, 356n82, 357nn83,95; *Letters,* 351n2

Stuart, Charles (Earl of Lennox), 68, 361n19

Stuart, Esmé, 15, 68, 69, 351n10

Stuart, Henrietta (Countess of Huntley), 21

Stuart, Lodovic (Duke of Lennox), 351n10

Summers, Claude, 343n37, 365n72, 368n119

Sussex, Earl of, 331n29

Swetnam, Joseph, 154–155, 159, 170, 173, 175, 225, 311, 313, 380n22, 382n43; *Araignment of Lewde, idle, froward, and unconstant women,* 154, 161–165, 167, 378n4, 379n5, 382nn40,43,46; *School of . . . Defence,* 379n4

Swetnam the Woman-hater, Arraigned by Women (Thomas Heywood?), 155, 158, 379n9, 380n21

Swift, Carolyn, 270, 306, 405n72, 406n74, 408n108, 411n131

Sylvester, Joshuah, 247; *Lacrymae Lachrymarum,* 403n31; *Little Bartas,* 346n55

Tacitus, 179, 203, 211, 310, 327n23, 292n84

Talbot, Gilbert (Earl of Shrewsbury), 67, 68, 69, 76, 78, 79, 82, 86, 248, 329n9, 331n30, 354nn49,51,52, 355n58, 356n69, 357n83, 358nn97,99

Talbot, Mary, Countess of Shrewsbury (Arbella Stuart's aunt), 67, 69, 76, 77, 78, 82, 83, 89, 90, 354nn45,49,51, 355nn56,68

(Talbot), Mary Herbert, Countess of Pembroke (daughter of Earl of Shrewsbury, wife of William Herbert), 248, 285, 377n89

Talbot, William, 80

Tanfield, Elizabeth, Lady (mother of Elizabeth Cary), 181, 185, 186, 187, 188, 384n13

Tanfield, Sir Lawrence (father of Elizabeth Cary), 181, 184, 188, 381n29

Tasso, Torquato, 9, 298, 409n112; *Aminta,* 297, 298, 299, 300, 409nn118,119, *Discoursi del poema heroica,* 408n113

Taylor, Anne, 137

Taylor, Dick, Jr., 363n51

Taylor, John (the Water Poet): *An Englishmans Love to Bohemia,* 349n89; *Heavens Blessing,* 344n42

Temple, Sir William, 98; *Works,* 360n12

Tenney, M. F., 327n23

Thomson, Patricia, 360n9, 365n72, 366n90, 367nn100,109

Thucydides, 203, 392n84

Tillney, Edmund, 332n37

Tom Tell-Troath, 63–64, 350n98

Tourneur, Cyril: *Atheist's Tragedy,* 391n77
Travitsky, Betty, 325n4, 327n17, 380n17, 383n3, 400n8, 406n73, 408n105
Trevor-Roper, H. R., 350n103
Tricomi, Albert, 327n23, 332nn36,37
Tris, Christian, 80
Triumph of Protestantism, The (engraving), 57
Trumbull, Mr., 331n26, 339n95, 342nn36,37
Tufton, John (Earl of Thanet), 129, 376n74
Tuvil, Daniel: *Asylum Veneris,* 378n3

Underdown, David, 327n16
Utley, Francis, 378n1
Uvedale, Sir William, 190

Valency, Maurice, 383n3, 389n58, 391n70
Van Somer, Paul, 178, 377n88
Vennor, Richard: *The Right Way to Heaven,* 374n60
Vere, Sir Horace, 61
Verulam, Lady (wife of Francis Bacon), 377n89
Veteripont family, 131
Vickers, Nancy, 324n1
Villiers, George. *See* Buckingham, George Villiers, Duke of
Vindiciae Contra Tyrannos, 191
Virgil, 38, 75, 286; First Eclogue, 235, 297
von Schomberg, Hans Meinhard, 55, 346nn57,58, 347n63
Vox Regis, 350n96

Waller, Gary, 244, 324n24, 400nn4,7, 402n30, 404n42, 405n69, 408n103, 409n110
Walpole, Michael: *English Catholikes,* 331n28
Walsingham, Ethelreda, 22, 23, 31, 33, 331nn29,31, 336n66
Walsingham, Sir Thomas, 69, 70, 331n31, 400n10
Ward, A. W., 330n25
Warnke, Retha M., 325n4
Warwick, Anne Dudley, Countess of, 136
Watson, Jeanie, 325n4, 383n3
Wayne, Don M., 399n59
Webb, George: *The Bride Royall,* 54, 345n50

Weber, Kurt, 384nn10,13,18, 385nn19,25, 388nn45,48,51
Webster, John: *The Duchess of Malfi,* 9, 200, 391n77
Weidemann, Heather, 408n103
Weigall, Rachel, 327n18
Weinberg, Bernard, 409n112
Weintraub, Karl, 8, 327n25, 375n70
Weller, Barry, 382n1
Weston, Lady Jane, 386n30
Weston, Sir Richard, 59, 387n40
Wharton, Lord, 126
Whately, William: *A Bride-Bush,* 382n45
Whigham, Frank, 325n6
Whitaker, T. O., 374n56
White, Allon, 325n6
White, Robert: *Cupid's Banishment* (masque), 42
Whitney, Isabella, 6, 326n13
Whittaker, John, Sr., 66
Whyte, Roland, 244, 360n14, 400n9, 401nn14,15
Wiffin, J. H., 359n1, 360n8
Wilbye, John, 81; *Cantus,* 355n65
Willet, Andrew, 16; *Ecclesia Triumphans,* 328n5
Williams, Ethel C., 328n1, 330n21
Williams, Franklin B., 359n1, 374n59, 397n36
Williams, Raymond, 399n59
Williamson, George, 368n1, 369nn7,9,11, 370nn20,21, 371n27, 373nn46,52, 374nn56,58, 375n64, 377n86
Wilson, Arthur, 329n9, 343n34
Wilson, E. C., 343n31
Windsor, Lady Catherine, 38, 337n80, 339n96
Wingfield, Sir John, 397nn35,42
Wingfield, Susan. *See* Bertie, Susan, Countess of Kent
Winter, Lady Anne, 38, 337n80, 339n96
Winwood, Sir Ralph, 31, 55, 90, 346n59; *Memorials,* 331n26, 332n38, 336nn71,72, 337n74, 339n95, 342nn23,24,27,28, 343n33, 346nn54,56,57, 356nn76,81, 358n107
Wither, George, 19, 54, 246; *Abuses Stript,* 330n19, 402n27; *Epithalamia,* 345n51, 350n97; *Wither's Motto,* 63, 350n97
Woodbridge, Linda, 150, 156, 324n1, 326n12, 327n27, 378nn1,3, 380nn17,19, 382n45

Woods, Susanne, 214, 325n5, 394n4, 395n10, 396n20
Woolf, D. R., 319, 393n94
Woolf, Virginia, 288
Worcester, Countess of, 331n29
Worcester, Henry Somerset, Earl of, 33
Wotton, Lady, 377n89
Wotton, Sir Henry, 54–55, 59, 62, 104; *Book of Architecture,* 138; *Letters,* 330n21, 342n24, 346n55, 347n60, 356n72; *Reliquiae Wottonianae,* 349n94
Wright, Louis B., 340n1, 378n1, 382n50
Wroth, James (son of Mary Wroth), 247
Wroth, Lady Mary, 2, 3, 7, 8, 10, 31, 101, 242, 243–307, 313, 314, 355n66, 364n58, 400n9, 401n14, 402n20; education of, 244–245, 401n15; marriage of, 245, 401n17; children by Earl of Pembroke, 248, 403n40, 408n99; portraits of, 242, 403n35; and Anne Clifford, 377n90; Denny controversy, 248–251, 404nn46–51; letters of, 402n22, 403n39, 404n46; poems of, 251–263,

325n5, 404nn53,54; *Love's Victory,* 7, 243, 251, 296–307, 310–311, 314, 400n2, 408nn104,108, 410nn125–129, 411nn130,131; *Pamphilia to Amphilanthus* 7, 243–263, 312, 400n1, 405nn62,64,67; *Urania,* 7, 243, 248, 249–251, 263–296, 297, 301, 306, 307, 310, 311, 314, 325n5, 370n17, 399n1, 400n2, 402n24, 404n46, 406nn76,77, 407nn84,95,97–99, 408nn101; *Urania,* Part I, 263–282, 399n1, 405n59; *Urania,* Part II, 282–296, 400n2

Xenophon: *Cyropaedia,* 46, 340n6

Yates, Frances B., 346n53, 350n103
Yelverton, Sir Henry, 393n93
Yelverton, Hobart, 146
York, Archbishop of, 206

Zolius, 163
Zouche, Lord, 330n21
Zwicker, Steven, 359n2